Managerial economics
Analysis and cases

Managerial economics
Analysis and cases

W. WARREN HAYNES
Late Dean of Business Administration
State University of New York at Albany

WILLIAM R. HENRY
Professor of Business Administration
Georgia State University

 THIRD EDITION · 1974

BUSINESS PUBLICATIONS, INC. *Dallas, Texas 75231*

Irwin-Dorsey International, London, England WC2H 9NJ
Irwin-Dorsey Limited, Georgetown, Ontario L7G 4B3

Additional credits

Figure 9–2 on page 396 is from Donald N. DeSalvia, "An Application of Peak-Load Pricing," *Journal of Business*, Vol. 42, No. 4 (October, 1969), p. 460. Copyright 1969 by the University of Chicago. Reproduced by permission of the University of Chicago Press.

Figure 20–1 on page 481 and Table 10–1 on page 482 are from CORPORATE STRATEGY by H. Igor Ansoff. Copyright 1965 by McGraw-Hill Book Company. Used with permission of McGraw-Hill Book Company.

Figure 10–3 on page 494 is from TECHNOLOGICAL FORECASTING AND LONG RANGE PLANNING by Robert V. Ayres. Copyright 1969 by McGraw-Hill Book Company. Used with permission of McGraw-Hill Book Company.

Figure 10–4 on page 499 is from THE AMERICAN ECONOMY TO 1975 by Clopper Almon, Jr. Copyright 1966 by Clopper Almon, Jr. Reprinted by permission of Harper and Row, Publishers, Inc.

Figure 10–5 on page 504 is reprinted from "Faculty Needs and Resources in American Higher Education," in Vol. 404 of THE ANNALS of the American Academy of Political and Social Science. Copyright 1972 by the American Academy of Political and Social Science. Used by permission of Allan Cartter and the American Academy of Political and Social Science.

Third Edition

First Printing, May 1974
Second Printing, November 1974
Third Printing, January 1975
Fourth Printing, April 1975

ISBN 0-256-01573-2
Library of Congress Catalog Card No. 73–93360

Printed in the United States of America

Preface

This text contains: (1) expositions of the theoretical and analytical tools of economics that are useful in managerial decision making; (2) reviews of empirical studies and illustrations of applications of the concepts from managerial economics; (3) cases involving actual managerial situations that call for economic analysis.

Half of the chapters in this third edition are either completely new or very substantially changed compared to the second edition. Larry D. Schroeder of Georgia State University collaborated with me in rewriting Chapter 4 (Business Conditions Analysis and Short Range Forecasting) and in preparing the entirely new Chapter 10 (Long Range Forecasting). Larry L. Dildine of Georgia State University collaborated with me in rewriting the topics of Chapter 6 (Production and Cost Analysis) and in producing the new Chapter 12 (Cost-Effectiveness and Benefit-Cost Analysis). E. Earl Burch of Clemson University was the collaborator on the new material of Chapter 7 (Selected Topics in Production Economics). The reconstruction of Chapter 11 (Capital Budgeting) was my own work.

Only minor changes from the second edition were made in chapters 1, 2, 3, 5, 8, and 9.

The book reflects several guidelines developed by the author of the two earlier editions: (1) The exposition of theoretical ideas should take the form of a cumulative flow from simple to complex with considerable repetition of the basic concepts to assist the learning process; (2) Each presentation of theoretical analysis should be immediately followed by practical applications to demonstrate relevance and help bridge the gap between theory and practice; (3) An abundance of problems and cases should be provided to let the student test his understanding of theoretical concepts and develop the judgment skills required in applications of managerial economics; (4) There should be enough institutional, psychological, and sociological material to give the student practice in coping with the influences of the changing environment upon decision processes of managerial units; (5) The underlying analytical structure from economics should be carefully related to concepts from accounting, finance, production, marketing, management, and business policy to help the student integrate his professional knowledge.

Quantitative approaches to applications of managerial economics have been given somewhat more emphasis than in the earlier editions. However, the exposition is not rigorous and the assumed mathematical and statistical preparation of students is at the sophomore level.

In the second edition, Warren Haynes acknowledged assistance from numerous persons in the development of this text. Carl L. Moore, Frederic A. Brett, Robert N. Anthony, Stanley I. Buchin, John V. Lintner, Henry B. Arthur, Bernard Davis, James L. Gibson, James Ledford, Dale Osborne, Martin B. Solomon, Jr., Ravi Matthai, K.L. Varshneya, and John I. Reynolds contributed cases or cooperated with Haynes in writing cases. Many of these have been brought forward to the third edition. I am grateful to these persons and to many others, not known to me, who helped Warren Haynes during his years at the University of Kentucky, the Indian Institute of Management, and the Harvard Graduate School of Business Administration, when he was writing the first and second editions.

This revision was improved through reviews of the manuscript by Donald W. Huffmire of the University of Connecticut, Jewell Rasmussen of the University of Utah, Michael Keenan of New York University, and Bruce White of Georgia State University. I also acknowledge several helpful suggestions from Bjarke Fog of Copenhagen School of Economics and Business Administration and Charles R. Long of Georgia State University.

Thanks are also due to Marteen Shea, Norma Henry, Becky Strickland, Eric Tweedy, and Ralph Allen for their assistance in producing the manuscript, illustrations, and problems. Finally, I am grateful to Dean Kenneth Black, Jr., Georgia State University School of Business, for his interest and support.

As work on this edition ends, the next revision is already underway. I shall be grateful for suggestions for improving the fourth edition from teachers and students who use this book.

April 1974   WILLIAM R. HENRY

Contents

**PART ONE / Introduction to
managerial economics**

Relation to other branches of learning: *Microeconomic theory. Macroeconomic theory. Statistics. The theory of decision making. Operations research.*
Profits: A central concept: *Theories of profit. Managerial economics and
alternative profit theories.* Models and suboptimization: *Models. Suboptimization.* Behavioral theory of the firm. The usefulness of managerial
economics.

Incremental reasoning: *Incremental reasoning versus marginal analysis.
Empirical studies and illustrations.* Opportunity cost: *Incremental cost
versus opportunity cost. Empirical studies and illustrations.* Contribution:
Empirical studies and illustrations. Time perspective on costs and revenues:
Empirical studies and illustrations. Diminishing marginal productivity and
equimarginal allocation: *An elaboration of the equimarginal principle. Constant marginal products. Empirical studies and illustrations.* Time value of
money—discounting: *Empirical studies and illustrations.* Some important
applications: *Make or buy. Product-line decisions. Other applications.*

List of figures

List of tables

PART ONE / Introduction to managerial economics

1 / The scope and method of managerial economics

Managerial economics is economics applied in decision making. It is a special branch of economics that bridges the gap between abstract theory and managerial practice. It emphasizes the use of economic analysis in clarifying problems, in organizing and evaluating information, and in comparing alternative courses of action. While managerial economics is sometimes known as business economics, it provides methods and a point of view that are also applicable in managing nonprofit organizations and public agencies.

Economics is sometimes defined as the study of allocation of scarce social resources among unlimited ends. Managerial economics is the study of the allocation of the resources available to a firm or other unit of management among the activities of that unit. Thus, managerial economics is concerned with choice—with the selection among alternatives. It is goal oriented and prescriptive. Managerial economics aims at maximum achievement of objectives.

Managerial economics is pragmatic: It is concerned with analytical tools that are useful, that have proven themselves in practice, or that promise to improve decision making in the future. Although it avoids some of the most difficult abstract issues of economic theory, it also faces up to some complications that are ignored in theory, for it must deal with the total situation in which decisions are made.

The relation of managerial economics to economic theory is much like that of engineering to physics, or of medicine to biology. It is the relation of an applied field to the more fundamental but more abstract basic disciplines from which it borrows concepts and analytical tools. The fundamental theoretical fields will no doubt in the long run make the greater contribution to the extension of human knowledge. But the applied fields involve the development of skills that are worthy of respect in themselves and that require specialized training. The practicing physician may not contribute much to the advance of biological theory, but he plays an essential role in producing the fruits of progress in theory. The managerial economist stands in a similar relation to economic and management theory, with perhaps the difference that the dichotomy between "pure" and "applied" is less clear in management than it is in medicine.

RELATION TO OTHER BRANCHES OF LEARNING

Managerial economics has a close connection with microeconomic theory, macroeconomic theory, statistics, the theory of decision making, and operations research. The fully trained managerial economist integrates concepts and methods from all of these disciplines, bringing them to bear on managerial problems.

Microeconomic theory

The main source of concepts and analytical tools for managerial economics is microeconomic theory, also known as theory of firms and markets, or price theory. This volume contains numerous references to such microeconomic concepts as the elasticity of demand, marginal cost, the short and long runs, and market structures. It also makes use of well-known models in price theory, such as the model for monopoly price, the kinked demand theory, and the model of price discrimination.

In taking a pragmatic point of view, managerial economics neglects some fine points that take up much space in the theoretical literature. For example, managerial economics (at least as developed in this book) makes little use of indifference curves, which are central in the modern theory of demand. Indifference curves have helped clarify some important conceptual issues in economics, such as the separation of the income effects and substitution effects of price change. But so far they have played no part in managerial decision, since measurement of the variables required in a practical application of indifference analysis is not feasible.

Macroeconomic theory

The chief debt of managerial economics to macroeconomic theory is in the area of forecasting. Since the prospects of an individual firm often depend greatly on business in general, individual firm forecasts depend on general business forecasts. These make use of models derived from theory. The most widely used model in modern forecasting, the gross national product model, is a direct product of theoretical developments in the past 40 years. Although applications bypass some fine points of interest to the theorist, actual use of these models requires an examination of details (the inventory situation in the automobile industry, excess capacity in chemicals, consumer attitudes) that the theory necessarily ignores.

Statistics

Statistics is important to managerial economics in several ways. First, it provides the basis for empirical testing of theory. While deductive reasoning has made a central contribution to economics, the results of that reasoning can never be fully accepted until they are checked against data from the world of reality. This volume presents statistical tests of some of the generalizations most important to managerial economics.

Statistics is important in a second way, in providing the individual firm with methods of measuring the functional relationships used in decision making. It is not enough, for example, to state that the firm should base its pricing decisions on considerations of demand and cost. To take such action, the firm needs statistical measurements of the shape and position of the demand and cost functions. As another example, it is not enough to know that linear programming can be used to determine best product mixes or least-cost input combinations. To apply linear programming, it is necessary to estimate numerous input-output relationships. Statistical approaches are not the only way to obtain estimates of the parameters for decision making. Other sources are accounting, engineering, and subjective managerial estimates. But statistical methods are often helpful.

The theory of decision making

The theory of decision making is a relatively new subject that has a significance for managerial economics. Much of economic theory is based on the assumption of a single goal—maximization of utility for the individual or maximization of profit for the firm. It also usually rests on the assumption of certainty—of perfect knowledge. In contrast, the theory of decision making recognizes the multiplicity of goals and the pervasiveness of uncertainty in the real world of management. The theory of decision making often replaces the notion of a single optimum solution with the view that the objective is to find solutions that "satisfice" rather than maximize. It probes into an analysis of motivation, of the relation of rewards and aspirations levels, of patterns of influence and authority.

The theory of decision making is concerned with the processes by which expectations under conditions of uncertainty are formed. It recognizes the costs of collecting and processing information, the problem of communication, and the need to reconcile diverse objectives of individuals and interests in the organization. It requires consideration of the psychological and sociological influences on human behavior.

Economic theory and the theory of decision making appear to be in conflict, each based on a different set of assumptions. Which theory shall we choose? It is unnecessary to make a black-and-white choice. This book is obviously based on the belief that economic analysis is useful in the achievement of better decisions. It does not claim that businessmen always can reach the optima indicated by theory, but it does argue that it is useful to have some idea of the direction of such optima. It admits that, while economic theory is easy to apply in simple, slow-moving situations with clear-cut objectives, it is much less able to handle more complex problems with multiple goals and high degrees of uncertainty.

One of the main benefits of the case method in managerial economics is that it indicates the strengths and weaknesses of economic analysis in actual decision-making situations. One of the skills to be learned from a book of this type is the ability to evaluate the relevance of particular conceptual tools in dealing with the problems faced by management. The manager must temper the refinements of theory with the requirements of decision making.

Operations research

There is some disagreement about the proper definition of operations research, but in any case it is closely related to managerial economics. Operations research is concerned with "model building"—with the construction of theoretical models that aid in decision making. Managerial economics also applies models; economic theorists were constructing "models" long before that expression became fashionable. Operations research is frequently concerned with optimization; economics has long dealt with the consequences of the maximization of profits or minimization of costs.

Some writers suggest that it is the "team approach" which makes operations research distinctive. Operations research workers have come from the natural sciences, from statistics, from mathematics, as well as from economics. The resultant pooling of diverse talents may be its distinctive feature. Probably more important is the heavy reliance on mathematics. Most of the best-known operations research techniques are quantitative in character, as opposed to the more subjective and qualitative techniques usually used by management. Since economics is now becoming more mathematical, this suggests another parallel development in the two related fields.

The best way to describe operations research is to identify its recurrent techniques and models. The best-known method is linear programming, which is applied to a variety of problems of choice. Operations research workers have also developed inventory models indicating optimum quantities to order and optimum ordering times. Other common techniques are waiting-line (queuing) models, bidding models, and applications of probability theory. Economic analysis involves a logic which is closely related to the logic of these models. For example, incremental or marginal reasoning of long application in economics is also applied in inventory models. Economists have also taken a great interest in the relation of linear programming to traditional theories of the firm. Some topics in operations research, such as replacement theory, have developed directly from the work of economists.

It is not important to determine where managerial economics begins and operations research ends. There is a close relation of the two subjects and each has a contribution to make to the other.

PROFITS: A CENTRAL CONCEPT

Profit maximization is the central assumption in managerial economics. The reasons for the stress on profits are several. Profits are, after all, the one pervasive objective running through all business situations; other objectives are more a matter of personal taste or of social conditioning and are variable from firm to firm, society to society, and time to time. The survival of a firm depends upon its ability to earn profits. Profits are a measure of its success.

Another reason for emphasizing profits has to do with convenience in analysis. It is easy to construct models based on the assumption of profit maximization; it is more difficult to build models based on a multiplicity of goals, especially when those goals are concerned with such unstable and relatively immeasurable factors as the desire to be "fair," the improvement of public relations, the maintenance of satisfactory relations with the community, the wish to perform a service to the community, the desire to increase one's personal influence and power, and so on.

It is therefore usual to proceed in the early analysis as though profits were the only goal. After the consequences of that assumption have been derived, it is possible to bring in other considerations. Economics has developed a systematic and sophisticated system of logic as long as the goal is one of profits; it becomes more awkward and cumbersome when it incorporates other objectives.

Theories of profit

One difficulty in defining profit is that no single theory has been able to explain profits in a simple way. Profit is a mixture resulting from a variety of influences. The result is a variety of profit theories. These theories fall into four categories: those emphasizing profit as a reward for taking risks; those stressing the effect of luck, frictions, imperfections, and lags in producing profits; those centering on the monopoly element; and those relating profits to the flow of innovations in the economy.

The first theory of profit explains it as a reward for taking risks and bearing uncertainty. Entrepreneurs are unwilling to assume risks unless a reward compensates for the chances they take. The greater the risk the greater the profit incentive which is required. Thus one would expect a higher rate of profit in unstable and unpredictable industries such as electronics than in those with steady, dependable rates of growth, such as electric utilities.

Another theory of profit interprets it as a result of good luck combined with imperfections in the market mechanism. Changes in tastes and preferences, technology, or institutions, not anticipated or initiated by the firm, generate profits for it. In a purely competitive economy without lags, such profits would quickly disappear. Entry of new firms and expansion of existing firms would create a downward pressure on prices and the excess profits would be wiped out. In the real world of imperfections and frictions, the squeezing out of excess profits takes time. Thus, there may be substantial profits that owe their existence to pure luck.

Monopoly because of restricted entry is itself a source of profits. The existence of monopoly permits a curtailment of production and the establishment of prices above the competitive level. Although relative profit in competitive industries is a socially desirable guide for production, since it stimulates expansion in those parts of the economy where expansion is desirable, monopoly profit may be socially undesirable, since it is a reward for curtailing expansion where such expansion is socially beneficial.

Another theory of profit warns against condemning all monopoly profit too hastily. The innovation theory notes that profits arise from the development of new products, new production techniques, and new modes of marketing. The innovator who develops these new products and methods deserves a reward for his contribution to progress. It is true that he earns excess profits from the monopoly which the superiority of his innovations provides, but this monopoly is temporary. Old innovations are replaced by new ones in a constant process of "creative destruction."[1]

The innovation theory of profit breaks away from the static equilibrium analysis which is usual in traditional economic theory. Innovation profits result from change—from the disruption of the equilibrium or status quo. Any theory which ignores innovation neglects the most important function of profits, which is to reward change and to stimulate the replacement of less valuable and productive activities with more vital ones.

Managerial economics and alternative profit theories

One paradox of managerial economics is that, while it makes use of the assumption of profit maximization, it makes little direct use of the

---

[1] Joseph Schumpeter, *Theory of Economic Development* (Cambridge, Mass.: Harvard University Press, 1934).

theories of profit. Uncertainty, lags, frictions, and innovations give rise to the alternatives with which managerial economics is concerned. But most of the analysis is in terms of cost, demand, revenues, and market structure rather than directly in terms of profits. Thus we shall be concerned with the measurements of incremental revenue and incremental costs which lie behind incremental profits. We shall consider the contributions to overhead and profits which result from the alternatives under consideration. We shall compute the present value of estimated streams of profit in the future. We shall compare discounted rates of return, which are measures of profitability, with costs of capital. But none of this analysis is a direct application of one theory of profit or another.

Let us consider the risk and uncertainty theory first. Businessmen have coped with it in a variety of ways, mostly subjective in character. In recent years, more formal techniques for the analysis of uncertainty have developed under the titles of "decision theory," "decision trees," "Bayesian statistics," "queuing theory," "the Monte Carlo method," and "Markov processes." Modern managerial economics has recognized these important ideas and has incorporated them as part of the apparatus required for economic analysis. It is no surprise that a book entitled *Probability and Statistics for Business Decisions* should use the language of economics in many places (incremental cost, incremental gain, marginal utility, opportunity cost, and so on). Nor is it surprising that a book entitled *Economic Analysis for Business Decisions* should be heavily concerned with probability models.

The present volume, however, relegates the topics of risk and uncertainty to a secondary position. There are several reasons for this treatment. One is that the student should become thoroughly familiar with the basic concepts of managerial economics before complicating the analysis with probabilistic models. Some books on the subject tend to displace the important ideas of demand, cost, pricing, and capital budgeting with discussions of normal curves, Bayes' theorem, and Bernoulli processes. This is unfortunate, for the concepts of managerial economics and of statistics are complementary rather than competitive. Both aspects deserve attention. However, since probability is covered in courses in statistics and operations research, it seems appropriate to have a course in managerial economics concentrate on the fundamental economic analysis.

Thus, while we recognize the importance of risk and uncertainty as a source of profits, we shall not make much direct use of this idea, except in a general way, until the last part of the book. The theory of profit as a reward for risk taking is a useful one to keep in mind, but its direct application is better postponed for more advanced work.

We must show similar restraint in relating managerial economics to the innovation theory of profits. Economic analysis cannot produce the innovations; they are dependent upon qualities of imagination and leadership and are influenced by the organizational environments and systems of incentives. Managerial economics does evaluate new alternatives once they are developed. The entire chapter on capital budgeting is concerned with that topic. No analysis of alternatives can produce profits unless some of the alternatives are themselves profitable.

This discussion of profits has enabled us to place managerial economics in its proper perspective. Economics is not and cannot be the source of imaginative ideas for change. It does not provide the tools for determining the appropriate organization for the search for innovations. It is appropriate only for the evaluation of alternatives which have somehow already been discovered. And it does not deal with problems of leadership, communication and human relations involved in carrying out decisions.

MODELS AND SUBOPTIMIZATION

The real economic world is a very complex environment. Complete description of the technological and institutional influences on a firm would fill many books. However, only a few characteristics of the environment can be considered in making most decisions. Even these characteristics must usually be represented approximately rather than exactly. Managers plan with models, or simplifications of reality.

Models

Suppose the quantities of 19-inch color television sets that a particular manufacturer expects to sell in future months are represented by equations relating sales quantities to price, unit cost (which increases as more features are added), per capita incomes, and the manufacturer's expenditures on advertising. Some influences that are difficult to estimate and that will have less effect upon sales are disregarded in the above model: competitors' prices, dealer markups, dealer advertising, changes in official rates of currency exchange with other countries, and so on. Clearly, the manufacturer's view of demand is an approximation.

Models are structures involving relationships among concepts. The concepts are often represented by symbols so that the relationships can be expressed in mathematical form. The mathematical form allows quick determination of expected results of changes in the variables. The television set manufacturer of the example above can quickly estimate effects upon sales of his changes in price or advertising outlay with the aid of the demand equation, or model of demand.

Although models do not match reality point by point, they are based on theories that hypothesize structural correspondence between the models and certain aspects of the real world. The purpose of a model is to represent characteristics of a real system in a way that is simple enough to understand and manipulate and yet similar enough to the more complicated operating system that satisfactory results are obtained when the model is used in decision making. Thus, the test of whether or not a model is satisfactory cannot be the degree to which it corresponds to the real world. The appropriate test is whether or not it provides successful predictions.

The concept of optimization is basic in both managerial economics and operations research. Throughout this volume are examples of models and principles based on the assumptions that the objective is profit maximization or cost minimization under conditions of full information. The practitioner must adopt a mixed attitude towards such assumptions. He knows that as a description of actual managerial behavior they are inaccurate and oversimplified. But he also knows that simplifying assumptions are essential if he is to create order out of chaos.

Suboptimization

Few managers actually seek the greatest attainment of a single goal; they settle for partial achievement of a variety of goals, recognizing that furtherance of one objective may mean partial sacrifice of another. Even if the manager could specify a single goal, he could not achieve the "true" optimum, for the number of relevant variables and the variety of interrelationships would be too large and complex for any system of thought. Even the most elaborate models are still abstractions from reality. Any model or theory must necessarily simplify. The result is a paradox: managerial economics often assumes a desire to optimize a given objective, but it then simplifies in ways that assure a failure to fully achieve the optimum.

Operations researchers use the term "suboptimization" to describe this process of decision making by abstraction from the total complexity of reality and from the wide variety of goals. They construct models which reflect only part of reality and which face up to the bounds of human rationality. Such models indicate optimal positions within the limits or assumptions on which they are constructed. The result may be imperfect but should be superior to decisions based on crude rule of thumb or simple repetitions of past decisions. Rules of thumb and rigid formulas are replaced by the point of view that "it depends." Decisions must be adapted to circumstances; they must be based on an analysis of the possibilities. The questions of managerial economics are always those of more or less, of this combination opposed to those combinations, or of this alternative rated against others—with adaptation to the environment and to the goals of management.

BEHAVIORAL THEORY OF THE FIRM

"Behavioral theory of the firm" is helpful in understanding processes of decision making with multiple objectives and incomplete information.[2] Only a few highlights of the behavioral theory can be summarized here. The theory views the organization as a coalition of individuals, most of these being further organized into subcoalitions. Goals of the organization are developed through more or less continuous bargaining among potential coalition members.

Organizational goals are stated as aspiration levels (e.g., "increase our market share to 25 percent"; "earn 12 percent after tax on total capital employed"; "spend 8 percent of our budget on research and 2 percent on executive development"). The goals established at any one time may be inconsistent in the sense that it is not possible for all of them to be fully and simultaneously realized.

According to the behavioral theory, organizational decisions and re-source allocations are based on information and expectations that usually differ appreciably from reality. The organization cannot and does not attempt to acquire complete information about alternatives that are open to it. Flexibility, the possibility of revoking or modifying decisions, is highly regarded. When there are gaps between aspiration levels and actual results, the firm initiates search procedures to uncover additional alternatives. In many instances, methods of closing the gaps are discovered, and it may even be possible to raise some aspiration levels. In other instances, the aspiration levels must be reduced.

The behavioral theory represents the firm as an adaptive institution. It learns from experience and has a memory. Organizational behavior that "works" is incorporated into decision rules and standard operating procedures. These may be modified over the long run as the firm reacts to "feedback" from experience. However, in the short run, decisions of the organization are dominated by its rules of thumb and standard methods.

THE USEFULNESS OF MANAGERIAL ECONOMICS

Managerial decision-making requires compromise between the need for simplification to make the analysis manageable and the need for complication to consider a variety of objectives and influences. Costs of completeness must be weighed against errors of simplification. Common sense and good judgement are needed.

Managerial economics provides a rich body of tools and techniques that enables the manager to become a more competent model builder.

---

[2] Richard M. Cyert and James G. March, *A Behavioral Theory of The Firm* (Englewood Cliffs: Prentice Hall, 1963).

Thus, he can capture the essential relationships that characterize the situation while eliminating the cluttering details and peripheral relationships. Although the model builder chooses not to look at all aspects of the environment, he is nevertheless developing a clearer view of his problems, opportunities, and alternatives.

Managerial economics is helpful in making decisions such as the following: Which products and services should be produced? What inputs and production techniques should be used? How much output should there be and at what prices? When should equipment be replaced? What are the best sizes and locations of new plants? How shall available capital be allocated?

Enough space has been given to introductory statements. The best way to develop an understanding of managerial economics is to begin using the subject matter. The chapters that follow explain many useful concepts and relationships and provide some case materials which are essential in learning how to use economic analysis in practical decision-making.

2 / Six fundamental concepts

This chapter introduces some concepts which are basic to all of managerial economics. These concepts may appear elementary—almost self-evident. However, their application requires care. Empirical studies and illustrations at the end of each section of this chapter provide some insight into the considerations that complicate uses of these principles in decision making.

INCREMENTAL REASONING

Incremental reasoning involves estimating the impact of decision alternatives on costs and revenues, stressing the *changes* in total cost and total revenues that result from changes in prices, products, procedures, investments, or whatever may be at stake in the decision. The two basic concepts in this analysis are incremental cost and incremental revenue. Incremental cost may be defined as the change in total cost resulting from a decision. Incremental revenue is the change in total revenue resulting from a decision.

A decision is obviously profitable if *net* revenue is increased; this will be the result if:

1. It increases revenue more than costs
2. It reduces costs more than revenue
3. It decreases some costs more than it increases others
4. It increases some revenues more than it decreases others

Before the reader dismisses incremental analysis as too elementary for his attention, he might consider some of its implications. Some businessmen take the view that to make an overall profit they "must make a profit on every job." The result is that they refuse orders that do not cover full cost (labor, materials, and overhead) plus a provision for profit. Incremental reasoning indicates that this rule may be inconsistent with profit maximization in the short run. A refusal to accept business priced below full cost may mean rejection of a possibility of adding more to revenue than to cost. The relevant cost is not the full cost but rather the incremental cost. A simple problem illustrates what is involved. Take a case in which a new order will bring in $10,000 *additional revenue*. The costs of filling the order are estimated as follows:

Labor	$ 3,000
Materials	4,000
Overhead (allocated at 120 percent of labor cost)	3,600
Selling and administrative expense (allocated at 20 percent of labor and materials cost)	1,400
Full cost	$12,000

The above order appears to be unprofitable. But suppose that there is idle capacity with which this order could be produced. Suppose that acceptance of the order will add only $1,000 of overhead (the incremental overhead, limited to the added use of heat, power, and light, the added wear and tear on the machinery, the added costs of supervision, and so on). Suppose also that the order in actuality requires no added selling costs, since the only requirement is a signature on the contract and no added administrative costs. In addition, only part of the above labor cost is incremental with the order, since some idle workers already on the payroll will be put to work without added pay.

It is possible that the *incremental cost* of taking the order will be as follows:

Labor	$2,000
Materials	4,000
Overhead	1,000
Total incremental cost	$7,000

While it at first appeared that the order would result in a loss of $2,000, it now appears that the result is an addition of $3,000 in profit.

Perhaps a brief comment will minimize a common misunderstanding about incremental reasoning. Incremental reasoning does not mean that the firm should price at incremental cost or should accept orders that cover merely their incremental cost. In fact, "charging what the market will bear" is consistent with incrementalism, for it implies increasing rates if the result is an increase in net revenue. Acceptance of the $10,000 order in our illustration is conditioned upon the existence of idle capacity that would otherwise go unused and the absence of more profitable alternatives. Incremental reasoning never leads to acceptance of a less profitable order in preference to one that is more profitable; in fact it leads to the opposite.

Incremental reasoning versus marginal analysis

A reader with any familiarity with elementary economics can see that incremental reasoning is closely related to the marginal analysis of economic theory. Similarities and differences between these two approaches should be understood. In some applications, incremental reasoning is more efficient; in others, marginal analysis gives better results.

1. Marginal analysis always deals with *unit-by-unit changes*, whereas incremental reasoning is not restricted to unit change. For example, marginal cost is amount added to total cost by the last unit of increase in output; incremental cost could be associated with a change of any number of units, or it could result from an improvement in quality with no change in quantity.

2. Marginal analysis is particularly useful in looking at tradeoffs that are determined by *curvilinear* functions. For example, if the cost function is curvilinear, marginal cost changes as output is increased. The concept of marginal analysis calls for unit-by-unit comparisons of marginal cost with marginal revenue as output is increased, until the best level of output is found at the point where marginal cost is the same as marginal revenue.

3. Some other examples where marginal (unit-by-unit) analysis may be superior to incremental reasoning are: (*a*) selecting best *level of input* when the input-output relationship exhibits diminishing returns; (*b*) selecting best *product mix* as limited by commonly required scarce resources where the products substitute at decreasing rates; (*c*) selecting least cost *combinations of inputs* where inputs are substitutable at decreasing rates; (*d*) selecting *optimum maturity of assets* that gain value at decreasing rates over time.

4. Incremental reasoning is particularly useful in looking at tradeoffs that are *linear*. For these instances, only the end points of a range need to be compared. For example, if both the cost function and the revenue function are linear for output over the range from zero to technical capacity of a plant, it is sufficient to determine the incremental result of producing at capacity compared to no output at all. (Since marginal analysis would give identical results for every unit examined, it would also eventually select output at one end or the other of the range, but the unit-by-unit movement to an optimum point could be tedious.)

5. If *discrete* alternatives are to be compared, only incremental reasoning can be used. For example, suppose the decision is a choice be-

tween two technical processes that may be used to produce the same level of output. We cannot compare the processes in terms of marginal cost of moving from one to the other. However, there is an incremental cost associated with the change and this can be examined.

6. Marginal analysis on a unit-by-unit basis as depicted above is a special case of incremental reasoning. However, it can also be carried out with the aid of techniques from calculus and algebra. These analytic techniques directly determine optimum conditions and are discussed and illustrated in chapters to follow.

Empirical studies and illustrations

Do managers actually use incremental and marginal reasoning? The answer is that some do and others do not. Managers are not always fully aware of the reasoning behind their own decisions; apparently many of them unconsciously do apply incremental principles. In any case, many of them are inarticulate on their decision-making processes, making it difficult to determine what logic they do apply.

Earley's study of "excellently managed" large firms suggests that progressive corporations do make formal use of incremental analysis, and make use of accounting methods that are consistent with marginalism.[1] Earley finds that most of the 88 firms covered by the study "employ marginal accounting extensively, including segmented variable-fixed cost differentiation and the determination of separable fixed costs ... Most of them follow essentially marginal principles, and eschew or subordinate cost allocations and full-costing, in their product selection, product investment, and both short- and long-range pricing decisions."[2]

A study of small firms by Haynes makes it clear that the use of incremental accounting methods is far from universal.[3] Of the 100 firms covered by the study, not one used the special accounting methods cited in the previous study. It is true that the managers were often aware of the distinction between fixed and variable costs, and it is also true that some of these managers made use of ad hoc cost analyses that helped them apply incremental reasoning. Other managers reached decisions consistent with incrementalism by trial and error or by experimentation. But none of these small firms had a programmed accounting method (a routine method automatically producing data period by period) that provided the kinds of cost figures required for decision making. The item in the accounts that had the greatest impact on decision making was the profit or loss figure on the income statement. If this figure seemed "low" in

---

[1] James S. Earley, "Marginal Policies of 'Excellently Managed' Companies," *American Economic Review,* March 1956, pp. 44–70.

[2] Ibid., p. 61.

[3] Warren W. Haynes, *Pricing Decisions in Small Business* (Lexington, Kentucky: University of Kentucky Press, 1962).

relation to some predetermined standard, the manager often sought ways of improving the situation. In other words, the income figure motivated the managers to make decisions but did not provide the analysis required by those decisions. Accounting performed its stewardship function, supplying data required by the owners, creditors, or tax collectors. It also performed the control function, providing measurements of actual performance that could be compared with earlier experience or with standards. But normally it did not provide incremental data that would be useful for decisions.

The failure of the accounting systems of many firms to supply incremental data is not necessarily a deficiency. In many cases ad hoc analyses are less expensive than programmed accounting systems that must be maintained period after period. Furthermore, what is an incremental cost varies from one decision to another, making it unlikely that a programmed incremental system would always produce the required information. A manager who is experienced in decision making may be able to make the necessary adjustments in the regular accounting data on the back of an envelope in a few minutes. Thus the absence of marginalist accounting methods does not necessarily imply the absence of incremental reasoning.

A few illustrations should help the reader picture the variety of actual practice.

A laundry and dry-cleaning establishment. The managers of this firm rejected an opportunity to make use of idle capacity in the summer months when business was slack. A large motel wished to make a contract that would supply the laundry with business that would not cover "full costs" but which would more than cover incremental costs, leaving a contribution to overhead and profit. Apparently the managers were so certain that the full-cost figure, including allocated overhead, was the correct figure for decision making that they rejected a profitable order. They were unable to give any other reasons for rejecting the order; they did not believe that acceptance of the order would have any effect on their other business either in the present or in the future.

An advertising firm. The managers of a billboard advertising firm paid little attention to their regular financial accounting figures in making decisions on advertising rates. Instead they made up ad hoc income statements for future periods under alternative assumptions about rates. By this method they reached conclusions that appear to be fully in accord with incremental reasoning, even though the managers were unfamiliar with the economic jargon one might use to describe their analysis. Other companies appear to approximate incrementalism by trial and error, learning from experience what policies are likely to be conducive to increased profits.

In a study of small business, most companies appeared to fall between the extremes already discussed. Their managers were concerned with full costs (in retailing they emphasized wholesale costs); they used those costs as a starting point in pricing. But they did not adhere to rigid mark-ups on costs; instead they varied markups on different lines of goods and revised markups over time. Thus the most common pattern was that of "partial incrementalism," with either full cost or wholesale cost serving as a reference point or resistance point, but with considerable flexibility in adjustments to market conditions.

This review of empirical studies and illustrations supports two conclusions:

1. It is impossible to generalize on the uses of incremental reasoning, actual practice being variable.
2. Some firms could profit by giving more attention to incremental analysis, whether or not they revise their accounts to reflect this analysis.

OPPORTUNITY COST

Opportunity cost of a decision is the *sacrifice of alternatives* required by that decision. Sacrifice of alternatives is involved when carrying out a decision requires using some or all of *a resource that is in limited supply* to the firm. *Other use of the scarce resource must be given up* in order to make it available for the particular use.

Here are some specific illustrations of the meaning of opportunity cost:

1. Opportunity cost of funds tied up in one's own business is the interest (or profits corrected for differences in risk) that could be earned if these funds were invested in other ventures.
2. Opportunity cost of the time a person puts into his own business is the salary he could earn in other occupations (with a correction for the relative "psychic income" in the two occupations).
3. Opportunity cost of using a machine to produce a particular product is the sacrifice of earnings that would be possible in using the machine to produce other products.
4. Opportunity cost of using an owned machine that is useless for any other purpose is nil, since the particular use requires no sacrifice of alternatives.

Closely related to the concept of opportunity cost is the distinction between explicit and implicit costs. Explicit costs are recognized in the accounts, as in the case of payments for raw materials and, usually, for labor. Implicit (or imputed) costs are sacrifices, such as the use of capital supplied by owners of the business, that are not recognized in the accounts. To complicate matters slightly, some explicit expenses may not involve sacrifices of alternatives. For example, a company may pay wages to idle labor in periods of slack activity. These wages are in the nature of a fixed cost; they would not be included in the opportunity cost of a special order in which this labor might be used.

Incremental cost versus opportunity cost

Incremental cost is not the same as opportunity cost. Incremental cost is *difference in cost due to a decision;* it is subtracted from *incremental* revenue in using incremental reasoning to determine whether or not there is gain from a proposed *change in business activity.* Opportunity cost is *all of the economic cost of a scarce input* (or bundle of inputs) ; it is subtracted from *total* revenue in determining whether or not there is an economic profit in a proposed *use of the inputs.*

Incremental cost. The concept of incremental cost is often called "differential cost" in accounting. Some accountants refer to it as "relevant cost." These terms focus attention on the *change in cost due to a change in business activity.* The incremental costs are contrasted with the firm's sunk cost, or cost that runs on regardless of the change in activity.

Incremental cost must be compared to incremental revenue in using incremental reasoning to make a decision. In a particular decision, incremental revenue or incremental cost could be zero or negative. If the algebraic difference between incremental revenue and incremental cost is positive, the proposed change in business activity is profitable.

Opportunity cost. The concept of opportunity cost focuses attention on the *net revenue that could be generated in the next best alternative use of a scarce input* (or bundle of inputs.) Opportunity cost is calculated as the full amount of revenue that could be generated in the alternative use, less any decrease in cost of other inputs that results from giving up the other use. Since this *net* revenue must be given up, or sacrificed, to make the scarce input available for some particular use, it is called opportunity cost of the input.

Opportunity cost may or may not contrast with explicit accounting cost. If the firm owns land, there is no cost of using the land (rent) in the firm's accounts. However, the firm is giving up the net revenue that could be realized by renting this land to another firm. Therefore, the firm has an opportunity cost of using this land, and opportunity cost is greater than the explicit cost. On the other hand, if the firm buys materials from an abundant supply in the open market, there is an explicit cost of the materials in the firm's accounts. The next best use of these inputs would be not to purchase them, thereby making the money available for any other desired use. In this case, opportunity cost is the same as explicit accounting cost.

Opportunity cost, rather than explicit accounting cost, should be used in calculating economic profit from a particular use of a scarce input. Economic profit is positive for the best use of such a resource and negative for all other uses. Economic profit in a particular use is calculated as full revenue less the opportunity cost of all inputs required.

An example using both approaches. The following example contrasts correct usage of the incremental cost concept and the opportunity cost concept. A firm owns a piece of machinery that has been fully depreciated. Remaining expected life of the machine is one year, at the end of which the machine will have no salvage value. The machine is presently used to produce widgets with revenues and expenses as shown in Figure 2–1.

FIGURE 2–1

ANNUAL REVENUES AND EXPENSES, WIDGET PRODUCTION

Revenue		
Sale of widgets		$5,000
Expenses		
Electricity	$ 100	
Materials	1,000	
Labor	2,000	
Total Expenses		3,100
Accounting Profit		$1,900

The firm is considering an alternative use of the machine, in which it will be modified and used to produce gadgets. In the alternative use, the annual revenues and expenses would be as shown in Figure 2–2.

FIGURE 2–2

EXPECTED ANNUAL REVENUES AND EXPENSES, GADGET PRODUCTION

Revenue		
Sale of gadgets		$6,000
Expenses		
Electricity	$ 100	
Materials	1,500	
Labor	2,500	
Conversion expense	500	
Total Expenses		$4,600

The firm is also considering outright sale of the machine to another firm that has offered $2,300 for it. Thus, the firm has three alternatives: (1) to continue producing widgets, (2) to convert to gadget production, and (3) to sell the machine. Alternative 1 is the present use of the machine and will be used as a base in illustrating incremental reasoning.

Appropriate calculations for comparing continued widget production (Alternate 1) with conversion to gadget production (Alternative 2) are shown in Figure 2–3.

FIGURE 2–3

INCREMENTAL REVENUE, COST, AND PROFIT
(change to Alternative 2)

Total Revenue in Alternative 2		*Less Total Revenue in Alternative 1*		*Equals Incremental Revenue*
$6,000	—	$5,000	=	$1,000

Total Cost in Alternative 2			*Less Total Cost in Alternative 1*		*Equals Incremental Cost*
Electricity	$ 100	—	$ 100	=	0
Materials	1,500	—	1,000	=	$ 500
Labor	2,500	—	2,000	=	500
Conversion	500	—	0	=	500
Total Incremental Cost					$1,500

Incremental Revenue		*Less Incremental Cost*		*Equals Incremental Profit*
$1,000	—	$1,500	=	—$500

Changing to Alternative 2 results in incremental loss of $500 and should not be carried out. Next, compare continued widget production (Alternative 1) to sale of the machine (Alternative 3). The results are shown in Figure 2–4.

FIGURE 2–4

INCREMENTAL REVENUE, COST, AND PROFIT
(change to Alternative 3)

Total Revenue for Alternative 3		*Less Total Revenue for Alternative 1*		*Equals Incremental Revenue*
$2,300	—	$5,000	=	—$2,700

Total Cost in Alternative 3			*Less Total Cost in Alternative 1*		*Equals Incremental Cost*
Selling expenses	$100	—	$ 0	=	$ 100
Electricity	0	—	100	=	— 100
Materials	0	—	1,000	=	— 1,000
Labor	0	—	2,000	=	— 2,000
Total Incremental Cost					—$3,000

Incremental Revenue		*Less Incremental Cost*		*Equals Incremental Profit*
—$2,700	—	—$3,000	=	$ 300

Changing to Alternative 3 has an incremental profit of $300 and is the best use of the machine. *Note that costs used in calculating incremental costs are accounting or explicit costs; the concept of opportunity cost is not needed in incremental reasoning.*

Another approach to the above decision is based on the opportunity cost concept. Consider giving up continued widget production (Alternative 1) to make the machine available for conversion to gadget production

(Alternative 2). Net revenue in Alternative 1 is $1,900 (Figure 2–1). If Alternative 2 is selected, this net revenue will be sacrificed; it is the opportunity cost of the machine for use in Alternative 2. Revenue, economic cost, and economic profit of Alternative 2 would be as shown in Figure 2–5.

FIGURE 2–5

REVENUE, ECONOMIC COST, AND ECONOMIC PROFIT
(Alternative 2)

Revenue		$6,000
Economic Cost		
Electricity	$ 100	
Materials	1,500	
Labor	2,500	
Conversion	500	
Opportunity cost of machine	1,900 *Net Rev. of Alternative 1.*	
Total Economic Cost		$6,500
Economic Profit		— $500

Obviously, Alternative 2 is not attractive; it has an economic loss of $500 if Alternative 1 is given up. Calculations to compare sale of the machine (Alternative 3) with continued widget production (Alternative 1) are shown in Figure 2–6.

FIGURE 2–6

REVENUE, ECONOMIC COST, AND ECONOMIC PROFIT
(Alternative 3)

Revenue		$2,300
Economic Cost		
Selling expense	$ 100	
Opportunity cost of machine	1,900	
Total Economic Cost		$2,000
Economic Profit		$ 300

Since the economic profit of Alternative 3 is $300 it is the best of the three machine uses considered. *Note that full revenues and full economic costs are used in economic profit calculations. Economic costs are based on opportunity costs rather than accounting costs if these are different for particular items. The concept of incremental cost is not needed in economic profit calculations.*

Incremental reasoning and economic profit calculations are alternative approaches; they lead to identical final choices among any given set of alternatives. If a scarce resource is involved, the concept of opportunity cost should be kept in mind; it reminds one that the best use of the resource may be an alternative that has not yet been considered.

Empirical studies and illustrations

It is obvious that most managers are continually weighing alternatives, which means that they are at least roughly making subjective evaluations of opportunity costs. Some modern mathematical methods used in larger firms incorporate opportunity cost considerations; this is true of linear programming techniques and replacement models.

Some managers fail to make correct analyses of opportunity costs. Conventional accounting does not accurately reflect opportunity costs. Cost accounting systems that allocate overhead in relation to some basis such as direct labor cost overestimate economic costs of activities that use otherwise idle capacity. The following example illustrates some uses of opportunity cost.

Optimal use of water in a hydroelectric system. Electric utilities that own hydroelectric dams also operate steam-generating plants. They face a choice of using hydro power or steam power or some combination of the two. It is relatively easy to measure the cost of generating power in a steam plant, though the correct handling of depreciation may present some difficulty. But the cost of producing hydro power is much more troubling. After all, the dams are already built; their costs of construction are sunk and are irrelevant in making decisions for the future. The same is true of expensive generators, on which wear and tear is probably a small cost relative to the original price of the generators. And water is a "free gift of nature." Why not run the water through the generators as rapidly as possible and minimize the use of the steam plants?

Merely posing the question should suggest the solution to the problem. The use of the water behind a dam is not cost free, for it does require a sacrifice. Water used today cannot be used tomorrow; its use today involves an opportunity cost. Looking at the matter another way, the water behind a dam has value based on its capacity to produce power in the future.

Suppose a utility owns one hydroelectric dam and three steam plants. The three steam plants vary in efficiency, the new plant burning less coal per kilowatt-hour than the old ones. To meet the peak-load requirements all three plants and the dam must operate near capacity. To meet lower loads it is possible to cut off either the high-cost plants or the hydroelectric dam, or both. Running the water through the generators in off-peak periods would run the risk of not having enough stored-up water for peak periods. The sacrifice (opportunity cost) would be a measure of the loss of revenue and customer dissatisfaction that might result. In addition, the operation of the high-cost steam plants involves a sacrifice in the inefficient burning of fuel. The flow of water should be regulated as to minimize this sacrifice.

If the utility has additional objectives, such as flood control or maintenance of navigation (as is true of some public power systems), the analysis becomes more complex but the basic principles are the same. The stored-up water has value; its use involves an opportunity cost.

CONTRIBUTION

The contribution concept overlaps incremental reasoning and opportunity cost. It focuses attention upon *contribution to overhead and profit by units of output.* It is helpful in making decisions such as whether or not to shut down a plant or accept an order. Where several products require services of scarce or bottleneck resources (output of some products must be cut back if output of others is expanded), the contribution concept is an aid in determining the most advantageous combination of products.

Consider a case in which the price of a product is determined by outside forces—by competition or regulation. Assume this price is $95. Within the firm, total unit cost including allocated overheads is $103, but incremental cost is only $75. Loss by conventional accounting is $8 per unit, but there is a contribution to overhead and profit amounting to $20 per unit. *Unit contribution is incremental revenue per unit less incremental cost.* The issue is whether or not to drop the product.

If the company has *excess capacity,* the decision is easy. The product can be made without reducing output of other products. *Any contribution is better than none.* The product should not be dropped.

However, suppose the company has a *backlog of orders* for other products requiring the same production time per unit. If these products earn contributions of $50 or $40 or $30, they should not be sacrificed to permit output of the product with a $20 contribution. *More contribution is better than less.*

Where products vary in amounts of "bottleneck" resource used per unit of output, simple comparisons of contribution per unit of output are inadequate. An item contributing $50 per unit of output can be less profitable than an item with a $20 contribution if the first item requires three times as much of the scarce input. This suggests that products should be compared on the basis of their *contributions per unit of scarce resource required* (i.e., choice of product mix is another way of looking at allocation of scarce resources).

If a company has only one bottleneck in production, let us say in machine hours available, we can convert the contributions per unit of output into contributions per machine hour. Table 2–1 presents such a situation in a company producing five products.

TABLE 2-1

CONTRIBUTIONS ON FIVE PRODUCTS IN A SINGLE PLANT

Product	Price	Incremental Cost	Contribution per Unit	Machine Minutes Requirements
A	$15.00	$10.00	$5.00	60 minutes
B	14.00	8.00	6.00	80
C	13.00	9.00	4.00	40
D	12.00	7.50	4.50	30
E	6.00	2.50	3.50	15

At first glance Product B appears to be best; it produces a contribution larger than that of the other products. But Product B uses up more capacity for each unit produced. Clearly we must convert the contributions to make them comparable in relation to their requirements of machine time. One way to do this is to convert them into contributions per hour of machine time. The results are as follows:

Product A .... $ 5.00 per machine hour
Product B 4.50
Product C 6.00
Product D 9.00
Product E 14.00

These results indicate that Product E, which at first appeared to be the lowest contributor, is in fact the largest. The product priorities are almost the opposite of those which appear at first glance. If this illustration seems farfetched, it should be stated that in actual practice the order of contributions is frequently quite different from those suggested by casual observation.

Suppose, however, that more than one capacity bottleneck appears. If all five products pass through four processes, each of which can be the bottleneck, it is no longer possible to compute simple contributions in terms of just one of the bottlenecks. The problem becomes one in linear programming. It is discussed briefly in the section below and at more length in Chapter 7.

Empirical studies and illustrations

Twenty years ago the expression "contribution to overhead and profits" was almost unknown, although many managers were in fact using the idea without giving it a name. Today the term has become part of the vocabulary of management; one can say that a manager who does not understand contributions is probably not very proficient in modern cost analysis. Probably the term is used most widely in product mix decisions and pricing decisions, but it is also applicable to making or buying and other decisions. The "cash flows" which are estimated in capital budgeting are closely related to the contribution concept, as we shall see in the chapter on capital budgeting.

As has been stated, the contribution concept is applicable when linear programming is used to solve product mix problems. A mathematical friend of Haynes once confessed that he applied linear programming in solving a textile mill's production problems without knowing the difference between full cost and incremental cost. The product profitability estimates he used in the solution were profits above full costs rather than contributions above incremental costs. His solution was wrong, for no mathematical technique can correct for incorrect data.

It may be useful to push the linear programming illustration a little further. By introducing the elements of linear programming in bits as the economic aspects are introduced, the reader will be in a better position to study the more comprehensive treatment of linear programming in later chapters. It is important to recognize that linear programming is not a subject completely independent of the concepts of incremental cost, contributions, or opportunity costs, but is in fact a sophisticated way to incorporate those concepts in a mathematical form.

The initial step in linear programming is to set up the fundamental equations of the problem. Let us use the same contributions shown in Table 2–1 but this time assume four bottleneck departments rather than one. These departments are the four constraints. The basic data are shown in Table 2–2.

We are now in a position to set up the "objective equation." If the objective is to maximize contribution to overhead and profits from the products, the objective equation is.

$$Z = 5.00X_A + 6.00X_B + 4.00X_C + 4.50X_D + 3.50X_E = \text{maximum}$$

in which

$$
\begin{aligned}
Z &= \text{total contribution} \\
X_A &= \text{output of Product A} \\
X_B &= \text{output of Product B} \\
X_C &= \text{output of Product C} \\
X_D &= \text{output of Product D} \\
X_E &= \text{output of Product E}
\end{aligned}
$$

TABLE 2–2

DATA ON FIVE PRODUCTS TO BE PRODUCED IN FOUR DEPARTMENTS

Product	Contribution per Unit	Machine Hours per Unit Dept.1	Dept.2	Dept.3	Dept.4
A	$5.00	1.00	.50	1.00	.50
B	6.00	1.33	.60	1.00	1.00
C	4.00	.67	.70	1.00	.50
D	4.50	.50	.80	1.00	1.00
E	3.50	.25	.90	1.00	.50

Next we set up equations for each of the constraints—for each of the bottleneck departments. Suppose that the capacities in the four departments are:

$$
\begin{aligned}
&\text{Department 1} \dotfill 18,000 \text{ machine hours} \\
&\text{Department 2} \dotfill 15,000 \\
&\text{Department 3} \dotfill 24,000 \\
&\text{Department 4} \dotfill 20,000
\end{aligned}
$$

The number of hours used up by all products in each department cannot exceed the capacity of that department. This condition can be expressed mathematically in the form of four inequations,

$$
\begin{aligned}
1.00X_A + 1.33X_B + .67X_C + .50X_D + .25X_E &\leq 18,000 \\
.50X_A + .60X_B + .70X_C + .80X_D + .90X_E &\leq 15,000 \\
1.00X_A + 1.00X_B + 1.00X_C + 1.00X_D + 1.00X_E &\leq 24,000 \\
.50X_A + 1.00X_B + .50X_C + 1.00X_D + .50X_E &\leq 20,000
\end{aligned}
$$

Each of these inequations states that the sum of the machine hours used up by the five products must be "less than or equal to" the capacity of each department.

It is not necessary for our purpose here to show how to reach a solution. The task from this point is a mechanical one which can be turned over to a clerk who is familiar with the simplex method, computer programming, or other methods of solving the problem. The point to note here is that the objective equation makes use of the same contribution concept which is applied in other applications of managerial economics. But one cannot maximize the contributions without taking *all* of the constraints into account. Linear programming provides a method of solving such problems when the outputs are interdependent because they use the same capacities.

TIME PERSPECTIVE ON COSTS AND REVENUES

So widely known are the economic concepts of the long run and short run that they have become part of everyday language. The economist uses these terms with a precision that is often missed in ordinary discussion. In the parlance of economics, a decision is *long run* if it involves *possible variations in quantities of all inputs*. Such would be the case in building an entirely new plant. Decisions are *short run* if *quantities of some of the inputs remain fixed while others may be varied*. An illustration is the increase in the output of a department that requires variation in the quantity of labor and materials but not the amount of floor space or the number of machines.

Expressing the distinction between the long run and short run by emphasizing different kinds of decisions is not usual in economic theory. But it fits the purposes of managerial economics; it brings out clearly that there are a variety of short runs according to what is fixed and what is variable. The neat dichotomy between the short and long runs breaks down in actual practice. What remains is an estimate of those costs that will and those that will not be affected by the decision under consideration.

Managerial economists are also concerned with the short-run and long-run effects of decisions on revenues. The line between short-run and long-run revenue (or demand) is even fuzzier than that for costs. The really important problem in decision making is to maintain the right balance between the long-run, short-run, and intermediate-run perspectives. Management should take a long-range view of effects on costs and revenues rather than merely a "shortsighted" view. A decision may be made on the basis of short-run considerations, but may, as time passes, have long-run repercussions that make it more or less profitable than it at first seemed. An illustration may make this clear.

Let us consider a firm with temporary idle capacity. A possible order for 10,000 units comes to management's attention. The prospective customer is willing to pay $2 per unit, or $20,000 for the whole lot, but no more. The short-run incremental cost (which ignores the fixed costs) is only $1.50. Therefore, the contribution to overhead and profit is $ .50 per unit ($5,000 for the lot). But the long-run repercussions of the order must be taken into account:

1. If the management commits itself to a series of repeat orders at the same price, in time the so-called fixed costs may become variable. For example, it eventually will become necessary to replace the machinery. In fact, the gradual accumulation of orders may require an addition to capacity, with added depreciation and top-level supervision.

2. Acceptance of this order might have other kinds of long-run repercussions. If other customers find out about this low price they may demand equal treatment. Such customers may object that they are being treated unfairly and may transfer to suppliers with firmer "ethical" views on pricing. The shading of prices under conditions of excess capacity may undermine the company "image" in the minds of the clientele, giving a picture of a cutthroat competitor rather than that of a stable, dependable supplier.

A decision should take into account both the short-run and long-run effects on revenues and costs, giving appropriate weight to the most relevant time periods. The real problem is determining how to apply this general principle in specific decision-making situations.

Empirical studies and illustrations

Several illustrations should suffice to indicate the rather complex interrelations between the short and long runs on both the cost and demand sides and how such considerations are important in decision making.

Tennessee Valley Authority rate reductions. The Tennessee Valley Authority introduced sharp rate reductions soon after its formation. Table 2–3 presents data on electricity consumption and revenues at a number of locations before and after the rate reductions. As the reader can verify by examining the data, consumption did rise (in fact it rose more than the national average) but the rise in consumption was not sufficient to offset the rate reduction. One might conclude from Table 2–3 that the rate reduction was unprofitable, with the data indicating clearly why the private utilities which preceded the TVA did not reduce rates. A longer-run perspective might, however, lead to quite a different conclusion, for the period covered by the data is too short to allow a full adjustment to the lower rates. It takes time to wire additional homes and to install new appliances. Data for a longer period show a much greater response to the rate reduction and thus contradict the conclusion implied by Table 2–3 (though it is clear that a rapid increase in consumption would have taken place in any case, the national trend being upward; it would be necessary to correct the data for trend to obtain the true response of consumption to rates).

A printing company's refusal to price below full cost. A printing company included in a study made by Haynes maintained a policy of never quoting prices below full cost despite the fact that it frequently experienced idle capacity and that the management was aware that the incremental cost was far below full cost. The management had given considerable thought to the problem and had concluded that the long-run repercussions of going below full cost would more than offset any short-run gain. The reduction in rates for some customers might have an undesirable effect on customer "goodwill," especially among regular customers who might not benefit from the price reductions. Secondly, management argued that the availability of idle capacity was unpredictable and that by the time the order became firm the situation might change, with an interference of low-price orders with regular-price business. The management wished to avoid the "image" of a firm that exploited the market when demand was favorable and that was willing to negotiate prices downward when demand was unfavorable.

It would be difficult to demonstrate that management's reasoning on pricing was correct, but at least the argument is plausible. On the other hand, there was evidence that the management did not always enforce its policy. It admitted that in special cases it regretfully broke away from its policy. And sometimes it performed special services (such as editing manuscripts) without charge, a practice which amounts to a hidden form of price reduction. Despite these reservations, this illustration does point up the need to consider the long-run as well as the short-run impact of price policy.

TABLE 2-3

Average Consumption, Number of Customers, Total Revenue, and Average Revenue per Kilowatt-Hour, before and after Introduction of TVA Rates

A	B	C	D	E	F	G	H	I	J	K	L	M
			Average Consumption per Customer (Kilowatt-Hours)		Number of Customers		Total Consumption (Kilowatt-Hours)		Total Revenue		Average Revenue (Cents per Kilowatt-Hour)	
Contractor	Date TVA Service Began	Months in TVA Rates in Effect at June 30, 1935	Month Prior to TVA	June, 1935	Month Prior to TVA	June, 1935	Month Prior to TVA	June, 1935	Month Prior to TVA	June, 1935	Month Prior to TVA	June, 1935
Tupelo, Mississippi	February 7, 1934	17	49	112	955	1,241	46,398	138,570	$3,436	$2,849	7.4	2.1
Alcorn County Electric Power Association	June 1, 1934	13	49	101	1,180	1,519	58,288	153,880	3,129	3,298	5.4	2.1
Athens, Alabama	June 1, 1934	13	51	112	521	712	26,589	79,667	1,464	1,655	5.5	2.1
Pontotoc County Electric Power Association	June 1, 1934	13	33	71	311	450	10,158	31,985	648	781	6.4	2.4
New Albany, Mississippi	November 12, 1934	7	43	75	539	577	22,896	43,021	1,553	1,028	6.8	2.4
Pulaski, Tennessee	January 4, 1935	6	49	84	477	531	23,581	44,431	1,370	991	5.8	2.2
Dayton, Tennessee	February 1, 1935	5	40	53	451	480	17,995	25,457	1,132	680	6.3	2.7

Source: Tennessee Valley Authority, *Statistical Bulletin No. VII*, December, 1935, as reprinted in M. P. McNair and R. S. Meriam, *Problems in Business Economics* (New York: McGraw-Hill Book Co., 1941), p. 94.

DIMINISHING MARGINAL PRODUCTIVITY AND
EQUIMARGINAL ALLOCATION

One of the most useful principles of economics is the proposition that *a scarce input should be allocated among competing uses in which the input exhibits diminishing marginal productivity in such a way that the value added by the last unit is the same in all uses.* We shall call this generalization the equimarginal principle.

Let us consider a case in which a firm has 100 units of some kind of skilled labor at its disposal. For purposes of simplicity we shall assume this amount to be fixed, so that the total payroll is predetermined. The firm is involved in five activities which require labor services—activities A, B, C, D, and E. It can increase any one of these activities by adding more labor, but only at the sacrifice of other activities.

If we add a unit of labor to activity C, an increase in output results. Let us call the value of this added output due to one more unit of labor the value of the marginal product of labor in activity C. Similarly we can estimate the value of the marginal product in activities A, B, D, and E. It should be clear that if the value of the marginal product is greater in one activity than another, an optimum has not been achieved. It would be possible to shift from low-marginal-value to high-marginal-value uses, thus increasing the total value of all products taken together. If, for example, the value of marginal product of labor in activity A is $10 while that in activity B is $15, it is profitable to increase activity B and reduce activity A.

An elaboration of the equimarginal principle

We need to clarify several aspects of the equimarginal principle. First, we must note that the values of the marginal products in our formula are net of incremental costs (the incremental costs do not include the cost of the input which is being allocated). In activity A we may add one unit of labor, with an increase in physical output of 100 units. Each unit is worth $ .25, so that the 100 units will sell for $25. But the increased production consumes raw materials, fuel, and other inputs, so that the variable costs in activity A (not counting the labor cost) are higher. Let us say that the incremental costs are $15, leaving a net addition of $10. The value of the marginal product which is relevant for our purposes is this $10.

Implicit in the discussion up to this point is diminishing returns to the inputs which are being allocated. This point deserves closer attention. One of the most fundamental of all generalizations in economics is the "law of diminishing returns" (also known as the law of variable proportions). It states that as quantities of variable inputs are added to fixed quantities of other inputs the marginal product eventually declines. To return to our earlier illustration, as more labor is added to activity A, we expect the value of the marginal product of labor to decline, as shown in Figure 2–7.

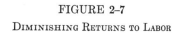

FIGURE 2–7

DIMINISHING RETURNS TO LABOR

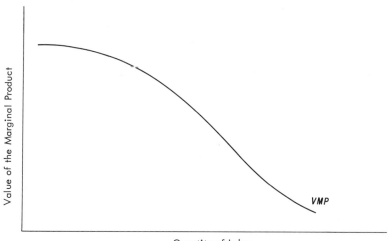

Quantity of Labor

We would expect the law of diminishing returns to apply to the other activities in the same way, though each marginal product curve will have a somewhat different shape depending on technology. Figure 2–8 shows the five marginal product curves simultaneously. Suppose that we allocate 20 units of labor to each activity, as shown in Figure 2–8. Clearly the values of the marginal products are not equal—the value in activity E is much higher than the others. It is profitable to transfer labor to E, away from A and C especially; the resulting addition to the value of E is higher than the necessary reductions in the values of A and C. By reshuffling labor in this way, we can reach an optimum in which the values of the marginal products are equal in all activities. The optimum is shown in Figure 2–9.

Several complications which are often important in practice can receive only passing attention in this introductory chapter. One is that the measurement of the value of the marginal product may have to be corrected if the expansion of an activity requires a reduction in the price of the output. If activity A represents the production of radios, but it is impossible to sell more radios without a reduction in price, it is necessary to adjust for the change in price. Another complication is complementarity of demand, when an increase in the availability of one product stimulates the sales of another. Similarly if products are complementary in produc-

FIGURE 2–8

MARGINAL PRODUCT CURVES FOR FIVE ACTIVITIES

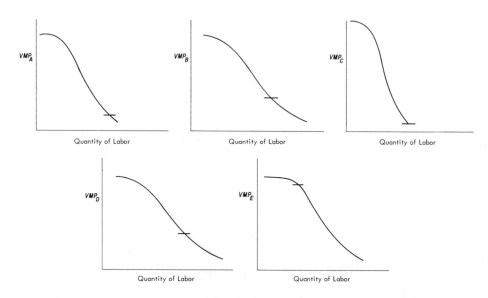

FIGURE 2–9

OPTIMAL ALLOCATION OF LABOR TO FIVE ACTIVITIES

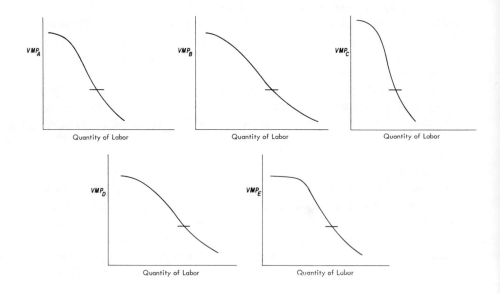

tion a more involved analysis is required. But the equimarginal principle still applies after the necessary adjustments are made.

Constant marginal products

In many cases the law of diminishing returns may not operate exactly as described so far. It may be possible for a firm to increase the quantity of labor in one department without encountering diminishing marginal production until some limit of capacity is reached or until all the labor is employed. The curve for the value of the marginal product is horizontal in such a case up to full capacity at which point it drops to zero. Figure 2–10 represents this situation for five activities.

FIGURE 2–10

CONSTANT MARGINAL PRODUCTS IN FIVE ACTIVITIES

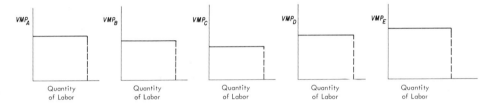

In this case we do not reach the situation in which the values of the marginal products are equal in all activities. Since the value of the marginal product is greatest in activity E, we prefer to use labor there rather than the other activities. Why not shift all of the labor to E? Some constraint, such as a limit of the capacity in E, or limits on other variable inputs required, may set a limit on the amount of labor that can be used in E, so that labor is also allocated to D, then A, and so on until the available labor is exhausted.

In linear programming models there is an implicit assumption that the values of the marginal products are horizontal as shown in Figure 2–10. But in linear programming we would not be allocating labor alone; we would also be allocating other inputs which are required along with labor but which are limited in total supply. For example, we might have a limited amount of floor space to distribute among the five activities, and a limited amount of assembly capacity. Linear programming does not equate the values of the marginal product of labor in the five activities, but does allocate labor and the other inputs to achieve a maximum contribution to profits.

The outcome of the discussion is this. We may retain the equimarginal principle as long as diminishing returns are relevant. But when the values of the marginal products are constant (horizontal), we need an alternative form of the principle, making use of inequalities rather than equalities. This form of the principle would read as follows: *We should apply inputs first to activities with higher marginal product values until these activities reach their limits before moving to lower values.*

Empirical studies and illustrations

The equimarginal principle is an extremely practical idea despite the abstract appearance of the preceding discussion. It is behind any rational budgetary procedure. The objective of budgeting is (or should be) to allocate resources where they are most productive. But it is productivity at the margin rather than average productivity which is relevant. Even when productivity is extremely difficult to measure, the equimarginal principle must be applied in at least a rough or general way if one wishes to avoid waste in useless activities.

One of the clearest cases of the application of the principle is in investment decisions. Whatever criterion is used in making such decisions—whether it is a crude measure like the payback period or a refined measure like the present value—the aim is to separate investments with high rates of return from investments with low returns, so that the funds can be allocated accordingly.

At the opposite extreme is the allocation of research expenditures. The productivity of research is notoriously difficult to measure. One can never tell when research that appears to be highly theoretical and remote from practicality will eventually pay off. Nevertheless, the equimarginal principle is relevant in research. After all, a company does not hire research men indiscriminately. It selects men who promise to make a contribution to the company's line of activity. The company is likely to expand research activities which are beginning to pay off and to contract activities which appear to have passed their peak of usefulness. No doubt mistakes are made in this process, but the failure to make any comparisons of potential productivity can only lead to diffusion of expenditure on nonessentials.

A recent study based on an analysis of research and development in 120 firms suggests that more systematic evaluations of research are possible.[4] While one must not expect pinpoint precision in estimating the worth of alternative lines of research—and in many cases only qualitative estimates are possible—it is nevertheless possible to rank different types of research. Many companies budget research as a given percentage of sales. Others follow a rule of increasing such expenditures by a fixed percentage, but it makes more sense to evaluate each research program individually.

One great enemy of the equimarginal principle is the stress on averages.

---

[4] J. B. Quinn, "How to Evaluate Research Output," *Harvard Business Review,* March-April, 1960, pp. 69–80; and "Long-Range Planning of Industrial Research," *Harvard Business Review,* July-August, 1961, pp. 88–102.

It is irrational, for example, to budget advertising expenditure on the basis of some average percentage of sales. Such a policy would result in lower advertising in poor times than in prosperity, when the opposite practice might be more profitable. There is no reason to suppose that advertising expenditures on one product must hold the same ratio to sales as for another product—the responsiveness may be quite different for one than for another. Similarly, the averaging of budget increases over all departments is unlikely to be consistent with the equimarginal principle. Some departments may actually be due for cutbacks of less essential activities.

Another enemy of the equimarginal principle consists of a variety of sociological pressures. Inertia is one—activities are continued simply because they exist. Empire building is another—activities expand to fulfill the needs of managers for power. Unfortunately, departments which are already overbudgeted often use some of their excess resources to build up propaganda machines (public relations offices) to win additional support.

TIME VALUE OF MONEY—DISCOUNTING

One of the fundamental ideas in economics is that a dollar tomorrow is worth less than a dollar today. This appears similar to the saying that a bird in the hand is worth two in the bush. This analogy might be misleading, implying that the reason for discounting the future dollars is the uncertainty about receiving them. *Even under conditions of certainty it would still be necessary to discount future dollars to make them comparable with present dollars.*

A simple illustration should make clear the necessity of discounting. Suppose you are offered a choice between a gift of \$100 today or \$100 next year. Naturally you will select the \$100 today. This is true, as has been stated, even if there is certainty about the receipt of either gift, since today's \$100 can be invested and can accumulate interest during the year. Let us suppose that you can earn 5 percent interest on any money you have at your disposal. By the end of the year it will accumulate interest to become a total of \$105.

There is another way of putting the matter that brings out the discounting principle more forcefully. We might ask how much money today would be equivalent to \$100 a year from now. Again assume a rate of interest of 5 percent. We discount the \$100 at 5 percent, which means that we divide it by 1.05. Thus:

$$V = \frac{\$100}{1+i} = \frac{\$100}{1.05} = \$95.24$$

where

V = present value
i = the rate of interest

As a cross check for those who are unfamiliar with the discounting principle, we can multiply the $95.24 by 1.05 to determine how much money will have accumulated during the year at 5 percent. The answer is $100.

$$\$95.24 \times 1.05 = \$100$$

This shows that $95.24 plus the interest on $95.24 will accumulate to an amount exactly equal to $100; a person who can earn 5 percent on his money should be indifferent in choosing between the two bundles of money: $100 a year from now or $95.24 today. The present value of $100 is thus $95.24.

The same kind of reasoning applies to longer periods. A sum of $100 two years from now is worth

$$V = \frac{\$100}{(1+i)^2} = \frac{\$100}{(1.05)^2} = \frac{\$100}{1.1025} = \$90.70$$

Again we can check by computing how much the cumulative interest on $90.70 would be after two years.

We can now establish a general formula for the present value of a sum to be received at any future date:

$$V = \frac{R_n}{(1+i)^n}$$

in which

$V =$ present value
$R =$ the amount to be received in the future
$i \ =$ the rate of interest
$n =$ the number of years elapsing before the receipt of R

If the receipts are spread over a period of years, the formula becomes:

$$V = \frac{R_1}{1+i} + \frac{R_2}{(1+i)^2} + \frac{R_3}{(1+i)^3} + \cdots + \frac{R_n}{(1+i)^n}$$

Another form of the same formula is:

$$V = \sum_{k=1}^{n} \frac{R_k}{(1+i)^k}$$

when k can take on any value from 1 through n.

It will be necessary to refer to and elaborate on these formulas, especially in the chapter on investment decisions. For present purposes, however, the need is not so much the memorization of a formula as it is the grasp of a fundamental concept. The main point in this section may be summarized in a principle, which we shall call the discounting principle: *If a decision affects costs and revenues at future dates, it is necessary to discount those costs and revenues to present values before a valid comparison of alternatives is possible.*

Empirical studies and illustrations

The practice of discounting is pervasive and observable in everyday business practice. The simplest case of discounting is that when one borrows on a note at the bank. If the note is for $1,000, the borrower does not receive the full amount but rather that amount discounted at the appropriate rate of interest. If the discount rate is 6 percent and the note for one year, the borrower will receive approximately $942. One might say that the present value to the bank of the borrower's promise to pay $1,000 in a year is only $942 at the time of the loan.

Real estate prices reflect the discounting principle, though in a more complicated and less obvious way. The rational way to determine what one will pay for a piece of property is to estimate the future returns he expects, which may in the case of a home be primarily subjective in character. One will discount those future returns at the opportunity cost of capital to reflect the sacrifice of alternative earnings. The market value of the real estate is determined by the interaction of such discounted present values set on the property by the various potential buyers and sellers. Even such rules of thumb as "an apartment house should sell at ten times annual rentals" are rough approximations of the discounting principle.

The same principle of discounting should apply to the operations of an individual firm, though considerable uncertainty about the future revenues and appropriate discount rates necessarily exists. If a firm is considering buying a new piece of equipment, it should estimate the discounted value of the added earnings from that equipment. If it is considering the purchase of another firm, or a merger, the same principle of valuation applies. And, as we shall see, if it produces outputs that mature at varying ages, it cannot compare the profitability of changing the product mix without invoking the discounting principle.

SOME IMPORTANT APPLICATIONS

This entire volume is devoted to applications of the foregoing analysis to a variety of decisions. It is possible at this point to introduce some elementary but significant applications of the basic concepts: incremental costs, opportunity costs, the long and short runs, discounting, and the equimarginal principle.

Make or buy

Decisions to make or buy are among the most pervasive in industry. The question of purchasing on the outside or producing within the firm requires a direct application of the principles discussed so far, but the issues are complicated by a wide variety of considerations, as we shall see.

The advice that one should make or buy depending on which alternative is cheaper is not very helpful; the term "cheaper" is ambiguous. The costs of making or buying can be measured in a variety of ways: the following are only partial lists of the possible cost measurements.[5]

The Cost to Make	*The Cost to Buy*
1. Labor and materials.	1. The purchase price.
2. Labor, materials, and other variable expenses.	2. Purchase price plus delivery expense.
3. Labor, materials, other variable costs, and factory overhead.	3. Purchase price, delivery expense, plus receiving and handling expense.
4. Labor, materials, other variable costs, factory overhead, and selling expense.	4. Purchase price, delivery expense, receiving and handling expense, plus buying costs.
5. Labor, materials, other variable costs, factory overhead, selling expense, and general overhead.	5. Purchase price, delivery expense, receiving and handling expense, buying costs, plus costs of inspection.

The fact is that some of these measurements are appropriate part of the time and others are needed in different circumstances. The problem is to determine the impact of the decision on costs—the estimation of the incremental costs. Professor Culliton, the leading writer on "make or buy," suggests three alternative methods of determining the impact of the decision: all three are variations on the incremental approach developed in this volume.

Complete budgets. This method projects the costs of the entire firm under the two alternatives. This would reveal the difference in costs, which is, of course, what is required in incremental reasoning. The method is rather cumbersome for decision-making purposes: time can be saved by narrowing attention to the cost areas most likely to be affected by the decision.

Localized budgets. This method restricts attention to the area of the business directly affected by the decision to make or buy. When the analysis within this area is complete, it is possible to adjust for changes in costs in other segments of the business.

Incremental cost method. This method requires estimates of changes in costs brought about by the decision to make or buy. It differs from the other methods in that it begins with estimates of the changes in particular costs, rather than totaling up costs before computing the differences.

Professor Culliton recommends that the analysis concentrate on changes in total costs rather than unit costs. Unit costs require an averaging that often obscures what is happening to the totals and thus confuses the decision maker.

---

[5] James W. Culliton, *Make or Buy* (Cambridge, Massachusetts: Harvard University, Bureau of Business Research, 1942).

The chief source of confusion in the analysis of costs is in the treatment of burden or overhead. In all probability some of the so-called overhead costs will be affected and others unaffected, creating the necessity of determining which fall into the changing or unchanging categories. To increase the complexity of the problem, some costs may be unaffected in the short run but may increase in the long run. For example, a decision to make a part may absorb short-run excess capacity, but if this capacity is needed for other purposes in the future, restriction of attention to the short run is in error. To put the matter in another way, it is necessary to consider the opportunity costs of each alternative, and the opportunity cost of making instead of buying is the absorption of capacity that may in the future be useful for other products.

The argument that a firm should make parts to fill in the excess capacity created by cyclical or seasonal fluctuations in demand is simply a special application of incremental-opportunity cost reasoning. Excess capacity means that the incremental overhead costs of manufacturing are small and that the sacrifices of alternative opportunities are limited. But the effect on supplier goodwill and the resulting difficulties of obtaining supplies in good times must be reckoned with.

Decisions to make or buy should take into account a variety of special considerations which complicate the analysis.

Quality. The firm may be able to achieve greater control over quality by manufacturing the part itself. The result is a reduction in assembly costs or an increase in customer goodwill and future sales which should be a part of a complete incremental analysis. Alternatively, the firm may not require as high a quality as outsiders are supplying and can bring quality and costs into line by manufacturing itself. On the other hand, the specialized knowledge of outside suppliers may exceed that within the firm, so that the firm cannot match the outside quality.

Assurance of supply. The firm may be able to coordinate the flow of parts more effectively by producing at home. Some suppliers are undependable and others are unable to keep up with demand. If the firm has access to several or many suppliers, this argument for making the part becomes less persuasive. In any case the total impact on costs, including the costs of disrupted production, and the total impact on revenue, including the effect of changed customer goodwill, should be estimated.

Defense against monopoly. A firm may manufacture parts to protect itself against a monopoly in supply. A mere threat to manufacture may in some cases suffice to restrain suppliers from overcharging, but threats must be backed up with demonstrations that the firm is competent to do the job.

Summary. Complete incremental reasoning requires the evaluation of a number of subtle considerations that might at first be overlooked: customer goodwill, supplier goodwill, internal know-how, administrative and technical skills, and the risk that the costs of unimportant sidelines in manufacture might not be controlled satisfactorily. Students of the make or buy problem think that there may be a tendency to overlook some of the less measurable advantages of outside supply and to exaggerate the economies of internal manufacture.

Product-line decisions

Most firms produce more than one product. They sometimes face problems of deciding whether to add new products, to drop old products from the product line, to change the relative proportions of products, to farm out part of the production to other firms, and so on. In the discussion at this point we shall deal with the short run, in which capacity is fixed; a longer-run analysis would require a discussion of investment analysis which is postponed to a later chapter. But we must not ignore the longer-run repercussions of the short-run decisions.

The short-run problem itself includes a number of variations. Let us consider first the case in which the firm has excess capacity: its present line of products is not absorbing the capacity. The question is whether to add another product. The first step is to compute the contribution of the new product to overhead and profits. This requires an estimate of the added revenue and of the incremental costs of the product. The normal overhead allocations should be avoided in such estimates; instead the estimates should measure the increase in each cost, direct or indirect, resulting from adding the product. If the contribution, the difference between the added revenue and the incremental cost, is positive, the analysis is favorable to adding the product.

A complete analysis, however, must check for other considerations. For example, the management should not introduce the new product if an even better new product is available. A search for all the available opportunities should precede making the final decision. Another way of expressing this idea is to say that the opportunity costs of alternative uses of the excess capacity must be estimated. Another factor is the possible impact of the new product on the products already produced. In some cases it may complement or "round out" the product line, increasing the sales of the other products. In such a case the contribution to overhead and profits of the new product is greater than the direct contribution of the product itself. In other cases the product may compete with items in the present line, so that the initial contribution estimates must be adjusted downward. Such adjustments in estimates should recognize both immediate and longer-run impacts of the new product. If, for example, the excess capacity is temporary, management must face the question of whether the new product can be abandoned when the demand for the other products recovers, or whether an expansion of facilities will be justified. Often it may be preferable to accept temporary excess capacity rather than to create production bottlenecks when the excess disappears. In addition, management must determine whether it has the know-how to produce and distribute the product.

If the situation is one of full use of capacity the analysis becomes even more complex. In this case management must not only determine the contribution of each product (and of products that might be introduced into the product mix) but must also determine how much the opportunity cost of increasing the output is in terms of the reduction of the contributions of the other products. This is exactly the kind of estimate made in the simplex method of linear programming, as we have already seen. The linear programming method of determining which products belong "in the solution" assumed limited capacity and makes use of both contribution estimates and estimates of opportunity costs. A management which does not use linear programming must nevertheless run through estimates analogous to those in the simplex method if it is going to approximate an optimal use of its resources.

Now we come to an even more complex situation: allocation of resources to a variety of slowly maturing products. An example would be a garden nursery with a fixed acreage of land and a wide variety of planting opportunities. Such a nursery faces the problem of determining which plants to propagate and grow, what ages to assume in such choices, what future prices should be assumed, as well as what prices to charge now on plants which are already mature. In addition, the nursery must determine when to mark down prices on plants tying up land needed for other uses, and when to destroy plant materials that are in the way. The solution to such a problem requires an estimate of the contributions of the various plants over time, which requires in turn estimates of revenues and incremental costs. It also requires the discounting of future revenues, costs, and contributions to arrive at the present value of such contributions at the time decisions on the use of the land are to be made. Estimates of the present value of the contribution for all plants on an acre basis would provide a basis for rational decisions. These estimates would make it possible to compare the contribution from rapidly maturing plants with those from slowly maturing plants.

Such complex models for decision making are open to the criticism that they are "impractical"; most managers do not have the data or the knowledge to apply the models. The trend, however, is toward a more systematic analysis of product mix problems. And even in firms where decisions continue to be qualitative and subjective, it can do management no harm to think through the logic required for rational decisions on which products to expand, which to contract, and which to abandon.

Other applications

The principles in this chapter apply to many other decisions, some of which we shall view briefly.

Decisions on allocation of space in a retail store.   The correct procedure would measure the contributions to overhead and profit above incremental cost for each commodity. The analysis is complicated by the fact that the space is not homogeneous; the space where the traffic flows is more valuable than space in remote parts of the store. The turnover of each product depends not only on its price but also upon its location.

Decision on advertising expenditures. While many firms have applied simple rules of thumb in their advertising expenditures, more refined techniques reflecting economic reasoning are coming into use. It does not make sense to budget advertising as a percentage of sales or on the level of the rival's expenditures. What is needed is a measure of responsiveness of sales to advertising along with measures of the added cost of production of a larger volume.

Figure 2–11 shows how sales and profits might respond to increased advertising outlays. This diagram assumes diminishing returns to adver-

FIGURE 2–11

RELATIONSHIP OF REVENUE AND PROFITS TO ADVERTISING OUTLAYS

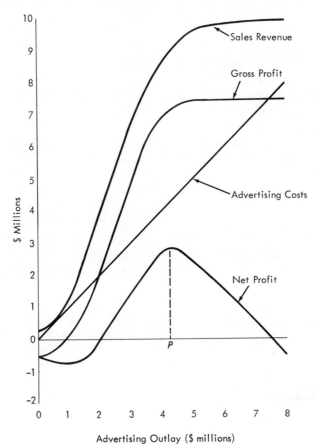

Advertising Outlay ($ millions)

tising—a reasonable assumption. The problem of measurement is extremely difficult in this case. Advertising has effects spread out over time. Competitors may change their advertising. Consumer tastes may change independently of the advertising. Research techniques are being developed which may overcome some of these problems.[6] But even in the absence of exact measurements, it is clear that the principles outlined in this chapter provide a more flexible and rational basis for determining advertising expenditures than do the usual rules of thumb.

PROBLEMS FOR CHAPTER 2

1. A manufacturing company is considering expanding production by 50 units.
   a. The revenue and costs involved are

Revenue	.... $2,500	Materials	.... $ 750
Labor	.... $1,500	Miscellaneous	.... $ 950

   The manager is also told that a third of the labor costs is already being spent on employing idle workers. Using incremental reasoning, should the firm expand?
   b. Show the same thing using marginal analysis. Assume constant marginal cost and marginal revenue.
   c. Assume it is learned that the MC is not constant but changes according to the following graph.

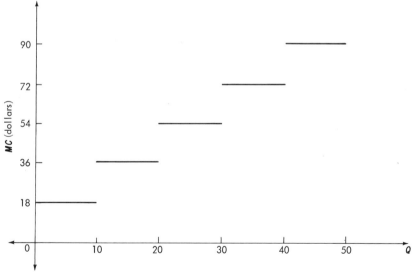

Will the firm expand and how much? Assume constant MR.

---

[6] R. J. Jessen, "A Switch Over Experimental Design to Measure Advertising Effect," reprinted in R. E. Frank, A. E. Kuehn, and W. F. Massey, *Quantitative Techniques in Marketing Analysis* (Homewood, Illinois: Richard D. Irwin, Inc., 1962), pp. 190–230.

d. Assume the market price of each unit of Q rises by $5. What is the best level of output?

2. A firm is using laborer A to produce product X, and laborer B to produce product Y. The expenses and revenues associated with these products are

X		Y	
Revenue	$1,500	Revenue	$1,000
Wages	$ 400	Wages	$ 300
Material	$ 100	Material	$ 400
Electricity	$ 50	Electricity	$ 100

The firm is considering using both laborers to produce product Z with the following revenue and costs. Assume these two laborers are the only ones available and capable of producing X, Y, or Z.

Revenue, $2,000

Cost associated with A		with B	
Wages	$400	Wages	$300
Material	$300	Material	$350
Electricity	$100	Electricity	$200
Total Costs	$800	Total Costs	$850

What is the economic profit in moving to produce Z?

3. A firm can use a limited supply of input I to produce any of the five products below.

Product	Price/Unit	*Incremental* Cost/Unit	Quantity of I/Unit
A	30	10	5
B	40	30	5
C	20	15	5
D	10	5	5
E	20	5	5

a. Determine the best product for production.

b. Assume the quantity of I required per unit of product is 5, 10, 5, 2.5, and 2.5, respectively. What is the best product?

c. Assume we have a limited amount of two resources I and II with the following per-unit requirements.

Product	Quantity of I per Unit	Quantity of II per Unit
A	5	10
B	10	2
C	5	2.5
D	2.5	10
E	2.5	10

Set up the objective equation and the corresponding restraints assuming a maximum of 30 units of I and 100 units of II.

d. Under the conditions of C determine the best single product and then determine the optimum product mix.

4. A firm producing machinery has a two-year lease on its plant at $10,000 a year and a six-month lease on its trucks at $100 a month. Each month the firm produces 40 machines, each one selling for $100. Its labor, electrical, and raw material costs per month are $100, $20 and $80 respectively. What are its fixed costs, variable costs per unit of output, and contribution per unit of output over the next three years?

5. A firm can produce three products using a limited resource X. Each product has a constant price, and the resource X is limited to 100 units.
Given the following information, what products and how much of each does the firm produce?

Product	Production	Limit	Prod. Price	Incremental Cost/X
A	$Q_A = 5X$	$Q_A \leq 600$	$10	$ 5
B	$Q_B = 15X$	$Q_B \leq 60$	$15	$ 50
C	$Q_C = 10X$	$Q_C \leq 160$	$40	$150

6. What is the present value of $1,000 received two years from now?
   a. Assume the discount rate is 5 percent.
   b. Assume the discount rate is 10 percent.
   c. Assume the gift is five years away instead of two years.

Cases for part one

THE CASE METHOD

The case method provides the most convenient way of acquiring skill in applying managerial economics short of actual decision making itself. Cases reveal the complexity of the environment in which decisions are made. Cases force the student to leave the ivory tower of abstract theory, to face up to the uncertainties of the "real world," and to make the simplifications required to create order out of the multitude of facts faced by management.

Many readers of this book will be unfamiliar with the case method. The best way to learn this method is to use it, but a few introductory comments may be helpful. The case method requires the development of an orderly analysis of the given situation. It involves the evaluation of facts, the organization of such facts into meaningful patterns, the separation of important facts from unimportant or irrelevant information, the formulation of alternative courses of action, the evaluation of those alternatives in terms of the facts and the goals of the undertaking, and final choice of a solution.

Procedure in analyzing a case

The steps in analyzing a case may vary from one student to another and from one case to another. It would be wrong to claim that only one procedure is appropriate. The following outline of steps should be taken merely as suggestive of one way of going about the analysis.

Definition of the central issue or issues. *A case may contain a variety of issues from the trivial to the significant. The analyst should focus on the key problems.*

Organization of the evidence. *When the analyst has determined what he considers to be the central issue or issues, he can then proceed to organize the facts around topics related to those issues. This requires the separation of the unimportant from the significant and the irrelevant from the relevant. Often it is necessary to organize the facts in a new form: in the form of a break-even chart or flow of funds statement, for example. The construction of charts and tables that clarify the situation requires imagination; it is one of the chief tools of orderly decision-making.*

Determination of the alternatives. *In some cases the alternatives are clear; in others the analyst must invent alternatives appropriate to the situation. The analyst cannot remain content with predetermined alternatives; he must strive for new and better solutions.*

Evaluation of the alternatives. *One of the best ways to organize the facts in a case is to relate them to the alternatives. Some facts become arguments in favor of or against an alternative; some of them suggest the probable consequences of choosing one alternative over another.*

It is necessary, finally, to appraise each alternative—to weigh its strengths and weaknesses. Weak alternatives are discarded in favor of strong ones.

The decision. *The manager must not evade making a final choice of the alternative which seems best to him. He must be decisive. He should be aware of the limitations as well as strengths of his choice, and he should beware of overstating his case. But the manager must decide, for inaction itself involves a choice.*

The case method applied in managerial economics

The cases in a managerial economics book have a special character; they are not the same as cases in accounting, finance, or policy. The cases are intended to provide an opportunity to apply the concepts of economics to the problems of management. Rather than being "representative" of all managerial decisions, they are chosen from those areas of management most amenable to economic analysis.

Nevertheless, these cases should be approached in the same way as other policy cases. The initial effort should go into determining the problems or issues, with secondary regard to whether or not these are economic problems. Some students make the mistake of organizing their case analysis around economic concepts instead of using the concepts as tools where appropriate in the analysis of the case. The objective is not to find out whether the case is one in opportunity costs or demand elasticities or valuation, but rather to determine the issues and then use whatever analysis is appropriate. Some of the cases, however, are intended as simple exercises in the use of economic analysis.

Almost all of the cases in this book are based on actual situations; a few are synthesized from the experience of several firms. Obviously none of the cases supplies "all of the facts." Management never has all the facts, though management is in a better position than is the student to search for answers to questions that arise during the decision-making process. Trying to make sense out of a situation without full knowledge may be frustrating, but it is part of the essence of management.

Normally there is no single "correct" solution to a case. Two managers of equal ability might select different alternatives; it is often difficult to say that one alternative is better than the other. It is possible to say, however, that some case analyses and some recommendations are superior to others. The criteria for making this determination are as follows:

1. *The extent to which the analysis and solution show an understanding of the real issues involved*
2. *The extent to which the analysis is based on the particular facts in the situation*
3. *The degree to which the solution appears to be workable under the circumstances*
4. *The extent to which the analyst is able to support his position*

This chapter consists of elementary cases. The fundamental concepts discussed in Chapter 2 should be helpful in making decisions in these cases. The objective should be to size up each situation, to organize and analyze the facts, to evaluate the alternatives, and to reach a solution— and to use economic concepts when they are helpful.

WHAT PRICE PROGRESS*

EFFICIENCY EXPERT: Joe, you said you put in these peanuts because some people ask for them, but do you realize what this rack of peanuts is *costing* you?

JOE: It ain't gonna cost. 'Sgonna be a profit. Sure, I hadda pay $25 for a fancy rack to holda bags, but the peanuts cost 6 cents a bag and I sell 'em for 10 cents. Figger I sell 50 bags a week to start. It'll take 12½ weeks to cover the cost of the rack. After that I gotta clear profit of 4 cents a bag. The more I sell, the more I make.

EFFICIENCY EXPERT: That is an antiquated and completely unrealistic approach, Joe. Fortunately, modern accounting procedures permit a more accurate picture which reveals the complexities involved.

JOE: Huh?

EFFICIENCY EXPERT: To be precise, those peanuts must be integrated into your entire operation and be allocated their appropriate share of business overhead. They must share a proportionate part of your expenditures for rent,

---

* Reprinted from *Lybrand Journal* (Lybrand Ross Brothers & Montgomery) whose editors note: "We have been unable to locate the source of this paper. If any of our readers can provide us with this information, we shall be delighted to acknowledge our indebtedness."

heat, light, equipment depreciation, decorating, salaries for your waitresses, cook . . .

JOE: The *cook?* What's he gotta do wit'a peanuts? He don' even know I got 'em!

EFFICIENCY EXPERT: Look Joe, the cook is in the kitchen, the kitchen prepares the food, the food is what brings people in here, and the people ask to buy peanuts. *That's* why you must charge a portion of the cook's wages, as well as a part of your own salary to peanut sales. This sheet contains a carefully calculated cost analysis which indicates the peanut operation should pay exactly $1,278 per year toward these general overhead costs.

JOE: The peanuts? $1,278 a year for overhead? The nuts?

EFFICIENCY EXPERT: It's really a little more than that. You also spend money each week to have the windows washed, to have the place swept out in the mornings, keep soap in the washroom and provide free cokes to the police. That raises the total to $1,313 per year.

JOE: (*Thoughtfully*) But the peanut salesman said I'd make money . . . put 'em on the end of the counter, he said . . . and get 4 cents a bag profit . . .

EFFICIENCY EXPERT: (*With a sniff*) He's not an accountant. Do you actually know what the portion of the counter occupied by the peanut rack is worth to you?

JOE: Ain't worth nothing . . . no stool there . . . just a dead spot at the end.

EFFICIENCY EXPERT: The modern cost picture permits no dead spots. Your counter contains 60 square feet and your counter business grosses $15,000 a year. Consequently, the square foot of space occupied by the peanut rack is worth $250 per year. Since you have taken that area away from general counter use, you must charge the value of the space to the occupant.

JOE: You mean I gotta add *$250 a year more* to the *peanuts?*

EFFICIENCY EXPERT: Right. That raises their share of the general operating costs to a grand total of $1,563 per year. Now then, if you sell 50 bags of peanuts per week, these allocated costs will amount to 60 cents per bag.

JOE: *What?*

EFFICIENCY EXPERT: Obviously, to that must be added your purchase price of 6 cents per bag, which brings the total to 66 cents. So you see by selling peanuts at 10 cents per bag, you are losing 56 cents on every sale.

JOE: Somethin's crazy!

EFFICIENCY EXPERT: Not at all! Here are the *figures.* They *prove* your peanuts operation cannot stand on its own feet.

JOE: (*Brightening*) Suppose I sell *lotsa* peanuts . . . thousand bags a week 'stead of 50.

EFFICIENCY EXPERT: (*Tolerantly*) Joe, you don't understand the problem. If the volume of peanuts sales increases, our operating costs will go up . . . you'll have to handle more bags with more time, more depreciation, more everything. The basic principle of accounting is firm on that subject: "The Bigger the Operation the More General Overhead Costs that must be Allocated." No, increasing the volume of sales won't help.

JOE: Okay, You so smart, *you* tell *me* what I gotta do.

EFFICIENCY EXPERT: (*Condescendingly*) Well . . . you could first reduce operating expenses.

JOE: How?

EFFICIENCY EXPERT: Move to a building with cheaper rent. Cut salaries. Wash the windows biweekly. Have the floor swept only on Thursday. Remove the soap from the washrooms. Decrease the square foot value of your counter. For example, if you can cut your expenses 50 percent, that will reduce the amount allocated to peanuts from $1,563 to $781.50 per year, reducing the cost to 36 cents per bag.

JOE: (*Slowly*) That's better?

EFFICIENCY EXPERT: Much, much better. However, even then you would lose 26 cents per bag if you only charge 10 cents. Therefore, you must also raise your selling price. If you want a net profit of 4 cents per bag you would have to charge 40 cents.

JOE: (*Flabbergasted*) You mean even after I cut operating costs 50 percent I still gotta charge 40 cents for a 10 cents bag of peanuts? Nobody's that nuts about nuts? Who'd buy 'em?

EFFICIENCY EXPERT: That's a secondary consideration. The point is, at 40 cents you'd be selling at a price based upon a true and proper evaluation of your then reduced costs.

JOE: (*Eagerly*) Look! I gotta better idea. Why don't I just throw the nuts out . . . put 'em in a ash can?

EFFICIENCY EXPERT: Can you afford it?

JOE: Sure. All I got is about 50 bags of peanuts . . . cost about three bucks . . . so I lose $25 on the rack, but I'm outa this nutsy business and no more grief.

EFFICIENCY EXPERT: (*Shaking head*) Joe it isn't that simple. You are *in* the peanut business! The minute you throw those peanuts out you are adding $1,563 of annual overhead to the rest of your operation. Joe . . . be realistic . . . *can you afford to do that?*

JOE: (*Completely crushed*) It'sa unbelievable! Last week I was a make money. Now I'm in a trouble . . . just because I think peanuts on a counter is a gonna bring me some extra profit . . . just because I believe 50 bags of peanuts a week is a easy.

EFFICIENCY EXPERT: (*With raised eyebrow*) That is the object of modern cost studies, Joe . . . to dispel those false illusions.

1. *What is incremental cost per bag of peanuts?*
2. *What is the weekly contribution of the peanut rack?*
3. *How would the case be changed if there were an alternate use for the space, such as a chewing gum display?*
4. *Does management need full cost including allocated overhead for some purposes, or can all management decisions be based on contributions above incremental cost?*
5. *Comment on the efficiency expert's principle that "the bigger the operation the more general overhead costs that must be allocated." Are there better criteria for allocating overhead costs?*

NEWVILLE BRANCH OF AJAX CLEANERS (REVISED)*

Mr. B. Fraley was manager of the Newville branch of the Ajax Cleaners. In this position he had considerable autonomy in making decisions affecting the branch. The central office of the company developed the accounting reports for each branch and occasionally made suggestions to the individual managers.

In June 1961 the ratio of wages and salaries of the Newville branch to sales was 46 percent. The company suggested that as a rule of thumb this ratio should never exceed 33⅓ percent. The president of the company recommended that Mr. Fraley discontinue the shirt laundry service, a minor adjunct to the dry cleaning business, in order to bring labor costs into line.

Mr. Fraley made an estimate of costs and revenues resulting from the shirt laundry in June. He accumulated data on labor costs and supplies. (He consulted Mr. Frederick, an accountant friend, who suggested the basis for allocating overhead. Exhibit 1 shows the estimate of overhead costs and direct costs for the shirt laundry department.) The result showed a small loss on the shirt laundry as follows:

Revenue	$740
Full cost	745
Loss	$ 5

EXHIBIT 1

COST COMPUTATIONS ON THE LAUNDRY—JUNE 1961
(including overhead allocation bases)

Manager's salary—Average time spent in the department	$155
Advertising—Sales	22
Telephone—Sales	16
Heat, light, power—Ratio of departmental heat, light, power costs	5
Employer's payroll tax—Ratio of departmental salary costs	9
Rent—Floor space	16
Amortization—Floor space	23
Insurance—Sales	24
	$270

Add direct costs

Salaries	$200	
Supplies	140	
Heat, light, power	25	
Payroll tax	10	
Depreciation	100	
		475
Total cost		$745

* This case was prepared by W. W. Haynes of the Harvard Business School and J. L. Gibson of the University of Kentucky as a basis for class discussion. All names and locations have been disguised. The case is a by-product of research for the Small Business Administration, which agency is in no way responsible for the discussion. The case was revised by W. R. Henry in 1973.

Mr. Frederick was not certain that the full cost figure was the appropriate one for Mr. Fraley's problem. He had been reading some articles on "incremental income accounting" and suggested that a variation on that approach might be helpful in clarifying the problem at hand and future decision-making issues. Obviously such an approach would have to be kept extremely simple and inexpensive to deal with Mr. Fraley's small operations.

The steps in establishing a system of incremental income accounting are as follows:

1. Segmentation of the business. Mr. Fraley's business might be broken into two segments—dry cleaning and shirt laundry.

2. Segregation of costs between fixed and variable costs. This would require that Mr. Fraley make qualitative judgments as to which costs were fixed and which were variable. A more elaborate statistical approach for segregating costs would be too expensive.

3. Separation of the fixed costs into assigned fixed costs and unassigned fixed costs. The assigned fixed costs would be those which were fixed for short-period fluctuations in activity but which were avoidable if the segment were permanently discontinued. Examples would be depreciation on specialized equipment and salaries of supervisors in the particular segment. The unassigned fixed costs would be those which did not vary with output and which could not be avoided by discontinuance of the segment.

The result of such an analysis would be a chart of accounts which would appear as in Exhibit 2. Such a system of accounts would break the data into four categories: revenue, variable costs, assigned fixed costs, and unassigned fixed costs. Mr. Fraley could easily prepare this report once the system had been established. The report indicated the "contribution" each segment was making to assigned and unassigned fixed costs and to profits.

Some particular expenses might overlap several categories, requiring an allocation. For example, heat, light and power would fall into both the variable cost and unassigned fixed cost categories. Mr. Fraley would have to determine which labor costs would in fact vary with output, which would be fixed as long as the segment was maintained, and which would be attributable only to the total operation. One danger of such a system is that it might not reflect the fact that a cost which had been variable had become fixed, or vice versa.

Mr. Frederick offered to assist Mr. Fraley without charge in preparing a report for June 1961 based on such a system of accounts because of his interest in the accounting problem it presented. The result is shown in Exhibit 3.

Mr. Fraley was then faced with consideration of both the full cost report and the incremental income report in making his decision about

EXHIBIT 2

CHART OF ACCOUNTS
MARGINAL INCOME ANALYSIS

Laundry	*Dry Cleaning*
1. Sales revenue	1. Sales revenue
2. Variable costs	2. Variable costs
a. Salaries	*a.* Salaries
b. Supplies	*b.* Supplies
c. Heat, light, power	*c.* Heat, light, power
d. Employer's payroll tax	*d.* Employer's payroll tax
e. Repair and maintenance	*e.* Repair and maintenance
f. Clothes lost and repaired	*f.* Clothes lost and repaired
3. Assigned fixed costs	3. Assigned fixed costs
a. Depreciation of equipment	*a.* Depreciation of equipment

4. Unassigned fixed costs
   a. Salaries
   b. Advertising
   c. Repairs and maintenance of plant
   d. Taxes
   e. Telephone
   f. Heat, light, power
   g. Employer's payroll tax
   h. Rent
   i. Depreciation of building, fixtures
   j. Amortization of leasehold improvements
   k. Insurance

EXHIBIT 3

MARGINAL INCOME ANALYSIS REPORT FOR JUNE 1961

	Dry Cleaning		Laundry	
Sales		$2,800		$740
Variable costs:				
Salaries	$ 790		$200	
Supplies	760		140	
Heat, light, power	150		25	
Employer's payroll tax	43	1,743	10	375
Contribution to assigned and unassigned fixed cost		$1,057		$365
Depreciation		200		100
Contribution to unassigned fixed cost	$1,122	$ 857		$265
Unassigned fixed costs:				
Salaries	$650			
Advertising	88			
Telephone	66			
Heat, light, power	35			
Employer's payroll tax	36			
Rent	100			
Depreciation	183			
Amortization	140			
Insurance	95	1,393		
Net loss for the period		$ 271		

abandonment of the shirt laundry. Exhibit **4** presents a summary of the income statement for the entire operation in June.

EXHIBIT 4
NET INCOME STATEMENT FOR JUNE 1961

Sales		$3,540
Salaries	$1,640	
Supplies	900	
Heat, light, power	210	
Employer's payroll tax	89	
Advertising	88	
Telephone	66	
Rent	100	
Depreciation	483	
Amortization of leasehold improvements	140	
Insurance	95	
Total expenses		$3,811
Net Loss		($ 271)

1. *Was the rule of thumb helpful? Why or why not?*
2. *Was the full cost estimate helpful? Why or why not?*
3. *Did the incremental income analysis help in making the decision? Why or why not?*
4. *What is accomplished by separating fixed costs from variable costs? What is gained by separating assigned from unassigned fixed costs?*
5. *Are the allocation bases in Exhibit 1 reasonable? Do they contribute to decision making in this firm?*
6. *Which is relevant in this case: the contribution to the unassigned fixed cost or the contribution to the assigned and unassigned fixed cost? Explain.*
7. *What is the relation between the variable costs in this case and the incremental cost concept? What is the relation of assigned fixed cost to the concept of time perspective?*
8. *What considerations result from viewing laundry sales in the light of longer time perspective?*
9. *What considerations result from thinking about possible effect on dry cleaning sales of closing the laundry?*
10. *What decision was correct on the shirt laundry business?*

ATHERTON COMPANY*

Early in January 1956 the sales manager and controller of the Atherton Company met for the purpose of preparing a joint pricing recommendation for Item 345. After the president approved their recommendation, the price would be announced in letters to retail customers. In accordance with company and industry practice, announced prices were adhered to for the year unless radical changes in market conditions occurred.

The Atherton Company was the largest company in its segment of the textile industry; its 1955 sales had exceeded $6 million. Company salesmen were on a straight salary basis, and each salesman sold the full line. Most of the Atherton competitors were small. Usually they waited for the Atherton Company to announce prices before mailing out their own price lists.

Item 345, an expensive yet competitive fabric, was the sole product of a department whose facilities could not be utilized on other items in the product line. In January 1954 the Atherton Company had raised its price from $1.50 to $2 per yard. This had been done to bring the profit per yard on Item 345 up to that of other products in the line. Although the company was in a strong position financially, considerable capital would be required in the next few years to finance a recently approved long-term modernization and expansion program. The 1954 pricing decision had been one of several changes advocated by the directors in an attempt to strengthen the company's working capital position so as to ensure that adequate funds would be available for this program.

Competitors of the Atherton Company had held their prices on products similar to Item 345 at $1.50 during 1954 and 1955. The industry and Atherton Company volume for Item 345 for the years 1950 to 1955, as estimated by the sales manager, is shown in Exhibit 1. As shown by this exhibit, the Atherton Company had lost a significant portion of its former market position. In the sales manager's opinion, a reasonable forecast of industry volume for 1956 was 700,000 yards. He was certain that the company could sell 25 percent of the 1956 industry total if the $1.50 price was adopted. He feared a further volume decline if the competitive price was not met. As many consumers were convinced of the superiority of the Atherton product, the sales manager reasoned that sales of Item

EXHIBIT 1

ATHERTON COMPANY
(prices and production, 1950–55, Item 345)

Year	Physical Volume of Production (Yards)		Price Charged by Most Competitors	Atherton Company Price
	Industry Total	Atherton Item 345		
1950	610,000	213,000 35 %	$2.00	$2.00
1951	575,000	200,000 35 %	2.00	2.00
1952	430,000	150,000 35 %	1.50	1.50
1953	475,000	165,000 35 %	1.50	1.50
1954	500,000	150,000 30 %	1.50	2.00
1955	625,000	125,000 20 %	1.50	2.00
1956	700,000	175,000 25 %		1.50

345 would probably not fall below 75,000 yards, even at a $2 price.

During the pricing discussions, the controller and sales manager had considered two other aspects of the problem. The controller was concerned about the possibility that competitors would reduce their prices below $1.50 if the Atherton Company announced a $1.50 price for Item 345. The sales manager was confident that competitors would not go below $1.50 because they all had higher costs and several of them were in tight financial straits.

The controller prepared estimated costs of Item 345 at various volumes of production (Exhibit 2). These estimated costs reflected current labor and material costs. They were based on past experience except for the estimates of 75,000 and 100,000 yards. The company had produced more than 100,000 yards in each year since World War II, and prewar experience was not applicable due to equipment changes and increases in labor productivity.

EXHIBIT 2

ATHERTON COMPANY

(estimated cost per yard of Item 345 at various volumes of production)

	75,000	100,000	125,000	150,000	175,000	200,000
Direct labor	$ .400	$ .390	$ .380	$ .370	$ .380	$ .400
Material	.200	.200	.200	.200	.200	.200
Material spoilage	.020	.020	.019	.019	.019	.020
Department expense:						
Direct*	.060	.056	.050	.050	.050	.050
Indirect†	.400	.300	.240	.200	.180	.150
General overhead‡	.120	.117	.114	.111	.114	.120
Factory cost	$1.200	$1.083	$1.003	$ .950	$ .943	$ .940
Selling and adminis- trative expense§	.780	.704	.652	.618	.613	.611
	$1.980	$1.787	$1.655	$1.568	$1.556	$1.551

* Indirect labor, supplies, repairs, power, etc.

† Depreciation, supervision, etc.

‡ 30 percent of direct labor.

§ 65 percent of factory cost.

1. *How, if at all, did the company's financial condition relate to the pricing decision?*
2. *Which price, $1.50 or $2, should have been recommended?*

FINCH PRINTING COMPANY

In December 1954 William Welch agreed to become a director of the Finch Printing Company, located in an eastern city with a population of over 300,000. He was a cousin of three majority stockholders in the company—Miss Mabel Finch, the company vice president, and her sister and brother, both of whom were inactive. He understood that one of his responsibilities was to represent the interests of these stockholders.

Background

The Finch Printing Company was founded in 1901 by Jacob Finch, father of the three major stockholders just mentioned. The company engaged in job printing of a high quality. The company had a city-wide reputation for fine workmanship, dependability, and strong managerial ethics. The firm did considerable printing for religious organizations, but its main customers were commercial firms. It printed several journals or trade magazines with a wide geographical circulation, but most of its business was local. The firm never reached a large size; maximum employment was 50.

Jacob Finch maintained several policies which undoubtedly limited the profits of the firm. He refused to do any printing for liquor firms even though opportunities to print for them were numerous. He tried to maintain employment for most of his employees during the depression of the 1930s despite the low level of business, a fact that weakened the financial structure of the company in that period.

Upon Jacob Finch's death in 1941, his daughter, Mabel Finch, took over the management of the company as president. It was not her intention to remain in that position, but she was unable to find a successor until 1953. The company was not particularly profitable during her presidency, despite the general improvement in business activity during World War II and the years that followed. Wartime restrictions limited the ability of the company to make profits.

In October 1953 Miss Finch succeeded in employing a new president, Mr. Arthur Yount, who was thoroughly familiar with the printing industry. Mr. Yount received a salary and was to share in the company profits on a prearranged basis. One of Mr. Yount's first acts was to sign a contract with a correspondence school, resulting in a 40 to 50 percent increase in sales (see Exhibit 1).

In 1954, when William Welch became a director, the firm was still located in an antiquated four-story building not entirely suited to modern printing techniques. The building had been largely written off; most of the balance sheet item "Building and building improvements" represented land and a new elevator installed in conformance with safety requirements. The building was located near the center of the city and undoubtedly was worth over $40,000 because of that location.

Developments in 1954, 1955, and 1956

In spite of the improvement in profits from 1953 to 1954 (see Exhibit 1), the company prospects did not appear favorable to Mr. Welch. He found that a serious difference had arisen between Mr. Yount, the president, and the vice president, Miss Finch. Miss Finch believed that Mr. Yount was not living up to certain agreements made orally when he was employed and that he was not carrying out some of the long-standing policies of the firm. Furthermore, she believed that he was limiting her authority to much narrower confines than was originally intended. Mr. Yount apparently believed that Miss Finch was interfering with his management of the business and that she was cutting across organizational channels. There was evidence of the formation of factions at lower levels in the firm.

The board of directors met once a month. In 1955 and 1956 it consisted of five members: Mr. Yount (the president), Mr. Welch, two members who represented the Bettsville Industrial Foundation which held mortgage bonds in the company, and Mr. Oswald (a minority stockholder). Miss Finch preferred not to hold a position as a director, but she attended meetings as secretary of the board. The majority of the directors appeared to be satisfied with the new presidency, partly because of the improved profit position which offered greater protection to the creditors.

The approximate division of the common stock in the company was as follows:

Mabel Finch	25%
Her sister	18
Her brother	17
Mr. Yount	10
Mr. Oswald	20
Others	10

The company had paid no dividends to the stockholders for over ten years up to late 1955, when the board voted a dividend of $1 per share. Mr. Welch had at first favored a larger dividend but was convinced that this would be unwise after examining a cash budget for the near future. The payments due on the mortgage, the accrued taxes, and the bonus due the president, and other obligations seemed to preclude a larger dividend at that time.

Miss Finch had always worked at a low salary, both as president and vice president. In 1956 the board approved an increase in her salary from $3,500 to $5,000. She had felt an obligation to her family to keep her father's business going. She also felt the same responsibility to the company employees that her father had exhibited in earlier years.

The situation in 1956

Mr. Welch became increasingly concerned with the company's situation as the years passed. The profit position deteriorated after 1954. The company appeared to be too dependent on a single customer, the correspondence school, and sales to that customer showed evidence of declining in 1956 (see Exhibit 1, p. 62). The tension between the president and vice president continued, and disharmony spread through the company. For example, the plant superintendent spoke rudely to Miss Finch and refused to let her "interfere" in his department even when it seemed necessary to her to check on the progress of some orders for which she was responsible. Several employees resigned, including one who showed considerable promise as a manager.

Mr. Welch was concerned about several risks facing the company: the risk of losing the correspondence business, with a resultant loss of profits; the risk of declines in "other sales"; the risk of the president's resignation with a probable loss of the correspondence business; and the risk that the internal friction would result in greater inefficiency and higher costs. Mr. Welch believed that most of the stockholders had long before assumed that their stock was almost worthless, and there was a possibility that Mr. Yount (who owned about 10 percent of the stock) might eventually be able to buy up a majority interest at low prices.

Several alternatives occurred to Mr. Welch as he thought about the problems of the company:

1. The company might lower prices to get fuller use of its idle capacity and labor force. Mr. Welch suspected that a high proportion of the costs were fixed, especially wage costs. Printing firms did not normally hire and fire printers as business increased and decreased; they found it necessary to maintain the work force during the lulls, with resultant idle labor during a substantial part of the year.

2. The company might raise prices to improve its margins, though Mr. Welch noted that there were at least 50 competitors in the city, some of which might win customers away if prices were raised.

3. The company might invest in improved equipment in order to cut costs. Mr. Welch knew little about printing equipment. The only proposal for new equipment that he could recall during his period on the board was one for a press like one the company owned. When Miss Finch pointed out to the directors that the existent press was idle a good part of the time, this proposal was abandoned.

4. The company might build or lease a new one-floor plant which would result in lower handling costs. Mr. Welch did not know what this would cost, but he learned from an acquaintance in the printing business that simply moving and rewiring the equipment might cost $60,000.

5. The company might add to its sales force, which consisted in 1956 of the part-time efforts of the president, the vice president, plus the sales manager, and one additional salesman. The sales manager and salesman were paid a 10 percent commission on sales.

Mr. Welch was not completely satisfied with any of these alternatives.

EXHIBIT 1

COMPARATIVE PROFIT AND LOSS STATEMENT FOR THE FISCAL YEARS ENDED SEPTEMBER 30, 1953, 1954, 1955, 1956

	1953		1954		1955		For the 6 Months Ended March 31, 1956	
	Amount	Percent to Net Sales	Amount	Percent to Net Sales	Amount	Percent to Net Sales	Amount	Percent to Net Sales
Net sales								
Correspondence school	$ 0	0	$ 64,712	27.55	$100,058	36.60	$ 25,530	20.08
Other	174,625	100.00	170,141	72.45	173,306	63.40	101,594	79.92
Total net sales	174,625	100.00	$234,853	100.00	$273,364	100.00	$127,124	100.00
Cost of sales								
Materials cost	$ 72,228	41.36	$ 87,591	37.30	$102,677	37.56	$ 50,867	40.01
Change in work in process	(508)	(.29)	(735)	(.31)	46	.02	(1,039)	(.82)
Direct department expenses	2,030	1.16	4,552	1.94	4,618	1.69	2,664	2.10
Wages—Direct	44,970	25.75	61,823	26.32	64,866	23.73	32,074	25.23
Wages—Indirect	15,266	8.74	14,244	6.07	15,383	5.63	7,454	5.86
Wages—Maintenance	3,449	1.98	3,234	1.37	3,469	1.27	1,878	1.48
Spoilage	1,155	.66	2,409	1.03	1,794	.66	720	.57
Payroll taxes	1,594	.91	2,043	.86	2,356	.86	895	.70
Power and light	1,256	.72	1,108	.47	1,141	.42	624	.49
Insurance—General	699	.40	765	.33	278	.10		—
Water	81	.05	130	.06	105	.04	36	.03
Fuel	747	.43	1,097	.47	991	.36	870	.68
Building maintenance	460	.26	1,377	.59	833	.30	147	.12
Depreciation—Building	655	.38	655	.28	655	.24	480	.38
Depreciation—Machinery	5,015	2.87	5,256	2.23	6,124	2.23	3,045	2.40
Cost of sales	$149,097	85.38	$185,550	79.01	$205,336	75.11	$100,715	79.23
Gross profit	$ 25,528	14.62	$ 49,303	20.99	$ 68,028	24.89	$ 26,409	20.77

Expenses								
Administrative, general	$ 22,339		$ 25,896		$ 31,382		$ 13,388	
Selling and delivery	12,295	19.84	12,807	16.48	19,570	18.64	11,450	19.54
Operating profit (loss)	$ (9,106)	(5.22)	$ 10,600	4.51	$ 17,075	6.25	$ 1,571	1.23
Other income	1,640	.94	8,999	3.83	1,377	.50	533	.42
Total	$ (7,466)	(4.28)	$ 19,599	8.34	$ 18,452	6.75	$ 2,104	1.65
Other deductions	+1,748	+1.00	−2,071	−.88	−2,068	−.75	−913	−.71
Profit (loss) before provision for taxes on income	$ (9,214)	(5.28)	$ 17,528	7.46	$ 16,384	6.00	$ 1,191	.94
Provision for taxes—Estimated	0	0	−2,561	−1.09	−5,356	−1.96	−389	−.31
Net profit (loss)	$ (9,214)	(5.28)	$ 14,966	6.37	$ 11,028	4.04	$ 802	.63

EXHIBIT 2

COMPARATIVE BALANCE SHEET

		Year Ending March 31	
ASSETS	*1954*	*1955*	*1956*
Current			
Cash	$ 15,028	$ 19,073	$ 4,152
Accounts receivable	16,188	18,467	29,995
Inventories			
Raw materials	10,598	10,361	9,682
Finished goods	329	537	189
Supplies	2,038	1,041	1,962
Work in process	4,329	4,284	5,322
Total current assets	$ 48,511	$ 54,662	$ 51,302
Other			
Cash surrender value—Life insurance (pledged)	$ 4,518	$ 4,750	$ 4,750
Accounts receivable—Officers and employees	119	739	44
Claim for refund of federal income taxes	—	892	892
Property, plant and equipment—(Mortgaged)			
Building and building improvements	23,637	24,291	24,291
Machinery and equipment	121,285	118,916	119,168
Delivery equipment	53	53	53
Office furniture and fixtures	6,544	6,667	6,707
Total depreciable assets	$151,517	$149,927	$150,219
Less reserve for depreciation	104,818	111,491	115,161
	$ 46,699	$ 38,436	$ 35,059
Land	9,115	9,115	9,115
Deferred charges	2,623	1,561	1,643
	$111,586	$110,155	$102,805

LIABILITIES AND CAPITAL

Current			
Notes payable (due within one year)			
Bettsville Industrial Foundation	$ 3,000	$ 3,000	$ 3,000
For equipment purchased	7,400	3,125	2,192
Accounts payable	21,310	20,534	21,062
Accrued expenses	1,084	1,363	1,861
Provision for taxes on income—Estimated	2,688	5,523	401
Provision for bonuses—Estimated	—	—	433
Total current liabilities	$ 35,482	$ 33,545	$ 28,950
Deferred indebtedness			
Mortgage notes payable maturing subsequent to September 30, 1954			
Bettsville Industrial Foundation	$ 17,000	$ 12,750	$ 10,500
For equipment purchased	3,200	—	—
American Type Founders, Inc.	—	806	—
Capital stock and surplus			
Common stock authorized and issued			
(500 shares—No par value)	$ 48,480	$ 48,480	$ 48,480
Surplus	7,423	14,573	14,875
	$111,586	$110,155	$102,805

But he believed that inaction could result in complete failure for the company.

Exhibit 2 presents a comparative balance sheet for the years 1954 through 1956.

1. *Do the profit and loss statements in Exhibit 1 show the economic profits of the firm? Do they reflect the full opportunity costs? Explain.*
2. *Break the expenses in Exhibit 1 into fixed and variable categories. (It may be necessary to split some categories. It will be necessary to use rough judgments in some of the separation of costs.)*
3. *What is the ratio of incremental cost to revenue (sales) according to your fixed-variable cost breakdown? What is the significance of this fact?*
4. *Does the capital stock and surplus category on the balance sheet show the economic worth of the firm? Explain.*
5. *What is the major issue in this case? (Beware of ignoring issues which are not listed in the case.)*
6. *Miss Finch continued to insist on the policy of refusing liquor business. Was she correct in this insistence? Was she rational? Was she ethical?*
7. *What action should Mr. Welch recommend?*

SELECTED DECISION-MAKING RULES AND PRACTICES

The following examples of practices, policies, and rules of thumb are taken from case studies of actual firms. Some of the examples may be consistent with the principles of managerial economics; others may represent a practical compromise with those principles, while still others are difficult to reconcile with incremental reasoning.

1. Some firms follow the rule that the annual budget for the replacement of equipment should equal the annual depreciation charges on equipment. The vice president of one manufacturing firm, for example, was considering such a policy to accelerate the replacement of equipment which he believed was lagging behind. Many of this company's machines were over 10 years or even 20 years old.

2. The owner-manager of a small printing firm follows the rule: "To make a profit, you must make a profit on every job." By this he means that each job must be priced to cover all the costs, including allocated overhead, and return a profit above those costs.

3. A dry cleaning and laundry firm considered the possibility of filling in its off-peak excess capacity with laundry service for motels. The company management, however, turned down this opportunity when it learned that the motels would not pay a high enough price to cover the overhead as well as the direct costs.

4. The plant manager of a branch of a large national firm was faced with a decision on making or buying a component. Up to the time of the decision the plant manufactured the part, but a potential supplier was willing to sell at a price below the plant's full cost. In spite of this

low price the manager decided to continue manufacture within the plant. His reasoning was as follows:

a. The overhead presently absorbed by manufacturing the component would have to be reallocated to other parts manufactured within the plant.

b. The reallocation of overhead would result in higher unit costs for other parts.

c. These higher unit costs would require higher prices for the company's products, placing it in a less favorable competitive position.

5. One owner-manager of a furniture company made the following statement: "Overhead must come first." By this he meant that price must cover the overhead costs and then cover as much of the variable costs as possible.

6. A garden nursery and landscaping firm refused to develop plants or trees which took more than eight years to mature. The management reasoned that the high prices of the slower maturing plants didn't compensate for the longer period they tied up the land.

7. Many firms maintain a policy of not buying new equipment or replacing old equipment unless the investment will pay for itself in less than three years (or some other predetermined number of years). This rule is known as the payback criterion.

8. The author of this book sometimes feels under pressure to attend athletic events because he already has tickets in his possession.

9. The Empire Room of the Waldorf Astoria Hotel in New York City is similar to other dining, dancing, and entertainment facilities in the Hilton Hotels chain. In 1955 the Empire Room was less profitable than its counterparts in the other Hilton hotels, with only a 5.7 percent return on sales (a loss of 5.5 percent in 1954) as compared with returns of from 7.1 percent to 34.4 percent in the other hotels.[1] In spite of this low profit level, Hilton Hotels spent more proportionately on advertising the Empire Room than it spent on the other rooms. In January and February, 1954, the advertising budget for the Empire Room was $11,779 and total sales amounted to $143,308. Similar figures for other Hilton hotels in New York were:

Room	Advertising Costs	Sales
Rendezvous Room (Plaza Hotel)	$1,905	$ 88,826
Persian Room (Plaza Hotel)	7,803	98,340
Grill Room (Roosevelt Hotel)	5,779	249,378
Cafe Rouge (New York Statler)	2,747	111,688
Lounge Room (Mayflower Hotel)	3,800	59,047

---

[1] See *Hilton Hotels Corporation (BR),* a case published by the Harvard Graduate School of Business Administration, copyright 1960, p. 15. The data are reproduced by permission of the President and Fellows of Harvard College and Professor John D. Glover.

1. *How do the rules and practices of these companies hold up under analysis in terms of the concepts in Chapter 2: incremental reasoning, time perspective, discounting, opportunity costs, and the equimarginal principle?*

PART TWO / Demand and
forecasting

3 / Demand analysis

Economic analysis usually begins with demand, or the consumer side of economic activity, and then transfers attention to the producer, or cost and supply side. After both demand and supply have been treated, the two sides are brought together in discussions of pricing and other types of decisions. Topics in this book are organized in the traditional sequence.

Demand analysis is one of the manager's essential tools in long-range planning. Prospects for growth of demand in various market areas should be carefully projected before choosing sizes and locations of new plants. If demand fluctuates, plants with flexible design (but higher average costs) may be desirable and considerable capital will be needed to carry inventories. If demand is sufficiently responsive to advertising, investment in market development may be justified.

Demand considerations also enter day-to-day financial, production, and marketing management. Sales forecasts provide some of the key assumptions used in projecting cash flows and net income by periods. Sales expectations affect production scheduling and inventory planning. Before prices are changed, probable reactions of customers and competing firms should be taken into account. The manager can make good use of economic concepts contained in demand analysis.

SOME BASIC CONCEPTS

It is important to recognize that the layman and professional economist sometimes use the term "demand" in different ways. To the layman demand usually means simply *one quantity* sold or to be sold. For example, one often hears an expression such as: "The demand for automobiles may be 7.25 million in the coming year." To the economist, demand is a functional relationship of *various quantities* of a product to such variables as price, consumer income, prices of substitutes, season, and availability of credit.

Quantitative expressions of demand

The economist can express his knowledge of demand in several ways. At the most abstract level he can use mathematical notation to indicate the *functional relationship* under study, such as:

$$Q_d = f(X_1, X_2, X_3, \ldots, X_n)$$

in which

Q_d is the quantity purchasers are willing to buy, and X_1, X_2, etc., are the influences on Q_d

Normally the Q_d in such an equation represents the quantity per unit of time (such as a week or year) of a particular product in a particular market (such as baby shoes in Boston, or all shoes in the United States), and the X's represent specific influences such as price, advertising expenditures, income, population, the availability of credit, and the prices of substitutes. Note that demand quantity is a *rate; i.e.,* quantity per unit of time.

Such a functional notation is of limited use to the manager, for it indicates the existence of a relationship without specifying the nature or magnitude of the influences of the independent variables on quantity. One cannot tell from such an abstract equation even whether the relationship is positive or negative—whether, for example, an increase in price has a stimulating or dampening effect on the quantity of sales. It is therefore desirable to express the relationship as a *specific equation;* for example:

$$Y = -2812.8 + 34.4X_1 + 35.6X_2 + 2024.3X_3$$

in which

Y = thousands of refrigerators sold annually
X_1 = disposable income in billions of 1939 dollars
X_2 = change in disposable income from the preceding year
X_3 = logarithm of time (1925 = 1)

This equation is based on an actual statistical study of refrigerator sales.[1]

The economist can also express demand relationships in the form of a *demand schedule.* Table 3–1 presents a hypothetical demand schedule.

---

[1] *Survey of Current Business,* June 1950, p. 8. An evaluation of this study appears in Joel Dean, *Managerial Economics* (Englewood Cliffs, N.J.: Prentice-Hall, Inc. 1951), pp. 213–14.

TABLE 3–1

DEMAND SCHEDULE (units per month)

Price	Income (dollars per year)		
	2,400	3,000	3,600
$10	100	125	150
9	120	150	180
8	150	187	224
7	200	250	300
6	260	325	390
5	340	425	510

Table 3–1 illustrates relationships of quantities to two variables, price and income. Demand schedules are unwieldy if effects of three or more variables upon quantities are to be shown simultaneously.

Part of the above information can be shown on a *graph* as in Figure 3–1. The economist is quite aware that such a graph is a simplification, limited to the effect of one or two variables, usually just price or income, and excluding information about other influences on quantity sold. But he often desires to focus attention on one influence, especially upon the price-quantity relationship.

FIGURE 3–1

A FAMILY OF DEMAND CURVES (hypothetical)

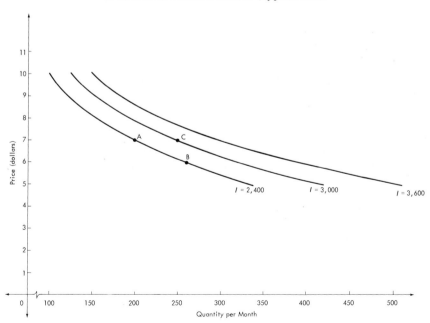

In business practice actual quantification of the demand function is probably the exception rather than the rule. Managers make subjective estimates of the influence of price and other variables on sales; without such estimates any rational approach to decisions would be impossible. The trend is toward quantification, though cost of the statistical analysis required may in some cases exceed the benefits. Subjective estimates may be quite practical when uncertainty is great or when volume is too small to provide a reasonable return on the cost of market research.

Meaning of "change in demand"

The important distinction between quantity change due to movement along a demand curve and quantity change associated with a change or a shift of demand can be seen in Figure 3–1. The quantity change from Point A to Point B is entirely due to a price reduction. It is a *movement along a demand curve*. On the other hand, the change from Point A to Point C is not accompanied by a change in price; it can be attributed entirely to a change in income. Thus, the latter change in quantity is due to a *shift in demand*. In other words, changes or shifts in demand are associated with changes in variables other than price, whereas movement along demand curves are associated with changes in price. "Change in demand," an increase or a decrease, means a shift of the demand curve.

Price elasticity of demand

Price elasticity of demand is a simple but useful idea. It is a measure of the responsiveness of quantity to price change (assuming all other variables constant). Price elasticity is roughly the ratio of percentage change in quantity sold to percentage change in price. Elasticity is the percent change in quantity that would accompany a *one* percent change in price. Such a comparison of percentages is independent of the particular units in which prices or quantities are measured. Thus, elasticity for a particular product allows meaningful comparisons with elasticities on other products that may be measured in dissimilar units or that have prices much greater or smaller. For example, the elasticity of demand for residential housing can be compared with elasticity for recreational travel.

A crude (and unsatisfactory) formula for calculating arc elasticity, which must be based on a *discrete* change in price, illustrated by a price decrease, is:

$$e_p = \frac{\dfrac{Q_2 - Q_1}{Q_1}}{\dfrac{P_2 - P_1}{P_1}} = \frac{\dfrac{\Delta Q}{Q_1}}{\dfrac{-\Delta P}{P_1}} \tag{3-1}$$

where e_p is elasticity of demand with respect to price

Q_1 is quantity sold in a specified market per unit of time before the change in price

Q_2 is quantity sold in a specified market per unit of time after the change in price

P_1 is the original price

P_2 is the final price

Formula 3–1 is the ratio of change in quantity, expressed as a percentage of original quantity, to change in price expressed as a percentage of original price.

Note that the change in quantity usually has an algebraic sign opposite to that of the change in price; thus, price elasticity of demand usually has a negative sign. Indeed, price elasticity is assumed negative unless otherwise specified. The negative sign is sometimes disregarded in economic literature; in such cases discourse is in terms of absolute values.

Formula 3–1 is ambiguous. It yields different values over the same interval, depending upon whether the price change is an increase or a decrease. Consider the effect of increasing price over the same range as the illustrative decrease in Formula 3–1. Absolute values of ΔQ and ΔP would still be the same; their signs would reverse, and the sign of the overall ratio would not be changed. However, the initial value of Q_1 (from the other end of the quantity range) would be smaller, so as to increase the value of the overall numerator in Formula 3–1. In contrast, the initial value of P_1 (from the other end of the price range) would be greater, which would increase the value of the overall denominator in Formula 3–1. Thus, if Formula 3–1 were used, calculated value of price elasticity would be smaller for a price decrease than for a price increase over the same interval. The ambiguity described above is eliminated in Formula 3–2:

$$ e_p = \frac{\dfrac{Q_2 - Q_1}{(Q_1 + Q_2)/2}}{\dfrac{P_2 - P_1}{(P_1 + P_2)/2}} \tag{3-2} $$

In Formula 3–2, changes in quantity and price are calculated as percentages of the *average* of their respective original and final values. Thus, Formula 3–2 yields the same result for either an increase or a decrease in price, over the same interval. Formula 3–2 can be simplified as follows:

$$ e_p = \frac{\dfrac{\Delta Q}{Q_1 + Q_2}}{\dfrac{\Delta P}{P_1 + P_2}} \tag{3-3} $$

Formula 3–3 is simple and unambiguous and should be used when arc elasticity is calculated for practical work. Note again that ΔQ and ΔP usually have opposite signs; if one is positive, the other is negative.

Formula 3–3 is a measure of *arc* elasticity. It measures responsiveness of quantity change to price change for a *finite movement* of price and quantity. Since it covers the entire distance from Q_1 to Q_2 and from P_1 to P_2, it averages elasticities at points in between.

Another measure of elasticity is available, known as *point* elasticity. It measures the responsiveness of quantity to price *at a given point* and requires calculus in its computation. The formula is:

$$e_v = \frac{dQ}{dP} \cdot \frac{P}{Q} \qquad (3\text{–}4)$$

in which

$P =$ the price at a given point on the demand curve
$Q =$ the quantity at that price

$\dfrac{dQ}{dP} =$ the first derivative of the demand equation with respect to price

Most readers will recognize that the elasticity of demand is *not* the same as the *slope* of the demand curve. The slope is given by:

$$\text{Slope of an arc} = \frac{P_1 - P_2}{Q_2 - Q_1}$$

$$\text{Slope of a point} = \frac{dP}{dQ}$$

While the slope of a straight-line demand curve is the same at all points, the elasticity for such a curve varies from one point to the next. For example, refer to Formula 3–4 and assume a move down and to the right on a straight-line demand curve. The *reciprocal* of slope (dQ/dP) would be constant, but value of P/Q would fall. Therefore, elasticity would decrease.

An elasticity of zero (perfectly inelastic demand) means there is no quantity response to price change. An elasticity of minus infinity (perfectly elastic demand) means that the firm can sell any quantity it wishes at the prevailing price, but none at all at slightly higher prices. An elasticity of minus one (unitary elasticity) means that the percentage change in quantity equals the percentage change in price. Figures 3–2, 3–3, and 3–4 illustrate demand curves with constant elasticities of zero, infinity and unity, respectively.

A demand curve with unitary elasticity through its range would be a rectangular hyperbola with an equation such as:

$$Q \cdot P = K, \text{ or } Q = K/P \qquad (3\text{–}5)$$

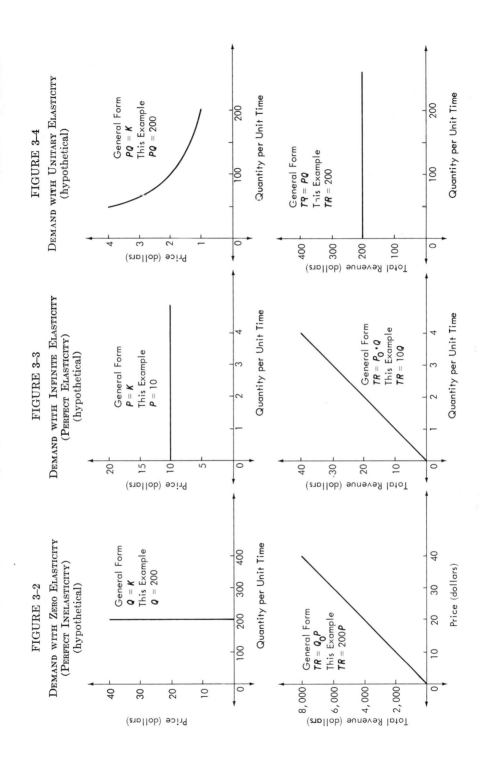

FIGURE 3-2

DEMAND WITH ZERO ELASTICITY
(PERFECT INELASTICITY)
(hypothetical)

General Form
Q = K
This Example
Q = 200

General Form
TR = Q₀P
This Example
TR = 200P

FIGURE 3-3

DEMAND WITH INFINITE ELASTICITY
(PERFECT ELASTICITY)
(hypothetical)

General Form
P = K
This Example
P = 10

General Form
TR = P₀ · Q
This Example
TR = 10Q

FIGURE 3-4

DEMAND WITH UNITARY ELASTICITY
(hypothetical)

General Form
PQ = K
This Example
PQ = 200

General Form
TR = PQ
This Example
TR = 200

FIGURE 3–5

LINEAR DEMAND CURVE WITH VARYING ELASTICITIES AND THE CORRESPONDING TOTAL REVENUE CURVE
(hypothetical)

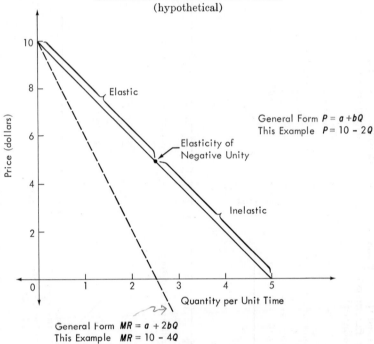

General Form $P = a + bQ$
This Example $P = 10 - 2Q$

Elastic

Elasticity of Negative Unity

Inelastic

General Form $MR = a + 2bQ$
This Example $MR = 10 - 4Q$

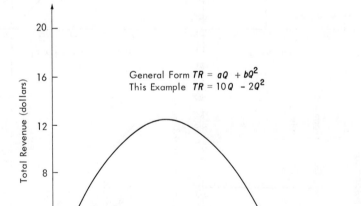

General Form $TR = aQ + bQ^2$
This Example $TR = 10Q - 2Q^2$

in which K represents total revenue, in this case a constant. Figure 3–4 is such a curve. It would be unusual to find an actual demand curve which would approximate unitary elasticity throughout its range. But many demand curves are elastic in the upper part of their range and inelastic in the lower part. This means they include an intermediate portion over which elasticity is approximately minus one. Such is the case for a straight-line demand curve sloping downward to the right, as shown in Figure 3–5. Most producer experience involves a limited movement on the relevant demand curve or curves. In such cases, it may be convenient and practical to assume either constant slopes or constant elasticities in demand estimation and in planning calculations.

If absolute value of elasticity is less than one, total revenue falls as price is reduced. If the absolute value exceeds unity, total revenue increases as price drops. It is important to learn these relationships among elasticities, price changes, and changes in revenues. They are shown in Figure 3–5.

Incremental revenue and marginal revenue

Incremental revenue (ΔR) is simply any change in total revenue resulting from a management decision. It is calculated as:

$$\Delta R = R_2 - R_1$$

where R_2 is total revenue if the decision is carried out and R_1 is total revenue if there is no change in activities of the firm. *Incremental revenue* could be associated with an output change (of any number of units) or with any other kind of change. As examples, incremental revenue could conceivably result from higher prices with increased advertising, or from higher prices with product improvement, without any change in output. Or, incremental revenue could be associated with an entirely new product. Incremental revenue can be positive or negative.

Marginal revenue is a special case of incremental revenue. It is always associated with a change in output. Furthermore, *marginal revenue* is the change in total revenue resulting from the *last unit* added to total sales. Relationships of marginal revenue to elasticity of demand are shown in Figure 3–5. Marginal revenue can be positive (elastic demand), zero (unitary demand), or negative (inelastic demand).

An average of marginal revenue for output changes (ΔQ) greater than one unit can be calculated as:

$$\text{Average } MR = \frac{R_2 - R_1}{Q_2 - Q_1} = \frac{\Delta R}{\Delta Q} \tag{3-6}$$

in which R_1 represents the total revenue before the price change that brought about the change in quantity and R_2 the total revenue after this change. The reason for dividing by the difference between the old quantity and the new quantity is to convert the incremental change in revenue to an average change *per unit* of change in output. Marginal revenues may be different at the various points within the range of incremental changes in quantity.

The formula for marginal revenue at a point is:

$$MR = \frac{dR}{dQ} \tag{3-7}$$

which is simply the first derivative of the equation for the total revenue curve with respect to quantity.

If elasticity is unity, marginal revenue is zero, for the price change produces no change in total revenue. If the demand is perfectly elastic, marginal revenue is equal to the price. Relationships of elasticity, marginal revenue, and total revenue along a straight line demand curve are depicted in Figure 3–5.

If one knows price and elasticity of demand at a point he can compute marginal revenue. A general formula for the relation of marginal revenue to price and demand elasticity is:

$$MR = P\left(1 - \frac{1}{e}\right) \tag{3-8}$$

Please note that the negative sign of e is ignored in this formula. An alternative formulation is $MR = P\left(1 + \frac{1}{e}\right)$ in which the negative sign is recognized.

For demand curves sloping downward to the right (which is true of most demand curves), the marginal revenue is less than the price. The reason for this is clear. If the price is reduced from $10 to $9 and sales increase from 1,000 units to 1,500 units, average marginal revenue over the last 500 units is less than $9. It is true that total revenue increases by $9 for each of the added 500 units. But total revenue is reduced by the fact that all of the original 1,000 units must now sell for $1 less. The marginal revenue is computed, as indicated in Formula 3–6, by dividing the change in revenue of $3,500 by the change in quantity of 500 units. The result is $7. Another way of arriving at the same figure of $7 is to recognize that for every additional $9 on added units one must in this case deduct a loss of $1 of revenue on each of two units formerly selling at $10.

Income elasticity of demand

Income elasticity of demand is a measure of the responsiveness of the quantity of purchases to changes in income. Purchases of some commodities respond very little to income changes. Examples would be salt and potatoes. Sales of other commodities increase or decrease rapidly with increases or decreases in income. Examples are motor yachts and private aircraft. Industries subject to rapid shifts in demand are known as "feast and famine" industries. In general, durable consumer goods are more responsive to changes in income than nondurable goods.

Income elasticity of demand for most commodities is positive, indicating higher purchases at higher incomes. Income elasticity for a few commodities is negative; such commodities are known as "inferior goods." Examples are salt pork and dried beans, which increase in popularity in periods of low income, then give way to more expensive foods in more prosperous periods.

The formula for average income elasticity over a discrete change in volume is:

$$e_I = \frac{\dfrac{Q_2 - Q_1}{Q_2 + Q_1}}{\dfrac{I_2 - I_1}{I_2 + I_1}} \tag{3-9}$$

in which I_2 and I_1 represent the new and old incomes.

The formula for income elasticity at a point is:

$$e_I = \frac{dQ}{dI} \cdot \frac{I}{Q} \tag{3-10}$$

in which I is income at a given point on the equation relating quantity to changes in income with no change in price or other variables in the demand function

Q is quantity at the same point

$\dfrac{dQ}{dI}$ is the first derivative of the demand equation with respect to income

Disposable personal income is the most common measure of income for such purposes, but other measures of income are also in use.

Knowledge of income elasticities is useful in forecasting the effects of changes in business activity on particular industries. If one has made a forecast of national income or disposable personal income, he can then apply income elasticities in estimating the changes in the purchases of individual commodities. Such forecasting is limited by the same difficulties to which the price elasticities are subject: sales are influenced by other variables not covered by the elasticity measure; and past relationships may not persist in the future.

Cross elasticity of demand

Cross elasticity of demand measures one of the most important demand relationships, the closeness of substitutes or the degree of complementarity of demand. The quantity of sales of one commodity or service is influenced by the prices of substitutes; the lower the prices of substitutes the lower the sales of the commodity under consideration. The formula for cross elasticity is:

$$e_c = \frac{\dfrac{Q_2 - Q_1}{Q_2 + Q_1}}{\dfrac{P_{s2} - P_{s1}}{P_{s2} + P_{s1}}} \tag{3-12}$$

in which P_{s1} and P_{s2} represent the new and old prices of the substitute commodity.

A *high cross elasticity* means that the commodities are *close substitutes*. A *cross elasticity of zero* means that they are *independent* of each other in the market. A *negative cross elasticity* means that the goods are *complementary* in the market—a decrease in the price of one stimulates the sales of the other. An example would be the sale of high-fidelity components and the prices of records. Reduced prices of records in recent years have no doubt stimulated the sale of high-fidelity components.

This ends the discussion of demand elasticity concepts. The concept of elasticity is a flexible tool that may be used to measure the influence of changes of any variable on another. The reader probably can work out himself the formulas for other elasticities that may be useful. Two examples are market share elasticity (responsiveness of the percentage share one firm has of the market to changes in the ratio of its prices to industry prices) and promotional elasticity (responsiveness of sales to changes in advertising or other promotional expenditure).

ESTIMATING DEMAND EQUATIONS

The *exact* nature of relationships of various influences to the quantity sold per period cannot usually be determined. It is not feasible to set up conditions under which each of the influences is varied, one at a time, as the others are held constant. A manager cannot hold weather constant, keep selling effort of competitors from changing, increase or decrease prices of competing goods, or change consumer incomes. Information about demand relationships is necessarily limited to *estimates* of the demand equations.

Models

An assumed relationship of quantity per period to price and other variables becomes a *model* when it is expressed in a mathematical form. One example of a model of demand is:

$$Q = b_0 - b_1 P + b_2 A + e$$

in which Q is quantity and is the *dependent* variable

P and A are independent variables
b_0, b_1, and b_2 are symbols for the *parameters* to be estimated
e is error, assumed to be normally and independently distributed with a mean of zero and constant variance

The above example assumes *linear* relationships of Q to the independent variables. Although the underlying relationships are usually believed to be curvilinear, linear approximations may be satisfactory over the *limited range* of available data and expected future experience.

A frequently used curvilinear model of demand has the form:

$$Q = b_0 \, P^{b_1} \, A^{b_2} \, e$$

in which the variables and parameters are as defined above.
The second equation assumes that the marginal effects of each variable are not constant but rather are dependent upon the value of that variable and of all other influences represented in the demand equation. An equation of the second form has *constant elasticities;* these elasticities are the exponents of the variables. The equation transforms to become *linear in logarithms;* the transformation is

$$\log Q = \log b_0 + b_1 \log P + b_2 \log A + e$$

Although there are other useful mathematical forms of demand equations, the linear form and the power form that becomes linear in logarithms have been used most because their parameters can be estimated by the least-squares methods of statistics. These methods are based on the following assumptions about the data: the variations of the exogenous (right-hand side) variables are independent of each other; error is normally distributed with zero mean and constant variance; also error is independently distributed—i.e., successive errors are not correlated. Three methods of obtaining data to be used in making demand estimates are discussed below.

Experiments

Experiments can be carried out either in a laboratory or in the market place. Laboratory experiments allow good control over the experimental conditions. Participants in the experiment can be carefully selected to have demographic characteristics of a population that is of interest. The form of the experiment usually provides a limited amount of money to the participants; they are then allowed to choose between brands of a product, and they get to keep both the product selected and the remainder of the money. The prices of the brands can be deliberately varied to determine the price elasticity of the brand that is of interest and its cross elasticities with competing brands.

Results of laboratory experiments cannot be extrapolated to provide forecasts for the market place unless the participants in the experiment are actually representative of the target population. Further, the experiment must be carried out in such a way that participants do not alter their behavior because of knowledge that they are under observation.

Experiments can also be carried out in actual markets. This is often done in connection with new products, where there may be interest in consumer responses to different packages and different advertising approaches as well as in effects of price changes. *Test marketing* is experimentation in a few selected market areas with the objective of obtaining estimates of demand relationships for a total market that contains many areas.

An excellent example of market experimentation is a study of demand for fresh oranges by University of Florida researchers in 1962.[2] Grand Rapids, Michigan, believed to be representative of the Midwest market, was the test market. Florida oranges from two areas (Indian River district and Florida interior) in two sizes (200 and 163) were evaluated against California size 138.

Nine supermarkets cooperated. Prices per dozen were systematically varied plus to minus 16 cents from a base price, in 4-cent increments. The base price was the average retail price of each type prior to the experiment. Thus, each of the types of oranges was offered at nine different price levels. The experiment ran 31 days and involved sales of over 9,250 dozens of oranges.

The researchers estimated price elasticities for each type of orange and were also able to estimate cross elasticities between the different types. Several of these estimates are shown in Table 3–2. The numbers on the diagonal in the table are elasticities with respect to own prices and the off-diagonal numbers are cross price elasticities.

TABLE 3–2

ELASTICITIES OF DEMAND FOR ORANGES
(Florida Valencia size 200 and California Valencia size 138)

A 1 percent change in the price of:	Produces these percentage changes in quantities of:		
	Florida (Indian River)	Florida (Interior)	California
Florida Indian River	−3.07	+1.56	+0.01
Florida Interior	+1.16	−3.01	+0.14
California	+0.18	−0.09	−2.76

[2] Marshall B. Godwin, W. Fred Chapman, Jr., and William T. Hanley, *Competition Between Florida and California Valencia Oranges in the Fruit Market,* Bulletin 704, December 1965, Agricultural Experiment Stations, Institute of Food and Agricultural Services, University of Florida, Gainesville, Florida, in cooperation with the U.S. Department of Agriculture and Florida Citrus Commission.

Experimentation in actual markets is very expensive. Retailers must be compensated for their cooperation and for any losses that they may have. Many observers are required to make counts of purchases and to relate these to such circumstances as customer traffic, time of day, location, etc. Costs also include possible permanent losses of customers who switch to competing products during the experiment and possible loss of information to competitors who may also monitor the experiment. Furthermore, competitors sometimes sabotage market tests through unusual price changes, sudden changes in advertising, special offers to consumers (coupons), and so forth.

Because of the expense and administrative and logistical problems of running a market test, along with the danger of revealing information to competitors and the vulnerability of the test to competitive sabotage, such experiments are usually carried out only for brief periods of time and only in a few markets. The brevity of the experiments tends to assure constant incomes and unchanging tastes and preferences but it also precludes estimates of long run effects of changes in price, package, advertising, etc. Only short run elasticities can be estimated.

Another limitation of market experimentation is that test markets must be selected very carefully to be representative of the whole market. Some cities have been favored for test marketing to the extent that there is concern that their populations have been "over tested"—i.e., subjected to so much experimentation that their reactions to variations in influences on demand are no longer representative of the larger market.

Household consumption surveys

Household consumption surveys provide data that are especially helpful in estimating relationships of incomes and demographic characteristics to the quantities of goods purchased per week. A consumption survey begins with selection of a sample of households that is representative of the population in the market or markets that are of interest. For example, the national market could be stratified into regions, then into rural and urban populations, and finally into income groups within each degree of urbanization.

A survey is usually designed to determine consumption of a selected set of commodities in a cross section of households during a short period, perhaps one week. Measurement of consumption involves going into the home and making an initial inventory of the amounts of each item that are on hand, obtaining the cooperation of the housewife in keeping a diary of her total purchases during the week, and returning to the home to make a final inventory of quantities on hand at the end of the period.

An excellent example of a household consumption survey is a study by the Institute of Home Economics and the Agricultural Marketing Service in the spring of 1955. This survey obtained detailed data on a week's consumption of about 250 commodities for households in four regions, with three urbanizations within each region, and by income group within each urbanization.

Some results from the 1955 Household Consumption Survey are shown in Tables 3–3 and 3–4. These results, as summarized by one of the principal investigators, suggest:

1. The quantity of all food per se, excluding marketing services, consumed per person varies with the level of income within each urbanization but has a quite *low* income elasticity (item 1, Table 3–3).

2. The value of food marketing *services* per person bought with food per se, both in retail stores and eating places, varies with the level of income two to three times as much as the *quantity* of food per se consumed among families within each urbanization category (item 2, Table 3–3).

3. Income elasticity of food expenditures is *less* among families with higher real incomes than for lower income groups (Table 3–4).[3]

TABLE 3–3

INCOME ELASTICITIES FOR FOOD AS ESTIMATED FROM CROSS-SECTION DATA

| | | Income Elasticity | | |
Item	All U.S.	Urban	Rural Nonfarm	Farm
1. Per person use of purchased farm foods	.24	.14	.26	.15
2. Value of food marketing services bought with food per person	.42	.33	.46	.26

TABLE 3–4

HOW EXPENDITURES ON FOOD INCREASE AS REAL INCOME OF
HIGHER-INCOME FAMILIES INCREASES

Income above Mean, Percent	Expenditures per Person, Percent
25	8
50	17
100	22
200	51

Household consumption survey data pertain to a very short period and may not permit adequate estimates for commodities with consumption that varies markedly from season to season. Quantity data cannot be obtained for consumption away from home; this consumption can be

---

[3] Marguerite C. Burk, "Ramifications of the Relationship Between Income and Food," *Journal of Farm Economics*, 44 (1), February 1962, p. 115.

3 / Demand analysis 87

measured only by expenditures. If there are regional price differences, it is not usually possible to separate the regional demographic influence from the price effects. (It would be possible if reliable estimates of price elasticities were available, such as those from experiments.) In spite of the above problems, household consumption surveys are the best sources of data for estimates of the influences of income and demographic factors. The principal drawback related to this method is the great expense involved.

Time series data

Time series data are observations of economic variables at various points through time. Such observations can be especially useful in estimating the influences of price changes on quantity sold per unit of time. However, great care must be taken in making and using estimates based on time series data.

An example that illustrates several problems encountered in time series analysis is a study of United States demand for coffee.[4] The demand model was

$$Q = F(Yd, rP)$$

Where Q is the quantity of unroasted coffee beans annually deflated by population

Yd is aggregate real disposable income deflated by population and consumer price index

rP is a weighted average of prices of regular and instant deflated by consumer price index

Estimates of the demand parameters are shown in Table 3–5 for the total populations for 1920–41 and 1947–66.

One problem encountered by the investigator was the postwar introduction of instant coffee. This product uses less green coffee beans per

TABLE 3–5

DEMAND EQUATIONS FOR COFFEE

Equation*	by†	Ey‡	brp†	Erp‡	R^2	DW
1. 1920–41, total population	4.21	.338	−.084	−.302	.758	7.25
2. 1947–66, total population	−5.05	.556	−.030	−.143	.74	1.86
3. 1947–66, Q', total population ...	−2.72	.290	−.033	−.150	.51	2.10

* The means of the Q's for equation 1 through 3 are: 17.6, 16.1, and 17.0. The Q's are per capita pounds in green (unroasted) beans annually.

† by and brp are regression coefficients for Yd and rP.

‡ Ey and Erp are the elasticities of quantity with respect to income and relative price, respectively, evaluated at the means.

<hr />

[4] John J. Hughes, "Note on the U.S. Demand for Coffee," *American Journal of Agricultural Economics,* 51, No. 4, November 1969.

cup than regular coffee because of greater efficiency of extraction, but the price also reflects the cost and the value of extra convenience built into the product. Instant coffee gradually increased its share of the market over the postwar period. The investigator estimated Equation 3 with quantities of green beans adjusted to what they would have been if the instant coffee consumed had been regular, but effects of the introduction and gradual acceptance of instant coffee are not clear. The form of the product changed over time. *Change of products* is a major problem in making estimates from data collected over any long period of time.

Another problem facing the investigator was the apparent switch of income elasticity from positive in the prewar period to negative in the postwar period. It is possible that coffee became an inferior good as incomes rose and consumption of distilled wines and spirits increased. However, the role of alcoholic beverages in the demand for coffee could not be determined. Their consumption over time is highly collinear with disposable income; as a result, per capita wine and spirit consumption and incomes could not be used as independent variables in the same equation. If the investigator attempted to do so, both of the two coefficients relating income to coffee quantity and alcoholic beverage consumption to quantity would be unreliable estimates. The only really satisfactory way of coping with two-variable *multicollinearity* is *to remove the effect of one of the collinear variables.* For example, if the effects of income upon consumption of coffee were already known (through household consumption surveys, for example), these could be removed and there would be no need to have income as a variable in the demand equation. Consumption of alcoholic beverages could then be used as a shift variable in the demand equation, thus picking up the effect of a specific trend in consumer tastes and preferences.

A third problem often encountered in deriving estimates from time series data is *autocorrelation,* in which the residuals (unexplained variations in the dependent variable) are serially correlated when plotted in the order of occurrence. The effect of autocorrelation is to make the standard errors unreliable. Autocorrelation was apparently not a problem in the study of the demand for coffee, since the tests for autocorrelation with the Durbin-Watson statistic were close to or above 2.0. This value indicates absence of serial correlation in the residuals.

Empirical studies and illustrations

The leading figure in demand measurement before World War II was Henry Schultz, whose *The Theory and Measurement of Demand*[5] is a classic. Schultz's findings on the demand for sugar are representative of

---

[5] Henry Schultz, *The Theory and Measurement of Demand* (Chicago: The University of Chicago Press, 1938).

his results. For the period from 1875 to 1929 he found that the price elasticity of the demand for sugar remained fairly constant, in the area of −0.40 or −0.30, with slight evidence of a downward trend in elasticity. That the demand for sugar is inelastic should not surprise the reader; the result is very much in line with what one would expect. Schultz also found that the increase in per capita consumption of sugar had slowed down in the 55 years covered by his study, suggesting a low income-elasticity and the absence of a shift in tastes toward sugar and products incorporating sugar.

Schultz's findings on other agricultural commodities are of interest, even though they are based on prewar data and on statistical methods that have since been refined. The elasticities in Table 3–6 are based on the period from 1914 or 1915 through 1929, often with the elimination of the years 1917 through 1921.

TABLE 3–6

ELASTICITIES OF PER CAPITA DEMAND FOR SELECTED AGRICULTURAL COMMODITIES

Commodity	Price Elasticity with Standard Errors	Comments
Corn	−0.4924 ± 0.1563	Earlier periods show somewhat higher elasticities.
Cotton	−0.1248 ± 0.0570	Considerable change in elasticity over time, partly because of the international character of the market.
Wheat	−0.1854 ± 0.0372	
Potatoes	−0.3073 ± 0.0285	Earlier periods show somewhat higher elasticities.
Barley	−0.3870 ± 0.2361	Earlier periods show somewhat lower elasticities.
Rye	−2.4444 ± 0.4569	Earlier periods show much lower elasticities.

Source: Henry Schultz, *The Theory and Measurement of Demand* (Chicago: The University of Chicago Press, 1938), pp. 551–53.

Schultz is careful not to attribute too much accuracy to his findings. He notes that the standard errors are relatively large, making it impossible to say with a high degree of probability that the difference between two elasticities is significant. The evidence, with a few exceptions like that of rye, suggests strongly that the demand for agricultural commodities is inelastic, a conclusion supported by more recent studies. This inelasticity means that a small crop has greater value to farmers as a whole than a large crop, a fact that accounts for various attempts to restrict agricultural output.

Richard Stone has conducted a similar study based on more recent

British experience.[6] Table 3–7 presents selected elasticities from his study, including income elasticities and cross elasticities, as well as price elasticities. The reader might find it an interesting exercise to try to estimate the elasticities before looking at Table 3–7, or at least to separate those commodities that he thinks will have extremely low price elasticities or low income elasticities from those with higher elasticities.

Low price elasticities for bread, margarine, tea (remember this is a study in the United Kingdom), and tobacco are what one would expect. The positive price elasticity for coffee and the negative cross elasticity of coffee related to tea prices run contrary to all expectations, and indeed Stone rejects them as unacceptable (note that the standard errors are high). That flour and margarine are "inferior commodities" (ones with negative income-elasticities) is understandable. To Americans the high positive income-elasticity of demand for fish may seem strange. The high substitutability of butter for margarine, of imported mutton and lamb for pork, of carcass meat for bacon and ham, and of other fresh fruit for apples is consistent with the usual observations. It is reassuring that most of these elasticities (but not quite all of them) come so close to *a priori* expectations.

Empirical measurements of price elasticities, income elasticities, and cross elasticities for manufactured commodities are less common than for agriculture. Studies of automobile demand both before and after World War II indicate that its price elasticity is not much more than 1.0, a fact that helps explain the reluctance of automobile manufacturers to reduce price to offset declines in demand.[7] The evidence is overwhelming that the elasticity of demand for cigarettes is extremely low in Western countries; in Great Britain, for example, enormous tax and price increases on cigarettes have done little to curtail the volume of purchases.[8] Both the price elasticity and the income elasticity of demand for public utility services are low, as one might expect. The income elasticity of demand for clothing and furniture is probably slightly greater than unity; the income elasticity of expenditures upon rent is probably less than unity.[9]

The best known of the U.S. demand studies of the 1960s was that of

---

[6] Richard Stone, *The Measurement of Consumers' Expenditure and Behavior in the United Kingdom, 1920–1938* (Cambridge, Eng.: Cambridge University Press, 1954), Vol. I.

[7] See, for example, C. F. Roos and V. von Szelski, *The Dynamics of Automobile Demand* (New York: General Motors Corporation, 1939), pp. 21 ff.

[8] A statistical study of the demand for tobacco in 14 countries found low price and income elasticities, but a high response to population growth. A. P. Koutsoyannis, "Demand Functions for Tobacco," *The Manchester School of Economic and Social Studies,* January 1963.

[9] Summaries of studies of the demand elasticities for these and other commodities appear in Aaron W. Warner and Victor R. Fuchs, *Concepts and Cases in Economic Analysis* (New York: Harcourt, Brace & Co., 1958), pp. 144–69.

TABLE 3-7

DEMAND ANALYSES FOR SELECTED PRODUCTS BASED ON BUDGET SURVEYS, 1937–39, OR TIME SERIES, 1920–38

Commodity	Income Elasticity	Own Price	Substitution Elasticity with Respect to — Price of Specified Commodities	
Flour (1924–38)	−0.15(±0.11)	−0.79 ± 0.21		
Bread	−0.05(±0.04)	−0.08 ± 0.07		
Home-produced beef and veal	0.34(±0.06)	−0.41 ± 0.18	Imported mutton and lamb price	0.50 ± 0.15
Pork	0.58(±0.24)	−0.67 ± 0.18	Home-produced and imported mutton and lamb price	0.85 ± 0.48
Bacon and ham	0.55(±0.09)	−0.88 ± 0.12	Carcass meat price	1.45 ± 0.43
Poultry	1.17(±0.22)	−0.27 ± 0.23	Home-produced mutton and lamb price	0.86 ± 0.35
Eggs	0.54(±0.07)	−0.43 ± 0.12		
Fish, fresh and cured	0.88(±0.07)	−0.74 ± 0.15	Carcass meat price	0.49 ± 0.22
Fresh milk	0.50(±0.18)	−0.49 ± 0.13	Home-produced beef and veal price	0.73 ± 0.15
Butter	0.37(±0.08)	−0.41 ± 0.13	Flour price	−0.21 ± 0.11
Margarine	−0.16(±0.11)	0.01 ± 0.17	Butter price	1.01 ± 0.17
Home-produced potatoes	0.21(±0.06)	−0.56 ± 0.06	Imported potatoes price	0.09 ± 0.06
Home-produced apples	1.33(±0.21)	−1.67 ± 0.20	Other fresh fruit price	2.77 ± 0.66
Oranges	0.92(±0.17)	−0.97 ± 0.24	Dried fruit price	0.63 ± 0.32
Sugar	0.09(±0.04)	−0.44 ± 0.10	Chocolate and confectionery price	1.06 ± 0.34
Tea	0.04(±0.04)	−0.26 ± 0.07	Coffee price	0.14 ± 0.08
Coffee	1.42(±0.30)	0.55 ± 0.42	Tea price	−0.54 ± 0.39
Beer	−0.05(±0.09)	−0.87 ± 0.06		
Tobacco as a whole	0.25(±0.07)	−0.27 ± 0.06		
Cigarettes	0.22(±0.10)	−0.39 ± 0.10		
Coal	0.26(±0.07)	−0.50 ± 0.19		
Electricity	0.15(±0.11)	−0.60 ± 0.14		

SOURCE: Richard Stone, *The Measurement of Consumers' Expenditure and Behavior in the United Kingdom 1920–1938*, pp. 322–27, 390, 400. The elasticities Stone has selected as most reliable are shown, by permission of the Cambridge University Press.

H. S. Houthakker and L. D. Taylor.[10] Their findings are not easily summarized, since they applied a variety of approaches to the different commodities in their study. In most cases they tried to apply a dynamic model
which recognizes that current expenditures depend upon preexisting inventories and upon habit formation. The short term effect of price or
income changes is distinguished from the long term result. For durable
commodities for which inventories are maintained the short term effect of
a change in income will be greater than the long term effect. For habit-
forming commodities, the long term effect is larger than the short term
effect, and income changes have a smaller effect than they do on durable
commodities.

One illustration of the Houthakker-Taylor study is the demand for
new cars and net purchases of used cars. The equation reached after considerable experimentation was:

$$f_t = .5183 \, f_{t-1} + .1544 \, \Delta \, y_1 + .0148 \, y_{t-1} - .4749 \, \Delta \, p_t - .0457 \, p_{t-1} + 14.0725 d_t$$

in which

f_t = per capita personal consumption expenditures on new and used
automobiles in the year t (1954 dollars)

y_t = total per capita consumption expenditure in year t

p_t = relative price in year t of the good in question (1954 = 100)

d_t = dummy variable used to separate post-World War II years from
earlier years; takes a value of 0 for 1929–41 and 1 for 1946–61.

According to this equation, the short-run relative price elasticity was
—.9578, while the long-run relative price elasticity was —.1525. The
short-run total expenditure elasticity (somewhat like the income elasticity) was .1937, while the long-run total expenditure elasticity was
.0308. An attempt to include consumer credit as a variable did not improve the equation.

The Houthakker-Taylor study covered 83 commodities. The authors
do not claim a high degree of accuracy for many of their equations and
suggest some ways in which research methods could be improved. It is
clear that the study of consumer demand is still in the developing stages.

These various measurements of demand are all subject to error. Obviously they do not have the degree of precision and accuracy of prediction sometimes achieved in the physical sciences. The difficulty of
conducting controlled experiments in which one could test consumer responses to given changes in price or income is a great handicap. Furthermore, statistical methods suited to available data on quantities and
prices are still under development. One British study which measured
predictive accuracy of demand analysis came to rather negative conclu-

[10] H. S. Houthakker and L. D. Taylor, *Consumer Demand in the United States,*
1929–1970 (Cambridge, Mass.: Harvard University Press, 1966).

sions on the subject.[11] Future improvements in the statistical methods used in measuring demand will undoubtedly increase the usefulness of demand estimates.

MARKET STRUCTURE

It is time to take notice of the distinction between two kinds of demand schedules or curves: the industry (market) demand and the demand facing the individual company. It is possible to compute price elasticities and income elasticities for either.

In general, one would expect price elasticity of individual company demand to be greater than that of industry demand, for the company faces competition from the similar products of rival firms. However, the precise relationship between industry demand and company demand depends on the nature of competition within the industry—on the structure of the market.

A classification of markets

Based on the relationship of individual company demand to industry demand there are four categories of market structure:

1. Monopoly
2. Pure competition
3. Monopolistic competition
4. Oligopoly

The case of *single-firm monopoly* is rare. It is approximated in public utilities, such as electric utilities, which are usually granted a monopoly privilege within a specified market area by government franchises. Even an electric utility faces some competition from substitutes (gas, fuel oil). Thus the concept of monopoly is not a neat one. If a single firm actually controls an entire industry, *the company demand curve and the industry demand curve are the same.*

The case of *pure competition* is equally rare. The conditions for pure competition are: (1) a homogeneous commodity for all firms in the industry; (2) numerous sellers and buyers, so that none has a perceptible influence on the total market; (3) free entry into and exit from the industry. The theory of pure competition also assumes perfect knowledge of the prevailing price on the part of buyers and sellers. Under these conditions the product of one firm is indistinguishable from that of another. Advertising, patents, brand names, and other features that separate one firm's product from that of another do not exist. While cases which meet all of these requirements are exceptional, some markets ap-

---

[11] Mark B. Shupack, "The Predictive Accuracy of Empirical Demand Analysis," *The Economic Journal,* September 1962, pp. 550–75.

proach pure competition closely enough that the theory is a useful approximation. Under such conditions, *the demand for the individual firm's product approaches perfect elasticity.* A perfectly elastic demand implies that the firm can sell all it wishes at the market price. It can sell nothing at a price that is higher, for buyers will transfer to other sellers.

Monopolistic competition refers to markets in which (1) the sellers are numerous and (2) the product of each firm is differentiated from that of the competitors. In such a situation *the firm's demand curve slopes downward to the right, with an elasticity greater than that of the industry demand. There is some question whether one may refer to the industry demand curve at all in such a case, for the product of each firm is to some degree different from that of the next.* Nevertheless, it is useful to retain the concept of the industry as long as one recognizes its limitations.

Oligopoly refers to markets with small numbers of firms; the Greek base of the word means "few sellers." The markets for steel and cement approximate the conditions of *homogeneous oligopoly,* for most buyers of standardized products care little about who the supplier is but are interested in minimizing the cost of an approximately standard product. *Differentiated oligopoly* is more widespread (automobiles, machinery, household appliances). In such conditions products are differentiated physically; advertising, salesmanship, trade names, and other devices also distinguish the product of one firm from that of another. It is more difficult to generalize about the shape or elasticity of the demand curve in oligopoly than in the preceding market situations. In fact, the *interdependence of the price policies of competing firms in oligopoly may preclude drawing a simple demand curve, showing the relationship between a firm's own price and the quantity it sells.*

OTHER INFLUENCES ON DEMAND ELASTICITIES AND DEMAND LEVELS

The preceding section dealt with the influence of market structure on demand. It is now appropriate to review a variety of other influences affecting demand. Most of these affect industry demand, but some operate directly on company demand.

Derived demand: producers' goods and consumers' goods

Some commodities and services are final goods, ready for direct use by consumers. Others are producer goods: materials, parts, services, or components that are to be used in further production. Demand for producer goods is *derived from demand for ultimate consumer goods* and thus is known as *derived demand.* Demand for steel is a derived demand; consumers do not buy steel directly, but rather they buy finished products that combine steel with labor and other inputs. Similarly, demand for labor services is usually derived from demand for the final products resulting from combining the labor with other inputs.

In general, derived demands are *less* elastic than final demands. The less costly the component in relation to the total cost of the final good, the more likely this is to be the case. For example, demand for glue used in binding books is probably quite inelastic, since a large percentage change in the price of glue will have little effect on the total cost of production. Some labor unions may try to take advantage of this "principle of unimportance" in demanding high wages for special skills that are a small proportion of total cost of products. However, a derived demand can still be subject to competition from close substitutes. If it is easy to replace a certain type of labor with machinery, for example, the elasticity of demand for that labor may be high.

Another factor distinguishes demand for producers' goods from that for consumer goods. Buyers of producers' goods are usually experts, less influenced than laymen by promotional activity and more influenced by a careful evaluation of the characteristics of the commodity. Expert buyers are often sensitive to small price differences.

If the demand for a final good increases, the derived demand for the *durable* producers' goods may rise more rapidly. The reason is that *the demand for increased capacity is likely to be large in ratio to the normal replacement demand.* This effect is called the *acceleration principle.*

Effects of attitudes and expectations: durable and nondurable goods

Demand for a durable good, consumers' or producers', is likely to be more volatile than demand for nondurable goods for two additional reasons: 1. It can be stored. 2. Its replacement can be postponed.

Storability of durable goods makes possible the expansion or contraction of inventories. In the recessions since World War II, the decrease in the size of inventories in billions of dollars has been almost the same magnitude as the decrease in the entire Gross National Product. Those industries dependent upon buildup of inventories as an important part of total demand suffer disproportionately in recessions. If a producer of durable goods wishes to forecast his demand he must give some attention to the probability that inventories of his product will be increased or decreased. This may require an evaluation of the current inventory-sales ratio and of buyers' attitudes toward increases in inventories.

Storability of the commodity also affects the short-run price elasticity of demand. If buyers believe that a reduction of price is temporary, they will tend to build up inventories. A price increase believed to be transitory may have the opposite effect. If, on the other hand, the buyers forecast that price decrease is merely a beginning of a trend, they may wait for even lower prices and use up their inventories, whereas a price in-

crease viewed as the start of a trend would stimulate stocking. Expectations are a central influence on demand for durable goods. Customers
buy not for the past or present but for the future and must make predictions of the state of future markets.

Another influence on demand for durable goods is the postponability
of replacement. In periods of recession, consumers postpone the replacement of automobiles, furniture, and other durable consumer goods. In
the great depression of the 30s, especially in 1932 and 1933, there was
little replacement of producers' goods, as is indicated by the fact that
the net investment was small or even negative. But in periods of expected shortages, such as the period just after the beginning of the
Korean War, replacement demand takes an upward leap.

Luxuries and necessities

It makes a difference whether a good or service is a luxury or necessity, with the demand for necessities being more inelastic. Whether or
not a particular commodity is a necessity depends in part on whether
substitutes are available. The economist is more hesitant to use the
luxury-necessity classification than is the layman, for the issue is largely
one of taste and culture. Some goods which appear now to be essential
to life were unknown 60 years ago: the mechanical refrigerator is an
example. Nevertheless, the analyst may find it useful to consider whether
under present conditions the good is likely to be considered a necessity
in his evaluation of demand. This will force him to consider some of the
sociological influences on demand.

Another hypothesis is that the demand for inexpensive items—items
that take up only a small part of the purchaser's income—is less elastic.
The reason is that consumers pay less attention to price changes on such
insignificant items. This is another factor making the demand for salt
inelastic, it is claimed. At the same time, many low-priced items are ones
purchased frequently by the consumer, who therefore may be more aware
of price change on such purchases than he is on less frequent purchases.
Perhaps the way to resolve this issue is to consider these two different
influences on demand: the ratio of the price of the item to income, and
the frequency of purchase of the item.

Long-run and short-run demand

In general, the short-run elasticity of industry demand is less than
the long-run elasticity (unless the change in price is considered to be temporary). The reasons for this are:

1. It takes time for buyers to become familiar with the new price and
to adjust to it, and to make the required changes in their consumption
habits.

2. It may take time to wear out durable items that are not to be

replaced. For example, reduced rates for mass transit systems may not have full effects until there has been some wearout of private automobiles.

Product improvements

Changes in the product itself will bring a change in its demand. In many industries, firms are constantly improving products. A large part of research and development activity is devoted to modifying products which already exist.

In the modern world, the constant flow of innovation—the development of new products, new distribution and selling techniques, and new modes of production—has a tendency to create new substitutes for old products. The result is what Schumpeter has called "creative destruction," which includes the destruction of demands for old goods and services. No evaluation of demand is complete until the analyst has examined the possible encroachment of new products on old markets. Since forecasting of technological change may go quite wide of marks, innovation is another factor creating uncertainty in predictions of demand.

Promotional activity

Management does not necessarily take the demand as given. It can act to shift the position and shape of the demand curve. A sales force can promote the product through *personal selling. Advertising* can create a greater awareness of a product and its attributes; it may develop tastes which were formerly unknown or unexpressed. Changes in distribution *channels* or in the *service* provided may help shift the demand curve upward.

Managers can sometimes manipulate the closeness of substitutes or degree of differentiation to some extent through advertising and other forms of sales promotion. The objective is to increase the degree of differentiation, with an increase in the monopoly power of the firm. But maximization of differentiation is not, and should not be, the objective of every firm. Many firms indeed profit from imitating competing products. Some furniture firms, for example, send representatives to furniture shows to copy the designs of leading firms. The objective in such cases is to minimize the degree of differentiation so that the imitating firms can take advantage of the resultant high elasticity of demand with somewhat lower prices. In such cases advertising may be aimed at demonstrating similarities to products of competitors, rather than emphasizing differences from these products.

Population changes

Population growth is another important influence on demand. Shifts in the age distribution of population bring about substantial changes in markets for a wide range of products. In most parts of the world the proportion of the population below 20 years of age and over 65 years of age is increasing sharply. The proportion of income under the control of these age groups is increasing even more rapidly. Demography, the study of population, will become increasingly significant in demand studies in the future.

Empirical studies and illustrations

This section will concentrate on studies of the volatility of demand and studies of the acceleration principle.

Studies of demand volatility. The Department of Commerce studied effects of income changes on demands for various commodities. Instead of measuring income elasticity of demand, these studies focus on income sensitivity, a slightly different concept. Income elasticities measure the ratio of percentage changes in quantity demanded to percentage changes in income; indexes of income sensitivity measure the ratio of percentage changes in expenditure (in dollars) to percentage changes in income. The study covers both prewar and postwar conditions. Some of the main findings are summarized in Table 3–8.

TABLE 3–8

INCOME SENSITIVITY OF SELECTED CONSUMER EXPENDITURES
(based on disposable personal income)

Commodity Group	Prewar	Postwar
Total personal consumption expenditures	0.8	1.0
Durable goods	2.1	1.2
Nondurable goods	.7	.9
Services	.5	1.0
Automobiles and parts	2.8	1.1

SOURCE: U.S. Department of Commerce, Office of Business Economics, as published in L. J. Paradiso and M. A. Smith, "Consumer Purchasing and Income Patterns," *Survey of Current Business*, March 1959, pp. 21–28.

These data support the hypothesis that demand for durable goods is more volatile than for nondurables, but differences between durables and nondurables since the war are much less than before. Probably increased liquidity of consumers and greater stability of business activity account for these changes in sensitivity; consumers are no longer at the mercy of current income in allocating their expenditures.

A few comments on income sensitivity of demand for individual commodities may be of interest. Postwar demand for street railway and bus services has shown a negative income sensitivity, suggesting that these are considered to be inferior services for most consumers; consumers apparently prefer to use more expensive automobile services if their income allows. Income sensitivity of demands for gas, electricity, water, and telephone services has shown a sharp increase from the prewar to the postwar period (from 0.2 to 1.3 and over), suggesting that public utilities are no longer insulated from the business cycle. Demand for physicians' and dentists' services has shown an increased income sensitivity (from around 0.8 to 1.1 and over), while that for alcohol has declined, perhaps indicating a shift in consumer attitudes on what are luxuries and what are necessities.

Status of the acceleration principle. Do statistical studies support the famous principle of intensified fluctuations in derived demand? The answer depends on how strictly one wishes to interpret that principle. If he expects it to provide precise predictions of demand fluctuations, he is going to be disappointed. Several factors complicate the operation of the principle:

1. If demand for a final good increases, but under conditions of excess capacity, no stimulation of derived demand may take place.

2. If expectations are optimistic, demand for a producers' good may increase even without an increase in final demand.

3. Addition of extra shifts or overtime work makes it possible to increase output without adding to facilities.

4. Technological developments may stimulate purchases of improved producers' goods without any change in ultimate demand; furthermore, technological progress may change the capital-output ratio.

Thus it should be no surprise that empirical support for the acceleration principle is meager. Econometricians have been engaged in testing the principle since the pioneer work of Tinbergen in 1938; their findings have been mostly negative.[12] Recent studies have attempted to verify more flexible interpretations of the acceleration principle, relating investment to changes in output over a series of previous periods and making an allowance for excess capacity.[13] These modifications, plus a recognition of the role of expectations, place the acceleration principle in a more favorable light.

Study of the acceleration principle produces mixed feelings. Despite the failure of most empirical studies to support the principle, it is a matter of common sense that changes in demand for final output must require varying levels of investment. It is also common sense to recognize that in a world of changing technology, shifting expectations, and excess capacity the principle could not work out in a neat, mathematical

---

[12] See J. Tinbergen, "Statistical Evidence on the Acceleration Principle," *Economica*, May 1938,, pp. 164–76; T. Hultgren, *American Transportation in Prosperity and Depression* (New York: National Bureau of Economic Research, 1948), pp. 157–69; and J. R. Meyer and E. Kuh, *The Investment Decision* (Cambridge, Mass.: Harvard University Press, 1957).

[13] L. M. Koyck, *Distributed Lags and Investment Analysis* (Amsterdam: North Holland Publishing Company, 1954), chap. IV, and Robert Eisner, "A Distributed Lag Investment Function," *Econometrica*, January 1960, pp. 1–29.

way. It probably is wise to retain the acceleration principle as a partial prediction of demand for producers' goods; the principle is not satisfactory as a explanation or as a mechanical device for predicting changes in demand.

PSYCHOLOGICAL AND SOCIOLOGICAL CONCEPTS OF CONSUMER BEHAVIOR

Traditional demand analysis takes price, income, and the availability of substitutes as the independent variables and the quantity purchased as the dependent variable. Economists are aware that human beings are involved in this relationship but they usually give little attention to the psychological and sociological motivations of these human beings. The question is whether the behavioral sciences are helpful in the analysis of demand. In this book it is possible only to list some major propositions along with some recent findings and some current directions of research.

A few major propositions

1. One of the basic propositions of psychology is that there is much more to human choice than the careful evaluation of alternatives. People make choices for a great variety of reasons, some of which are observable (such as a reaction to a change in price), some of which the individual may not wish to reveal in an interview, and some of which the decision maker may not realize himself.

2. Behind patterns of consumer behavior that appear on the surface to be straightforward are deeper causes and motives which are difficult to observe and to measure. Accordingly, research into such behavior is a difficult task, involving techniques that go behind and beyond the simple correlation of prices, incomes, and quantities purchased.

3. Consumer behavior is socially conditioned. Economists themselves have long recognized the inadequacies of the traditional approach of adding together individuals' demand curves to obtain market demand curves. This approach implicitly assumes the independence of each individual's demand for a product. Such an assumption ignores such notions as:

a. Veblen's "conspicuous consumption," which views people as buying not merely to satisfy inner wants but also to impress others.

b. Duesenberry's "demonstration effect," which portrays individuals coming under the influence of the consumption patterns of those with whom they come into contact. A family moving into a wealthy neighborhood is running the risk that the "demonstration" of higher consumption patterns there will set a higher goal of spending. Studies have shown, for example, the major importance of neighborhood influence in the purchase of air conditioners.

c. The notion that commodities serve as status symbols. The drop in automobile sales and the introduction of compact cars in the late 1950s was attributed by some to the reduced prestige value of the automobile. Some observers argued that homes were taking the place of automobiles as status symbols.

4. Interviews may reveal shifts in consumer expectations and attitudes which help explain changing consumption patterns. In particular, it is claimed that optimism or pessimism about the future will determine the level of purchases of durable consumer goods, such as furniture, appliances, and automobiles.

Empirical studies and illustrations

Recent research in consumer behavior is voluminous; only a few examples may be presented here. The following studies focus attention on psychological and sociological demand influences:

1. A study of the purchases of instant coffee, reported by Mason Haire,[14] suggests the difficulties of structured interviews. A questionnaire included the question, "Do you like instant coffee?" Those who answered no were asked, "What do you dislike about it?" Most of those with negative responses stated that they did not like the flavor. The research workers were skeptical of this answer. They found upon deeper probing that many respondents thought that the purchaser of instant coffee was lazy. To housewives who place a high value on the art of making coffee, such considerations are probably more important than the simple matter of flavor. But it is difficult for housewives to verbalize these motives; they find it difficult to say that they reject instant coffee because they wish to avoid being classified as lazy.

2. Sociological studies indicate that buying habits are correlated with social positions and conceptions of role. Isolated city dwellers prefer to buy in small stores because of the personal contacts possible there. Concepts of "fashion" vary from one social class to another. Sewing at home has a higher value as a prestige symbol in some social classes than in others.

3. Cartoon devices have been used by psychologists to probe the deeper reasons for consumer behavior. Such an approach was used to determine reasons for decline of a grocery store's sales.[15] A cartoon showed two women drinking coffee at a table. The balloon above the first woman shows her saying: "Well, I feel I have to buy food where the price is lower—that's the main thing as far as I'm concerned." The sec-

---

[14] Mason Haire, "Projective Techniques in Marketing Research," *Journal of Marketing,* April 1950, pp. 649–56. Republished in Robert Ferber and Hugh G. Wales, *Motivation and Market Behavior* (Homewood, Ill.: Richard D. Irwin, Inc., 1958), pp. 93–103.

[15] Martin Zober, "Some Projective Techniques Applied to Marketing Research," *Journal of Marketing,* January 1956, pp. 262–68. Reprinted in Ferber and Wales, *Motivation and Market Behavior,* pp. 197–206.

ond woman answers: "Art and I agree that I should shop where . . . ."
The respondent is supposed to fill in the rest of the statement, thus indicating attitudes about grocery stores. In this case, a series of seven car-
toons produced a pattern indicating the high importance of the quality
of meat in the selection of a grocery. The store in question had in fact
sold meat of variable quality when it opened, giving an unfavorable first
impression. As a result of the survey, the store concentrated on advertising high quality of its meats.

4. An interesting study of the market for air conditioners supports the
importance of sociological influences on demand. Some neighborhoods
have gone in for air conditioning on a large scale; other neighborhoods
with the same socioeconomic status have not experienced this upsurge in
demand. The demand for air conditioners spreads by means of neighborhood contact, with certain families taking a role of leadership. Thus
neighborhood group pressures serve as major influences on the purchase
of these durable goods; "it is the group that determines when a luxury
becomes a necessity."[16]

5. Unfortunately validity tests on some devices used to probe into
psychological motives do not support a high level of confidence in the
findings. The best-known of the projective techniques, the Rorschach
inkblot test, has shown little validity as a personnel screening device.[17]
Validation experiments involving the Thematic Apperception Test, another well-known projective technique, have also shown low correlations.
While such tests have not involved the study of consumer behavior, they
suggest extreme caution in using these techniques in forecasting demand.
Recent developments in projective techniques indicate that progress in
the future is likely. A more careful experimental foundation is required
before the validity of this approach can be assured.

Some current hypotheses

There are at present two competitive approaches to consumer behavior.
One approach tries to avoid the rather undefined area of psychology and
sociology by relating purchasing outcomes to relatively measurable variables, such as income or price. The other approach makes a more direct
attack on the intervening psychological and sociological variables. The
managerial economist takes an interest in these alternative attacks on
the problem despite the inconclusive state of present research, for these
studies should eventually increase our ability to predict changes in demand.

---

[16] W. H. Whyte, Jr., "The Web of Word of Mouth," in L. H. Clark (ed), *The
Life Cycle and Consumer Behavior* (New York: New York University Press, 1955).

[17] For a review of statistical study of the Rorschach test see D. B. Lucas, "Can
the Clinical Techniques be Validated," in Ferber and Wales, *Motivation and Market
Behavior,* p. 127.

Earlier sections developed measures (such as income elasticities) that related purchases to the absolute level of income. Two alternatives to the absolute income hypothesis have been proposed: the relative income hypothesis, which stresses the relative position of the consumer on the income scale, and the permanent income hypothesis, which suggests that consumption is related to average income or anticipated income over a number of periods.[18]

The permanent income hypothesis has important implications for the purchase of durable consumer goods. It separates current income into two components: "transitory" income and "permanent" income. The transitory income includes any fluctuations in short-run income that are not expected to persist in the long run. An increase in transitory income, according to this hypothesis, is more likely to flow into durable goods purchases which are intermittent in character. Transitory income appears to be closely related to the concept of "discretionary" income which has long been used in studies of the demand for durable goods. Discretionary income is that part of income left over after deduction of regular, re-current expenses; it is available for the purchase of durable goods. One weakness in this approach is the difficulty of drawing the dividing line between that part of income which is permanent and that part which is transitory or discretionary. Nevertheless, the permanent income hy-pothesis promises to lead to a deeper understanding of consumer behavior.

Other studies are attempting to relate consumption to recent changes in income, to increases in household wealth, and to the size of liquid assets. The heavy purchases of durable goods after World War II, for example, are claimed to relate not only to the difficulties of purchasing such goods during the war, but also to the high levels of liquid assets.

Another approach focuses on expectations, attitudes, and other psy-chological and sociological variables. George Katona has long argued that attitudes such as optimism about the future and the willingness to buy are important determinants of consumer behavior. These changes in attitudes may bring about shifts in consumption patterns long before income and wealth changes take place. Data on attitudes provide an in-sight into underlying motives and thus lead to a deeper understanding of behavior.

At the same time that Katona and his associates at the Survey Re-search Center were collecting attitudinal data, they were also surveying consumer intentions to buy, which are on a somewhat different plane from the underlying psychological motives. Close relations between in-tentions to buy and actual purchases were discovered. Some observers have argued that success of predictions based on intentions to buy makes

---

[18] See Robert Ferber, "Research on Household Behavior," *American Economic Review,* March 1962, pp. 19–63, for an excellent survey of the literature. Much of the present section is based on Ferber's survey.

deeper probing into motives unnecessary, since the data on expectations and attitudes appear to add little to the predictive power of this type of analysis.

Other research workers are focusing attention on consumer decision-making processes. For example, attention is being devoted to the extent to which consumers deliberate on the purchase of durable goods. Deliberation appears to be more frequent among consumers with more education and higher incomes.

Such a wide variety of hypotheses and research approaches is confusing to the practitioner. In time this type of analysis should lead to a deeper understanding of consumer behavior and a higher predictive power in dealing with broad consumption aggregates and with the demand for individual commodities.

A STUDY OF DEMAND FOR DURABLE GOODS

Durable goods offer an especially difficult challenge to the research worker, since the consumer is able to build up or contract his stock of durables at various rates over time. The problem is one of determining the major influences on rates of change in purchasing. One must decide at the outset whether he is going to measure the influences on the consumption of the services produced by durable goods or is going to try to measure influences on the goods proper. In addition, the researcher faces the following problem:

1. There are no well-defined units in which the quantity of durable goods can be measured. The quantity of wheat is measured in bushels, but in what units do we measure the quantity of automobiles?

2. Great differences exist in the quality of durables at a given time and quality changes over time, complicating the measurement problem.

3. Related to the preceding problems is the difficulty of obtaining adequate price data for durables. What is the price of an automobile? The problem is compounded by the fact that the published "suggested prices" are not always the prices at which the goods are sold.

4. The existence of a secondhand market for durable goods creates a problem of relating the demand for new units to the demand for old units. It is necessary to consider both the "stock demand" (such as the demand for automobiles both new and old) and the "flow demand" (the demand for new automobiles). But the data on the stocks of durable goods are usually inadequate.

5. The most difficult problem in measuring the stock of existing durable goods is that of depreciation. Only rough approximations of depreciation are possible. The possibility of repairing the durable good means that there is more than one way to increase the stock.

All of these difficulties are illustrated in a study of the demand for household refrigeration.[19] The researcher, M. L. Burstein, attempted to overcome inadequacies of the suggested list prices by constructing a price index based on the Sears, Roebuck mail order catalog data. He considered a variety of depreciation patterns, both of the declining balance and straight-line varieties, with a preference for assuming a depreciation rate of 10 percent per annum.

Burstein used two different measures of income in his analysis: (1) disposable personal income, which is in line with the absolute income hypothesis, and (2) expected income (based on a complicated weighted average of income over a period of eight years), which reflects the permanent income hypothesis. Thirty-eight different equations were fitted to the data, to reflect different income concepts, different treatments of depreciation, different statistical techniques, and so on.

While each of the 38 equations gave somewhat different estimates, Burstein concluded that the price elasticity for refrigeration was between -1.0 and -2.0 and that the income elasticity was between 1.0 and 2.0. It is interesting to note that Burstein made no use of psychological or sociological concepts or data in his analysis, placing his analysis in sharp contrast with the studies discussed earlier in this section. We can expect a continued development of these two kinds of research. While the economist may continue to prefer approaches stressing variables (such as price and income) which can be expressed in monetary units, Burstein's study shows that the measurement of such variables may be every bit as difficult as the measurement of psychological or sociological factors.

PROBLEMS FOR CHAPTER 3

1. Complete the following table:

Price	Quantity	AR	TR	MR	Arc e_p
100	1				
80	2				
60	3				
50	4				
30	5				
20	6				

[19] M. L. Burstein, "The Demand for Household Refrigeration in the United States," in Arnold C. Harberger (ed.), *The Demand for Durable Goods* (Chicago: The University of Chicago Press, 1960), pp. 99–145.

2.

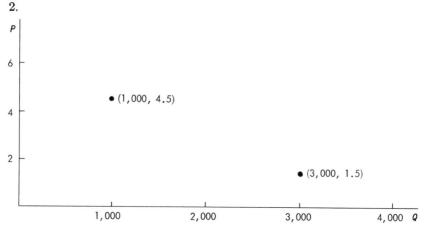

a. Determine the linear demand equation passing through the two points marked.
b. What is the equation for marginal revenue?
c. Find the point of unitary elasticity.

3. Suppose $Q = 360 - .5P$ is the demand equation for widgets.
   a. Find the equation for total revenue.
   b. Find the equation for marginal revenue.
   c. Find the point coefficient of price elasticity at $Q = 200$.

4. Assume $P = .0005(Q-100)^2$ is the demand function for some market.
   a. For what range could the function be valid? What law is involved?
   b. At $Q = 75$, is the demand elastic or inelastic with respect to price?

5. Consider the following demand equation for product A with respect to the prices of products A and B, and income I:

$$Q_A = 500 - .6P_A + 20I + .4P_B$$

   a. Find the price elasticity of A at $Q_A = 600$, $I = 20$, and $P_B = 100$.
   b. Find the income elasticity of A at $Q_A = 550$, $P_A = 60$, and $P_B = 130$.
   c. Find the cross elasticity of A relative to the price of B at $Q_A = 1000$, $I = 20$, and $P_A = 70$. How are A and B related?

6. The demand equation for product XYZ is:

$$P = 50 - .05Q$$

   a. Find the equations for total revenue, average revenue, and marginal revenue.
   b. Show that $MR = AR$ where AR is maximum.
   c. What is MR when TR is maximum?
   d. Compute the coefficient of price elasticity for $Q = 25$ units and $Q = 75$ units.

7. The demand equation of a certain product is:

$$P = \frac{55}{Q}.$$

a. Does this equation agree with the Law of Demand? Explain the relationship in terms of elasticity.

b. Find the equations for marginal revenue and average revenue. Explain these results in terms of elasticity.

8. The demand function for A is:

$$\log Q_A = \lambda + 5 \log I \qquad .5 \log P_A + 9 \log P_B$$

where Q_A is quantity of A demanded, I is per capita income, P_A is the price of product A, P_B is price of product B, and λ is a constant.

a. What is the price elasticity of A, the income elasticity, the cross elasticity of A and B?

b. What do the elasticities say about the demand for A?

c. What is the MR at $P_A = \$15$?

9. Given the demand function $Qx = \lambda \ Py^5 \ Px^{-2} \ I^{-5}$, where Qx is the amount of X demanded, Px is the price of X, Py is the price of a commodity Y, and I is per capita income, calculate the MR at $Px = \$15$.

4 / Business conditions analysis
and short-range forecasting

Short-range forecasts—approximately one to two years into the future —are essential in planning product mix, pricing, level of output, inventories, financial needs, and net income. This chapter discusses methods for making such forecasts. Business conditions analysis, which develops the outlooks for the general level of business activity and for major sectors of the economy, is considered first. Business conditions, such as consumption spending and investment spending, are viewed as influences that shift demand as the chapter moves on to methods of forecasting particular industry demand and capacity. Next, the chapter takes up methods of making forecasts for the specific products and inputs of individual firms. The chapter concludes with examples of forecasting for a particular commodity and for a particular firm.

The objective of this chapter is not to produce sophisticated general business forecasters. The purpose is more modest: to provide a survey of commonly used forecasting methods that will be helpful in evaluating and using forecasts made by others. Few businessmen make their own *general business forecasts;* most depend upon forecasts from outside sources. On the other hand, many managers do make internal forecasts of the *short-range outlook for particular products and inputs of individual firms.*

FORECASTING GENERAL BUSINESS CONDITIONS

This section begins with a brief description of how general business activity and its major components are measured. It then turns to various methods of forecasting changes in business conditions. These include simple barometric methods, survey methods, and opportunistic forecasts.

Finally, the section provides a brief discussion of more sophisticated methods of forecasting using econometric models.

Measuring business conditions

The best-known measure of *business activity* is *gross national product* (GNP), which measures total market value of all final goods and services produced within an economy during a time period, usually one year. Note that this definition specifies that *market values* are to be used in computing GNP and also that only *final goods and services* are to be measured. The first provision means that certain forms of activity—for example, housewives' services—are not measured in the national income accounts.[1] Limitation of the measure to final goods and services means that intermediate outputs in the production process are not counted separately. This is reasonable, since value of final output will encompass the value of intermediate goods; to measure both would be double counting of production.

The basic circularity of income-product flows, as illustrated in Figure 4–1, shows that it is possible to measure economic activity from two viewpoints—the total output or the total inputs. *Total output* is *the sum of the amounts spent on all final goods.* Similarly, *total inputs* are measured by the *total incomes which accrue to their owners.*

As indicated in Table 4–1, *demand for aggregate production* can be specified as consumption, investment, government, and net exports (the value of exports minus the value of imports). Although personal consumption constitutes the largest component, private investment is the most volatile component and thus the most crucial one in determining accuracy of forecasts.[2]

On the input side of the ledger, *national income* consists of compensation of employees, proprietors' incomes, rental incomes of persons, corporate profits and net interest. The factor cost of everything produced in the economy would equal the incomes earned, if it were not for indirect business taxes and capital consumption allowances; i.e., depreciation of equipment used up in the production process. From national income accounts it is quite simple to derive such components as personal income and disposable personal income, as shown in Table 4–2.

Further discussion about national income accounts is beyond the scope of this book. However, it is important to be aware of sources of such income information. Probably most important is the monthly publication

---

[1] There have been attempts to quantify such nonmarket output. See, for example, Ismail Abdel-Hamid Sirageldin, *Non-Market Components of National Income* (Ann Arbor: Institute for Social Research, 1969).

[2] It is important to keep in mind that for national income purposes, investment means only expenditures on plant and equipment and does not include "investments" in land or the stock market, for these transactions do not involve the actual production of new goods or services but are only transfer transactions.

FIGURE 4–1

CIRCULAR FLOW OF NATIONAL PRODUCT*

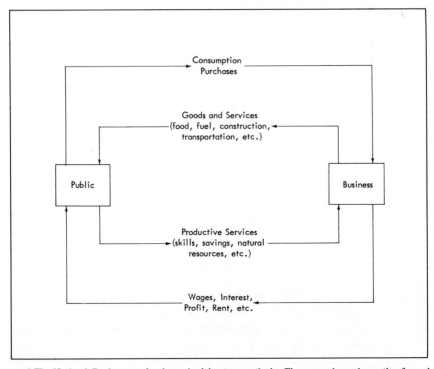

* The National Product can be determined by two methods. The upper loop shows the *flow of final goods and services* from the business to the public sector. The total dollar value of these goods and services per year is one measure of the National Product. The lower loop shows the *flow of productive services* from the public to the business sector. The total dollar amount that the business sector pays per year for these services is an alternate (and equal) measure of the National Product.

TABLE 4–1

EXPENDITURES ON 1972 GROSS NATIONAL PRODUCT
(billions)

Personal consumption		$ 726.5
Durable goods	$117.4	
Nondurable goods	299.9	
Services	309.2	
Gross private domestic investment		178.3
Nonresidential fixed investment	118.2	
Residential structures	54.0	
Change in business inventories	6.0	
Net exports of goods and services		−4.6
Exports	73.5	
Imports	78.1	
Government purchases of goods and services		255.0
Federal	104.4	
State and local	150.5	
Total GNP		$1,155.2

TABLE 4–2

NATIONAL INCOME, 1972

Type	Amount (billions)
Compensation of employees	$705.2
Business and professional income	55.6
Farm income	19.6
Rental income	25.6
Corporate profits and inventory valuation adjustment (IVA)	87.7
Net interest	41.3
Total national income	934.9
Less corporate profits and IVA, contributions for social insurance, wage accruals less disbursements	
Plus government transfers, interest paid by government, dividends, business transfers	
Equals	
Personal income	935.8
Less personal tax and nontax payments	
Equals	
Disposable personal income	795.1

FIGURE 4–2

GROSS NATIONAL PRODUCT

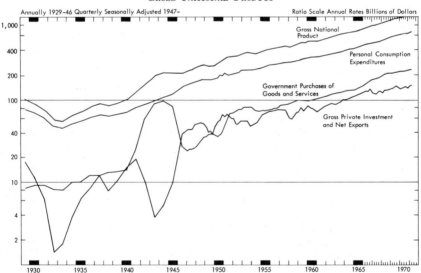

Source: Board of Governors, Federal Reserve System, *Historical Chartbook*, p. 73.

by the Commerce Department entitled *The Survey of Current Business.* This publication contains updated income accounts as well as many other data concerning the state of the national economy. Statistical supplements to the annual *Economic Report of the President* also contain national income tables. Finally, the *Federal Reserve Bulletin* is another public source of current economic data. The components of national income fluctuate over time, a fact quite visible in Figure 4–2 above. Forecasting such fluctuations is one objective of business conditions analysis.

Probably the simplest way of forecasting business conditions is to look at past changes in various measures of business activity and base predictions on this history. This is the barometric or *indicator* method of forecasting.

Indicator forecasts

Just as one can observe the levels of GNP or national income over time, many other time series of economic measurements are available. Particular economic time series can be determined to have systematic timing differences in their changes relative to changes in general business activity. There is particular interest in those series with movements that lead (occur before) changes in GNP. This type of research has been a major output of the National Bureau of Economic Research, especially Wesley C. Mitchell, Arthur Burns, Geoffrey Moore, and Julius Shiskin.[3]

The basic idea behind the indicators approach is that certain types of activities usually begin to slow down *before* the general level of economic activity turns downward. If such activities also speed up before the level of economic activity turns upward, then a data series measuring the activities is a *leading indicator*. It reaches its peak in the cycle before GNP reaches a peak and it goes through a trough before gross national product turns up. The other two types of series are the *roughly coincident series* and the *lagging indicators*. The former usually move *with* the general level of economic activity while the latter usually change direction only *after* the general level of business has already made a change. All three of these possibilities are shown in Figure 4–3.

Economists at the National Bureau have devoted much effort to the classification of large numbers of series into these general categories. Further, they have compiled lists of series which are easily accessible to the forecaster. The current "long list" includes 88 U.S. series: 72 monthly and 16 quarterly. Of these, 36 are classified as leading indicators, 25 are roughly coincident, 11 are lagging and 16 are unclassified by timing.[4] The

---

[3] The National Bureau of Economic Research is a private nonprofit research organization with the object to "ascertain and to present to the public important economic facts and their interpretation in a scientific and impartial manner." The four individuals mentioned constitute the nucleus of the group at the National Bureau which has been studying business cycles over the past 40 years.

[4] In their book, *Indicators of Business Expansions and Contractions,* Geoffrey H. Moore and Julius Shiskin (New York: Columbia University Press for the National Bureau of Economic Research, 1967) briefly review previous efforts in classifying series and note that Mitchell and Burns studied nearly 500 monthly or quarterly series in preparing *Statistical Indicators of Cyclical Revivals,* Bulletin 69, (New York: National Bureau of Economic Research, 1938). They also report that Moore investigated about 800 such series in preparing his book, *Statistical Indicators of Cyclical Revivals and Recessions,* Occasional Paper 31, (New York: National Bureau of Economic Research, 1950).

FIGURE 4–3
LEADING, LAGGING, AND COINCIDENT INDICATORS

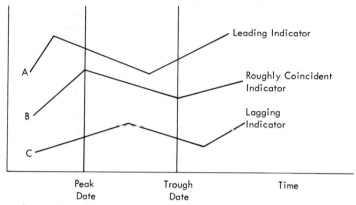

SOURCE: Roger K. Chisholm and Gilbert R. Whitaker, Jr., *Forecasting Methods* (Homewood, Ill.: Richard D. Irwin, Inc., 1971), p. 42.

"short list" is a subset of the long list and includes 25 U.S. series—12 leading, 7 coincident, and 6 lagging. Four of these are quarterly; the remainder are monthly. The short list including median leads (—) or lags (+) in months is shown in Table 4–3.[5]

A set of 36 leading indicators, or even just the short group of 12 leaders, usually contains conflicting signals. A method of summarizing their *net* indication is needed. The National Bureau has developed such a method called the *diffusion index*. The diffusion index is the *percentage* of members of a set of series *that is moving upward*. It ranges from zero (when all are moving downward) to 100 (when all series are moving upward).

A diffusion index is an indicator of the extensiveness of an expansion or contraction. Further, it may provide information about forthcoming changes in direction of the set. For example, if during an expansionary period the diffusion index for all leading indicators stands near 90 for several months, but then begins to fall, it warns the forecaster that some of the leading series are beginning to turn downward; a general decline in economic activity may be forthcoming.

Individual indicators of economic activity may be of interest not only because they have uses in general economic forecasting but also because they directly provide some information about specific business conditions that can possibly be related to demand shifts for particular goods or services. For *current* information on these indicators, a good source is

---

[5] Moore and Shiskin, ibid., p. 34. Note that this book revised the lists of indicators to include new series. It includes an appendix and the 862 series they examined as well as the sources for each.

TABLE 4–3

"Short List" of Economic Indicators

Classification and Series Title	First Business Cycle Turn Covered	Median Lead (—) or Lag (+) in Months
Leading indicators (12 series)		
Average work week, production workers, manufacturing	1921	— 5
Nonagricultural, placements, BES	1945	— 3
Index of net business formation	1945	— 7
New orders, durable goods industries	1920	— 4
Contracts and orders, plant and equipment	1948	— 6
New building permits, private housing units	1918	— 6
Change in book value, manufacturing and trade inventories	1945	— 8
Industrial materials prices	1919	— 2
Stock prices, 500 common stocks	1873	— 4
Corporate profits after taxes, Q	1920	— 2
Ratio, price to unit labor cost, manufacturing	1919	— 3
Change in consumer installment debt	1929	—10
Roughly coincident indicators (7 series)		
Employees in nonagricultural establishments	1929	0
Unemployment rate, total (inverted)	1929	0
GNP in constant dollars, expenditures estimate, Q	1921	— 2
Industrial production	1919	0
Personal income	1921	— 1
Manufacturing and trade sales	1948	0
Sales of retail stores	1919	0
Lagging indicators (6 series)		
Unemployment rate, persons unemployed 15+ weeks (inverted)	1948	+ 2
Business expenditures plant and equipment, Q	1918	+ 1
Book value, manufacturing and trade inventories	1945	+ 2
Labor cost per unit of output, manufacturing	1919	+ 8
Commercial and industrial loans outstanding	1937	+ 2
Bank rates, short-term business loans, Q	1919	+ 5

Source: G. H. Moore, and J. Shiskin, *Indicators of Business Expansions and Contractions* (New York: National Bureau of Economic Research, 1967).

Business Conditions Digest published monthly by the Commerce Department. Data can also be obtained monthly from the Commerce Department's *Survey of Current Business* and the Federal Reserve Board's *Federal Reserve Bulletin,* mentioned previously. Before using these series, especially the various leading indicators, the forecaster may find it helpful to consult the various National Bureau of Economic Research (NBER) publications.

Substantive criticisms can be made of the indicators approach. Four weaknesses cited by Lewis are: (1) the indicators give *no indication of the magnitude* of future changes in economic activity; (2) they are *very short range* with probably only six months' advance warning; (3) the *individual series seldom move together,* whereas the diffusion index hides specific series; (4) for leading series to be useful *there must be no major structural changes in the economy* which might shorten or lengthen their lead time.[6]

Various empirical investigations of predictive accuracy of the indicators approach have been made. One such study by Michael Evans is reported in his book *Macroeconomic Activity.*[7] Although he sees the NBER approach as providing a good picture of the economy and as a valuable collector and verifier of data, Evans concludes that leading indicators cannot be used effectively or accurately as the core of a practical method of forecasting. Nevertheless, economic indicators are often used in conjunction with other methods. McKinley, Lee, and Duffy suggest, "Best results are obtained when the indicators are used together with other data, such as the national income accounts and anticipation surveys."[8] The indicators approach is viewed more favorably by Lempert in *How Business Economists Forecast.*[9]

Surveys of attitudes and plans

Among the leading indicators noted in Table 4–3 are new orders in durable goods industries and new building permits for private housing. These orders and permits represent earlier plans and intentions that are in the process of being carried out. Information about attitudes toward the future and plans for the future may have relatively long lead compared to actual producer or consumer behavior. One method of measuring attitudes and plans simply asks managers or consumers what they expect the future to bring. This is the method of surveys.

This section is limited to a brief review of survey methods: it covers the general approaches used, several sources of this type of forecast and an overall evaluation of the method. More complete information can be found in Lansing's and Morgan's book *Economic Survey Methods* and the many references they cite on specific techniques; these include designing the survey, sampling the population, collecting the data, and analyzing the results.[10] Basically, there are two areas for use of survey

---

[6] John P. Lewis, "Short-term General Business Conditions Forecasting, Some Comments on Method," *Journal of Business,* 35 (October 1962), pp. 347–48.

[7] Michael K. Evans, *Macroeconomic Activity* (New York: Harper and Row, Publishers, 1969), p. 460.

[8] David H. McKinley, Murry G. Lee, and Helene Duffy, *Forecasting Business Conditions* (American Bankers Association, 1965), p. 176.

[9] Leonard H. Lempert, "Leading Indicators," in William F. Butler and Robert A. Kavesh, eds. *How Business Economists Forecast* (Englewood Cliffs, N.J.: Prentice Hall, 1966).

[10] John B. Lansing and James N. Morgan, *Economic Survey Methods* (Ann Arbor: Survey Research Institute, 1971).

methods—producer's behavior and consumer behavior; these will be taken up in order. However, first consider a sometimes neglected area of survey forecasting—plans of governments.

Since government expenditures approximate 30 percent of GNP, planned activity in this sector must always be considered in business forecasting. *Governments' intentions* are available earlier than reliable information about consumer or producer plans for activities during the corresponding period. For example, in January of 1973, the Budget of the United States for the fiscal year July 1, 1973–June 30, 1974 (called the 1974 budget) was published for the federal government. Similarly, state governments publish their full-year spending intentions well in advance of the fiscal year. Budgets of governments can be surveyed to determine what the public sector of the economy is planning to do.

Producer expectations regarding investment expenditures, sales, and inventory levels are all subjects of survey research. There are three major surveys of investment anticipations—the Commerce Department–Securities and Exchange Commission (SEC) survey, the McGraw-Hill survey and the National Industrial Conference Board survey. In the Commerce–SEC survey, firms are queried about their previous quarter's investment and also their anticipated investment during the next quarter. Anticipations and realizations can be compared quarter by quarter. The results of this survey are published the third month of each quarter in the *Survey of Current Business*. The March 1973 issue carried an additional forecast for the entire year (already one-fourth gone).

The McGraw-Hill survey appears twice yearly in *Business Week* and concentrates on *investment plans,* especially of larger firms. The first survey is taken sometime in October; the results are published early in November and cover the following year. A resurvey is taken in early spring and published in April.

The National Industrial Conference Board survey concentrates on *capital appropriations* of 1,000 manufacturing firms. Because of the focus on appropriations, this source of "anticipatory data" is likely to be firmer than simple expectations, as measured in the two surveys mentioned above.

In addition to investment anticipations, the Commerce–SEC survey also obtains *sales* and manufacturing *inventory* expectations. The results of these surveys appear quarterly in the *Survey of Current Business*.

Predictive accuracy of the yearly Commerce–SEC anticipations results has been shown to be approximately equal to that of more complex models (such as those discussed in the section on econometric models below).[11] However, the McGraw-Hill survey and the quarterly surveys of the Commerce–SEC were not found to be as accurate as the more complicated forecasting methods.[12] There is still much controversy about the

---

[11] Evans, *Macroeconomic Activity,* pp. 468–70.

[12] Ibid., pp. 470–79.

effectiveness of anticipations data in predicting plant and equipment expenditures.[13]

Turning to *consumer expectations* surveys, there are several groups that compile such data. Perhaps the best known of these is the Survey Research Center at the University of Michigan. The approach taken by this group is more complicated than simply asking an individual whether or not he plans to purchase an automobile or appliance sometime during the next six months, although questions about *buying plans* are a part of the survey. In addition, there are several queries into the *attitudes* of consumers, which advocates of this forecasting method believe to be as important as actual plans. An example of an attitudinal question is: "Now, about things people buy for their house—I mean furniture, house furnishings, refrigerator, stove, TV, and things like that—do you think now is a *good* or bad time to buy such large household items?"[14] Answers to questions such as these are then classified as being optimistic, neutral, or pessimistic, and are used in an index of general attitudes. The results of these surveys are reported annually in the Survey Research Center's *Survey of Consumer Finances* and in business news outlets such as *The Wall Street Journal.*

Predictive accuracy of consumer surveys is subject to much dispute. Forecasters directly related to institutions conducting such surveys claim good accuracy and have provided evidence to show the strength of their position.[15] These advocates point out that consumer purchase action requires more than just ability, as might be suggested by a simple relationship of personal consumption to income. In addition, there must be willingness to buy; this is what the surveys purportedly measure.

On the other hand, those who do not agree with the surveying method of forecasting usually argue that directly measurable variables such as credit conditions are the root cause of the behavior. Therefore, in their view surveys add nothing to ordinary econometric models of the economy. Evans notes that attitudinal surveys have not predicted very well nor does their predictive record ". . . appear to have improved in the recent past."[16]

---

[13] See, for example, Irwin Friend and William Thomas, "A Reevaluation of the Predictive Ability of Plant and Equipment Anticipations," *Journal of the American Statistical Association,* 65 (June 1970), and the references cited therein.

[14] One of several questions cited in F. Gerard Adams, "Consumer Attitudes, Buying Plans, and Purchases of Durable Goods: A Principal Components, Time Series Approach," *Review of Economics and Statistics,* 46 (November 1964), p. 348.

[15] See, for example, Eva Mueller, "Ten Years of Consumer Attitude Surveys: Their Forecasting Record," *Journal of the American Statistical Association,* 58 (December 1963), or I. Friend and F. G. Adams, "The Predictive Ability of Consumer Attitudes, Stock Prices and Non-Attitudinal Variables," *Journal of the American Statistical Association,* 59 (December 1964).

[16] Evans, *Macroeconomic Activity,* p. 466.

A more moderate view may be advisable. The forecaster may decide that it is better to utilize additional information about attitudes than to ignore it completely. The approach of using all available information is really the cornerstone of the next forecasting method to be discussed.

Opportunistic forecasting

"Opportunistic" is not meant to have a derogatory connotation. Rather, it means that the forecaster takes advantage of all opportunities: he will use *all sources of information* which present themselves, and he is *not restricted to a particular model or technique*. Thus, an opportunistic forecaster might use some basic macroeconomic theory, results of attitudinal surveys, and current changes in the leading indicators. Many business forecasters likely use such an ad hoc approach; the primary source of information regarding the technique is a book by John Lewis and Robert Turner.[17] The discussion of opportunistic forecasting in this section is necessarily brief; only a few high spots are touched.

The opportunistic method requires a certain amount of economic theory (in fact a large portion of Lewis's and Turner's book is devoted to the theoretical basis of macroeconomic behavior). Further, a working knowledge of the national income accounts is necessary. This is because the method of forecasting deals with various sectors of the economy, one at a time, viewing the level of activity in some sectors as given, or *exogenous* (e.g., government spending), and conceiving the level in some other sectors as determined within the system, or *endogenous* (e.g., consumption). The method is iterative, requiring much cross checking and adjustment, with considerations of internal consistency, sector capacities, and so on.

Opportunistic forecasting is a large, catchall category; it excludes only those forecasts made explicitly and solely from survey data, leading indicators, or econometric models. The opportunistic approach is widely used. The so-called consensus forecasts found in various publications (usually near the first of the year) are summaries of forecasts from various sources; most of these individual forecasts fall in the opportunistic classification.

Because of its ad hoc nature, generalized evaluation of opportunistic forecasting is rather difficult. The diversity of the approach is both a strength and a weakness. By use of all sorts of information, the method may be able to perform as a predictor "better than" other specific techniques of forecasting. However, the accuracy of the method apparently varies with the intuition and judgment of the particular forecaster. Forecasts prepared by the opportunistic method may be nearly perfect in one year and contain large errors in the following year. Such variance is

---

[17] John P. Lewis and Robert C. Turner, *Business Conditions Analysis,* 2d ed. (New York: McGraw-Hill Book Co., 1967).

reduced by using a *partially specified* model such as the **GNP** model described below.

Opportunistic forecasting with a GNP model

The basic assumption in GNP model building is that demand governs business activity; if total spending increases, business activity increases. The problem of forecasting is thus one of *forecasting components of aggregate demand.*

For this purpose it is desirable to break the GNP into several parts, each of which represents an important segment of total expenditure. Some of these components are much larger than others, as is shown in the data for 1972 in Table 4–1. The time spent on analyzing a component may not be proportional to its dollar magnitude; inventory investment and consumption of durable consumer goods are more volatile than other components and require attention out of proportion to their share of the total.

The problem of consistency. The procedure is to forecast the components of the GNP and to sum. But the components are interdependent, so that *cross checking and adjustment* is required. The level of consumption, for example, depends in large part on the level of the gross national product itself. Purchases of plant and equipment depend on many factors, but among them is the rate at which the GNP is increasing and the extent to which demand is exerting pressure on capacity. Inventory investment depends on the rate of current purchases as well as on the accuracy with which this rate has been anticipated. Net foreign investment depends in part on the rate of growth in the domestic gross national product as compared with that of foreign national products.

It might be objected that the problem is circular and is insoluble. If each component depends on others or on the total, where does one start? A mathematician would find no difficulty with such a situation; he could construct a series of simultaneous equations to reflect the kinds of interdependence under discussion. In fact, this is exactly what the econometrician does. Even without the system of equations, it is possible to make adjustments in one component to bring it in line with a forecast of another, and to make a series of adjustments of this sort until the forecast as a whole appears *consistent.*

Federal government expenditures. The forecaster usually starts with estimates of government expenditures because they are more likely to be independent of other components. While it is true that the government sometimes adjusts some spending according to the level of business activity, most of it must be planned in advance; the forecaster can make use of the budgets, proposed legislation, and presidential messages that indicate the direction of federal spending.

The simplest procedure is to start with the latest figure on federal government expenditures and to concentrate on probable *increases or decreases* from that figure. What are the sources of information about future government spending? The President's budget message and state of the union message early in the year provide information on what he proposes for the next budget period. The Bureau of the Budget publishes more detailed reports on spending plans. Newspapers and weeklies provide information on how the President's program is progressing in Congress and on other changes in expenditure that may emanate from Congress. Commentators try to evaluate the probabilities of certain programs succeeding in getting through the legislative mill and others' failing. Again, it should be stressed that the forecast must be in terms of *spending on current production*. Appropriation of funds by Congress does not assure that those funds will be spent in the period under consideration.

Forecasting federal government spending requires political as well as economic astuteness. In the cold war, one main difficulty is in predicting shifts in military requirements. But, as demonstrated in the Korean War, even under crisis conditions shifts in military spending may be slow. The Department of Commerce publication, *Defense Indicators*, is a useful source of data about military spending.

State and local government expenditure. The task of aggregating the expenditures of thousands of separate state and local governments is beyond the resources of most forecasters. The simplest solution is to deal with probable *changes* in the aggregate. Since World War II, state and local government expenditures have exhibited an upward trend so consistent from year to year that many forecasters simply project the trend into the future. Extrapolation of trends is normally a risky venture; structural forces that accounted for the trend in the past may not endure in the future. In the case of state and local government expenditures, however, pressures for expansion of road programs and for building of schools would appear to guarantee continued yearly increments in spending. The trend projection should recognize that state and local government expenditures are increasing at an increasing rate; the increment in spending tends to grow over the years.

Expenditures on plant and equipment. If one knew nothing about recent levels of spending, forecasting expenditures on new plant and equipment would be extremely hazardous. Again it is simpler to forecast *changes* in the total based on knowledge of current attitudes, plans, and conditions. However, it is well to remember that this category of spending has gone through rather dramatic fluctuations in the past (a fact quite apparent in Figure 4–2). Investment is based on expectations of future sales and profits, and expectations are prone to change sharply. Investment is also sensitive to rates of change in other categories of spending and in current or expected pressures on capacity. Fortunately, several surveys of business plans for investment are available to assist the forecaster. (They are discussed briefly in the section on survey methods, above.)

The forecaster of investment must be aware of a wide variety of influences. Current profits and stock prices no doubt influence future expectations. Current monetary conditions partially determine the ability of firms to finance expansions (though heavy reliance on plowed-back earnings blunts this influence). Relationships of production rates to designed capacities (operating ratios) helps form expectations of the need for new plant and equipment. The rate of technological change determines obsolescence of old equipment and thus influences the rate of replacement. It is no use pretending that analysis of such diverse influences is easy and a high degree of accuracy is not to be expected. Fortunately, the supply of data for investment forecasting is constantly increasing. The *Survey of Current Business*, for example, now publishes data on anticipated changes in sales, on manufacturers' evaluations of their capacity, and on the carry-over of plant and equipment projects. ✕

Residential construction. An evaluation of monetary conditions—of the availability of credit, of interest rates, and of the terms on which mortgage loans may be obtained—is more important in forecasting residential construction than in forecasting for any other sector. Changes in financial conditions *lead* changes in construction expenditures. The size of down payments required in purchasing new homes and the length of time for repayment influence the magnitude of construction. Pegged Federal Housing Administration and Veterans Administration interest rates have been major factors in fluctuations in new housing. When those rates are far below current market rates, availability of FHA and VA loans diminishes sharply. Privately financed housing starts have been more stable. Among the other influences are: the level of vacancies in homes and apartments already built; the rate of formation of new families, which depends on the age structure of the population; and consumer attitudes towards future income prospects.

The forecaster of residential construction should give attention to several statistical series. The F. W. Dodge Corporation publishes data on construction contract awards which give an idea of building that is in prospect about five months in the future. Data are also available in the *Survey of Current Business* and elsewhere on housing starts and on construction already under way. Since it takes a number of months to complete buildings that have been started, figures on housing starts provide some insight into the level of construction in the future. The problem of seasonal variations is a handicap in interpretation of data on construction awards and starts. A rise in one of these indexes may merely reflect the usual spring and summer increase in building activity. It is desirable to correct data for seasonal variations, but the methods used for such corrections have difficulty in separating cyclical from seasonal influences.

Inventory investment.   Inventory investment is highly volatile, sometimes rising to a positive $20 billion (annual rate) in prosperity and falling to a negative $10 billion in recession. Since World War II no other sector has had a greater influence in determining the pace of expansion or contraction in short-run business activity.

One important influence on inventory investment is the ratio of inventory levels to sales. In short-run forecasting it is reasonable to assume that the businessman intends to maintain a certain ratio of stocks to sales or to production rates in the cases of raw materials and goods in process. Inventories below these levels are inadequate to meet production and customer requirements. Inventories above this level involve unnecessary interest and storage expenditures and risks of obsolescence. Over long periods, technological change and improvements in inventory management may permit changes in these ratios, but in short-run forecasting such trends can be ignored.

The level of inventory investment depends also on expectations of businessmen. If they expect sales to increase they will build up inventories, and vice versa. Thus the forecasting of inventory investment must rest on an evaluation of business expectations, which in turn depends on expected changes in the other sectors. *Fortune* magazine and other publications attempt to evaluate inventory-sales ratios and sales expectations and to convert these into estimates of inventory changes.

Some forecasters find it useful to distinguish between voluntary and involuntary inventory investment or disinvestment. Inventories may increase because businessmen want them to take care of anticipated improved business. In such a case, a present rise in inventory investment is a favorable indicator of future levels of investment. An increase in inventories may, however, result from a failure of sales to reach anticipated levels, in which case an eventual contraction of the inventory buildup may be expected as firms cut back their orders for replacements. Similarly, inventories may contract because managers planned it so or because of an unexpected increase in sales; the one cause has the opposite significance of the other. It is true that data on inventory investment do not reveal whether the investment or disinvestment is voluntary or not. But it is not difficult in practice to determine whether the present inventory expansion or contraction is one planned by business or instead one that is likely to experience a reversal in the near future.

The big problem in estimating inventory investment is one of timing. One may know that a present expansion of inventories is temporary but may be unable to specify exactly when the reversal will take place. He may be aware that a present inventory disinvestment results from a desire to bring stocks back in line with sales, but he may not know how long the correction will continue, especially if a continued decline in sales means a continued failure in the restoration of the desired ratio.

The excess of exports over imports. The prospect for the excess of exports over imports is extremely complex, involving an evaluation of both the import and export situations, which requires an investigation of the progress of foreign economies as well as the domestic scene, international comparisons of price and wage changes, revisions in tariffs and other policies affecting trade, and the study of the markets for particular commodities important in international trade. Changes in trade have been *very* important in some recent years. A background in international economics would be helpful in analyzing this sector.

Consumption. The Keynesian tradition is to consider consumption to be relatively passive. If the main determinant of consumption is income, then the forecast of the other segments should lead to the required forecast of consumption. One need merely apply the multiplier theory, which says that given change in the other segments (investment and government spending) should result in an induced change in consumption because of the changes in income that result. We do not yet have a precise idea of what the magnitude of the multiplier is, though we are quite certain that it is less for decreases in nonconsumption spending than it is for increases in such spending.

One simple rule which provides fairly accurate forecasts of consumption is as follows: in normal recoveries from mild recessions the increase in consumption is approximately equal to the increase in nonconsumption spending; in mild recessions consumption remains at the prerecession level or increases slightly. This rule requires modification for more severe recessions or depressions and for inflationary periods or periods (like the beginning of the Korean War) when shortages are expected. In any case, the forecaster should modify his estimates for special influences on consumption in the period under study. In particular he should make a separate study of the demand for durable consumers' goods, which tends to be more volatile and more subject to special influences that will be discussed shortly.

A more sophisticated approach makes the forecast of consumption a part of the solution of at least two simultaneous equations which reflect the relations between disposable personal income and the GNP, between consumption and disposable personal income, and which might treat the increase or decrease in nonconsumption spending as an independent variable. This approach begins to move in the direction of the econometric models to be discussed shortly. These approaches to handling the problem of induced changes in consumption will be developed more fully in a few pages.

No one (and certainly not Keynes himself) ever really believed that forecasting of consumption was a simple matter of estimating income. The forecaster must contend with autonomous as well as induced changes in consumption. There is reason to believe that consumer attitudes and expectations influence their expenditures. And a multitude of factors help determine spending on particular types of commodities and services.

The forecaster may forecast consumption of durable goods separately, for durable goods more than nondurables are subject to special influences. In fact, the careful forecaster will break durable goods into subcomponents, such as purchases of automobiles, of household appliances, of furniture, and so on. In the forecasting of the consumption of durable consumer goods one should take into account the present levels of installment debt; high debt may mean a reluctance of lenders to permit future increases in indebtedness and also a reluctance of consumers to obligate themselves further. One should also evaluate present holdings of consumer durables.

Individual components: sources and suggestions.   The sketch of gross national product model building presented so far provides a framework for the forecaster. Filling in the detail requires a knowledge of sources of information, supported by skills in using that information to best effect. Table 4–4 lists some of the most important sources of data and indicates their uses.

Some awkward problems.   In using the gross national product model, the forecaster must face some difficulties which are mentioned here only briefly. The two most serious problems are those related to price changes and to induced effects of changes in one segment of the economy on other segments.

Forecasting would be much simpler if one could assume stability in prices. But in some years the increase in the gross national product in current dollars may be as much a result of inflation as of changes in "real" product. The forecaster should provide separate estimates of changes in production and changes in prices.

One simple procedure is to make an initial forecast, using the framework already described, without any attention to potential price changes, temporarily making the assumption of stable prices. The forecaster can then examine the implications of the initial forecast, making adjustments where necessary. If, for example, the initial forecast is one of a great increase in aggregate demand which will place considerable pressure on capacity, the forecaster may anticipate considerable inflation resulting from the competition for scarce resources. In any case, the forecaster must take care in separating his analysis in real terms from that in terms of current dollars. An extrapolation of past increases in state and local government spending which reflects both inflation and increases in volume does not make sense if one is forecasting only the physical increase in output.

TABLE 4-4

SOURCES AND USES OF KEY FORECASTING INFORMATION

Component of GNP	Type of Information	Source and Date	Uses of the Information
Federal government spending	1. President's budget message to Congress.	Newspapers carry summaries in January. Also published by government.	Provides the most important information on federal expenditures for the next fiscal year, starting on July 1. Is subject to revision by Congress.
	2. Summary of the budget message.	*The Budget in Brief* (Government publication in January).	Presents a summary of the budget message.
	3. Review of the economic situation with emphasis on the federal budget.	President's *Economic Report* (Government publication in late January).	Presents an interpretation of the budget and its economic implications.
	4. Review of the economic situation with emphasis on the federal budget.	*Midyear Budget Review* (Government publication in August).	Presents a review of the federal spending program for the current fiscal year, reflecting congressional revisions of the budget.
	5. Reports on congressional action on presidential spending plans.	Newspapers and weekly magazines throughout the sessions of Congress.	Provides information on the success or failure of the President's program in Congress, as well as predictions of future plans both of the President and Congress.
State and local government spending	1. Data on the levels of state and local government spending in recent periods.	The national income accounts in the *Survey of Current Business* (monthly).	The usual procedure is to extrapolate the recent trend into the future, with possible revisions based on newspaper reports on expedited programs or on financial difficulties.
Investment in plant and equipment	1. Surveys of intentions to invest.	McGraw-Hill Book Company (*Business Week* in November); also Department of Commerce and SEC (*Survey of Current Business*, November, March, and other issues).	These surveys provide excellent information in business investment plans for the coming year (or quarter). The past record of these surveys is good for most periods.

TABLE 4-4—Continued

Component of GNP	Type of Information	Source and Date	Uses of the Information
	2. New orders for durable goods.	*Survey of Current Business* (monthly).	Since orders usually lead actual production and sales, this series provides suggestions on future changes in investment.
	3. Nonresidential construction contracts (F. W. Dodge Index).	*Survey of Current Business* (monthly) and *Business Conditions Digest* (monthly).	Since construction awards should normally lead actual construction, this series suggests potential changes in the building of factories, office buildings, stores, etc.
Residential construction	1. Family formation.	Intermittent projections by the Bureau of the Census.	Provides information of a key segment of the potential market for new housing.
	2. Residential construction contracts awarded or housing starts.	*Survey of Current Business* (monthly) and *Business Conditions Digest* (monthly).	Provides an indication of potential changes in housing construction before those changes take place.
	3. Mortgage terms and ease of securing loans (down payments, interest rates, monthly payments).	Newspapers provide intermittent reports. *Federal Reserve Bulletin* (monthly).	Information on the terms of FHA, VA, and regular mortgages indicates the financial restraints on the purchase of new homes.
	4. Vacancy rate.	Bureau of Labor Statistics.	Indicates the extent of saturation of the housing market.
	5. Home-building survey.	*Fortune* magazine (monthly).	Indicates developments in residential construction.
Inventory investment	1. Ratios of inventories to sales on the manufacturing, wholesaling and retailing levels (requires computations involving series on inventories and series on sales).	*Survey of Current Business* (monthly).	Indicates whether inventories are high or low in relation to a "normal" ratio. Must be interpreted with caution in the light of recent changes in final sales and the attitude of businessmen toward inventories.
	2. Manufacturers' inventory expectations.	*Survey of Current Business* (monthly).	Indicates extent to which businessmen expect to expand or contract inventories.
	3. Inventory surveys.	*Fortune* magazine (monthly).	On the basis of sales expectations and assumed inventory-sales ratios, estimates amount of inventory change.

Category		Sources	
Consumer durable goods	1. Surveys of consumers' intentions to spend and save (including intentions to buy automobiles).	Survey Research Center, University of Michigan and Federal Reserve Board. *Federal Reserve Bulletin* (quarterly).	Indicates intentions to purchase durable goods. There is considerable correlation between these intentions and actual purchases.
	2. Rate of housing construction.	*Survey of Current Business* (monthly).	The building of new houses has an important influence on sales of furniture and appliances.
	3. Installment credit outstanding (in relation to the disposable personal income).	*Federal Reserve Bulletin* (monthly).	A high level of installment credit already outstanding may mean a lower willingness to incur new debt or a lower willingness to lend.
	4. Buying-plan surveys.	National Industrial Conference Board *Business Record.*	Suggests potential changes in the purchase of consumer goods.
	5. Projected consumer outlays on durable goods and housing.	*Consumer Buying Indicators* (quarterly).	Covers surveys of plans of consumers to purchase automobiles, appliances, furniture, and housing.
Nondurable consumer goods and services	1. Regression lines relating the past consumption of nondurable goods and services to the past disposable personal income.	Past issues of the *Survey of Current Business* provide the necessary data. Special articles in the *Survey of Current Business* review findings on such relationships.	Past relationships to disposable personal income show considerable stability, though the rate of sales to income rises in recession.
Comprehensive collection of indicators	1. Charts covering most of the best known indicators.	*Business Conditions Digest* (monthly).	A compact collection of charts covering indicators of income, production, prices, employment, and monetary conditions.

As has already been noted, various segments of the gross national product are interdependent. Forecasted changes for one segment may have important implications for another. The econometrician gets around the problem by using simultaneous equations reflecting these interdependencies. The forecaster using the more qualitative model under discussion must somehow make adjustments in his initial forecasts which will perform, at least roughly, the function served by the simultaneous equations. Suits provides a good (and simple) way of dealing with multiplier-accelerator effects.[18]

The two most important kinds of induced effects are (1) effects of changes in investment and government spending on consumption and (2) effects of the changes in demand for total output on investment. The first is the problem of the *multiplier;* the second the problem of the *acceleration effect.* The present discussion deals only with the multiplier.

The multiplier is the ratio of a change in income to the change in investment or government spending. It may be expressed as:

$$m = \frac{\Delta Y}{\Delta(I+G)}$$

where $\Delta(I+G)$ is the cause, the change in investment and government spending, and ΔY is the effect, the change in income.

The forecaster may proceed as follows. He may initially make an estimate of consumption based on the assumption that disposable personal income remains the same. At this stage he takes into account surveys of consumer attitudes and intentions to buy, financial considerations such as the size of liquid assets and the extent of consumer debt, and any other influences on consumption which he is able to uncover. In later stages of his forecast he drops the assumption of the constancy of income. He examines his estimates of changed nonconsumption spending (investment and government expenditure) to see whether these indicate a rise or fall in incomes which will induce a change in consumption.

The crudest way to handle this problem is to make a rough estimate of the multiplier effect based on past experience and apply it to the data. If the change in nonconsumption spending is positive (an increase), the forecaster may take the multiplier to be approximately 2.0, which would suggest induced increases in consumption approximately equal to the increases in nonconsumption spending. If, instead, the forecast indicates a decline in nonconsumption spending, he will apply a much smaller multiplier, for the evidence is strong that short-run declines in income do not affect consumption as much as increases in income. Consumption is "sticky" in the downward direction; in fact, consumption has declined very little in each of the recessions since World War II, suggesting that the multiplier is closer to 1.0 than to 2.0 in such periods. A major decline

---

[18] Daniel B. Suits, *Principles of Economics* (New York: Harper, 1970), pp. 193–209.

in investment or government spending would probably have a greater multiplier effect, for consumers would find it more difficult in such circumstances to resist a decline in their standards of living.

A more sophisticated approach involves use of several simultaneous equations which treat the gross national product and consumption as unknowns and take investment and government expenditures as exogenous variables. On the basis of past experience one might assume that consumption is 80 percent of disposable personal income and that disposable personal income is 69 percent of the gross national product. In such a case the simultaneous equations would appear as follows:

$$GNP = I + G + C$$
$$C = .80 \ (.69 \ GNP)$$

where

GNP = gross national product
I = investment (including the excess of exports over imports)
G = government spending (including state and local spending)
C = consumption

These two equations contain two unknowns (both I and G having been estimated already) and are easy to solve. More advanced approaches would use more complex equations, which might include marginal propensities to consume rather than average propensities, which would separate the effects of increases in nonconsumption spending from the effects of decreases, and which would separate the purchases of durable consumer goods from those of nondurable goods and services.

Any further elaboration of the use of simultaneous equations would bring us to econometrics, the next major topic of this chapter.

Checks for consistency. The final step in gross national product model building is to check the various components for consistency. Among the questions that are appropriate are the following:

1. Is the forecast level of government expenditure consistent with the total forecast? If the overall forecast indicates heavy unemployment, a reduction in taxes or an increase in public works might be in prospect. If the overall forecast indicates inflationary pressures, an increase in taxes or curtailment of spending might be imminent.

2. Are the assumptions on monetary sector consistent with the overall forecast? If the overall forecast indicates heavy unemployment, an easing of money by the Federal Reserve System may be imminent, with possible repercussions on residential construction or other sectors.

3. Are prospective profits consistent with other parts of the forecast? We have not discussed the forecasting of profits, but the thorough forecaster will check to see that prospective profits are in line with estimates of investments.

4. Is the level of personal saving consistent with the rest of the fore-

cast? Again, we have not developed the forecast of personal saving, though it is directly related to the forecast of consumption. A complete forecast would devote special attention to the savings forecast.

5. What magnitude of government surplus or deficit is likely under the conditions indicated? Some forecasters pay particular attention to the prospective deficit or surplus. A large deficit would be a stimulant to the economy that should already be reflected in government expenditure. But one can argue that the real point of interest is the net contribution of the government above its intake of taxes. If government expenditures are increasing but tax collections are increasing even faster, the stimulating effect of expenditures will be much less than they seem at first.

6. Is the forecast of total output and prices consistent with the available capacity? A strong pressure on capacity might mean that some investment or consumption plans might not materialize and that inflationary pressures will exceed those in the initial forecast.

Recapitulation. The foregoing discussion of gross national product model building has deliberately avoided some of the technical issues the forecaster must face in practice. But an understanding of this approach should be a big help to a decision maker in evaluating published forecasts. The reader should now be aware of the kinds of assumptions that go into such forecasting and, consequently, of the limitations of the forecasts. The following section discusses econometric models. Such models must be *completely* specified.

Econometric models

To begin the discussion of econometric models and to define several terms, consider the following very simple model of the macro economy.

$$Y = C + I + G + X \tag{1}$$
$$C = a + bY + dC_{-1} \tag{2}$$
$$I = e + fi \tag{3}$$
$$G = G' \tag{4}$$
$$X = X' \tag{5}$$
$$i = i' \tag{6}$$

Y: gross national product

C: consumption expenditures with C_{-1} denoting consumption expenditures in the previous period.

I: investment expenditures

G: government expenditures

i: an interest rate

X: net foreign exports

a, b, d, e, and f: unknown parameters or constants; i.e., unknown numbers

The above equations are either behavioral equations or identities. The behavioral equations are those which contain unknown parameters (i.e., Equations 2 and 3). The term "behavioral" stems from the fact that these equations specify how economic groups, such as consumers and producers, behave. The remaining equations are identities, either equilibrium conditions (1) or definitional identities (4, 5, and 6). Variables within the set of equations can be classified as "endogenous" or "exogenous." Values of *endogenous* variables are *determined within the system of equations.* In this example, they include GNP, consumption expenditures, and investment expenditures. Values of exogenous variables are *specified from outside the system* by the forecaster. These latter variables include expected government spending, net exports, and interest rate. C_{-1} is a *predetermined* variable.

Steps in forecasting with an econometric model consist of the following. First, a model such as the one indicated above must be *specified.* Economic theory determines the appropriate functional relationships (specification becomes a point of contention when the basic theory differs among forecasters). In the above example, a simple "consumption function" hypothesizes that current consumption depends upon current income and also upon consumption in the previous period. Each equation is an explicit statement of how the forecaster believes some of the sectors of the economy are interrelated; as a group these equations comprise what he believes to be the important behavioral characteristics of the economy.

The second step in the forecasting process is *estimation* of the unknown parameters; i.e., the values of a, b, d, e, and f. This requires two bits of expertise—knowledge of data and their sources and intimate knowledge of statistical estimation methods. The most commonly used form of estimation is some type of regression technique. Of course this technique must take into account the fact that the model is an interdependent one; i.e., consumption is a major portion of income (Y) but is in turn affected by the level of income.

The third step in forecasting is *simulation.* The forecaster "plugs in" values for the exogenous variables to get forecasts of the endogenous ones. For instance, assume that the following behavioral equations had been estimated.

$$C = 44 + .35Y + .7C_{-1}$$
$$I = 400 - 9620\ i$$

Further assume that the forecaster is willing to assume the following values for the exogenous variables:

$$C_{-1} = 510$$
$$G = 300$$
$$X' = 30$$
$$i' = .05$$

He would then forecast the level of Gross National Product to be 1,000.

Note that the structure of the above simple model includes an inter-period feedback effect through lagged consumption that would keep this model going if initial values of G', X', and i' were assumed to hold constant for several periods into the future. Or, a more interesting simulation could be carried out by plugging in expected changes in these "predetermined" variables. Projections more than one period into the future may be of much interest even though these become less and less reliable as the horizon is extended.

In appraising the basic four-step procedure for forecasting—constructing a model, estimating the parameters, choosing values for the exogenous variables, and simulating the future—several possible weak links are obvious. First, there is the *possibility of incorrectly specifying the model*. For example, perhaps interest rates actually have little bearing upon investment expenditures whereas profits of earlier periods are a good predictor of investment. In such a case, predictions will not be very accurate and the forecaster finds he needs to modify his model.

A second possible weakness relates to any attempt to extrapolate into the future based on past experience. *A change in the structure of the economy cannot be measured immediately* even though it may be having important effects on the level of income and employment. This problem can be encountered even in short-run forecasts. Therefore, it would involve really heroic assumptions to project GNP as much as 15 years into the future using a quarterly model of the U.S. economy tested for the period 1945–72.[19]

A third possible weak link in the procedure involves choice of values for exogenous variables. In the more complex models discussed below, these *guesses about the future can be crucial*.

Perhaps the most important positive feature of econometric model forecasting is that it *requires the forecaster to completely specify the assumptions* underlying his forecasts. This allows thorough examination of all aspects of the model, and this may lead to improvements in the approach.

Another strength of econometric models is their *capability for simulation of a great variety of possible environments*. For example, the impact of a possible major railway strike can be predicted. Such information can possibly lead to more intelligent policy-making than would otherwise be possible.

Of course, practical econometric models are much more sophisticated than the naive model presented above. During the past 20 years, econometric model building and forecasting has been a "growth industry." One of the early models of the U.S. economy was constructed and esti-

---

[19] An analogous procedure would be to "backcast" GNP for 1930 based on the same model and compare predicted with observed values.

mated by Lawrence Klein.[20] It was followed by the Klein-Goldberger model, which was the forerunner of the 32-equation econometric forecasting model used in the early 1960s at the University of Michigan.[21]

The basic structure of another model constructed during the 1960s is shown in Figure 4–4. This is a pictorial representation of a 49-equation model constructed by economists at the Office of Business Economics of the Department of Commerce, often called the O.B.E. model.[22] Note the basic interrelationships and the classification of variables into exogenous, endogenous and lagged endogenous.

The first truly large-scale project was necessarily a committee undertaking; economists were assigned to various sectors of the economy— e.g., demand for consumer durables or the housing construction sector— and each came up with a sectoral model which was then linked to the overall model.[23] The result was the Brookings model; tests have shown that this model contains substantial weaknesses.[24]

Lawrence Klein helped construct another large-scale model which is still being used (in revised form) by the Econometric Forecasting Unit of the Wharton School. Evan's book contains much information regarding the structure of this model.[25] The most recent version of the Wharton model is documented by McCarthy.[26] Detailed forecasts made with this model are available on a subscription basis.

In the above models, a major role is played by the so-called *real* sector of the economy. Little attention is given to the *monetary* sector of the

---

[20] *Economic Fluctuations in the United States,* 1921–1941 (New York: John Wiley and Sons, 1950).

[21] Lawrence R. Klein and Arthur S. Goldberger, *An Econometric Model of the United States, 1929–1952* (Amsterdam: North-Holland Publishing Co., 1955). For a discussion of the University of Michigan model being used in the early 1960s as well as a very lucid description of the techniques of forecasting from econometric models, see Daniel Suits, "Forecasting and Analysis with an Econometric Model," *American Economic Review,* 52 (March 1962), pp. 104–132. A more up-to-date discussion of the Michigan model is in Michael D. McCarthy, *Wharton Mark III Quarterly Economic Forecasting Model* (Philadelphia: Wharton Series on Quantitative Economics, 1972).

[22] M. Liebenberg, A. H. Hirsch and J. Popkin, "A Quarterly Econometric Model of the United States: A Progress Report," *Survey of Current Business* (May 1966), pp. 13–20.

[23] James S. Duesenberry, Gary Fromm, Lawrence R. Klein, and Edwin Kuh, *The Brookings Quarterly Econometric Model of the United States* (Chicago: Rand, McNally, 1965). Further results are found in a book edited by the same authors entitled *The Brookings Model: Some Further Results* (Amsterdam: North-Holland Publishing Co., 1969).

[24] See Z. Griliches, "The Brookings Model Volume: A Review Article," *Review of Economics and Statistics,* 50 (May 1968), pp. 215–34, or R. J. Gordon, "The Brookings Model in Action: A Review Article," *Journal of Political Economy,* 78 (May/ June, 1970), pp. 489–525.

[25] Evans, *Macroeconomic Activity.*

[26] Michael D. McCarthy, *Wharton Mark III Quarterly Economic Forecasting Model.*

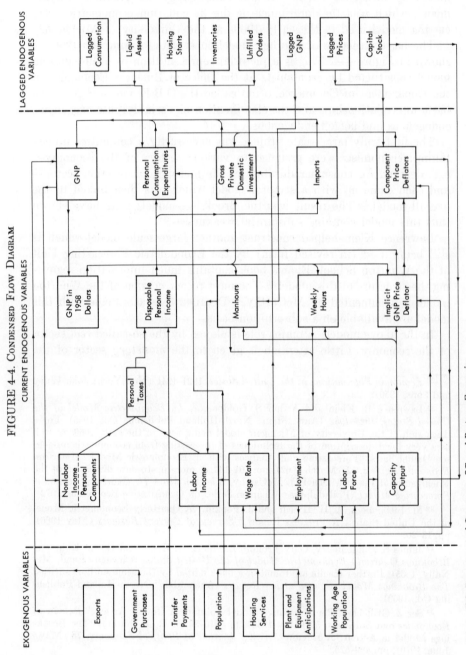

FIGURE 4-4. CONDENSED FLOW DIAGRAM

CURRENT ENDOGENOUS VARIABLES

LAGGED ENDOGENOUS VARIABLES

Lagged Consumption

Liquid Assets

Housing Starts

Inventories

Unfilled Orders

Lagged GNP

Lagged Prices

Capital Stock

GNP

Personal Consumption Expenditures

Gross Private Domestic Investment

Imports

Component Price Deflators

GNP in 1958 Dollars

Disposable Personal Income

Manhours

Weekly Hours

Implicit GNP Price Deflator

Personal Taxes

Nonlabor Income Personal Components

Labor Income

Wage Rate

Employment

Labor Force

Capacity Output

EXOGENOUS VARIABLES

Exports

Government Purchases

Transfer Payments

Population

Housing Services

Plant and Equipment Anticipations

Working Age Population

Source: U.S. Department of Commerce, Office of Business Economics.

economy. During the late 1960s, a model was developed jointly by the Board of Governors of the Federal Reserve System and economists at the Massachusetts Institute of Technology in which there is much more emphasis on the financial sector.[27] This model is currently known as the MPS model (MIT; Pennsylvania; Social Science Research Center) and is used by monetary authorities in predicting effects of their possible policy changes.

Numerous other econometric models are currently turning out either quarterly or annual forecasts of the state of the economy. The results of many of these forecasts are annually summarized by at least two organizations—The Federal Reserve Banks of Richmond and of Philadelphia. To gain insight into possible short-run developments in the national economy during the coming year, one would do well to study these summaries along with the leading indicators and then possibly undertake some opportunistic forecasting for himself. (Additionally, for the producer selling in a regional market, several local or regional econometric models are currently being developed.)

Experience with the forecasting methods

Judging the relative accuracy of econometric forecasts is a difficult task, since the problem is not well defined. For example, should one look at the predictive accuracy of total GNP forecasts or should one also look at the forecasts of the components of GNP? Further, as was indicated above, expected values for exogenous variables must be included whenever a forecast is made. In judging the accuracy of the predictions, should one use the "guesses" of the forecasters (and in a sense rank their abilities to guess what fiscal and monetary policies will be), or should one use actual past values for the exogenous variables and test only the predictive ability of the model as such. In one attempt to test the relative accuracy of the OBE and Wharton models, it was found that using *actual values* of the exogenous variables produced *larger* errors than using the *original forecasting assumptions*.[28] This points out that forecasting is both an art and a science. Forecasters continually "fine tune" their models, using judgment.[29]

---

[27] See Frank de Leeuw and Edward M. Gramlich, "The Channels of Monetary Policy: A Report on the Federal Reserve-MIT Model," *Journal of Finance,* 24 (May 1969), pp. 265–90.

[28] See Michael K. Evans, Yoel Haitovsky, and George I. Treqz, "An Analysis of the Forecasting Properties of U.S. Econometric Models," in *Econometric Models of Cyclical Behavior,* Bert G. Hickman, ed. (Columbia University Press for the National Bureau of Economic Research, 1972), pp. 949–1139.

[29] The usual method of "fine tuning" a model consists of adjustments of the constant terms in various equations. Thus, in the simple example above, the forecaster might reduce the value of e in the investment equation (3) if his first simulation of the model showed investment much greater than the forecaster "feels" it would be. This type of action indicates that even econometric models are "opportunistic" in the

Finally, note that econometric forecasts and opportunistic forecasts often differ. At the beginning of 1973, consensus forecasters were predicting a strong economy all year. Three months later, they were beginning to hedge somewhat and point to possible recessionary movements during late 1973. On the other hand, the Wharton econometric group, which had also predicted a strong economy at the beginning of the year, revised its predictions in March to indicate that an even greater expansion in the economy was to be expected. It is further notable that there are at times wide differences *within* both the econometric group and the opportunistic group.

FORECASTING INDUSTRY DEMAND AND CAPACITY

The focus of discussion now narrows to short-run forecasts of industry demand and capacity. Such forecasts are important to the firm for several reasons. First, projected business conditions in the firm's own industry determine expected sales and profit opportunities and are needed in decisions about product mix, pricing, and inventories. Second, expected relationships of demand to capacity in other industries are needed in forecasting their pricing and levels of production; the outlook for other industries may be important to the firm because they supply inputs or because they are its markets. Third, near-term prospects for another industry may be basic considerations in timing an entry into it.

The discussion to follow provides brief treatments of survey methods and statistical analyses of historical data. It then goes over input-output analysis in some detail. Finally, it explores forecasting of near-term changes in industry capacity.

Surveys

Surveys used in forecasting industry demand range from informal to sophisticated. A common technique, especially for sales forecasting, is polling of the sales force. Sometimes selected outside consultants are asked for estimates of future industry demand. For some industries, consumer anticipation surveys of the Survey Research Institute or the Census Bureau can be used. For example, a supplier who needs intentions of consumers to build houses during the next three months can simply look at the Census Bureau's *Current Population Reports* "Consumer Buying Indicators" (Series P-65) to obtain an extremely low-cost estimate. Of course, for a firm concerned only with regional markets, this approach may not be sufficient. Finally, there are surveys of consumers or retailers that incorporate random sample designs and pretested, sophisticated questionnaires.

Major problems with random sample surveys are their cost plus some

---

sense that the forecaster will use additional information to make such adjustments. See McCarthy, *Wharton Mark III Quarterly Forecasting Model.*

conceptual problems in handling nonrespondents and evaluating the true intent of those who do respond. Nevertheless, surveys are and will continue to constitute an important research tool in demand forecasting.

Statistical forecasts

This rather vague heading includes a wide spectrum of somewhat mechanical forecasting methods based upon various statistical techniques. Probably the most naive method of statistical projection is to assume constancy—either no changes, constant absolute changes, or constant rate of change. A stationary state forecast in period t of the level of the variable X in period $t + 1$, denoted X_{t+1}, would specify

$$X_{t+1} = X_t$$

where X_t denotes the value of X during the forecast period.

Constant absolute change can be predicted using the formulation

$$X_{t+1} = X_t + (X_t - X_{t-1})$$

That is, the expected next period change in the value of X is equal to the past period's absolute change in this variable. Finally, a constant relative change can be forecast as

$$X_{t+1} = [(X_t - X_{t-1})/(X_{t-1})] \, X_t$$

Thus, if the variable grew at a 5 percent rate during the past period relative to period $t - 1$, this growth rate will continue during the next period.

Each of the above methods of forecasting has one overriding advantage—a low cost. Their weakness is the rigidity in assumptions about the nature of changes over time. Because of this rigidity, they are not capable of predicting turning points in a series of data. However, for certain uses they may be quite useful.

A more complex forecasting method is *time series analysis*. "Decomposition of time series data" is described in many business statistics textbooks and will not be detailed here. Basically it breaks the changes in values of a time series into seasonal movements, cyclical movements, trends, and erratic events. Differences among the various decomposition methods are mainly in the assumption about how the various components interact; e.g., multiplicatively or additively. Chisholm and Whitaker review several of these methods and provide a list of further references which could be studied before choosing any of these methods.[30] The technique called *exponential smoothing* is particularly useful in making sales forecasts for an item based only on its own past history of sales.[31]

---

[30] Roger K. Chisholm and Gilbert R. Whitaker, Jr., *Forecasting Methods* (Homewood, Ill.: Richard D. Irwin, Inc., 1971), pp. 16–27.

[31] See Robert G. Brown, *Smoothing, Forecasting, and Prediction of Discrete Time Series* (Englewood Cliffs, N.J.: Prentice-Hall, Inc., 1963).

Still more sophisticated forecasts can be made with the aid of correlation and regression techniques. *Correlation* analysis implies no causal relationship, but specifies the direction and strength of association between two variables. However, such a measure can be of use to the forecaster if the variable in which he is interested is highly correlated with some other variable for which he has a forecast. For example, if demand for building materials is found to be highly correlated with housing starts during the previous quarter and there is a major drop in such starts, it is reasonable to forecast that demand for building materials will fall.

Regression analysis requires more detailed *a priori* assumptions than correlation analysis. In regression analysis, an explicit functional relationship between one or more independent variables and the dependent variable is hypothesized and estimated. Given this estimated relationship and forecasts of values for the independent variables, values of the dependent variable can be projected. For example, assume that the forecaster has specified that the level of total quarterly sales of a particular product in the building materials industry, D, was a linear function of housing starts in the previous quarter, S, and the level of GNP, Y. Using past observations of these variables, he can estimate the regression coefficients. Assume the following regression equation is estimated:

$$D = 40.35 + 50.13S + .000000045Y \qquad R^2 = .943$$

The coefficient of determination, R^2, indicates the percent of the total variation in the dependent variable which can be attributed to variations in the independent variables. Thus, in this example, it appears that the two chosen variables account for over 94 percent of the changes in industry demand—an encouraging sign when one wishes to use regression analysis for predictive purposes.[32]

If the forecaster has values of the independent variables for the prediction period, he merely "plugs in" these values to determine a forecast value for the dependent variable. For example, in the regression equation above, if the value of housing starts in the current period were 3,000, and if the predicted value of GNP for the next period were 1,200 billion, then the forecast value of the dependent variable would be 204,-430. Two practical points are illustrated in the above example. First, the use of lagged values, when appropriate, makes forecasting easier; observed values from an earlier period do not have to be predicted. Second, if one must use predicted values, it is helpful if these values are already being forecast by others; e.g., GNP.

---

[32] Note that the absolute size of R^2 may *not* be important in other uses of regression analysis. For example, if the primary purpose of the technique were to *test hypotheses* about the theorized relationships between the independent and dependent variables, one would be more concerned with the sizes of the standard errors of the coefficients relative to values of the coefficients themselves. Further discussion of these topics is beyond the scope of this book.

Success in using regression techniques for prediction depends upon constancy of the structural relationship between the independent and dependent variables. Also, several assumptions about the nature of the variables must hold for the estimated coefficients to have desirable properties and for the predictions to be accurate. These regression problems are beyond the scope of this book. A user of regression analysis should make himself aware of them.[33]

One of the real advantages of regression analysis for prediction is that this technique allows a more "scientific" or systematic approach to forecasting. By starting with those variables which theoretically influence the dependent variables, the forecaster is building upon a somewhat more solid foundation than if he were simply looking at the situation and making ad hoc prognostications. Advantages of carefully built theoretical foundations are even more evident in the industry forecasting technique discussed below—input-output analysis.

Input-output analysis

The conceptual idea behind input-output analysis is really quite simple. It merely explicitly recognizes that *industries are interrelated.* For example, the steel industry, rubber industry, electrical power industry, and many others supply inputs used by the automobile industry. Thus, some of the *outputs* of each of the above-listed industries are required as *inputs* to produce automobiles. On the other hand, automobiles are used as inputs by the above-listed industries (automobiles may even be used as inputs by the automobile industry). Input-output analysis quantifies interindustry relationships by showing estimated flows of intermediate goods used in production of final goods and services.[34]

To aid the understanding of input-output analysis, the four industry example in Table 4–5 has been constructed. All flows are measured in dollars; flows of *inputs* are listed *down* an industry's *column* and the flows of *outputs* are shown *across* an industry's *row.* For example, the entry in the third column of the second row shows that Industry B produced 40 units of output which were used as inputs by Industry C. Note that the diagonal entries show the amounts of goods produced by an industry for its own use—for example, automobiles by the auto industry. The last two rows show that not only are the processed outputs of other industries used as inputs in production but also labor, management,

---

[33] A brief review of these problems, including autocorrelation, multicollinearity, etc., are found in Chisholm and Whitaker, *Forecasting Methods.* For even more complete descriptions of the technical nature of these problems, see any basic econometrics book; e.g., J. Johnston, *Econometric Methods,* 2d ed. (New York: McGraw-Hill Book Co., 1972).

[34] For a more detailed discussion of the basics of input-output analysis, including its use in forecasting, see William H. Miernyk, *The Elements of Input-Output Analysis* (New York: Random House, 1965).

TABLE 4–5

INPUT-OUTPUT TABLE
(hypothetical example)

		Inputs to Industry				Final Demand		
		A	B	C	D	Persons	Government	Total
Output of Industry	A	20			5	90	15	130
	B			40	10	10	40	100
	C		80	10	10	100		200
	D	30		90				120
Value Added	Wages	50	15	30	75			170
	Other	30	5	30	20			85
	Total	130	100	200	120	200	55	

TABLE 4–6

OUTPUT DISTRIBUTION TABLE
(hypothetical example)

		Industry				Final Demand		
		A	B	C	D	Persons	Government	Total
Output of Industry	A	.15			.04	.69	.12	1.00
	B			.40	.10	.10	.40	1.00
	C		.40	.05	.05	.50		1.00
	D	.25		.75				1.00

and other nonprocessed inputs. These are the "value added" amounts for each industry. The rightmost columns of the table show the several final users of industry outputs.

Other useful tables can be derived from a basic input-output table. For example, an *output distribution table* can be derived by dividing each entry in the basic table by its corresponding *row* total.[35] Such a table is shown in Table 4–6 for the hypothetical example. The table shows the proportions of an industry *sales* that go to each of the other industries and to final demand sectors. The forecasting implications of an output distribution table are easy to see. For example, if a firm in Industry D feels that firms in Industry C are in for a hard time in the near future, it must prepare for derived decreases in demand. Likewise, if Industry B is highly dependent upon sales to the public sector, estimates of the political situation may be the most important ingredient in its market planning.

Direct requirements tables are regularly provided in national input-output tables. A requirements table, shown in Table 4–7 for the hypo-

---

[35] Chisholm and Whitaker, *Forecasting Methods,* p. 66, provide another example of such a table and note that such tables are not regularly published by authors of national input-output tables but are quite useful for individual firms.

TABLE 4–7

DIRECT REQUIREMENTS
(hypothetical example)

| | | *Industry* | | | | | |
		A	B	C	D	*Persons*	*Government*
Industry Source	A	.15			.04	.45	.27
	B			.20	.08	.50	.73
	C		.80	.05	.08	.50	
	D	.23		.45			
Value Added	Wages	.39	.15	.15	.63		
	Other	.23	.05	.15	.17		
	Total	1.00	1.00	1.00	1.00	1.00	1.00

thetical example, is found by dividing each entry in the original table by the corresponding *column* sum. The resulting coefficient shows what proportion of an industry's *inputs* are required from each of the other industries as well as from itself. For example, a firm in Industry B would realize that it was almost totally dependent upon inputs from Industry C; if a large industry-wide strike were anticipated in C, it would do well to build up inventory of the threatened items.

From the direct requirements table, one might expect that to increase output in Industry C by $1,000, output in Industry B would need to expand by $200. This is only partially true. Note that for Industry C to expand it must also increase its own output simply to supply itself and must rely upon industry D to increase output as well. Industry B must increase output in excess of $200 to meet the *indirect* requirements in C and D. The above scenario indicates the complex interactive nature of even the simple hypothetical four-industry economy. It is summarized in the *total requirements* or direct *and* indirect requirements table as shown in Table 4–8. For example, the entry in the first column of the first row indicates that if final output of Industry A is to increase by $1, total output of the industry must be increased by $1.19. The total requirements is obtained by matrix operations on the input-output matrix and the vector of final demands.[36]

Basically, short-run forecasting with an input-output model involves projecting the level and composition of the final demand sector and determining what kind of impact this final demand would have on those industries that are of interest.

Five crucial points constitute possible weaknesses of input-output analysis as a forecasting technique. First, there is the *important role played by the forecast of final demand and its composition.* Errors in

---

[36] For a further discussion of these manipulations see either Chisholm and Whitaker, *Forecasting Methods,* pp. 69–71, or Miernyk, *The Elements of Input-Output Analysis,* pp. 24–28.

TABLE 4–8

DIRECT PLUS INDIRECT (TOTAL) REQUIREMENTS
(hypothetical example)

		Inputs to Industry		
	A	B	C	D
Outputs of Industry A	1.190	.035	.054	.298
B	.024	1.261	1.104	.502
C	.030	.326	1.380	.628
D	.052	.128	.201	1.102

this forecast will, of course, show up in the implications drawn from the input-output table. Second, perhaps the greatest potential weakness of input-output forecasting is the *avoidance of any explicit recognition of prices,* either input or output prices, although the construction of the table is based on total dollar value of outputs in the several industries and must utilize some price level. For example, the most complete table now being used in the United States is based on 1963 prices. Because of the lag between base year and forecast year, current relative price levels in the several industries may not be the same as the ones implied in the table. Third, the basic assumption in construction of the technical coefficients is a linear homogeneous production function. This assumption implies that *as output within an industry increases, input proportions remain constant, with constant input price ratios.* Further, a doubling of output will require exactly a doubling of all inputs. It is easy to see the importance of such an assumption; if it does not hold, expansion in one industry may not have the impacts upon other industries that are forecast by the input-output table.

Fourth, the constant input-output formulation *ignores the possibility of industry outputs reaching capacity with the resulting changes in relative prices of intermediate goods and perhaps a change in input proportions in other industries.* This assumption of constant technical coefficients goes counter to the usual arguments of economics concerning substitutions of input factors. Fifth, an obvious shortcoming of the input-output method of forecasting for specific firms within industries is that *even the most complicated table thus far constructed contains only 370 industries.* Such a breakdown may not be fine enough for many forecasting purposes. Further, many firms have markets that do not correspond to any of the industry groupings used in constructing input-output tables.

A final drawback to the use of the input-output method of forecasting industry demand is the *high cost.* For this reason, most firms will have to rely on analyses published by the government.[37] The most recent such

---

[37] Chisholm and Whitaker, *Forecasting Methods,* p. 75, indicate that several firms are undertaking construction of specific-output tables tailored especially for their own needs.

publication appeared in the *Survey of Current Business* in November of 1969.[38] This article contains a verbal description of the 1963 Input-Output Table of the United States, which was constructed as a matrix of 370 industries. Three additional volumes contain supplementary data that may be of use to the forecaster.

Note that input-output forecasting techniques can also be used for regional or even local markets. In fact, one of the more active fields within input-output analysis has been the construction of regional models. If the relevant market is really regional in nature, use of the national table may require untenable assumptions about the homogeneity of the regional and national economics.[39] When used for a single industry, the input-output approach is reasonably simple.[40] Many large-scale econometric models now have integrated input-output structure.[41]

In conclusion, input-output techniques are unique among forecasting methods in that they reflect interindustry relationships, and therefore are really the only form of internally consistent industry forecasting available. Unfortunately, their cost and rigid structural assumptions make them less than the perfect forecasting tool.[42]

Forecasting industry capacity. This section is concerned with potential rate of real output (capacity) in an industry and how it may be constrained by various factors. Industry capacity forecasts are compared with demand projections to make judgments about an industry's short-term prospects for pricing and profits.

If *labor* is readily available—i.e., there exists a pool of unemployed within the labor market area—it cannot be a constraint on capacity and capital is the relevant restriction. However, in cases of full or nearly full employment in the labor market, increased employment in an industry can occur only via three paths, all of which might increase costs. First,

---

[38] U.S. Department of Commerce, *Survey of Current Business,* 49 (November 1969). Note also that three supplemental volumes were also published for these tables. They include Volume 1: *Transactions Data for Detailed Industries;* Volume 2: *Direct Requirements for Detailed Industries;* and Volume 3, *Total Requirements for Detailed Industries.*

[39] For examples of the use of input-output analysis in state or regional forecasting see Charles M. Tiebout, "An Empirical Regional Input-Output Projection Model: The State of Washington, 1980," *Review of Economics and Statistics,* 60 (August 1969), or William H. Miernyk, "Long Range Forecasting with a Regional Input-Output Model," *Western Economic Journal,* 6 (June 1968).

[40] C. Richard Long, "Textiles in Transformation," *Monthly Review,* Federal Reserve Bank of Atlanta, 51(5), May 1966.

[41] Ross S. Preston, *The Wharton Annual and Industry Forecasting Model* (Philadelphia: Wharton School), 1972.

[42] Although not a recent contribution to the literature, a set of papers contained in the volume *Input-Output Analysis: An Appraisal* (Princeton University Press, 1955) for the National Bureau of Economic Research provides detailed arguments for and against input-output forecasting. See especially the paper by Carl F. Christ, "A Review of Input-Output Analysis," pp. 137–69, and the comment by Milton Friedman, pp. 169–74.

current workers may be employed for longer hours per week. Second, workers currently employed in other industries may be attracted away from their position. Finally, individuals not in the labor force may be attracted into the labor force. The first two possibilities, of course, involve higher labor costs, either overtime rates or higher wages to attract mobile workers. The third, an increase in labor force participation, requires higher wages and also involves new labor force entrants who are likely to be less productive than the general labor force.

Capital (plant and equipment) is also important in determining an industry's potential output. In the very short run, plant and equipment cannot be increased except in the rare cases in which there are both unoccupied floor space and new equipment available from stocks. Thus, for industries using specialized capital equipment, the forecaster should usually not expect an immediate increase in new capital even if the firms are willing to invest. However, one possibility for short-run increases in capital levels is utilization of previously unemployed capital such as putting into service older machines which had been retired before they were worn out. Of course, productivity of such machinery is likely to be lower than currently used machines or newly produced machinery, and costs are likely to be higher.

In the slightly longer run where it is physically possible to increase capital through investment, one must consider the *willingness of firms* to add to capital. Expected profitability is the underlying motivation for such expenditures. A final point, closely tied to the concept of capital expansion, is the *ease of entry* into the industry. For certain industries where there are few unique real capital requirements—e.g., management consulting—firms may spring up very rapidly in response to increased demand, thus making capacity constraints very weak. On the other hand, in cases where inputs are unique and require time for production—e.g., the lumber industry—new firms may not find entry easy.[43]

Forecasting of industry capacity will require certain kinds of data. For information about current situations in labor markets one can consult various documents by the U.S. Department of Labor, especially the publication titled *Employment and Earnings Statistics in the United States and Selected Labor Market Areas*. Current levels of industrial production in various industries are compiled by the Board of Governors of the Federal Reserve System. Also, McGraw-Hill periodically publishes in *Business Week* an index of production compared to capacity in various industries. This index is based on surveys of manufacturers.[44] Finally, a forecaster interested in a particular industry will do well to consult

---

[43] For a more specific discussion of the question of industrial capacity, especially the importance of capital expenditures, see Robert C. Yost, "The Capacity Concept and Economic Forecasting," *Mississippi Valley Journal of Business and Economics* (Spring, 1968), pp. 16–30.

[44] Ibid., p. 30.

FIGURE 4–5
WHY CEMENT USERS ARE GETTING SQUEEZED

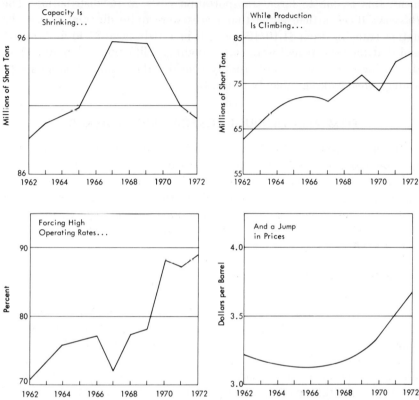

Source: Data, Standard & Poor's, Bureau of Mines, Commerce Department; Chart, Robert Mc Auley, *Business Week.*

industry trade publications; these often provide valuable insight into the current state of the industry, and they may report plans for expansions by individual firms that will substantially change industry capacity.

An example of the impact of capacity upon profitability was observed in the cement industry during the early 1970s. As discussed in *Business Week*,[45] cement producers experienced large demands during the 1950s and responded with large-scale expansions of plant and equipment that increased capacity tremendously. Demand decreased during the 1960s and cement prices also decreased. Low product prices combined with increasing costs decreased profits and resulted in little subsequent expansion of capital within the industry. Because of capacity limitations, cement makers were hard pressed to meet increased demands during the early 1970s and cement prices rose sharply. These changes are shown graphically in Figure 4–5.

[45] March 10, 1973, pp. 130 a-d.

A second interesting aspect of the above example is that cement, like many other goods, is produced for regional markets. In the case of cement, this is due to large transportation costs in its distribution. The *Business Week* article noted that prices were quite different across the nation (ranging from $1.10/100 pounds in Pittsburg to $1.40 in Atlanta) and that the "shortages" were correspondingly different regionally. Thus, the business forecaster must usually consider the regional markets separately when making capacity forecasts.

FIRM AND PRODUCT FORECASTS OF DEMAND

We have discussed forecasts for major sectors of the economy and then for particular industries. Attention can now be turned to the individual manager's usual objective in economic forecasting—namely, prediction of demand for his own product or products. The discussion begins with estimates of *market potential*, first for producer's goods, then consumer's goods. Next it moves to forecasts of *market share for an individual firm*.

Market potential for producer's goods

Producer's goods are goods that will be used by other firms in their production process. One common technique of predicting demand for such goods is the "build-up" approach to market potential forecasting.[46] This relatively simple method uses . . . "one or more series of marketing data weighted by the relative importance of the various industries having use for the product." The method includes these steps: (1) determining the industries that purchase the product and the percent of the total market that is attributable to each of these industries; (2) adjusting these percentages to account for changes or trends in market structure; (3) ascertaining the importance of an industry in a particular geographic area relative to that industry nationwide—this involves construction of weights based on published data; (4) calculating weighted market potentials for specific areas. Such steps are carried out for a hypothetical machine tool manufacturer in Table 4–9.

This method of forecasting market potential can be used for markets defined in ways other than spatially. For example, the buildup approach could be based on types of customers, demographic groups, and types of outlets.

Probably the greatest weaknesses of the method are the importance of judgments in adjusting the weights and problems with lack of data.

---

[46] This technique and others are discussed in Francis E. Hummel, *Market and Sales Potentials* (New York: The Ronald Press, 1961).

TABLE 4–9

MARKET AREA BUILDUP METHOD OF ESTIMATING A PRODUCER'S GOODS'
MARKET POTENTIAL
(hypothetical example)

Industry*	SIC†	SIC weight unadjusted‡	SIC weight adjusted§	Percent SIC‖	Weighted Proportion#
Mining machinery ..	3532	40	30	.080	2.40
Industrial furnaces and ovens	3567	45	50	.035	1.75
Truck and bus bodies	3713	15	20	.60	1.20
			100		5.35

Market Potential: 5.35% of National Market

* Industries in area which might purchase goods.
† Standard industrial code of industry.
‡ Past relative importance of industries as purchasers of product.
§ Expected relative importance of industries as purchasers.
‖ Relative importance of area in U.S. market. May be found as

$$\text{(i)} \quad \frac{\text{No. Production Workers in SIC in area}}{\text{No. Production Workers in SIC in U.S.}}$$

$$\text{(ii)} \quad \frac{\text{Value added in SIC in area}}{\text{Value added in SIC in U.S.}}$$

or by some other weighing method.
SIC weight adjusted *times* percent SIC.

Market potential for a consumer's good

Techniques similar to the method discussed above can also be used for forecasting market potential for a consumer's good. One approach to consumer goods market potentials is through the use of consumer "buying-power" estimates. Probably the best-known generally available index of buying power is published by *Sales Management* magazine in its "Annual Survey of Buying Power." Indices of buying power are estimated for all counties and larger cities in the United States. Each indice is a weighted average of three factors with the relative weights being .5: .3: .2 for the area's percentage of total national income, percentage of total national retail sales, and percentage of total national population, respectively. The index numbers range from 6.5438 in New York City and 3.9719 in Chicago to levels like .0005 in Issaquena County, Mississippi, or .0002 in Arthur County, Nebraska. After estimating total national consumer sales potentials for a product, the forecaster would simply multiply this total by a given area's index of buying power to get its market potential.

Market share forecasting

After forecasting market potential for the nation or for a regional market, a firm must estimate what share of this total it will obtain.

Probably the most often used approach conceives the firm's market share as depending upon various decision variables such as advertising expenditures, other distribution policies, price and "effectiveness" of marketing effort. Upon hypothesizing the variables of importance in this process, the forecaster sets up the general behavioral equation $S_i = f(X_1 \ldots X_n)$ which "explains" the ith firm's share. Of course, an explicit functional form with parameters that specify exactly how the Xs act to determine S_i is hypothesized. The parameters can then be estimated from market data by statistical methods.

In his *Marketing Decision Making: A Model-Building Approach,* Kotler discusses several different models of market share determination including simple linear models, nonlinear models, and models specifying that the effects or actions occur only with certain time lags.[47] Among the types of explanatory variables mentioned are relative prices, relative advertising expenditures as well as the effectiveness of these expenditures, product quality and levels of service provided. The models as presented provide a systematic yet flexible way of considering various market share determinants.

Doyle Weiss reported a study somewhat along the lines described above. His approach was to use four determinants of market shares for four brands of competing products within the class of "low-cost consumer foods."[48] These determinants were hypothesized to be (1) price, (2) advertising, (3) retail availability, and (4) physical characteristics of the product. Using several different functional forms, Weiss found each to yield coefficients of determination, R^2, which were significantly different from zero and always near .9.

Another example of forecasting of market shares is provided in the book *Mathematical Models and Marketing Management* by Robert Buzzell.[49] Buzzell discusses use of regression analysis by E. I. du Pont De Nemours and Co. (Inc.). In forecasting market shares, the basic approach was similar to that used by Weiss; however, the data were obtained from surveys both of households using the product *and* of firms supplying the product. In this way, it was possible to utilize the linear model

$$S_i = a + b_1 AVL + b_2 DP + b_3 ADV$$

where the independent variables are

---

[47] Philip Kotler, *Marketing Decision Making: A Model-Building Approach* (New York: Holt, Rinehart and Winston, 1971), pp. 92–99.

[48] Doyle Weiss, "Determinants of Market Share," *Journal of Marketing Research,* 5 (August 1968), p. 290. Because of restrictions by the cooperating company, Weiss was not allowed to specify the product or brands under study.

[49] Boston: Harvard University Press, 1964.

AVL: a proxy for availability of the product and defined as the proportion retail outlets stocking the product under investigation

DP: a proxy for "dealer push" which was measured as the proportion of sales persons specifying the product by name

ADV: a proxy for advertising thrust measuring the percentage of change in advertising before and during the experiment.

The final variable was included because the experiment was designed primarily to determine the relative effectiveness of different levels of advertising. In some areas a 300 percent increase in advertising was used. The results of the experiment highlighted the importance of availability of the product; increased emphasis upon this factor was planned.

In evaluating the regression approach to market share forecasting, it must be remembered that any unit increase in value of an independent variable that has a positive coefficient in a linear function will result in a constant increase in market share. Such a relationship is unreasonable if the value of the variable is carried too far. Thus, either the applications of the equations should be restricted by appropriate limits, or nonlinear forms of the functions should be estimated.

Some useful ideas

A number of interesting ideas which have been applied in actual forecasting for firms or products deserve attention.

Population changes. Some demands are closely related to population growth and demographic changes. The producer of baby foods profits from projections of increased birth rates. The publisher of textbooks studies the potential changes in college enrollment in the near future. Real estate investors pay attention to the growing proportion of the population over 65 in age and the special housing needs of this group. Forecasters are using estimates of the rate of family formation to help determine the potential market for residences. Bureau of Census publishes population projections periodically.

Discretionary income. Some forecasters make use of measurements of discretionary or supernumerary income rather than the usual measures of GNP or disposable personal income. There is evidence that the sale of consumer durables relates more closely to income after the deduction of certain regular expenses than it does to total income. Discretionary income is disposable personal income (personal income after income tax but including transfer payments) less necessary living costs (such as food and clothing) and less fixed commitments (payments on debt). The National Industrial Conference Board has developed a discretionary income series.

Discretionary buying power. Indexes of discretionary buying power start with discretionary income and add cash balances, near liquid assets, and new consumer credit. Obviously a wide variety of such measurements is possible. (The purist may raise questions about the addition of flows, such as income, to stocks, such as cash, but both stocks and flows are sources of liquidity that may influence consumption.)

Consumer credit outstanding. A forecaster may wish to consider the status of consumer debt outstanding before estimating the demand for a durable consumer good. A high ratio of outstanding consumer debt to current income may suggest a slowdown of purchases based on new debt for two reasons: lenders will become more cautious about risks, and the consumers themselves will reduce additions to debt. The forecaster may also take into account any changes in the regulation of installment debt by the Federal Reserve Board.

Saturation levels. Some forecasters give attention to the concept of a limit or saturation level in the particular market. This consideration is especially important for durable consumer goods, such as automobiles or household appliances. As we approach a point at which close to 100 percent of the households have refrigerators, the potential market for additional refrigerators becomes limited; the demand becomes mainly a replacement demand (which may be bolstered by planned obsolescence through the use of new designs and colors).

The size and age distribution of existing stocks. For many consumer durables the size of existing stocks must have a considerable influence on additions to stocks. In a way this repeats the point already made about saturation levels. The age distribution of the outstanding durables may be of particular importance. For example, the automobile market in 1957–58 was depressed by the existence of large numbers of automobiles of recent vintage resulting from the peak sales of 1955–56.

Replacement demand versus new-owner demand. The demand for durables falls into two parts: the demand for replacements on the part of those who already own the item and the demand of entirely new owners. Some forecasters separate these two demands, recognizing that the influences on each are different. New household formation, for example, will have little effect on replacement demand, but may be a major influence on new-owner demand.

More complex patterns of behavior. While it seems that the expectation of price increases should stimulate the purchase of consumer durable goods, such is not always the case. Katona's studies at the University of Michigan show that bad news about the rising cost of living, as in 1966 and 1967, may discourage discretionary purchases.[50] Increases in disposable income resulting from one-time tax cuts are likely to have an impact different from increases which may be expected to be repeated.

---

[50] George Katona, "On the Function of Behavioral Theory and Behavioral Research in Economics," *The American Economic Review,* March 1968, pp. 146–49.

Katona's studies also suggest that studies of consumer sentiment will improve forecasts of their discretionary expenditures.

An example of industry demand forecasting: nonmonetary demand for gold

In 1971, Michalopoulos and Van Tassel made a forecast of commercial (nonmonetary) uses of gold in the United States in 1975.[51] There are four classes of such uses: jewelry, electronics manufacturing, other industrial uses, and dentistry.

In the case of jewelry, the use of gold was expected to depend upon (1) shifts in the demand for jewelry, (2) changes in the price of jewelry relative to other prices, and (3) changes in the price of gold relative to other inputs (particularly other precious metals) used in producing jewelry. The demand function for jewelry was estimated from time series data as:

$$Vj = -4.0692 + 1.6715M + 0.3591 \ Hg$$
$$(12.8600) \quad (.0006) \quad (13.7517)$$
$$N = 15 \qquad R^2 = .9808 \quad DW = 1.6105$$

in which

Vj = value added annually in the jewelry industries
M = annual marriages
Hg = annual high school graduations

Although per capita income had been hypothesized as one of the explanatory variables, the income series was found to be collinear with marriages and graduations and this variable was dropped from the demand equation.

The prediction equation for the use of gold in jewelry was then estimated from time series data as

$$Gj = 15682.080 + 0.0040Vj - 162.9524 \ P_c$$
$$(12.8600) \quad (.0006) \quad (13.7517)$$
$$N = 15 \qquad R^2 = .9808 \quad DW = 1.6105$$

in which

G_j = thousands of ounces of gold used annually in jewelry
V_j = value added annually in the jewelry industry
$$P_c = \frac{Pg_0}{CPI} + \frac{K \ (Pg_t - Pg_0)}{(CPI_t - CPI_0)}$$

Pc is a variable that reflects changes in the price of jewelry relative to other prices because of changes in the relative price of gold. The market

---

[51] Constantine Michalopoulos and Roger C. Van Tassel, "Gold as a Commodity: Forecasts of U.S. use in 1975," *Western Economic Journal,* Vol. 9, No. 2, pp. 157–71.

price of gold was deflated by the consumer price index (*CPI*) and the
resulting index of gold price was adjusted by a constant (*K*) to account
for the fact that gold cost is on the average only 38.9 percent of the
total value of end product. Subscripts *o* and *t* refer to base and given
time periods, respectively. The model assumes no changes in other elements of cost of jewelry production relative to the national average.

Gold use in electronics manufacturing and in other industrial applications was estimated from time series data by the two equations:

$$G_e = 1369.4027 + 16.158\ E$$
$$(16.3863)\qquad (1.6706)$$
$$N = 15\quad R^2 = .9781\quad DW = -1.6825$$

$$G_n = 8/.2734 + .0010\ V_n$$
$$(1.4414)\qquad (.0001)$$
$$N = 14\quad R^2 = .9277\quad DW = 2.0041$$

in which

G_e = annual gold use in electronics in ounces
E = value added annually in the electronics industry
G_n = annual gold use in other industrial applications in ounces
V_n = value added annually in other industrial applications.

The price elasticity of demand for gold in industrial uses was considered
to be so highly inelastic that it could be ignored, since gold content in
electronics ranges from 1 to 4 percent of total value of end products.
However, the sensitivity of gold use to changes in its price relative to
other precious metals was estimated by means of data from a questionnaire sent to a sample of industrial firms. The arc elasticity of demand
for a change of gold price to $50 was —.17 and $70, —.30.

Use of gold in dentistry was estimated from time series data as

$$G_d = 345.3557 + 1.453\ Y$$
$$(3.8234)\qquad (.2672)$$
$$N = 14\quad R^2 = .711\quad DW = 1.5887$$

in which

G_d is gold used annually in dentistry, in ounces
Y is real disposable per capita income

Projections of gold use for nonmonetary purposes in 1975, shown in
Table 4–10, were made as follows:

Jewelry: projections were based on projected marriages and graduations and alternative assumptions about the price of gold.

Industry: projections were based on independent projections of the
output of electrical machinery and the FRB industrial output index and
alternative assumptions about the price of gold.

TABLE 4–10

PROJECTED U.S. COMMERCIAL USE OF GOLD IN 1975 IN OUNCES

Relative Gold Price	Jewelry	Industry	Dental	Total
No Change	5,285	3,569	1,541	10,396
Price = $50	4,544	3,425	1,100	9,069
Price = $70	1,902	3,013	1,100	6,015

Dentistry: projections were based on projected personal disposable income.

An example of demand forecasting for a firm: a bank's demand for loans

This example is based upon a case example provided by Data Resources, Inc.[52] Demand at a particular bank for commercial loans was estimated from quarterly time data as:

$$D_c = -21266.3 + 1318.6M + 2763.2\ S$$
$$(-0.8) \quad\quad (4.5) \quad\quad\quad (3.3)$$
$$+9088.7\ CP{-}BL + 1091.8\ CI$$
$$(2.3) \quad\quad\quad\quad (2.4)$$
$$\text{R}^2 = 0.985 \quad\quad\quad\quad \text{DW} = 1.736$$

in which

D_c is commercial loan demand in dollars

M is national money supply

S is quarter to quarter change in sales of the nonelectrical machinery industry (an industry served directly by the bank).

$CP{-}BL$ is difference between commercial paper interest rate and the short-term business loan interest rate (a measure of relative attractiveness of these two sources of funds to commercial borrowers).

CI is total U.S. commercial and industrial loan demand (the bank average "share" is approximately .11 percent of the national market).

The equation was econometrically corrected for first order autocorrelation.

The bank's demand for mortgage loans was estimated from quarterly time series data as:

$$D_m = 37350.40 + 0.61\ M_{-1} - 155.74\ C$$
$$(3.5) \quad\quad (5.5) \quad\quad\quad (-2.8)$$
$$+19934.7\ H - 5354.9\ U + 5317.61\ I$$
$$(4.5) \quad\quad\quad (-3.9) \quad\quad\quad (2.7)$$
$$\text{R}^2 = 0.897 \quad\quad\quad\quad \text{DW} = 1.301$$

---

[52] Data Resources, Inc. is an economic information services firm located in Lexington, Massachusetts.

D_m is mortgage loan demand in dollars

M_{-1} is seasonally adjusted mortgage loans outstanding during the previous period

C is deposits at mutual savings bank and savings and loan associations (competing sources of funds)

H is average housing starts

U is the state's rate of unemployment (a proxy for ability of residents to buy new homes and for the state's attraction to new residents)

I is the conventional mortgage loan interest rate (entering positively because down payment terms are the rationing mechanism rather than interest rates and because banks can compete more effectively as interest rates rise toward legal ceilings)

The bank's demand for installment loans was estimated from quarterly time series data as:

$$D_i = 19207.3 + 0.85\ I_{t-1} - 2899.4U$$
$$(18.3) \quad (38.3) \quad\quad (-9.7)$$
$$+92.69C \quad\quad + \quad\quad 215.3A$$
$$(4.9) \quad\quad\quad\quad (3.4)$$
$$R^2 = 0.999 \quad\quad\quad DW = 1.099$$

in which

D_i is demand for installment loans in dollars

I_{t-1} is installment loans outstanding during the previous period

U is the state's unemployment rate

C is the number of charge cards outstanding

A is national spending on automobiles and parts

The above equations, combined with externally developed forecasts of the national, regional, and industry variables, comprise a loan-demand forecasting system for the bank. The forecasts of exogenous variables are provided by Data Resources, Inc. Sensitivity analysis, the simulation of effects of assumed changes in these variables, is perhaps the most useful application of the forecasting system, since it is helpful in making contingency plans in the face of uncertainty. This example shows how the cost of using and analyzing external data can be brought within the reach of medium size firms by using vendor services.

AN EXERCISE FOR CHAPTER 4

*GNP forecast for 1970**

PART I

Prepare a forecast of the GNP and its principal components for each quarter through 1970, using the data for 1969, third quarter (*Survey of Current Business,* July 1971) as follows:

	Billions
Gross National Product	$940.2
Change in GNP from previous period	18.4
Personal income	759.3
Disposable personal income	643.2
Personal outlays	600.9
Personal consumption expenditures	584.1
Interest paid by consumers and transfer payments to foreigners	16.8
Change in business inventories	10.4
Corporate profits before tax (adjusted)	78.0
Corporate profits taxes	38.2
Corporate profits after taxes	39.8
Capital consumption allowances (depreciation)	82.1
Indirect business taxes, etc.	87.1
Contributions for social insurance	54.7
Transfer payments, etc.	95.7
Dividends	24.7
Change in dividends from previous period	0.5

It is important to know the following relationships: Net national product = GNP − Capital consumption allowances. National income = Net national product − Indirect business taxes. Personal income = National income − Corporate profits + Dividends − Contributions for social insurance + Transfer payments. Disposable income = Personal income − Personal income taxes. Gross private domestic investment = Fixed investment + Net change in inventory investment

Assume that the following data are given:

	Annual Rates in Billions of Dollars				
	1969:4	*1970:1*	*1970:2*	*1970:3*	*1970:4*
Government expenditures on goods and services					
Total	$213.0	$217.3	$216.5	$220.1	$223.7
Federal	99.5	100.2	96.8	96.1	95.9
Defense	78.4	78.9	75.1	74.2	73.2
Nondefense	21.1	21.3	21.6	21.9	22.7
State and local	113.5	117.1	119.7	124.0	127.9
Fixed Investment	132.3	130.8	132.1	133.5	133.6
Nonresidential investment	102.2	100.8	102.1	104.8	100.8
Residential investment	30.1	30.0	29.9	28.7	32.8
Net exports	2.7	3.5	4.2	4.0	2.7

Source: *Survey of Current Business,* July 1971.

---

* Note: This case is a modification of one written by Professor John Lintner of

Assume also that:

1. Personal outlays in each quarter are equal to .95 of disposable income in the preceding quarter. The portion of personal outlays represented by interest paid by consumers and personal transfer payments by foreigners increases by $0.3 billion in each quarter and the balance represents consumer expenditures on goods and services. Personal consumption expenditures are "personal outlays" less such "transfers."

2. Examine past inventory behavior and make your own estimates, taking into account what you know, or can find out, about current conditions in the economy.

3. The quarter-to-quarter change in corporate profits before taxes in billions of dollars is equal to:

$$0.4 \ (\Delta GNP)_t + 0.3 \ (\Delta Inv.)_t - 0.2 \ (\Delta GNP)_{t-1} - 1.0 \text{ billion}$$

4. The change in corporate profits taxes equals 45 percent of the current change in the corporate profits before taxes.

5. Dividends change by 30 percent of the current change in corporate profits after taxes plus 50 percent of the change in dividends in the previous quarter.

6. The change in contributions to social security (payroll taxes) amounts to 10 percent of the change in GNP.

7. The change in indirect business taxes is equal to 15 percent of the change in GNP.

8. The change in transfer payments by government and certain interest payments increases $1.3 billions per quarter.

9. The change in personal income taxes is equal to 15 percent of the change in personal income.

10. Capital consumption allowances increase by 1.5 billions in each quarter.

PART II

After you have completed mechanical projections based on the above assumptions, consider how reasonable they seem in the light of all the other information you have at your disposal. What assumptions do you believe should be changed? How, how much, and for what reasons? What would be the order of magnitude of the changes induced in your first projection? Has this approach given adequate attention to the multiplier and accelerator? Explain the basis for your conclusion.

PART III

Compare your forecast for 1970 with the actual changes in the GNP and its components during that year. How great was the error in your forecast? What are the apparent reasons for those errors?

(Note: Statistical data will be found in issues of the *Survey of Current Busi-*

---

the Harvard Graduate School of Business Administration. The case has been influenced greatly by the Duesenberry-Eckstein-Fromm econometric model. This simplified form of the latter material was developed for classroom use to illustrate some of the more fundamental relationships which need to be taken into account in forecasting in the simplest possible way. In itself, it was not intended to provide a model which would be fully adequate for forecasting business conditions in practice.

ness and in *Economic Indicators.* Current business literature such as *Business Week, Fortune,* monthly letters of the leading commercial banks and Federal Reserve Banks, the monthly issues of *Economic Indicators,* and the publications of the leading investment services will supply information which may enable you to form an opinion on the reasonableness of the given assumptions and data to be used in the mechanical projections.)

Forecast for the coming year: mechanical model

The "mechanical" model used in the GNP forecast for 1970 may be adapted for use for any short period in the 1970s. This approach would start with forecasts of federal expenditures quarter by quarter using the sources mentioned in Chapter 4. Next the forecast would move on to state and local government expenditures and to the components of investment. The forecast of inventory investment would proceed as in the 1970 forecast. Then the most tedious task is to forecast consumption using the assumptions listed in the 1970 forecast.

Forecast for the coming year: GNP "judgmental" model

On the basis of the discussion in Chapter 4, you may forecast the GNP and its principal components for the coming year. In such a forecast you will wish to use many of the sources mentioned in Chapter 4. This exercise is best done as a team effort, with part of the team concentrating on plant and equipment, part on residential construction, part on government expenditure, and so on. After preliminary estimates are made of the investment and governmental components, the team as a whole can cooperate in making estimates of consumption which will take the multiplier into account. Various degrees of mathematical sophistication are possible. The simplest approach is to assume that the induced increase in consumption will be roughly equal to total increase already estimated for all the other components, but as Chapter 4 points out, consumption is stickier in the downward direction and is influenced by factors other than income change.

After this forecast is made, the results may be compared with those in the more subjective approach in the preceding case. The question which then arises is whether the extra work required by the "mechanical" model produces results in the form of superior forecasts which compensate for the extra effort.

Forecast for 1970: leading indicators

In late August 1972 the 12 most important leading indicators shown in *Business Conditions Digest* appeared as in Exhibits 1 and 2.

What kind of forecast for 1970 would you make on the basis of movements in these indicators in 1969? How much confidence would you have in this forecast?

EXHIBIT 4–1

CYCLICAL INDICATORS: SELECTED INDICATORS BY TIMING
(leading indicators)

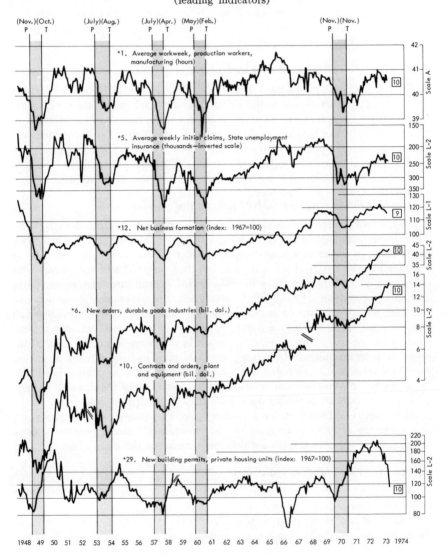

(Nov.)(Oct.)   (July)(Aug.)   (July)(Apr.) (May)(Feb.)   (Nov.)(Nov.)
P   T   P   T   P   T   P   T   P   T

*1. Average workweek, production workers, manufacturing (hours)

*5. Average weekly initial claims, State unemployment insurance (thousands—inverted scale)

*12. Net business formation (index: 1967=100)

*6. New orders, durable goods industries (bil. dol.)

*10. Contracts and orders, plant and equipment (bil. dol.)

*29. New building permits, private housing units (index: 1967=100)

1948 49 50 51 52 53 54 55 56 57 58 59 60 61 62 63 64 65 66 67 68 69 70 71 72 73 1974

EXHIBIT 4–2

CYCLICAL INDICATORS: SELECTED INDICATORS BY TIMING—CONTINUED

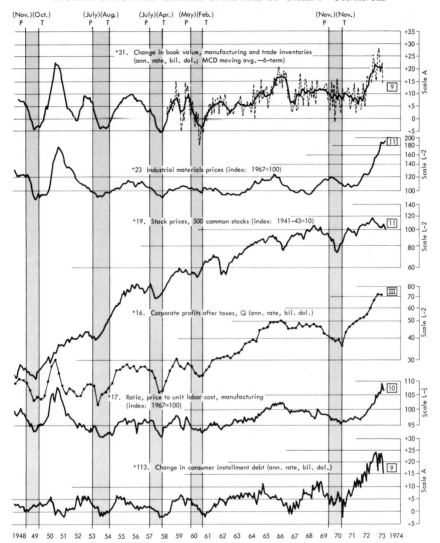

Cases for part two

This section includes two types of case material. The first consists of cases in which the considerations in Chapter 3, such as elasticity of demand, are paramount. The second concentrates on the introduction of a new product with all the attendant uncertainties which must be forecast. The cases vary from extremely broad ones dealing with nationally distributed products under conditions of extreme uncertainty to ones dealing with specific problems in a small firm.

Because of the decision-making orientation of this text the majority of the cases do not require statistical estimation of demand. No advanced statistical techniques are required; the student must interpret certain statistical results but is not required to do computations of his own.

The Bausch and Lomb, Inc., case is one which can be studied at a relatively low level. However, it is also a case which the well-prepared student will find extremely interesting and which can be used to illustrate the use of some of the more powerful statistical techniques.

THE PRICING OF AUTOMOBILES

In 1958, Walter Reuther, the President of the United Automobile Workers, suggested a reduction in the price of automobiles averaging $100 a car. The automobile market was weak in 1958, with resultant unemployment; lower prices would lead to greater sales and would stimulate employment. Mr. Reuther believed that a $100 reduction in prices, about 4 percent, would increase sales by 16 percent.

In testimony before the Senate Subcommittee on Antitrust and Monopoly, Mr. Theodore O. Yntema, Vice President of the Ford Motor

Company, disagreed with Mr. Reuther's estimation.[1] Mr. Yntema cited studies which indicated price elasticities ranging from 0.5 to 1.5. Mr. Yntema made it clear that he was referring to the elasticity of demand in response to a permanent price change of all manufacturers; he admitted that the elasticity to a temporary price cut might be greater. The studies to which Mr. Yntema referred included the well-known prewar volume by Roos and von Szeliski, which found elasticities ranging from .65 to 1.53. (Apparently the Roos-Szeliski findings are interpreted in somewhat different ways by various students of automobile demand, but all interpretations fall within the range of .65 to 1.53.)

Perhaps more recent studies would be more relevant than that of Roos and Szeliski. A Department of Commerce study of automobile demand resulted in several estimating equations, one of which was

$$Y = 0.0003239 \ X_1{}^{2.536} \ X_2{}^{2.291} \ X_3{}^{-1.359} \ 0.932^{X_4}$$

where

Y = new private passenger car registrations per million households
X_1 = disposable personal income per household in 1939 dollars
X_2 = current annual disposable income per household as a percentage of the preceding year in 1939 dollars
X_3 = percentage of average retail price of cars to consumer prices measured by consumer price index
X_4 = average scrappage age in years[2]

Similar equations based on slightly different assumptions resulted in price elasticities close to the one implied by the above equation, as do studies by Chow.[3]

1. *What is the significance of Mr. Reuther's demand estimate?*
2. *What is the significance of Mr. Yntema's demand estimate?*
3. *What is the price elasticity of demand for automobiles according to the Department of Commerce demand estimate?*
4. *How would the relevant conditions differ between an automobile firm with excess capacity and one with a high ratio of output to capacity?*
5. *How does long-run demand for automobiles relate to the short-run pricing decision which is the center of controversy in the case?*

[1] Statement before the Subcommittee on Antitrust and Monopoly, Committee on the Judiciary, U.S. Senate, February 4–5, 1958. Extracts from this statement appear in A. W. Warner and V. R. Fuchs, *Concepts and Cases in Economic Analysis* (New York: Harcourt, Brace & Co., 1958), pp. 147–48.

[2] *Survey of Current Business*, April 1952, p. 20. This study is cited in F. E. Nemmers, *Managerial Economics: Text and Cases* (New York: John Wiley & Sons, Inc., 1962), pp. 102–7.

[3] G. C. Chow, "Statistical Demand Functions for Automobiles and Their Use for Forecasting," in A. C. Harberger (ed.), *The Demand for Durable Goods* (Chicago: University of Chicago Press, 1960).

PRICE CUTTING AT MACY'S[4]

A United States Supreme Court decision in 1951 freed many firms from the restriction of "fair trade" legislation and opened the way to more aggressive price policies.[5] This Schewegmann decision freed firms that had not signed state "fair trade" contracts on merchandise which had been transported in interstate commerce. R. H. Macy and Company was a nonsigner firm and was also a proponent of free pricing. Macy's slogan was: "We endeavor to save our customers at least 6 percent for cash, except on price-fixed goods." Therefore it is not surprising that Macy's proceeded to cut prices only eight days after the Schewegmann decision. Macy's ran a two-page advertisement announcing 6 percent price reductions on 5,978 items which were formerly fixed in price under the "fair trade" legislation.

Macy's faced strong competition from other department stores, including Abraham and Straus, Bloomingdale's, Namm's and Gimbel's, whose motto was "Nobody—but nobody—undersells Gimbel's." These stores took retaliatory action against Macy's. One hour after the Macy's reductions took effect, Gimbel's began to cut prices. Abraham and Straus followed a few hours later with cuts of 10 percent or more. As Macy's learned of this retaliation, it proceeded to cut to 6 percent under the new low prices of competitors. By the end of the day all the other stores mentioned were engaged in a full-scale price war. Some price cuts were as much as 30 percent in the first day.

The price cuts involved well-known branded items, such as Underwood typewriters and Palm Beach suits. Only a small percentage of the original 6,000 items on which Macy's had cut price became involved in the deeper price cuts. A few items were cut below wholesale cost (Bayer aspirin slipped in price from 59 cents to 4 cents). The tempo of price cuts varied from item to item. Price cuts in the competing stores were not identical but tended to be similar.

The volume of business done by the stores engaged in price cutting increased sharply. While normally Macy's sold less than 3.5 percent of Sunbeam Mixmasters sold in New York, its proportion rose to 56 percent in the 10 weeks following the beginning of the price war. Abraham and Straus increased its share of Brooklyn sales from 2.5 percent to 60 percent. In June 1957, the total sales of 13 New York and Brooklyn department stores were 14 percent above those of the previous June, with one store recording a 33.4 percent increase. The largest increases in volume were in major appliances and housewares.

The Fifth Avenue stores did not participate in the price cutting. Many

---

[4] This case is based on Ralph Cassady, Jr., "New York Department Store Price War of 1951: A Microeconomic Analysis," *Journal of Marketing,* national quarterly publication of the American Marketing Association, July 1957, pp. 3–11.

[5] *Schewegmann Bros.* v. *Calvert Distilleries Corporation,* 314 U.S. 384 (1951).

neighborhood hardware stores did cut prices, and price reductions spread to the Bronx and to Jersey City. But the price war came to a close in August 1951, about six weeks after it started. The impact of the price cuts on volume began to diminish rapidly, and the stores wished to bring the war to an end. Gradually prices were restored to their former levels. One way this was done was for the aggressor to run out of stock until competitors restored the old price.

The chief question raised by the events of 1951 is whether the executives of Macy's made a correct evaluation of the elasticity of demand in initiating its price reductions. Some observers have suggested that Macy's might have done better to cut price-fixed items by 6 percent without publicizing this cut.

1. *What was Macy's estimate of elasticity of demand for the "fair trade" goods?*
2. *What was the actual elasticity of demand?*
3. *How do the possible actions of competitors affect the elasticity of demand in this case?*
4. *How does the short-run elasticity of demand compare with the long-run elasticity for the "fair trade" items?*
5. *Would you describe the industry structure of department stores in New York City as "perfect competition"? Explain.*

THE BOSTON AND MAINE RAILROAD

On Sunday, January 6, 1963, the Boston and Maine Railroad instituted a new rate schedule for commuters into Boston. A federal and state subsidy of $2.2 million, part of a program to aid mass transportation, made this experiment with reduced fares possible. The objective of the federal program of subsidies was to determine whether lower commuter rates would relieve the problem of congestion on highways. The Boston and Maine experiment was to last one year, unless the railroad became discouraged with the results and terminated the program in six months.

In 1946 the Boston and Maine had carried 40,000 commuters a day to and from branches to the west, north, and east of Boston. In the following years it had modernized commuter equipment but had lost passengers steadily. It raised fares to cover the higher costs per passenger, with the result of further reductions in traffic and the curtailment of schedules. Expressways into Boston had stimulated commuting by automobile but had also accentuated traffic and parking problems in downtown Boston. By January of 1963 the Boston and Maine passenger count had fallen to 11,000 per day and the passenger deficit had reached $3.8 million per year.

The federal and state subsidies (two-thirds federal and one-third Massachusetts) made possible the reduction of fares by 25 percent to 40 percent and the increase in the number of daily trains from 187 to 391. The railroad spent $170,000 cleaning and refurnishing 101 diesel cars and

EXHIBIT 1

Passenger Counts, Boston and Maine Railroad
(comparable weeks in 1962–63)

New Hampshire District (Boston to Woburn)

	Week Ending Feb. 15, 1962			Week Ending Feb. 14, 1963	
Day	No. of Trains	Passenger Count	Day	No. of Trains	Passenger Count
Fri. 9th	37	2,758	Fri. 8th	55	2,833
Sat. 10th	29	794	Sat. 9th	36	1,132
Sun. 11th	21	285	Sun. 10th	19	397
Mon. 12th	37	2,616	Mon. 11th	55	3,163
Tues. 13th	37	2,660	Tues. 12th	55	3,186
Wed. 14th	37	2,627	Wed. 13th	55	3,280
Thur. 15th	36	2,325	Thur. 14th	55	2,981

Portland District (W) Reading

	Week Ending Feb. 15, 1962			Week Ending Feb. 14, 1963	
Day	No. of Trains	Passenger Count	Day	No. of Trains	Passenger Count
Fri. 9th	54	6,765	Fri. 8th	112	7,535
Sat. 10th	36	1,575	Sat. 9th	36	1,846
Sun. 11th	24	447	Sun. 10th	20	808
Mon. 12th	54	6,625	Mon. 11th	112	8,121
Tues. 13th	54	6,693	Tues. 12th	112	7,872
Wed. 14th	54	6,939	Wed. 13th	112	8,087
Thur. 15th	54	6,830	Thur. 14th	112	8,022

New Hampshire District

	Week Ending Feb. 15, 1962			Week Ending Feb. 14, 1963	
Day	No. of Trains	Passenger Count	Day	No. of Trains	Passenger Count
Fri. 9th	25	3,159	Fri. 8th	46	3,868
Sat. 10th	22	1,080	Sat 9th	27	1,467
Sun. 11th	16	1,052	Sun. 10th	18	1,199
Mon. 12th	25	2,543	Mon. 11th	46	3,699
Tues. 13th	25	2,478	Tues. 12th	46	3,876
Wed. 14th	25	2,686	Wed. 13th	46	4,978
Thur. 15th	25	2,450	Thur. 14th	46	3,703

Fitchburg Division

	Week Ending Feb. 15, 1962			Week Ending Feb. 14, 1963	
Day	No. of Trains	Passenger Count	Day	No. of Trains	Passenger Count
Fri. 9th	24	2,221	Fri. 8th	42	3,112
Sat. 10th	10	449	Sat. 9th	22	1,060
Sun. 11th	8	200	Sun. 10th	8	331
Mon. 12th	24	2,456	Mon. 11th	42	3,368
Tues. 13th	24	2,318	Tues. 12th	42	3,419
Wed. 14th	24	2,426	Wed. 13th	42	3,414
Thur. 15th	24	1,380	Thur. 14th	42	3,175

EXHIBIT 1—*Continued*

PORTLAND DISTRICT—EASTERN ROUTE

	Week Ending Feb. 15, 1962			*Week Ending Feb. 14, 1963*	
Day	*No. of Trains*	*Passenger Count*	*Day*	*No. of Trains*	*Passenger Count*
Fri. 9th 41		5,169	Fri. 8th 92		6,855
Sat. 10th 33		1,299	Sat. 9th 35		1,969
Sun. 11th 21		644	Sun. 10th 19		1,188
Mon. 12th 41		4,690	Mon. 11th 92		6,939
Tues. 13th 41		4,841	Tues. 12th 92		6,803
Wed. 14th 41		4,991	Wed. 13th 92		6,924
Thur. 15th 41		4,526	Thur. 14th 92		6,786

PORTLAND DISTRICT—WESTERN ROUTE

	Week Ending Feb. 15, 1962			*Week Ending Feb. 14, 1963*	
Day	*No. of Trains*	*Passenger Count*	*Day*	*No. of Trains*	*Passenger Count*
Fri. 9th 26		2,817	Fri. 8th 40		3,221
Sat. 10th 25		1,212	Sat. 9th 27		1,813
Sun. 11th 15		869	Sun. 10th 13		870
Mon. 12th 26		2,590	Mon. 11th 38		3,041
Tues. 13th 26		2,518	Tues. 12th 38		2,786
Wed. 14th 26		2,528	Wed. 13th 38		2,909
Thur. 15th 26		2,282	Thur. 14th 38		2,836

EXHIBIT 2

COMMUTER FARE CHANGES, SELECTED POINTS
BOSTON AND MAINE RAILROAD

	1962	*After Jan. 6, 1963*
New Hampshire District		
North Chelmsford, Mass.	$16.80	$11.13
Lowell, Mass.	15.82	10.72
Woburn	9.83	7.70
Portland District (Reading)		
Reading	10.69	8.12
Portland District—Eastern		
Salem	12.75	8.88
Portland District—Western		
Andover	14.85	10.13
Fitchburg Division		
Fitchburg	23.60	15.47
Concord	14.20	9.70

an additional $43,000 to set up a canopy at North Station in Boston. The railroad hoped to reduce passenger revenue deficits despite the reduction of fares and the improvement in service.

Exhibit 1 presents passenger counts for comparable weeks in 1962 and 1963, before and after the fare reduction. Each passenger is counted both on the inward and on the outward trip; this explains the fact that the totals for 1962 are about double the figure of 11,000 passengers mentioned above.

Exhibit 2 shows some of the fare changes from selected points on the Boston and Maine. The rates are quoted for 20-ride commuter books.

1. *What is the elasticity of demand for commuter services of the Boston and Maine Railroad on weekdays? What is the elasticity of demand for commuter services on Saturdays and Sundays? (Calculate the elasticities route by route.)*
2. *What is the overall elasticity of demand? How should the various elasticities be weighted in determining overall elasticity—by passenger count or by amount of fare?*
3. *How do you account for differences among elasticities by routes and by days of the week? Do these have practical implications?*
4. *How does time perspective affect your view of this case?* lower in short-run p·96
5. *Was the rate reduction profitable, considering all elements of the case?*
   no. inelastic demand. decrease in demand → decrease in π,

THE STATE UNIVERSITY PRESS (A)

The State University Press published a work in American history in November 1962. It priced the book at $8.50 and estimated that sales would approximate 1,800 copies. After discounts by distributors the Press expected to receive about $5.70 per copy—barely enough to cover its unit costs.

The manager of a retail store claimed that the price of $8.50 was too high. He believed that at a price of $5 the Press could expect substantial gift sales of the book, with perhaps a doubling or tripling of volume. The editors of the Press believed, however, that sales would be only 50 percent higher at the lower price.

The costs of publishing the book are shown in Exhibit 1. These costs were accumulated after publication but include some estimates. (A pre-publication forecast of costs had estimated them at $4,881; the higher actual costs resulted from a substantial number of author's changes in the galley proof and page proof stages.)

1. *Estimate the elasticity of demand, incremental revenue, and marginal revenue under the following assumptions: (1) a doubling of sales at the lower price; (2) a tripling of sales; (3) a 50-percent increase in sales. (Assume that the proportion of the retail price going to the Press is about the same at various prices.)*

EXHIBIT 1

ESTIMATED COST OF HISTORY BOOK
(publication date—November 28, 1962)
Quantity—1,000 bound copies plus 1,000 unbound sheets

Text

Stock	$ 774.50	
Composition	2,305.90	(354.8 hours)
Press	740.40	(106.9 hours)
Ink	22.34	
Art	40.00	
Cuts	64.66	
Miscellaneous	36.50	
Overhead (15% of above)	597.00	
Total text costs		$4,581.30

Jacket

Stock	$ 28.50	
Composition	13.00	(2 hours)
Press	58.30	(8.3 hours)
Ink	7.26	
Art	107.00	
Cuts	39.00	
Overhead (15% of above)	38.00	
Mailing	3.94	
Total jacket costs		$ 300.00
Binding (1,000 copies)	724.00	
Freight (estimated)	120.00	
Total cost		$5,725.30

2. *Assuming that the demands can be approximated by straight lines and sales will double at the lower price, estimate the marginal revenue at a number of prices between $8.50 and $5—for example, at $8, $7.50, and $7. Is the assumption of straight-line demands reasonable?* it's an average. the syst we've got to work with.

3. *Estimate the marginal cost or incremental cost per book for quantities exceeding 1,800. For this purpose assume that the press run would be increased upward from 2,000 to take care of the extra demand at the lower prices. Note that the composition costs are fixed for a single run. Binding costs include a fixed element of, say, $150 per lot, but the remaining binding costs are proportional to volume. Make any other assumptions which seem appropriate. (While a full discussion of costs appears in Chapter 5, the incremental reasoning presented in Chapter 2 should suffice for this purpose.)*

4. *Would a price of $5 be sound if the Press were a private company operated for profit? Discuss.* $6.28 Maximum Rev. (see note).

5. *Would a price of $5 be sound for the University Press, recognizing that the objective is not maximum profit but that heavy losses on this book would cut down on funds available for other books?*

BAUSCH AND LOMB, INC.*

The following excerpts are taken from a brokerage firm's evaluation published in mid-1971:

Bausch & Lomb, one of the oldest and strongest names in the American optical industry now stands on the threshold of one of the most important developments in its corporate life—the introduction of the soft contact lenses. These lenses, made from materials sublicensed under patents originating from work done in Czechoslovakia, are now being gradually introduced to professionals across the country.

B&L is the nation's second largest producer of ophthalmic products, ranking behind the American Optical Division of Warner-Lambert. See our discussion of the "Ophthalmic Industry" for our interpretation of overall industry trends.

B&L has experienced reasonably satisfactory growth from this market, although we believe that it has lost share to American Optical over the last two or three years. The market for frames and lenses increased at least 6.4 percent and 14.3 percent, respectively, in the 1963–70 period; this pattern of growth probably slowed somewhat in the 1967–1970 period. However, gains were relatively better maintained in frames than in lenses, reflecting a trend toward higher priced products, stimulated by a greater emphasis on the fashion aspect of eyeglasses.

We believe that eyeglass sales have been restrained by the poor economy. As the economy turns upward, and particularly as the consumer becomes more interested in discretionary medical spending, B&L should experience a strong surge in its ophthalmic business. The leverage in this operation is believed to be substantial and, on a 10 percent sales move, we estimate that earnings could increase by 25 percent or so.

We believe that the soft lenses, tradenamed Soflens, constitute a significant advance over the traditional hard contact lenses due mainly to a high degree of comfort obtained with the lens even in the initial wearing stages, as well as a closer fit with the eye, reducing the possibility of losing the lens or of having dirt particles lodge under the lens. In addition, and obviously most important, the lenses provide excellent vision correction—fully satisfactory in the substantial majority of patients.

We believe that the lenses are unique and that the market will be relatively uncrowded for some time. Among the significant bars to competition are the following: (i) the lens is covered by both product and process patents; these patents may not guarantee the total absence of competition, but, on the other hand, as the patents are enforced we believe that they will at least hinder the development of alternate products; (ii) B&L has made a number of improvements in both the lens itself and in the manufacturing process; (iii) the lenses

---

*This case was prepared at Georgia State University by Eric Tweedy under William R. Henry. It is based upon Hearings of the Senate Select Committee on Small Business in connection with soft contact lenses.

have been judged to fall under the Food and Drug Act and, as such, require elaborate premarketing testing procedures and ultimately governmental approval; passage through this process took B&L more than four years and (iv) the name and reputation of Bausch & Lomb—both at the consumer and professional levels —will support a preference for B&L's products even in a strongly competitive market.

Defense against scientific criticism

The soft contact lenses are open to several criticisms. Of primary concern are the possibilities of infection and poor visual performance. The porous structure of the HEMA polymer is thought by some to provide a breeding place for pathological organisms or fungi tendrils. Dr. Chester Black, past president of the Contact Lens Association of Ophthalmologists, appeared in Senate testimony to defend Soflens™ from these charges. Results of clinical studies were provided that tended to be favorable toward the efficacy and safety of the Bausch and Lomb lens:

Extract from Statement of Chester J. Black, M.D.
Before the
Government Regulation Subcommittee
of the
Senate Select Committee on Small Business,
July 7, 1972

SOFLENS CLINICAL TRIAL RESULTS, FEB. 15, 1971—ACTIVE PATIENTS

Slit-Lamp Examinations	*All Investigators*	*C. J. Black*
Total eyes fitted	2,512	250
Less initial visit only	152	11
Eyes with slit-lamp finding on last visit	2,360	239

Slit-Lamp Findings	*Number Negative*	*Percent*	*Number Negative*	*Percent*
Edema	2,191	93	239	100
Vascularization	2,360	100	239	100
Staining	2,304	98	239	100
Injection	2,302	98	232	97
Other Complications	2,357	100	239	100

Visual Acuities	*All Investigators*	*C. J. Black*
Total eyes fitted	2,512	250
No acuity reported	34	0
Eyes with acuity reported	2,478	250

SOFLENS CLINICAL TRIAL RESULTS—Continued

Visual Acuities	Number	Percent	Number	Percent
20/20 or better	1,311	53	82	33
20/25 or better	2,265	91	243	97
20/30 or better	2,410	97	244	98
Less than 20/30	68	3	6	2

Wearing Time	All Investigators	C. J. Black
6 months or less	185	25
7 to 12 months	368	50
13 to 18 months	335	21
18 months or more	373	30

Although Dr. Black's testimony was favorable, some other work has indicated some problems in both areas, acuity and infection.

Competition

Bausch and Lomb's major competition in the soft contact lens market comes from Naturalens™, a product of Griffin Laboratories, a subsidiary of Frigitronics. The Griffin lenses are composed of basically the same material as the Soflens™, but they are more hydrophilic, somewhat harder and thicker, and come in a wider range of fitting parameters. Additionally, the Griffin Naturalens™ has been shown in clinical studies to have better optical properties, to be better suited as a bandage lens and drug dispenser, and to have other valuable therapeutic uses. The Naturalens™ has FDA approval for therapeutic use only.

Extract from a
Statement of Aran Safir, M.D., Mount Sinai School of
Medicine, Department of Ophthalmology, New York City,
Before the Government Regulation Subcommittee of the
Senate Select Committee on Small Business

The B&L lens is easier to fit. There are few choices for the clinician to make. He has little or no control over lens thickness, diameter, and curvature, but can choose from a variety of refractive powers. He can often determine at one sitting whether or not the patient will obtain reasonably good visual acuity. The lenses can then be dispensed directly and the patient scheduled for a re-visit so that his adaptation to the lenses can soon be evaluated.

The Griffin lens is available in a variety of diameters, thicknesses, and curvatures, as well as refractive powers. It has therefore not been possible to keep a stock of lenses that allow for direct dispensing. Considerable time can be spent in trial and error manipulation of these variables. When the prescription is determined, the lens is ordered by mail. One of the greatest difficulties with Griffin lenses has been the lack of predictability of delivery of the lenses ordered. When the lenses have arrived, they have not always performed in the manner expected based on the trial lenses fitted. Precise checking of all the lens variables has not been possible for reasons already given.

However, the Griffin lens has some advantages as a refractive device. Because he can manipulate the lens characteristics, the practitioner can achieve satisfactory vision in a somewhat higher percentage of patients with this lens than he can with the B&L lens. Nevertheless, a significant number (19 percent) of our patients abandoned the Griffin lens because of unsatisfactory acuity.

It is our opinion that the Griffin lens is more comfortable than the B&L lens. We suspect that this is due to the larger diameter of the Griffin lens, because the smallest Griffin lenses feel very much like the B&L lenses. Some patients notice no discomfort with either, but some are aware of mild sensations of a foreign body in the eye, especially with the smaller diameter lenses.

Pricing

Marketing of the B&L product is discussed in this excerpt from the 1971 brokerage study:

Price.—The B&L lenses have been priced initially at $65 per pair. This price compares with a typical price from a hard lens manufacturer of $15–$20 per pair. However, the price to the dispenser is a relatively minor portion of the price of the fitted lens to the patient. It appears that the price of the soft lens to the patient, at least at the outset, will be $300 per pair or so, compared with about $200 for the hard lens. In time, we believe that dispensers—particularly optometrists who have been losing share of the contact lens market to ophthalmologists in recent years—will reduce prices to the patient. This will be facilitated by the relative ease with which the soft lens is fitted to the patient, particularly compared to the hard lens, as well as the probability that the time involved in fitting the soft lens will be substantially reduced.

The present price for the Soflens adopted by B&L will, in our opinion, be reduced by perhaps 25 percent over the next three years. This will largely reflect the probable lower cost structure once B&L enters longer production runs but will also reflect the existence of either real or potential competition.

The brokerage firm's study also considers the pipelining of the specialists who will dispense the lenses:

Pipelining and Reordering.—B&L is selling the lenses to the dispenser in a kit containing 72 lenses, each pair costing $65, five sterilizers, each costing $21, a professional sized sterilizer and a film projector. The kit is priced at $2,905. The extent of the initial acceptance of the kits will obviously influence the development of sales from B&L to the dispenser for the next year or so. For example, if 20 percent of the nation's 18,000 dispensers—roughly 3,600 dispensers—order kits during 1971, this would result in sales to B&L of about $10.5 million. However, this would also place about 130,000 pairs of soft contact lenses in the hands of the dispenser and act as a brake to additional sales in subsequent months. The extent of this restraint will depend basically on the relationship of the size of the pipe-line to the consumer acceptance rate. For example, 130,000 pairs of lenses is equal to only about three months sales if the market for soft lenses reaches 500,-000 pairs per year.

Apart from the pipelining consideration, B&L will be shipping lenses to dispensers as they are sold to the consumer. As the dispenser fits each patient, he will reorder the specific lenses used in the fitting, thus maintaining a relatively complete inventory of most popular sizes. In this way, B&L's sales will eventually reach a close relationship to retail demand, but this relationship will be warped initially by the pipelining.

The situation in mid-1972 is detailed in this excerpt from Mr. Dodd's Senate testimony:

The original fitting set offered for sale contained 72 lenses. Some practitioners have adjusted their inventories to meet the specific needs of their practice simply by purchasing additional quantities of lenses or by not re-ordering lenses as they are dispensed. Many practitioners with large contact lens practices carry inventories well above the 72 lenses they received initially, while others stock fewer. A recent survey showed that the average number of lenses in the fitting sets of our accounts was 67.3.

Appendix A
Extracts from a Brokerage Firm's Analysis

The following table shows the total number of people, distributed by age groups, wearing corrective lenses, as of June 1966 (000 omitted):

Age	Persons 3 years and over	No corrective lenses	With corrective lenses		
			Total	Eyeglasses only	Contact lenses
Total 3+	178,907	92,693	86,020	84,247	1,773
3–16	55,037	46,652	8,263	8,110	153
17–24	22,393	13,039	9,310	8,474	835
25–44	45,185	26,250	18,914	18,314	599
45 and over	56,292	6,743	49,533	49,348	185
45–54	21,850	4,112	17,732	17,636	97
55–64	16,864	1,337	15,526	15,469	57
65 +	17,578	1,294	16,275	16,244	——

Source: National Center for Health Statistics.

As indicated, the use of corrective lenses increases proportionately with age. Furthermore, the proportion of people wearing contact lenses is centered primarily in the 17–24 age group, where about 10 percent of all corrective lens wearers used contact lenses, and in the 25–44 groups, where 3 percent (of a far larger group) wore contact lenses.

We estimate that the number of people wearing contact lenses in 1970 reached

3.0 million, somewhat less than double the number four years ago. Although not shown in the above table, the usage rate of contact lenses among females is more than twice as frequent as among males (1,242,000 compared with 530,000). The usage of contact lenses, relative to eyeglasses, is relatively heavy in the Western part of the United States, among people with incomes over $5,000 per year and among white collar workers. These segments of the population are each growing as a percentage of the total. Further, based on Department of Commerce data, as well as trade estimates, we estimate that sales of contact lenses (in pairs) traced the following approximate pattern over the past five years (in millions):

The table below includes both new patients—those purchasing a pair of contact lenses for the first time—and patients reordering a pair of lenses either due to a change in vision or loss of the initial pair. We estimate that the number of different people who have purchased a pair of contact lenses is now approaching 10.0 million. Of these, we believe that about 3.0 million continue to wear the lenses with a high degree of regularity and 7.0 million people either wear them infrequently or not at all.

Year	Contact lenses sold (in pairs)	Eyeglass lenses (in pairs)
1965	0.8	36.0
1966	1.0	37.0
1967	1.2	38.0
1968	1.2	44.0
1969	1.3	45.0
1970	1.0	44.0

Sources: Bureau of the Census, Optical Goods Manufacturers Association and FD&S.

The following discussion is directed at the size of the potential total corrective lens market and, within that, the segment likely to be directed towards contact lens.

According to government data, cited earlier, about 42 percent of all people 17 to 24 years of age wear glasses; similarly, 42 percent of all people 24 to 44 wear glasses. The onset of vision defects is typically at a relatively early age. The following table shows the age at which each segment of the population first obtained corrective lenses (000 omitted):

Present age		Age when first obtained corrective lenses[1]			
		Under 17	17–24	25–44	45 +
All ages	86,020	—	—	—	—
3–16	8,263	8,263	—	—	—
17–24	9,310	6,533	2,531	—	—
25–44	18,914	6,778	4,654	6,571	—
45 +	49,533	4,400	4,021	15,550	22,592

[1] Totals may not add due to small number of people in categories above age 17 who did not recall when they first obtained correction.

Source: National Center for Health Statistics.

As indicated, of the 86 million people wearing glasses at the date of the census, 30 percent of these obtained vision correction before the age of 17 and another 13 percent before the age of 24. The substantial majority of these people were nearsighted, a vision defect well suited to the use of contact lenses. Based on this data, it appears that about one out of seven people under the age of 17 and two out of five people in the 17–24 age category wear some type of corrective lens.

The following table presents the age of the population of the U.S. at the end of 1969 and shows the likely distribution of the population by 1975 and by 1980 (000 omitted):

Year	Total	Under 5	5–14	15–24	25–44	45 +
1969	203,216	17,960	41,345	35,054	47,994	60,863
1975[1]	217,557	19,968	38,565	40,011	53,928	65,086
1980[1]	232,412	23,245	38,104	41,736	62,302	67,024

[1] Assumes fertility rate of 2,775 per 1,000 women of childbearing age (known as series C in census projections).

We further assume that contact lens usage has increased modestly as a percentage of all corrective lenses worn over the past four years and, furthermore, that contact lens usage will continue to increase over the next five and ten years. Specifically, we believe the contact lens usage will conform to the following usage rate:

Year	Percent of all corrective lenses
1966	2.1
1969	2.4
1975	7.2
1980	12.2

(i) As indicated, we believe that 6.0 million people either now wearing eyeglasses or not yet wearing any type of corrective lenses will be converted to contact lenses between 1969 and 1975 and another 5.9 million between 1975 and 1980. Of these, we estimate that the conversion rate to soft lenses will start slowly but build up significantly as the decade proceeds (in millions):

Year	Soft, as percent of total
1971	16.7
1972	50.0
1973	63.3
1974	70.0
1975	73.7
1976	76.3
1977	78.7
1978	81.1
1979	85.8
1980	85.3

The above estimates assume that about 4 million people a year are passing the age of 24, approximately half of whom are wearing some type of corrective lens. Of these, probably half will be attracted to contact lenses, producing a new market of 1 million pairs of contact lenses per year. The balance will be derived from the substantial group of eyeglass wearers attracted to contact lenses for the first time.

(ii) We believe that the conversion of existing contact lens wearers to the soft lenses will probably be relatively minor. The only reasons for switching from a reasonably acceptable product would be either due to the high discomfort associated with dirt and grime lodging under the lens, typically in a city environment, or due to the ability of the wearer to use the soft lens on a less regular schedule, not now available to the hard lens wearer due to the discomfort normally associated with readapting to the lens. The barrier to conversions from hard lenses to soft lenses will be the substantial price of being refitted with soft lenses. We estimate that about 5 percent per year of the existing hard lens population will be attracted to the soft lens—or roughly 150,000 pairs per year. This will build up gradually over the next few years.

(iii) We believe that a substantial number of people who had purchased hard lenses and subsequently dropped out of the market will purchase a pair of soft contact lenses.

The primary reasons for not using the pair of hard lenses, even after spending something in the area of $200, is the high degree of difficulty which most people encounter in adapting to the lens. Many people—probably half—eventually give up this effort and revert to eyeglasses. However, all of these people were motivated at one time to wear contact lenses and, if the adaptation period is eased—as it is with the soft lenses—a significant number may come back to the market. We believe that roughly 5 percent per year of the dropout population, or about 350,000 people, will be attracted back to the market. This will start slowly but build up across the next four years.

1. *Using the information from Appendix A and whatever other information is available, update for 1975 and 1980 the projected distribution of population by age groups as presented in Appendix A.*
2. *Using the projection in Question 1, project the usage of corrective lenses by age groups in 1975 and 1980.*
3. *Appendix A contains estimates of the relative usages of contact lenses in 1975 and 1980. These projections were made on the basis of growing discretionary income and improving popularity of the soft lenses. Using whatever information is available, revise these projections. Use the new projections to calculate projected distributions among age groups for usage of contact lenses.*
4. *Appendix A also contains projections of soft-lens' share of the market. Revise these estimates and project the share of the total corrective lens market which will belong to soft lenses in 1975 and 1980.*
5. *On the basis of Question 4, and any other information available, predict the share of the soft lens market which will be enjoyed by Bausch and Lomb in 1975 and 1980.*

Note: Good sources of information include the Funk and Scott indexes on corporations and industries, trade and medical journals, Moody's, and other specialized industry or corporate surveys.

PART THREE / Production
and cost

5 / Break-even and volume-profit analysis

INTRODUCTION: FIXED AND VARIABLE COSTS AND OTHER COST CLASSIFICATIONS

Short-run cost analysis deals with behavior of costs when *some inputs are fixed* and *others are varied* in quantity. Short-run cost analysis is one of the most useful toolkits in managerial economics. It is indispensable in the discussions of pricing which come later in this book. It is necessary for rational decisions about abandoning a product line or establishing a new product line with existing facilities. It is useful in determining whether or not to increase rates of specific outputs, to use idle capacity, or to rent facilities to outsiders.

Fixed and variable costs

Short-run cost analysis starts with a distinction between fixed costs and variable costs. Most readers already know that *fixed costs are unrelated to changes in volume* and *variable costs are dependent upon volume.* Yet it is desirable to warn against several possible misunderstandings.

1. The *dividing line* between fixed costs and variable cost is *not the same for all decisions.* Elementary treatments put material costs and direct labor costs in the variable cost category, they include depreciation expense and indirect labor and administrative charges in a fixed cost category, and they leave little scope for judgment. Such an approach is far too simple. Take direct labor cost, for example. It makes a difference whether a decision to accept a particular order requires additional overtime or can be managed with the use of available idle time. Another example is depreciation, often assumed to be entirely a fixed expense that

runs on regardless of the level of output. A little reflection will suggest that the wear and tear component of depreciation is related to the output; this component of depreciation is known as user cost. It is also possible that increased output may increase depreciation not only by increasing user cost on existing equipment but also by requiring additional machinery.

2. Some costs are a *mixture of both fixed and variable elements.* We have already noted the case of depreciation. The *obsolescence* component of depreciation is a function of time and thus runs on regardless of decisions about the level of output from the plant and equipment already on hand. The *wear and tear* element of depreciation is related to output, often in a complicated way. Depreciation may be accelerated by overtime or extra shifts. On the other hand, some types of equipment may actually deteriorate faster when not in use. For example, an automobile left in a garage for a long period suffers deterioration.

Other expenses are also a mixture of fixed and variable components. Such costs may be called *semivariable expenses.* Utility bills, for example, frequently include a fixed charge and a charge based on consumption; this is known as a two-part tariff. Salesmen may be paid both a straight salary and commissions based on volume. Supervisors may be paid bonuses based on output, in addition to fixed salaries.

3. Some expenses increase in a *stairstep* fashion. For example, foremen's salaries may remain constant as output increases until management adds an additional foreman, causing the expenses of supervision to rise to a higher level. Stairstep costs are probably not usual in practice, for management can overcome such sudden jumps in cost. It is possible to change the ratio of foremen to labor, or to put foremen on overtime.

4. Some students interpret the expression "variable cost" to mean any cost that varies over time. For example, they take the fact that a machine may cost more to purchase today than five years ago as evidence that depreciation on such machines is variable. This is a complete misinterpretation of what "variable" means. The term does not refer to variations in prices over time, but rather to *cost-output (or decision-cost) relationships in a given period of time.*

5. Another confusion results from the difference between costs as totals and as averages. Figures 5–1 through 5–5 illustrate *total* and *unit* cost-output relationships for several kinds of cost behavior. An understanding of these models will be essential in practical work to follow. Carefully study all five pairs of figures.

6. The expression "completely fixed expense" is open to diverse interpretations. We need to distinguish among the following kinds of costs:

a. Costs which are fixed as long as operations are going on, but which are escapable if operations are *shut down.* An example might be the salaries of the supervisory staff.

FIGURE 5–1 (a)

A LINEAR TOTAL-COST FUNCTION, WITH ALL COSTS VARIABLE

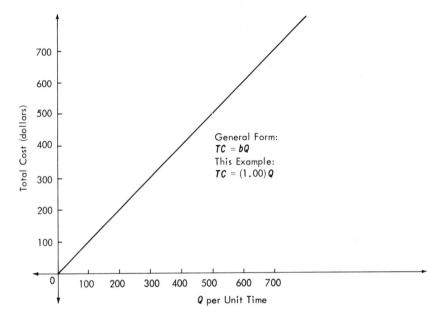

General Form:
$TC = bQ$
This Example:
$TC = (1.00)Q$

FIGURE 5–1 (b)

A CORRESPONDING AVERAGE COST FUNCTION

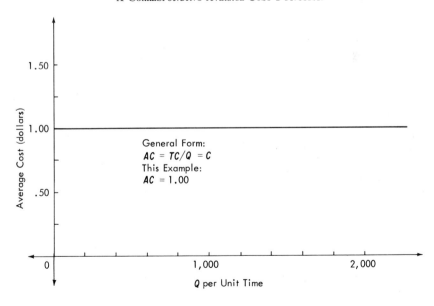

General Form:
$AC = TC/Q = C$
This Example:
$AC = 1.00$

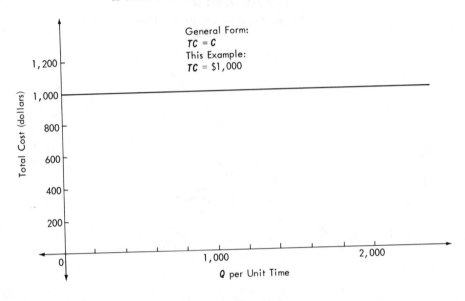

FIGURE 5-2 (a)

A TOTAL COST FUNCTION WITH ALL COSTS FIXED

General Form:
$TC = C$
This Example:
$TC = \$1,000$

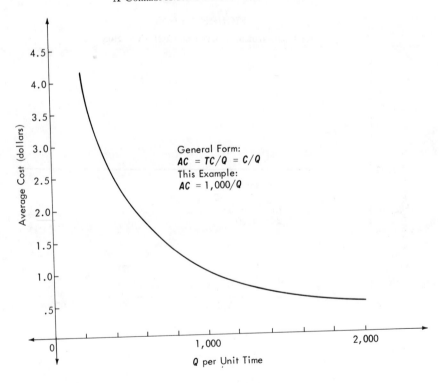

FIGURE 5-2 (b)

A CORRESPONDING AVERAGE COST FUNCTION

General Form:
$AC = TC/Q = C/Q$
This Example:
$AC = 1,000/Q$

FIGURE 5–3 (*a*)

A LINEAR TOTAL COST FUNCTION WITH FIXED AND VARIABLE COSTS

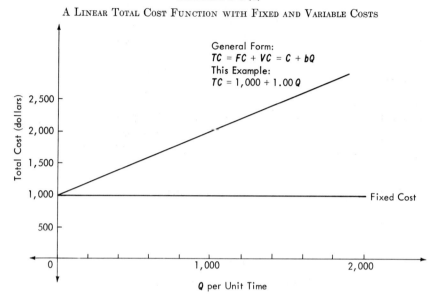

General Form:
$TC = FC + VC = C + bQ$
This Example:
$TC = 1,000 + 1.00\,Q$

FIGURE 5–3 (*b*)

A CORRESPONDING AVERAGE COST FUNCTION

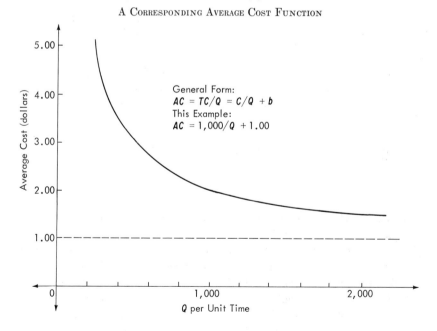

General Form:
$AC = TC/Q = C/Q + b$
This Example:
$AC = 1,000/Q + 1.00$

FIGURE 5–4 (*a*)

A Stairstep Total Cost Function

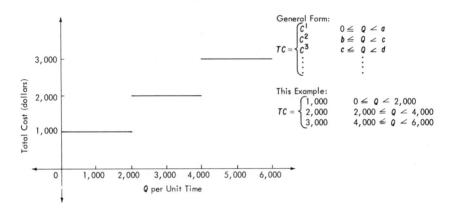

FIGURE 5–4 (*b*)

Corresponding Average Cost Function

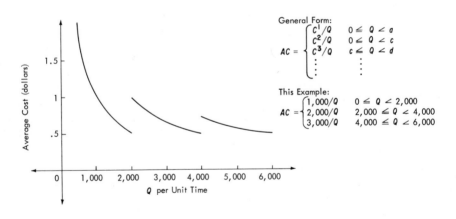

b. Costs which run on even if production is halted but which are escapable if the company is *liquidated*. These costs are inescapable in the short run but escapable in the long run. An example might be the wages of watchmen or the minimum heating expense required to prevent the freezing of pipes. We shall call these expenses *standby fixed costs.*

c. Costs which are not the result of output but which are at the *discretion of management.* Examples are advertising expense, research expense, and consultants' fees. This category may sometimes include a substantial part of wages and salaries. These expenses go under the name of *programmed fixed costs.*

FIGURE 5–5 (a)

A More Complicated Total Cost Function
(for example, an electric utility expense on which there is a fixed
charge with blocks of use at decreasing charges per unit)

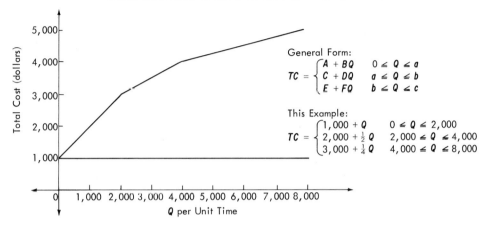

General Form:

$$TC = \begin{cases} A + BQ & 0 \leq Q \leq a \\ C + DQ & a \leq Q \leq b \\ E + FQ & b \leq Q \leq c \end{cases}$$

This Example:

$$TC = \begin{cases} 1{,}000 + Q & 0 \leq Q \leq 2{,}000 \\ 2{,}000 + \frac{1}{2}Q & 2{,}000 \leq Q \leq 4{,}000 \\ 3{,}000 + \frac{1}{4}Q & 4{,}000 \leq Q \leq 8{,}000 \end{cases}$$

FIGURE 5–5 (b)

Corresponding Average Cost Curve

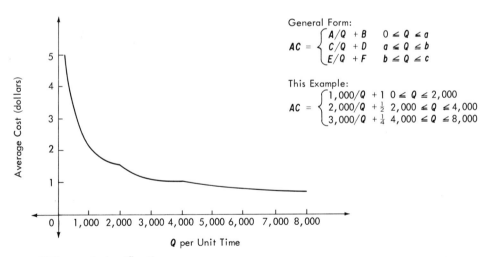

General Form:

$$AC = \begin{cases} A/Q + B & 0 \leq Q \leq a \\ C/Q + D & a \leq Q \leq b \\ E/Q + F & b \leq Q \leq c \end{cases}$$

This Example:

$$AC = \begin{cases} 1{,}000/Q + 1 & 0 \leq Q \leq 2{,}000 \\ 2{,}000/Q + \frac{1}{2} & 2{,}000 \leq Q \leq 4{,}000 \\ 3{,}000/Q + \frac{1}{4} & 4{,}000 \leq Q \leq 8{,}000 \end{cases}$$

Other cost classifications

The fixed-variable classification is inadequate to deal with all of the
cost relationships involved in managerial decisions. The following additional classifications will be useful, each classification pointing up a
different aspect of decision making.[1]

---

[1] This section is heavily influenced by Joel Dean, *Managerial Economics* (New
York: Prentice-Hall, Inc., 1951), pp. 257–72.

⤬ *Incremental costs versus sunk costs.* A cost is incremental *if it results from a decision;* costs which do not arise from the particular decision but which run on anyway are excluded from incremental costs. A decision to drive an extra 1,000 miles should take into account the extra fuel costs and wear and tear on tires but can ignore the portion of depreciation which marches on regardless of usage. A decision to buy a second car, in contrast, must reckon with the added depreciation expenses resulting from having two cars aging rather than one.[2] It is necessary to determine which costs are actually incremental for any given decision.

Marginal costs versus incremental costs. Marginal costs are always related to changes in *output;* incremental costs may relate to any decision affecting costs. Marginal costs are always computed for *unit* changes in output; incremental costs are more flexible in that they may relate to *any* change, whether it is a one-unit change in output, a thousand-unit change in output, or a decision that leaves output unaffected but changes costs in other ways.

Opportunity costs versus "costs" requiring no sacrifice. A cost is not really a cost from the point of view of economics (or decision making) unless it requires a *sacrifice of alternatives*—unless it is an *opportunity* cost. Determining what an opportunity cost is or, more important, determining the level of opportunity costs requires the measurement of what is given up by foregoing the best alternative use. The use of idle space which has no alternative use is cost-free for a particular purpose, regardless of the amount of depreciation being charged on the space.[3] The use of a machine which has been written off the books completely does involve a cost if its use for the purpose under consideration requires giving up alternative opportunities.

Escapable costs versus inescapable costs (avoidable versus unavoidable costs). A cost is escapable *if the decision frees the enterprise from an outflow of funds that would have been required otherwise.* If cutting back production by 10 percent will free the firm from material costs of $10,000 per month and labor costs of $5,000 per month, those costs are escapable. But if no foreman can be laid off as a result of this decision, foremen's salaries do not enter into the escapable costs.

Whether certain costs are escapable varies according to the decision. Some costs that cannot be escaped as a result of reductions in output may be escaped by closing down the department completely. The part of depreciation which relates to wear and tear (the user cost) is escaped by reducing output, but the part which flows on over time regardless of

---

[2] This illustration is developed by W. J. Vatter in "Tailor-Making Cost Data for Specific Uses," *N.A.C.A. Bulletin,* 1954 Conference Proceedings as reprinted in W. E. Thomas (ed.) *Readings in Cost Accounting, Budgeting and Control* (Cincinnati: South-Western Publishing Company, 1955), pp. 316–18.

[3] This statement must be qualified to recognize that additional wear-and-tear may result from putting the idle space to work.

output is escapable only if the machine or building is sold, and even then only if there is a market for such assets. (A fuller discussion of depreciation must be postponed until the next section.)

The antithesis of the escapable cost is the inescapable or sunk cost— the *cost that runs on whether the alternative is chosen or not.* Again what is or is not sunk depends on the decision under consideration. If I am considering leasing my house during the summer while on leave, I must consider the depreciation on the house—the payment for mowing the lawn and the fixed charge on my telephone and other utilities—to be inescapable. But I can escape from all of these expenses by selling the house, at the cost of incurring considerable inconvenience and expenses of other types. The terms avoidable and unavoidable are often used as substitutes for escapable and inescapable. These terms will be used interchangeably in the discussion which follows.

Common costs versus separable costs. Most firms produce more than one product and thus run into the problem of common costs. Often it is difficult to attribute costs to particular products since they result *from the mix of products* rather than from one product taken at a time. In decision making much of the confusion of trying to determine which costs are common and which are traceable to a particular product can be resolved by applying incremental reasoning. It is often easier to determine how much a change in the output of a single product changes a particular cost than it is to determine the product's total "fair share" of that cost.[4] In any case, it is the change in cost rather than the traceability of cost which is relevant. But it is necessary to face up to more complex situations in which an increase in the output of product A brings an increase (or decrease) in the marginal cost of product B. Such problems are important in determining the product mix in the oil industry or other industries in which the same raw materials or processes result in a variety of end products.

Other cost concepts

A few additional terms appear in business literature. Frequently businessmen refer to *out-of-pocket costs.* Strictly speaking the term should refer to *cash outlays to outsiders.* Payments for raw materials are an out-of-pocket cost, but depreciation is not. Often managers use the term to mean incremental costs. But the salary of a supervisor requires a cash outlay to outsiders which may not be incremental for a given increase in output. Often the phrase "out-of-pocket" is ambiguous as to what is really intended.

A similar confusion surrounds the term *direct cost.* Some accountants apparently define direct costs to be the same as variable costs. One ac-

---

[4] Once the accountant has adopted a routine for allocating overhead costs it may be easy to determine the "full cost" of a product. But the result of this computation is not relevant for most decision making.

counting research study states, "Direct costs are those which vary directly with volume (raw material, direct labor, and direct supplies) plus certain costs which vary closely with production and can be allocated to a product or group of products on a reasonably accurate basis."[5] But the expression "direct" seems to refer more to the ease with which a particular expense may be *traced to an individual department or product.*[6] Traceability and variability are not the same thing; the ambiguity on just which is being measured results in confusion. And, as we have seen, even if we restrict direct costs to mean variable costs, its meaning depends on just what decision is being made. A completely programmed system of direct costing cannot provide the exact incremental cost figure required for every kind of decision.[7]

The distinction between *controllable* and *noncontrollable* costs is important in management, which must be concerned with fixing responsibility for keeping costs in line with predetermined standards. This book, however, is less concerned with control than it is with decision making, so that there will be few, if any, references to this dichotomy on the pages which follow.

The term *imputed* or *implicit* costs refers to costs which are relevant in decision making but which are not recorded in the accounts. Implicit cost is the *difference* between opportunity cost and the nominal or explicit cost of an input. Examples of implicit costs are the interest and dividends that could be earned by capital elsewhere, the difference in salary a sole proprietor might earn in an outside position, and the rental that could be earned on property in other undertakings.

The term *differential cost* appears in some accounting literature to mean approximately the same thing as incremental cost in this volume. The differential cost may be computed as a total or on a unit of output basis.

Recent articles and books on accounting have stressed the need for *relevant costs*—that is costs which are needed to reach an optimal decision.[8] Relevant costs and revenues are also emphasized in managerial economics.

---

[5] N.A.A. Research Report No. 37, January 1, 1961, p. 11.

[6] In fact, Gordon Shillinglaw, *Cost Accounting: Analysis and Control* (Homewood, Ill.: Richard D. Irwin, Inc., 1961), p. 102, defines a direct cost as one "that is specifically traceable to a particular costing unit." Some books appear to relate "direct costing" to the collection of variable costs but use "direct costs" to mean traceable costs, a distinction which is confusing to the layman.

[7] Support for this position appears in Howard C. Greer, "Alternatives to Direct Costing," in William E. Thomas (ed.), *Readings in Cost Accounting, Budgeting, and Control* (Cincinnati: South-Western Publishing Co., 1955), pp. 300–312.

[8] See Charles T. Horngren, "Choosing Accounting Practices for Reporting to Management," *N.A.A. Bulletin,* September 1962, pp. 3–15; and G. R. Crowningshield, *Cost Accounting: Principles and Managerial Application* (Boston: Houghton Mifflin Co., 1962), pp. 481–82.

Empirical illustrations

Uses of fixed and variable costs and the relevance of some of the other cost concepts are illustrated below in an operation familiar to everyone. Even this simple example demonstrates the *need for flexibility* in adapting cost measures to particular problems.

The independent corner grocery store would seem to offer a simple situation for the analyst. However, it presents a number of borderline issues. Let us consider some particular expenses to see whether they fit into the fixed or variable categories.

Cost of goods sold. The sums paid at wholesale for the groceries are the clearest illustrations of variable costs. The greater the volume of sales the greater these expenses. The complications are relatively insignificant: The firm may benefit from quantity discounts which would keep this cost from being exactly constant per unit of sales; changes in the sales mix, with various commodities selling at different markups, might cause a shift in the cost of goods sold per unit of sales; the sale of an item that has become obsolete and has been sitting on the shelves a long time may involve no real sacrifice, or at least not one equal to the original whole-sale cost.

Rental on the building. Rental expense would appear to be the clearest case of a fixed expense, running on without regard to the level of sales. Yet a decision to close down would affect costs in different ways depending on the length of the rental contract and on possible alternative uses of the property. The availability of convenient storage space on the outside might enable the firm to vary warehousing rentals according to volume. If the firm actually owns the store property, the true cost of using is the sacrifice of opportunities for earnings from alternatives.

Employees' wages. Variability of wages in such a store depends on how short a run one has in mind. If one is looking at the variation within a day, such costs are only partially variable. The store may be able to employ extra help for anticipated rush hours, but may have to keep some help to meet unpredictable peaks in activity. Under contemporary employment conditions it is doubtful that clerks will work only during peak periods unless they are relatives of the owner. Grocery stores meet this problem in part by shifting clerks from cash registers to stocking tasks; their ability to transfer workers from jobs that have to be done at particular (but not always predictable) times to fill-in jobs helps control costs. The opportunity to keep employees on overtime also increases the ability to adjust wages to volume but, of course, produces the complication of time-and-a-half for overtime.

Storage costs. Interest on minimum inventories takes on a fixed character. Remaining interest costs, along with associated handling costs and costs of deterioration and obsolescence, might be treated as a variable cost dependent on volume, since the firm can vary size of inventory with the volume of sales and output. The cost of the storage space, on the other hand, would be included in the rental expense already discussed—usually a fixed cost. One complication is that handling costs, deterioration, and obsolescence depend on the mix of products, which might vary from time to time.

Utilities. The costs of heating, lighting, and water are probably as close to fixed costs as one could find. Even if the charges for electricity include both fixed and variable components (as is true in the case of a two-part tariff), the manager of a grocery store will have little opportunity to relate the total charges to volume; he will not turn off the lights simply because the traffic is low.[9] At the same time, they are costs that are escapable if the store is closed down completely, for the utilities can be disconnected.

Depreciation on equipment. Depreciation on refrigerators and other specialized grocery equipment is handled as a fixed expense in usual accounting practice. From the standpoint of short-run decisions it might be ignored, since resale or salvage value of this equipment is probably negligible. No sacrifice is involved in its continued use. In either treatment the cost is excluded from short-run variable costs and from incremental cost.

Advertising expense. Advertising presents a peculiarly difficult conceptual problem in the classification of costs. Suppose management were to adopt the policy of varying advertising with sales volume; it might then appear that advertising is a variable cost, rising and falling directly with sales. But advertising expense is not a result of volume; it is an attempt to manipulate volume. Thus the policy of basing such expenses on volume is arbitrary and usually unsound. Two solutions present themselves: (1) to treat advertising as a fixed expense budgeted by management in advance and thus unrelated to short-run volume or (2) to leave such expenses out of the fixed-variable classification, placing them in a special category of manipulable expenses, which we have called "programmed expenses." The literature does not give as much attention to the distinction between such programmed costs and fixed costs as seems warranted.

ACCOUNTING COSTS AND ECONOMIC COSTS

Accountants did not originally develop their cost concepts for the same purposes that the economists have in mind; the difference in purposes led

---

[9] A decision to carry or abandon frozen foods will affect the electricity bill. This is another illustration of the variety of short runs encountered in practice, since the electricity consumed by frozen foods is fixed in the extremely short run but may be varied by changing the physical facilities.

to differences in definitions. Concepts of cost must serve the purposes at hand. When it comes to analysis for decision making, economists and accountants are in close agreement. "Managerial economics" and "managerial accounting" have profited from mutual contributions of each subject to the other, so that the two are now almost inseparable.

Limitations of traditional accounting data for decision making

Originally accounting had only an indirect relationship to decision making. The main function of accounting has been that of reporting—of recording what has happened to income and wealth during a given period. The profit and loss statement (income statement) attempts to tell how well the firm has done. Data required to determine past profitability are not those needed to select among alternatives for the future. Another main function of accounting closely related to that of reporting is stewardship—the presentation of information that will protect the interests of the stockholders, creditors, or tax collectors. But again stewardship and decision making are quite different objectives.

Accounting has had still another objective—that of control—of providing standards against which performance can be judged. Classifications of accounts according to areas of responsibility and data most suitable for control purposes are not necessarily appropriate in choosing among alternatives for the future.

The main principle followed in the collection of data for reporting, stewardship, or control has been to use *historical* costs. In measuring the cost involved in the use of resources such as materials or equipment, the accountant concerns himself with acquisition costs of those resources. But decision making is necessarily concerned with *future* costs and revenues; the past is not always an accurate guide for the future.

Data from traditional accounting procedures for reporting or control are often deficient for decision making for the following reasons:

1. *Historical cost data do not always reflect the opportunity costs of decisions.* Raw materials acquired at $1,000 last month may be worth more today because they could be sold for more. Or, to take another illustration, in periods of slack business, opportunity costs fall far below the depreciation based on historical costs; in periods of high activity, the sacrifice in selecting one alternative over another may be far above depreciation.

2. *Traditional accounting procedures ignore certain items which are costs from the economic point of view.* The most obvious examples, discussed in Chapter 2, are the failure of accounting for sole proprietorships or partnerships to record the sacrifice of the owners' time which may be useful for other purposes, or to record the earnings possible if the funds were invested elsewhere.

3. *Traditional accounting classifications do not usually measure ex-*

actly the incremental costs or escapable costs required in the analysis of a decision-making problem. The breakdown between fixed costs and variable costs moves in this direction but may not provide the flexibility in classification required by decision making. As already noted, a cost that is fixed or sunk for one kind of decision may be variable or escapable for another. Decision making requires tailor-made cost classifications.

4. *Traditional procedures for overhead allocation often lead to confusion in decision making.* Accountants may allocate overhead on the basis of direct labor costs in a department, or some similar basis. Perhaps past results suggest that overhead should be allocated at the rate of 150 percent of direct labor cost. Suppose that management is considering introduction of a labor-saving machine which will cut direct labor costs $12,000 per year. One might be tempted to assume that overhead costs will be cut by $18,000 (150 percent of $12,000). In this case, the allocation rate is actually irrelevant.

Accountants themselves recognize that the bases for overhead allocations are arbitrary. One classical statement on the subject is: ". . . cost allocation at best is loaded with assumption and in many cases, highly arbitrary methods of apportionment are employed in practice. Certainly it is wise not to take the results of the usual process of internal cost computation too seriously."[10]

Remember that traditional accounting procedures were developed for purposes other than what we have in mind. Remember also that accounts are our main source of data for decisions. The skilled manager must learn how to *interpret* accounts and how to ask accountants for data and classifications of data which *suit his needs.*

The special problem of depreciation

Accepted accounting practice is to base depreciation on original cost and to allocate that original cost over time. The objective is to spread acquisition cost over the time periods in which the asset is to be used. Depreciation in accounting is thus "a procedure for spreading the cost of a long-term asset over its useful life in a more or less equitable manner." Many students believe that the accountant's depreciation charge is intended to provide a fund for the replacement of assets, but this is *not* the purpose.

In decision making, we need a depreciation figure which reflects the *sacrifices* in selecting one alternative over another. Measurement of this sacrifice requires considerable judgment (accountants traditionally try to avoid such judgment) and varies according to the decision.

1. Suppose that a machine has broken down completely, beyond any hope of repair. The management wishes to decide whether to buy a new

[10] W. A. Paton and A. C. Littleton, *An Introduction to Corporate Accounting Standards* (Chicago: American Accounting Association, 1940), p. 120.

machine or to purchase on the outside the parts that have been produced by the machine. In this case, *reproduction* or replacement cost of the machine is the relevant basis for depreciation—*historical* cost of the old machine is irrelevant.

2. Suppose an old machine appears to have four years of physical life remaining. The issue is whether to sell the machine now and start buying the parts on the outside at once. Original cost of the machine was, let us say, $50,000. Book value net of depreciation is $20,000 and annual *depreciation for accounting purposes* is $5,000 per annum. However, the measurement of *depreciation needed in the analysis of this problem* is expected loss in market value of the machine in the future. If the machine is worth $7,000 now but is expected to be worth $5,500 a year from now, the sacrifice in retaining it a year is $1,500. Economic depreciation is $1,500 rather than $5,000—it measures the sacrifice of an opportunity of selling the machine now rather than later.

3. Suppose the machine has no market value but still is productive. The economic depreciation is *nil* regardless of the book value or the accountant's depreciation charge.

4. Now consider a decision to increase output by 50 percent. What is needed is a measure of the increase in depreciation. Managerial economists often assume that this increase is negligible, for obsolescence is unaffected by use and machines or buildings tend to deteriorate over time whether used or not. A more refined approach is to try to measure the added wear and tear resulting from use—to measure the user cost. In many cases user cost may be safely ignored, but in others it may be a significant consideration.

Variations on these situations appear in practice, sometimes requiring a complex analysis. Some cases may require a mixture of short-run and long-run considerations. Taxes complicate the issue. But enough has been said to indicate the *opportunity cost* basis for the economist's measurement of depreciation and to indicate that financial accounting is usually concerned with quite a different problem.

Empirical studies and illustrations

Traditional techniques of financial and cost accounting often are at variance with the requirements of economics. But accountants have developed special approaches for purposes of decision making which go under various names, such as direct costing, marginal income analysis, differential costing, merchandise management accounting, cost-volume-profit analysis, and contribution accounting.

How extensive are these approaches in actual practice? Chapter 2 cited a study by James S. Earley of a sample of large firms which suggests that differential accounting is becoming widespread. Earley states, "leading cost accountants and management consultants are currently advocating principles of accounting analysis and decision making that are essentially 'marginalist' in character and implications."[11] Earley finds a widespread separation of fixed and variable costs and other procedures moving in the direction of incremental reasoning. It appears doubtful, however, that all of the firms in his sample face up to the full implications of managerial economics. Do they tailor-make costs to meet the varying requirements of different decisions? Do they adjust cost estimates to reflect changes in opportunity costs with variations in the use of capacity?

A study of small businesses suggests that their accounting procedures seldom reflect incremental reasoning.[12] Chapter 2 cited cases from the study in which the accounting systems encouraged the managers to use full costs (including allocated overhead) when incremental costs would have been more appropriate. Many of the managers made little use of accounts in decision making. Most of them resorted to highly subjective ad hoc analyses varying in thoroughness. Some made fairly careful pencil-and-paper calculations which used some accounting data but were mainly based on estimated values.

Actual practice, therefore, appears to vary from situations in which accounting and economics are closely interwoven in providing the information needed for decisions to the opposite extreme in which overhead allocations, past costs, historical depreciation, and similar accounting conventions actually confuse management. Every manager would profit from thinking through the relationships between accounting and economic concepts.

BREAK-EVEN CHARTS

Up to this point we have been mainly concerned with *classifications* of particular expenses (salaries, depreciation, etc.). We now turn to the *relationships of costs to output* per unit of time.

Form of the break-even charts

Figure 5–6 illustrates a typical break-even chart. The horizontal axis on such a chart represents output; the purpose of the chart is to show the effects of changes in rate of output upon cost, revenue, and profit. It should be noted that revenues as well as expenses are shown on the vertical axis, usually with total revenue drawn as a straight line through the origin. A linear revenue function assumes that the price is constant regardless of output. This assumption is appropriate under conditions of

---

[11] James S. Earley, "Marginal Policies of 'Excellently Managed' Companies," *The American Economic Review,* March 1956, p. 44.

[12] J. L. Gibson and W. W. Haynes, *Accounting in Small Business Decisions* (Lexington: University of Kentucky Press, 1963).

FIGURE 5–6

A Typical Break-Even Chart

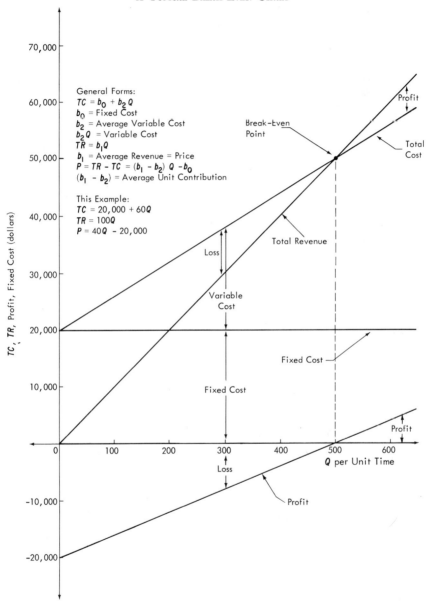

General Forms:
$TC = b_0 + b_2 Q$
b_0 = Fixed Cost
b_2 = Average Variable Cost
$b_2 Q$ = Variable Cost
$TR = b_1 Q$
b_1 = Average Revenue = Price
$P = TR - TC = (b_1 - b_2) Q - b_0$
$(b_1 - b_2)$ = Average Unit Contribution

This Example:
$TC = 20,000 + 60Q$
$TR = 100Q$
$P = 40Q - 20,000$

FIGURE 5–7

Break-Even Chart: Contribution to Profit Form

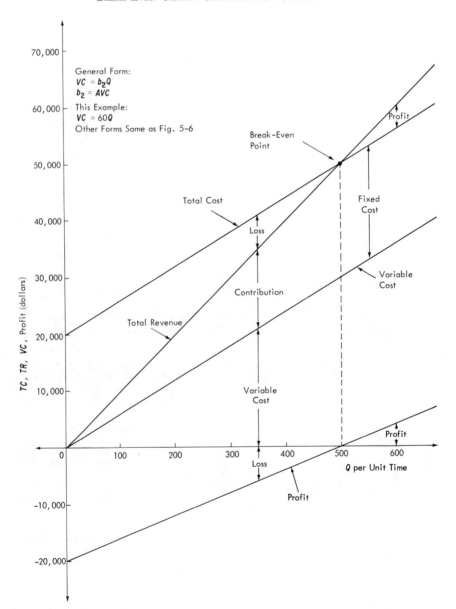

pure competition, in which the firm sells all output at the market price, but it is not suitable when the demand curve of the firm slopes downward to the right. Total cost is also usually shown as a straight line; it is the sum of the fixed costs which are horizontal on the chart and the variable costs which are assumed to rise linearly.

The student should not jump to the conclusion that the purpose of the break-even chart is to determine the break-even point—the point at which total revenue equals total cost. The break-even point is of some interest, but the chart also shows what happens to profits (or losses) at outputs greater or less than the break-even volume. The principal objective of the chart is to indicate *what happens to total costs, total revenues, and profits as output and sales change from one rate to another.*

Contribution to overhead and profit

Sometimes the information shown on Figure 5–6 is presented in an alternative form with variable costs shown first on the vertical axis; fixed costs are added to the variable costs. Such a form is shown in Figure 5–7. Figure 5–7 has the advantage that one can read on it the *contribution* to overhead and profit quite readily. Decision making in the short run is more concerned with this contribution to both overhead and profits than it is to the profit figure alone.

The contribution form of the break-even chart is closely related to the incremental reasoning described in Chapter 2. The stress is on the changes in total revenue and changes in total cost as output varies. Fixed costs appear in a subordinate position. The interesting point about an increase in output and sales of 10 percent, for example, is the additional contribution to overhead and profit; this involves a simple comparison of the increase in revenue with the increase in cost.

It should now be clear why break-even analysis is sometimes called "profit contribution analysis." In the pages which follow we shall examine a number of other types of analysis which apply the contribution concept.

Construction of break-even charts

Where does one obtain the information for plotting a break-even chart? There are two usual ways of undertaking this task, both based on the income statement.

1. One approach, which is called the *analytical* or engineering approach, is to take a single income statement for the firm (or department) and to use judgment in classifying costs into those that are fixed and those that are variable. A manager of a small firm who is intimately familiar with output-expense behavior should have little difficulty with such a classification, though there are inevitably some borderline problems, as in the case of semivariable expenses already described. The

manager simply asks himself whether he would actually increase this expense if output were to increase, and he estimates the amount of the increased spending. He may find it necessary to abandon the linearity assumption upon which break-even charts are usually constructed and introduce stairstep costs and other semivariable expenses. The resultant chart might look like Figure 5–8 rather than take the usual linear form.

FIGURE 5–8

A COMPLEX BREAK-EVEN CHART

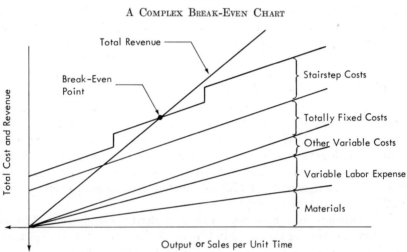

2. A second approach, the *statistical* or historical approach, compares a series of income statements for succeeding periods which reflect varying levels of output and costs. By plotting the output-cost relationship on a scatter diagram, one can estimate the position of the total cost line. If one assumes that the costs are linear, he can extrapolate the total cost line back to the vertical axis (at which output is zero), thus estimating the level of the fixed costs.

Figure 5–9 illustrates this approach. The dots on the diagram show the relation between the cost and output for particular periods. These dots will not fall exactly on a single line, for other influences inevitably affect costs. It is hoped, however, that the dots will be arranged in enough of a pattern that a line of best fit may be located. The *slope* of this line is an estimate of the *marginal costs* (or unit variable costs under conditions of linearity). The *intercept* on the vertical axis is an estimate of the *fixed cost*. It is then possible to draw in an appropriate total revenue line and to find the break-even point.

More refined statistical techniques for estimating the total cost line are possible. For example, one may correct the data for changes in input prices over time, or for changes in ratios of inputs to output.

FIGURE 5–9

ESTIMATING THE TOTAL COST LINE FROM A SCATTER DIAGRAM

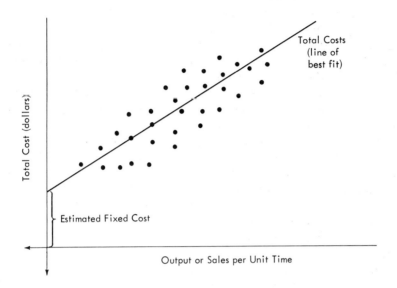

Scale of the output axis

The discussion so far has failed to define precisely what measure of output is plotted on the horizontal axis of the break-even chart. If the firm produces one standard product, one simply plots the volume of *physical output* (in pounds, tons, cubic feet, or whatever the appropriate unit is). The total cost line then provides an estimate of the cost at any level of physical output.

If, however, the output is not homogeneous, the measurement of output is more complex. How can one add together quantities of refrigerators and stoves? One solution is to compute an *index number* of output which will give proper weight to the various products. Another solution is to measure output as a *percent of capacity*. A simpler, and more widely known approach is to use *sales dollars* as a measure of output. Sales dollars automatically weight the various products according to their sales value. In this case, the total revenue line becomes a 45-degree diagonal, provided that the same scale is used on both axes of the break-even chart. The use of sales dollars does not completely overcome the conceptual difficulties involved in measuring output. Suppose, for example, that the price of one product is increased and another decreased. Does it follow that the relative importance of the two products is actually different as far as costs are concerned?

Limitations of break-even analysis

Some of the major limitations of break-even analysis are clear from the preceding discussion.

1. The charts usually are not corrected for changes in factor prices. If a break-even chart is based on past data, those data should be adjusted for changes in wages and for changes in the prices of raw materials. Such adjustments are cumbersome. The analytical approach avoids the necessity of making these adjustments.

2. The charts usually assume that the price of the output (or the set of prices of the outputs) is given. In other words, they assume a horizontal demand curve that is realistic only under conditions approximating pure competition. A simple way of attempting to overcome this limitation is to draw a series of total revenue lines on the chart, each based on the assumption of a different price. One can then estimate the volume that will be sold and produced at each price and can read from the diagram the expected profits. Figure 5–10 illustrates this form of the chart. Of the prices shown, that of $5 is the most profitable. Unfortunately, the estimation of the volume at various prices is itself difficult and subject to error.

3. The charts ignore other influences on profits. They assume that profits are a function of output alone, neglecting the obvious fact that they are also a result of technological change, improved management, changes in the scale of the fixed inputs, and many other forces.

Break-even charts are static. They are drawn on the assumption of given relationships between costs and revenues on one side and output on

FIGURE 5–10

Break-Even Chart with Alternative Revenue Lines for Alternative Prices

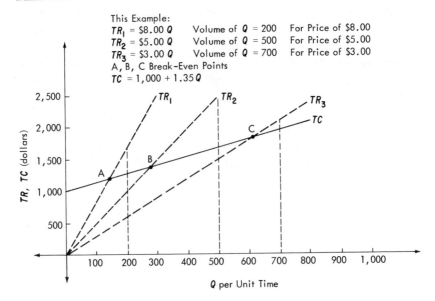

This Example:
$TR_1 = \$8.00\,Q$ Volume of $Q = 200$ For Price of $8.00
$TR_2 = \$5.00\,Q$ Volume of $Q = 500$ For Price of $5.00
$TR_3 = \$3.00\,Q$ Volume of $Q = 700$ For Price of $3.00
A, B, C Break–Even Points
$TC = 1,000 + 1.35\,Q$

Q per Unit Time

the other. Costs and revenues may, however, shift over time in such a way that projections based on past data may be misleading.

4. As has already been indicated, break-even charts are based on rather arbitrary assumptions as to the relative importance of different products in multiproduct firms. A change in the sales mix may mean that the revenue-output relationship shown on the chart is no longer applicable. As Dean says: "Changes in the composition of demand impair the accuracy of the static sales line and may vitiate the profit projection. Whenever products differ in contribution margin and there is variation in product-mix from period to period, profits will vary at a given output rate. . . . Under these circumstances, the constant-price sales line is inaccurate, even as a static function."[13]

5. When break-even charts are based on accounting data, as they usually are, they suffer from all the limitations of such data, such as neglect of imputed cost, arbitrary depreciation estimates, and inappropriate allocations of overhead costs.

6. The carryover of inventory from one period to the next presents another difficulty. What is the value of output produced in one period to be sold later? Normally this difficulty is glossed over in break-even analysis, though it is possible to make adjustments that will correct most of the error.

7. Selling costs are peculiarly difficult to handle in break-even analysis. Selling cost changes are not a result of output changes; they are a cause of changes in sales and output. Furthermore, the relationship between output and selling expenses is unstable over time, reducing the accuracy of the projection of past relationships into the future.

8. Costs in a particular period may not be a result exclusively of the output in that period. Maintenance expenses, for example, are especially hard to attribute to a given time period, being a result of past output or a preparation for future output. Maintenance costs are usually not perfectly matched with output, resulting in an error in profit projections.

9. The simple form of the break-even chart shown so far makes no provision for taxes, particularly the corporate income tax. One may develop the chart to show part of the profit going to the government in taxes and the remainder going to the stockholders or being retained for expansion. If the company suffers alternating years of profit and loss or if it falls into varying tax brackets, this adjustment for taxes is somewhat difficult to show on the chart.

Evaluation of break-even charts

It is easy to build up a formidable list of limitations of break-even charts. Some writers are skeptical of their usefulness unless they are

---

[13] Joel Dean, *Managerial Economics* (Englewood Cliffs, N.J.: Prentice-Hall, Inc., 1951), p. 334.

made much more complex than is usual.[14] At the same time, break-even analysis is simple, easy to understand, and inexpensive.

Usefulness of break-even charts undoubtedly varies from industry to industry. Those industries experiencing frequent changes in input prices, rapid improvements in technology, and many shifts in product mix will profit little from break-even analysis. In other industries, break-even analyses may be quite useful to managers who are familiar with their limitations and simplifications. Management depends heavily on analytical tools that cut through the complexity of reality and focus attention on fundamental relationships.

PROFIT-VOLUME ANALYSIS

Many authors have adapted break-even analysis to the situation of the multiproduct firm. They construct break-even charts for the individual product, individual department, or "sector." One variation is what Bergfeld, Earley, and Knobloch call the profit-volume (P/V) technique or cost-volume-profit analysis.[15] The main concepts used in the P/V technique are:

——P/V Income = Sector's sales volume in dollars minus sector variable costs.

——Profit Contribution = P/V income minus specific programmed costs.

——Specific Programmed Costs = Cost of selling the output of the sector or other costs of promoting that sector (as opposed to programmed cost for the firm as a whole).

——P/V Ratio = The ratio between the unit P/V income and unit price; i.e., unit contribution, or slope of the P/V line.

This variation on the break-even chart is shown in Figure 5–11. The function begins at specific programmed cost below the zero contribution line. The upward sloping line shows the Profit Contribution; its *slope* is the P/V ratio or *contribution per dollar sales*. One moves along the sloping line to the point representing the expected sales volume. The vertical distance between this point and the zero line is the profit contribution for the sector. Such a chart ignores overheads that cannot be definitely allocated to this sector. It shows whether a product is covering its own variable and programmed costs; it shows what contribution the product is making to overall company overhead and profit. The chart

<hr/>

[14] Ibid., pp. 337–38.

[15] Albert J. Bergfeld, James S. Earley, and William R. Knobloch, *Pricing for Profit and Growth* (New York: McGraw-Hill Book Co., 1957). Modern cost accounting books frequently include a chapter on this type of analysis.

thus permits an evaluation of product profits at varying levels of sales, and also provides information for the comparison of contributions from one product to another.

Figure 5–12 shows two products, permitting a comparison of both the break-even points and the contributions. Product B on this chart has a

FIGURE 5–11

PROFIT-CONTRIBUTION CHART

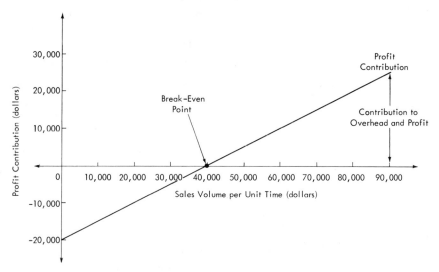

FIGURE 5–12

PROFIT CONTRIBUTION ON TWO PRODUCTS

This Example:

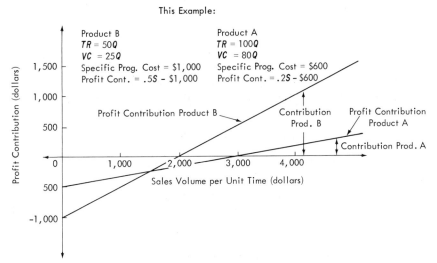

lower break-even point and makes the greater contribution. This approach is helpful in making decisions on the product mix.

Profit-volume analysis is applicable to still other decision-making problems. The charts may be modified to analyze the impact of price changes by showing different revenue lines for different prices. Suppose a price decrease is under consideration. The chart will show whether the increased volume will offset the reduction in unit price. Figure 5–13 illustrates this. The dots on the revenue lines indicate the expected volume at each price.

FIGURE 5–13

PROFIT CONTRIBUTION CHART WITH ALTERNATIVE ASSUMPTIONS ABOUT PRICE

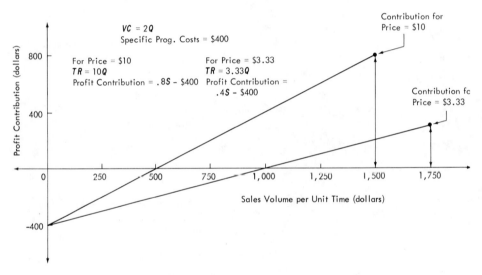

Similar modifications in profit-volume charts can show the impact of changes in wages or other input prices. None of these modifications completely overcomes the static character of break-even charts.

CURVILINEAR FUNCTIONS

Break-even analysis and profit-volume analysis are often concerned with results over relatively short ranges of output. Maximum sales expected at a given price and minimum sales expected at the same price may set the upper and lower limits, respectively, to the relevant range of output. In another setting, sharply rising costs beyond the designed capacity of a plant may set the upper limit to output, and a break-even point that is not far away may set the lower limit. In such cases as

FIGURE 5-14

A CURVILINEAR TOTAL-COST FUNCTION AND CORRESPONDING MC FUNCTION

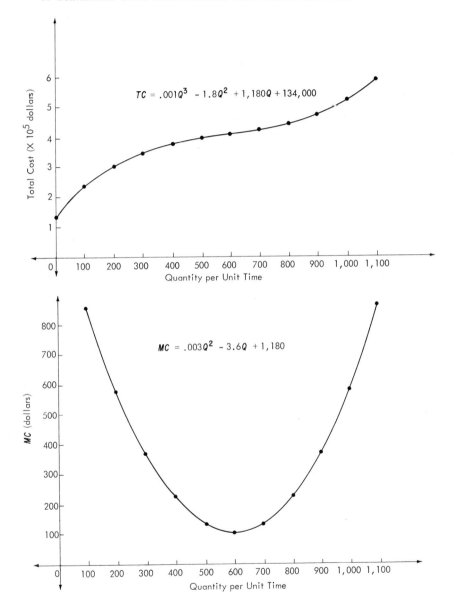

these, the assumption that cost and revenue are linear functions of output may be quite close to the true relationships.

On the other hand, if a relatively wide range of output is to be considered, the total cost function will often be curvilinear because of the law of variable proportions. This law, sometimes called the "law of diminishing returns," applies when variable inputs are added to fixed inputs. It asserts that increases in total output per unit of additional input may initially be increasing but must eventually be decreasing. A total cost function corresponding to an input-output relationship that is subject to the law of variable proportions will have decreasing marginal costs and then increasing marginal costs, so as to be S-shaped, as depicted in Figure 5–14. These matters are discussed more fully in Chapter 6.

A firm with a curvilinear total cost function would face a linear total revenue function if product price were independent of output of the firm (perfect competition). This situation produces a break-even chart like the one depicted in Figure 5–15. Note that there are two break-even

FIGURE 5–15

A BREAK-EVEN CHART WITH CURVILINEAR TOTAL-COST FUNCTION

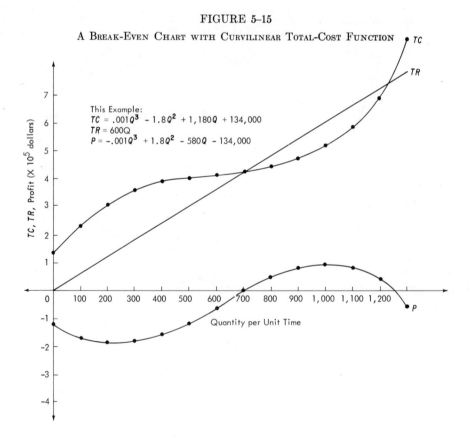

This Example:
$$TC = .001Q^3 - 1.8Q^2 + 1,180Q + 134,000$$
$$TR = 600Q$$
$$P = -.001Q^3 + 1.8Q^2 - 580Q - 134,000$$

points. Note also that profit is maximum at that particular level of output where the vertical distance between the cost and revenue curves is greatest.

If the firm faces a demand curve that slopes down and to the right (monopoly or monopolistic competition), the total revenue function rises to a peak and then declines (this was discussed in Chapter 3). In this case, both the cost curve and the revenue curve are curvilinear and the break-even chart is similar to Figure 5–16. As before, there are two break-even points and a particular level of output that produces maximum profit.

FIGURE 5–16

A Break-Even Chart with Curvilinear Total-Cost and Total-Revenue Functions

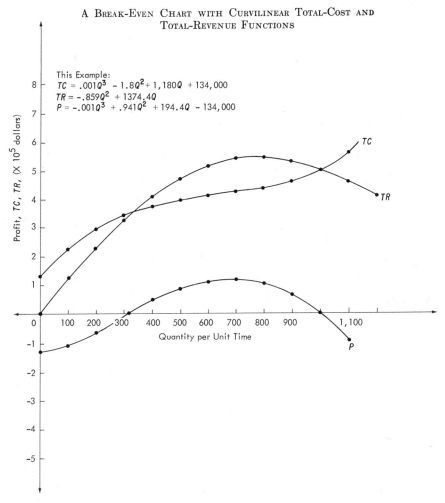

This Example:
$TC = .001Q^3 - 1.8Q^2 + 1,180Q + 134,000$
$TR = -.859Q^2 + 1374.4Q$
$P = -.001Q^3 + .941Q^2 + 194.4Q - 134,000$

ALGEBRAIC TECHNIQUES

Break-even analysis, profit-volume analysis, and choice of optimum level of output (in instances of curvilinear functions) are unnecessarily tedious if graphical techniques are used. The managerial economist needs clear mental images of the *relationships* depicted by these figures. Thus, it may be useful to make quick, approximate sketches of the relevant graphs. However, the desired *numerical results* can be obtained more precisely and far more easily by using algebraic techniques, as explained below.

Algebraic form of break-even analysis

Algebraic execution of break-even analysis is illustrated by reference to Figure 5–6. The total revenue and total cost functions in this figure are:

General form:
$$TR = b_1 \cdot Q$$
$$TC = b_0 + b_2 \cdot Q$$

This example:
$$TR = \$100 \cdot Q$$
$$TC = \$20,000 + \$60 \cdot Q$$

where

TR is total revenue per unit of time
TC is total cost per unit of time
Q is output per unit of time
b_1 is price of the product
b_0 is fixed cost per unit of time
b_2 is marginal and average variable cost per unit of output

To determine the break-even level of output, set the expression for revenue equal to the expression for total cost, as follows:

General form:
$$b_0 + b_2 \cdot Q = b_1 \cdot Q$$

This example:
$$\$20,000 + \$60 \cdot Q = \$100 \cdot Q$$

The solution is:

General form:
$$Q = \frac{b_0}{b_1 - b_2}$$

This example:
$$Q = 500$$

In words, break-even output is fixed cost divided by unit contribution.

Suppose we wish to calculate profit at some stated level of output, say 650 units. Profit (P) is total revenue less total cost, as follows:

General form:
$$P = (b_1 \cdot Q) - (b_0 + b_2 \cdot Q)$$

This example:
$$P = (100 \cdot Q) - (\$20,000 + \$60 \cdot Q)$$

The solution is:

General form:
$$P = -b_0 + Q (b_1 - b_2)$$

This example:
$$P = \$6,000$$

In words, profit is the product of output and unit contribution minus fixed cost.

The convenience of algebraic analysis can be verified and understanding of the above explanations can be reinforced by calculating break-even outputs for alternate values. Work the above example with price increased 10 percent; with price decreased 5 percent; with price unchanged and variable cost per unit increased 5 percent; with variable cost decreased 10 percent; with price and variable cost unchanged and fixed cost increased 25 percent. Using the original data, calculate profit at an output of 400 units; at an output of 600 units.

Algebraic form of profit-volume analysis

Profit-volume analysis by the algebraic technique is explained with the aid of Figure 5–11. The profit-contribution function is determined as follows:

General form:

$$P/V = S - SVC = b_1Q - b_2Q = (b_1 - b_2)Q$$

$$PC = P/V - SPC = \frac{b_1 - b_2}{b_1} S - SPC$$

where

P/V	$= P/V$ Income
S	$=$ Sales Volume on Total Revenue
SVC	$=$ Sector's Variable Cost
b_1	$=$ Product Price
b_2	$=$ Sector's Average Variable Cost
$b_1 - b_2$	$=$ Contribution per unit of Q
$\dfrac{b_1 - b_2}{b_1}$	$=$ Contribution per dollar of Sales or P/V ratio
PC	$=$ Profit Contribution
SPC	$=$ Specific Programmed Costs

To determine the sector's break-even sales volume, set the expression for PC equal to O, as follows:

$$\frac{b_1 - b_2}{b_1} S - SPC = 0$$

The solution is:

$$S = \frac{SPC}{\dfrac{b_1 - b_2}{b_1}}$$

In words, sector break-even volume is obtained by dividing specific programmed costs by sector contribution per dollar of sales. To determine results at any given sales volume, simply substitute that level of sales in the PC equation and determine the value of PC.

This example:

Price = \$100, Sector's Average Variable cost = \$50, and SPC = \$20,000;

$$P/V = \frac{100 - 50}{100} S = .5S$$

$$PC = .5S - 20{,}000$$

Break-even points:

$$.5S - 20{,}000 = 0$$

$$S = 40{,}000$$

Understanding of the above explanation can be verified by calculating sector break-even for other values. Work the example assuming a price increase of 5 percent; with price the same and variable cost per unit increased 10 percent; with no change in price or variable cost and specific programmed cost decreased 15 percent. Using the original data, calculate PC for sales volume of \$90,000.

Algebraic determination of optimum output

If there is a curvilinear form of the cost function (or of both the cost and the revenue functions), there is a particular level of output that yields maximum profit. This level can be determined analytically by algebraic techniques. The method is explained by reference to Figure 5–16.

The equation for the revenue (R) function in Figure 5–16 is a quadratic form:

$$TR = -.859\ Q^2 + 1374.4Q$$

in which

TR is total revenue per unit of time
Q is output per unit of time

The equation for the cost function in the figure is a cubic form:

$$TC = .001Q^3 - 1.8Q^2 + 1{,}180Q + 134{,}000$$

The equation for profit (P) is the expression for total revenue less the expression for total cost:

$$P = -.859Q^2 + 1374.4Q - .001Q^3 + 1.8Q^2 - 1{,}180Q - 134{,}000$$

Combining terms: $P = -.001Q^3 + .941Q^2 + 194.4Q - 134{,}000$

At its maximum point, the slope of the profit function is zero. Since the slope of this function is its first derivative with respect to Q, a general expression for the slope can be found by methods of differential calculus.

$$\frac{dP}{dQ} = -.003Q^2 + 1.882Q + 194.4$$

Let this expression be set equal to 0:

$$0 = -.003Q^2 + 1.882Q + 194.4$$

The resulting equation can be organized in the general quadratic form:

$$0 = aQ^2 + bQ + c$$

The general quadratic form has two solutions, the two values of Q. These two roots are determined by the general equation:

$$Q = \frac{-b \pm\sqrt{b^2 - 4ac}}{2a}$$

For the example, the equation for the roots of Q and two solution values are:

$$Q = -90.33$$
$$Q = 717.7$$

The negative value cannot be the solution, so the second value is the answer sought.

In words, in the case of a curvilinear cost function, the quantity corresponding to maximum profit can be obtained by:
1. Subtracting the cost function from the revenue function to obtain the profit function
2. Determining the first derivative of the profit function with respect to Q
3. Setting the expression for the first derivative equal to zero
4. Solving the resulting equation for the value of Q

Although the above procedure pinpoints a particular value for "optimum" output, two cautions should be kept in mind. First, expected value of profit may not change much over a considerable range of values for output; i.e., profit may not be very sensitive to changes in output in the vicinity of optimum. Secondly, cost and revenue functions used in analysis are estimates; the true functions may be shaped and positioned somewhat differently.

CHOOSING BETWEEN LINEAR AND CURVILINEAR COST MODELS

Either the linear or the curvilinear form could describe the relationship of cost to changes in output over a specified range in a particular firm. However, analyses based on these forms do not have the same results. In the case of curvilinear cost and/or revenue functions, profit reaches a peak at a particular level of output; this output is optimum.

Cost behavior determines the appropriate form to use in a particular case. Both linear and curvilinear forms can be observed in practice.

Empirical studies and illustrations

J. Johnston's *Statistical Cost Analysis* reviews findings from a number of cost studies.[16] Johnston starts with Joel Dean's pioneer studies in a furniture factory, a leather belt shop, and a hosiery mill; all indicate constant marginal cost and linear total cost functions. A similar study by Dean in a department store is inconclusive on whether total costs are linear, but Dean thought that the curvature, if any, would be slight.

Johnston reviews two studies in the steel industry, one of which shows constant marginal cost while the other suggests a decline in marginal cost throughout the output range.[17] There is doubt that the latter study succeeded in separating short-run costs from long-run factors such as changes in capacity. Johnston also reviews a study of railway operating costs in Great Britain and a study of costs in the American rayon industry, both of which are consistent with constant marginal costs.

Some critics have alleged that statistical methods used in these studies have a bias toward linear estimates of marginal cost. Johnston denies this and even suggests that the bias, if any, may be toward curvilinearity. Stigler argues that findings of constant marginal costs up to capacity are inconsistent with observed behavior of firms.[18] He offers evidence that most of the short-run variations in output over business cycles are variations in rate of output of plant rather than variations in number of plants. Constant marginal costs at varying levels would imply variations in numbers of plants. This controversy goes beyond the scope of this chapter; details can be found in the publications by Stigler and Johnston.

Earl Heady cites several studies that showed increasing marginal costs and curvilinear total cost functions in agriculture.[19] These studies are concerned with relationships of crop yields per acre to amounts of fertilizer per acre. However, Heady also suggests that many marginal cost curves in agriculture are similar to those of industry; i.e., horizontal with a sharp upturn at capacity of fixed plant.

A British study of five factories found that marginal and average variable cost per unit fell, slightly and unevenly, over the range of output.[20]

---

[16] John Johnston, *Statistical Cost Analysis* (New York: McGraw-Hill Book Co., 1960).

[17] Johnston, *Statistical Cost Analysis,* p. 168.

[18] George J. Stigler, *The Theory of Price,* rev. ed. (New York: Macmillan Co., 1952), p. 167.

[19] Earl Heady, *Economics of Agricultural Production and Resource Use* (Englewood Cliffs, N.J.: Prentice-Hall, Inc., 1952).

[20] F. Troughton, "The Teaching Concerning Costs of Production in Introductory Economics", *The Journal of Industrial Economics,* April, 1963, pp. 96–115.

In contrast, a study of several automobile laundries shows strong evidence of gradually diminishing marginal products, resulting in gradually rising marginal costs.[21] A study of production of transformers also shows gradually diminishing marginal products with increased hours of work per day in a plant where machinery and supervision are held constant.[22]

Implications for decision-making

We should avoid oversimplified generalizations about the relationship of cost to output in the short run. It appears that short-run cost functions are quite close to linear over the usual range of output in many industries. On the other hand, rising marginal costs are sometimes encountered.

A reasonable way for the manager to estimate the effects of alternative actions upon cost is to use his own judgment in determining how the different categories of cost will be affected by these actions. Changes in cost for the various items can then be aggregated to provide cost information that is relevant for the decision. This "flexible" approach can be applied to decisions about product introduction and abandonment, as well as to choice of level of output with plant regarded as given.

The manager should be especially careful not to overlook the possibility of rising marginal costs as output per unit of time is increased. Causes of rising marginal cost can be subtle: gradual declines in labor productivity as work force is increased, creeping managerial inefficiency as the ratio of supervisors to workers falls, and increases in waste of materials and user cost as production presses harder against the designed capacities of machinery and equipment.

PROBLEMS FOR CHAPTER 5

1. A porcelain figurine is made and sold by White Rock Statuary at a variable cost of $500 per unit. The fixed costs per period are $1,000. Each unit is sold at a price of $750.
    a. Draw a break-even chart, labeling all lines, the axes, profit (loss), and the break-even point.
    b. Redraw the graph with a fixed cost of $2,000 per year.

2. Cost and related data are shown below for the Acme and Bettre Corporations:

	Acme	*Bettre*
Fixed costs	$800,000	$400,000
Discretionary costs	$120,000	$240,000
Variable costs/unit	$ 3	$ 7
Sales price/unit	$ 8	$ 10

[21] Milton H. Spencer and Louis Siegelman, *Managerial Economics: Decision Making and Forward Planning* (Homewood, Ill.: Richard D. Irwin, Inc., 1959), pp. 204–9.

[22] E. E. Nemmers, *Managerial Economics* (New York: John Wiley and Sons, Inc., 1962), pp. 166–67.

a. Compute the break-even point for each company.

b. The Acme Company is thinking of increasing advertising expenditures by $100,000. Recompute the break-even point. If the increased expenditure yields 25,000 more units of sales, is it wise?

c. Which company is more susceptible to adverse economic conditions?

3. The Bloom Company has recently purchased a plant to manufacture a new product. The following data pertain to the new operation:

```
Estimated annual sales ....................... 24,000 units
Estimated costs:
    Material  ............................... $4.00/unit
    Direct Labor ...........................   .60/unit
    Overhead  .............................. $24,000 per year
    Administrative expenses ................. $28,800 per year
    Selling expenses ........................  15% of sales
```

a. If profit per unit is to be $1.02, what will be the selling price?

b. Compute the break-even point, both in dollars and in units.

4. The Pacem Company manufactures and sells a line of slot-car tracks, cars and accessories. The company's sales department provides the following data.

Product	Demand (est.) for 1973
Dare-Devil	$Q = 100,000 - 10,000\,P$
Speed-Demon	$Q = 50,000 - 5,000\,P$

The production standards per unit are:

Product	Material	Labor
Dare-Devil	$1.40	$.80
Speed-Demon	$ .70	$.50

Fixed overhead is $100,000 and variable overhead is estimated at 50 percent of direct labor costs.

a. Compute the profit contribution for each product if the output of Dare-Devil is 50,000 units and of Speed-Demon is 40,000 units.

b. Given the production levels in (*a*) what is the contribution per labor dollar expended on that product?

5. The Arthur Corporation has the following budget for the coming year:

```
Fixed costs ........................................ $40,000
Subcontracting costs (variable) ...................... $2/unit
Other variable costs .............................. $1/unit
Sales price ........................................ $5
Budgeted production and sales ..................... 30,000 units
```

As an alternative to subcontracting, a plant can be leased for the year for $51,200. Total variable cost under this arrangement would be $1.20 per unit.

a. Find the break-even point under the initial budget.

b. Compute the break-even point under the lease arrangement.

c. Should the lease of plant be undertaken?

d. How sensitive is the Arthur Corporation's profit figure to sales volume under each alternative?

6.

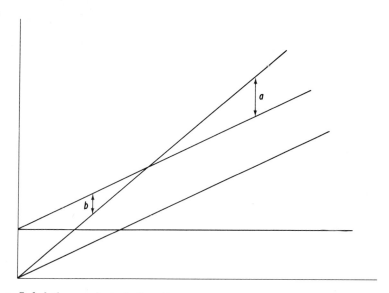

a. Label the graph, including the axes.

b. Identify quantities a and b as shown.

7. Mr. Brighton has worked in a machine shop all his life. He has saved and invested wisely and now wishes to start a business of his own. He has decided to manufacture screws in his garage on a one-man shop basis. Apart from the initial installation of power lines, and a machine, all costs of production will be variable. The initial power installation will be written off in the first year.

Three equipment alternatives are open to Mr. Brighton. He may choose to equip with either a manual, semi-automatic, or fully automatic lathe. The production costs under these alternatives are presented below:

Lathe	*Fixed/Year*	*Variable/Unit*
Manual	$ 2,500	$.00400
Semi-automatic	$ 5,000	$.00150
Fully automatic	$12,000	$.00025

Mr. Brighton feels that he can sell virtually any number of screws for 50 cents a hundred. The limiting factor will be the number of screws he will be able to produce. Production data for the three machines is presented below:

Lathe	*Output (100s/hr)*
Manual	.3
Semi-automatic	1.8
Fully automatic	6.0

a. How many hours per year must Mr. Brighton work under each alternative in order to break even?

b. If Mr. Brighton could work only 2,000 hours a year, what would be the break-even price under each alternative?

c. Which alternative is optimal under the original conditions? Should Mr. Brighton quit his job? (It pays $5.00 per hour.)

8. A firm's total cost and total revenue functions are given by $TC = (Q - 50)^3 + 200,000$ and $TR = 800,000 - 20 (Q - 200)^2$. How much should the firm produce to maximize profit? What is the profit at this point?

6 / Production and cost analysis:
short run, finite runs, long run

This chapter provides tools needed in decisions about methods of production, rates of output and product pricing, and future sizes and locations of plants. First, physical relationships of the rate of output to quantities of inputs per unit of time are developed. Next, these physical relationships are combined with input and product prices to determine: optimum rate of input (and output) with one input variable; least-cost combinations of multiple variable inputs at various rates of output; short-run cost functions; and optimum rates of output with multiple variable inputs. Third, economics of producing a finite total output are examined: interest centers on tradeoffs between rate of production and total running time with particular attention to start up costs, learning, and opportunity costs. Finally, the planning horizon is extended to the very long run in which sizes and locations of plants become fully variable; the effects upon cost of changes in plant sizes, numbers, and locations are explored.

PRODUCTION FUNCTIONS

Production includes any process that transforms one or more inputs into an output. In agriculture and manufacturing, inputs are combined to produce goods through changes in the *form* dimension. In producing transportation, inputs are combined to change goods availability in the dimension of *space*. In producing storage, inputs are combined to change goods availability in the dimension of *time*. Changes in the form, space, and time dimensions of goods increase their values by giving consumers the goods that they want, in the place that they are needed, and at the time that they are desired. Production is not restricted to transforming inputs into physically tangible outputs, as in manufacturing or construction; it is *any activity that increases consumer usability of goods or services*. Principles of production economics are fully applicable in goods marketing and in providing personal services, such as medical care and police protection.

Inputs are combined to produce output using the best available technology or known methods of production. A typical manufacturing process might employ several classes of labor, a number of machines, land and buildings, several types of manufactured inputs, and a variety of raw materials in order to produce a single product line. *For any given combination* of quantities of each of these inputs, *the best technology* is that which *provides the highest rate of output*. The relationship between various *combinations of inputs* and the resulting *maximum rates of output* is called the *production function*. In mathematical notation, a production function for a process with five inputs may be expressed generally as:

$$Q = f\ (X_1,\ X_2,\ X_3,\ X_4,\ X_5)$$

where Q is the maximum *rate of output* (quantity per unit of time) and each X refers to the *rate of use* of a type of input (for example, manhours per week, or vehicle miles per year). Assume there is *one best way* to combine any given combination of inputs, so that the function is single-valued.

The long run and the short run

Consider the possibility of varying the amounts of inputs currently used in a production process. Some inputs will be subject to this kind of change on very short notice. Workers may be put on overtime, orders may be placed for increased materials deliveries, and perhaps machines may be speeded up or shifts added. On the other hand, such changes as increasing warehouse space or adding to the number of machines would normally require a considerable amount of time and could be considered only if planning were done well in advance of production. A planning horizon that is advanced far enough to allow *all* inputs to be *varied* in amount, including the number of managers or the size and location of plants, extends across a planning period called the *long run*. In the long run, production is restricted by available technology, but not by past choices. The production function that is relevant in week-to-week or month-to-month decision-making may be regarded as having some inputs that are variable in amount, and some which must be taken as fixed. Any period in which *some* inputs are *fixed* is called the *short run*.

The short-run production function

A short-run production function with only two variable inputs is depicted in three dimensions in Figure 6–1. *Rates of output* are measured by the *height* of the production surface *OLPC*, which has the shape of a hill. *Alternative combinations of rates of application of the two inputs* (called capital and labor) are measured *in the horizontal plane.* For example, if labor is used at rate *OA* and capital at rate *OB*, then the maximum possible rate of output is *E*, the height of the production surface above *D*.

FIGURE 6–1

A Short-Run Production Function Sliced Vertically

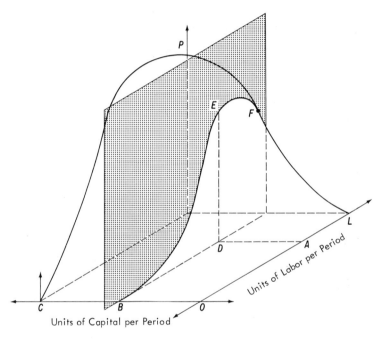

Units of Capital per Period

PRODUCTION WITH ONE INPUT VARIABLE

Now consider what happens to output as the rate of labor use is increased without changing the rate of employment of capital. This is illustrated in Figure 6–1 by slicing the production surface *vertically* and parallel to the *L* axis. The curve *BEF* is formed by one such slice and represents various rates of output obtainable with a constant *OB* units of capital and increasing amounts of labor. At every point along *BEF*, therefore, the *proportion* of labor to capital is increasing.

The detailed effects of increasing the proportion of labor to capital (while holding the rate of capital use at *OB*) are shown in two dimensions in Figures 6–2*a* and 6–2*b*. The total product curve in 6–2*a* is the same as *BEF* in Figure 6–1. It depicts the rate of output as first *increasing at an increasing rate* as labor is added, then *increasing at a decreasing*

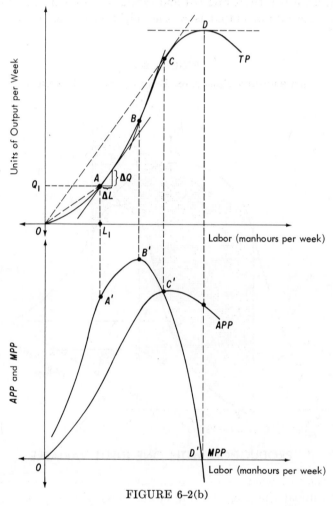

FIGURE 6-2(a)

A TOTAL PRODUCT CURVE

FIGURE 6-2(b)

THE CORRESPONDING MARGINAL AND AVERAGE PRODUCT CURVES

rate, and finally *decreasing absolutely* as still more labor is added (perhaps because so many workers are stumbling over one another, or trampling the product).

Marginal product

For decision-making purposes, the most useful way of looking at a total product curve is to observe the changes in the rate of output as successive equal increments are added to the rate of input use. Notice that such incremental output changes are different in every part of the curve. One example is shown in the diagram, in which one 40-hour per week employee is added to an existing 200 man-hours per week of labor. This labor increment ΔL brings forth additional output of ΔQ units per week. The ratio $\Delta Q/\Delta L$ is the addition to rate of output per added unit of labor per week. By considering *very small* increments of labor input, it can be seen that $\Delta Q/\Delta L$ can be measured *at any given point* by the slope of a tangent to the total product curve. Mathematically, the *marginal physical product* (*MPP*) (corresponding to the slope of these tangents) is simply the *partial* derivative of the production function with respect to the rate of input L.

Figure 6–2b shows the marginal physical product curve corresponding to the total product curve of Figure 6–2a. Notice that the slopes of tangents to *TP* increase with movements to the right up to point B; thereafter the slopes decline, becoming negative after point D. Hence marginal physical product is highest at point B (as indicated directly below by B') and falls to zero at point D (as shown by D').

"Law" of variable proportions

What accounts for the shape of the *MPP* curve? Between O and B, labor is so sparsely applied to the fixed inputs that these existing machines, buildings, acres of land, etc., cannot be properly tended. One might imagine, for example, two persons for every three stations on an assembly line. Adding the third worker may add more to output than adding the first and second ones did. In the range from O to B, *increasing marginal productivity* is observed. Once point B is reached, more output may be obtained by overtime, added shifts, more supervisory personnel, etc., but now *diminishing marginal physical product* is encountered. Additional input in the range beyond D is subject to *absolutely decreasing output*. The observation that diminishing returns are a pervasive feature of production processes is stated formally as the *law of variable proportions*. This "law" (or empirical regularity) states that as the rate of one input (labor in this case) is increased *relative to others,* the marginal physical product of that input will eventually decline. Points to the right of D in Figure 6–2a are obviously to be avoided, since these additional workers actually hinder production. Optimum input rate is in the range of decreasing marginal productivity, and is determined by the method described in the next section.

Optimum rate of input (one input variable)

If the marginal physical product of an input (X) is multiplied by that product's marginal revenue at the corresponding rate of output, the result is called the *marginal revenue product* of the input.

For an output (Y) sold in a perfectly competitive market:

$$MRP = \frac{\Delta Y}{\Delta X} \cdot P_y \qquad\qquad (6\text{--}1)$$

For an output (Y) sold in a market with a sloping demand curve:

$$MRP = \frac{\Delta Y}{\Delta X} \cdot P_y \, (1\text{--}1/e) \qquad\qquad (6\text{--}2)$$

Marginal revenue product is simply the *addition to revenue* per additional unit of *input*. Therefore, it pays to increase the rate of use of the input if this marginal revenue product is greater than the market price of the input.[1] Since marginal product is decreasing with increases in the rate of use, a rate which equates MRP to price of the input is eventually found. This is the *optimum* rate of *input;* of course, there is a corresponding rate of *output*.

Managers constantly carry out the kind of reasoning described above. For example, farmers use it to make decisions about the amounts of fertilizer per acre, irrigation water per acre, and insect or disease control materials per acre. Manufacturers use it to make decisions about the numbers of workers per shift, line speeds, and so on. The reasoning involves comparisons of the effects upon cost and revenue of small changes in labor, machine use, materials, and so on, in which these inputs are considered *one at a time* and in *unit-by-unit increments*. Although determination of optimal input is a relatively simple decision process, this process (along with some nearly as simple reasoning involving input substitution, which is to be discussed shortly) is responsible for much of the efficiency of present-day production.

Average product

The total product curve can also be related to *average productivity*, or output per unit of input. An average physical product (APP) curve is defined as Q/L for every level of L. Referring again to the arbitrarily chosen point A, average physical product is OQ/OL which will also be recognized as the *slope* of the ray OA. Hence, we may derive the APP curve of 6–2b by a means similar to the derivations of MPP, this time by measuring the changing slopes of *rays* from the origin to the TP curve. Observe that the steepest of such rays is the one tangent to TP at $C;$ i.e., average physical product (output per man-hour) is greatest at C.

PRODUCTION WITH TWO INPUTS VARIABLE

We began the discussion of the production function illustrated in Figure 6–1 by choosing arbitrarily the point E corresponding to the combi-

---

[1] If the firm faces a rising supply curve for the input, *marginal* supply price must be used instead of the input's market price in making this comparison.

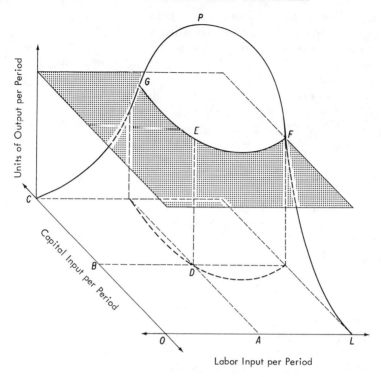

FIGURE 6–3

A PRODUCTION SURFACE SLICED HORIZONTALLY

P

G

E

F

C

B

D

Units of Output per Period

Capital Input per Period

O   *A*   *L*

Labor Input per Period

FIGURE 6–4

VIEW OF PRODUCTION SURFACE FROM DIRECTLY ABOVE

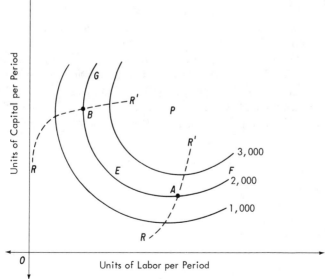

Units of Capital per Period

G

R'

B

R'

P

R

E

F

3,000

A

2,000

R

1,000

O

Units of Labor per Period

nation of capital and labor at point D. But point D is not the only combination of rates of labor and capital use that will produce DE amount of output. Other points on the production surface that are in the same horizontal plane as E represent the same level of output. These points of equal output are on the curve FEG, in Figure 6–3, formed by a *horizontal* slice through the production surface. This curve is called an isoquantity curve or an *isoquant*, since it connects points of the same quantity of output. One could readily imagine other horizontal slices through the production hill, some representing greater and others representing smaller rates of output. Since some inputs are fixed, there is an *absolute limit* on output as shown by point P. Viewed from overhead, the isoquants project to the labor-capital plane, where they look like contours on a relief map, as in Figure 6–4. If the level of output represented by each possible isoquant (6–4 shows only few) is known, then all of the production choices facing the firm are shown in such a diagram. In Figure 6–4, the quantities of output are given as 1,000, 2,000, and 3,000 to indicate the direction of change in output for movement from isoquant to isoquant.

Substitution among variable inputs

A little consideration of Figure 6–4 will show that some input combinations are not desirable. For example, in going to the right from point A an addition to variable capital must be combined with added labor to maintain the *same* output. A choice to the right of A along the 2,000-unit isoquant would never be made by an efficiency-conscious firm. The same type of situation pertains to the employment of capital beyond point B at the 2,000-unit level of output. The only production choices that are relevant for the firm, therefore, are along those portions of isoquants that slope downward to the right. These points lie *between* the two curves RR′. These curves are boundaries of the efficient use of inputs, called *ridge lines*.

Elimination of those combinations of inputs that lie outside the ridge lines still leaves a very large number of choices of input combinations at each output level. Along each isoquant in the region between the ridge lines, increase in use of one input allows reduction in the required amount of the other. There will ordinarily be a *least-cost combination* for any given amount of output. To determine this combination requires knowledge of both the production function *and* the prices of inputs.

Least cost combinations of inputs

The determination of the lowest-cost combination of inputs is illustrated in Figure 6–5. In accordance with our broad view of what constitutes production, the production process in this figure is "selling." The product to be sold is this book. Suppose the publisher wishes to sell this book at the rate of 2,000 copies per month, by means of some combination of (X_2) efforts of sales persons and (X_1) mailing of free examination copies to professors. This target is indicated by the single isoquant curve.

FIGURE 6–5

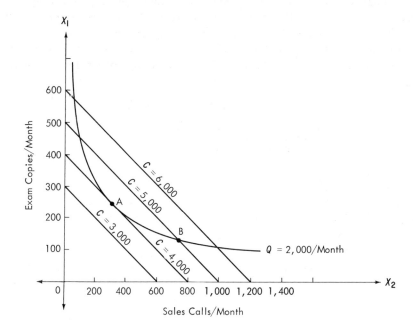

Each straight line in the diagram represents a monthly cost. These *isocost lines* connect all input combinations that require the same expenditure as determined by

$$C = P_1 \ X_1 + P_2 \ X_2$$

where X_1 refers to number of examination copies given away, X_2 refers to number of sales calls made, and the Ps are the effective prices; i.e., marginal costs, associated with each input. Suppose, for example, that each additional book costs $10.00 to manufacture and mail to prospects while each additional call by a salesman on behalf of the book costs $5. So long as these input prices may be taken as fixed the isocost curves will be straight lines. The lowest possible cost at which 2,000 units per month may be sold is given by the point A in Figure 6–5, at which approximately 300 sales calls are made and 250 examination copies are given away at a total monthly cost of $4,000. Any other combination that will produce 2,000 sales per month, such as point B, results in higher cost.

Now, let us examine this solution in some detail. The 2,000-unit isoquant is drawn as a smooth curve that is *convex* to the origin. The *slope of the isoquant* is of particular interest because it represents the *rate* at which examination copies can be replaced by sales effort and still maintain the given sales level. Since the slope changes along the curve, the slope at any single point, such as A, applies only to trade-offs involving *small* changes in X_1 and X_2; hence, this slope (strictly speaking, its absolute value) is called the *marginal rate of technical substitution* (MRTS). From point A, a small reduction in gift copies, $- \Delta X_1$, will reduce sales (output) by $\Delta X_1 \cdot MPP_1$. To stay on the same isoquant requires a change in X_2, ΔX_2, that will increase output by the same amount;

$$\text{so } \Delta X_1 \cdot MPP_1 = \Delta X_2 \cdot MPP_2$$

$$\text{or } \frac{\Delta X_1}{\Delta X_2} = \frac{MPP_2}{MPP_1}$$

(This provides another interpretation of MRTS as the *ratio of marginal products* of the inputs.)

Notice that the slope of the isoquant decreases as sales effort is increased; i.e., the number of examination copies that can be replaced by increasing sales effort by one call becomes smaller with increases in the total amount of sales effort already employed. This characteristic of diminishing marginal rates is common to most production processes; it accounts for the convex shape of isoquants, which in turn assures that there will be a single minimum-cost input combination for any output level.

The expansion path

A set of cost-minimizing input combinations for *various* output levels is shown in Figure 6–6 by the points A, C, D, E, and F. Each combination is a point where an isoquant has the same slope as an isocost curve. Now the equation for an isocost curve can be written as

$$X_1 = C/P_1 - (P_2/P_1) X_2$$

where

C is cost
P_1 is price of input 1
P_2 is price of input 2
X_1 is quantity of input 1
X_2 is quantity of input 2 of the isocost curve

The slope of the isocost curve is the inverse ratio of input prices, P_2/P_1 and tangency means that

$$MRTS = P_2/P_1$$

or that

$$MP_2/MP_1 = P_2/P_1$$

FIGURE 6–6

EXPANSION OF OUTPUT

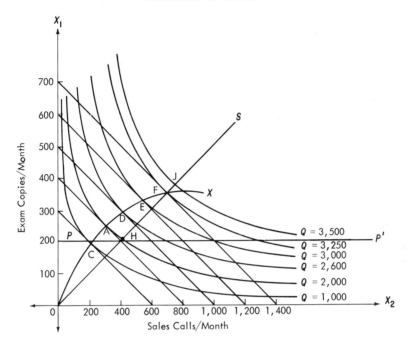

Another way to arrange this equation is

$$\frac{MP_1}{P_1} = \frac{MP_2}{P_2}$$

which gives one a working rule for trading off among inputs: *adjust the combinations of rates of input use* until the *marginal product per dollar spent is equal for all inputs.* If, for example, an extra ten dollars spent to provide a free examination copy is expected to bring a greater increase in sales than $10 spent for two more sales calls, the number of free copies should be increased (thereby reducing MP_1 because of diminishing returns) and sales calls should be reduced (thereby increasing MP_2); substitution around the isoquant continues until marginal products per dollar are equalized. Managers are constantly searching for ways to reduce cost of a given rate of output through input substitution. When many inputs and substitution possibilities are to be considered, linear programming, discussed in Chapter 7, is useful.

It can be seen that the set of points A through F are on the path of output expansion with each rate of output being achieved at least cost. Thus, the function OX is called the *expansion path.*

Contrasts: law of variable proportions, decreasing returns to scale, expansion path

Figure 6–6 also illustrates the relationships among three often confused characteristics of production. The horizontal line PP' illustrates the *law of variable proportions,* and is simply a "top view" of Figure 6–1. Following this line to the right, one encounters *diminishing returns* to successive units of sales effort as the proportion of sales effort to sample copies is increased. However, when inputs are increased *in the same proportion,* as along line OS, the firm is said to be increasing the scale of production activity. This particular set of isoquants exhibits *decreasing returns to scale,* since increasing the rate of use of *both* inputs by some common factor increases *output* by a smaller factor. For example, doubling both inputs from their levels at H raises output from 2,000 to 3,500, a factor of 1.75, as shown by the isoquants at H and J. Had the expansion of output represented by these isoquants exactly doubled, production would be said to exhibit *constant returns to scale* in that range, and similarly an output expansion greater than proportional to the increase in inputs is called *increasing returns to scale.* A single production process may exhibit decreasing, constant, and increasing returns to scale over various ranges of output.

Returns to scale and returns to variable input proportions are *purely technological relationships* used to describe the available production processes. By contrast, the curve OX represents the *expansion path* of a firm which chooses the *least-cost* input combinations to achieve successively higher levels of output. This path depends upon *relative prices* of the inputs as well as upon the technology of production. Investigation of the expansion path will provide us with information about *costs of various rates of output* that is needed to determine the best level of output for the firm.

SHORT-RUN COST FUNCTIONS

A cost function is a relationship between the *value of production inputs* that are *used by the firm in each period* and the *rates of output* attained. In the case of the production function illustrated in Figure 6–6, five different levels of cost are represented by isocost curves, and the maximum rates of output associated with those costs are shown by the isoquants at points C, A, D, F, and G. Graphing the levels of cost represented by each isocost line against rates of output given by the corresponding isoquants at the points of tangency indicates five points along a *total cost function.* This function is shown in Figure 6–7a.

Notice that this total cost curve is curvilinear. After an output level of 1,200 units is reached, costs increase with output at an increasing rate. In general, the behavior of costs with increases in rate of output is de-

FIGURE 6-7(a)

A SHORT-RUN TOTAL COST FUNCTION

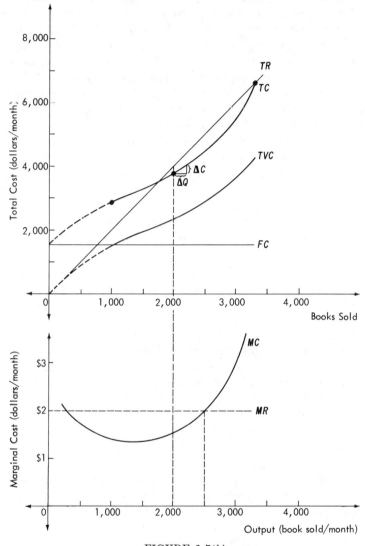

FIGURE 6-7(b)

A SHORT-RUN MARGINAL COST FUNCTION

termined by a combination of (1) decreasing returns to scale, (2) increases in input prices, and (3) changes in input proportions. In our specific example, decreasing returns is the principal determinant, since input prices are fixed, but cost-saving changes in input proportions also affect the shape of the total cost curve. As Figure 6–6 showed, total costs would be greater along the scale line OS, at every point except O and F, as compared to the actual expansion path OX.[2]

Since we have been discussing short-run production decisions, total cost will include some expenses that are incurred regardless of the output level. In our example, suppose a monthly cost of $1,500 is incurred to sell this book even if no sample copies are sent out or sales calls made. These *fixed costs* would include the monthly values of warehouse space, packaging and mailing equipment, and at least a share of the time of sales office personnel. The difference between total cost and fixed cost is shown on Figure 6–7a by the *total-variable-cost* curve, TVC. Although rates of output below 1,000 units cannot be derived directly from previous isoquant diagrams, the dashed line in 6–7a indicates possible behavior of costs in this range, reflecting increasing returns to scale at these low output rates. (An explanation of this might be that sales calls and examination copies are taken more seriously by a prospective user if he finds that more of his colleagues have also heard of the book.)

The *marginal-cost curve* shown in Figure 6–7b may be derived from either the TC curve or the TVC curve. Marginal cost is the addition to cost that results from a *unit* increase in output, so that fixed costs have no effect on the marginal cost curve. Marginal cost is measured by the *slope* of either TC or TVC at each output level. For example, at 1,000 units of output a small increase in output, ΔQ, brings about an increase in cost, ΔC, at the rate of about $1.30 per additional book sold. Mathematically, marginal cost is the first derivative of the total cost curve, with respect to quantity, as discussed in Chapter 5.

Inspection of slopes of the TC or TVC curve at various output levels shows that marginal costs fall with increased output for low-output levels, then the total curves have an inflection point at which MC is minimum, and thereafter marginal costs increase with output. The reasons for this general shape have already been noted; namely, increasing returns due to "lumpy" inputs or grossly oversized plants at low-output level, followed by diminishing returns due to increased use of standby equipment, increased maintenance, and the like at higher rates of output. Furthermore, short-run increases in output often require payment of overtime wage rates or increases above standard wages to attract the necessary additional work force. MC in Figure 6–7 is drawn with a smooth "U" shape to illustrate all of these possible effects. Actual production processes often have an initial stage of falling MC, and, in some cases, MC is very flat over a wide range of output.

In most decisions about the rate of output, the most useful description of costs is the marginal-cost function. The reason for this is shown in Figure 6–7b. If the firm wishes to maximize the profits from its selling

---

[2] The student should be able to demonstrate that it is possible for total-cost curve not to be a straight line even if returns to scale *and* input prices are constant.

efforts, it must compare addition to cost with addition to revenue as selling effort is increased, continuing to increase selling effort until the rising marginal cost becomes equal to marginal revenue.

Suppose that the authors' royalties, production, and shipping of the book cost $10 altogether and the publisher sells it for $12. Selling effort thus produces a contribution of $2 per book, which may be said to be the *price* or marginal revenue of *selling*. This is the slope of line *TR* and the height of line *MR* in Figure 6–7. Increases in selling achieved at the cost of more free copies and sales calls, in optimal proportions, will be profitable up to 2,500 units of output. This rate of output is optimum, since any reduction therefrom will subtract more from revenue than from cost and any further sales volume will cost more to obtain than it returns. As a general rule, where price of output is unrelated to output rate, output should be adjusted to the point where price is equal to marginal cost; i.e.

$$P = MC$$

The above approach to determining optimum rate of output, based on marginal conditions, is an alternate to the method based on maximization of the profit function that was shown in Chapter 5. Both approaches are useful. Managers often need to determine level of output where production is subject to diminishing returns.

While problems of maximization require knowledge of the *marginal cost curve,* it is sometimes helpful to know other cost-output relationships. Figure 6–8 illustrates the relationship of marginal cost to *average*

FIGURE 6–8

RELATIONSHIPS OF MARGINAL COST TO AVERAGE COST

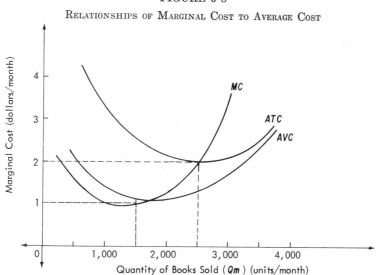

total cost, or *unit cost,* and to *average variable cost.* Average total cost, *ATC,* is the total cost of production *per unit of output;* i.e., $ATC = TC/Q$. Average variable cost is total *variable* cost per unit of output.

$$AVC = \frac{TVC}{Q} = \frac{TC - FC}{Q}$$

The *vertical difference* between *ATC* and *AVC* may be called *average fixed cost, AFC,* which, of course, becomes smaller as the output rate increases.

Notice that both of these average cost curves cross *MC* at their respective low points. This, as we have shown earlier in this chapter, is always true of any "marginal" and "average" curves derived from the same "total" curve.

Average costs cannot be used to find an optimum rate of output. However, *ATC* will prove useful later to show *how much* profit is attained at the maximum profit rate of output, and *AVC* is relevant in deciding *whether production (any production) should be undertaken.* As Figure 6–8 shows, if only $1 were added to revenue per book sold instead of $2 as before, then 1,500 units of output per month would be the optimum (in this case, *loss-minimizing*) rate of output, if *any* output is to be produced. (We know there is a loss, since cost per unit [*ATC*] is over $2.) However, in this case, even the *variable cost* would not be met by sales revenue, so the firm would be better off not to try to sell the book at all! (Note: students should refrain from writing wisecracks here.)

COST FUNCTIONS FOR FINITE PRODUCTION RUNS

In the previous discussion of relationships among production techniques, costs, and rates of output, the length of time over which activities are dependent upon the decision at hand has been characterized simply as "short run." At this point, we take into account the possibility that the rate of output may affect the length of time over which production of a given type of product needs to continue. If the total *volume* of output is *finite,* as with much production to order (e.g., a building, a printing job, or a given number of aircraft of a particular type), then there is an exact relationship between the average *rate of output, X,* and the *length of time, L,* over which production will be carried out.

This relationship is simply $XL = V$, where V is the total desired *volume* of output.

Increases in costs with increases in rate of production

Consider the production of 25 commercial airliners to customer specifications. Volume of output is fixed by the contract, but the manufacturer may vary the *rate* of output by choosing to produce the planes in a *shorter or longer period of time* (up to the maximum period set by the agreement). For reasons discussed in the previous section (diminishing returns, overtime wages, increased maintenance cost, and the like), one would expect total *variable* cost of the 25 units to increase as their production rate is speeded up in a given plant.

Costs associated with plant and equipment, total *fixed* cost, may also be increased by producing the finite output at a higher rate. For example, in aircraft production, increases in output rate will be more and more difficult within the capacity of a single assembly line. So producing the same number of aircraft more rapidly may be more cheaply accomplished by setting up a second line. The corresponding increase in *capital outlays* and *start-up costs* will normally result in a larger total fixed cost of producing the given volume. (Start-up costs differ from capital outlays by being *one-time* outlays for any given production run, no matter how long this run may be; they do not depreciate with use. Initial planning, setup of machines, and initial slow running are examples of start-up costs.) Most of the additional physical capital required is long lasting and some of it may be specialized to the assembly of the particular type of aircraft. Capital costs are not *necessarily* higher as a result of adding another assembly line; the equipment *may* be sufficiently general in its applications that it can be sold at the end of the production run for original cost less actual depreciation or that it may be used to produce other products. However, start-up costs are *surely* greater if a second assembly line is added, since start-up has no salvage or conversion value. Hence, as a general rule, speeding up the production rate *may* involve *higher capital costs* and *will* involve *greater start-up costs* for any given total volume of output.

The response of costs to increases in the *rate of output* for *finite volume* is usually characterized by *increasing marginal cost*, where marginal cost is the *change in total cost for a unit increase in output per unit of time*. For example, if increasing the rate of manufacture of 25 aircraft from 5 per year to 6 per year raises the cost of producing all 25 by $1 million, then a further rate increase to 7 per year may result in a further increase in total cost of *more than* $1 million. (This comparison is based on constant price levels: inflation would have practical implications that are ignored here).

Then what are the "economies of large-scale production"? In the case of finite runs, these are the result of increases in *volume* through increased *length of production run*. If our aircraft manufacturer can secure another contract for 10 more planes, to be built at the same rate per year as the first 25, the result may be *lower average unit costs* for the 35-plane production run. There are basically two reasons for this: (1) learning by doing, and (2) reduction of capital costs and start-up costs per unit of output.

The learning curve

Learning refers to the reduction in *labor input per unit of output* as the total volume of output is increased using a particular process. The regular pattern of learning over successive units of output is called the *learning curve*. This relationship is usually expressed as a constant fraction, which is the proportion by which the amount of input required for the *marginal* unit is reduced each time output is *doubled*. The use of this measure implies that the effect of learning on the cost of successive units of output is as shown in Figure 6–9.

FIGURE 6–9

A LEARNING CURVE

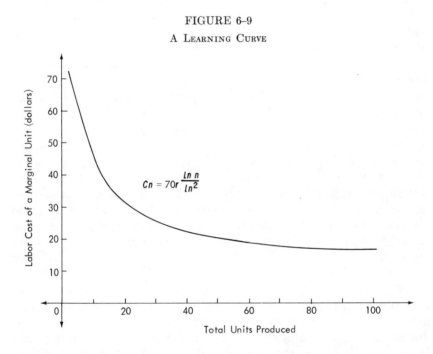

This diagram is drawn for a *learning rate* of .8. It shows a process which requires $70 worth of labor to produce the first unit of output. The second unit costs $70 (.8) = $56, the fourth costs $70 (.8)^2 = $44.80, the eighth costs $70 (.8)^3 = $35.84.

There is evidence that the learning rate in the aircraft manufacturing industry is indeed about .8, which, as Figure 6–9 shows, implies a very dramatic reduction in cost for at least 50–60 units of output. An airplane is a very complex product that requires much labor in assembly. The manufacturing operation is paced by people rather than by machines, and so there is great opportunity for learning. Aircraft manufacture is, therefore, an extreme case.

Note that the learning phenomenon is probably applicable in some degree to practically all production process. In addition to improvement in scheduling and coordination that reduces labor needed in assembly work, materials costs will decline as means are found to avoid mistakes in cutting, forming, etc.; selling techniques will be improved as personnel become more familiar with both product and customers; maintenance costs are reduced as operating procedures on machine and tools become more routine; and so on. Estimation of costs for increased *volume* of production should, therefore, never ignore the possibility of further learning. Learning can be expected with increases in volume involving either increased rate or longer production run, but is more closely associated with the latter.

Spreading of capital and start-up costs over longer production runs

Lengthening the production run does not have just the benefits of additional learning; it also ordinarily reduces capital costs per unit and always reduces start-up costs per unit. For example, consider the production of submarines according to government specifications. As in the aircraft example earlier, necessary total capital and start-up costs will depend primarily upon the *rate* of output and will involve primarily long-lived, specialized equipment associated with shipyards. The capital and start-up cost per unit of output will be reduced by increasing the *volume* (and thus the length of the production run) over which these costs are spread. (In addition, increases in volume may make it economical to further reduce *operating* costs by replacing hand labor, or by more efficiently using materials, or by avoiding bottlenecks, all with the aid of additional specialized capital, which, of course, involves a greater *initial outlay*.)

One major consideration may limit unit-cost reduction through increases in production volume. This is the cost of holding output in inventory. In cases such as book printing, where the most economical rate of production normally exceeds the rate of sales and increasing the length of run will also reduce unit costs by spreading start-up costs, consideration of production costs alone would call for producing output equal to the total anticipated sales for all time in the first production run. But reduced marginal *production* costs with increases in lot size must be balanced against rising marginal costs of holding *inventories*, and the latter effect will often limit the volume of any given production run to less than total anticipated sales. Production decisions involving inventory management are discussed in Chapter 7.

Simultaneous expansion of volume and rate

The preceding discussion suggests that expansion of *volume* of a product will be cheaper, in terms of current costs, if it is accomplished by expanding the *length* of the production run rather than by increasing the *rate.* However, to do the latter also involves postponing revenues (even if it does not result in loss of sales). The firm is therefore confronted with the necessity of considering a trade-off between *earlier realization of benefits* through an increase in *rate* and *reduction in total costs* through an increase in *length* of production run. Determination of the *best* mixture of rate increase and increased length of production run is a difficult type of capital-budgeting problem that is beyond the scope of this book. However, we will consider the effect upon *cost* of simultaneous expansion of volume and rate.

A manufacturer of small appliances perceives a 50 percent increase in rate of sales which is expected to hold throughout the annual model year. If the firm does not wish to alter the annual cycle of product changes, then it will accommodate this change by increasing the rate of output by 50 percent and leaving the length of the run unchanged. Notice that this means a *proportionate* increase in both rate *and* volume. Because of the increase in volume, additional learning may be expected, capital and start-up costs, although greater, will be spread over a larger output, and additional labor-saving or materials-conserving techniques may become economical. It is also possible that *plentiful* inputs may be obtained at lower prices, or on better credit terms, or with lower shipment costs because they are purchased in greater quantities.

All the above factors suggest *declining* marginal costs because of greater output *volume*. On the other hand, increasing the *rate* of production in order to obtain this volume will undoubtedly tend to *increase* the marginal costs. *Scarce* inputs such as labor, raw materials, and land may increase in price as the firm competes for additional units against other uses. (For labor, this may take the form of overtime pay.) At the same time, these additional inputs will likely be of lower quality. As pointed out earlier in the chapter, increasing the rate will also require higher capital and start-up costs, and there will be additional likelihood of production bottlenecks, equipment breakdown, and other symptoms of diminishing marginal productivity.

A summary of the offsetting effects of rate and volume increases has been given by Jack Hirshleifer, using the diagram in Figure 6–10.[3] Curve I shows increases in marginal cost as the rate of output is progressively increased, while *length of run is shortened* to maintain the *same volume of output*. Curve III represents the decreases in marginal cost with successive increases in output achieved by *extending production over a longer time period*, but *at a constant rate*. The cost effects *when both volume and rate are increased proportionately*, holding *length of production run constant* as in the appliance example, are given by Curve II. The U-shape of Curve II indicates that economies of mass production are important

---

[3] Jack Hirshleifer, "The Firm's Cost Function: A Successful Reconstruction?" *Journal of Business,* 35 (July 1962).

FIGURE 6–10

EFFECTS UPON COST OF INCREASING THE RATE, INCREASING THE VOLUME,
AND INCREASING BOTH IN CONSTANT PROPORTION

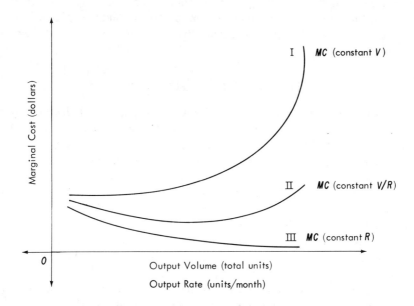

at low output levels but that diseconomies of increasing the rate eventually come to dominate as production is expanded. This is so because advantages of greater volume tend eventually to be exhausted (quantity discounts, learning, etc., have their limits), while the disadvantages of increased rate (overtime, plant expansion, increasing the flow of raw materials, and so on) tend to be more and more aggravated by expansion.

The reader will recognize that the behavior of cost in Curve II of Figure 6–10 is similar to the traditional *short-run* marginal-cost curve which is discussed in a more formal way in the first part of this chapter. The major differences are that in the appliance example we have been explicit about the length of the time period involved, and, more importantly, it is understood that the production run will *stop* at the end of that period. By contrast, the traditional *short run* defines a time horizon for the effects of decisions, but it assumes that production will continue *indefinitely*. If production is assumed to continue indefinitely, then all capital will be fully depreciated.

Now consider extending the anticipated length of a production run from one year through an ever-increasing number of years. Eventually, *all* capital equipment used to produce any continuing rate of current output will need to be replaced at approximately the same time, so that further extension of the *length of the run* cannot yield further reductions in *capital* costs. On the other hand, *start-up costs* and *product develop-*

ment costs continue to be spread over greater volume as the length of run is increased; there is no limit to this effect. If the production run (however broadly defined) is expected to continue indefinitely, and if the planning horizon is also beyond maximum life of plant and equipment that is affected by the planning, then we pass to the case of *long-run* planning.

LONG-RUN COST FUNCTIONS

Long-run cost analysis is concerned with the economies or diseconomies of scale that apply to a single plant or firm. In some industries unit cost reductions due to increased scale may be insignificant; in such cases, it is possible for large and small firms to coexist on relatively equal terms. Such is apparently the case in a great deal of agriculture and certain kinds of personalized retailing; the *survival* of small firms in these industries is evidence that their average costs are not sharply different from those of larger firms. In other industries, inability of small firms to survive suggests that they do not benefit from some substantial cost advantages available to larger firms. An example is the automobile industry.

Note that some of those industries that are dominated by giant *firms* may be characterized by insignificant economies (or even diseconomies) of large *plant* size. In such cases, production is decentralized, even though coordinated by large parent firms. At the plant level, the situation is almost certainly a combination of economies of scale at low levels of output and diseconomies at large sizes, with the optimum at some intermediate size. The analysis of long-run cost is important, therefore, both for understanding the competitive environment of a firm and for choices involving the scale of plants within a firm.

Many sources of economies of scale have already been explored in connection with the discussions of effects of large *volume* of output. In general, the cost advantages of *firm* size may be classified as those arising from (1) indivisibility of inputs, (2) market power, (3) input specialization, and (4) diversity. In many cases where output per dollar of cost can be increased by a change in production technique, the more efficient technique involves *inputs which cannot be scaled down without loss of productivity.* Examples are advertising in national media, and transportation in railroad box cars. In addition, large firms can often obtain *lower input prices* by taking advantage of their status as a major customer of most suppliers. Third, a large firm can afford to hire *men and machines that are especially suited for specialized tasks* and thus more proficient at those tasks than inputs that are more versatile. Finally, *diversity of products* may enable a large firm to support fundamental research which is uncertain of application to any specific product, or to obtain cheaper finance because of the pooling of risk, or to keep fixed facilities more nearly in full use by substituting production of items that have increasing demands for those that are declining.

This is an appropriate point at which to consider the distinction between the plant and the firm. Management must distinguish between those economies available to the *firm* as it increases in size and what happens to cost as each *plant* is expanded. *Within* the individual plant, long-run economies of scale are also to be expected. In manufacturing, a larger plant may be able to take advantage of the *line* (product) principle of plant layout using more specialized equipment and labor; while smaller plants may be dependent upon the *functional* principle of layout with its greater flexibility, but with longer lines of transportation and greater problems of production control. In general, there are economies of scale arising from indivisibility of persons and major items of equipment, from the advantages of specialization, and from various economies of lot size.

On the other hand, transporting inputs to the plant and distributing its outputs often involve increasing costs as more production is carried out at a given location. One large plant, as compared with several smaller ones, has the disadvantage of longer distances to customers if the market is geographically distributed. Similarly, if inputs must be assembled from geographically scattered sources, transportation costs to large plants will be greater. For example, increasing long-run marginal cost due to distribution of inputs (feed) and assembly of intermediate product (live broilers) has been shown for the broiler chicken industry.[4] Expansion of a single plant may also encounter higher labor costs if the plant is a major employer in the area.

Are there diseconomies of scale for the *firm?* One important bit of indirect evidence indicates that such diseconomies exist—the fact that more than one firm is able to survive in most industries. If economies of scale persisted throughout all ranges of output, one firm would drive out all others because of the advantages of its lower unit costs. For example, the public utilities are often called "natural monopolies" in recognition of the apparent inability of small firms to compete with the low costs of large enterprises. Where long-run cost curves merely become horizontal, it would appear that the horizontal portion of the curves should be lower for some firms than for others, resulting in a tendency toward monopoly. Thus, some economists deduce from the absence of monopoly in most industries the conclusion that, in these industries, costs eventually rise with increases in sizes of firms.

Since diseconomies of large *plants* may be overcome by decentralizing, what could account for diseconomies of scale for the *firm?* The usual reasons given for such diseconomies are related to management. Some

---

[4] William R. Henry and James A. Seagraves, "Economic Aspects of Broiler Production Density," *Journal of Farm Economics*, 42, No. 1 (February 1960), pp. 1–17.

writers argue that, even in the long run, management is a relatively unique and limited factor; it is impossible to increase management as rapidly as the other inputs, so that eventually it is spread too thin and organizational effectiveness declines. Other writers provide quite a different analysis. They claim that the managerial staffs increase more rapidly than output because of the growing cumbersomeness of the firm and greater problems of communication and coordination.

The critics of such generalizations about the inefficiency of management for larger-scale organization point out that the industry has many ways of overcoming the problems of communication and coordination just noted. Large firms can decentralize, providing a great deal of autonomy for smaller units within the firm.

This controversy leaves us with two competing generalizations about long-run cost curves of *firms:*

1. The traditional view that they are U-shaped, with definite diseconomies at large and small outputs. In most cases the U will take on a saucer shape with a long stretch of constant costs.

2. The view that the curves are L-shaped, declining at first and then becoming horizontal. Under such conditions large and small firms exist together; the mixture of firm sizes depends on the history of the industry.

Relation of short-run cost curves to the long-run cost curves

It is time to be somewhat more explicit about the relation between short-run and long-run costs of *plants*. The long-run cost curve is sometimes known as the "planning" curve, since it involves only the long-range choices of the firm. After the manager has selected a scale of output, he must then operate along the short-run cost curve which is consistent with that plant.

Figure 6–11 illustrates the relationship between the U-shaped short-run and long-run curves, assumed here to be U-shaped also. It should be clear why the long-run cost curve (planning curve) is sometimes called an *envelope* curve. Only a few short-run cost curves are shown. Each is associated with a particular plant. Conceptually, there could be an infinite number of such curves, each reflecting a slightly different scale. However, indivisibilities in some of the inputs will usually limit the number of feasible plant sizes in actual practice.

Another way of describing the relationship under consideration is to state that the long-run cost curve (LRAC) is the curve *tangent to all of the possible short-run cost curves*. In the long run the manager can select whatever plant size will minimize the costs for the output that he expects to produce in the future. In the short run he must operate along the particular short-run curve he has selected, even though some of the other short-run cost curves might have allowed lower costs.

One complication is worthy of consideration. The manager knows that

FIGURE 6–11

THE LONG-RUN PLANNING (ENVELOPE) CURVE

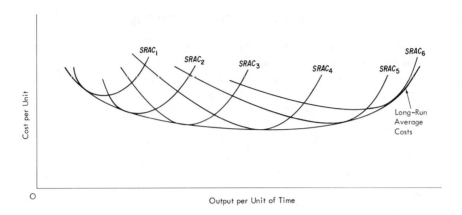

his forecast of future sales and output is uncertain. Rather than select a technology that gives the lowest cost for a given output, he might select a more flexible technology that will minimize costs over a range of outputs. Figure 6–12 shows two cost curves, one of which gives the lowest cost for output *OA,* but which because of the inflexibility of the plant means high costs at outputs *OB* or *OC.* The other curve is more horizontal, so that the penalties for wrong guesses about the appropriate scale are less severe. The tendency of managers to shun inflexible plants, such as the one depicted in Curve 1, may help account in part for some empirical

FIGURE 6–12

SHORT-RUN COST CURVES FOR PLANTS DIFFERING IN FLEXIBILITY

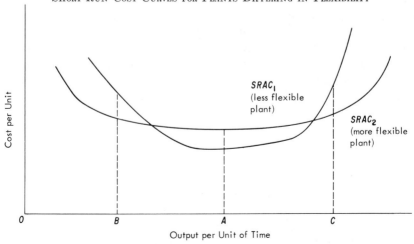

findings of constant short-run marginal costs over firms' normal operating ranges of output.

ESTIMATING COST FUNCTIONS

It is useful to classify the various empirical estimates of cost curves according to (1) the main source of data, and (2) whether estimates are for the short run or for the long run. One common source of data is observations of actual costs or related measures for firms of different sizes (or for firms of changing size). These data are analyzed by statistical techniques to estimate the cost-output relationship. An alternative method is to calculate probable costs using technological and input price information to simulate cost behavior at different rates of output. The first method will be referred to as the *statistical* method; the second as the *engineering* (or synthetic) method. A third method which has also been investigated for long-run studies is to infer the shape of the cost curve by comparing the competitive success of firms of different sizes. This method is known as the *survivor technique*. Examples of these methods are discussed below.

Statistical estimates of cost functions

The best method of using historical production and cost data in estimating cost functions is to employ multiple regression analysis. The most common approach is to fit an equation of the form

$$C_i = a + b_{1i} X_{1i} + b_2 X_{2i} + b_3 X_{3i} + \cdots + b_n X_{ni} + U_i$$

where the dependent variable C_i is total cost in the accounting period for the ith observation, and the Xs are all measurable cost-determining variables, one or more of which will be measures of output rate. The variable U is the sum of unspecified factors, or disturbances, and these are assumed to be randomly distributed with zero mean and constant variance. Estimates of the bs derived from such a model are measures of marginal costs associated with each of the determining factors. Hence, if the data are accurate and complete, if the chosen form of the function is correct, and if future costs will behave on average as they did in the past, the estimated marginal costs may be used as guides in the firm's decisions.

Accuracy and applicability of the available data will depend upon the nature of the cost-accounting systems of the firm or firms to be analyzed. All costs (at least all those that may *vary with output*) and all other *factors that affect cost* should be measured over the *same unit of time,* and that period should be *short enough* to pick up the effects of any significant variations in rates of output. The data may consist of observations on each variable *for a single firm over a number of time periods.* Only if the cost relationship stays unchanged through time will such a statistical *time series* provide data suitable for estimating *future* costs associated with various output levels or scales of plant. Another possible source of data are observations on the variables *for each member of a group of firms producing at various rates within the same period of time.* Such observations are called *cross-section* data.

What variables should be included in the analysis? As a general rule, any variable which could cause a cost curve to shift should be included in addition to measures of output. Factor price changes, changes in production methods, and seasons of the year are likely candidates. Other factors that are commonly found to affect costs are changes in design capacity—i.e., plant size—and simply the passage of time, as a proxy for learning. Observations on each of these must, of course, match the dependent variable in terms of time period over which they are measured.

A number of cross-section and time series regression studies have been made to estimate short-run and long-run cost behavior. In accordance with economic theory, *short-run* studies seek to relate total cost to *variations in output rates* in firms designed for least cost at a *given scale* (or capacity). *Long-run* studies attempt to relate total costs to *variations in plant or firm scales* where each production rate is *at the minimum cost level for each plant.* For example, consider the following regression equation derived from actual cross-section data for firms in the feed mill industry:

$$C = 10018 + 6.8193V + 0.3051K$$

where V stands for total annual volume (tons) of feed mixed and K is annual capacity of each mill; C is *annual* cost.

When K is 10,000 tons per year, *unit* cost varies with output rates as in Curve I of Figure 6–13. This curve is simply calculated from the above cost equation substituting the value of K and dividing by V; hence, $C/V = 13069/V + 6.8193$. Marginal costs for this size of plant become nearly constant up to the level of capacity. (At capacity, costs of further expansion are assumed to increase rapidly, although this is not indicated in the equation.) However, plants with larger capacities have lower average costs at capacity, as in Curve II of Figure 6–13, which represents a 20,000-ton capacity plant. Connecting the low point of each short-run curve gives the long-run average cost, or envelope, curve.

The above example illustrates a much-discussed feature of most statistical cost studies that have been reported. These studies have typically indicated flat, or nearly flat, marginal cost curves after an initial stage of rapid cost decline. This so-called L-shaped cost curve has received much attention because it implies that average and marginal costs are equal in the normal operating range of the firm, that firms of various sizes may coexist in the market, and that there is no "natural limit" to a single firm's share of any market in the absence of government regulation.

FIGURE 6–13

PLANT CURVES AND ENVELOPE CURVE

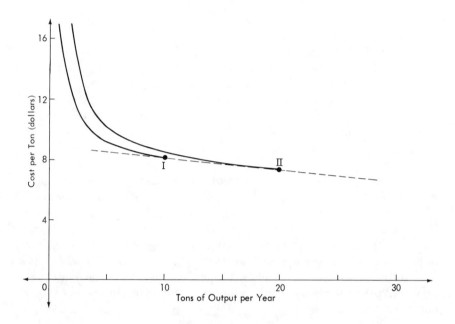

Table 6–1 reports the accumulated evidence from a large number of short-run (S) and long-run (L) studies using both cross-section (CS) and time-series (TS) data. You will note that only two studies, Nordin's 1947 study of a light plant, and Nerlove's 1961 study of the United States electric generating industry, clearly show increasing MC over any range of output.

Despite the near uniformity of the results of statistical cost studies, the findings of constant or declining MC are still a subject of lively debate. Critics of the statistical cost studies have pointed out both methodological and logical flaws in these studies that may make their results misleading.

The methodological criticisms are mostly concerned with: (1) inadequacy of the data used, and (2) improper statistical analyses of the data. *Accounting data* have been criticized on grounds that the annual accounting period is usually longer than the economists' short run and, therefore, much of the cost variation with short-run changes in rate of output is obscured. In addition, it is argued with respect to *cross-section data* that accounting rules for valuing depreciation and capital assets, for allocating joint costs in multiproduct firms, and for measuring changes in input prices may all lead to biases in the shape of long-run cost curves.

TABLE 6–1

RESULTS OF STUDIES OF COST CURVES

Name	Industry	Type	Period	Result
Dean (1936)	Furniture	TS	S	MC constant. SRAC "failed to rise."
Dean (1941)	Leather belts	TS	S	Significantly increasing MC. Rejected by Dean.
Dean (1941)	Hosiery	TS	S	MC constant. SRAC "failed to rise."
Dean (1942)	Dept. Store	TS	S	MC declining or constant.
Dean and James ... (1942)	Shoe stores	CS	L	LRAC is U-shaped (interpreted as *not* due to diseconomies of scale).
Ezekiel and Wylie (1941)	Steel	TS	S	MC declining but large standard errors.
Yntema (1940)	Steel	TS	S	MC constant.
Ehrke .... (1933)	Cement	TS	S	Ehrke interprets as constant MC. Apel (1948) argues that MC is increasing.
Nordin (1947)	Light plant	TS	S	MC is increasing.
Lomax .... (1951)	Gas (U.K.)	CS	L	LRAC of production declines (no analysis of distribution).
Gribbin (1953)	Gas (U.K.)	CS	L	'' ''
Lomax (1952)	Electricity (U.K.)	CS	L	'' ''
Johnston .... (1960)	Electricity (U.K.)	CS	L	'' ''
Johnston .... (1960)	Electricity (U.K.)	TS	S	SRAC falls, then flattens tending towards constant MC up to capacity.
McNulty .... (1955)	Electricity (U.S.)	CS	L	Average costs of administration are constant
Nerlove (1961)	Electricity (U.S.)	CS	L	LRAC excluding transmission costs declines, then shows signs of increasing.
Johnston .... (1960)	Coal (U.K.)	CS	L	Wide dispersion of costs per ton.
Johnston .... (1960)	Road passenger tpt. (U.K.)	CS	L	LRAC either falling or constant.
Johnston .... (1960)	Road passenger tpt. (U.K.)	TS	S	SRAC decreases.
Johnston .... (1960)	Life Assurance	CS	L	LRAC declines.
Borts (1952)	Railways (U.S.)	CS	L	LRAC either constant or falling.
Borts (1960)	Railways (U.S.)	CS	L	LRAC increasing in East, decreasing in South and West.
Broster (1938)	Railways (U.K.)	TS	L	Operating cost per unit of output falls.

Source: A. A. Walters, "Production and Cost Functions; An Econometric Survey," *Econometrica*, January–February 1963, pp. 49–54.

For example, if the smaller firms in an industry tend to be those with older machinery and equipment, the valuation of assets by historical, rather than current, prices will give a flattening bias to cross-section estimates of the long-run cost curve. Another problem of cross-section studies is that any advantage due to size of a firm will tend to be capitalized in merger and acquisition valuations and thus enter into the book value of the assets used, so that measured costs subsequently appear to be constant for firms of all sizes. Time series studies avoid this problem by relating costs to changes of output for a single firm; however, they require more additional variables to account for changing technology, prices, seasonality, and the like, and one or more of these variables may tend to be collinear with changes in output.

Some problems of the second type, *improper analysis of the data,* may be illustrated by further reference to the feed mill example introduced above. Stollsteimer, Bressler, and Boles have calculated a number of regressions using the *same data* on costs of 29 feed mills with *various forms* of the cost equation.[5] The method in all cases is least-squares multiple linear regression, but each of the forms implies a different shape of the long- and short-run cost curves. The estimated equations are given in Table 6–2, and the implied long-run cost curve is shown in Figure 6–14. Notice that it is the form of the function, not solely the data, that

TABLE 6–2

ALTERNATIVE COST EQUATIONS DERIVED FROM IDENTICAL ANNUAL DATA ON TOTAL COSTS, PLANT VOLUME, AND PLANT CAPACITY, 29 MIDWESTERN FEED MILLS*

Model	Total Cost Equation†	R^2
1c	$C = 70.042V^{0.8} + 0.30140\,(K - V)$ (16.80)oo (1.86)	.96
1d	$C = 22.702V^{0.9} + 0.30001\,(K - V)$ (20.53)oo (2.25)o	.98
1f	$C = 2.229V^{1.1} + 0.41178\,(K - V)$ (18.10)oo (2.83)o	.97
3a	$C = 10018 + 6.8193V + 0.3051K$ (15.05)oo (2.27)o	.98
3c	$C = 7.1080V + 0.4458K - 0.00000182VK$ (15.16)oo (3.22)o (1.75)	.98
3d	$C = 5799 + 6.5445V + 0.2578K + 0.00000083K^2$ (6.22)oo (0.43) (0.32) $+ 0.00000365VK - 0.000000000012VK^2$ (0.61) (0.73)	.98
4a	$C = 0.004122K^{1.4} + 109.3V/(K^{0.27} - 6.01)$	.94

* Basic data for all models and the results for 1c and 1d were made available by Professor Richard Phillips, Iowa State University, Ames, Iowa.

† In all equations, C represents total mill costs in dollars per year, V represents annual mill volume in tons, and K represents computed annual mill capacity in tons. Figures in parentheses are t ratios: o indicates significance at 5 percent level, while oo indicates significance at the 1 percent level.

Source: J. F. Stollsteimer, R. G. Bressler, and J. N. Boles, "Cost Functions from Cross Section Data—Fact or Fantasy?" *Agricultural Economics Research* (July 1961), p. 84.

[5] J. F. Stollsteimer, R. G. Bressler, and J. N. Boles, "Cost Functions from Cross Section Data—Fact or Fantasy?" *Agricultural Economics Research* (July 1961), pp. 79–88.

determines whether an estimated cost curve is U-shaped, flat, or even (as with curve 1*f*) upward sloping.

Choice among statistical estimates is customarily made by comparing measures of goodness of fit of the regression line. The most common measure of goodness-of-fit is the coefficient of determination, or R^2, which is reported for each of the feed mill industry regressions in Table 6–2. In this example, there is very little to choose among any of the alternative formulations, or even between the two "extreme" cases, 1*f* and 4*a*, because of the fact that *all* of these equations have a very close fit to the data; each "explains" 94–98 percent of the variance in costs.

The culprit in this case is the high correlation between the independent

FIGURE 6–14

SEVEN LONG-RUN COST CURVES STATISTICALLY ESTIMATED FROM THE
SAME SET OF DATA FOR 29 MIDWESTERN FEED MILLS

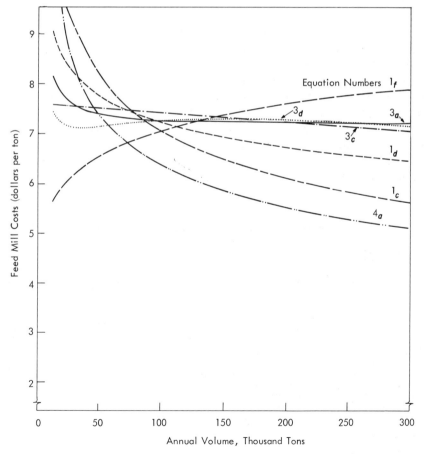

variables. Used together, these two variables "explain" the data well, but the *actual* shapes of the cost curves depend upon the *true* independent influence of each variable, and this is impossible to sort out without added information because the explanatory variables are collinear. Empirical cost curves can be very useful but they must be estimated and evaluated carefully to avoid misleading results.

The persistent empirical finding of L-shaped cost curves has been subject to conceptual scrutiny in addition to the above methodological challenges. Stigler has argued that the increasing cost portion of long-run curves will simply not be observed, at least not for very long, in a market with rival firms. Instead of estimating cost curves from observed cross-section data, Stigler advocates the "survivorship technique."[6] The technique requires the following steps: (1) classification of the firms in the industry into size classes and (2) determination of *which size classes are increasing or decreasing their share* of the total output. As Stigler states: "If the share of a given class falls, it is relatively inefficient, and in general is more inefficient the more rapidly the share falls."[7]

Stigler has applied this technique to the study of the making of steel ingots by open-hearth or Bessemer processes. His findings appear in Table 6–3. He translates these findings into the long-run average cost curve of Figure 6–15. This figure does not pretend to measure *how much* higher costs are at lower and higher scales, but it reflects the smaller shares of the total produced by small and large companies.

Stigler makes a similar analysis of the automobile industry. In this case the smallest companies show a consistent decline in their share of output but there is no evidence of diseconomies of large size (at least in normal peacetime).

TABLE 6–3

DISTRIBUTION OF OUTPUT OF STEEL INGOT CAPACITY BY
RELATIVE SIZE OF COMPANY

Company Size (percent of industry total)	1930	1938	1951
Under ½	7.16	6.11	4.65
½ to 1	5.94	5.08	5.37
1 to 2½	13.17	8.30	9.07
2½ to 5	10.64	16.59	22.21
5 to 10	11.18	14.03	8.12
10 to 25	13.24	13.99	16.10
25 and over	38.67	35.91	34.50

Source: *Directory of Iron and Steel Works of the United States and Canada*, 1930, 1938; *Iron Age*, January 3, 1952, as reprinted in George J. Stigler, "The Economics of Scale," *The Journal of Law and Economics*, (October 1958) pp. 57–71.

[6] George J. Stigler, "The Economics of Scale," *The Journal of Law and Economics*, October 1958, pp. 57–71.

[7] Ibid., p. 56.

FIGURE 6–15

LONG-RUN COST CURVE CONSISTENT WITH DATA ON STEEL INGOTS

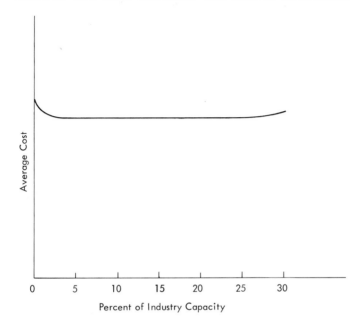

Another conceptual explanation for falling or constant empirical marginal cost curves is related to the earlier discussion in this chapter of the relationship of cost changes to changes in production volume and rates. Hirshleifer has pointed out that the statistical cost studies have made no attempt to measure changes in these two dimensions separately and, hence, have simply captured the largely offsetting effects of simultaneous change in rate and volume. Note that the U-shaped cost functions of traditional theory are based on changes *only in rates,* since the length of the production run and volume are both implicitly assumed to be infinite.

Engineering estimates of cost functions

The engineering approach to estimation of cost functions consists of the following steps: (1) selecting the *rates of operation* for which the various *plants* are to be *designed;* (2) breaking the production process flow into *stages* (in each stage the product undergoes some transformation), *transportation links* that move the product from stage to stage, and *temporary storage points;* (3) determining *least-cost combinations* of labor, materials, and equipment *at each stage* for *each of the design rates of output;* (4) synthesizing these optimally designed stages into complete *plants;* and (5) *estimating costs* for each plant at the designed rate of

FIGURE 6–16
Process Flow Diagram for Pear-Packing Plants

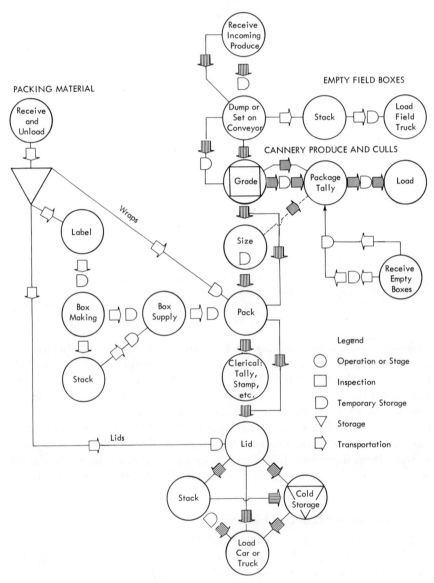

output and at other rates (so as to produce short-run cost curves for each of the plants as well as several points on the long-run cost curve).

Advantages of the engineering method are: (1) it standardizes technology, factor prices, plant efficiency, operating ratios and other factors affecting costs, thus enabling isolation of the effects of changes in rates of output and sizes of plants; (2) costs can be simulated by use of expected

FIGURE 6–17

FIVE METHODS OF SUPPLYING PACKERS WITH EMPTY BOXES

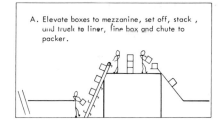

A. Elevate boxes to mezzanine, set off, stack, und truck to liner, line box and chute to packer.

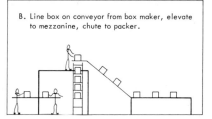

B. Line box on conveyor from box maker, elevate to mezzanine, chute to packer.

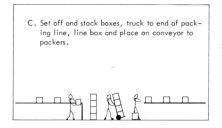

C. Set off and stack boxes, truck to end of packing line, line box and place on conveyor to packers.

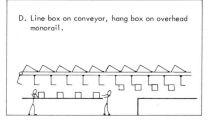

D. Line box on conveyor, hang box on overhead monorail.

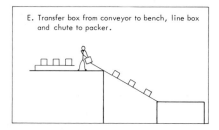

E. Transfer box from conveyor to bench, line box and chute to packer.

future factor prices and other assumed future conditions, thus possibly generating especially useful information for decision making. The disadvantages of the method include the time required and the great cost if careful estimates are made.

A study of pear packing. A University of California study of costs of pear packing provides excellent insight into the nature of the engineering method.[8] Figure 6–16 shows a process flow diagram for pear packing. The researchers determined the best method of carrying out the work in each of these twenty stages at three rates of processing (15, 40, and 70 thousand pounds per hour).

For example, at the stage labeled "box supply," the five methods depicted in Figure 6–17 were compared. Labor requirements shown in Table 6–4, equipment requirements and costs shown in Table 6–5, and costs of

---

[8] B. C. French, L. L. Sammet, and R. G. Bressler, "Economic Efficiency in Plant Operations with Special Reference to the Marketing of California Pears," *Hilgardia*, 24, No. 19 (July 1956).

TABLE 6–4

Unit Labor Requirements and Production Standards for the Types of Jobs Performed in the Distribution of Empty Boxes to the Packers

Operation	Net Unit Time, Man-Minutes per Box	Production Standard,* Boxes per Hour
Bring package of pads and liners from nearby supply point	.014	3,860
Place bottom pad and side liners		
Fold and place one pair of side liners	.110	490
Place one pair of side liners (no folding required)	.036	1,500
Place bottom pad	.036	1,500
Nest boxes on conveyor, set off, and stack	.048	1,130
Transfer empty boxes—for example, from conveyor to elevator, conveyor to chute, conveyor to monorail hook, conveyor to bench		
One box per transfer	.066	820
Two boxes per transfer	.054	1,000
Four boxes per transfer	.030	1,800
Truck empty boxes (standard pear boxes)		
Fork truck: distance 30 feet	.007	7,700
distance 60 feet	.009	6,000
Hand truck: distance 30 feet	.022	2,460
distance 60 feet	.031	1,740

* Based on net time plus allowance for rest and delay of 10 percent of total work time.

TABLE 6–5

Equipment Requirements for Distribution of Empty Packing Boxes with Different Methods

	Method				
Item	A	B	C	D	E
Work table and box chute per 250 boxes per hour, each	1	..	1*	..	1
Gravity conveyor per 100 boxes per hour, feet	32	32	32	..	32
Hand truck per 100 boxes per hour, each	.1	..	.5	..	..
Box elevator per 2,000 boxes per hour	1	1	..	..	..
Box mezzanine, floor area per 100 boxes per hour, square feet	300	300	..	..	..
Monorail conveyor per 100 boxes per hour, feet	..	..	..	70	..

* Work table only.

box supply in relation to rate of output as shown in Table 6–6, were estimated. All 20 stages, optimally designed at each of the three rates of operation, were synthesized into complete plants as shown in Table 6–7. Variable and fixed costs were then estimated for each plant at various rates of output; Table 6–8 shows the resulting estimates for the middle-sized plant.

TABLE 6–6

EMPTY BOX AND MATERIALS SUPPLY—LABOR, OPERATING, AND EQUIPMENT
COSTS IN RELATION TO RATES OF PACKED OUTPUT

Volume Range Boxes per Hour	Number of Workers	Direct Cost * ($ per Hour)			Equipment ($)	
		Labor	Equipment Repair and Operation	Total	Replacement Cost	Annual Fixed Cost†
Method A						
0–190	2	2.10	0.05	2.15	1,060	130
191–245	3	3.15	0.05	3.20	1,240	150
490	4	4.20	0.07	4.27	2,010	240
735	5	5.25	0.09	5.34	2,780	330
790	6	6.30	0.09	6.39	2,950	350
820	7	7.35	0.10	7.45	3,050	360
980	8	8.40	0.11	8.51	3,620	430
1,225	9	9.45	0.13	9.58	4,390	520
1,470	10	10.50	0.15	10.65	5,160	610
1,580	11	11.55	0.16	11.71	5,510	660
1,640	12	12.60	0.16	12.76	5,760	690
Method B						
355	2	2.10	0.06	2.16	1,520	180
625	3	3.15	0.08	3.23	2,370	280
730	4	4.20	0.09	4.29	2,700	320
820	5	5.25	0.10	5.35	2,980	360
1,250	6	6.30	0.13	6.43	4,340	520
1,460	7	7.35	0.15	7.50	5,000	590
1,640	8	8.40	0.16	8.56	5,570	660
Method C						
225	2	2.10	0.01	2.11	290	40
445	3	3.15	0.03	3.18	580	80
660	4	4.20	0.04	4.24	860	110
870	5	5.25	0.06	5.31	1,130	150
1,075	6	6.30	0.07	6.37	1,400	180
1,130	7	7.35	0.08	7.43	1,530	200
1,290	8	8.40	0.08	8.48	1,690	220
1,505	9	9.45	0.10	9.55	1,970	260
1,720	10	10.50	0.12	10.62	2,250	300
Method D						
355	1	1.05	0.09	1.14	1,450	190
625	2	2.10	0.14	2.24	2,390	320
820	3	3.15	0.16	3.31	2,580	340
1,250	4	4.20	0.21	4.41	3,700	490
1,640	5	5.25	0.27	5.52	4,830	640
Method E						
245	1	1.05	0.02	1.07	370	50
490	2	2.10	0.04	2.14	740	100
735	3	3.15	0.06	3.21	1,110	150
980	4	4.20	0.08	4.28	1,470	200
1,225	5	5.25	0.10	5.35	1,840	250
1,470	6	6.30	0.12	6.42	2,210	300
1,715	7	7.35	0.14	7.49	2,580	350

* Direct costs are based on the following: wage rate of $1.05 per hour; power costs $0.03 per motor horsepower per hour; direct repair, 0.5 percent of replacement cost per 100 hours of use.

† Estimated as 13.2 per cent of replacement cost. See table 36 for additional details.

TABLE 6-7

LABOR AND EQUIPMENT REQUIREMENTS FOR THREE EFFICIENT PLANTS WITH 70 PER CENT PACKED AND A 200-HOUR SEASON*

Stage or Cost Component	Job	Crew Organization — Number of Workers, Plant Capacity, 1,000 Pounds per Hour			Equipment Requirements† — Type of Equipment	Number of Units, Plant Capacity, 1,000 Pounds per Hour		
		15	40	70		15	40	70
1. Dump	Dumper	1	—	—	Dumping table and elevator to grading table	1	1	2
	Set off empty lugs	—	2	3	Stack dumping machine	—	1	2
					Empty lug conveyor:			
					Power—40 feet	—	1	2
					Gravity—48 feet	—	1	2
2. Grade	Sorters	9	16	30	Grading table—28 feet	—	1	2
					17½ feet	1	—	—
					Distribution belt, 30 feet	—	1	2
3. Pack	Packer	17	45	71	Tub packing line, 80 feet	1	—	—
					Belt packing line, 60 feet	—	3	5
					Packing stands	17	45	71
4. Tally	Packer tally	1	1	2	Tally desk, forms, pencils	1	1	2
5. Lid-stamp weigh	Lidder operator	1	1	1	Stitcher type lidder	1	1	1
	Check-weigh, stamp	—	—	—	High speed lidder	—	1	2
					Bench scales	1	1	2
	Place top pad	1	4	6	Stamp stand and stamps	1	1	2
6. Carload	Carloaders	1	3	5	Car squeeze	1	1	1
					Ramps	1	2	4
					Hammers (in miscellaneous equipment)	—	—	—
7. Boxmaking and label	Assumed to be on contract basis	—	—	—		—	—	—

Item	Labor				Equipment			
8. Empty packing box supply	Box men	1	2	5	Monorail conveyor—100 feet	--	4.2	--
					Gravity conveyor—35 feet	2.2	--	10
					Work table and box chute	1	--	4
9. Package cannery	Box fillers	2	5	8	Cannery and cull conveyors	‡	‡	‡
10. Transportation	Truckers	5	10	16	Hand trucks	5	10	16§
	Set off packed boxes	1	--	--	Power conveyor—lidder to car	--	‖	‖
	Conveyor men	--	1	1	Gravity conveyor—lidder to car	--	‖	‖
11. Miscellaneous labor	Foremen	2	3	4	No equipment	--	--	--
	Nightmen	1	1	2				
	Seasonal office clerks	2	2	3				
	Weighmaster‖	1	1	1				
	Utility	1	2	3				
12. Office and administrative labor	Manager	1	1	1	No equipment	--	--	--
	Bookkeeper	--	1	1				
13. Miscellaneous equipment	No labor	--	--	--	Small tools, office equipment, etc.	**	**	**
14. Building	No labor	--	--	--	Floor-space—sq. feet††	15,900	30,900	48,600
15. Miscellaneous general costs	No direct labor	--	--	--	No equipment‡‡	--	--	--
16. Accounting to growers for fruit received	Sampling labor	2	4	7	Sampling table	1	1	1
					Bench scales	1	1	1
					Hand truck	1	1	1
Total crew		50	105	170				

* Of the total output, 10 per cent is No. 1 cannery and 20 per cent No. 2 cannery and culls. For purposes of conversion from pounds to lugs, field lugs are figured at 44 pounds each.

† Includes only the major items and specifications.

‡ For more detailed specifications, see L. L. Sammet, and I. F. Davis, *Building and Equipment Costs, Apple and Pear Packing*, California Agricultural Experiment Station, Giannini Foundation of Agricultural Economics, Mimeographed Report No. 133, 1953, p. 37.

§ Fork trucks might be used in this plant to advantage with little increase in cost—see discussion in text. Equipment requirements would, of course, differ.

‖ Details on the types of conveyors and transportation distances are given in L. L. Sammet, *In-Plant Transportation Costs as Related to Materials Handling Methods, Apple and Pear Packing*, California Agricultural Experiment Station, Giannini Foundation of Agricultural Economics, Mimeographed Report No. 142, 1953. p. 10 and p. 50.

¶ Combined with the duties of a trucker in small plants.

** For more detailed specifications, see Sammett and Davis, *Building and Equipment Costs*, p. 37.

†† See Sammet and Davis, *ibid.*, for further details.

‡‡ Includes office and general supplies, auditing and legal expense, and insurance on inventories.

TABLE 6–8

TOTAL VARIABLE COSTS FOR A PLANT OF 40,000 POUNDS PER HOUR CAPACITY,
70 PER CENT PACKED, AND A 200-HOUR SEASON (TECHNOLOGIES ARE
AS SPECIFIED FOR THIS POINT ON THE LONG-RUN COST CURVE)

Stage or Cost Component	Average Annual Fixed Cost	Rate of Total Output—1,000 Pounds per Hour						
		10	15	20	25	30	35	40
		Cost per Hour—Dollars						
1. Dump	641	1.40	1.40	1.40	1.40	2.50	2.50	2.50
2. Grade	280	8.56	9.61	10.66	11.71	13.81	14.86	16.96
3. Pack	1,722	22.94	34.58	45.88	57.19	68.82	78.13	91.43
4. Packer tally	2	1.05	1.05	1.05	1.05	1.05	1.05	1.05
5. Lid, stamp, etc.	495	2.47	2.47	3.52	3.52	3.52	4.57	5.62
6. Carloading	137	1.45	1.45	2.90	2.90	2.90	4.35	4.35
7. Boxmaking and label	– –	3.65	5.47	7.29	9.12	10.94	12.76	14.59
8. Box supply	320	1.14	1.14	1.14	2.24	2.24	2.24	2.24
9. Package cannery	200	1.40	2.60	2.60	3.80	3.80	5.00	6.20
10. Transportation	320	5.14	6.39	7.65	8.90	11.40	12.66	13.91
11. Supervision and miscellaneous	– –	7.82	10.42	10.42	11.96	11.96	11.96	14.56
12. Miscellaneous equipment	1,578	– –	– –	– –	– –	– –	– –	– –
13. Office and administration	7,150	– –	– –	– –	– –	– –	– –	– –
14. Building costs	5,488	– –	– –	– –	– –	– –	– –	– –
15. Miscellaneous general costs	659	– –	– –	– –	– –	– –	– –	– –
16. Sampling	153	1.10	1.65	2.20	2.75	3.30	3.85	4.40
Total	19,145	58.12	78.23	96.77	116.54	136.24	155.93	177.81

Figure 6–18 summarizes the findings of the California study of pear packing costs. Both the short-run (plant) cost curves and the long-run (envelope) curve are L-shaped.

Studies of broiler processing. Plant cost curves obtained by the engineering method are usually L-shaped with lowest unit cost at the design rate of operation. However, there are cases in which plant operating rates can be either increased or decreased from the design rate, but the result of moving in either direction is to increase the unit cost. Figure 6–19, from a New Hampshire study of broiler chicken processing costs, is an example of U-shaped *plant* cost curves derived by the engineering method.[9] However, note that the L-shape is still generated for the long-run, or envelope, curve.

The New Hampshire study dealt only with *internal* costs of broiler processing plants. A North Carolina study subsequently showed that the above-described L-shaped long-run cost curves would be U-shaped if

[9] George B. Rogers and E. T. Bardwell, *Economies of Scale in Chicken Processing*, New Hampshire Agricultural Experiment Station Bulletin 459, April, 1959.

FIGURE 6-18

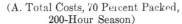
(A. Total Costs, 70 Percent Packed, 200-Hour Season)

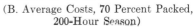
(B. Average Costs, 70 Percent Packed, 200-Hour Season)

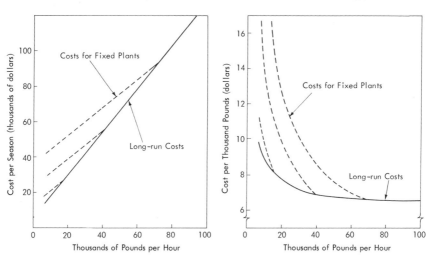

costs of *distributing* feed to broiler farms and *assembling* live broilers to the plant were added to the processing costs.[10] The amount of transport cost to be added to processing cost depends upon average length of haul, which in turn depends upon both the plant size and the "effective production density" of the broiler growing area in birds per square mile per year. Figure 6–20 shows combined processing and transport costs for plants of various sizes at one level of effective production density, and Figure 6–21 shows the combined curves at six different levels of production density.

Managerial uses of empirical cost curves

Estimates of cost curves enter into many important decisions. These include short-run choices of rates of output and prices and long-run decisions about numbers, sizes, and locations of plants.

In the case of decisions about rates of output for competitive firms, the optimum rate is the one that makes marginal cost equal to price. Firms with sloping demand curves can choose an optimum combination of price and output at the rate that makes marginal cost equal to marginal revenue. Pricing decisions are discussed in more detail in Chapter 8.

Decisions about output and pricing are so important to the firm that

---

[10] William R. Henry and James A. Seagraves, "Economic Aspects of Broiler Production Density," *Journal of Farm Economics,* 42, No. 1 (February 1960).

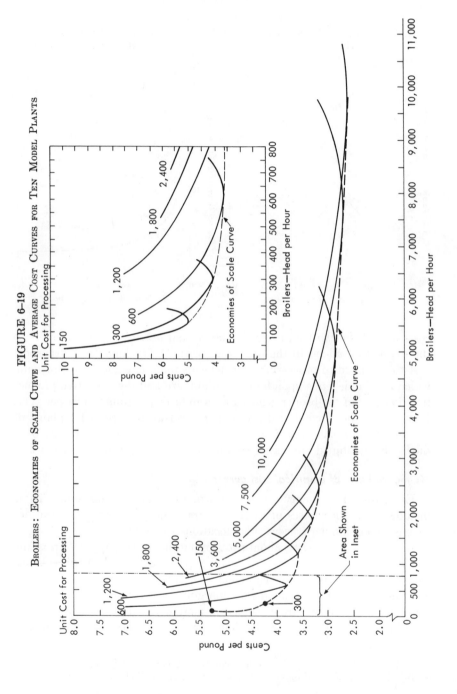

FIGURE 6-19

BROILERS: ECONOMIES OF SCALE CURVE AND AVERAGE COST CURVES FOR TEN MODEL PLANTS

FIGURE 6–20
SELECTED TRANSPORT COSTS, PROCESSING COSTS AND COMBINED COSTS, FOR
EFFECTIVE PRODUCTION DENSITY OF 500 BIRDS PER SQUARE MILE PER YEAR,
AVERAGE LENGTHS OF HAUL, IN MILES, POSTED ALONG TRANSPORT COST CURVE

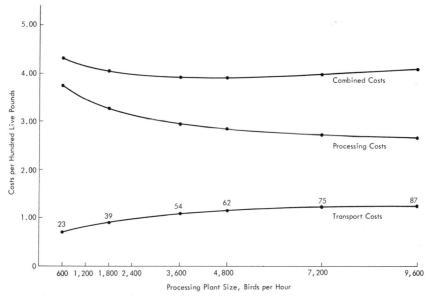

Source: William R. Henry and James A. Seagraves, "Economic Aspects of Broiler Production Density," *Journal of Farm Economics*, 42, No. 1 (February 1960), p. 7.

FIGURE 6–21
RELATIONSHIP OF PROCESSING PLANT SIZE TO COMBINED COSTS OF TRANSPORTATION
AND PROCESSING FOR DIFFERENT EFFECTIVE PRODUCTION DENSITIES

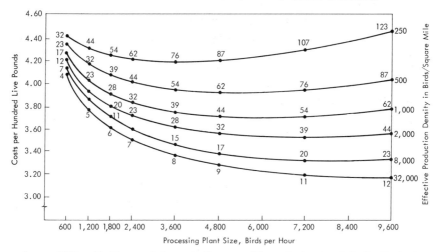

Source: William R. Henry and James A. Seagraves, "Economic Aspects of Broiler Production Density," *Journal of Farm Economics*, 42, No. 1 (February 1960), p. 9.

reliable estimates of cost functions are worth considerable effort and expense. And managers obviously cannot make these decisions without using some kind of estimates or assumptions about the *short-run* cost functions.

A firm considering plant construction or expansion needs estimates of *long-run* cost functions in determining whether or not to make the investment and what size of plant to build. In a situation with unvarying demand and constant structure of factors affecting cost (factor prices, technology, etc.), the decision rule would be simple: build the plant that makes long-run marginal cost equal to marginal revenue. Under actual conditions, the decision is more complex because demand is usually expected to shift over time, the structure of factors affecting cost may also be expected to shift, and there are construction economies that make it advisable to build or expand plants in substantial increments of capacity. Thus, the plan for expansion of capacity should be optimal through time in the face of dynamic changes; enumeration of projected results under alternative expansion plans may be the best approach.

Decisions about plant construction or expansion are especially difficult in multiplant firms. A model that is helpful for such decisions has been developed by Stollsteimer.[11] The problem of simultaneously determining the number, size, and location of plants that minimize the combined transportation and processing costs for raw material produced in varying amounts at scattered production points is handled by the model.

The following data are used as input:

1. Estimated or actual amount of raw material to be assembled from each point of origin
2. Cost of transporting a unit of material between each point of origin and each potential plant site
3. A plant-cost function which permits determination of the cost of processing any fixed total quantity of material in a varying number of plants
4. Specification of potential plant locations.

The form of each plant's total cost function is assumed to be linear with respect to total output and to have a positive intercept. Equal factor costs are assumed for all locations. Stollsteimer's procedure determines approximately optimum numbers, sizes and locations of plants for the problem described above.

---

[11] John F. Stollsteimer, "A Working Model for Plant Numbers and Locations," *Journal of Farm Economics* 45 (August, 1963), pp. 631–645.

7 / Selected topics in production economics

This chapter shows how some of the concepts from the economic theory of production have been developed into powerful production planning techniques. The following topics are discussed: the conceptual framework of product mix problems; an introduction to linear programming with an application to a product mix problem using a graphic approach and an algebraic approach; a discussion of sensitivity (or postoptimality) analysis as applied to the product mix problem; the conceptual framework of problems involving least-cost input combinations as these are formulated for linear programming; empirical examples of the use of linear programming in feed and sausage formulation; an introduction to inventory problems; an introduction to techniques for determination of optimum inventories that take into account both the economies of lot size and the economies of buffering against uncertainties associated with timing of materials deliveries, work disruptions, and fluctuations in customer demands.

THE PRODUCT MIX PROBLEM: CONCEPTUAL FRAMEWORK

Consider a situation in which a farmer can produce two basic crops, corn and soybeans. He also raises cattle. The farmer has 1,000 acres of land available and employs four helpers; each of these works 40 hours per week. The farmer measures his output in bushels of corn, bushels of soybeans, and number of cattle produced and sold at market per year. The farmer may produce one of any number of combinations of products per year. For example, he may produce all corn and no soybeans and no cattle; or, for that matter, he may choose to produce all of any one of the products and none of the others. More realistically, he may choose

261

to produce some of each product (i.e., x bushels of corn, y bushels of soybeans, and z cattle). However, the number of possible combinations is practically unlimited. How should he go about choosing the best combination to produce; i.e., how many bushels of corn, how many bushels of soybeans, and how many cattle? His choices are many but are limited by his limited resources, land and labor. In view of these limits, a decision to produce one more bushel of corn affects the number of bushels of soybeans that he can produce and the number of cattle, and so on. If the farmer is rational, he will try to produce the optimum mix of products. But how should optimality be defined? What should his objective be?

The general nature of product mix problems

Product mix problems only occur when two or more resources are limited and there are two or more products that require at least one of the limited resources. (If only one resource is limited, it is appropriate to use equimarginal allocation based on marginal revenue product, as discussed in Chapter 2.) A business firm or a nonprofit organization producing goods or services has limited resources in the short run. There are only so many hours of labor available each week; there are only so many units of each required raw material available; only a certain number of hours of use per week are available at each piece of equipment, and so on. Although many different combinations of products may be produced, a decision to produce one unit of any particular product requires the sacrifice of some quantity of at least one of the other products. Any particular combination of products will be called a product mix. The basic problem is then: *within the constraints imposed by the limited resources, select from all possible combinations of product mixes the "optimum" product mix.* In order to solve this problem it is necessary to develop several additional concepts and to define optimality.

Production possibility curves

Consider again the situation the farmer faces. For simplicity we will assume he is considering only two enterprises: corn and cattle. He has only 1,000 acres of land and a fixed number of hours of labor per week. Figure 7–1 is a hypothetical *production possibility curve*. It shows various combinations of corn (bushels) and cattle (number) that could be produced per year using 1,000 acres of land. A maximum quantity of corn (Y_2) can be grown if there is no raising of cattle (Y_1). By giving up some corn production, land can be made available for use as pasture for cattle. This process substitutes cattle for corn in the product mix.

The production possibility curve in Figure 7–1 is concave to the origin. This curvature reflects the assumption of a *diminishing marginal rate of substitution* of Y_1 for Y_2 for movement from point to point down and to the right. The absolute value of the slope of the curve $(\Delta Y_2/\Delta Y_1)$ is in-

FIGURE 7–1
PRODUCTION POSSIBILITY CURVE
(heterogeneous inputs)

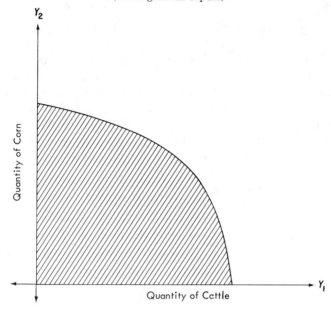

FIGURE 7–2
PRODUCTION POSSIBILITY CURVE
(homogeneous inputs)

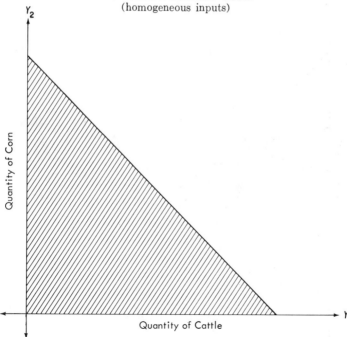

creasing. To obtain one more unit of Y_1, more and more Y_2 must be fore-gone as Y_1 is increased.

Diminishing marginal rates of product substitutions are often observed in practice; they are explained by heterogeneity of fixed inputs. In the example of Figure 7–1, the land is not uniform in quality. It ranges from rich and level to poor and hilly. All of the land can be planted in corn or grazed by cattle, or there can be various combinations of corn and cattle production. As the farmer increases cattle production, more and more corn must be given up to obtain land for one cow. Increasingly fertile land is being withdrawn from corn production and reallocated to cattle.

How many product mixes are possible? Each point on the curve represents a *feasible product mix* that will utilize all available land. Each point in the shaded region of Figure 7–1 also represents a feasible product mix that will leave some land unused, or *redundant*.

A production possibility curve can be drawn for each of the limited resources. Figure 7–2 is another such curve showing the various combinations of corn and cattle production possible assuming a fixed supply of

FIGURE 7–3

PRODUCTION POSSIBILITY CURVES
(superimposed)

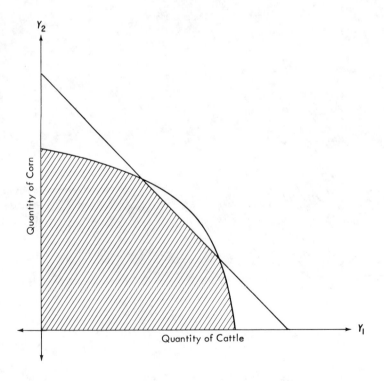

labor. This curve is linear if the labor is homogeneous. Each point on the curve and in the shaded region represents a feasible product mix, considering only the limited supply of labor.

Figure 7–3 shows both of the production possibility curves discussed above. The shaded region is a set of points common to both curves. Since the farmer is limited by both resources, land and labor, only those product mixes in the shaded region are feasible.

Now that the set of feasible product mixes has been determined, several other questions must be answered. How much product substitution is advantageous in such a case? What is the optimum product mix? The solution depends upon *relative contributions* of the two products. These contributions are determined by *prices of the products* and by *prices and amounts of the corresponding variable inputs.*

Isocontribution lines

Changes in product combinations with contributions constant are depicted by the three *isocontribution lines* in Figure 7–4. For example, all product combinations on Isocontribution Line $3,000 would contribute exactly $3,000.

Relative positions of the isocontribution lines are determined by the absolute amounts of contribution per unit of each product. The slope of the lines depends upon relative contributions and therefore upon both prices and variable costs of the products. Isocontribution line $3,000 is established as follows. First, the contribution per unit of Y_2 (Cy_2) is calculated: it is price less variable unit cost. It should be noted that *if contribution is considered constant, several economic assumptions are implicit*. To assume that price does not change according to level of output is to assume a *horizontal demand curve*. It is also assumed that variable cost per unit is constant. This implies both *constant prices of inputs* and *constant marginal productivity of inputs* over the range considered.

Constant variable unit cost, although sometimes observed in actual production, is a special case. Diminishing marginal productivity of variable inputs as output of either product is increased, resulting in increasing marginal cost for that product, would be more generally encountered. This would make the isocontribution lines *convex* to the origin rather than straight lines. Although such a change in form of the curves would not affect the general results of this exposition, it makes determination of product mix very difficult if there are numerous products to consider. Constant marginal productivity is often assumed because constant contributions make the problem easier to handle. (If *decreasing* marginal productivity *must* be taken into account it can be approximated through *stepwise reductions* that allow it to remain constant over successive ranges of output. If output over each range is then formally treated as

FIGURE 7–4
ISOCONTRIBUTION LINES: TWO OUTPUTS

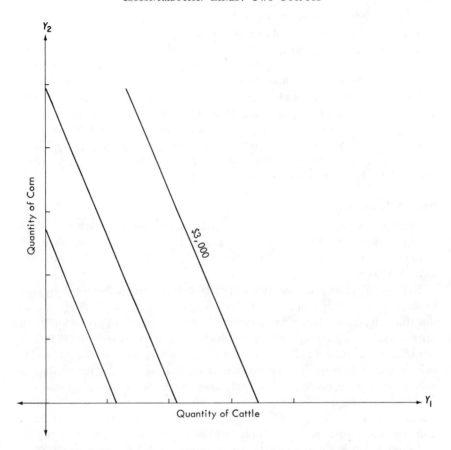

a different product, one can still use the approach to product mix determination that is discussed in the following sections.)

The next step in establishing Isocontribution Line $3,000 is to calculate the number of units of Y_2 produced alone that would provide a total contribution of $3,000 (e.g., $3,000/Cy_2 =$ number of units of Y_2); the result is the value of the Y_2 intercept. The third step is to calculate the Y_1 intercept using the above procedure and the contribution associated with each unit of Y_1 (Cy_1).

Finally, a straight line connecting the two intercepts completes this particular isocontribution line. Any point on the line segment represents a combination of bushels of corn and number of cattle which would result in a total contribution of $3,000. Infinitely many other isocontribution lines can be generated in a similar fashion. One such line exists for each value of total contribution.

Optimum product mix

In Figure 7–5 the isocontribution lines from Figure 7–4 have been superimposed on the production possibility curve of Figure 7–3. The objective is to find that combination of products, or that product mix, which yields *maximum total contribution*.

FIGURE 7–5

OPTIMAL COMBINATION OF TWO OUTPUTS WITH A GIVEN QUANTITY
OF INPUTS AND A GIVEN PRICE OF OUTPUTS

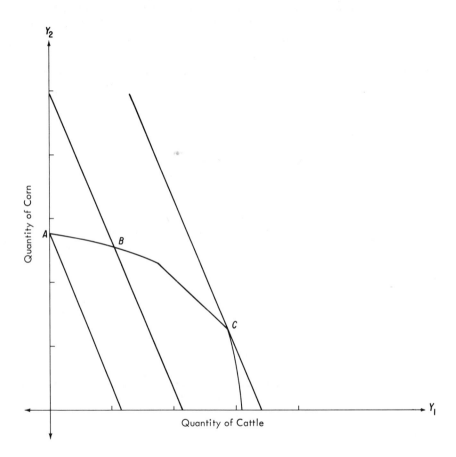

Consider Point A on the production possibility curve. Is it advantageous to move around the curve to Point B? Since the change results in a move to a higher contribution line which implies greater total contribution, the product substitution is clearly desirable. However, contribution can be increased still more by moving around to Point C. In contrast, any move from Point C would result in a product mix falling on a lower isocontribution line and therefore would reduce total contribution. Point *C* is the optimum product mix in this illustration, because it is the one that produces the greatest total contribution.

AN INTRODUCTION TO LINEAR PROGRAMMING

A particular case of the product mix problem involves the assumptions that all of the various physical product-substitution possibilities and iso-contribution lines are linear. The advantage of the assumptions of linearity is that it allows the use of powerful mathematical techniques, known as *linear programming*, or LP. If one is going to employ these tools, he must be careful that he understands the economic implications of this assumption of linearity. This section considers the formulation of a product mix problem into the LP framework. The necessary assumptions and their implications are discussed as well as the techniques employed in solving this class of problems.

An example will be used throughout this section in order to explain the formulation and solution of product mix problems. Assume a manufacturer produces two products, desks and bookcases. Both products must be processed through two work stations. At work station 1, the wood is sawed and sanded. At work station 2, the products are assembled and stained. Because of a limited amount of labor and a limited number of machines only 126 hours are available weekly at work station 1. For similar reasons only 96 hours are available at work station 2. Sawing and sanding of desks requires 6 hours; 3 hours are needed for bookcases. Assembling and staining desks and bookcases requires 2 and 4 hours, respectively.

Assuming that contribution per desk is $8 and contribution per bookcase is $6, we wish to determine the optimum number of desks and bookcases to produce and sell. Table 7–1 summarizes the pertinent information.

TABLE 7–1
Problem Information

Work Center	Hours Required for One Unit of Product		Total Hours Available
	Desks	Bookcases	
1	6	3	126
2	2	4	96
Contribution per unit	$8	$6	

Formulation of an LP problem

1. *The objective of the firm must be stated explicitly as a linear function of the activities.* It is necessary to define explicitly in measurable

terms the activities that are competing for the limited resources. In our example the two activities are desk production and bookcase production. We will represent the level of these activities (if a rate, quantity per unit of time) by the number of desks (D) produced and sold and the number of bookcases (B) produced and sold.

After the outputs of the competing activities have been explicitly defined, it is necessary to determine the objective the firm wishes to achieve. The rational firm wishes to select and produce that combination of products which will maximize total contribution. In our example then, the firm wishes to determine that number of desks and that number of bookcases which if produced and sold will maximize total contribution. Mathematically the firm's objective may be stated as:

Maximize $8D + 6B$

If we let Z represent total contribution, then $Z = 8D + 6B$ is known as an *objective function*.

Of what significance is it that the objective function must be linear? For the objective function to be linear requires that the contribution per unit of each product be constant. In our example, no matter how many desks are produced, each desk sold returns a contribution of $8. No matter how many bookcases are produced, each bookcase returns a contribution of $6. Since contribution per unit is defined as the difference between price and variable cost per unit, both price and per-unit variable cost must be constant. Constant price implies a horizontal demand curve which in turn implies pure competition. Strictly interpreted, constant variable cost per short-run unit implies a horizontal marginal cost curve and therefore constant returns rather than increasing or diminishing returns.

2. *The restrictions placed on the firm by limited resources must be stated explicitly as linear equalities or inequalities.* If these restrictions did not exist, maximum contribution would be achieved by an "infinite amount of production." It is only because resources are limited that a problem exists. These limits constitute the *constraints* of the problem. For our example there are two constraints, one imposed by a limited number of hours available at work station 1 and another imposed by the limited number of hours available at work station 2. Stated mathematically the constraints are:

(1) $6D + 3B \leq 126$ (work station 1)

(2) $2D + 4B \leq 96$ (work station 2)

Let us closely examine these two constraints. First consider constraint 1. The coefficients 6 and 3 are *technological coefficients*. Each desk produced requires 6 hours at work station 1. Each bookcase requires 3 hours. There are only 126 hours available. Since D represents the number of desks processed at work station 1, $6D$ represents the total amount of the available time at work station 1 used in producing desks. Similarly, $3B$ represents the total amount of available time at work station 1 that will be used in producing bookcases. It follows that $6D + 3B$ would be the total number of hours used at work station 1 for the production of D desks and B bookcases. Since there are only 126 hours available, then $6D + 3B$ must be less than or equal to ($\leq$) 126. The "less than" is included since we are not required to use all the hours available, but in no case may we use more than 126 hours. Any product mix (D, B) that the firm produces must be determined so that it does not violate $6D + 3B \leq 126$. Constraint 2 may be similarly interpreted.

Of what significance is it that these inequalities must be linear? Linearity implies that the amount of each resource required is the same for the nth unit of the activity as it is for the first. Implicit assumptions are that: (1) the resource is homogeneous and (2) the relation of the resource to the output is characterized by constant returns. Another way of expressing the same thing is to say that constant marginal rates of substitution are assumed. For example, to process one desk at work station 1 requires 6 hours and one bookcase requires 3 hours. It follows, then, that the marginal rate of substitution between desks and bookcases is 2 (6/3); i.e., the decision to process one more desk at work station 1 requires the sacrifice of processing two bookcases. Similarly, the marginal rate of substitution at work station 2 would be ½ (2/4). Since each desk requires only two hours at work station 2 while each bookcase requires four hours, the decision to produce one more desk requires the sacrifice of only ½ bookcase.

3. *Nonnegativity requirements must be recognized.* There is no physical meaning to negative production levels, such as $D = -4$, and so we do not allow production to be "negative." We must constrain each unknown production level to be either zero or positive; i.e., to be *nonnegative*, $D \geq 0$ and $B \geq 0$.

An additional assumption inherent in the preceding assumptions is generally referred to as the assumption of *divisibility*. The divisibility assumption simply implies that the activity levels are permitted to assume fractional values as well as integer values. For example, we admit the technological possibility of $D = 2.5$ and $B = 4.41$.

Now that our problem has been formulated as an LP problem and the necessary assumptions and their implications discussed, it is perhaps appropriate to present the formulation here in its entirety.

D = number of desks
B = number of bookcases } variables

(1) Maximize $Z = 8D + 6B$} objective function

subject to:

$$(2) \ 6D + 3B \leq 126$$
$$(3) \ 2D + 4B \leq \ \ 96$$
$\Big\}$ constraints

and

$$(4) \ D \geq 0, \ B \geq 0 \ \} \ \text{nonnegativity requirements}$$

Management's problem is to find values for D and B that satisfy the relations (2), (3), and (4), and also maximize total contribution (1).

Methods of obtaining solutions are presented in following sections. However, since it should be evident by now that the assumption of linearity has far-reaching economic implications, the reader may even be wondering if LP can be used in "real-life" problems. Although one would rarely consider the LP model to be a perfect representation of real-life problems, it can often be a sufficiently accurate approximation for practical purposes. For example, short-run marginal cost curves may not be horizontal as is required by the linearity assumption of LP. They are often U-shaped because of increasing and decreasing returns. However, as illustrated in the empirical examples of Chapter 6, the curves are often "flat" enough over wide ranges to permit linear approximations. The point is this: it is often justifiable to assume linearity as an approximation, but one should always remain aware of the implications of the assumption.

A graphic solution

Graphic methods of linear programming can be used only when there are no more than three variables involved because we can draw in no more than three dimensions. However, the graphical approach is most helpful in demonstrating the underlying logic of LP. In this section, the graphical method of LP is illustrated by use of an example. The basic problem discussed in the preceding section will be solved graphically. It is presented below as previously formulated:

D = number of desks
B = number of bookcases
$\Big\}$ variables

$$(1) \ \text{Maximize} \ Z = 8D + 6B \ \} \ \text{objective function}$$

subject to:

$$(2) \ 6D + 3B \leq 126$$
$$(3) \ 2D + 4B \leq \ \ 96$$
$\Big\}$ constraints

and

$$(4) \ D \geq 0, \ B \geq 0 \} \ \text{nonnegativity requirements}$$

Step 1: plot the constraints in the problem on a graph. Figure 7–6 is such a graph. The horizontal axis represents number of desks and the vertical axis represents the number of bookcases. It should be noted that we are concerned only with the first quadrant. This fact is the obvious result of the nonnegativity requirements (4).

FIGURE 7–6

FEASIBLE REGION FOR A SIMPLE LP PROBLEM

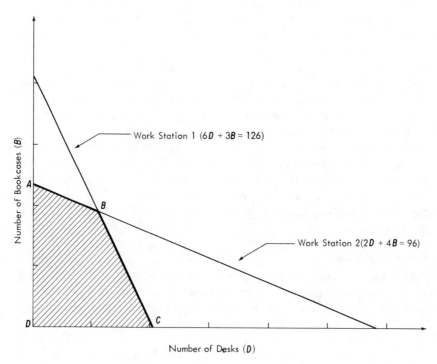

The steepest line in the graph represents the constraint imposed on production by the limited number of hours available at work station 1. It was found by plotting the equation

$$6D + 3B = 126$$

Since the actual constraint (2) is an inequality, each point on the line and every point to the left of the line represents a product mix which satisfies this constraint. This line is in fact simply a production possibility curve. The fact that it is linear derives from the assumptions previously discussed.

Similarly, in Figure 7–6 the constraint imposed by work station 2 is plotted. Every point on the line and to the left of the line represents a product mix which satisfies the constraint

$$2D + 4B \leqq 96$$

Since both work-stations must be used in order to produce a desk or a bookcase, only those product mixes which fall in the shaded areas of Figure 7–6 are possible. For a combination to be feasible, the available time at neither work station may be exceeded. The shaded area represents all those product combinations that satisfy both constraints.

$$6D + 3B \leqq 126$$

$$2D + 4B \leqq 96$$

This area is called the *feasible region* because every point which lies within it or on its boundary represents a combination of values of the variables (the output levels of *D* and *B*) which does not violate either constraint. Every point in the feasible region is called a *feasible solution*. Note that each constraint has decreased the size of the area within which solutions may exist. The *solution space* has been reduced from the entire plane to the feasible region as depicted in Figure 7–6.

Step 2: calculate all the coordinates of each *corner point*. A corner point is any point in the feasible region which occurs at the intersection of two or more of the constraints. For example, in Figure 7–6 there are four corner points which are labeled *A, B, C,* and *D*. Point *A* occurs where the nonnegativity requirement $D \leq 0$ and the constraint for work station 2 intersect. *C* occurs at the intersection of $B = 0$ and the constraint for work station 1. To calculate point *B*, the following two equations are solved simultaneously:

$$(1) \ 6D + 3B = 126$$

$$(2) \ 2D + 4B = \ \ 96$$

We multiply the second equation by -3 and add the results to equation 1.

$$
\begin{array}{r}
6D + 3B = 126 \\
-6D - 12B = -288 \\
\hline
-\ 9B = -162 \\
B = 18
\end{array}
$$

Substituting $B = 18$ in equation 1:

$$
\begin{array}{l}
6D + 3(18) = 126 \\
6D = 72 \\
D = 12
\end{array}
$$

Point *B* is then (12, 18). Point *D* is the origin (0,0), which is always a corner point.

Step 3: with all feasible product mix alternatives delineated, select the one that meets the objective of maximizing contribution. The basic theorem of linear programming tells us that *the optimum solution must always lie at a corner of the feasible region.* Although no attempt will be made to prove this theorem here, the student may intuitively understand the reason for this by studying Figure 7–7. Figure 7–7 is simply the feasible region as depicted in Figure 7–6 with a set of isocontribution lines superimposed on it. The line closest to the origin (*R*) is simply the set of all product mixes which return a total contribution of $120. It was found by plotting the line for the equation

$$8D + 6B = 120$$

Should the firm produce one of the product mixes shown on this line? Before answering, consider the next isocontribution line *S*. It was found by plotting the equation

$$8D + 6B = 168$$

It should be noted that there are an infinite number of possible isocontribution lines, one for each possible value of total contribution. Since the contribution per unit of each product is unchanging, the isocontribution lines form a series of parallel straight lines. Obviously the firm would be better off to produce a product mix on the second line *S* because

FIGURE 7–7
GRAPHIC SOLUTION FOR A SIMPLE LP PROBLEM

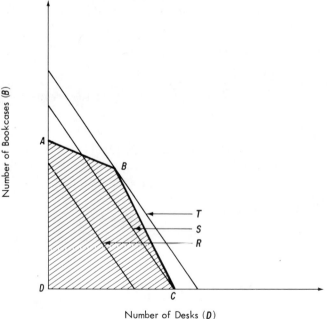

Number of Desks (*D*)

the total contribution is greater for each product mix on this line than it was for line R. In fact the firm should continue to the highest (farthest from origin) line which still has at least one point in common with the feasible region. It should be obvious that this point will always be a corner point as shown by isocontribution line T in Figure 7–7. Any move to a higher isocontribution line results in product mixes which are not feasible. Any move to a lower line results in less than maximum contribution.

For this reason, we need only to compare the value of the total contribution at each corner point. The one resulting in the greatest contribution is the optimum product mix.

Corner Point		*Total Contribution*
$(0, 0)$	$8 (0) + 6 (0)$	$ 0
$(0, 24)$	$8 (0) + 6 (24)$	\$144
$(21, 0)$	$8 (21) + 6 (0)$	\$168
$(12, 18)$	$8 (12) + 6 (18)$	\$204

Thus the optimum product mix is to produce 12 desks and 18 bookcases. Neither the time constraint at work station 1 nor the constraint at work station 2 is violated since:

$$6(12) + 3(18) = 126$$
$$2(12) + 4(18) = 96$$

The resulting contribution is \$204.

An algebraic solution

We have thus far examined the basic structure of linear programming problems and have solved a simple example by the graphical method. However, as previously noted, the graphical solution is only a first step in explaining linear programming. We shall now introduce a less restricted approach, the algebraic method. It is not the most efficient method but is introduced here for pedagogical reasons. It is a bridge which leads to the procedure known as the *simplex method*, which is the quickest and easiest method for arriving at optimum solutions.

The algebraic solution to a linear programming problem will be demonstrated with the same problem that we used in the graphic method. The problem was stated mathematically as

Maximize $8D + 6B = Z$

Subject to:

$6D + 3B \leqq 126$

$2D + 4B \leqq 96$

and

$D, B \geqq 0$

We begin by modifying the constraints which at present are inequalities. By adding a *slack variable* to each inequality, we convert each inequality into an equality.

$$6D + 3B + S_1 = 126 \qquad (7\text{–}1)$$

$$2D + 4B + S_2 = 96 \qquad (7\text{–}2)$$

S_1 represents the idle time (or slack time) at work station 1. S_2 represents the idle time at work station 2. Generally we rewrite the equations in the following form

$$S_1 = 126 - 6D - 3B \qquad (7\text{–}3)$$

$$S_2 = 96 - 2D - 4B \qquad (7\text{–}4)$$

The next step is to find a feasible solution which is a corner point. The origin is always trivially such a solution. Therefore our first solution is:

First Solution

$$D = 0$$
$$B = 0$$
$$S_1 = 126 - 6(0) - 3(0) = 126$$
$$S_2 = 96 - 2(0) - 4(0) = 96$$

This solution obviously yields no contribution since

$$\text{Total contribution} = 8D + 6B$$
$$= 8(0) + 6(0)$$
$$= 0$$

The question then arises, "Can we do better?" Examining the objective function,

$$8D + 6B = Z$$

we see that the obvious answer is yes. Each desk added to our solution will increase total contribution by $8. Each bookcase will add $6. We select the variable that will add the most, which in this case is desks (D). Now the question arises, "How many desks?" Assume all time available at each work station is used for the production of desks. Equation 7–3, $S_1 = 126 - 6D - 3B$, shows that in work station 1 we have 126 hours available and each desk requires 6 hours. Thus, considering only work station 1, we can make

$$\frac{126 \text{ hours}}{6 \text{ hours per desk}} = 21 \text{ desks}$$

The constraint for work station 2, equation (7–4) $S_2 = 96 - 2D - 4B$, shows that there are 96 hours available and each desk requires 2 hours. Therefore, we can make:

$$\frac{96 \text{ hours}}{2 \text{ hours per desk}} = 48 \text{ desks}$$

Obviously, since each desk must be processed at each work station, we can make only 21 desks. Our second solution is therefore:

Second Solution

$$D = 21$$
$$B = 0$$
$$S_1 = 126-6(21) - 3(0) = 0$$
$$S_2 = 96-2(21) - 4(0) = 54$$

$$\begin{aligned} \text{Total contribution} &= 8D + 6B \\ &= 8(21) + 6(0) \\ &= \$168 \end{aligned}$$

Obviously the change was advantageous. Can we do even better? Before trying to answer this we must alter each of our equations to represent what we have done. The slack time in work station 1 was reduced to zero. Equations 7–3 and 7–4 must be changed to reflect this.

Solving 7–3 for D, we obtain

$$\begin{aligned} S_1 &= 126 - 6D - 3B \\ 6D &= 126 - 3B - S_1 \\ D &= 21 - 1/2B - 1/6S_1 \end{aligned} \qquad (7\text{–}5)$$

Substituting this value for D into 7–4 we obtain

$$\begin{aligned} S_2 &= 96 - 2D - 4B \\ S_2 &= 96 - 2(21 - 1/2B - 1/6S_1) - 4B \\ S_2 &= 96 - 42 + B + 1/3S_1 - 4B \\ S_2 &= 54 - 3B + 1/3S_1 \end{aligned} \qquad (7\text{–}6)$$

Finally, substituting for D in our objective function we obtain

$$\begin{aligned} \text{Total contribution} = Z &= 8D + 6B \\ Z &= 8(21 - 1/2B - 1/6S_1) + 6B \\ Z &= 168 - 4B - 4/3S_1 + 6B \\ Z &= 168 + 2B - 4/3S_1 \end{aligned} \qquad (7\text{–}7)$$

Summarizing, we now have:

Objective function

$$Z = 168 + 2B - 4/3S_1 \qquad (7\text{–}7)$$

Constraints

$$D = 21 - 1/2B - 1/6S_1 \qquad (7\text{–}5)$$

$$S_2 = 54 - 3B + 1/3S_1 \qquad (7\text{–}6)$$

It is probably worth while at this point to consider the coefficients in each of these equations and try to understand their meaning. Consider the objective function

$$Z = 168 + 2B - 4/3S_1$$

The constant 168 simply means that if $B = 0$ and $S_1 = 0$, as they do in the second solution, then total contribution will be $168. The coefficient 2 in front of B says that each unit of B added to the solution will increase total contribution by $2. This may seem strange, since we originally stated the contribution per unit of B to be $6. However, remember that in the second solution all of the time available at work station 1 was utilized producing D (desks). If we produce one unit of B (bookcase), we must give up some amount of desks. Since each desk requires 6 hours at work station 1 and each bookcase requires 3 hours, to produce a book-case requires sacrificing ½ (that is, ³⁄₆) desk. Since the contribution per desk (D) is $8, we lose ½ ($8) $= $4 contribution from the ½ desk we sacrifice. Thus the *net* contribution for adding one bookcase to our solution is $6 − ½ ($8) $= $2.

Now consider the coefficient $-4/3$ of S_1. This simply means for each unit of S_1 added to our solution we would lose $4/3 contribution. Why? Remember S_1 is slack time at work station 1. Since all the time at work station 1 is being used to produce desks, to get a unit of S_1 means we sacrifice an hour of desk production. Since each desk requires 6 hours, we would sacrifice ⅙ desk. Contribution per desk is $8, so that we would sacrifice ⅙ ($8) $= $4/3.

Now consider equation 7–5

$$D = 21 - 1/2B - 1/6S_1$$

The constant 21 tells us that if $B = 0$ and $S_1 = 0$, as they do in the second solution, then $D = 21$. The coefficient $-½$ of B simply says that for each unit of B added to the solution ½ unit of D must be sacrificed. The reason for this was given previously. S_1's coefficient can be explained similarly.

The other constraint, equation 7–6,

$$S_2 = 54 - 3B + 1/3S_1$$

may be similarly interpreted. The constant 54 means that there will be 54 hours of idle time at work station 2 if solution 2 is implemented. The co-efficient of B means that each unit of B added to the solution will decrease the idle time by 3 hours. This may seem contradictory, since each book-case requires 4 hours at work station 2. However, remember that each unit of B added to the solution requires the sacrifice of ½ unit of D at work station 1. This means that the time required for ½ unit of D at work station 2 will also be freed. Since each desk requires 2 hours at work sta-tion 2, the sacrifice of ½ desk will free 1 additional hour at work station 2.

Thus the processing of 1 additional bookcase at work station 2 requires only a net of 3 hours of the idle time available (4 hours for processing of bookcase — 1 hour freed for $\frac{1}{2}$ desk less to be processed). The coefficient of S_1 may be similarly interpreted.

We are now ready to answer the question posed earlier, "Can we do better than solution 2?" Since the revised objective equation

$$Z = 168 + 2B - 4/3S_1$$

has a positive coefficient 2 in front of B, the answer is yes. We should add some B to our solution because each unit added will increase our total contribution by \$2. How much B? We must consider our revised constraints to answer this.

Equation 7–5 shows us that for each unit of B added we must give up $\frac{1}{2}$ unit of D. Since in our second solution we produce 21 desks (D), we are limited to

$$\frac{21 \text{ desks now produced}}{1/2 \text{ desk given up for 1 bookcase}} = 42 \text{ bookcases}$$

Equation 7–6 for work station 2

$$S_2 = 54 - 3B + 1/2S_1$$

tells us that we now have 54 hours of idle time available at work station 2 and each bookcase will take 3 hours; thus we are limited to

$$\frac{54 \text{ hours available}}{3 \text{ hours for 1 bookcase}} = 18 \text{ bookcases}$$

Since both work stations must be utilized to process bookcases, we are limited to 18 bookcases. Our third solution is therefore:

Third Solution

$$B = 18$$
$$S_1 = 0$$
$$D = 21 - 1/2B - 1/6S_1 = 21 - 1/2(18) - 1/6(0) = 12$$
$$S_2 = 54 - 3(18) + 1/3S_1 = 0$$

$$\text{Total contribution} = 6B + 8D = 6(18) + 8(12)$$
$$= \$204$$

The process from here on is simply a repeat of the steps we have already carried out. We alter the objective function and the constraint equations to reflect what we have done. They are presented below before alteration

Objective function

$$Z = 168 + 2B - 4/3S_1 \qquad (7\text{–}7)$$

Constraints

$$D = 21 - 1/2B - 1/6S_1 \qquad (7\text{--}5)$$

$$S_2 = 54 - 3B + 1/3S_1 \qquad (7\text{--}6)$$

The slack time in work station 2 was reduced to zero. Equations 7–5 and 7–6 must be changed to reflect this.

Solving 7–6 for B we obtain

$$S_2 = 54 - 3B + 1/3S_1$$
$$3B = 54 + 1/3S_1 - S_2$$
$$B = 18 + 1/9S_1 - 1/3S_2 \qquad (7\text{--}8)$$

Substituting this value for B into Equation 7–5 we obtain

$$D = 21 - 1/2B - 1/6S_1$$
$$D = 21 - 1/2(18 + 1/9S_1 - 1/3S_2) - 1/6S_1$$
$$D = 21 - 9 - 1/18S_1 + 1/6S_2 - 1/6S_1$$
$$D = 12 - 2/9S_1 + 1/6S_2 \qquad (7\text{--}9)$$

Finally, substituting for B in our objective function we obtain

$$Z = 168 + 2B - 4/3S_1$$
$$Z = 168 + 2(18 + 1/9S_1 - 1/3S_2) - 4/3S_1$$
$$Z = 168 + 36 + 2/9S_1 - 2/3S_2 - 4/3S_1$$
$$Z = 204 - 10/9S_1 - 2/3S_2 \qquad (7\text{--}10)$$

Summarizing, we now have:

Objective function

$$Z = 204 - 10/9S_1 - 2/3S_2 \qquad (7\text{--}10)$$

Constraints

$$D = 12 - 2/9S_1 + 1/6S_2 \qquad (7\text{--}9)$$

$$B = 18 + 1/9S_1 - 1/3S_2 \qquad (7\text{--}8)$$

To determine whether we can do better we consider the objective function. It is noted that all coefficients are negative. This means that if either S_1 or S_2 were increased total contribution would decrease. Our third solution is therefore the optimum solution.

It should be obvious that we have established an iteration procedure (i.e., a set of steps that are repeated over and over until some criterion is met). The procedure is quite simple and direct. It was from the above iteration procedure that the *simplex algorithm* was developed.

SENSITIVITY ANALYSIS

A user of linear programming should not confine his interest to the numerical values of an optimum solution. Since each of the coefficients in the linear programming model is an estimate and thus subject to error and/or change, the user needs to know how much the coefficients can vary without causing changes in a computed optimal solution.

Such an analysis is termed *sensitivity analysis* or postoptimality analysis. In some cases, a small variation in one of the coefficients may result in a new optimal solution with a significantly different value for the objective function. In other cases, a large change in a coefficient may result in no change in the optimal product mix and little change in the value of the maximum.

In this section, variations of the three following types will be discussed:

1. Variations in objective function coefficients
2. Variations in requirements coefficients
3. Variations in technological coefficients

Additionally, the effects of the addition or deletion of constraints, as well as the addition or deletion of variables can be studied, but these analyses are beyond the scope of this book.

Variations in objective function coefficients

In order to illustrate the use of sensitivity analysis, we will return to the problem discussed in the preceding section. Table 7–1 is a summary of the important data for this problem.

The problem was formulated in the LP framework as:

Maximize:

$$Z = 8D + 6B$$

Subject to:

$$6D + 3B \leq 126$$
$$2D + 4B \leq 96$$
$$D, B \geq 0$$

where D represented the number of desks produced and B the number of bookcases; the optimal production schedule was found to be:

$$D = 12$$
$$B = 18$$

This production schedule results in an optimal profit of $204.

Contribution per unit for each of the products is a function of their selling price, cost of materials, direct labor and other variable costs. Since each of these estimates is subject to error and to future changes, we wish to determine *how much variation each contribution per unit may have in each direction without causing a change in the present optimal solution.*

For example, how much can the contribution per desk vary from \$8 without changing the optimal product mix? In answering the question raised above, we may utilize our initial model (designated as I below) as well as our final set of equations designated as F.

I:	$Z - 8D - 6B$			$=0$	Row 0
	$6D + 3B$	$+ \ S_1$		$=126$	Row 1
	$2D + 2B$		$+S_2$	$=96$	Row 2
F:	Z	$+10/9S_1 \ +2/3S_2$		$=204$	Row 0
	D	$+2/9S_1 \ -1/6S_2$		$=12$	Row 1
	B	$-1/9S_1 \ +1/3S_2$		$=18$	Row 2

The first set of equations is the set used at the outset of the process of deriving the algebraic solution. The other set is the final set of equations derived in determining the algebraic solution.

In order to answer our question, suppose that Row 0 of I is changed such that the contribution of D becomes (\$8+δ). Row 0 of I becomes

$$Z - (8+\delta) \ D - 6B = 0 \qquad (7\text{-}11)$$

It can easily be shown that Row 0 of F would become

$$Z - \delta D + 10/9S_1 + 2/3S_2 = 204 \qquad (7\text{-}12)$$

In order to draw any conclusions about the critical range of δ, we must recreate a coefficient equal to 0 for D in Row 0. This may be done by multiplying Row 1 of F by δ and adding it to Equation 7-12 to give

$$Z + (10/9 + 2/9\delta)S_1 + (2/3 - 1/6\delta)S_2 = 204 + 12\delta \qquad (7\text{-}13)$$

Careful analysis of Equation 7-13 reveals that the current solution is optimal for

$$- 5 \leqq \delta \leqq 4 \qquad (7\text{-}14)$$

If δ is less than -5, the coefficient of S_1 becomes negative. If δ exceeds 4, the coefficient of S_2 becomes negative. Consequently, as soon as δ falls outside the range in Equation 7-14 the present solution is no longer optimal.

Another way of stating the result is that as long as the contribution of one desk is between \$3 and \$12 *and all other data of the problem remain constant*, the optimal product mix is unchanged. Note that the maximum contribution would change however. For example, if the contribution per desk increased to \$10, we would still produce 12 desks and 18 bookcases. However, the total contribution would increase to \$228 as opposed to \$204. This example serves to illustrate the difference between optimal schedule sensitivity and optimal contribution sensitivity.

Similar analysis shows that if the contribution per bookcase changes by δ where

$$- 2 \leqq \delta \leqq 10$$

there will be no change in the optimal product mix, provided all other data of the problem remain constant. Monetarily, as long as the contribution per bookcase is between $4 and $16, optimal contribution will be attained with the present product mix. This result is interesting in that contribution per unit may *increase* as much as $10 without changing the optimal product mix. However, a *decrease* of more than $2 will change the optimal product mix.

The above information would be beneficial to the decision maker in evaluating alternative pricing structures as well as in assessing the impact of changes in costs on production schedules. It also demonstrates that even though the contribution estimates are in fact estimates, the results for the model are not extremely sensitive to relatively large errors.

A word of warning: we considered a change in only one coefficient at a time, assuming that the other coefficient was constant. Coefficients could change simultaneously. Analysis of simultaneous changes in coefficients is called *ranging analysis;* the scope of the book allows no further discussion of this more general case of sensitivity analysis or of the techniques used.

Variations in requirements coefficients

We will now investigate whether the optimal solution is changed if a constant on the right-hand side of the constraints is changed. For example, suppose the number of hours available at work station 1 changes; how far can it vary without affecting our optimal solution? In order to answer this question we must investigate Row 0 of F,

$$Z + 10/9S_1 + 2/3S_2 = 204$$

Since, in our final solution, $S_1 = 0$, there was no unused time (slack time) in work station 1. Obviously then, if the number of hours available at work station 1 were decreased the number of desks and bookcases produced would be affected. The coefficient of S_1, $10/9$, represents the decrease in total contribution associated with making one less hour available. Similarly an increase of one additional hour would increase total contribution by $10/9$. Following the same reasoning, the incremental contribution from one additional hour available at work station 2 is $2/3.

It is obvious that the optimal product mix as well as the corresponding level of contribution may be quite sensitive to changes in the right-hand constants. It is not possible to change a right-hand constant without affecting the optimal product mix unless the corresponding slack variable is nonnegative.

The increases in contribution by additional hours at each of the work stations can be recognized as the marginal revenue products of these limited resources; i.e., the maximum worth of one more unit to the firm, assuming all other data of the problem remains constant.

Variations in technological coefficients

The technological coefficients are the coefficients on the left-hand side of the constraints. They are generally based on work standards. For example, the coefficient of D in Row 1 of I means that production of one desk requires 6 hours of processing time at work station 1. In actual practice a figure such as this would probably be determined by careful analysis of past experience and the application of time and motion studies. Since each such coefficient is an estimate, we would be interested in determining the effect of variations in any one of these coefficients on the optimal solution. For example, the actual number of hours of processing time at work station 1 for a desk could vary considerably from 6 hours because of the skill and experience of the workers, the age and conditions of the machines, or any number of other variables.

We will not make an effort here to discuss methods of assessing the impact of changes in technological coefficients. Such analyses require the development of concepts beyond the scope of this book.

Conclusion

The primary point made in this section on sensitivity analysis is that the linear programmer is not finished with his work when he has determined an optimal solution. The linear programming model is commonly referred to as an optimizing model, but it optimizes if and only if one assumes that all relevant variables have been included and that the values of the coefficients are sufficiently accurate. Since the decision maker is often faced with uncertainties as to such factors as future demand, prices, costs, technological change, and so forth, no experienced user of LP would be satisfied without carrying out careful sensitivity or post-optimality analyses of the types described above.

Linear programming and some basic economic concepts

That linear programming has a close relationship to traditional economic analysis should now be apparent. *In a two-product example the boundary of the feasibility area not only looks like a production possibility curve; that is precisely what it is. The isocontribution lines are the same isocontribution lines that appeared before.* The major difference between LP and the traditional analysis is that the curvilinear production possibility curve of traditional analyses is made up of straight-line segments in the LP formulation.

Linear programming relates to traditional economic analysis in other ways:

1. *Linear programming recognizes the irrelevance of fixed costs and focuses attention on the excess of incremental revenue over incremental costs*—and, in particular, on the contribution to overhead and profits.

In this way it is consistent with the principles of incremental reasoning introduced in Chapter 2.

2. *Implicitly linear programming takes opportunity costs into account.* This is quite clear in the simplex method (not described here), in which the procedure is one of comparing the additional revenue resulting from bringing a new product into the solution with the sacrifice of earnings from the products that must be given up.

3. *Linear programming also provides a basis for estimating the value of the marginal products of the inputs required.* It is interesting that this modern mathematical technique, which developed independently of economics, supplies those measures of marginal product which economists all along have insisted provide the correct criterion for decisions on the quantities of inputs to employ.

Joel Dean's pioneer book in managerial economics (published in 1951) ignored linear programming, which was then in its infancy. It is now apparent that linear programming provides a means for bridging the gap between traditional theory and the needs of management.

Empirical studies and illustrations

Perhaps the oil industry has gone farther than any other in the application of linear-programming techniques. The four main categories of the oil business are: (1) exploration, (2) drilling and production, (3) manufacturing, and (4) distribution and marketing. Linear programming has made important contributions to the last three. In production, linear programming is used to find the optimal use of alternative reservoirs available to a company along with the use of crude oil from the outside.[1]

Applications in manufacturing (refining) are more numerous. For example, it is used to find the optimal combination of products to be produced from given crude oil, to find the optimal blend of crude oils with varying characteristics to produce certain end products, or to solve some combination of these problems. Similarly, linear programming is used to determine the blend of various stocks coming from a refinery which will give the minimum cost of gasoline with required specifications. This blending program is complicated by the fact that the relation between tetraethyl lead content and octane rating is nonlinear, but a method of getting around the problem has been developed.

Oil companies have also used linear programming to minimize transportation costs from refineries to bulk terminals and to determine which refineries and bulk terminals should be expanded. They have also used the method to reduce costs from bulk terminals to service stations.

---

[1] W. W. Garvin, H. W. Grandall, J. B. John, and R. A. Spellman, "Applications of Linear Programming in the Oil Industry," *Management Science* (July 1957), reprinted in E. H. Bowman and R. B. Fetter, *Analyses of Industrial Operations* (Homewood, Ill.: Richard D. Irwin, Inc., 1959), pp. 3–27.

Similar applications are spreading to other industries, including scheduling of railway freight movements, the allocation of aircraft to alternative routes, and the determination of the optimum mix of products within a given plant. Each application presents its special difficulties, requiring considerable versatility in adapting the general method of linear programming to the specific problems at hand.

LEAST-COST COMBINATION OF INPUTS

The least-cost combination problem will be introduced by examples. Determination of least-cost combinations of inputs is a frequently encountered management problem. For example, petroleum refiners can obtain a final product with the desired properties (lubricants, heating oils, gasolines, etc.) through blending various combinations of basic petroleum distillates. Frankfurter manufacturers can use varying proportions of pork, beef, chicken, and dried milk. Breakfast cereal manufacturers can vary the proportions of different grains. The general problem of least-cost input determination was considered in Chapter 6. Under certain conditions, least-cost input combinations can be found through the use of linear programming.

Formulation of least-cost linear programming problems

An interesting example illustrates the use of LP in finding least-cost combinations of inputs. The Arion Company manufactures a particular animal feed from a grain and an oilseed meal. The buyers of this feed mix have specified that it must meet at least the following minimal nutritional requirements: it must contain at least 800 units of nutritional component P (protein) and 1,200 units of nutritional component E (energy). The product is sold in 110-pound bags. Ingredient G (a grain) contains 5 units per pound of nutrient P and 15 units per pound of nutrient E. Ingredient OM (an oilseed meal) contains 10 units of nutrient P and 10 units of nutrient E per pound. The Arion Company must pay 3¢ per pound for ingredient G and 4¢ per pound for ingredient OM. The Company wishes to determine the amount of each ingredient they should

TABLE 7–2

PROBLEM INFORMATION
(hypothetical least-cost problem)

Nutrient	Amount contained		Minimal Requirement
	Ingredient G (Grain)	Ingredient OM (Oilseed Meal)	
Component P (Protein)	5	10	800
Component E (Energy)	15	10	1,200
Cost/pound	3¢	4¢	

include in each 110-pound bag in order to meet the nutritional requirements while minimizing their expenditures. Table 7–2 summarizes the pertinent information.

Requirements for LP formulation. The requirements for formulating a least-cost input problem into the LP framework are basically the same as the requirements for product mix problems. They are presented below with only brief discussion since the reader should now be familiar with the basic approach.

1. *The objective function of the firm must be stated as a linear function of the cost of the inputs.* We define our two basic inputs as follows:

G = number of pounds of grain included in the mixture

OM = number of pounds of oilseed meal included in the mixture

Since the firm wishes to minimize its total cost for the mixture, the objective function may be stated mathematically as:

$$\text{Minimize } 3\text{¢ } G + 4\text{¢ } OM = \text{total cost}$$

The linear objective function infers constant marginal costs of inputs. No matter how many pounds of G are used in the mixture, the cost per pound is 3¢. The cost per pound of OM is 4¢ regardless of the quantity used.

2. *The restrictions placed on the blend must be stated explicitly as linear equalities or inequalities.* These restrictions again constitute the *constraints* of the problem.

For our example there are three constraints. Two are imposed by the necessary minimum nutritional requirements and one is due to the requirement that each sack contain at least 110 pounds. Stated mathematically the constraints are:

$$(1) \quad 5\, G + 10\, OM \geqq \quad 800$$

$$(2) \quad 15\, G + 10\, OM \geqq 1{,}200$$

$$(3) \qquad G + \quad\;\; OM \geqq \quad 110$$

The first constraint insures that the final mixture will contain at least 800 units of nutrient P. Each pound of G contains 5 units of nutrient P and each pound of OM contains 10 units of nutrient P. Therefore the total number of units of nutrient P is $5\, G + 10\, OM$, which must equal at least 800. The "greater than" ($>$) is used since we could feasibly include more than 800 units of nutrient P. Constraint 2 may be interpreted similarly for nutrient E. The third constraint ($G + OM \geq 110$) simply states that the total number of pounds in each bag must be at least 110. The reader should take care that he understands the significance of the linearity assumptions built into the constraints. If in doubt, he should refer to the corresponding section of the product-mix discussion.

3. *Nonnegativity requirements must be recognized.* We must constrain

each input to be either zero or positive, since a negative level of input has no physical meaning. Therefore we require that:

$$G \geqq 0 \text{ and } OM \geqq 0$$

Additionally, the assumption of divisibility is made; i.e., input levels may assume fractional values.

The entire problem is summarized below and formulated in an LP framework.

G = number of pounds of ingredient G included in final mixture $\Big\}$ variables
OM = number of pounds of ingredient OM included in final mixture

(1) Minimize $C = 3\textit{¢ } G + 4\textit{¢ } OM$ } Objective function

Subject to:

(2) $5\ G + 10\ OM \geqq\ \ \ 800$
(3) $15\ G + 10\ OM \geqq 1{,}200$ } constraints
(4) $G +\ \ \ \ OM \geqq\ \ \ 110$

and

(5) $G \geqq 0,\ OM \geqq 0$ } nonnegativity requirements

Management's problem is to find values for G and OM that satisfy the relations (2), (3), (4) and (5), and also minimize total cost.

The graphic solution

This problem may be solved algebraically or by the use of the simplex method mentioned earlier. However, since there are only two variables, we will solve it graphically. The basic steps laid out for solving product mix problems are appropriate for the solution of least cost combination of input problems also.

Step 1. Plot the constraints in the problem on a graph. Figure 7–8 is such a graph. The horizontal axis represents the number of pounds of feed ingredient G, while the vertical axis represents the number of pounds of feed ingredient OM. Because of the nonnegativity requirements (5), we may restrict our search for a solution to the first quadrant.

The line in the graph represents the constraint imposed by the minimum requirements for the number of units of nutrient P per bag of the final mixture. It was found by plotting the equation

$$5\ G + 10\ OM = 800$$

Since the actual constraint (2) is an inequality, each point on the line and every point *to the right* of the line represents an input combination which satisfies this constraint.

Similarly, in Figure 7–9 the constraint imposed by minimum require-

FIGURE 7–8

FEASIBLE REGION FOR NUTRIENT COMPONENT P

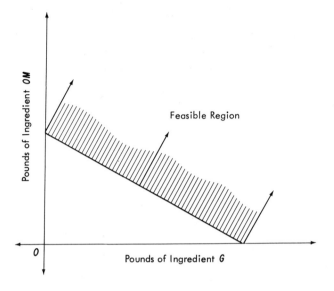

FIGURE 7–9

FEASIBLE REGION FOR NUTRIENT COMPONENT E

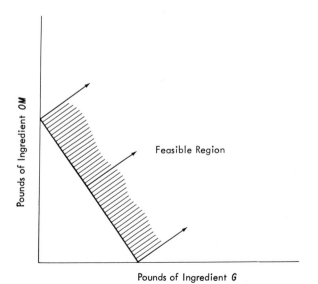

ments for nutrient E is plotted. Every point on the line and to the right of the line represents an input combination which satisfies the constraint

$$15\ G + 10\ OM \geqq 1{,}200$$

Finally, in Figure 7–10 the constraint $G + OM \geq 110$ is plotted. This line is an isoquant showing all possible combinations of both inputs which total to 110 pounds in the final mixture.

FIGURE 7–10

FEASIBLE REGION FOR BAG WEIGHT

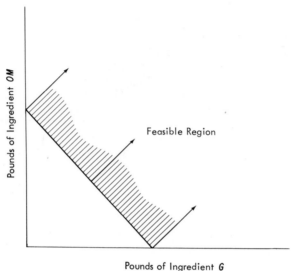

In Figure 7–11 all three constraints are plotted on the same graph. Only those points that lie in the shaded area satisfy all three constraints. This set of points then comprises the feasible region. The problem is to select a point from this set of points that minimizes total cost.

Step 2. Calculate the coordinates of each corner point, i.e., each point at which two or more constraints intersect (including the non-negativity constraints). It is obviously only necessary to calculate the corner points that are feasible. In this example, there are four such points labeled A, B, C, and D on Figure 7–11.

Point	Coordinates
A	(0,120)
B	(20,90)
C	(60,50)
D	(160,0)

FIGURE 7–11

FEASIBLE REGION WITH ALL CONSTRAINTS

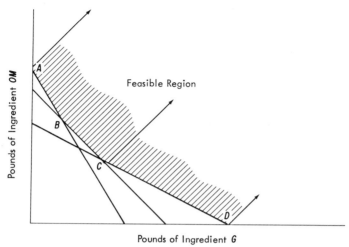

Pounds of Ingredient OM

Feasible Region

Pounds of Ingredient G

Step 3. With all feasible input combinations delineated, the remaining task is to select the one that meets the objective of minimizing cost. The optimum solution must lie at a corner point of the feasible region.

The student may intuitively understand the reason for this by studying Figure 7–12. Figure 7–12 is the feasible region as depicted in Figure 7–11 with a set of isocost lines superimposed on it. Since the cost of each

FIGURE 7–12

FEASIBLE REGION WITH ISOCOST CURVES

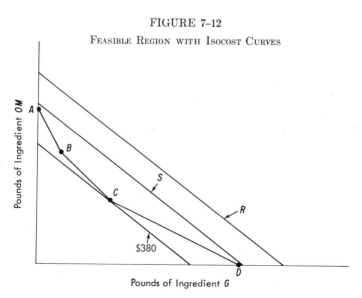

Pounds of Ingredient OM

$380

Pounds of Ingredient G

pound of G is 3¢ and each pound of OM costs 4¢, the total cost of the mixture is $3\ G + 4\ OM$ (our objective equation). By plotting $3\ G + 4\ OM = TC$ and varying TC, a set of parallel isocost lines is generated. For example, the line R was formed by plotting the equation

$$3\ G + 4\ OM = \$6.00$$

All points on this line represent input combinations resulting in a total cost of \$6.00. The isocost line S was found by plotting the equation

$$3\ G + 4\ OM = \$5.00$$

All input combinations on this line result in a total cost of \$5.00. Since the firm is trying to minimize total cost, a shift to the left of the isocost curve is advantageous. The rational firm will use an input combination found by shifting the isocost curve as far to the left as possible. However, since the constraints must be met, the isocost curve must have at least one point in common with the feasible region. It should therefore be obvious that the optimal solution will occur at a corner point of the feasible region.

The total cost for the input combination at each corner point is calculated below.

Corner Point		Total Cost
(0,120)	3 (0) + 4 (120) =	\$4.80
(20,90)	3 (20) + 4 (90) =	\$4.20
(60,50)	3 (60) + 4 (50) =	\$3.80
(160,0)	3 (160) + 4 (0) =	\$4.80

Thus the optimum input combination is 60 pounds of Ingredient G and 50 pounds of Ingredient OM. The total cost will be \$3.80 for each 110 pound sack of the final mixture. The reader should satisfy himself that such a mixture satisfies the minimum nutritional requirements.

Empirical illustration: Computone Systems, Inc.

Computone Systems, Inc., a firm with headquarters in Atlanta, Georgia, provides a service which the firm has named "Instant Linear Programming." This service is used by numerous animal and poultry food companies in formulating rations. A specialized console is provided to the user. At any time, night or day, seven days a week, the feed company nutritionist can quickly set up the ingredient costs and other data of a least-cost linear programming problem by flipping switches on the face of the console. He then dials the number of the company's central computer, waits for a tone, and presses a switch to send the problem inputs. Within minutes, the solution to the problem is printed at the feed company's console.

Figure 7–13 is an example of a Computone Systems, Inc. computer

FIGURE 7–13

LEAST-COST FORMULATION OF A POULTRY RATION

LEAST COST FORMULA

PLANT............COMPUTONE SYSTEMS, INC. #2
PRODUCT NO. 104
PRODUCT NAME......BROILER FINISHER
DATE AND TIME......04/10/73 18.06.21

AMOUNT NUM INGREDIENT NAME	SCALE READING	COST	LOW RANGE	HIGH RANGE	INGREDIENT MIN	INGREDIENT MAX
1060.94 061 CN GR YL 9.0/12	1060.9	3.20		4.47		
560.81 283 SOYBEAN ML S-49	1621.7	10.00	9.17	16.38		
141.95 072 CN GL ML-60/125	1763.7	13.20	11.79	28.88		
120.91 092 FAT AN&VEG HYDR	1884.6	9.00	3.67	26.35		140.0
43.17 217 PHOS DEFLUOR	1927.8	4.10	.45	18.93		
36.37 098 FEATHER ML HYD	1964.2	6.20	3.91	8.39		60.0
10.95 146 LIMESTONE	1975.1	.60		5.01		
10.00 125 FIXED INGRED	1985.1	18.00			10.0	10.0
6.00 107 FISH ML ANCHOVE	1991.1	19.50		20.73		6.0
2.91 251 SALT	1994.0	1.50		33.06		
2.00 319 VIT PMX BROIL-5	1996.0	48.00			2.0	2.0
1.00 053 COPPER SULFATE	1997.0	3.00			1.0	1.0
1.00 299 TR-MIN BROIL-DM	1998.0	10.10			1.0	1.0
1.00 050 COCCIDIOSTAT	1999.0	100.00			1.0	1.0
98 310 VIT A 30,000	2000.0	30.00		230.06		

④ $129.14 PER TON

⑤		
002 ALFA.DHY 17-516	4.00	1.09
156 MT&BONE SCRP-50	12.50	8.30	200.00
057 CN GR YL 8.0/12	99.00	3.01
060 CN GR YL 8.9/12	99.00	3.18
147 LYSINE-L 50PCT	999.00	84.99

① FORMULA SPECIFICATIONS
② OPTIMUM FORMULATION
③ INVENTORY RESTRICTIONS
④ FORMULA COST
⑤ OPPORTUNITY PRICES FOR UNUSED INGREDIENTS

computone
SYSTEMS, INC. 361 E. Paces Ferry Road, N.E. Atlanta, Georgia 30305

① RESTRICTION NAME	MINIMUM	ACTUAL	MAXIMUM	NUTRIENT COST
WEIGHT	1.00	1.00	1.00	4.0367
MET ENERGY POULTRY	1500.00	1500.00	1500.00	.0035
PRODUCTIVE ENERGY		1082.96		
CRUDE PROTEIN	20.50	24.72		
DIGESTABLE PROTEIN		21.65		
ARGININE	1.15	1.55		
LYSINE	1.10	1.10		1.7805
METHIONINE	.45	.45		3.5642
METH & CYSTINE	.84	.84		1.3610
TRYPTOPHANE	.21	.28		
GLYCINE		1.17		
HISTIDINE		.57		
LEUCINE		2.41		
ISOLEUCINE		1.18		
PHENYLALANINE		1.31		
PHENYL & TYROSINE		2.27		
THREONINE		.99		
VALINE		1.28		
CRUDE FAT		8.55		
CRUDE FIBER		2.51		
MOISTURE		8.81		
ASH		5.34		
CALCIUM	1.00	1.00	1.05	.1203
PHOSPHORUS-AVAIL	.55	.55	.57	.2031
PHOSPHORUS-TOTAL		.78		
SALT		.24		
SODIUM	.20	.20	.30	.1403
POTASSIUM		.70		
MANGANESE		40.60		
ZINC		31.50		
IRON		118.70		
COPPER		62.61		
IODINE		.12		
XANTHOPHYLL	10.00	15.24		
CAROTENE		1.54		
VITAMIN A	4.00	4.00		.0076
VITAMIN E		2.68		
THIAMIN		1.27		
RIBOFLAVIN		1.98		
NIACIN		18.15		
PANTOTHENIC ACID		5.46		
CHOLINE		524.40		
PYRIDOXINE		2.93		
FOLACIN		.25		
BIOTIN		.06		
VITAMIN B-12		4.21		

PRODUCT PRICING OPTION

PLANT............COMPUTONE SYSTEMS, INC. #2
DATE AND TIME......04/11/73 11.38.54

		LAST FORMULA ORIG $ TON	NEW FORM ACT $ TON	ACT $ TON	PURCH MARGIN	LAST FORM MARKET $ TON	MARGIN TON	TOTAL MARKET VALUE	CWT
PROD NUM	DATE								
102	04/04/73	128.33	130.54	130.54	4.61	135.15	10.00	145.15	7.26
104	04/11/73	129.14	130.20	128.27	6.51	136.71	6.00	142.71	7.14
112	03/15/73	131.05	122.54	122.54	6.29	128.83	18.00	146.83	7.34
601	03/28/73	123.03	123.71	123.71	11.18	134.89	32.00	166.89	8.34
653	03/15/73	83.19	78.67	78.67	1.94	80.61	23.00	103.61	5.18
664	04/03/73	77.53	81.86	78.09	-1.62	80.24	14.00	94.24	4.71
803	03/28/73	98.76	93.50	92.95	-1.02	92.48	22.00	114.48	5.72
822	04/11/73	75.39	76.50	74.25	-.87	75.63	16.00	91.63	4.58
841	04/11/73	82.31	82.31	82.31	-1.38	80.93	25.00	105.93	5.30
851	03/02/73	63.25	69.05	66.41	-.22	68.83	20.00	88.83	4.44
		①	②	③	④	⑤	⑥	⑦	

① Least Cost Amount from Last Solution
② Last Solution at Actual Costs
③ New Least-Cost Solution at Actual Costs
④ Column ③ minus Column ②
⑤ Last Solution at Market Costs
⑥ Margin Value Previously Stored
⑦ Column ⑤ plus Column ⑥

SIXTY NUTRIENT VALUES FOR EACH INGREDIENT
SOLVES PROBLEMS WITH UP TO
40 INGREDIENTS AND 40 NUTRIENT RESTRICTIONS

For Additional Information Phone: Area Code (404) 261-0070
or write COMPUTERIZED FORMULATION DIVISION

COMPUTONE SYSTEMS, INC.
361 East Paces Ferry Road, N. E.
Atlanta, Georgia 30305

INVENTORY OPTION

PLANT............COMPUTONE SYSTEMS, INC. #2
DATE AND TIME......04/11/73 11.43.46
OPTION...00 INGREDIENT USAGE REPORT

NUM NAME	POUNDS	TONS	COST TONS
2 ALFA.DHY 17-516	28481.49	14.2500	1139
4 ALFA.DHY 20-660	1463.47	.7300	73
50 COCCIDIOSTAT	199.99	.1000	200
53 COPPER SULFATE	119.99	.0600	3
61 CN GR YL 9.0/12	859641.68	429.8200	28368
69 CORN GLUTEN FD	12000.00	6.0000	540
72 CN GL ML 60-125	18590.81	9.3000	2453
79 COTSD ML SOL-44	46087.73	23.0400	3433
86 DIST DR SOL CN	52221.47	26.1100	2611
92 FAT AN&VEG HYDR	82593.53	41.3000	7433
98 FEATHER ML HYD	11645.29	5.8200	722
107 FISH ML ANCHOVE	720.00	.3600	140
113 FISH ML MENHADN	11608.09	5.8000	2553
125 FIXED INGRED	5799.99	2.9000	1044
138 HOMINY FD YL	4812.17	2.4100	141
146 LIMESTONE	31770.29	15.8900	190
160 METH DL 98	590.01	.3000	590
161 METH 100	313.46	.1600	329
163 MILO-9	219815.45	109.9100	6374
172 MOLASSES. CANE	32000.00	16.0000	1020
201 PH 18.5.20 CA22	1581.14	.7900	69
217 PHOS DEFLUOR	18585.77	9.2900	762
231 POUL BY-PROD ML	20000.00	10.0000	3300
244 RICE MILL FEED	2368.62	1.1800	33
251 SALT	5480.97	2.7400	82
283 SOYBEAN ML S-49	286108.76	143.0500	28610
299 TR MIN BROIL-DM	119.99	.0600	12
308 UREA 281 45PCT	11547.83	5.7700	665
310 VIT A 30.000	623.04	.3100	186
319 VIT PMX BROIL-5	240.00	.1200	115
328 VIT PMX SWN 769	353.14	.1800	70
340 WHEAT MIDDS STD	260014.37	130.0100	9750
734 DICALCIUM PHOSPHATE	21226.29	10.6100	1252
961 VIT PX LAY 5.7	1275.00	.6400	255
TOTALS	2049999.83	1025.0000	104529

PROD	POUNDS	TONS	PROD	POUNDS	TONS
102	160000.00	80.00	104	240000.00	120.00
112	400000.00	200.00	601	200000.00	100.00
653	80000.00	40.00	664	60000.00	30.00
803	170000.00	85.00	822	240000.00	120.00
841	240000.00	120.00	851	260000.00	130.00
TOTAL	2050000.00	1025.00			

FIGURE 7–14

Least-Cost Formulation of a Sausage

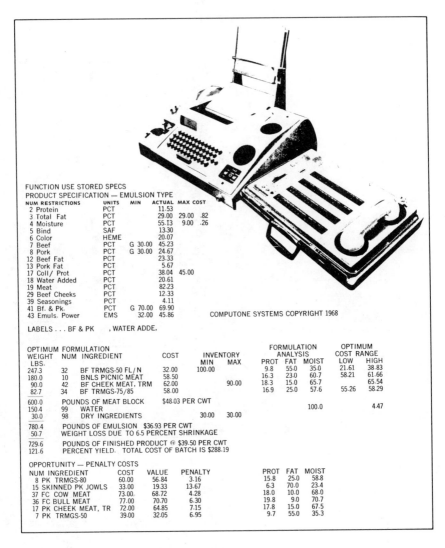

FUNCTION USE STORED SPECS
PRODUCT SPECIFICATION — EMULSION TYPE

NUM RESTRICTIONS	UNITS	MIN	ACTUAL	MAX	COST
2 Protein	PCT		11.53		
3 Total Fat	PCT		29.00	29.00	.82
4 Moisture	PCT		55.13	9.00	.26
5 Bind	SAF		13.30		
6 Color	HEME		20.07		
7 Beef	PCT	G 30.00	45.23		
8 Pork	PCT	G 30.00	24.67		
12 Beef Fat	PCT		23.33		
13 Pork Fat	PCT		5.67		
17 Coll/ Prot	PCT		38.04	45.00	
18 Water Added	PCT		20.61		
19 Meat	PCT		82.23		
29 Beef Cheeks	PCT		12.33		
39 Seasonings	PCT		4.11		
41 Bf. & Pk.	PCT	G 70.00	69.90		
43 Emuls. Power	EMS	32.00	45.86		

COMPUTONE SYSTEMS COPYRIGHT 1968

LABELS . . . BF & PK   , WATER ADDE,

OPTIMUM FORMULATION

WEIGHT LBS.	NUM	INGREDIENT	COST	INVENTORY MIN	INVENTORY MAX	FORMULATION ANALYSIS PROT	FAT	MOIST	OPTIMUM COST RANGE LOW	HIGH
247.3	32	BF TRMGS-50 FL/N	32.00	100.00		9.8	55.0	35.0	21.61	38.83
180.0	10	BNLS PICNIC MEAT	58.50			16.3	23.0	60.7	58.21	61.66
90.0	42	BF CHEEK MEAT, TRM	62.00		90.00	18.3	15.0	65.7		65.54
82.7	34	BF TRMGS-75/85	58.00			16.9	25.0	57.6	55.26	58.29
600.0		POUNDS OF MEAT BLOCK	$48.03 PER CWT							
150.4	99	WATER						100.0		4.47
30.0	98	DRY INGREDIENTS		30.00	30.00					
780.4		POUNDS OF EMULSION $36.93 PER CWT								
50.7		WEIGHT LOSS DUE TO 6.5 PERCENT SHRINKAGE								
729.6		POUNDS OF FINISHED PRODUCT @ $39.50 PER CWT								
121.6		PERCENT YIELD. TOTAL COST OF BATCH IS $288.19								

OPPORTUNITY — PENALTY COSTS

NUM	INGREDIENT	COST	VALUE	PENALTY	PROT	FAT	MOIST
8	PK TRMGS-80	60.00	56.84	3.16	15.8	25.0	58.8
15	SKINNED PK JOWLS	33.00	19.33	13.67	6.3	70.0	23.4
37	FC COW MEAT	73.00	68.72	4.28	18.0	10.0	68.0
36	FC BULL MEAT	77.00	70.70	6.30	19.8	9.0	70.7
17	PK CHEEK MEAT, TR	72.00	64.85	7.15	17.8	15.0	67.5
7	PK TRMGS-50	39.00	32.05	6.95	9.7	55.0	35.3

formulation for a poultry ration. Note that the printout includes complete nutritional specifications for the ration, the optimal formulation with price ranging for each ingredient, forcing and limiting of ingredients to reflect inventory and nutritional considerations, and the calculation of opportunity prices at which each unused ingredient would enter the formulation. Product pricing and perpetual inventory options are also available, as shown in the figure.

Computone Systems, Inc. provides a similar service for meat companies, in which linear programming is used to determine least-cost combinations of ingredients for various sausages. Figure 7–14 shows a Computone "mini-terminal" (it is smaller than the company's standard console) and an example of a least-cost sausage formulation. The printout includes incremental cost for each effective restriction (reduction in cost if the restriction is relaxed by one unit), price ranging for each ingredient included in the least-cost formulation, and opportunity prices for each ingredient that does not enter the formulation.

These are examples of highly sophisticated planning techniques that are economically available to medium and small firms from vendors of management services. Computone Systems, Inc. has over 60 of these specialized consoles installed nationwide.

INVENTORY OPTIMIZATION

Let us begin by posing the question, "What is inventory?" In general, inventory is an idle resource. It is a stock, as contrasted to resources that are flowing. There are three main types of inventories: raw materials and purchased parts and supplies, work-in-process, and finished goods.

1. Raw materials and purchased parts and supplies: Items in this type of inventory are generally purchased by the firm from an outside source. It includes such things as sheets of metal, bottles of chemicals, small tools, and office supplies. *Raw materials and purchased parts and supplies* are items that will be used up or transformed in the production press.

2. Work-in-process: Transformation from raw material to finished product does not usually take place in one continuous flow. Instead, the raw material is partially processed at one work station, then moves to another work station for further processing, and so forth. Partially processed material that accumulates between work stations or departments is known as *work-in-process* inventory.

3. Finished goods: Generally, when the transformation process is completed and the final product is obtained, it is not shipped out immediately. It is stored in a warehouse until someone requests it or until transportation is available. Accumulations of finished goods or products are known as *finished goods* inventory.

The functions of inventory

The fact that inventory is an idle resource does not imply that it serves no purpose. There are several functions of inventory. Although any particular inventory does not necessarily have all of the following functions, it may simultaneously fulfill more than one of them:

1. Lot-size inventories. Consider the situation in which a firm needs only one-half box car of an item a month. Because of the high freight charges for partial box car loads, the firm may find it advantageous to order a full box car. This larger order size increases the average stock of the item at the plant. The firm is willing to carry the increased stock or inventory in order to reduce transportation costs. Similar situations may occur when the firm's own cost of setting up machines for a production process is very high. The firm may produce more of the product than is required for immediate usage or shipments in order to save on setup costs. Inventories generated for either of these reasons are known as *lot-size* inventories.

2. Seasonal or anticipations inventories.   These inventories also facilitate a smooth production flow. For example, toy manufacturers expect the greatest demand for their products in the Christmas season. In *anticipation* of this seasonal demand, they spread the work over earlier months; i.e., they produce more than is demanded during these months. They are willing to carry the seasonal inventories in order to have smoother annual production schedules; fluctuating production schedules that are matched to seasonally varying sales rates result in very high costs for hiring, training, overtime, layoffs, and so forth.

3. Decoupling (buffer) inventories.   Probably the most important function of inventories is to decouple successive operations. The production process is made up of successive stages or activities; production moves from ordering and receiving raw materials to partial processing of the raw materials at one work station to further processing at the next work station and so forth. Inventories can *decouple (buffer)* each pair of activities in this process, so that the required operations can be somewhat independent. Raw material inventories, for example, buffer the production process from the uncertainty of material deliveries. Work-in-process inventories buffer successive stages in product development from work disruptions in prior stages; and, finally, finished goods inventories insulate the production process from the uncertain demands of customers.

4. Transit inventories.   *Transit* inventories exist because material must be moved from one place to another and this move requires time. Although this inventory is not being used, someone owns it and such costs as insurance and taxes are being experienced. This inventory must therefore be considered if one is to carry out a thorough analysis of inventory problems and costs.

The objectives of an inventory system

Before designing any system, one must know the objectives which the system is to meet. Inventory systems are no exception. We must now consider the question, "What is the objective of any inventory system?"

Here we run into conflicting objectives because the way inventory is viewed by a member of an organization depends in large part on the department to which the individual belongs. Most firms have at least three basic departments or functional areas: marketing, finance, and production.

Frequently the marketing department views inventory as an unlimited resource. Its objective is to maximize customer service. It can do this by having short delivery times, and therefore it feels that the production department has failed if any item is not available when an order can be taken. In general, *maximizing customer service* requires relatively *high* levels of finished goods inventory.

On the other hand, the finance department views inventory as a necessary evil. Inventory ties up capital that could be used elsewhere, thus generating an opportunity cost. High levels of inventory also increase costs of such items as storage, taxes, insurance, pilferage, and deterioration. Since the finance department generally has an objective to *minimize the level of investment costs,* the finance department desires relatively *low* levels of all types of inventory.

Finally, the production department's objective is to *maximize production efficiency.* They desire inventory levels sufficient to insulate successive steps in the production process and to allow larger production runs with fewer setup costs. In general, the production objective requires *high* levels of all types of inventory.

Objectives of the departments are obviously conflicting. Is it possible to devise an inventory system that can strike a satisfactory balance among these conflicting objectives?

Inventory associated costs and their nature

In order to answer the preceding question, it is first necessary to pose another question: Is there a common denominator among the conflicting objectives? The answer is yes. Each of the objectives is related to certain costs. For example, from the point of view of the sales department, too little inventory results in back orders and stockouts and their associated costs. The finance department, however, views the costs from a different point of view. Too much inventory results in such costs as insurance costs, taxes, storage costs, and capital investment. The production department is concerned with costs associated with changes in the production level such as hiring, training, laying off workers, overtime, idle time, and setup costs.

It is evident that some of these costs *rise* with increases in inventory levels and some *decrease* with larger inventory levels. What then should be the objective of an inventory system? *The objective should be to establish inventory levels that minimize total inventory-associated costs.* It is the purpose of this section to explore the nature of these costs using four broad classifications.

1. Inventory-carrying costs. This classification includes all costs directly incurred by the company because of the level of inventory on hand. As the level of inventory increases, these costs will increase.

a. Cost of capital: Some businessmen make the mistake of assuming that cash tied up in inventories costs nothing. However, money invested in inventory is not available for other purposes. It has an "opportunity cost," and inventory can tie up large amounts of capital. It is not uncommon for a manufacturing firm to have as much as 25 percent of its total capital in the form of inventories.

How does a firm estimate the cost of capital for inventories? Some firms use the bank interest rate to estimate this element of carrying costs. However, very few businessmen would be satisfied with uses of their firm's capital which do not earn more than a lender's rate of return. For this reason, many firms use the rate of return which the firm expects to realize on the average from its total capital investment. The theoretically correct rate is the firm's *marginal cost of capital,* which is discussed in the capital-budgeting chapter of this book. It would usually be somewhat higher than the firm's average rate of return.

This element of carrying cost is often expressed as a percentage of the value of average inventory on hand.

b. Storage and handling costs: Inventory must be stored. If storage space is rented or could be used for other productive purposes (opportunity cost) a charge for the storage space should be considered. However, if storage space is in a state of excess capacity that cannot be used for other productive purposes, such a charge is not justified. In either case, the cost of moving items to and from storage, including damages, wages and equipment expense, should be included.

c. Costs of obsolescence, deterioration, pilferage: Any one of these costs may be major or minor depending on the nature of the inventory under consideration. For example, in style goods industries, the problem of obsolescence is acute; because of changing sales patterns and customer desires, some inventory may be no longer salable. Likewise, items such as fresh fruits and vegetables may have extremely high costs due to partial spoilage and deterioration. Other items may get dirty from handling, may dry out, may get damp, or may deteriorate in other ways.

The total of these costs can usually be obtained by dividing their actual costs, as determined by cost accounting, by average value of inventory.

d. Taxes and insurance costs: Many states and cities have inventory taxes. These may be based on inventory investment at a particular time of the year or on average inventory investment for the entire year. Most companies also carry insurance on their inventories. Tax and insurance charges are usually expressed as a percentage of average inventory investment, and thus require no additional calculations.

It should be evident that *all of the costs under the general heading of inventory-carrying costs vary directly with the size of inventory.* There is no general rule as to how an aggregate figure for carrying cost should be calculated. The specific components which are important in this calculation vary from case to case depending on the nature of the specific inventory under consideration. For example, as has been previously pointed out, obsolescence as a part of inventory-carrying cost varies widely with time and is not the same for different items in an inventory. The same is true for most of the other costs composing carrying cost. This would perhaps indicate the desirability of calculating a different carrying cost for each item in the stock list. Since this is generally impractical, average figures for all inventory or for broad classes of inventory are usually chosen. For manufacturing companies, annual carrying costs average about 20 percent of average annual inventory investment. For other types of firms, the figure varies from 5 to 65 percent. However, for reasons pointed out above, one must not rely too readily on averages.

2. Ordering and setup costs. This classification of inventory costs is composed of costs that vary inversely with the size of orders and thus inversely with the size of inventory. The term *order cost* applies to the expense of issuing an order to an outside supplier. When material is ordered, orders must be written and invoices processed. The lots received must be inspected and delivered to stores or production stations. Order costs include the fixed cost of maintaining an order department and the variable costs of preparing and executing purchase requisitions. Perhaps writing a purchase order does not sound expensive. However, some companies estimate the cost to run from $5 to $15 per order. The cost may be hundreds of dollars if bids must be requested and processed. As an estimate, to be used with considerable judgment, the cost of the procurement operation, including overhead charges, divided by the number of orders placed, may be used to approximate order cost.

The term *setup cost* refers to the physical work incurred in preparing for a production run (setting up equipment and adjusting machines) and the clerical costs of shop orders, scheduling, and expediting.

Setup costs and ordering costs per order remain relatively constant regardless of the size of the order.

3. Out-of-stock costs. This cost is perhaps the most difficult one to estimate. If an item is not available when a customer orders it, sales may be lost or extra costs may be incurred. If it is possible to expedite a rush delivery, the cost may be identified as the difference between the usual cost of delivery and the extra cost for accelerated service. The cost of processing a back order as well as overtime required should be included. Some firms estimate the out-of-stock cost as simply the loss of contribution from the sale of the item. This approach is applicable only when there is no loss of future business.

The most difficult part, however, is to estimate the cost of possible customer dissatisfaction. Because of this difficulty, firms sometimes designate a "reasonable" level of customer service by specifying the percent of time they are willing to experience a stockout. Such an inventory policy has a cost that increases as probability of stockout is reduced.

4. Capacity-associated costs. When it becomes necessary to alter the rate of production, certain costs are incurred. These costs include such items as overtime, idle time, hiring, training, and layoff costs and can often be calculated by using data from accounting records.

A clear understanding of the functions of inventory and the nature of the associated costs is essential in designing an inventory system. Some of the costs are difficult to estimate and their relationships to level of inventory should be subjected to careful analysis. In the following section, a simple inventory model, one that can serve as a basic building block in more complex systems, is explained.

The economic order quantity (lot size) model

In this section a basic inventory model is developed. It is concerned with inventories that take advantage of the economies of lot size. Such inventories are advantageous even under conditions of certainty. In order to develop this model a number of simplifying assumptions are made.

1. Demand is known and constant. The total number of items required for one year is known exactly. Additionally it is assumed that the usage rate of the items is uniform over time.
2. Lead time is known and constant. *Lead time* is simply the time elapsing between the time an order is placed and the order is received.
3. Orders are received instantaneously, i.e., the entire order is received at the same time. For example, if lead time is known to be two weeks and an order is placed, we are assuming that at the end of two weeks the entire order is received.
4. The purchase price is constant. This is to say that the price of each item is constant and does not change because of order size. This assumption rules out quantity discounts.
5. The ordering (setup) costs are constant. The cost per order does not vary with changes in the number of units ordered.

There are two basic questions, (1) how much should be ordered each time an order is placed and (2) when should an order be placed.

Before trying to answer these questions, it will be helpful to consider the behavior of inventory level under conditions 1–5. Figure 7–15 is a graphical representation of inventory level under the assumed conditions. In this figure, Q represents the quantity that is ordered each time an order is placed. We designate it as EOQ or Economic Order Quantity. The sloping lines represent the inventory level declining as the items are used. Rate of use is constant and therefore inventory declines in a straight line. Each line has the same slope due to assumption (1). When the inventory drops to the level ROP (Reorder Point), an order is placed. Exactly when the level drops to zero, the new order is received. It should

FIGURE 7–15

INVENTORY LEVEL UNDER ASSUMPTIONS 1–5

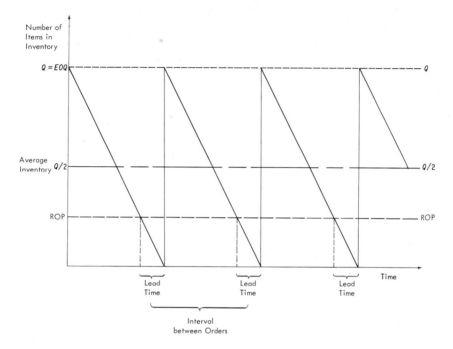

be noted that under these conditions stock-outs will not occur. The ROP is determined by noting the lead time, which is constant, and calculating the number of items used during this time. Since demand is constant and lead time is constant, the ROP is easily calculated and does not change. The average inventory level is $(Q + 0)/2$ or simply $Q/2$.

The remaining problem is to determine the EOQ. We only need to be concerned with two basic costs, ordering costs and carrying costs. Because of the simplifying assumptions, other costs such as purchase costs and stock-out costs are not dependent on the decision.

Trial and error approach. An example illustrates the trial and error method of determining EOQ. Assume that a firm is ordering a basic stock item from an outside supplier. The firm uses 1,000 of these items per year at a price of $2 per unit. The firm has estimated the cost per order to be $2.50 and the carrying cost to be 25 percent of the value of average inventory. The firm wishes to determine a quantity to order which will minimize total inventory-associated costs. One order per year (1,000 items) would obviously minimize yearly ordering cost but would also result in maximum carrying costs because of the large resulting average inventory. The average inventory level could be substantially reduced by ordering 50 times a year, but this would result in high annual ordering costs.

The example highlights the basic tradeoffs in an economic order quantity problem. In general, carrying costs can be kept low by ordering frequently but the resulting ordering costs will be high. Similarly ordering costs can be kept low by ordering infrequently but the resulting carrying costs will be high. The determination of economic order quantities requires finding the quantity which results in the lowest *total* cost.

This tradeoff is depicted graphically in Figure 7–16. In this figure as the number of units per order increases, carrying cost increases. However, the ordering cost decreases.

FIGURE 7–16

GRAPHICAL EOQ DETERMINATION

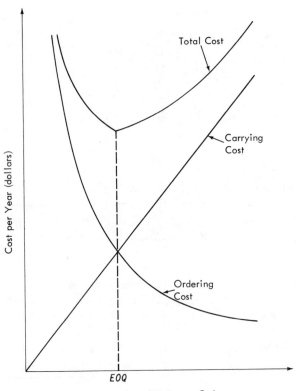

The total cost for any point is simply the sum of ordering cost and carrying cost at that point. The resulting total cost curve is U-shaped. The objective is to determine the number of units per order that corresponds to the minimum point on this total cost curve.

Returning to the example, the approximate order quantity can be determined by trial and error, and is shown in Table 7–3.

$$\begin{array}{ll} \text{Carrying costs} \\ \text{per Year} \end{array} = \begin{pmatrix} \text{Number of units} \\ \text{in inventory on} \\ \text{average} \end{pmatrix} \times \begin{pmatrix} \text{Value of} \\ \text{1 unit} \end{pmatrix} \times \begin{pmatrix} \text{Carrying cost} \\ \text{Percentage} \end{pmatrix}$$

$$= Q/2 \times P \times C$$
$$= QCP/2$$

$$\begin{array}{ll} \text{Ordering costs} \\ \text{per Year} \end{array} = (\text{number of orders}) \times (\text{cost per order})$$
$$= R/Q \times S$$
$$= RS/Q$$

$$\text{Ordering Costs} = RS/Q$$
$$\text{Carrying Cost} = QCP/2$$
$$\frac{QCP}{2} = RS/Q$$
$$Q^2 CP = 2RS$$
$$Q^2 = 2RS/CP$$
$$Q = \sqrt{2RS/CP}$$

The final formula above can be used to solve directly for *EOQ*. Values of the variables in the previous example are given below and the formula is utilized to solve directly for the EOQ.

$$R = 1,000 \text{ units (annual requirements)}$$
$$S = \$2.50/\text{order (costs/order)}$$
$$C = .25 \ (25\%) \text{ (carrying cost as percent)}$$
$$P = \$2/\text{unit (purchase cost/unit)}$$
$$Q = \sqrt{2RS/CP}$$
$$= \sqrt{\frac{2(1,000) \ (2.50)}{2(.25)}}$$
$$= \sqrt{\frac{5,000}{.50}}$$
$$= \sqrt{10,000}$$
$$= 100 \text{ units}$$

The final result is the same as found by the trial and error approach. Total costs are minimized by ordering 100 units each time an order is placed.

Initial assumptions of this simple model are relatively restrictive. Although they may be met in a few real world situations or at least approximated, generally one or more of them does not hold true. In the following sections there are methods for dealing with situations in which some of the simplifying assumptions are relaxed. Although the following treatment is far from exhaustive, it indicates the basic strength of this method of analysis.

Variable purchase costs. Suppliers are often willing to offer a smaller

TABLE 7–3
DETERMINATION OF EOQ BY TRIAL AND ERROR

Number of Orders	Units per Order	Units in Average Inventory	Value of Average Inventory	Annual Carrying Cost	Annual Ordering Cost	
1	1,000	500	$1,000	$250.00	$ 2.50	
2	500	250	500	125.00	5.00	
4	250	125	250	62.50	10.00	
8	125	62.5	125	31.25	20.00	
10	100	50	100	25.00	25.00	
12	84	42	84	21.00	30.00	
14	72	36	72	18.00	35.00	

Annual usage is 1,000 items; purchase price, $2 per item; cost per order, $2.50; inventory-c
cost, 25 percent.

It should be noted that as carrying costs decline, ordering costs incr
Total costs decrease initially but then beyond some point begin to
crease. Minimum total costs occur when 100 units are ordered each t
*Minimum total costs are incurred at the point where ordering costs e
carrying costs.* Under the initial assumptions, this is always the
The student may wish to plot the calculated relationships of order
to ordering costs, carrying costs, and total costs. The relationships
as generally depicted in Figure 7–16.

The economic order quantity having been determined, attention tu
to the inventory level at which an order should be placed. Assume t
there are 50 work weeks in a year and that lead time is two weeks. Si
a constant usage rate has been assumed, 20 units, i.e., $\dfrac{1000 \text{ units/year}}{50 \text{ weeks/year}}$,
used weekly. Therefore 40 units, 20 wks × 20 units/wk, are used dur
lead time. The ROP is 40 units. The complete decision rule is: When
inventory level drops to 40 units, an order should be placed for 100 un
It should be noted that stock-outs will never occur, since lead time
exactly two weeks. During the two weeks of waiting for the order to
received, the 40 units in inventory are used up. At the point when i
ventory level drops to zero, the new order is received; the invento
level becomes 100 units; and the cycle begins again.

Algebraic solution. By taking advantage of the fact that minimu
total costs are incurred at the point where carrying costs equal orderir
costs, a direct algebraic solution for the EOQ is easily obtained. Th
following symbols will be utilized in deriving the algebraic solution:

Q = Economic order quantity in units
R = Annual requirements in units
S = Cost to place one order or setup cost in dollars
C = Carrying costs as a percentage of the value of average inventory
P = Per unit cost of each item

per unit cost if the buyer will purchase larger quantities. These reductions in purchase costs are generally known as quantity discounts.

The buyer must decide whether the savings he receives on his purchase costs *and* from ordering fewer times each year compensate for the additional carrying costs he will experience because of purchasing larger quantities. This type decision calls for careful incremental reasoning. One method for analyzing such a problem is presented below. The following symbols will be utilized:

A = Annual requirements in dollars
S = Cost/order
C = Carrying cost as a percent of the value of average inventory
Q = Quantity presently being ordered in dollars
D = Discount/unit being offered
X = New order quantity in dollars

First, we will express symbolically the relevant costs for the decision under the ordering system presently in use.

Ordering costs = (Number of Orders) × (Cost/Order)
$$= A/Q \times S$$
$$= AS/Q$$

Carrying costs = $\left(\begin{array}{c}\text{Value of average}\\ \text{Inventory}\end{array}\right)$ × (Carrying cost as percent)
$$= Q/2 \times C$$
$$= QC/2$$

Purchase costs = (Annual requirements in $)
$$= A$$

Similar costs are expressed symbolically under the proposed system:

Purchase costs = Previous annual cost − Discount
$$= A - A \times D$$
$$= A(1-D)$$

Ordering costs = (Number of Orders) × (Cost/Order)
$$= [A(1-D)/X] \times S$$
$$= AS(1-D)/X$$

Carrying costs = $\left(\begin{array}{c}\text{Value of average}\\ \text{Inventory}\end{array}\right)$ × (Carrying cost as percent)
$$= X/2 \times C$$
$$= XC/2$$

We now wish to express the incremental savings the firm would experience in changing from its present system to the proposed system. It would experience two types of saving: saving on purchase costs and savings on ordering costs.

Incremental savings:

$$\text{Purchase savings} = \text{Present purchase costs} - \text{Proposed purchase costs}$$
$$= A - A(1-D)$$
$$= A - A + AD$$
$$= AD$$

$$\text{Ordering savings} = \text{Present ordering costs} - \text{Proposed ordering costs}$$
$$= AS/Q - \frac{AS(1-D)}{X}$$

The firm would, however, experience incremental carrying costs, since a larger order size would result in larger inventory levels.

Incremental costs:

$$\text{Carrying costs} = \text{Proposed carrying costs} - \text{Present carrying costs}$$
$$= XC/2 - \frac{QC}{2}$$

By equating the incremental savings to the incremental costs we may determine the value X, which is the largest amount(s) that the firm would be willing to purchase in each order, in view of the quantity discount.

$$XC/2 - QC/2 = AD + AS/Q - \frac{AS(1-D)}{X}$$

We first multiply through by X.

$$X^2 C/2 - XQC/2 = ADX + ASX/Q - AS(1-D)$$

We now convert to the quadratic equation form $(ax^2 + bx + c)$.

$$(C/2)X^2 - \left(\frac{QC}{2}\right)X - (AD)X - (AS/Q)X + AS(1-D) = 0$$

Simplifying we obtain:

$$(C/2)X^2 + \left(-\frac{QC}{2} - AD - \frac{AS}{Q}\right)X + AS(1-D) = 0$$

The solution to the general quadratic equation is:

$$X = \frac{-b \pm \sqrt{b^2 - 4ac}}{2a}$$

In our case:

$$a = C/2$$
$$b = \left(-\frac{QC}{2} - AD - AS/Q\right)$$
$$c = AS(1-D)$$

Therefore the solution to our equation is:

$$X = \frac{\left(\frac{QC}{2} + AD + \frac{AS}{Q}\right) \pm \sqrt{\left[-\left(\frac{QC}{2} + AD + \frac{AS}{Q}\right)\right]^2 - 4\left[\left(\frac{C}{2}\right)\right]\left[AS(1-D)\right]}}{2\ (C/2)}$$

$$= \frac{\frac{QC}{2} + AD + \frac{AS}{Q} \pm \sqrt{\left(\frac{QC}{2} + AD + \frac{AS}{Q}\right)^2 - 2CAS\ (1-D)}}{C}$$

To illustrate, suppose the supplier in our previous example offered the firm a 2 percent discount if it would order \$333 worth of the items per order.

$A = \$2,000$ (1,000 units $\times$ \$2/unit) — annual requirements
$S = \$2.50/$order (costs/order)
$C = .25$ (carrying costs as percent)
$Q = \$200$ (100 units $\times$ \$2/unit) — present order quantity
$X = $ largest amount to buy at one time to get discount
$D = .02$ (2%) — discount

$$X = \frac{\frac{QC}{2} + AD + \frac{AS}{Q} \pm \sqrt{\left(\frac{QC}{2} + AD + \frac{AS}{Q}\right)^2 - 2CAS(1-D)}}{C}$$

$$= \frac{\frac{\$200(.25)}{2} + \$2,000(.02) + \frac{\$2,000}{\$200}\ (\$2.50)}{}$$

$$\pm \frac{\sqrt{\left[\frac{\$200(.25)}{2} + \$2,000(.02) + \frac{\$2,000\ (2.50)}{\$200}\right]^2}}{}$$

$$\frac{- 2(0.25)\ (\$2,000)\ (2.50)\ (1-.02)}{.25}$$

$$= \frac{\$25 + \$40 + \$25 \pm \sqrt{(\$25 + \$40 + \$25)^2 - \$2,450}}{.25}$$

$$= \frac{\$90 \pm \sqrt{(90)^2 - \$2,450}}{.25}$$

$$= \frac{\$90 \pm \sqrt{(\$8,100 - \$2,450)}}{.25}$$

$$= \frac{\$90 \pm \sqrt{\$5,650}}{.25}$$

$= \$660.80$ or \$59.20 (but the smaller value is not relevant, since this amount will not earn the discount).

Therefore *$660.80* is the largest amount that the firm can afford to order to take advantage of the discount. Ordering this quantity would just equate incremental savings with incremental costs. If the firm can obtain the discount by ordering less than this amount, incremental saving will be greater than incremental costs. In this case, the firm should accept the proposed plan, since they receive the discount for orders of $333.

Although the introduction of quantity discounts often results in more complex problems than the one we have just discussed and thus calls for different methods of solution, each of the methods of analysis relies on the use of incremental reasoning of the type just described.

Inventory models under conditions of uncertainty

The models discussed above are appropriate for situations in which economies of lot size make it advantageous to build up (and then deplete) inventories under certainty. It is often desirable to recognize uncertainty in demand for the product and in its supply. Although many such models are available to fit specific situations, this section discusses only one basic model.

In the models previously discussed we have assumed that demand was known and constant, or uniform, over time. We also assumed that lead time was known and constant. Figure 7–15 illustrated the inventory level over time under these assumptions.

However, these assumptions are not always realistic. Lead time may vary because the supplier has run into production difficulty or because of transportation delays. Furthermore, there is usually some fluctuation in demand from period to period.

The concept of stockouts. When an order cannot be filled for an item a *stockout* is said to have occurred. Fluctuations in lead time or in usage rate can lead to stockouts. Figure 7–17 depicts a stockout caused by a lead time longer than expected. Note that in the first period, demand and lead time were as expected and no stockout occurred. However, in Period 2, although the usage rate did not vary, lead time was longer than expected. The result was a stockout.

Figure 7–18 depicts a stockout caused by an increase in usage rate. Again in Period 1, lead time and usage rate were as expected and no stockout occurred. However, in Period 2, although the lead time did not vary, the usage rate increased resulting in a stockout.

The concept of safety stock. Safety stocks afford a method of buying short-term protection against the uncertainties of customer demand and the uncertainties of lead time. *Safety stocks* are increases in inventories that decrease the probability of stockouts.

Safety stocks, as other types of inventory, have certain costs associated with them. Since stockouts decrease as the level of safety stock is

FIGURE 7–17

INVENTORY LEVEL WITH VARYING LEAD TIME

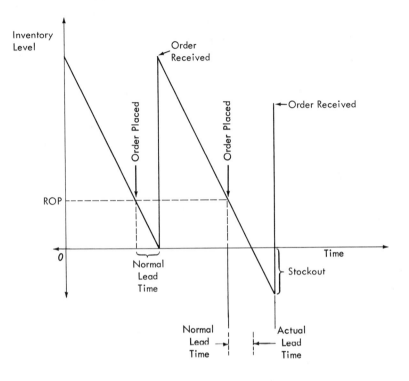

FIGURE 7–18

INVENTORY LEVEL WITH VARYING USAGE RATES

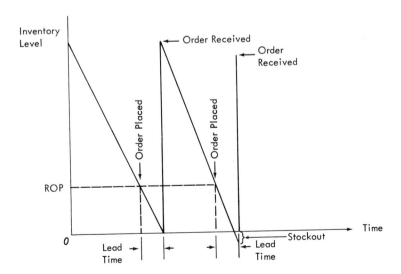

increased, out-of-stock costs are inversely related to the safety-stock level. However, additional safety stock will increase carrying costs. The basic question to be answered then is: How much additional inventory (safety stock) can be economically justified?

Determination of optimum safety stock levels. To illustrate the type of analysis needed to determine an appropriate level of safety stock, the following example will be used. Through analysis of its inventory records the XYZ Company has accumulated the following information about the usage rate of a particular item during lead time or during a reorder period.

TABLE 7–4
USAGE DURING REORDER PERIOD

Number of Units Used During Reorder Period	Number of Times This Quantity Was Used	Probability of This Usage	$P(d>r)$
0	5	.05	.95
50	10	.10	.85
100	10	.10	.75
150	15	.15	.60
200	25	.25	.35
250	15	.15	.20
300	10	.10	.10
350	10	.10	.00
	100	1.00	

The last column simply gives the probability that demand d will be greater than the value in column 1. For example the probability that demand during the reorder period will be greater than 0 is .95. For simplicity, items are required in batches of 50 units. This, however, does not affect the generality of the method we will employ.

Assume that the firm has also estimated the following values:

K = Cost of carrying one unit in inventory for 1 year = $4
π = Stockout cost/item out of stock = $2
R = Annual demand in units = 1,000 units
Q = Economic order quantity = 100 units

The XYZ Company now wishes to determine its ROP; i.e., the number of units in inventory at the time a new order is placed. The larger this value, the smaller will be the probability of a stockout and therefore the smaller the stockout-associated costs. However, as the ROP value is increased, the carrying costs will increase. The firm is faced again with conflicting costs and wishes to resolve this conflict in order to minimize inventory-associated costs.

The alternative values of ROP are the values in Column 1 of Table 7–4. How does the firm decide on which value to use as its ROP? As long as the incremental carrying costs are less than the expected incremental reduction in stockout costs, the firm should continue to add units to its ROP.

For example, in determining whether to raise ROP from 0 units to 50 units, the following incremental analysis is appropriate.

$$\text{Incremental carrying costs} = 50 \text{ units} \times K$$
$$= 50 \text{ units} \times \$4 \text{ unit}$$
$$= \$200$$

$$\text{Expected stockout costs} = 50 \text{ units} \times \pi \ P(d{>}0) \times \text{number of orders periods per year}$$
$$= 50 \text{ units} \times \$2 \times .95 \times 10 \text{ orders per year}$$
$$= \$950$$

Obviously, it is to the firm's advantage to add these 50 units, since the expected stockout costs from not making the 50 units is greater than the incremental cost for carrying the 50 units.

Should the firm add 50 more units? Again the incremental costs must be compared.

$$\text{Incremental carrying costs} = 50 \text{ units} \times K$$
$$= 50 \text{ units} \times \$4 \text{ unit}$$
$$= \$200$$

$$\text{Expected stockout costs} = 50 \text{ units} \times \pi \ P(d{>}50) \times \text{number of orders per year}$$
$$= 50 \times 2 \times .85 \times 10$$
$$= \$850$$

The second increase of 50 units is also to the firm's advantage, since incremental costs are less than savings. It should be noted that the multiplication by the number of orders per year in the expected stockout cost calculation is necessary to convert expected stockout cost to an annual figure instead of a per-reorder-period cost, since carrying costs are expressed as annual costs.

It should be obvious that the firm will continue to add units up to the point where the incremental carrying costs equal expected stockout costs. Beyond this point incremental costs are greater than incremental savings. Expressed symbolically, the firm should continue to add units until

$$50 \ K = 50\pi \ [P(d{>}r)] \ R/Q$$

Solving this for $P(d{>}r)$ we obtain

$$P(d{>}r) = \frac{KQ}{\pi R}$$

In our example, solving for $P(d>r)$ we obtain

$$P(d>r) = \frac{4 \times 100}{2 \times 1,000}$$
$$= 4/20$$
$$= .20$$

The XYZ Company should continue adding units until $P\ (d>r) = .20$. This occurs where ROP $= 250$ units (Table 7–4). If the firm sets its ROP less than 250 units it will lose more money from stockouts than the incremental carrying cost necessary to avoid these stockouts. If the firm sets its ROP greater than 250 units, the incremental carrying costs will be greater than the savings from avoiding the stockouts.

Notice that *expected* usage during lead time is 190 units (expected usage $= 0$ units $\times$ .05 $+$ 50 units $\times$ .10 $+$ 100 units $\times$ .10 $+$ ... $+$ 300 units $\times$ .10 $+$ 350 units $\times$ .10). Thus the ROP is greater than the expected usage. In general ROP $=$ expected usage during lead time $+$ safety stock. Therefore, the safety stock is 60 units in this example.

Sensitivity analysis. Since we are forced to make rather difficult estimates in order to employ the EOQ formula, it is of interest to determine how sensitive the model is to changes in the basic parameters. For example, in Table 7–5 we have calculated the EOQ for four different levels of annual demand. The other parameters retained the same values as in our original EOQ calculations.

TABLE 7–5

SENSITIVITY OF EOQ TO CHANGES IN DEMAND

Annual Requirements Units	EOQ Units
1,000	$\sqrt{\dfrac{2\,(1,000)\,(\$2.50)}{\$2\,(.25)}} = \$100.00$
1,100	$\sqrt{\dfrac{2\,(1,100)\,(\$2.50)}{\$2\,(.25)}} = \$104.89$
1,210	$\sqrt{\dfrac{2\,(1,210)\,(\$2.50)}{\$2\,(.25)}} = \$110.02$
1,331	$\sqrt{\dfrac{2\,(1,331)\,(\$2.50)}{\$2\,(.25)}} = \$115.40$

$S = \$2.50/\text{order}$
$C = .25$
$P = \$2.00/\text{unit}$

What is the significance of these results? In each case the new demand figure was found by increasing the prior demand figure by 10 percent;

i.e., the prior demand figure was multiplied by 1.10. It should be noted that the EOQ value was changed only by a multiple of 1.0488 (the square root of 1.10). The implications of these calculations should be quite clear. The size of an order, and thus the average inventory level, rises only by the square root of the increase in demand. It is additionally meaningful to know that the EOQ value is not very sensitive to changes in demand, since we are using estimates. The student should be able to see that similar results can be found by experimenting with the other parameters.

Conclusions. It has been the purpose of this section to introduce the student to the nature of inventory problems. The necessity for careful cost analysis has been stressed. The student should have gained an appreciation of the practical uses of cost analysis and incremental and marginal analysis, and some of the other concepts presented in this text.

It must be emphasized that no attempt has been made to cover the entire area of inventory analysis or to introduce anything but the simplest approaches to inventory problem solutions.

PROBLEMS FOR CHAPTER 7

1. A manufacturer produces two types of fasteners. One of the fasteners is sold under the Royal brand name and the other under the Acme brand name. The Royal fasteners sell for $10 per package, while the Acme fasteners sell for $9.50 per package. The variable cost of the Royal fasteners is $5 per package. The Acme fasteners have a variable cost of $5.50 per package. Both the Royal and Acme fasteners must go through the stamping department and the plating and packaging department. The stamping department has 9,600 minutes per day available, and the plating and packaging department has 12,000 minutes per day available for use. Each package of Royal fasteners takes four minutes in the stamping department and two minutes in the plating and packaging department. Each package of Acme fasteners takes two minutes in the stamping department and ten minutes in the plating and packaging department.

   a. Solve for the optimum product mix and contribution both graphically and algebraically.

   b. Set this problem up as a linear programming problem.

   c. Determine what would happen if the prices and variable costs changed so that the contribution was $7 per package from the Royal brand and $3 per package from the Acme brand.

2. The Artistic Ardvark, Inc., manufactures two art statues for sale to the general public. The "antediluvian" work contributes $8 per unit to overhead and profit, while the "Futuristic" work contributes $6 per unit to overhead and profit. Each type of statue must pass through three departments: mixing, molding, and finishing. The following information has been gathered on the hours each type of statue requires in each department and the capacities of the departments.

TIME REQUIREMENTS
(hours)

	Antediluvian	Futuristic	Capacity, Hours
Mixing	2	4	1,500
Molding	5	2	2,000
Finishing	1	1	500

a. Determine the optimum product mix and the optimum contribution using the graphic method.

b. What would be the optimum product mix if the contributions changed to $5 for both types of statues? What would be the optimum contribution in this case? Does this situation violate the rule that an optimum solution will always be found at a corner point?

c. Formulate the original example as an LP problem.

3. The Acme Cleaning Chemical Company produces an industrial cleaner for carpets. This chemical is made from a mixture of two other chemicals which both contain cleaning agent A and cleaning agent B along with some inert ingredients. Their product must contain 175 units of agent A, 150 units of B and weigh at least 100 pounds. Chemical X_1 costs $4 per pound while chemical X_2 costs $10 per pound. Chemical X_1 contains one unit of agent A, three units of agent B, and some inert ingredients per pound. Chemical X_2 contains seven units of agent A, one unit of agent B, and some inert ingredients per pound.

a. Determine the least cost mixture with regard to total weight, the weight of each chemical $(X_1 + X_2)$ and the minimum cost. Do this graphically.

b. Set this problem up in the LP format.

4. The NP Growright Company manufactures a liquid plant fertilizer from mixing two chemical solutions together. With the exception of two key ingredients, N and P, all of the ingredients are found in two solutions so that regardless of how the solutions are mixed their percentage contents will be satisfactory. The company sells tanks which are guaranteed to contain a minimum of 500 gallons of the fertilizer. Furthermore, in addition to the other ingredients, the fertilizer in the tank units must contain at least 1,000 units of ingredient N and 750 units of ingredient P. Solution X_1 has been found to contain 1 unit of N per gallon and 3 units of P per gallon. Solution X_2 contains 4 units of N per gallon and 1 unit of P per gallon. The costs of solution X_1 and X_2 are $4 and $3 per gallon respectively.

a. Solve this problem graphically.

b. Set the problem up in the LP format.

5. The Dudway Company has determined that it utilizes 5,200 units of the Mark 30 Widget each year. The usage rate is approximately constant throughout the year. Studies by the industrial engineering department indicate that it costs $18.50 to place an order. It has been estimated that carrying costs are approximately 20 percent of the average inventory. The price of the Mark 30 Widget is $10 per unit. What should the economic ordering quantity be?

6. Boxkahn, Inc. purchases approximately 50,000 rolls of tape per year from Strongfasten, Inc. This tape is utilized at a constant rate throughout the year. Currently the company estimates that each order to suppliers costs $10 and that its carrying costs are approximately 15 percent. At present, Boxkahn pays $5 per roll of tape. Strongfasten has offered Boxkahn a 10 percent discount if they will order at least 1,200 rolls at a time. Should Boxkahn accept this offer? If so, how many units should they order?

7. Terry, Inc., is concerned about the cost of stockouts for a consumer goods product which they sell. Because many customers will purchase a similar product elsewhere rather than return, they estimate the cost of a stockout to be $4 per unit. Their annual demand for this product is 5,000 units, and it has been determined that the EOQ is 500 units per order. The cost for carrying one unit in inventory for one year is estimated to be $2. From past history Terry has found the distribution of sales during the reorder period to be as given below.

Number of Units Used During Reorder Period	Number of Times This Quantity Was Used	Probability of This Usage	$P(d > r)$
0	5	0.05	0.95
25	25	0.25	0.70
50	25	0.25	0.45
75	30	0.30	0.15
100	10	0.10	0.05
125	5	0.05	0.00

a. Determine the ROP (reorder point).
b. Determine the expected usage during lead time.
c. Determine the safety stock.

Cases for part three

Cost analysis is an integral part of most problem-solving situations in which a manager becomes involved. This is true regardless of whether the decision maker is a profit-seeking businessman or a government-agency manager concerned with satisfying certain public needs. The cases in this section focus on cost analysis in making decisions on product mix and on the abandonment or expansion of activities.

The student will have the opportunity to determine the classifications of cost, to use incremental analysis, and to study the use of various accounting systems for managerial decision-making. Some of the cases make use of break-even analysis and have information so that break-even charts can be developed using both the statistical method and the engineering method. One case allows the student to visualize the problems and opportunities which are involved because of varying capital investments and varying contributions per dollar of revenue through the use of the profit-volume contribution analysis.

It is not possible to find cases which isolate cost considerations from other economic variables. The cases in this section require some attention to the demand concepts covered in Chapters 3 and 4. Some of the cases foreshadow the discussion of pricing which is treated more formally later in the text. Marketing considerations are important throughout. No attempt is made here to isolate one aspect of the analyses from the rest of the business considerations.

RANDOLPH STONE COMPANY

The Randolph Stone Company was a partnership engaged in stone quarrying and the paving of roads. The company sold primarily to state

EXHIBIT 1

PROFIT AND LOSS STATEMENT 1956 THROUGH 1961

	1956	1957	1958	1959	1960	1961
Net sales	$131,758.71	$248,025.45	$404,037.72	$196,432.41	$84,574.65	$433,658.51
Operating expenses						
Salaries and wages	19,186.50	35,196.48	41,484.90	24,543.03	17,379.57	46,598.01
Travel expense	114.00	529.26	308.79	171.96	54.90	204.60
Stationery and office supplies	67.35	126.12	78.18	78.66	.36	94.14
Auditing and legal	1.89	469.50	226.14	40.50	4.20	4.59
Dues and subscriptions	325.32	1,541.10	2,248.77	582.39	439.92	1,499.46
Repairs of equipment	2,157.24	2,933.19	7,496.79	4,475.01	1,294.83	9,559.05
Freight, in	8,104.29	13,779.39	10,270.02	5,315.64	2,763.69	12,542.07
Hired truck expense	13,513.08	27,204.21	39,039.69	15,553.44	7,897.17	42,546.69
Miscellaneous expense	508.41	424.59	1,621.26	569.10	4.65	606.00
Truck repair expense	207.42	456.24	1,981.56	1,082.22	317.94	1,814.10
Gas, oil, and lubricants	8,127.39	6,222.00	12,842.70	5,502.57	3,135.36	6,805.20
Stone purchased and sand	26,895.42	46,092.93	94,143.48	58,066.53	16,924.95	134,154.18
Oils and asphalt	29,425.35	53,740.89	80,837.55	22,336.02	11,076.18	46,041.87
Rent	514.29	……	6,972.51	6,804.60	2,345.34	3,682.26
Insurance expense	300.27	1,135.08	8,874.36	4,402.89	245.19	1,057.95
Utilities	814.38	1,706.19	2,123.79	464.82	245.55	333.18
License and fees	90.66	471.00	739.14	1,033.71	563.25	766.98
FICA expense	342.54	763.98	1,004.40	670.38	451.05	1,375.62
Kentucky unemployment contributions	344.01	831.39	1,345.29	744.48	452.91	1,249.77
Interest expense	1,592.01	4,795.50	4,852.20	3,533.55	1,863.54	1,350.84
Bonding expense	520.35	1,156.05	256.89	713.64	371.19	2,420.46
Depreciation of equipment	6,075.39	12,144.33	15,988.59	17,354.13	17,221.83	31,498.68
Telephone and postage	……	84.69	36.99	42.42	15.39	6.00
Taxes	……	3.81	33.15	263.55	15.75	315.00
Commissions	……	750.00	……	……	……	……
Advertising	……	……	402.15	440.43	37.50	52.89
Federal unemployment insurance	……	……	74.16	80.94	73.35	91.77
Sales tax	……	……	……	2,260.89	2,319.72	6,926.25
Bad-debt expense	……	……	……	1,042.41	42.18	274.80
Road construction supplies	……	……	……	……	……	911.31
	$119,227.56	$212,557.92	$335,283.45	$178,169.91	$87,557.46	$354,783.72
Net profit (loss)	$ 12,531.15	$ 35,467.53	$ 68,754.27	$ 18,262.50	$(2,982.81)	$ 78,874.79

and local governments; its gravel was purchased for road construction in nearby sections of the state.

The company owned and operated five stone quarries located within 100 miles of each other. In addition, it owned a paving operation in the same vicinity.

The quarries were generally profitable, returning on the average a book profit of from 10 to 20 percent of the book value of the partners' property. Occasionally one of the quarries operated at a loss, though this resulted partly from the fact that special repairs were charged off as a current expense.

The most unstable part of the business was the paving operation. Its instability resulted from the variations in road construction activities of the state government involved. In election years paving activity was high; in other years it tapered off. The result was that the paving activities of the firm fluctuated sharply from high to low profits.

Exhibit 1 covers data on paving revenues and expenses for the years from 1956 through 1961.

1. *Classify the expenses into fixed expenses and variable expenses based on the 1961 profits and loss statement. Use judgment in determining whether the expense is fixed or variable. Some expenses, such as advertising and rent, might be classified in a separate category, since they are more in the nature of programmed or manipulable expenses which are neither fixed nor a result of changes in output.*
2. *On the basis of your answer to Question 1, construct a break-even chart.*
3. *Plot a scatter diagram relating total cost to sales. Complete a break-even chart based on this approach.*
4. *Compare your two break-even charts (the one based on the classification of accounts; the other on a rough "statistical" analysis). Do they provide approximately the same estimate of fixed costs? How do you account for the differences in the two charts?*
5. *What limitations would a statistician find in the "statistical" chart constructed as an answer to Question 3?*

Consider possible effects of the following: price changes over time, changes over time in ages of major items of plant and equipment, and changes over time in ratio of capital to labor.

M AND H COMPANY (B)

The M and H Company invited a management consultant to advise them on the use of the company's accounts in decision making. The consultant's report* is reproduced below:

---

*Editorial changes are made in the original version for the purpose of classroom discussion and to disguise the original company.

This report presents the accounts of the M and H Company in the form of marginal income accounting—also known as differential accounting, cost-volume-profit analysis, or incremental analysis. The method is closely akin to direct costing, but does not require the tie-in with the day-to-day financial accounts or the change in inventory valuation required by direct costing.

Purposes of marginal income accounting

The objective of marginal income accounting is to aid in decision making rather than the reporting of past performance. It supplements the financial reports. If M and H were to adopt a permanent system of marginal income accounting, it would need special analyses of the acccounts only twice a year. These could be kept in a form which is relatively inexpensive—the work could be done in the slack periods in the accounting department.

In the case at instance, marginal income accounting would help achieve the following objectives:

1. Separation of the results of the Boonville and Dorchester operations: As we have seen there has already been a tendency to mix the Boonville and Dorchester accounts in such a way that the results are confusing and misleading. It is imperative for a business man to know how much each operation is contributing to the business.

2. Separation of the results of the poster, paint, and commercial departments: At present one cannot tell whether any of these departments is contributing adequately to the business to justify its existence. Nor can one tell which branches are the most profitable and thus the most appropriate for expansion.

3. Determination of the incremental costs of each activity: While at the present time one has a notion that the variable costs are much less than the fixed costs—and that the incremental costs are perhaps only 30 to 40 percent of the billings—that such is the case has not been determined in a systematic way. The incremental costs vary from one activity to another. In fact, they vary from one type of decision to another. Any system which helps to determine incremental costs should assist the executives in future decisions about the business.

It might be noted here that marginal income accounting tries to avoid arbitrary allocations of overhead. If some costs are common costs of the company as a whole, and are not a result of any particular activity (Boonville or Dorchester) as such, these costs are marked as company overhead. If some other costs are clearly related to Boonville activity or Dorchester activity but cannot be shown to be a result of a particular department (poster, paint or commercial), such costs are marked as Boonville overhead or as Dorchester overhead. One of the primary objectives of marginal income accounting is to determine how much Boonville and Dorchester are separately contributing to the company's overhead and profits and how much poster, paint, and commercial departments are contributing to local overhead, company overhead and profits. Thus a central concept throughout is the *contribution to overhead and profits*.

Arrangement of the accounts

I have identified each major account classification in a way which should be almost self-explanatory. The classes are shown in Exhibit 1. A code has been established for each class.

EXHIBIT 1

M AND H COMPANY (B)
(marginal income—classification of accounts)

B–PO–1   Booneville income from poster plant
B–PO–2   Booneville variable costs in poster plant
B–PO–3   Booneville poster plant contribution to poster fixed costs, local and company overhead, and profit.
B–PO–4   Booneville poster plant fixed costs
B–PO–4A   (Part of B–PO–4) Booneville poster plant sunk costs.
B–PO–4B   (Part of B–PO–4) Booneville poster plant escapable fixed costs.
B–PO–5   Boonville poster plant contribution to local and company overhead and profit (after deduction of poster plant fixed costs).

B–PA–1
B–PA–2
B–PA–3
B–PA–4   } The same for the Boonville paint plant
B–PA–4A
B–PA–4B
B–PA–5

B–C–1
B–C–2
B–C–3
B–C–4   } The same for the Boonville commercial plant
B–C–4A
B–C–4B
B–C–5

D–PO–1	D–PA–1	D–C–1	
D–PO–2	D–PA–2	D–C–2	
D–PO–3	D–PA–3	D–C–3	The same for the Dorchester poster plant,
D–PO–4	D–PA–4	D–C–4	Dorchester paint plant, and Dorchester com-
D–PO–4A	D–PA–4A	D–C–4A	mercial plant, respectively.
D–PO–4B	D–PA–4B	D–C–4B	
D–PO–5	D–PA–5	D–C–5	

In addition there are three overhead accounts, two local contribution accounts, and one company profit account.

B–OH   Boonville overhead
D–OH   Dorchester overhead
B–6   Boonville contribution to company overhead and profit
D–6   Dorchester contribution to company overhead and profit
O   Company-wide overhead
P   Company profit

Marginal income analysis for July 1967 through December 1967

The operational results for the six months from July through December 1967 appear in Exhibit 2. These results are based on a close study of each individual expense item to determine whether it is fixed or variable, sunk or escapable, and attributable to Boonville, Dorchester, or the company as a whole.

EXHIBIT 2

M AND H COMPANY (B)

B–PO–1	$355,230.92	B–PA–1	$206,261.48
Less B–PO–2	107,621.19	Less B–PA–2	72,305.19
Equals B–PO–3	247,609.73	Equals B–PA–3	133,956.29
Less B–PO–4A	96,155.16	Less B–PA–4A	32,343.98
Less B–PO–4B	89,651.49	Less B–PA–4B	51,502.33
Equals B–PO–5	61,803.08	Equals B–PA–5	50,109.98

B–C–1	$81,361.56
Less B–C–2	54,718.73
Equals B–C–3	26,642.83
Less B–C–4A	—
Less B–C–4B	2,299.83
Less B–C–5	24,343.00

D–PO–1	$99,898.50	D–PA–1	$23,318.21
Less D–PO–2	40,619.18	Less D–PA–2	3,866.94
Equals D–PO–3	59,279.32	Equals D–PA–3	19,451.27
Less D–PO–4A	13,608.73	Less D–PA–4A	4,068.32
Less D–PO–4B	15,937.68	Less D–PA–4B	5,517.93
Equals D–PO–5	29,732.91	Equals D–PA–5	9,865.02

D–C–1	$14,514.51
Less D–C–2	9,883.79
Equals D–C–3	4,630.72
Less D–C–4A	—
Less D–C–4B	591.66
Equals D–C–5	4,039.06

Total Boonville contribution to local and company overhead and profits ($61,803.08 + $50,109.98 + $24,343.00)	$136,256.06	
Less B–OH (Boonville overhead)	89,482.10	
Equals D–6 Boonville contribution to company overhead and profits)		$ 46,773.96
Total Dorchester contribution to local and company overhead and profits ($29,732.91 + $9,865.02 + $4,039.06)	$ 43,636.99	
Less D–OH (Dorchester overhead)	31,011.46	
Equals D–6 (Dorchester contribution to company overhead and profits)		$ 12,625.53
Total contribution to company overhead & profits		$ 59,399.49
Less O (Company-wide overhead)		100,011.60
Equals company's loss		(40,611.11)

Break-even charts: Boonville

The results can also be shown in the form of a series of break-even charts. Rather than construct a break-even chart for the company as a whole it makes more sense to construct individual charts for each segment of the business separately. An overall break-even chart would add together differing elements, thereby obscuring the outcome of particular operations.

The special break-even chart required to be constructed is known as the profit/volume chart. On it is plotted first of all the fixed costs (both sunk and escapable) resulting from the particular segment. Then is plotted what is called the P/V line (the profit-volume line) which is the incremental income at various volumes of sales. It is, in other words, the added income *minus* the added (variable) costs. The slope of the P/V line is the P/V ratio—the added contribution per unit of sales. Where the P/V line crosses the zero horizontal line is the break-even point. At this point, the income less the variable costs is enough to cover the segment's fixed costs. *But* at this point the segment makes *no* contribution to the company's overhead and profits.

Take Exhibit 3, for example. The specific fixed costs of the Boonville poster department amount to $185,806.65. The P/V ratio is .70, which means that every $1 of Boonville poster sales adds $.70 more income. It takes billings of $266,580 in each six-month period to break even in the poster plant—that is, to cover the specific fixed costs. Beyond that point the contribution to profit increases rapidly, reaching a level of $61,803.08 at billings of $355,230.92. At billings of $450,000 it would appear that the contribution would be over $127,500.

EXHIBIT 3

M AND H COMPANY (B)
(P/V [break-even] chart, Boonville poster department—
July through December, 1967)

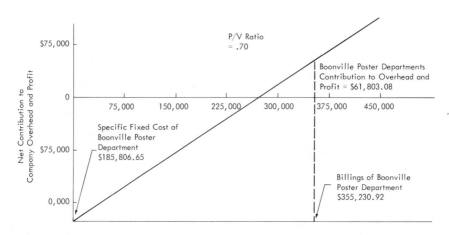

However, one qualification is necessary. Exhibit 3 probably exaggerates the added profits *beyond* present levels of sales in one respect. Remember that the salesmen's earnings have been treated partly as a fixed cost and partly as a variable cost. As billings push on beyond present levels and the salesmen become relatively more dependent upon commissions, the proportion of variable costs will rise, with a reduction in the P/V ratio. Thus, a completely accurate drawing of the charts would show a kink in the P/V ratio line somewhere beyond the present level of sales. This error is probably not serious—it might reduce the ratio from .70 to .65 beyond the sales level of $420,000 (or something of that magnitude).

Which of the three Boonville departments is the most profitable? The paint department made the largest contribution in ratio to its revenue in the six months under study. (See Exhibit 4.) The contribution of $50,109.98 on sales of $206,261.48 appears to be more favorable than the poster department's contribution of $61,803.08 on revenues of $355,230.92. This comparison is misleading, however. The results for the poster department are for its poorest six months. It will make a much larger contribution in the other six months, while the paint department will remain relatively stable. In addition, the poster department's P/V ratio is somewhat higher, which means that its contribution will respond rapidly to sales increases.

The Boonville commercial department's high ratio of contribution to sales certainly indicates that it is a desirable adjunct of the business. (See Exhibit 5.)

EXHIBIT 4
M AND H COMPANY (B)
(P/V [break-even] chart, Boonville paint department—
July through December, 1967)

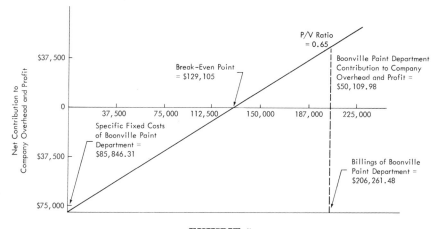

EXHIBIT 5
M AND H COMPANY (B)
(P/V [break-even] chart, Boonville commercial department—
July through December, 1967)

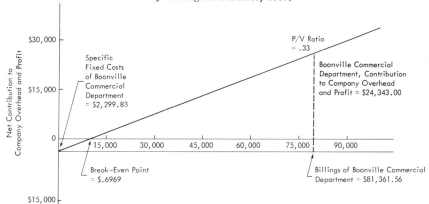

Its main advantage is its low proportion of fixed costs. Its main disadvantage is its low P/V ratio, which would preclude it from ever making the kind of profit which is possible in the poster department.

The fact appears to be that all three Boonville operations are profitable in every sense of the word—even though the overall company income statement shows a loss for the six months from July through December, 1967.

Break-even charts: Dorchester

The analysis for the Dorchester operations runs along similar lines. For some reason the poster department P/V ratio is lower (.59) in Dorchester than in Boonville—its variable costs are proportionally higher than in Boonville (Exhibit 6). But the billings are high enough to give a high ratio of contribution ($29,732.91) to billings ($99,898.50). Of course, the contribution should be considerably higher in the summer months.

The Dorchester paint department's P/V ratio of .83 is extremely high (Exhibit 7). One wonders whether all the variable costs for this segment have been discovered. Perhaps some of the poster department's variable costs should be shifted to the paint department. I have checked over the original worksheets and have found that M and H's accounts show $12,714.21 of labor for the poster department but only $1,181.56 for the paint department. Perhaps this allocation of labor costs should be rechecked.

If the present allocations are correct, the Dorchester paint department is extremely profitable in relation to sales and would be fantastically profitable if volume could be increased.

EXHIBIT 6

M AND H COMPANY (B)
(P/V [break-even] chart, Dorchester poster department—
July through December, 1967)

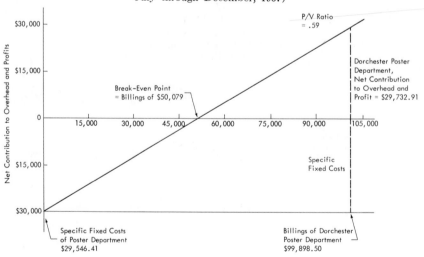

The Dorchester commercial department also makes a satisfactory contribution to overhead and profit (Exhibit 8). In this case the contribution results from the high volume in relation to fixed costs rather than to the P/V ratio which is relatively low. The low P/V ratio of .32 results, of course, from the

EXHIBIT 7

M AND H COMPANY (B)
(P/V [break-even] chart, Dorchester paint department—
July through December, 1967)

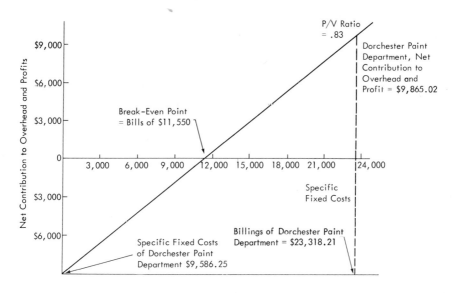

EXHIBIT 8

M AND H COMPANY (B)
(P/V [break-even] chart, Dorchester commercial department—
July through December, 1967)

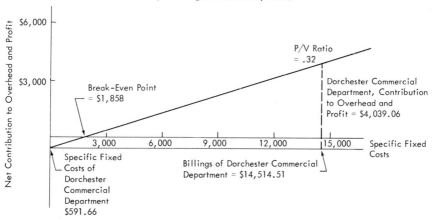

fact that commercial work takes proportionally more labor and materials (outright sales cost).

Future marginal income reports

I have tried to think of methods by which the analysis could be simplified so that future marginal income reports could be constructed with less effort. Accountants often use shortcuts which assume all costs of one type are variable and of another type are fixed, and so on. I think that such simplifications would not be appropriate in your business for several reasons:

1. It is desirable to separate specific fixed costs from local overhead and company-wide overhead. It is unlikely that any simple formula will do this exactly.

2. Costs which are fixed in one period may become variable and vice versa. Therefore a periodic review of the classification is desirable.

3. As you change your business—buying new property and perhaps selling off old property—you will need flexibility in changing the classification.

I am returning the original worksheets showing the classification of accounts. It will serve as a useful guide for future marginal income reports. But it will not provide automatic answers to all problems of classification which might arise.

1. *What is the purpose of separating sunk fixed costs from escapable fixed costs? What is the meaning of these terms? How is this breakdown relevant?*

2. *What is the meaning of the term "specific fixed costs" as used in the consultant's report?*

3. *Would an overall break-even chart for the company as a whole serve the purpose just as well as the individual P/V charts?*

4. *What is the meaning and significance of the break-even points shown on the P/V charts?*

5. *Three types of "contribution" are shown in Exhibit 2. What is the significance of each?*

6. *What purposes could be served by this type of analysis?*

JANET LEE'S DEPARTMENT STORE*

Janet Lee's store was a moderately small department store, with annual sales of $5,000,000. The store was organized into 60 departments, each of which is expected to contribute to the profitability of the entire operation. The merchandise ranged from candles and ready-to-wear goods to home furnishings and heavy appliances.

In the years from 1958 to 1961, the managers of the store had read and heard a great deal about a new system of accounting for retail stores, Merchandise Management Accounting. They doubted that this system would be suited to their business. They used the Contribution Plan

---

* This case was prepared by W. W. Haynes and J. L. Gibson of the University of Kentucky as a basis for class discussion. It is a synthesis of the situations in several stores rather than a case based on a single store. All names are disguised.

EXHIBIT 1

DEPARTMENT STATEMENT

Merchandise Statement

1. Inventory at cost—First of period
2. Merchandise received at invoice cost
3. Transportation cost ($\% = 3 \div 2$)
4. Transfers at cost ($+$ in, $-$ out)
5. Cumulative cost ($\% = 5 \div 10$ for year)
6. Inventory at retail—First of period
7. Merchandise rec'd at retail ($\% = 2 \div 7$ from 100%)
8. Additional markups, less cancellations
9. Transfers at retail ($+$ in, $-$ out)
10. Cumulative retail (markon $\% = 5 \div 10$ from 100%)
11. Gross sales
12. Less returns ($\% = 12 \div 11$)
13. Net sales
14. Markdowns, less cancellations ($\% = 14 \div 13$)
15. Employee discounts ($\% = 15 \div 13$)
16. Shrinkage—Estimated or actual ($\% = 16 \div 13$)
17. Total retail deductions (13 to 16 incl.)
18. Inventory at retail—End of period ($10 - 17$)
19. Inventory at cost—End of period ($18 \times \%$ 5 yr. to date)
20. Gross cost of goods sold ($5 - 19$) ($\% = 20 \div 13$)
21. Cash discounts on merchandise ($\% = 21 \div 13$)
22. Net cost of goods sold ($20 - 21$) ($\% = 22 \div 13$)
23. Workroom and other costs ($+$ or $-$) ($\% = 23 \div 13$)
24. Total cost of sales ($22 +$ or $- 23$) ($\% = 24 \div 13$)
25. Gross margin ($13 - 24$) ($\% = 25 \div 13$)

Expense Statement

Direct—Fixed plant and equipment charges
  Newspaper space costs
  Other direct advertising
  Buying salaries
  Other direct buying
  Selling salaries
  Delivery—Prorate (sales)
  Other direct
  Interest expense (.5% on inventory investment)
  Travel
    Total direct (also as % of 13)
Indirect—Administrative
  Occupancy
  Handling
  Publicity
  Buying
  Selling
    Total indirect (also as % of 13)
Total expenses (direct and indirect) (also as % of 13)
Net profit (gross margin—total expenses) (also as % of 13)

Accounting system, and saw no reason to change it. In any case, management made little use of the accounts for the analysis of alternatives in
decision making. The managers believed that the successful operation of
a department store depended on the accumulated knowledge and subjective judgment of store officials and that no programmed system of data
collection could be very helpful. The managers admitted that they did
not always understand the information provided by their present system
of accounting and that much of this information was probably irrelevant
for decisions. However, the accounting system was important for indicating areas which require management's attention.

The present accounting system

The Contribution Plan Accounting system used by the store accumulated and recorded expenses of the individual departments. Exhibit 1
illustrates a standard department statement. The top part of the statement
shows the computation of the cost of sales and the gross margin for the
department. The next section shows the so-called direct expenses, which
are the expenses that were attributable directly to the department. For
example, the item "fixed plant and equipment charges" refers to depreciation on such furnishings as display counters in the particular department. Therefore, the expression "direct expense" in this store did not
necessarily mean "variable expense," for some of the expenses were
fixed in the short run. The item "delivery expense" was included among
the direct expenses, even though it was prorated on the basis of sales.

The sections of the report discussed so far provided two important
percentages: (1) the gross margin as a percentage of net sales; and
(2) the direct expenses also as a percentage of net sales. Subtracting (2)

EXHIBIT 2
BASES FOR ALLOCATING INDIRECT EXPENSES

Expense	Bases for Allocating*
Administrative offices	Sales
Sales audit branch	Sales transactions
Personnel division	Average number of employees
Store maintenance	Area occupied
Buying and stock control	Purchases
Advertising	Sales
Credit branch	Credit transactions
Accounts payable branch	Number of invoices
Plant and equipment	Dollar value of space occupied
Heat, light, and water	Area occupied
Window display	Space points used
Institutional advertising	Radio time used
Receiving, checking, marking	Invoices handled
Contributions	Equally to all departments

can be other — they as well. arbitrary allocation. an admin. decision.

* Expense distributions are made according to suggestions of *Standard Expense Center Accounting Manual, NRMA,* 1954.

from (1) gave the "contribution" of the department to the indirect expenses and profit.

The last section of Exhibit 1, called the "indirect expenses," involved such items of administrative costs, occupancy, publicity, and indirect buying and selling expenses. These expenses were obtained by prorating the company-wide expenses to each department on the bases shown in Exhibit 2. Deduction of the indirect expenses plus the direct expenses from the gross margin resulted in the net profit for the department. This figure, like the others, appeared both in dollars and percentages and could be compared with similar figures for other departments. In addition, trade association literature included average percentages of similar stores which could be used for comparison.

Merchandise management accounting

In the late 1950s several experts on accounting for retail stores developed a more elaborate system called Merchandise Management Accounting—M.M.A. Some writers claim that this is an inappropriate title for an accounting system which aims at providing information for decisions in the future rather than the recording of historical data. One critic suggests that a more appropriate name might be *Merchandising Cost Analysis* or *Controllable Profit Merchandising*.

The central tool of M.M.A. is the cost pattern. In theory such a pattern might be constructed for each commodity carried by the store; in practice it may be desirable to combine some items to reduce the amount of record keeping. It is possible to maintain the system by departments rather than by commodities, reducing the cost of the system with a loss of detailed information. But one of the objectives of M.M.A. is to give more attention to individual items rather than to treat departments as homogeneous units.

Exhibit 3, taken from an article by one of the developers of M.M.A.,[1] illustrates a hypothetical cost pattern on one item in a major appliance department. The cost of receiving this item was estimated at $.65 per unit, and the cost of warehousing at $1.45 per unit. Some costs vary with dollar sales rather than with physical volume and are thus shown as percentages; illustrations are selling (if salesmen are paid on a percentage commission) and markdowns. The other cost estimates may be read from the chart.

Some duplication of cost patterns would exist within a department. There might be only 12 basic patterns in an appliance department because of similarities in items. This fact reduces the amount of record keeping.

---

[1] Robert I. Jones, "Merchandise Management Accounting in Practice," Arthur Andersen & Co., 1957.

varies w/ type of ~~produc~~ item. (i.e. easy to receive $.37, hard to receive $.92) etc.

EXHIBIT 3

MAJOR APPLIANCE DEPARTMENT
(variable cost centers—unit computations)

Receiving	$ .37	$ .50	$ .65	$ .78	$ .92
Warehousing	$ .75	$1.19	$1.45	$1.80	$2.25
Selling	6.0%	——	——	——	——
Advertising	2.5%	——	——	——	——
Carrying charges	(1.05%)	(1.95%)	(2.75%)	(3.77%)	(4.90%)	(8.25%)
Credit expense	$1.35	$1.60	$2.00	$2.40	$2.90	$4.25
Delivery	$1.40	$2.20	$2.95	$3.63	$4.40	$5.10
Installation	$3.50	$5.10	$5.50	$6.40	$7.25	——*
Warranty	$ .75	$1.20	$1.82	$2.10	$2.95	$5.25
Markdowns	3.50%	4.00%	4.50%	10.00%	——	——
Other costs	.70%	.90%	1.17%	——	——	——

　　* Customer pays.

EXHIBIT 4

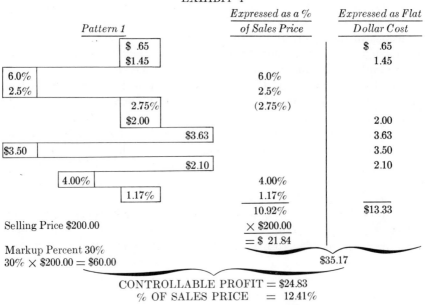

	Pattern 1	Expressed as a % of Sales Price	Expressed as Flat Dollar Cost
	$ .65		$ .65
	$1.45		1.45
6.0%		6.0%	
2.5%		2.5%	
	2.75%	(2.75%)	
	$2.00		2.00
	$3.63		3.63
$3.50			3.50
	$2.10		2.10
4.00%		4.00%	
	1.17%	1.17%	
		10.92%	$13.33

Selling Price $200.00　　　　　　　　　　× $200.00
　　　　　　　　　　　　　　　　　　= $ 21.84

Markup Percent 30%
30% × $200.00 = $60.00　　　　　　　　　　$35.17

CONTROLLABLE PROFIT = $24.83
% OF SALES PRICE　　= 12.41%

Exhibit 4, also taken from Jones' article shows how one might use the cost pattern on an appliance with a $200 selling price. Some of the expenses are expressed as percentages of the $200, others as "flat" dollar costs. The markup on the retail price of 30 percent ($60) can then be compared with the expenses obtained from the cost pattern of $35.17, leaving a "controllable profit" of $24.83.

EXHIBIT 5
Conversion Table of Controllable Profit to Return on Total Investment

Controllable Profit as a Percent of Cost	Return on Total Investment at Indicated Inventory Turnover Rates									Each Turnover of .1 Equals
	2	3	4	5	6	7	8	9	10	
2%	1.7 %	2.6 %	3.5 %	4.3 %	5.2 %	6.1 %	7.0 %	7.8 %	8.7 %	.09%
4	3.5	5.2	7.0	8.7	10.4	12.2	13.9	15.7	17.4	.17
6	5.2	7.8	10.4	13.0	15.7	18.3	20.9	23.5	26.1	.26
8	7.0	10.4	13.9	17.4	20.9	24.3	27.8	31.3	34.8	.35
10	8.7	13.0	17.4	21.7	26.1	30.4	34.8	39.1	43.5	.44
12	10.4	15.7	20.9	26.1	31.3	36.5	41.7	47.0	52.2	.52
14	12.2	18.3	24.3	30.4	36.5	42.6	48.7	54.8	60.9	.61
16	13.9	20.9	27.8	34.8	41.7	48.7	55.7	62.6	69.6	.70
18	15.7	23.5	31.3	39.1	47.0	54.8	62.6	70.4	78.3	.78
20	17.4	26.1	34.8	43.5	52.2	60.9	69.6	78.3	87.0	.87
24	20.9	31.3	41.7	52.2	62.6	73.0	83.5	93.9	104.3	1.04
28	24.3	36.5	48.7	60.9	73.0	85.2	97.4	109.6	121.7	1.22
32	27.8	41.7	55.7	69.6	83.5	97.4	111.3	125.2	139.1	1.39
36	31.3	47.0	62.6	78.3	93.9	109.6	125.2	140.9	156.5	1.57
40	34.8	52.2	69.6	87.0	104.3	121.7	139.1	156.5	173.9	1.74
44	38.3	57.4	76.5	95.7	114.8	133.9	153.0	172.2	191.3	1.91
48	41.7	62.6	83.5	104.3	125.2	146.1	167.0	187.8	208.7	2.09
Each 1% of cost equals	.87%	1.30%	1.74%	2.17%	2.61%	3.04%	3.48%	3.91%	4.35%	

Source: Robert I. Jones, "Objective and Basic Principles of M.M.A.," *Journal of Retailing*, Spring, 1958, p. 4.

Mr. Jones suggests a number of ways in which the cost patterns would be useful. The analysis (1) could indicate the effects on profit contribution of an increase in markup, or of carrying a more expensive item with the same markup; (2) could be useful in negotiating cost prices with suppliers by indicating the profit contribution on each individual item; (3) could aid in the analysis of alternative methods of buying (direct shipment versus warehouse handling, for example); (4) could indicate which items might receive more sales emphasis because of their high profit contributions; (5) could suggest areas in which handling costs are excessive, stimulating investigation of why such costs are out of line; and (6) could lead to elimination or reduction of some services. In fact, any decision requiring consideration of variable costs could be aided by the information developed by this system.

One additional refinement in M.M.A. is the computation of the return on invested capital. Exhibit 5 shows how the controllable profit may be converted into percentage returns, depending on the inventory turnover rate. For example, the 12.41 percent of sales price on the $200 appliance in Exhibit 4 would provide a 20.9 percent (actually slightly higher) return on investment if the turnover were four times per year. The comparison of returns on investment provides a sounder basis for merchandising decisions than comparison of only controllable profit.

Some representative decisions

The managers of Janet Lee's Department Store were involved in the kinds of decisions that are usual in retailing. One of these was pricing. The usual method of pricing was to add a predetermined markup to wholesale price, the markup varying with the line of merchandise. The markups were based on what was traditional or normal in the industry. Markdowns were common on items that did not move; the final price might even fall below wholesale cost, though this was the exception. The managers adhered to manufacturers' suggested prices on many items. They followed the practice of "price lining" on other goods.

Sometimes special cost studies were made for particular decisions by the management of the store. For example, an unusual type of glassware was introduced in the store; the managers had no previous experience with such merchandise. They estimated the incremental costs of handling the glassware, finding that delivery expense would be unusually large. On the basis of the cost estimates, a price was initiated and a small bonus was paid to sales clerks whose customers carried the glassware out of the store rather than have it delivered.

Another kind of decision problem was the opening and closing of a department or the change of its location. One example was the candies department, which in 1957 was located on the main floor. The managers believed that more profitable items could be located in that space and moved the candy counter to the basement. Later the store made an agreement with a national firm which handles high quality, high price candies to carry its merchandise on the main floor. The national firm guaranteed the sale of the candy, agreeing to take back all unsold candy. It also agreed to pay 50 percent of the advertising cost. The manufacturer's representative prepared a "profitability study" which compared the costs and revenue of the candies with that of the merchandise then occupying the space. This study was instrumental in persuading the management to invest in the required refrigerator cases and to move the candy department back to the first floor.

1. *Would Janet Lee's Department Store benefit from introduction of M.M.A.?*
2. *Should the store make greater use of accounting in decision making?*
3. *What are the deficiencies of the present accounting methods used in the store?*
4. *Discuss the bases of indirect expenses allocation shown in Exhibit 2.*
5. *Evaluate the cost pattern used in M.M.A. Does it give an estimate of incremental cost? Should it do so?*
6. *Does M.M.A. give all the information required for pricing?*

DIRECT COSTING*

One of the most controversial issues in the accounting profession in recent years has been that concerning direct costing. The concept of direct costing was first developed in 1936 but was not placed into use in many firms until the 1950s. A survey in 1953 revealed only 17 companies using the method; by 1962 the number had increased to over 250.[1]

The controversy over direct costing has centered on two major issues: the measurement of period income for purposes of financial accounting, and the use of accounting data in decision making. This case is more concerned with the decision-making aspects, since they are closer to the subject matter of managerial economics.

The measurement of income

The advocates of direct costing like to think of costs as falling into two categories: direct costs and period costs. The direct costs are those which vary with volume; the period costs are constant for a given period. The main effect of direct costing in the area of financial accounting is on the valuation of inventory. A change in the valuation of inventory

---

* Most of this case is based on Wilmer Wright and Felix P. Kollaritsch, "A Management Consultant and a Professor of Accounting Look at the Concept of Direct Costing," *The Controller* (now known as *Financial Executive*), July, 1962, pp. 322–29, 354–57. The Case is intended as an introduction to direct costing and to its relation to economic analysis. For a full discussion of the issues the reader is referred to texts on cost accounting and to research bulletins of the National Association of Accountants.

[1] *Business Week*, March 24, 1962, p. 46.

means a change in the reporting of period income. Direct costing would eliminate the allocation of fixed overhead costs to inventory which is characteristic of absorption accounting. In periods of excess production over sales, the effect would be to avoid including overhead in inventory values and thus to prevent the "overstatement" of income. In periods when sales exceed production, the effect is to prevent the "understatement" of income.

An illustration from an article in *Business Week*[2] on direct costing shows how standard absorption accounting might distort income. (See Exhibit 1.) In this case sales increased by 50 percent from January to February, but the absorption accounting system showed a profit of $2,000 in January and a loss of $5,000 in February. The reason for this was the inclusion of $6,000 of period costs in the January inventory— costs which were charged to the cost of sales in February. Direct costing resulted in a restatement of profits, with a $4,000 loss in January and a $1,000 profit in February. The supporters of direct costing would claim that the second result is more reasonable, since February is the kind of month which is profitable, while a long sequence of months like January could only lead to bankruptcy.

The advocates of absorption accounting would uphold the allocation of overheads to production. They insist that the production process involves a conversion, not only of material and labor into the values of the product but also a conversion of overhead into such values. They argue that machines as well as labor produce values. It seems to them illogical that replacement of labor by machines should lead to a neglect of part of the conversion costs. According to one writer on the subject, "a product is the result of all expenditures made in its manufacture. In establishing accountability, the product should be charged with those expenses."[3] The same writer notes that it is possible to convert depreciation from a period cost to a direct cost by shifting from straight-line depreciation to unit production depreciation; it seems unreasonable to him that such an arbitrary change in costing should determine whether or not depreciation should enter into unit cost. He also notes that the shortening of the length of the accounting period results in a higher proportion of period costs—if the period is made short enough even wages become a period cost.

One strong argument against direct costing applies when inventories are deliberately built up in one period for sale in another period. It seems logical that a substantial part of the overhead should be deferred until the final sale of the product. Direct costing would not permit the deferment of overhead in the period of inventory build-up and thus,

---

[2] "Direct Costing to the Rescue," *Business Week*, March 24, 1962, p. 45.

[3] Felix P. Kollaritsch, in Wright and Kollaritsch, "A Management Consultant and a Professor of Accounting Look at the Concept of Direct Costing," p. 325.

as shown in Exhibit 1, would avoid any recognition of the values in the inventories other than the direct cost. It would seem important to determine the cause of excess production in any particular period. If the purpose of the excess production in one period is to provide for seasonally high levels of sales in the future the absorption of overhead would appear to be reasonable; values in the production period do exceed the direct costs and should be recognized on both the balance sheet and income statement. If, however, the excess production is due to an error of scheduling the absorption of overhead might seem improper.

EXHIBIT 1
Two Methods of Measuring Income

1. *Standard Absorption Accounting*	January	February
Sales @ $10	$20,000	$30,000
Cost of sales @ $8 per unit	16,000	24,000
($5 direct cost plus $3 standard overhead)		
Unabsorbed "burden" or overhead	——	9,000
($12,000 minus $3 per unit produced)		
Gross profit	4,000	(3,000)*
Selling and administrative expenses	2,000	2,000
Net operating profit	2,000	(5,000)*

2. *Direct Costing*	January	February
Sales @ $10	$20,000	$30,000
Direct cost of sales @ $5	10,000	15,000
Gross profit	10,000	15,000
Overhead expenses	12,000	12,000
Selling and administrative expenses	2,000	2,000
Net operating profit	(4,000)*	1,000

* Loss.

Source: *Business Week*, March 24, 1962, p. 45.

The movement to direct costing for the reporting of income has been slowed by the opposition of the public accounting profession and by the requirements of the Securities and Exchange Commission. The Internal Revenue Service requires the use of full costs in the valuation of inventory for tax purposes. It seems unlikely that these agencies will soon change their opposition to direct costing for financial reporting.

Decision making

Even if one agrees that direct costing is not appropriate for the reporting of income, he may still recommend it for decision-making purposes. It is possible to adopt direct costing and then to convert the final figures to a full-cost basis in the financial reports.

The advocates of direct costing claim that it is better suited to providing data for decisions than is absorption accounting. For example, the system shows the effects of an increase in the volume of sales on costs and on profits. In combination with information about price-volume relationships, it indicates the effects of price change on profits. Wilmer Wright, one of the best-known consultants on direct costing, has constructed a comparison of direct costing and absorption costing for a single product (Model #1971) in the form of a table. (See Exhibit 2.) He claims that the information provided by direct costing is much more useful for profit planning, pricing, make-or-buy decisions, or for decisions on product mix. Note that Exhibit 2 shows that direct costing does not preclude the allocation of overhead (period costs). In fact the overhead is allocated in two parts: those costs which would be eliminated if the product line were dropped (specific period expense) and those which would continue on even if the line were dropped. The period costs are not allocated to particular units but are handled as totals.

Some accountants and other authorities deny that direct costing has

EXHIBIT 2

Cost Analysis—Model 1971
(direct costs)

	Dollars per Unit	Profit Plan
Planned volume—units	——	5,000
Net sales	$165.00	$825,000
Direct cost		
Material	$ 46.00	$230,000
Variable labor	45.50	227,500
Other direct expense	24.00	120,000
Total direct cost	$115.50	$577,500
Margin	$ 49.50	$247,500
Percent P/V	30%	30%
Specific period expense	——	150,000
Model contribution	——	$ 97,500
Allocated period expense	——	90,000
Operating profit	——	$ 7,500

Cost Analysis—Model 1971
(absorption costs)

	Dollars per Unit	Profit Plan
Planned volume—units	——	5,000
Net sales	$165.00	$825,000
Manufacturing cost		
Direct labor	$ 35.00	$175,000
Material	46.00	230,000
Manufacturing overhead	58.50	292,500
Total manufacturing cost	$139.50	$697,500
Gross profit	$ 25.50	$127,500
Percent	15.4%	15.4%
Selling and administrative costs	$ 24.00	$120,000
Operating profit	$ 1.50	$ 7,500

Source: Wilmer Wright and Felix P. Kollaritsch, "A Management Consultant and a Professor of Accounting Look at the Concept of Direct Costing," *The Controller* (now known as *Financial Executive*), July 1962, p. 326.

these advantages. The Committee on Distribution Costs and Efficiency of the American Marketing Association had this to say:

If all overhead is not absorbed, it will not be possible to show net profits by products or customer classes. Without these net profit figures, it is difficult to make full application of the results to management decisions.[4]

One writer on the subject has argued that fully allocated costs are superior to direct costs in pricing. His argument is as follows:

If the full unit cost is not recovered in the price, production will be abandoned. . . . Intelligent pricing necessitates full unit cost information. The establishing of prices without the inclusion of the related pro rata fixed manufacturing expenses would appear to be unrealistic and complicated. *How much, for instance, should a regular price be set above the marginal cost? 10 percent, 20 percent, or more?* Without the knowledge of the pro rata fixed expenses applicable to a product, any price decision would be arbitrary and probably unsound. In pricing products, consideration should be given to the amount of capital invested in production facilities, particularly in the case of multiproduct plants where varying capital investments are needed for different products.[5]

The same author has also criticized the emphasis of direct costing on contribution margins in these words:

Under direct costing only those items which sell below their direct cost are considered actual loss items. The higher the contribution margin the more profitable is the item, say those who believe in direct costing—without further analysis of those fixed expenses originated with the production of the item. It is doubtful whether the true profitability of a product or department can be measured without first determining its corresponding fixed expenses. Contribution margins and profit are not synonymous. The product with the highest contribution margin could easily be responsible for the occurrence of fixed expenses far in excess of the returns that the price of this product yields above direct costs. On the other hand, a product with a small contribution margin might not only cover its direct fixed expenses but may also render a satisfactory profit. Under direct costing it would be possible for some truly profitable items to be neglected by management because of low contribution margins.[6]

Conclusion

The debate over direct costing has also gone into the issue of cost control, a subject which is of less interest in this case. The position in favor of direct costing can be summarized in the following quotation:

---

[4] The Committee on Distribution Costs and Efficiency, The American Marketing Association, "The Values and Uses of Distribution Cost Analysis," *Journal of Marketing,* Vol. 21 (April 1957). Reprinted from the *Journal of Marketing,* national quarterly publication of the American Marketing Association.

[5] Felix P. Kollaritsch, in Wright and Kollaritsch, "A Management Consultant and a Professor of Accounting Look at the Concept of Direct Costing," p. 329.

[6] Ibid., p. 357.

[I]t may be stated with little fear of contradiction that the use of direct costing will continue to grow because it meets the needs of operating executives for internal management accounting and at the same time can accommodate almost any requirement for external reporting. Controllers who have taken the lead in converting their accounting system to direct costing are extremely enthusiastic. They report that since the conversion operating people have been turning to them more and more for guidance before important decisions are made. Operating executives, on the other hand, report that their financial men have learned to talk in terms that nonaccounting people can understand.[7]

The position against direct costing has been summarized in the following statements:

Its effectiveness is limited to special purposes which cannot be considered as the primary functions of cost accounting.

The exclusion of fixed manufacturing expenses from inventories is unrealistic. Fixed expenses are as much a part of the creation of new values as are labor and material.

Intelligent pricing and aggressive competition can only be exercised when complete information as to the cost of a product, product line, or department is available.

Profitability cannot be measured by the contribution margin.

Fixed costs are not best controlled in total, but rather in their relationship to the unit.

Simplifications, although a desirable objective in accounting, must be foregone where they lead to a distortion of facts or result in vagueness.[8]

1. *What production schedule is implicit in Exhibit 1? What number of units is produced in January? In February?*
   a. *Is this production schedule likely in actual business operations?*
   b. *Could such a schedule ever be a reasonable adaptation to conditions?*
   c. *Would it make any difference whether the excess production in January was deliberately planned for February sales or was a result of erroneous scheduling?*
2. *When is income or wealth created: at the time of production or at the time of sale? What bearing does this have on the issue of direct costing versus absorption accounting?*
3. *Would reported profit fluctuate more widely under direct costing or absorption accounting? Discuss.*
4. *Why might the U.S. Treasury oppose direct costing for tax purposes?*
5. *Does direct costing bring the costs of idle capacity to the income statement more promptly than absorption accounting? Explain.*
6. *Do you agree that profitability cannot be measured by the contribution margin? Does your answer depend upon whether it is short-run or long-run profitability which is under consideration?*
7. *Does direct costing lead to lower prices? Discuss.*
8. *What is your position on the direct costing controversy? Explain.*
9. *One writer has argued that instead of emphasizing direct costing or conven-*

---

[7] Wilmer Wright, ibid., p. 357.

[8] Kollaritsch, ibid., p. 357.

tional costing, we should stress "relevant costing." (C. T. Horngren, Cost Accounting: A Managerial Emphasis, *1962.) What do you suppose he has in mind?*

THE MINERVA OXYGEN VENT VALVE*

In March 1959, Mr. H. R. Deming, president of Dem-A-Lex Dynamics Corporation of Lexington, Mass., called a meeting of the executive committee to consider a proposal which would establish improved quality control over an item produced by Dem-A-Lex as subcontractor for several prime contractors. The item was an oxygen vent valve used in the "Minerva," a rocket-powered missile.

This valve had been adopted by several large missile manufacturing companies during 1958 for use in the recently developed Minerva missile. In early 1959, however, the Department of Defense announced that the Minerva missile had been designated as an operational first line weapon and that all prime contractors of the Minerva missile were to enter crash production programs. Because of the increased urgency of the program and the importance of the oxygen vent valve to the Minerva's proper functioning, an executive committee meeting had been called to consider a proposal, submitted by Mr. Massey, the company's production manager. Mr. Massey's proposal recommended the utilization of a newly introduced piece of testing equipment which would greatly reduce the number of defective vent valves delivered by Dem-A-Lex to the various prime contractors.

Company history

Mr. Deming, a graduate electromechanical engineer, had left his position with a large electrical products manufacturing company in 1948 and started a small research service organization in an Army surplus Quonset hut. He stated, "I had always wanted to tinker around with my own ideas and push them to completion, and when I saw the chance to obtain a research grant for the development of a high temperature pressure indicator, I couldn't resist the temptation to apply for the grant. I was completely fed up with all the red tape, required reports, and voluminous records associated with my previous job."

Since 1948, the company had grown rapidly, and net sales in 1958 had exceeded $6 million (see Exhibits 1 and 2). As the company had expanded, Mr. Deming, considered by most of his associates as an inventive genius, decided to devote his time and energy to research and

---

* This case was prepared by Andrew McCosh under the direction of Stanley I. Buchin of the Harvard University Graduate School of Business Administration as a basis for classroom discussion rather than to illustrate either effective or ineffective handling of administrative situations. Copyright © 1965 by the President and Fellows of Harvard College. Used by specific permission.

EXHIBIT 1

THE MINERVA OXYGEN VENT VALVE
(balance sheet as of December 31, 1958, in thousands of dollars)

ASSETS

Cash and marketable securities	$378	
Accounts receivable (net)	954	
Inventories	685	
Notes receivable (employees)	126	
Total current assets		$2,143
Land and buildings (net)	$360	
Machinery and equipment (net)	680	
Prepaid expenses	6	
Other assets	13	
Total fixed assets		1,059
Total assets		$3,202

LIABILITIES AND NET WORTH

Accounts payable	$250	
Notes payable to bank @ 6%	700	
Dividends payable	35	
Other accruals	315	
Total current liabilities		$1,300
Mortgage payable on real estate	$120	
Long-term bonds (7% coupon)	500	
Common stock (40% owned by Mr. Deming, Sr., and his son)	410	
Earned surplus	872	
Total fixed liabilities and net worth		1,902
Total liabilities and net worth		$3,202

development of new products and had turned the actual operating management of the business over to his son Stephen Deming, a former Air Force jet pilot and a recent graduate of a well-known business school. Mr. Deming, Sr., had developed several unique and commercially saleable products since 1948, among which were: metal and fabric strain gauges which signaled a condition of overload on the material; special high pressure intensifiers and pressure transducers; solenoid-triggered butterfly valves; ultralow temperature liquid pumps and flow regulators; high tension circuit breakers; and most recently the oxygen vent valve. Patents had initially been obtained on each of these items, but, after they had been a few years on the market, similar devices, but different enough to avoid patent infringement, had been developed by the larger manufacturing companies in the industry. Because of their size and volume production methods, these companies could generally produce the item more cheaply than could Dem-A-Lex.

As a result of this, Dem-A-Lex did not attempt to compete on a volume-price basis with the larger firms in the industry, but instead,

EXHIBIT 2

THE MINERVA OXYGEN VENT VALVE

(statement of profit and loss for year ending December 31, 1958,
in thousands of dollars)

Gross sales	$6,193	
Less allowances given for defective valves	143	
Net sales		$6,050
Cost of goods sold:		
Direct labor	$1,010	
Materials	2,030	
Factory burden	1,362	
Cost of goods sold		4,402
Gross Profit		$1,648
Operating expenses:		
Selling expense*	332	
Administrative expense*	198	
Research expense*	350	
Interest expense	93	
Total operating expenses		$ 973
Net profits before tax		$ 675
Federal taxes (52%)		350
Net income after tax		$ 325
Dividends on common stock		30
Net addition to retained earnings		$ 295

    * See Exhibit 3 for an analysis of this expense.

exploited each product as fully as possible before the larger concerns developed a similar item. After the loss of the high volume customer to the larger producers, Dem-A-Lex then concentrated its efforts on modification and adaption of the item to the customer with unique or special requirements who could not obtain the special adaptation from the high volume producer, or whose requirements were too small to interest such a producer.

Flexible production scheduling and the ability of the research department to modify standard production models to meet unusual product specifications, had given Dem-A-Lex the ability to capture a specialized portion of the total market for most of its products. Mr. H. R. Deming commented, "We are not trying to butt heads with the big boys. Our policy is to sell our real assets—our research and development skills, and our productive flexibility."

Sale of vent valves accounted for nearly 25 percent of Dem-A-Lex's total sales during 1958, while the other 75 percent was made up of the sale of strain gauges, pressure gauges, intensifiers, and transducers, various types of electrically and hydraulically operated valves, regulators, circuit breakers, and other electrical and mechanical devices. Sales revenue from these items had been increasing at an annual rate of 8 percent since 1951. All of these items were manufactured in the general production department with general purpose equipment, while the vent valve was produced in a separate department on specialized equipment. This specialized equipment had been purchased or built by Mr. Deming himself during 1957 and 1958 at a cost of about $525,000. However, Mr. Deming commented that if he had to replace all this equipment today by purchase from outside vendors, it would probably cost him over $950,000.

Oxygen vent valve

In November 1956 Mr. H. R. Deming had begun work on the development of an improved oxygen vent valve. He had been motivated to experiment with this type of valve because of the high number of failures (nearly 60 percent defective) of valves which were then being used by missile producers. By January 1958 he had designed a valve which was lighter in weight and more resistant to extreme temperature and pressure than any valve then on the market. A new missile designated the Minerva was also introduced in early 1958, and by coincidence Dem-A-Lex's new vent valve met the missile's more rigid technical requirements. Because of this, Dem-A-Lex received subcontracts from several missile manufacturers to produce the oxygen vent valve for the Minerva missile.

The oxygen vent valve was a critical component to the proper functioning of any liquid rocket engine. A liquid rocket engine was basically a very simple mechanism. It consisted of a fuel tank, an oxygen tank, a pressure tank, a combustion chamber, and a number of valves for regulating the flow of material from the various tanks into the combustion chamber. Nitrogen gas from the pressure tank was used to force liquid oxygen and a liquid fuel (generally alcohol or kerosene and LOX) through propellent control valves into injector nozzles and thence into the combustion chamber where the mixture was ignited to provide the rocket's thrust.

Most missiles had four vent valves located on either side of the airframe just below the nose cone or warhead; the Minerva missile, however, had eight vent valves. In order to fill the oxygen tank these vent valves were opened and liquid oxygen at $-220°$ F. was pumped into the oxygen tank through filler valves at the base of the tank until the tank was full. When the tank was completely filled, liquid oxygen spewed out the four vent valves in heavy white streams. These valves then had to be closed before the system could be pressurized. Pressurization was accomplished by pumping nitrogen gas through a second chamber of the oxygen vent valve into the oxygen tank. If the vent valves did not close (because of the very low temperature), all pressure would be lost, and no oxygen could be forced into the combustion chamber.

These valves had to withstand not only temperatures of $-220°$ F.,

EXHIBIT 3

THE MINERVA OXYGEN VENT VALVE
(analysis of selling, administrative, and research expenses
for year ending December 31, 1958, in thousands of dollars)

Selling expense

Advertising	$ 33	
Salesmen's salaries and commissions	251	
Traveling expenses	24	
Supplies	7	
Heat, light and power (allocated on basis of floor space utilized by sales department)	2	
Samples	13	
Depreciation (allocated on basis of floor space utilized by sales department)	2	
Total Selling Expense		$332

Administrative expense
Officers' salaries (included half of

Mr. Deming, Sr.'s, salary)	$ 62	
Office wages	81	
Office expenses	14	
Legal and accounting	6	
Telephone and telegraph	3	
Miscellaneous expenses	7	
Depreciation (allocated on basis of floor space utilized by the office. Also included direct depreciation computed on various articles of office equipment)	4	
Bad debt losses	16	
Heat, light, and power (allocated on basis of floor space utilized by the office)	5	
Total Administrative Expense		$198

Research expense*
Officers' salaries (included half of Mr. Deming,

Sr.'s, salary)	$ 25	
Laboratory supplies and expendable equipment	45	
Depreciation (allocated on basis of floor space utilized by the research laboratory)	4	
Heat, light, and power (allocated on basis of floor space utilized by the research laboratory)	4	
Salaries of research personnel	186	
Materials used in development of operational prototypes	79	
Machinery and equipment depreciation	4	
Liability insurance	3	
Total Research expense		$350

* During 1958, the research staff spent approximately 75 percent–80 percent of its time on the development and testing of an oxygen vent valve constructed of "Berylitt," a metal alloy recently perfected by Dem-A-Lex.

but also those of +500° F. generated by the missile in flight as well as the great pressure caused by the expansion of nitrogen gas as it was forced through the valve chamber into the oxygen tank. Mr. Deming had developed an alloy of beryllium and titanium, referred to as "Berylitt," which was designed to withstand both extreme temperature and pressure. Mr.

EXHIBIT 4

THE MINERVA OXYGEN VALVE
(analysis of projected factory burden for fiscal 1959 in thousands of dollars)

	Budgeted for 1959 Assuming No Change in Production Procedures	Budgeted for 1959 Assuming Plating-Polish- ing Operation Added for 2,000 Vent Valves	Budgeted for* 1959 Assuming Testing Equip- ment Rented
Fringe benefits†	$ 354	$ 358	$ 359
Supervision	213	213	213
Inspection	147	150	149
Purchasing and receiving	123	128	128
Repair to tools and equipment	99	102	100
Clerical, trucking, and cleanup	90	90	90
Maintenance	43	43	48
Valve replacement parts	$ 17	$ 0	$ 5
Small tools	41	43	40
Spoiled work	69	65	67
Supplies	83	84	85
Department indirect	52	54	54
Heat, light and power	23	26	26
Test machine rental			24
Depreciation (allocated on basis of floor space utilized by the production facilities)	44	44	44
Total Factory Burden	$1,403	$1,400	$1,432

* These budgeted figures did not include any expected change in overhead costs associated with the addition of the plating-polishing process to the vent valve production operation.

† This item was composed of the cost of unemployment compensation, social security, a company-sponsored health insurance plan, and vacation payments, for all direct and indirect labor. It averaged 20 percent of labor costs annually.

Deming felt the vent valves had been quite successful because only 450 vent valves had proved defective out of the total 1958 sale of 1,500 valves. Previous valves had failed, on the average, 60 percent of the time.

Under the terms of various subcontracts which Dem-A-Lex held, the prime contractor was permitted to charge Dem-A-Lex $300 for each vent valve which was found defective. Of this, $250 was the cost of removing the defective valve from the missile and the installation of a new valve, while $50 was allowed for repairing the defective valve with parts supplied by Dem-A-Lex. These repair parts had cost Dem-A-Lex an average of $25 per defective valve in 1958 and had been charged to the burden account (Exhibit 4) by the accounting department, while the charge of $300 for each defective valve was recorded as a deduction from gross sales (Exhibit 2). Thus, each defective valve cost Dem-A-Lex an additional $325. Because of the urgency of the missile program, the prime contractor repaired the valves at the missile site, rather than sending them back to Dem-A-Lex for replacement.

The standard price which Dem-A-Lex received for each oxygen vent valve was $975. The cost accounting department computed the factory cost of each vent valve as follows:

Direct materials		$139
Direct labor:		
Machining time	$175	
Assembly time	100	
Inspection and packaging time	25	
Total direct labor		$300
Overhead: 135% of direct labor		405
Total product cost per valve		$844

The 135 percent overhead rate was based on the relationship of overhead costs to direct labor costs in 1958 (Exhibit 2). The factory cost accountant itemized the costs charged to the factory burden account as shown in Exhibit 4.

Quality control of the oxygen vent valve

Dem-A-Lex, in early 1959, had no way of subjecting its vent valves to operational temperatures and pressure before the valve was assembled into the missile. Each component part of the valve was carefully inspected for size, required tolerances, and surface before assembly, and the assembled valve was hydraulically tested before shipment to the missile manufacturer, but this did not prevent valve failure when the rocket engine was statically fired at the launching site (a test firing with the missile securely fastened to its launching pad).

One of two types of failure might occur when the engine was statically fired; first, the valve might freeze in the open position because of the frigid temperature of the liquid oxygen, or second, after it was closed, a butterfly valve (inside the vent valve) might freeze in the closed position and as the nitrogen gas was forced into the chamber of the vent valve, pressure would build up until the vent valve ruptured, thus depressurizing the oxygen tank. If either of the above conditions occurred, the valve had to be removed and rebuilt by the replacement of tension springs, the butterfly valve, and various pressure seals and diaphragms. Both types of valve failure were caused by a common factor, the expansion or contraction of the metal components in the valve as it was subjected to operational temperatures. Even the most accurate measurement of specified tolerances could not eliminate these failures, since the internal molecular structure of the metal in each valve was slightly different and thus each valve would be affected differently by the operational temperatures. Mr. Stephen Deming stated that it was much cheaper to have the prime contractor repair the defective valve than it was to junk it and that the cost of a valve failure ($300) charged by the prime contractor did not depend upon the type of defect that occurred. The subcontract did not permit the prime contractor to charge Dem-A-Lex $300 for the failure of a valve which had been rebuilt by the prime contractor. Thus, Dem-A-Lex could never be held financially responsible for more than one failure on each valve produced.

Mr. Stephen Deming pointed out, however, that the research department had developed a vanadium electroplating and polishing process which, if used, would guarantee that every vent valve would function perfectly. This process would eliminate all defects by reducing the expansion or contraction of any metal surface which had been treated with vanadium. The plating and polishing procedure would require $110 of material and three hours of labor at $3 per hour for each valve produced.

The company currently had excess capacity on the electroplating and polishing equipment located in the general production department and thus would not have to purchase additional equipment to perform this operation. However, there was no excess labor time available in the department, and Mr. Deming estimated that two or three new men would have to be hired to run the plating and polishing equipment. Mr. Massey stated that this equipment was currently being used by the general production department about 20 hours per week and that the processing of the vent valves on this equipment would consume another 14 to 15 hours per week, thus loading the equipment to nearly 90 percent of its total capacity. These pieces of machinery occupied approximately 800 square feet of the total factory space of 20,000 square feet and were being depreciated at the rate of $2,100 per year. This equipment would be fully depreciated by December 31, 1963. However, Mr. Deming, Sr., commented that he did not feel the additional cost was justified since he thought it was cheaper to "let your customers do your testing for you, and then all you have to do is pay for *just* those valves that have to be repaired. It's nonsense to incur the cost of plating when we don't have to!"

Mr. Massey, on the other hand, was in favor of renting a "revolutionary" piece of testing equipment which had just been put on the market. He had recently been approached by the National Machinery and Testing Equipment Co., of Zanesville, Indiana, about newly developed testing equipment which could be used to test each valve before its shipment to the prime contractor. Mr. Massey had loaned National Machinery 100 vent valves to test on this new equipment and had been told that 40 of these valves were defective while 60 were operationally perfect. The 60 valves which had tested "good" were especially marked and sent to one of the prime contractors by Dem-A-Lex. Later this prime contractor informed Dem-A-Lex that twelve of the valves which had tested "good" failed to operate and hence had to be rebuilt. The 40 vent valves which tested defective were sent to the general production department for electroplating and polishing. The National Machinery and Testing Co. stated that they could not guarantee complete accuracy in that a few valves which tested good would prove defective, while some which tested bad would in fact be operationally perfect. However, the equipment was reliable in that it would produce consistent readings on successive tests for any given valve. Mr. Massey was very much in favor of renting the testing equipment because he stated "It's obvious that it's going to save us money. By testing the valves we had only 12 rejects in a hundred, while if these same valves had been shipped directly to the prime contractor we would have incurred the cost of making good on about 42 (30 + 12) rejects. Thus, you see, the testing equipment would reduce our number of rejects by 70 percent; this would mean a cash saving of $300 as well as a reduction in the cost of repair parts for each potential reject which could be detected before shipment."

The testing equipment would cost Dem-A-Lex $24,000 a year for rental, and this figure would be a flat rate. There would be no additional installation charge, and the shakedown testing that would be required would be done at the expense of National Machinery. Mr. Massey proposed that the testing equipment be installed in a room recently vacated by the office staff. "If we do this," he said "we won't have to charge any overhead to the testing operation, since the space was vacant anyway." The office staff had just recently moved to quarters (2,400 square feet) which rented for $250 per month, across the street from the factory in order that the supplies storeroom could be expanded for the purpose of increasing its operational efficiency. The space which was vacated by the office staff consisted of 2,000 square feet of the total factory area of 20,000 square feet. The valve department occupied approximately 5,000 square feet of the total factory area. However, expansion of the storeroom was not critical and thus could be delayed for an extended period of time. This testing equipment would require the addition of two men to the payroll who would operate and load the equipment as a team. Because of union regulations these men would not be permitted to perform any other operation in their slack time. These specially trained employees would be paid $3.50 per hour. The National Machinery and Testing Equipment Co. estimated that the testing equipment could handle 2,500 vent valves annually working a 40 hour week. The machinery was also capable of operating under overtime conditions. The period of the initial rental contract would be one year, though this could be extended at Dem-A-Lex's option. The company also estimated that an annual expense of $3,500 could be expected for normal maintenance of the testing equipment including bimonthly replacement of the freon gas used in the equipment. Mr. Massey had also been informed that National Machinery was working on an improved testing machine which would probably be put on the market in 1961 or 1962.

Neither Mr. H. R. Deming nor his son, Stephen, was at all convinced of the advisability of renting the special testing machine. Mr. H. R. Deming did not feel that the anticipated volume of vent valve production would be enough to justify the rental charge, and further was concerned over the possibility that one of the large manufacturing companies might develop an improved oxygen vent valve which would replace Dem-a-Lex's valve. However, since solid fuel rockets were expected to make their entrance by 1965, at which time the production of liquid fuel rockets would be drastically curtailed, Mr. Sears (sales manager) did not feel that any competitor would be interested in spending a lot of time and money developing an improved oxygen vent valve unless he was specifically requested to do so by a major prime contractor. He did not think that any competitor was working on an oxygen vent valve at that time, and he estimated it would take at least two years and $400,000 for a competitor to develop an improved valve. Mr. Sears further pointed out that the increased urgency of the missile program might encourage missile manufacturers to look elsewhere for more reliable vent valves, but he did not think this too likely as long as the number of defective valves did not exceed a "reasonable" level. Dem-A-Lex was well liked by its prime contractors and had built up good rapport with them in past associations. Mr. Sears estimated that 2,000 oxygen vent valves would be demanded annually through 1965. Because of the complexity of the vent valve and because of expected increases in labor and material costs, Mr. Sears could foresee no reason for the biannually negotiated price of the valve to fall below the current contract price of $975. All of Dem-A-Lex's vent valve two-year subcontracts came up for renewal in January to April, 1960.

Stephen Deming was not sure whether the rental of the testing equipment could be justified, but he felt very strongly that all vent valves should be vanadium plated and polished by the newly developed production process. He commented, "Why should we spend $2,000 a month on fancy testing equipment when all we really need to do to solve our problem is to just plate the valves on existing equipment with only a small additional cost per valve?"

After extensive discussion of each of the above points of view, Mr. Deming adjourned the executive committee meeting until the afternoon of the following day, when he expected Mr. Swen's (the company controller) return from an out-of-town trip. He instructed Stephen Deming to fill Mr. Swen in on the discussion which had taken place at the committee meeting and to ask him to be prepared to submit his recommendations relative to quality control of the vent valve to the committee the following afternoon.

1. *Calculate the cost of continuing with payments of $300 plus $25 for parts for each failure.*
2. *Calculate the cost of the vanadium process.*

3. Calculate the cost of renting the new equipment.
4. Which of the above alternatives is preferable?

THE STATE UNIVERSITY PRESS (B)

The State University Press is engaged in producing scholarly books and monographs for which the demand is relatively limited. The objective is not profit; if it were the Press would select more popular works with a wider market. The Press must operate within the limits of its budget, including subsidies from outside foundations, and must therefore control costs.

One important decision affecting costs is the length of run for each publication. If the first run of a book is too small, the Press takes the risk of running out of stock and losing sales. It also must meet the extra setup costs required by a second run. But if the run is too large, the Press encounters storage costs and losses from unsold books.

Before publication of each book, one of the Press's editors makes an estimate of costs based primarily on past experience with similar books. For example, the cost of publishing 1,000 copies of a monograph in business administration planned for November 15, 1962, was $1,300 for composition and printing, $550 for binding, and $40 for freight.

Sometimes the estimates were considerably in error, especially if the author's alterations were numerous. The estimates tended to be on the low side. In the case of the business monograph under discussion, however, the actual costs were close to the estimates, as is shown in Exhibit 1 (many of the figures have been rounded).

The stock cost was a completely variable cost. The composition and press costs were a mixture of direct labor costs and allocations of equipment and space charges.

A second run of 1,000 copies would be considerably cheaper than the first run. A second run of the text would require 11 offset lithographic plates, costing $18 per plate. The stock would cost about $138, as before. The offset press run would take about 11 hours at $9 per hour. The ink would be $3.10. The jacket would require $10 for stock, $2 for ink, $18 for one offset plate, $9 for one offset press run, and $7 for one letterpress run. Binding costs would again be approximately $507. If the second run were smaller than 1,000 copies, the costs would be about the same except for the stock and binding costs. The stock costs would be proportional to the run, but the binding costs include a fixed element of about $100 per run.

Sometimes the Press would print extra sheets of a book in the first run, postponing binding the sheets until the first batch of bound copies were sold. On the business monograph under discussion no extra sheets were printed.

EXHIBIT 1

ACTUAL COSTS ON MONOGRAPH
(publication date—November 15, 1962)

Text

Stock	$138.00	
Composition	638.00 (98 hours)	
Press	141.40 (20 hours)	
Ink	3.10	
Miscellaneous	10.00	
Overhead (15% of above)	140.50	
Total cost of text		$1,071.00

Jacket

Stock	$ 10.00	
Composition	39.20 (5 hours)	
Press	37.80 (5.4 hours)	
Miscellaneous	1.50	
Ink	2.00	
Overhead (15% of above)	13.50	
Total cost of jacket		104.00
Binding		506.83
Freight		40.72
Total actual cost		$1,722.55

Decisions on the length of run were influenced by the shortage of storage space. No one had made an estimate of storage costs. Probably the rental value of the space used for storage would be $1,000 per annum. The space had a capacity for about 16,000 volumes and was constantly overcrowded. Copies of some old books were stored in a basement room and finally discarded after any hope of further sales had passed.

The retail price of the monograph was set at $3. The Press could expect to receive an average of $2.10 per copy after discounts to distributors. The greatest uncertainty concerned the level of sales. One purchaser had guaranteed to buy 500 copies. The Press had no previous experience with monographs in the business area and thus had little basis for estimating sales beyond the 500 copies. Sales of monographs in other subject matter areas usually ran below 500, and sometimes as low as 200. The Press could make fairly accurate estimates of sales of books on historical subjects and of monographs in archeology and anthropology, because it had published a number of works in those areas, but its estimates on other books were subject to considerable error.

1. *Construct a model for the determination of the economic length of run on books.*
2. *What economic principles are incorporated in your model?*
3. *Apply your model as best you can to the problem of the business monograph.*
4. *Did the Press make a sound decision in running off 1,000 copies? Explain. Should it have run some extra sheets?*
5. *Is a formal analysis of uncertainty helpful in this case? Discuss.*

PART FOUR / Pricing and output

8 / Pricing

The best place to start a discussion of pricing is with price theory. This theory has been developed for prediction of the effects of broad economic changes and evaluation of social controls. It is too much to expect that tools designed for social economics would be exactly suitable for managerial economics; managerial economics requires adaptation of the concepts to meet the needs of the individual undertaking. Nevertheless the theory is a convenient starting point.

THE THEORY OF PRICE FROM THE VIEWPOINT OF THE INDIVIDUAL FIRM

The basic assumption of price theory is the desire of entrepreneurs to maximize profits. Another assumption, which may be removed in more complete models, is that the firm produces only one output. It is also assumed that managers know the shapes and positions of their demand and cost functions. Under these conditions determination of optimal price is complicated only by variation in market structures.

Pure competition

In pure competition the firm can have no price policy. It must sell at a market price which it cannot control. The market price tends to move to a position that will clear the market—that will equate quantities sellers are willing to offer with quantities buyers are willing to take. The product of any one seller is identical to the product of any other seller. Each individual firm participates in the movement to market equilibrium through adjustments in its own output, but these adjustments are so small relative to total supply that they have negligible influence on market price.

The demand curve facing the firm is horizontal. At the market price the firm can sell all it desires; at any higher price it can sell nothing. Figure 8–1 illustrates pure competition. The demand curve (average revenue curve) is also the marginal revenue curve. *The only decision to be made by the firm is quantity to produce.* Under the conditions that have been specified, the firm will produce the quantity that equates marginal cost with price. Up to this point an increase in output adds more to revenue than to cost. Beyond this point it adds more to cost than to revenue.

FIGURE 8–1

DEMAND AND COST CONDITIONS IN PURE COMPETITION

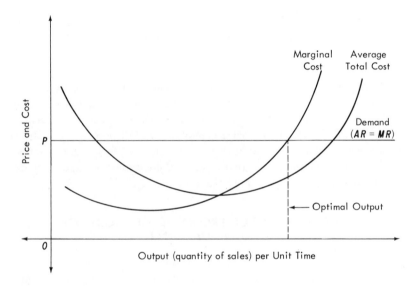

The price shown in Figure 8–1 permits the firm to earn profits exceeding normal profit. Figure 8–1 is a short-run solution; in the long run the excess profits will attract additional firms into the industry, and will encourage the existing firms to expand, thus exerting a downward pressure on price. In the long run, price tends to be equal to the minimum average cost of each firm. The forces determining price tend to squeeze out any excess profits.

Few firms operate under conditions of pure competition. The stock and bond markets and the markets for most agricultural commodities approximate these conditions. The seller of a common stock listed on the New York Stock Exchange cannot be sure of a sale if he demands a specific price, but normally he can sell as much as he wishes if he is willing to take the highest price offered. It is true that a large corporation, like the American Telephone and Telegraph Company, is in a somewhat different position in floating a new issue of common stock, for the issue may be large enough to have an impact on the market. But this is the exception; in most cases the individual stock buyer or seller is at the mercy of the market.

In a discussion of price policy of the individual firm, the theory of pure competition has limited relevance; it does emphasize the impersonal market forces that play a role even under semimonopolistic conditions. The theory is useful in social economics, for it permits the kinds of broad prediction needed there, such as the effect of an excise tax, of price control, or of rationing. But a chapter on price policy must focus on the more usual market situations in which firms have some control over price.

Monopoly

The theory of monopoly is more pertinent in discussions of price policy, not because monopoly is prevalent but because the theory is a convenient starting point in dealing with more complex markets. *In monopoly the firm's demand curve slopes downward to the right, for it is the industry demand curve.* The negative slope such as that shown in Figure 8–2 reflects the fact that purchasers take more at lower prices than at high. The marginal revenue curve lies below the demand (average revenue) curve, for reasons already developed. The way to maximize profits is to choose an output that equates marginal revenue and marginal cost. The firm may reach this position in two ways: it may offer the quantity *OA* which will sell at the price *AB;* or it may set the price at *AB* and let the

FIGURE 8–2
PRICE DETERMINATION UNDER CONDITIONS OF MONOPOLY

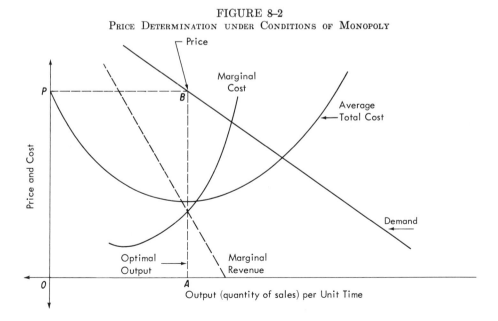

buyers decide how much they will take at this price, which turns out to be quantity *OA. The firm can choose price or quantity but not both.* In actual practice it is usual for the firm to establish the price and let the market set the quantity.

Barriers to entry are the foundations of monopoly. Some examples of such barriers are: (*a*) *control of supplies of raw materials,* such as Alcoa's control of bauxite supply prior to World War II; (*b*) *patents,* such as Polaroid's patents on instant photographic devices and materials; (*c*) *economies of scale,* such as those of most public utilities; and (*d*) *franchises.* Under conditions of monopoly excess profits are probable, but not inevitable. Presumably barriers to the entry of new firms protect the position of the monopolist from an erosion of profits. If, however, the demand curve is tangent to the cost curve, the firm must remain content with normal profits (which are included in the average cost curve).

So far, the diagrams have shown the cost curves in their traditional U-shapes. The chapter on costs presented evidence that marginal cost curves are often horizontal, with a consequent decline in average costs over the whole range of outputs. Such a redrawing of the graph, as in Figure 8–3, does not change the theory, for the optimum is still at the point at which marginal cost equals marginal revenue.

The theory of monopoly price, like all theories, is a simplification. No

FIGURE 8–3

PRICE DETERMINATION UNDER CONDITIONS OF MONOPOLY—CONSTANT MARGINAL COSTS

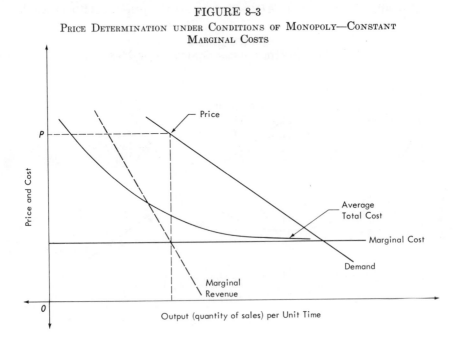

firm has complete protection from the entry of substitutes. No firm has exact information on the position and shape of its demand curve. *The curve can be shifted by sales activity. Management must make simultaneous decisions about price and promotion.* The theory of monopoly is therefore only a step in understanding pricing even in those industries in which the monopoly position is strong.

Monopolistic competition

Chamberlin's theory of monopolistic competition starts by considering each firm a monopoly with *a downward sloping demand curve* and marginal revenue curve. The demand curve does not have a steep slope, for *each product faces the competition of close substitutes.* But differentiation of the product assures that demand is not perfectly elastic, thus providing scope for price policy.

Where does competition enter into this theory? As already suggested, the competition of substitutes makes the demand curve more elastic than it would be otherwise. In addition, *barriers to entry are absent,* so that excess profits attract new competition, with a consequent long-run tendency for excess profits to diminish. Lastly, the firm faces such a *large number of competitors* that it ignores any impact its price policy may have on others, for its actions are imperceptible to competitors. *The result is price, quality, and advertising competition that tends to wipe out excess profits despite the individual firm's control over price.*

Rather than develop the intricacies of the theory of monopolistic competition (the reader may wish to read Chamberlin on the subject) it will suffice for our purposes to indicate the final equilibrium suggested by the theory. Figure 8–4 shows long-run equilibrium for the individual firm, which cannot earn excess profits because of entry of new competitors and because of price competition with close substitutes. Chamberlin did not insist that the equilibrium must necesarily be of the tangency variety shown in Figure 8–4, with zero excess profits. *Special advantages of patents and trademarks that cannot be wiped out completely by competition may permit a situation as in Figure 8–5, in which the demand curve is not pushed completely back to tangency with the cost curve.* In any case, the firm selects output that equates marginal revenue and marginal cost, the only position consistent with the objective of maximizing profit.

The relevance of the theory of monopolistic competition is sometimes questioned. The tangency solution, with a long-term tendency toward excess capacity, is disputed by some economists. We have already seen in earlier chapters reasons for doubting that the cost curves will have the U-shape usually assumed in the theory. The theory in the usual form is static and ignores the constant changes in product characteristics and shifts in marketing activity and competition which characterize markets for differentiated products. Most firms produce a line of products rather

FIGURE 8–4
Equilibrium under Conditions of Monopolistic Competition

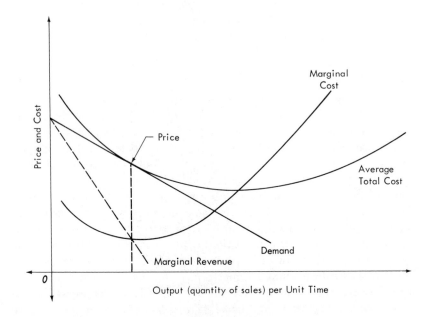

FIGURE 8–5
Price in Monopolistic Competition—Nontangency Case

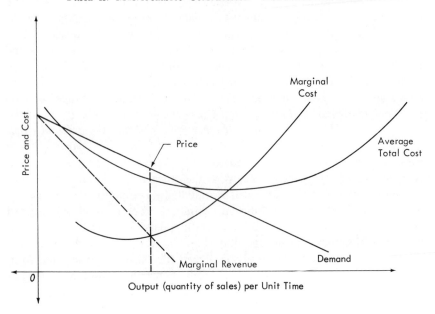

than the single product shown on the graphs. Many firms, rather than settling for a comfortable tangency equilibrium, appear to be engaged in a constant struggle to reduce excess capacity through marketing effort, through changes in the product mix, and through the introduction of new products.

Nevertheless, several features of the theory are clearly relevant. Most firms do face downward sloping demand curves; they can sell more at lower prices than at higher ones. They have scope for price policy. Their products are differentiated from products of competitors, but substitutes are close enough to reduce monopoly positions. They may at times have demand curves lying considerably above costs and allowing unusually high profits. But they face constant erosion of profits by entry of competitive products and marketing tactics of other firms. They are not perfect competitors without control over price; but also they are not monopolists who can earn comfortable profits without facing competition.

Oligopoly

Oligopoly refers to markets with small numbers of firms; the Greek base of the word means "few sellers." Two kinds of oligopoly may be distinguished; *homogeneous* oligopoly in which the *product is standardized;* and *differentiated* oligopoly in which the *product of each firm is somewhat distinct from that of the next.* The markets for steel and cement approximate the conditions of homogeneous oligopoly, for most buyers of those products care little about who is the supplier but are interested in minimizing the cost of an approximately standard product. Differentiated oligopoly is more widespread (automobiles, machinery, household appliances). Many such products are differentiated physically; advertising, salesmanship, trade names, and other devices may also distinguish the product of one firm from that of another. It is more difficult to generalize about the shape or elasticity of the demand curve in oligopoly than in the preceding market situations. In fact, the interdependence of the price policies of competing firms in oligopoly may preclude drawing a simple demand curve, showing the relationship between a firm's own price and the quantity it sells. Economists have dealt with this problem of interdependence in a variety of ways.

In the late 1930s Sweezy and other writers hypothesized that the demand curve of the firm in oligopoly is kinked. The kinked demand theory is controversial but is worthy of consideration. According to the theory the firm's demand curve appears as in Figure 8–6. The kink is at the existing price. Above that price the demand is highly elastic. Below, it is less elastic. The result is a sharp break in the marginal revenue curve, as is illustrated in the figure.

It should be made clear that the kinked demand is the demand as perceived by the seller who, on the basis of past experience, predicts the

FIGURE 8-6
A KINKED DEMAND CURVE

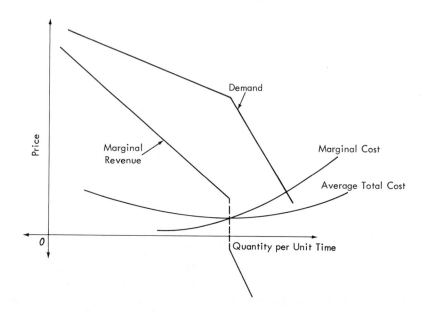

probable reactions of competitors to his price changes. He expects that if he raises price the competitors will not follow, resulting in an elastic demand as his customers transfer to other suppliers. He expects that if he reduces price, the competitors will retaliate, taking away most of the gains of the lower price. As a consequence, the incentive to change price is reduced, which should mean that prices in oligopoly are relatively sticky even in the face of general increases or decreases in average and marginal cost.

The empirical studies that will be cited raise doubts about the relevance of the kinked demand theory. Nevertheless, it is clear that the demand curves of the firms in oligopoly are interdependent. *The individual entrepreneur will not normally change price without evaluating the probable reactions of competitors.*

Rather than present a survey of various theories of oligopoly, it might be better to list some patterns of behavior that have been observed in oligopolistic markets.

Price cuts to drive out competition. A financially strong firm, disliking the insecurity of oligopoly, may try to drive out competitors by deliberately cutting price. A classic example was the reduction of price on kerosene by John D. Rockefeller. In practice, this variety of behavior may be difficult to distinguish from the next.

Price wars. In price wars each competitor shades price below that of the other, sometimes to the point that price falls below variable costs. Normally price wars are not planned but are a consequence of one firm's cutting price and starting off a chain of reactions.

Price leadership. One way of avoiding the unpleasantness of price retaliation is to develop a pattern of price leadership, in which competitors follow the price changes of one firm established as the traditional leader. Price leadership may take several forms: leadership by a dominant firm or barometric price leadership in which a smaller firm tries out a new price, which may or may not be confirmed by the larger firms.

Collusion. Another way of avoiding price retaliation is to agree formally on price or to divide up the market. Such arrangements convert oligopoly into monopoly, though there is always a risk of a firm's breaking the agreement. Collusion is usually illegal under the antitrust laws but is still with us, as is evidenced by recent suits against manufacturers of electrical equipment.

Nonprice competition. Because of the dangers of price competition, the firms in oligopoly may prefer to compete in advertising, style, sales activity, brand names, and so on. No doubt competitors retaliate to such activity, but presumably the danger of destructive competition is less.

Secret price concessions. It may be safer to engage in secret price concessions for selected customers than to reduce price openly, with the possibility of retaliation.

All past attempts to generalize such wide variety of behavior have fallen short. This is true of the Stackleberg solution, which assumes that oligopolists explicitly recognize the interdependence of their actions, the kinked demand theory, which claims that the seller will distinguish the reactions to a price increase from those to a price decrease, or the theory of games, which tries to apply sophisticated mathematical models to oligopoly. These theories all provide insights into oligopoly behavior, but none can claim to be "the" theory of oligopoly.

Traditional theory: its strengths and weaknesses

All of the foregoing theories of pricing behavior, with the possible exception of the theories of oligopoly, fall under the heading of marginalism. All of them assume an entrepreneur who compares added gain with added cost of increasing output, and works toward the position at which added gain and loss are equal. Such theories recognize that both cost and demand conditions do influence pricing. They portray the firm as adjusting to changes in market forces, revising output and price as demands shift or as costs change. They picture the manager as a rational human being who can analyze the implications of changes in conditions. Throughout this book we accept marginalism as a useful way of organizing one's thoughts about pricing decisions.

At the same time, the managerial economist must learn to distinguish between what traditional theory can and cannot do. The theory suffers from serious limitations when it comes to prescriptive analysis for individual firm behavior.

1. The theory usually rests on the assumption of profit maximization. In the real world profit maximization is no doubt a primary objective, but research indicates clearly that entrepreneurs are also guided by other motives. Some managers may be more interested in maximizing sales or increasing market share than in profits. Some may strive for personal power or prestige. Many managers are guided by strong convictions of what is ethical and what is not. Managers of small firms often care a great deal about how the community reacts to their practices. Managers of large firms are often aware of their responsibilities to the public. The cynic may claim that the alleged ethical motives are merely rationalizations of long-run profit-making; that the managers are really trying to avoid costly antitrust suits or other forms of regulation; or that they are endeavoring to build up public goodwill which gradually reflects itself in increased demand. It is difficult to draw the line between profit-seeking and other goals, but there can be little doubt that some managers sacrifice profits, even long-run profits, to maintain policies they feel are fair and just.

Increasingly, the view of social scientists is that businesses do not and cannot take profit maximization as the single objective. Several writers like R. A. Lester and R. A. Gordon challenged the profit maximization assumption in the 1940s, but the major attack on the assumption came in the 1950s and 1960s under the leadership of H. A. Simon and his associates at the Carnegie Institute of Technology (now Carnegie-Mellon). They have argued that the appropriate assumption is a goal of satisfactory profits which represent levels of managerial aspiration influenced by the organization and a variety of influences on management.[1] They would replace the profit maximization asumption with a more complex study of decision-making process, organizational structure, corporate strategies, and decision rules.

2. The theory does not distinguish clearly between long- and short-run effects of price change. In particular, the theory has little to say about the effect of today's prices on future profits. The usual graphs for short-run pricing show today's demand curve (and marginal revenue curve) and today's cost curves (including the marginal cost curve) and suggest that the manager adjusts prices to equate marginal revenue and marginal cost. The manager may, however, try to consider the discounted effect of today's price on future revenues. If he wants to build up an image of a

---

[1] Representative of the literature on the subject are J. G. March and H. A. Simon, *Organizations* (New York: John Wiley & Sons, Inc., 1958), and R. M. Cyert and J. G. March, *A Behavioral Theory of the Firm* (Englewood Cliffs, N. J.: Prentice-Hall, Inc., 1963).

low-price outlet, he may not charge as much as the immediate market would permit, sacrificing current profits for future profits. The economic theorist has always known this to be the case, but the formal tools of analysis that he has developed do not usually deal with this problem explicitly.

3. The theory usually assumes a single-product firm. The real world is mainly composed of firms producing several or many products. The theorist has good reasons for concentrating on the one-product case, but in managerial economics these reasons no longer dominate. The managerial economist must deal explicitly with interdependence of products both in sales and in production.

4. The theory does not face up to the problem of uncertainty. As we have seen, economic theory usually assumes that the entrepreneur knows his demand and cost functions. In the world of business this is hardly ever the case. Tools for dealing with uncertainty are still under development. But whether or not the managerial economist makes formal use of modern statistical and operations research techniques for dealing with uncertainty, he must take uncertainty into account.

5. The theory does not take into account that pricing decisions are influenced by a variety of persons with varied objectives and motives. The information that influences prices comes from many directions: the firm's accounting system, the firm's sales forces, news about competitor's actions and plans, and various policies and decision rules established within the firm.

In conclusion, the theory of pricing in the individual firm is an important step in understanding pricing. The managerial economist is, however, faced with the problem of bridging the gap between theory and practice. Thus, he must constantly check the relevance of theory against actual facts and must revise his analytical tools to meet the particular needs at hand.

Two shortcuts in pricing

Prescriptive literature on pricing sometimes contains two shortcuts that seem to bypass difficulties of applying marginalism in the uncertain world of business. The better known of these alternatives is full-cost pricing; the other is "going-rate" pricing. Each deserves consideration as a possible way of simplifying the pricing problem; each has serious limitations.

Full-cost pricing. One difficulty in discussing full-cost pricing is the absence of a generally accepted definition. In this book full-cost pricing means pricing at a level covering total costs, including overhead, plus a predetermined markup. The view that full-cost pricing must assure profitable business operations is widespread. Some writers and trade associations consider the method to be a "scientific approach" to pricing, presumably because it substitutes a formula for subjective judgments. Other writers claim that the method is a reasonable way of dealing with uncertainty and ignorance.

If the manager does not know the shape or position of his demand curve, he may find it convenient to adopt a technique that does not require such knowledge. If he is strongly motivated by questions of fairness and justice in pricing, he may adopt a formula that treats all categories of customers alike at all times regardless of conditions of the market. Full-cost pricing may help assure prices that are related to long-run cost in such a way as to discourage the entry of new competition into the industry. Lastly, full-cost pricing may, if adopted by all members of the industry, help protect the firms against price wars and cut-throat price competition, at the same time providing some flexibility in adjusting prices to cost changes.

It might be contended that overhead allocations and profit markups of full-cost pricing help assure that facilities are not allocated to products that fail to carry their share of overhead and produce their share of profit. If firms always operated at full capacity, the logic of this argument would be more appealing. In a world of cyclical change, of seasonality in demand, of varying price elasticities, and of complementary relations in demand, it is difficult to see how full-cost pricing can approach optimal profits.

In addition, it should be noted that full-cost pricing accepts the accountant's definition of costs, with its stress on original costs, with its questionable treatment of opportunity costs, and with its arbitrary allocations of overhead. It seems unlikely that a price formula based on an inflexible and (for economic purposes) an erroneous view of costs can lead to profitable operations.

This discussion of full-cost pricing does not state that the method is entirely without merits. It does suggest, however, that the manager should consider carefully whether it meets the needs of his situation before accepting it.

"Going-rate" pricing. Another shortcut to pricing, avoiding the effort of analysis, is to charge the "going rate." As is true of full-cost pricing, this approach is not necessarily unsound; in an oligopolistic price leadership situation it may be a reasonable way to stabilize prices. But analysis is necessary to indicate when such an approach to pricing is justified. The trouble with some of the literature on the subject is that it does not tell the manager when he should adopt the going rate and when he should make exceptions.

The distinction between "price takers" and "price makers" is related to the topic of going-rate pricing. Some sellers—those who operate in highly competitive conditions approaching pure competition—cannot determine prices but must accept those established by relatively impersonal market forces. Such sellers are "price takers"—they must take prices which are given. Examples are sellers of shares in the stock market, farmers selling their crops, or those who sell basic commodities like tin, rubber, or copper in world markets. The sellers with which we are mainly concerned in the chapter are "price makers"—those who have scope for discretion about prices. Since this book is concerned primarily with decision making, it inevitably focuses on enterprises that can make choices. Therefore, the remainder of this chapter will ignore "price takers" and "going-rate pricing."

Empirical studies and illustrations

The major issue in research on pricing has been the extent to which practice has followed mechanical procedures such as full-cost pricing, or, alternatively, has followed the more flexible and more demand-oriented precepts of marginalism. The findings are mixed and still somewhat a matter of controversy.

The best-known questionnaire survey on pricing is that of R. L. Hall and C. J. Hitch, who were concerned primarily with oligopoly.[2] They found a great majority of the 38 covered firms applying a full-cost policy. Most of them started with direct cost, added a percentage to cover overhead, and then added another percentage for profit. Hall and Hitch suggest a variety of reasons for adoption of full-cost pricing, among which are considerations of "fairness," ignorance of demand, ignorance of potential reactions of competitors, the belief that the short-run elasticity of market demand is low, the belief that increased prices would encourage new entrants, and the administrative difficulties of a more flexible price policy. Hall and Hitch use the kinked demand analysis to help explain full-cost pricing: this analysis emphasizes the belief that competitors follow a decrease in price, reducing the profitability of such decreases, but do not follow an increase. Hall and Hitch summarize their findings as follows:

1. A large proportion of businesses make no attempt to equate marginal revenue and marginal cost in the sense in which economists have asserted that this is typical behavior.

2. An element of oligopoly is extremely common in markets for manufactured products; most businesses take into account in their pricing the probable reaction of competitors and potential competitors.

3. Where this element of oligopoly is present, and in many cases where it is absent, there is a strong tendency among businessmen to fix prices at a level which they regard as "full cost."

---

[2] R. L. Hall and C. J. Hitch, "Price Theory and Business Behavior," *Oxford Economic Papers*, No. 2 (May 1939), pp. 12, 18–22, 25–27, 29–33; reprinted in T. Wilson and P. W. S. Andrews, *Oxford Studies in the Price Mechanism* (Oxford Clarendon Press, 1951), pp. 107–38.

4. Prices so fixed have a tendency to be stable. They will be changed if there is a significant change in wage or raw material costs, but not in response to moderate or temporary shifts in demand.

5. There is usually some element in the prices ruling at any time which can only be explained in the light of history of the industry.[3]

The Hall and Hitch conclusions have come under attack. Critics have noted that firms in the study varied margins from product to product; this suggests some attention to market forces. The critics have also suggested that inability to measure marginal revenue and marginal cost precisely does not require abandonment of marginalism, which must be interpreted to include subjective estimates and trial-and-error approaches to maximum profits.

George J. Stigler's study of price statistics raises doubts about the kinked demand theory.[4] Stigler finds greater price stability in monopoly than in oligopoly, contrary to the implications of the kinked demand theory.

A study in the 1950s by James S. Earley lends support to marginalism.[5] Earley's study covers large firms which are claimed to be "excellently managed," and thus is not necessarily representative of practice in general. Earley finds that these firms are adopting accounting methods that move in the marginalist direction, with breakdowns between fixed and variable costs and separation of fixed costs that can be attributed directly to particular segments. He also finds differentiation of margins on different product lines, with attention to competitive pressures and demand elasticities.

The best-known collection of case studies in pricing, that of Kaplan, Dirlam, and Lanzillotti, covers 20 of the largest industrial corporations in the United States.[6] The authors stress these patterns:

1. Considerable concern with "fairness" of prices, with attention to public responsibilities
2. Establishment of "target returns," stated as percentage returns on investment, consistent with what is considered "fair"
3. Attention to market share, with improvement in the firm's market position a major objective

---

[3] Ibid., p. 125.

[4] George J. Stigler, "The Kinky Oligopoly Demand Curve and Rigid Prices," *The Journal of Political Economy* (October 1947), pp. 432–49.

[5] James E. Earley, "Marginal Policies of 'Excellently Managed Companies'," *The American Economic Review* (March 1956), pp. 44–70; and James E. Earley, "Recent Developments in Cost Accounting and the 'Marginal Analysis,'" *The Journal of Political Economy* (June 1955), pp. 227–42.

[6] A. D. H. Kaplan, Joel B. Dirlam, and Robert F. Lanzillotti, *Pricing in Big Business* (Washington, D.C.: The Brookings Institution, 1958). Also see Robert F. Lanzillotti, "Pricing Objectives in Large Companies," *The American Economic Review* (December 1958), pp. 921–40.

4. A preference for stable prices or for stable margins
5. Stress on full costs in the mechanics of pricing, with widespread use of standard costs as the relevant full-cost data
6. Adjustments of margins on particular commodities to market conditions
7. Price leadership of both the dominant firm and barometric varieties
8. Restraint in charging what the market will bear in periods of market shortages
9. Occasional use of simple and crude rules of thumb in determining price changes, such as doubling the increase in labor costs in a new wage agreement

Individual cases show considerable diversity in behavior. Some firms, like International Harvester, may give especially strong attention to target returns, but still compute incremental costs when faced with severe competition. Other firms, such as the A&P, may place maintenance or improvement of market share ahead of target returns. The firms vary in willingness to delegate discretion over prices to subordinate officials. One firm follows a policy of pricing to meet competition: the National Steel Corporation follows prices set by U.S. Steel, with stress on control of costs to return a profit at those prices.

Kaplan, Dirlam, and Lanzillotti recognize certain limitations in their approach. They have difficulties in evaluating information released by company officials; they cannot be certain, for example, that stated objectives are not sometimes rationalizations rather than descriptions of actual goals. Critics of the study are particularly unconvinced by the authors' dismissal of profit maximization as a useful concept; they doubt that the firms are as bound by "target returns" as the authors suggest; they note evidence that the "targets" may be estimates of what the traffic will bear, which means that they are subject to market forces.

A study of small firms conducted by Haynes reaches conclusions somewhat different from those already cited.[7]

1. It does not find adherence to full-cost pricing, but rather some flexible attention to costs as resistance or reference points. Small businesses do adjust prices to market forces. They seek, through subjective evaluations of demand and through trial and error, prices that will help them achieve their objectives, one of which is profit maximization.

2. On the other hand, small firms have not adopted the incremental accounting techniques mentioned by Earley. Accounting appears to have a limited role in their pricing decisions, and when it does play a role it leads to stress on full costs and averages, rather than on incremental costs. The extent to which small businessmen are marginalists results

[7] W. W. Haynes, *Pricing Decisions in Small Business* (Lexington: University of Kentucky Press, 1962).

not from their use of accounting but from their experimentation in the market, their willingness to evaluate demand and costs subjectively, or their imitation of the practices of other firms.

3. Small firms do not appear to give the attention to "target returns" found in big business.

4. Small firms are often concerned with the ethics of pricing, and with community relations, as well as with the impact of prices on profits.

A more complete review of the literature would reveal even greater diversity of practice. This is what one would expect when he examines decision making in detail, for pricing must be adapted to the structure of the market, to the availability of information, to the competence of management, and to the variety of goals and community pressures. This survey of empirical studies indicates that narrow generalizations about pricing behavior are oversimplified. Most firms appear to practice "partial marginalism," but this covers a wide variety of behavior.

INCREMENTAL REASONING IN PRICING

Neither the traditional theory of the firm, with its high level of abstraction and generalization, nor the widely known shortcut formulas, with their inflexibility, provide the complete answer to the pricing problem. The present section attempts to provide a general framework within which the manager can formulate a pricing policy. This framework or point of view might best be called incremental reasoning. It obviously leans heavily on economic theory, but it reformulates the theory in a form more suitable for decision making.

Incremental reasoning in its most general form states: If a pricing decision leads to a greater increase in revenue than in costs it is sound; if it leads to a greater reduction in costs than in revenues it is favorable. What incremental reasoning amounts to, therefore, is the comparison of the impact of decisions on revenues and costs. Such reasoning does not, however, require a restriction of attention to revenues, costs, and profits; it permits, indeed it requires, consideration of the extent to which the decision contributes to or detracts from other goals. Recognition of multiple goals requires weighting of objectives, and, at the present state of knowledge, considerable subjective judgment. One way of handling this difficulty is to concentrate first on the impact of the decision on profits and later to adjust for other considerations.

Guidelines

Incremental reasoning requires a full play of the imagination to make certain that all repercussions of the decision are taken into account. The following guides should be helpful:

1. In evaluating the cost impact of the pricing (and output) decision,

the stress should be on the changes in total revenue and total cost rather than on average costs. Overhead allocations are irrelevant and should be ignored. Incremental reasoning requires statistical measurement of incremental costs or judgment about which costs are affected and by how much.

2. The method requires *attention to long-run* as well as short-run impact of the decision. A decision to increase prices now may increase immediate profits, but it may gradually undermine the firm's reputation for low prices and destroy customer goodwill. Or it may attract new competition.

3. The method requires consideration of *possible complementary relations in demand* between one product and another. The major reason for "loss leaders" in retailing is that they attract customers who will purchase other items. Any time the price decision on one item has an impact on the sale of other items, these additional effects on revenue must be equated.

4. The incremental method takes into account demand elasticities or, more simply, *price-volume relationships.* The decision maker must have some way of determining the impact of price change on volume. Sometimes a statistical or experimental approach to measuring demand may be justified. Other times, the manager may estimate responsiveness of sales to price by evaluating past experience and by considering various factors that might influence demand for this particular product.

5. The method requires attention to *market structure.* In some cases, the closeness of a large number of substitutes may mean that the firm has little control over price. In other cases, differentiation of the product may provide some scope for price policy, though it may require a careful coordination of pricing with sales promotion activity. In still other cases, the possible retaliation of competitors should be taken into account.

6. The method requires some way of dealing with *uncertainty.* The manager never knows the exact consequences of his pricing decisions. The degree of uncertainty may vary from one decision to another. No general rules govern optimal behavior in such circumstances, for attitude toward risk varies from one individual to the next. In a large impersonal corporation, individual attitudes toward uncertainty may be ignored; decisions can be based on the aim of maximizing expected profits (average profits). In small firms, the greater willingness of some managers than others to take chances is often a perfectly reasonable reflection of different attitudes toward possible gains or losses. Thus it is impossible to generalize that a manager should always say "yes" to a decision that offers a 0.7 probability of adding $100,000 to profits with a 0.3 probability of losses of $120,000. One manager may be attracted by the fact that this is better than a fair gamble. Another manager may be concerned that it offers the possibility of complete bankruptcy.

7. Incremental reasoning requires attention to *changing business conditions*. Instead of a mechanical application of formulas through good times and bad, it suggests the possibility of flexibility of prices to meet changing markets. This is not to say that flexibility is always wise, but rather to stress that it is always worthy of consideration.

8. Incremental reasoning implies *individualization of pricing* on the various products of a multiproduct concern. It is true that mechanical formulas simplify pricing decisions. In a firm with thousands of products such a simplification may cut managerial costs. But demand and competitive conditions facing the products are likely to be diverse; rigid pricing formulas prevent adjustment to that diversity. This is again a question of benefits versus costs. Will the firm gain enough in added profits or in furtherance of its other goals to justify the added management costs?

Note that incremental reasoning implies both cross-sectional flexibility and flexibility over time. By cross-sectional flexibility is meant the willingness to adapt prices to the special conditions of demand and cost that face each product. Flexibility over time has to do with the ability to adapt pricing to changing market conditions, to shifts in demand, to changes in price elasticities, and to the availability of excess capacity.

It is more important to develop a way of reasoning about pricing than it is to learn specific rules. Correct reasoning can be tailor-made to particular circumstances; rules frequently are applied when they no longer fit.

Empirical studies and illustrations

The major empirical issue that the preceding section raises is whether business does in fact follow the kind of incremental reasoning that has been outlined. The obvious answer is that some firms approximate such reasoning and others do not. Studies previously cited indicate that some firms adopt accounting methods that help them apply marginal reasoning; others tend to apply mechanical full-cost formulas. The study of small firms conducted by Haynes indicates considerable variation in the degree of sophistication in pricing policies and practices.

That firms with small staffs can apply incremental reasoning with only a minimum familiarity with the formal principles involved is illustrated by one case from this study, the case of a billboard advertising firm. This firm is aggressive in raising rates on its billboards to the level that traffic will bear. The managers seek information on what other firms are charging. They are not content with imitation, however, for they experiment with pricing to determine whether higher rates actually lead to lower volume. By such a procedure they find the point at which advertisers are likely to abandon billboard advertising in the towns in which this firm is located. The managers have bought out other firms with the intent of raising rates to the range that they have found feasible. The evidence suggests that the managers have been highly successful in increasing profits from their undertaking through price policy.

At the same time many other firms are using pricing practices that appear to fall far short of the incremental approach. Many firms consider full cost to be a floor below which they should not reduce prices. They accept the view that making a profit on every job assures profits for the firm as a whole. On the other hand, most small firms that claim to base prices on full costs do take demand into account in their actual pricing. They adjust prices to changing market conditions as long as the prices are above full cost. Some firms, such as garden and landscape nurseries which find it extremely hard to determine costs of individual products, make no formal reference to cost in their pricing. Still other firms simply imitate the prices of others. Many firms prefer to follow the suggestions of manufacturers or wholesalers rather than to make their own decisions on prices. Thus a great variety of behavior is observable, falling into the following patterns:

Full cost plus predetermined markups. This pattern is rare in small business and is probably less prevalent in large firms than some writers assume.

Full cost plus variable markups. This pattern is much more common than is the extreme type of full-cost pricing. It is clear that the determination of the markups requires an evaluation of market conditions.

Pricing using programmed costs and markups. Predetermined markups are used widely in retailing, but they are markups on wholesale cost; furthermore, such markups are variable from commodity to commodity, and are often flexible over time.

In large firms pricing decisions are often related to estimates of marginal or incremental costs. Sometimes these estimates are obtained from programmed systems of accounting which provide direct costs, differential costs, or other approximations to marginal costs.

Pricing based on ad hoc estimates of costs and demand. Few small firms make extensive use of their accounting data in pricing decisions. When they do make analyses for the purposes of pricing, they usually rely on ad hoc (back-of-the-envelope) estimates. Large firms also frequently make use of special studies, but are more likely than small firms to depend on technical specialists or consultants to aid them in analyzing pricing situations.

Pricing with little reference to costs. In some industries costs are so nebulous that they have little meaning to management in determining prices. An example is the garden nursery industry in which it is impossible to determine the "cost" of a particular plant or variety of plants. In such cases, managers may claim they consider costs in pricing, but in practice they refer only to the overall costs and profits on their income statements. Their pricing is based more on an evaluation of competition and the prices customers are willing to pay.

Perhaps the main point to stress is that even small firms with limited staffs and training can apply incremental reasoning in pricing. Such reasoning is consistent with subjective use of past experience, rough estimation of the impact of price changes, and experimentation with prices to determine the results of change.

SOME SPECIFIC GUIDES

The reasoning presented so far in this chapter has been general, so as to be applicable in a wide variety of situations. It is desirable now to review some ideas which have been suggested as specific guides to pricing. Such guides do not enable the manager to bypass incremental reasoning; he still must determine when and where the ideas are applicable. The guides do, however, provide hints that may aid in bridging the gap between the theory and its application.

Loss leaders

The use of loss leaders, which is widespread in retailing, is an application of ideas already discussed. It is a little difficult to define the expression "loss leader," for the idea is not to produce losses but rather to increase profits. One might define it as a product priced below wholesale cost, but such a definition might be both too broad and too restrictive. It is too broad in that it would cover pricing to clear the counter of unsold style goods and other special sales of overstocked items. It is too narrow in excluding the possibility of a price that does cover wholesale cost but which nevertheless is "low" in its direct contribution to overhead. As a result, a complicated definition is required: *a loss leader is an item which produces a less than customary contribution or a negative contribution to overhead but which is expected to create profits on increased future sales or sales of other items.*

An illustration of a loss leader is reduced introductory magazine subscription rates aimed at creating familiarity with the magazine, leading to future subscriptions at regular rates. Another illustration of a loss leader is coffee sold by a grocery at wholesale cost. Holdren lists some characteristics desirable in commodities which are to serve as loss leaders in a grocery store.[8]

1. *The buyer should know the prices of the commodity in other stores.*
2. *The price differential should be large enough to be perceptible.*
3. *The buyer's purchases of the commodity should be large enough to make a price cut important to him.*

---

[8] Bob R. Holdren, *The Structure of a Retail Market and the Market Behavior of Retail Units* (Englewood Cliffs, N.J.: Prentice-Hall, Inc., 1960), p. 140.

4. The buyer's demand for the commodity should be inelastic.

5. A price reduction should not signify a reduction in quality.

Turnover and pricing

One widely accepted view is that high turnover items should carry lower markups than those with lower turnover. One reason is that high turnover items are often high frequency-of-purchase items on which the customer is familiar with prices and willing to transfer trade if he sees better bargains elsewhere. The correlation is not exact, however, for turnover is measured from the point of view of the seller while frequency of purchase concerns the buyer. Nails may be a high turnover item for the hardware store but a low frequency purchase for the ordinary amateur carpenter.

A second reason for lower markups on high turnover goods is related to opportunity costs. High turnover goods occupy space for a shorter period and thus require lesser sacrifice of space that could be devoted to other goods. Furthermore, high turnover items may require less selling effort per dollar of sales, with a lower opportunity cost of selling time. If the firm has excess space and excess selling time, these reasons become less compelling.

It would be a mistake to rely on a formula relating markup to turnover alone. Turnover is itself a function of price. It might be possible to increase the turnover, and thus reduce the unit opportunity cost of space and selling effort, by reducing price. Furthermore, there is not a close correlation between turnover and space occupancy; jewelry may turn over slowly but occupies little space. The decision maker should consider the whole range of effects of price change and not just a single factor such as turnover.

Pioneer pricing: skimming price versus penetration price

Joel Dean's *Managerial Economics* is a rich source of useful distinctions worthy of consideration in pricing. Some of these distinctions are concerned with the life cycle of the product. Dean argues that the analysis of pricing in the early stages, when the product first appears on the market, is quite different from that in the late stages, when the product is suffering from encroachment from new products and from shifts in taste. But he wisely does not generalize about each stage, finding diversity within each of the stages of the life cycle. The problem is to determine for each product at each stage of its cycle both the short-run and long-run elasticities of demand.

Consider first a new product. Dean distinguishes between two kinds of policy for such a product: (1) a *skimming price* policy, with *initial high prices;* and (2) a *penetration price* policy, with *low prices at the beginning.* Each deserves separate attention.

The strategy of *skimming price* is most suitable when (1) the short-run demand is relatively inelastic and (2) undesirable effects of high present prices on future sales or sales of other products are not large. The demand is more likely to be less elastic for a product that is sharply differentiated from previous products, so that the possibility of substitution and of price comparisons is limited. In such a case, a high level of promotional activity may be appropriate, for it is necessary to make the public aware of the product.

It requires considerable judgment to determine when initial high prices are appropriate. Hula hoops sold initially at high prices to that segment of the market that cared enough for the novelty to buy anyway. It is doubtful that those who purchased hula hoops later at lower prices were at all deterred by the previous high prices; if anything the effect was the opposite, one of feeling that the low price was a real bargain. Similarly a high price on a "spectacular" movie in its first year should have little negative impact on those customers who can afford only the lower price and are willing to wait.

Dean makes the point that skimming price policy is safer. It gives the firm an opportunity to sell the product on a small scale at a price that is almost certain to cover costs. Later the firm can explore the possibility of tapping lower-price segments of the market. Perhaps this kind of reasoning influenced the setting of tolls on the San Francisco Bay Bridge, on which the initial rate was 60 cents per automobile, followed by a reduction to 50 cents, 40 cents, and finally to 25 cents. At each rate the traffic exceeded expectations, reducing the risk of lower rates. It is necessary to point out, however, that the objective of the bridge was not to maximize profits—the short-run demand was probably inelastic enough that a rate of 50 cents or 40 cents would have produced more revenue than the lower rate. The high revenues at high rates did reduce the risk of exploring the effects of lower rates.

A *penetration price* sacrifices the maximization of short-run profits for long-run objectives. Some products are introduced at prices below those intended for the long run to create familiarity with the product. Such apparently was the case with Tang, a powdered substitute for orange juice which appeared at first at cut-rate prices (two jars for the price of one, coupons offering discounts, etc.). After the public had gained familiarity with the product these special price cuts were removed. Apparently the producers of Tang believed that the initial price elasticity was high, but that those who tried out and liked the product would be willing to pay a higher price.

The conditions most favorable to penetration pricing are: (1) high short-run price elasticities with lower long-run elasticities, as in the case just discussed; (2) economies of scale in production; (3) the threat of new substitutes which may require restraint in profit making to discourage entry (Dean calls this "stay-out pricing"); and (4) a favorable impact of sales of the product under consideration on the sales of other company products and on customer goodwill.

In the selection of a skimming price or penetration price (or some compromise), the firm might well consider the prices of substitutes. If the prices of substitutes permit pricing of the new product at a high profit or if substitutes are too remote to be worthy of consideration, a skimming price may be appropriate. If the problem is one of taking business away from fairly close substitutes, a penetration price may be necessary to establish the new product on the market.

Pricing mature products

In an economy of rapid innovation and changing tastes such as ours, many products can expect a limited life on the market. The market for hula hoops and Davy Crockett caps may last a year or less; passenger services on the railroads are suffering curtailment after a century of consumer acceptance. The length of the life cycle is not easily predicted. Even when the deterioration has clearly set in, no general rules govern the optimal policy. In some cases a low price policy may delay the encroachment of new substitutes. In other cases low prices may instead set off price retaliation. Let us consider the case of motion picture theaters in the 1950s. That the market had declined was incontestable. But it does not follow that the appropriate reaction was price reduction. It may be that the demand had shifted to the left without any pronounced change in elasticity. In other words, the availability of television has cut into the market, but it does not follow that consumers' decisions to go or not to go to a movie were more price oriented than before. It seems unlikely that movies would enjoy a great revival if their prices were halved; in fact, the practice in the 1960s seems to have been to raise prices substantially.

A case in which a low-price policy seems to have delayed market decline is that of books. If book prices had increased as much as prices in general in the last two decades with novels selling at $7 to $10 rather than $3.50 to $5, the book industry might well be in great difficulty. Indeed, the appearance of high-quality paperbacks selling from $.75 to $2.50 has helped a great deal to bolster the industry, though this development is better considered as an introduction of a new product than a price reduction. Perhaps it is wrong to classify book publishing as a mature industry, but the book industry does appear to be adjusting both price and product to the changing times and taste.

Odd-number and round-number pricing

Some sellers believe that odd-number prices are more attractive to buyers than even numbers. A price of 43 cents may, for some strange reason, be more appealing than 42 cents or even 40 cents. Such a situation would indicate a jagged demand curve. The problem for management would be to determine which numbers have the greater appeal. Research so far provides little help on this score.

More widespread and plausible is the belief that demand is quite elastic to price reductions slightly below some round number. The sale of gasoline at 38.9 cents or 42.9 cents, the pricing of long-playing records at $3.98, $4.98, or $5.98, and similar practices give evidence that customers are heavily influenced by reductions of price below round numbers or, at least, of a widespread belief that such is the case. Again, present research is inconclusive on the effectiveness of such pricing. Perhaps the real impact is in price comparisons among products: the customer may be quite sensitive to the difference between 42.9 cents on one gasoline and 43.0 cents on another, but insensitive to the difference between 42.8 and 42.9. This creates an incentive to settle at 42.9.

Some sellers follow the opposite policy, with a preference for round numbers. For example, the management of a nursery with a reputation for quality believes that prices of $4 or $4.50 are more consistent with that reputation than prices like $3.99 or $4.23 that have a cut-rate appearance. This nursery does experiment with special prices at its annual sale, but, in general, resists pricing practices that might give the impression of a low-quality, mass-volume operation.

Imitative pricing and suggested prices

Another approach to pricing is simply to imitate prices of others. The reasons for such a policy in oligopoly are already familiar to the reader. But the practice appears even when the oligopolistic reasoning is not applicable. Imitation is easy on the decision maker. He may get the benefit of another firm's market analysis without worrying about demand elasticities and incremental costs.

Similarly the practice of following suggested prices of manufacturers or wholesalers gives the manager time to devote to other decisions. Some managers prefer to minimize the time devoted to pricing and go out of the way to find prepriced items. The suggested price is probably one that the manufacturer or wholesaler has found feasible under the market conditions and thus permits the retailer to gain the benefit of analysis without having to engage in it himself. This policy limits flexibility in meeting local conditions, but some sellers prefer to escape the pain of analyzing those conditions.

In the case of resale price maintenance, especially when it is supported by legislation, the choice of the seller is limited. He can sell the item only at the price established by the manufacturer. Some small retailers believe that such practices protect them from unfair competition from large outlets. Some manufacturers apparently prefer the control and stability of price that resale price maintenance provides. But in recent years, especially with the advent of discount houses and with court rulings unfavorable to price maintenance, the hold of this pricing practice has diminished.

Price lining

Another practice that is claimed to simplify the pricing problem is that of price lining, which consists of deciding for a considerable period of time (at least several years) on a limited number of price levels for different qualities of the same product. For example, a store may carry lines of summer dresses at $12.95, $15.95, $19.95, and $24.95. As each new season approaches, the buyers must decide on which dresses to fit into those predetermined price lines.

Department store managers apparently believe that price lining simplifies setting of prices, releasing time for sales promotion, inventory control, and other activities. Maximization of profits still requires equating marginal cost and marginal revenue, which in this case requires recognition of the fact that improved qualities normally increase volume but also increase the cost not only on the last unit but also on the intramarginal units. Figure 8–7 illustrates this reasoning. The marginal cost curve lies above the average cost curve for the same kind of reason that the marginal revenue curve lies below a downward sloping demand curve. Suppose, for example, that management is considering a choice between a dress that costs $11 and one which costs $12. The selling price is predetermined to be $15.95 whichever dress is selected. It is expected that the $11 quality

FIGURE 8–7

PRICE LINING

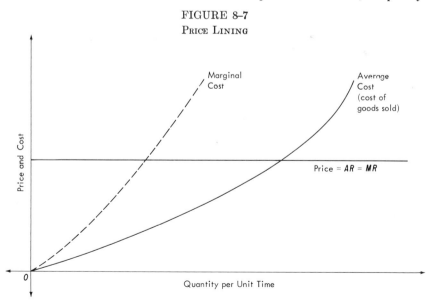

TABLE 8–1

Prices in Eight Supermarkets on Selected Items
(July 1954 prices)

Items	Average Price (in Cents)	Average Deviation as a Percent of Average Price	Average Price of Customary Unit Purchase (in Cents)	Wholesale List (in Cents)	Percentage Margin of Wholesale List
Cereals and bakery products					
Flour, wheat, 5 lbs.	52	4	52	49.5	4.8
Biscuit mix, 20 oz.	24	7	24	21.5	10.4
Corn flakes, 12 oz.	24	4.5	24	18.1	24.6
Rolled oats, 20 oz.	18.5	3	18.5	15.0	18.9
Corn meal, 1 lb.	14	11.5	14	13.5	3.6
Rice, 1 lb.	45	2	45	34.04	24.4
Meats, poultry and fish					
Round steaks, lb.	85	10	85	--	--
Rib roast, lb.	55	0	55	--	--
Canned luncheon meat	49	0	49	39.6	19.2
Canned salmon	75	2	75	61.4	18.1
Canned tuna fish	39	12	39	29.6	24.1
Dairy products					
Milk, evaporated	13	3	78	12.5	3.8
American cheese, lb.	67	2	67	--	--
Other fruits and vegetables					
Canned orange juice, 46 oz.	34	7	34	30.3	10.9
Peaches, #2½	29	13	29	25.96	10.5
Sliced pineapple, #2½	33	3	33	26.9	18.5
Fruit cocktail, #2½	31	21	31	32.9	.3
Cream style corn, #303	17	4	34	14.7	13.5
Peas, canned, #303	21	4	21	16.6	21
Tomatoes, canned, #2	23	7	23	19.1	17
Strained baby food, 4½–5 oz.	10	6	60	9	10
Dried prunes, lb.	33.5	7	33.5	25	25.4
Navy beans, lb.	16	6	16	12.8	20
Other foods					
Vegetable soup, 11 oz.	14.5	18	29	11.97	17.4
Beans with pork, 16 oz. ...	15	13	30	14.90	.7
Tomato catsup, 14 oz.	26	20	26	16.10	38.1
Coffee, lb.	118	3	118	123.50	– 4.7
Tea, ½ lb.	39	6	39	30.20	22.6
Vegetable shortening, lb. ...	30	3.5	90	33.4	–11.3
Peanut butter, lb.	48	12	48	45.1	6
Sugar, white, 5 lbs.	51.5	4	51.5	50	2.9
Corn syrup, 24 oz.	32	3	32	17.5	45.3
Grape jelly, 12 oz.	25	14	25	16.75	33
Chocolate bars, 1 oz.	5	0	5	3.50	30
Flavored gelatin dessert, 3–4 oz.	8.5	6	34	7.3	14.1

Source: Bob R. Holdren, *The Structure of a Retail Market and the Market Behavior of Retail Units* (Englewood Cliffs, N.J.: Prentice-Hall, Inc., 1960), pp. 76–79.

will sell in a volume of 200 dresses; The $12 quality in a volume of 300. The marginal cost (unit incremental cost) of the added dresses is $14, which is still below the selling price. Marginal reasoning would lead the manager to a still higher quality that would equate the marginal cost to the price of $15.95.

Empirical studies and illustrations

Only one of the pricing devices just described will be illustrated from empirical findings—the use of loss leaders. Holdren's outstanding study of supermarkets presents evidence on the commodities selected as price leaders. His study is limited to one city at one period of time, so that the findings may not be exactly reproduced in similar studies elsewhere. Table 8–1 reproduces his data on the average price, wholesale list price, and percentage margin in eight supermarkets.

Several products are quite clearly loss leaders, for their prices do not even cover wholesale cost. These are coffee, selling at that time at five cents below wholesale cost, and vegetable shortening, selling at over 10 percent below cost. But the low margins on a number of other commodities qualify them for inclusions as loss leaders: flour, corn meal, evaporated milk, fruit cocktail, strained baby food, beans with pork, peanut butter, and sugar.

Coffee is apparently a "natural" loss leader, being relatively high in price and purchased frequently, so that the consumer is quite aware of price differentials. Holdren points out, however, that the margin was unusually low in 1954 because of the high level of wholesale coffee prices at that time; in fact, coffee prices had fallen to as much as 30 percent below wholesale cost and margins were undergoing a recovery at the time the study was made.

OPTIMUM "MARKETING MIX": PRODUCT, PROMOTION, PRICE

In previous sections, attention has focused on the firm's possibilities for changing sales quantities through variations in price. If a product can be differentiated, potential effects of variations in product quality and promotion effort should also be taken into account. Variations in product quality can include changes in physical properties, packaging, services, and availability. Variations in promotion effort can include changes in advertising, selling, and publicity. The objective is to determine the best combination of product, promotion, and price.

The topic of price lining in the preceding section was concerned with choice of optimum product quality (measured by average cost per unit) with price and promotion taken as given. A similar analysis could be carried out for selection of optimum promotion effort (again measured by average cost per unit) with price (and product quality) taken as given.

Note that these independent analyses could not incorporate the probable interactions or complementarities among product quality, promotion effort, and price.

This section is a theoretical formulation of optimum choice of marketing mix. Figure 8–8 depicts a family of isoquants. Each isoquant shows the various combinations of total promotion cost and total product cost that will sustain *a given rate of sales* per unit of time *at some given price*. Curvature of the isoquants reflects complementarity of promotion effort and product quality. Greater distances from isoquant to isoquant as sales rates are increased are due to the steadily increasing difficulty of getting more sales at the same price.

FIGURE 8–8

OPTIMAL COMBINATIONS OF PRODUCT QUALITY AND PROMOTION
EFFORT FOR VARIOUS RATES OF SALES AT A GIVEN PRICE

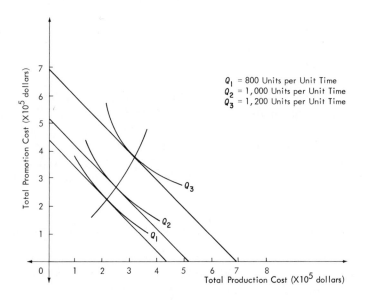

A family of isocost lines is also depicted in Figure 8–8. At points of tangency of these isocost lines and the various isoquants, the sales expansion path is developed. Each point on this expansion path shows the lowest total cost of promotion and product at which a given rate of sales can be achieved.

Figure 8–9 is derived from the path of sales expansion at lowest cost. It shows total optimized combination cost of promotion and product at various rates of sales. Total revenue at the given price is also shown in Figure 8–9. The optimum sales rate is found where the vertical distance

FIGURE 8–9

OPTIMAL AVERAGE COST AND SALES AT A GIVEN PRICE

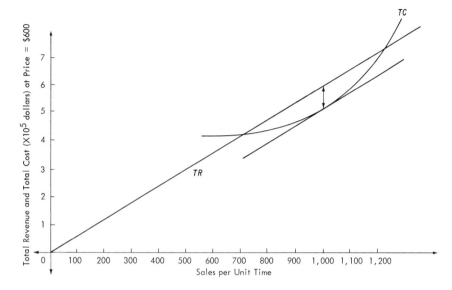

FIGURE 8–10

OPTIMAL AVERAGE COST AND SALES RATE AT A GIVEN PRICE

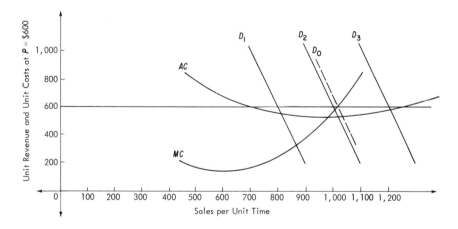

between total cost and total revenue is greatest. Figure 8–10 shows the parallel analysis using average and marginal costs and price (price if held constant is marginal revenue). Figure 8–10 depicts demand shifting and unit cost increasing due to product improvement and more promotion. Optimum sales rate is found where marginal cost becomes equal to marginal revenue.

The above analysis can be carried out for higher or lower prices so as eventually to determine the best combination of product quality, promotion effort, and price.

THE PRICING PROCESS

The pricing process is complex. Many influences and considerations must be taken into account. These are highlighted in the following discussion of parties involved in pricing, a multistage approach in which early decisions simplify subsequent ones, and a pricing checklist that summarizes considerations in pricing decisions.

Parties involved in pricing

The manager responsible for pricing decisions must consider a variety of individuals concerned with price. Oxenfeldt lists seven main parties to the pricing process: those responsible for sales promotion, the ultimate customers for the product, rival sellers, potential rivals, middlemen, suppliers, and the government.[9] Economic theory usually stresses only two of these parties: the buyers and the sellers. The pricing process in practice must take all of them into account, for they all are involved in the pattern of communication and influence which determines the final outcome.

The case of the *middleman* brings out the complexity of the pricing environment. Most manufacturers distribute their products through middlemen rather than directly. The mutual interests of the manufacturer and the middleman are obscure. The manufacturer would like the middleman to carry his product at a minimum markup, but the margin must be large enough to stimulate a desire to carry and "push" the product. The manufacturer would like a variety of middlemen to provide a wide coverage of the market, but middlemen often want to handle products on an exclusive basis. The manufacturer may wish to control prices charged by the middlemen and even the retail price; but the middlemen may wish to expand their sales by cutting price or to obtain a larger margin than the suggested price provides. A reduction of price by the manufacturer may reduce the value of middlemen's inventories, a fact that may lead to resentment unless some adjustment is made. Many of these issues are resolved by reference to trade policies and customs.

The relation of the *government* to pricing decisions is an especially painful one to many businessmen. Especially difficult is the problem of avoiding price discrimination of the sort deemed illegal under the Robinson-Patman Act. Most multiproduct firms, especially those with widespread

---

[9] The following discussion makes considerable use of ideas in Alfred R. Oxenfeldt, *Pricing for Marketing Executives* (Belmont, Calif.: Wadsworth Publishing Co., Inc., 1961).

markets, engage in price discrimination in a broad sense. The problem is to determine when such discrimination becomes illegal in the sense of the statutes. The criteria of legality require a determination of whether the pricing practices injure rivals or tend to lessen competition. They also require consideration of whether price differences reflect cost differences—for example, the lower costs made possible by supplying large quantities to certain customers. Similar difficulties arise in the interpretation of statutes and court decisions governing resale price maintenance, sales below cost, basing point systems of pricing, and a variety of other pricing practices.

A multi-stage approach to pricing

A. R. Oxenfeldt has outlined what he calls a "multi-stage approach to pricing."[10] This approach breaks the pricing process into a series of successive steps; decisions on the early stages facilitate subsequent decisions. Oxenfeldt outlines six stages, as follows:

Selection of market targets. The firm should determine the character of the market it expects to reach with the product under consideration. It may try to find segments of the market in which it has a special advantage, such as some insulation from competition. It may decide it wishes to sell to a particular income group or to those with special tastes. It may stress winning a larger share of the market. It may wish to develop markets which are complementary to those for the company's existing products. Such a decision requires an evaluation of the firm's capabilities, goals, and resources.

Selection of the firm or brand image. Management should decide what kind of reputation for the firm and brand names it is trying to build up in the public's mind. Some firms establish a reputation for high quality which may justify their high prices. Others may wish to be known as economical outlets for mass-produced commodities. Still others may wish to be known as innovators. The point is that management should make product, packaging, advertising, and pricing decisions which are consistent with the image it is trying to create.

Composition of the marketing mix. Management should coordinate advertising decisions with pricing. For example, if it is trying to increase sales by reducing price, its advertising should aim at increasing the elasticity of demand to such price decreases. Such advertising would stress the price advantage of the company's product. On the other hand, an increase in price might be accompanied by advertising which stresses the quality and distinctiveness of the firm's product. Similarly, decisions

---

[10] Alfred R. Oxenfeldt, "Multi-Stage Approach to Pricing," *Harvard Business Review* (July–August, 1960), pp. 125–33. Oxenfeldt's discussion is similar to Dean's "Steps in Pioneering Pricing" in *Managerial Economics* (Englewood Cliffs, N.J.: Prentice-Hall, Inc., 1951), pp. 413–19.

on the quality of service, styling, and packaging should relate to the pricing decisions.

Selection of the specific price policy.   The firm should next determine an overall price policy within which it can establish individual prices. Some illustrations of such policies are: to follow the price of the leader; to set prices at 10 percent below those of the leader; to determine the best price for each product individually; to follow the practice of marking up by a predetermined percentage on full cost; to follow the prices suggested by manufacturers or wholesalers; to maintain uniform prices throughout all markets; or to differentiate price according to the characteristics of particular markets.

Selecton of a price strategy.   The firm should choose current prices that are consistent with its long-term objectives. We have already presented illustrations of such strategies. For example, a penetration price strategy may aim at the creation of familiarity with the product as rapidly as possible, with subsequent dominance of the market. Prices may aim at discouraging the entry of new competition into the market. In other situations the strategy may be one of avoiding "rocking the boat," with restraint in changing prices in a way that will provoke retaliation.

Setting specific prices.   The previous steps provide a framework for establishing the prices of individual products. Some of the previous steps reduce this final step to a mere mechanical routine which can be delegated to clerks. But the choice of policies and strategies which call for flexibility will require considerable high-level analysis before prices are determined.

Pricing checklist

The following checklist of considerations in pricing is based on several works which attempt to bridge the gap between abstract theory and needs of the individual firm:

1. Consideration of price-volume relationships (elasticities of demand) to determine what happens to total revenue at various prices
2. Comparison of those price-volume relationships with incremental costs to determine the most profitable price on each item.
3. Estimation of the contribution to overhead and profits on each product that can be produced with the given facilities.
4. Selection of those products and sale at prices that will assure the largest contributions to overhead and profits
5. Investment in new facilities according to the estimated profits in the future of alternative products at optimum prices, taking costs into account
6. Flexibility of prices over time to meet changing market and cost

conditions, unless there are *strong* arguments against flexibility (possible retaliation, high costs of changing decisions, etc.)

7. Consideration of the impact of price changes on the "image" of the company in the market, on customer goodwill, and on the firm's reputation for "fair" prices

8. Consideration of the impact that price changes on one commodity may have on the sales of other items.

9. Experimentation with price changes, when this is not too costly, to determine what customer responses are likely to be

10. Determination of how much customers will benefit from price reductions, for this will give some clues as to the response to price changes

11. Comparison of the long-range implications of price changes against the immediate impact of those changes.

12. Consideration of the life cycle of the product, with different price strategies for new products than for mature products facing a decline in demand

13. Consideration of competitors' reactions to price changes

14. Evaluation of the impact of price changes on the entry or exit of competitive rivals

15. Coordination of price policies with other marketing policies, so that these are consistent and complementary

16. Determination of the incremental costs or marginal costs of each product, even when full-cost pricing is applied, in order to evaluate the impact of full-cost pricing from time to time

17. Avoidance of overestimating how much can be accomplished by pricing alone; it is only one phase of management and cannot guarantee profitable operations.[11]

---

[11] This list is based primarily on the following works: Joel Dean, *Managerial Economics;* A. R. Oxenfeldt, *Pricing for Marketing Executives;* and W. W. Haynes, *Pricing Decisions in Small Business.*

9 / Selected topics in pricing

This chapter is concerned with advanced topics in pricing. It begins with a discussion of price discrimination, in which differences in prices of a product in its various markets do not match differences in costs. It then takes up peak load pricing, in which price of a nonstorable good is increased and decreased with changes in demand over short periods of time. The next topic is utility rate regulation, in which particular attention is given to the choice between average cost and marginal cost pricing of output of a decreasing cost industry. The chapter moves on to price and output determination for multiple products; i.e., products that are technically interdependent in production. The final topic is interdivisional transfer pricing in large, multiple-product, multiple-process companies.

PRICE DISCRIMINATION

Two definitions of price discrimination are necessary for our purposes. One is a tight, narrow definition, useful for analytical purposes. The other is looser and broader, but closer to the realities of business. The two definitions are:

1. The practice of charging different prices to different segments of the market for the same commodity or service.[1]

2. The practice of charging prices with differences that do not correspond to differences in marginal costs of slightly differentiated goods or services.

---

[1] Joan Robinson's classic definition of price discrimination is "the act of selling the same article, produced under a single control, at different price to different buyers." See *The Economics of Imperfect Competition* (London: Macmillan & Co., Ltd., 1933), p. 179.

The first definition presumes a homogeneous commodity. The second definition recognizes that differentiation of price is likely to accompany differentiation in characteristics of the commodity. *To determine whether price discrimination exists one must compare price differentials with cost differentials.* The absence of price differentials may be discriminatory, as is the case when the same commodity is sold at the same price over a wide territory in which transportation costs vary. The existence of price differentials may, on the other hand, be nondiscriminatory, as would be the case if price differences match differences in transportation costs.

Some writers prefer the term "differential pricing" to "price discrimination," for the latter term may carry unintended connotations. Price discrimination is actually a neutral, technical term describing a particular business practice rather than something that is evil by definition.

Conditions necessary for price discrimination

Two conditions are necessary for profitable price discrimination:

1. Segmentation of the market. *It must be possible to segment the market and to prevent resale from one segment to another.*

2. Differences in the elasticity of demand. *The elasticity of demand in one segment of the market must be lower than in another if discrimination is to be profitable.*

Segmentation of the market and differences in elasticity both imply that competition must be imperfect. In a highly competitive market, new sellers would move rapidly into those market segments in which high prices are charged, driving down the price differentials and destroying the segmentation. Specialists would engage in arbitrage—buying in the cheap segments and selling in the dear markets—until the price differentials disappear.

How is segmentation of the market achieved? A great variety of methods are in use. It is best to present specific illustrations.

1. Doctors can separate patients with high incomes from those with low. The fact that the product is a direct personal service prevents its resale.

2. Railroads can separate high-value commodities from those with low value per unit of volume or weight. A simple inspection of commodities ensures that they do not travel at the wrong rate.

3. Manufacturers frequently offer quantity discounts, thus separating large purchasers from small ones. If the quantity discounts are explained by differences in marginal costs of selling to large and small buyers, no discrimination results. However, if the quantity discounts also reflect differences in bargaining power of the buyers or urgency of their demand, price discrimination is present.

4. State universities usually charge higher tuition rates to out-of-state

students than to residents of the state. Such universities require evidence of residence, sometimes calling in legal advice in borderline cases.

5. Some firms sell approximately the same product under different brand names at widely differing prices. Consumer ignorance of the similarity in quality prevents a large-scale transfer of customers from one brand to the other.

6. Some producers charge different prices to different trade channels. For example, they may charge more in the replacement market than in the original-equipment market. Replacement demand is likely to be less elastic, permitting a higher charge.

7. Firms sometimes sell abroad at prices lower than domestic prices, a practice known as "dumping." Tariffs and cost of shipping the product back to the exporting country help maintain segmentation of the market.

8. One simple way of segmenting customers, with some leakage to be sure, is to offer the commodity at a "regular" price most of the year and then reduce the price at times of special sales. Some customers are not patient enough or price conscious enough to wait for the sales; others are bargain hunters and will wait. Such a policy makes it possible for the seller to tap both kinds of market.

9. Professional journals usually carry lower student subscription rates. They require evidence of a student status. The presumption is that student demand for journals is more elastic; in addition, students may acquire a long-term desire for the journal, adding to long-run demand.

10. Faculty members can buy books at discounts below student prices. Their demand is more elastic for books they do not use directly in their courses; furthermore, they may adopt the books in the future. On the other hand, elasticity of student demand is reduced by the practice of requiring texts.

11. Theaters usually charge children lower prices even though they occupy just as much space as adults and may actually be somewhat more costly in wear and tear. In most cases it is easy to determine the age category of the customer, but some leakage seems likely on children at ages close to the dividing line.

The reader can no doubt supply other illustrations. We might classify these examples of market segmentation into broad categories:

1. Segmentation by income and wealth
2. Segmentation by quantity of purchase
3. Segmentation by social or professional status of the customer
4. Segmentation by location
5. Segmentation by time of purchase
6. Segmentation by preferences for brand names
7. Segmentation by age of the customer
8. Segmentation by convenience to the buyer

The theory of price discrimination

For purposes of the exposition of the theory of price discrimination, it is desirable to start with a homogeneous commodity. This makes it possible to consider only one marginal cost curve. After the basic problem is understood it is not difficult to extend the theory to differentiated products.

Figure 9–1 presents the standard diagram of price discrimination. The market consists of two segments, one with a more elastic demand curve than the other. Demand in the more elastic segment is indicated by D_1; in the less elastic segment by D_2. The corresponding marginal revenue

FIGURE 9–1

PROFIT MAXIMIZATION WITH PRICE DISCRIMINATION

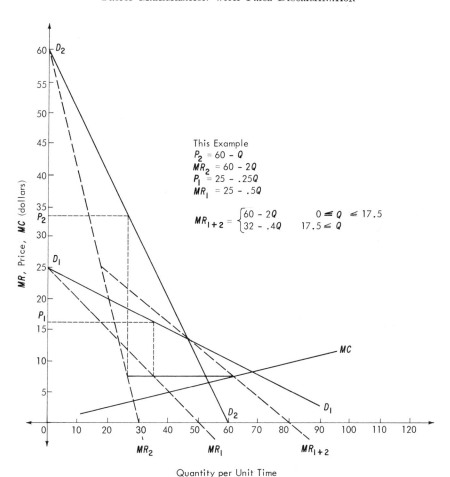

This Example
$$P_2 = 60 - Q$$
$$MR_2 = 60 - 2Q$$
$$P_1 = 25 - .25Q$$
$$MR_1 = 25 - .5Q$$

$$MR_{1+2} = \begin{cases} 60 - 2Q & 0 \leqq Q \leqq 17.5 \\ 32 - .4Q & 17.5 \leqq Q \end{cases}$$

Quantity per Unit Time

curves are indicated by MR_1 and MR_2. The aggregate marginal revenue curve is derived by *horizontal* summation of the *quantities* in both curves at each of the marginal revenues. The reader should note that it is the quantities that are summed and not the marginal revenues *themselves*.[2]

On the cost side of the analysis only the marginal cost is relevant; the other cost curves are not shown. It should be clear that only one marginal cost curve exists under the conditions specified; it makes no difference from the cost point of view whether the product sells in market 1 or market 2, since it is the same product. The marginal cost is governed by the total output.

The problem in maximizing profits is one, as before, of choosing an output that equates marginal revenue and marginal cost. At the same time, total input must be allocated between the markets in such a way that their marginal revenues are equal. Optimum total output is found when the *aggregate* marginal revenue intersects the marginal cost curve.[3] *The horizontal line from the point of intersection intersects the two marginal revenue curves, thus indicating how the total output should be allocated between the two markets. Market prices are found on the demand curves, directly above the intersections of the horizontal line with the marginal revenue curves.* As one would expect, the price in the more elastic segment, P_1, is considerably lower than the price in the second, P_2.

As a check on his understanding of the diagram, the reader might note that the solution equates the marginal revenue in the two segments, as well as equating marginal revenue to marginal cost. If MR_1 were greater than MR_2, or vice versa, the firm could increase profits by transferring units from one segment to the other. This is an illustration of the equimarginal principle. From another point of view, if either MR_1 or MR_2 were greater than marginal cost, an expansion of output would be profitable. Optimization requires that $MR_1 = MR_2 = MC$. The difference between P_1 and P_2 is not explained by difference in marginal cost. Thus, we can be sure that this is an example of price discrimination.

Price discrimination in practice: legal issues

It is not always possible to determine whether observed price differences are explained by price discrimination. The first difficulty is in determining whether two or more products are really differentiated versions of the same product or, instead, two different products on which price comparisons are inappropriate. A second difficulty is in measuring mar-

---

[2] This point is stressed to distinguish price discrimination from the pricing of joint products in which the vertical addition of marginal revenues is appropriate.

[3] The solution would not be affected by redrawing the marginal cost curve to be horizontal. Earlier chapters have presented evidence of horizontal marginal cost curves; but it is clearer for purposes of exposition to draw a rising marginal cost curve.

ginal costs of the various products, which requires some way of dealing with common costs.

The legal status of differential pricing is uncertain. This book avoids the legal intricacies of antitrust and price discrimination legislation and rulings. *In general, the Federal Trade Commission and the courts have permitted price differentials that reflect differences in cost;* our earlier discussion of costs should explain why this criterion has been so troublesome in such cases. The courts tend to rely on average costs rather than marginal costs in measuring cost differentials, with consequent difficulties in the treatment of overhead. The courts have upheld larger discounts to retailers than to wholesalers and have upheld quantity discounts that could be justified in terms of cost differentials. But the courts have ruled against basing point systems of pricing and have ruled against quantity discounts that may injure or suppress competition. *A major criterion of illegality is injury to competitors.*

The position of the manager in this area of differential pricing is a complex one. On one hand he is challenged to use imagination in finding more profitable ways of adjusting prices to market conditions. But he may be concerned with his obligations to the public and with avoidance of price differentials that might be considered unfair or harmful to competition. In addition, the manager must consider the legal consequences of his pricing behavior, with the possibility, in view of the complexity of the problem, that his ideas of equity may not always conform to those of the Federal Trade Commission or the courts.

Empirical studies and illustrations

Many illustrations of price discrimination could be presented, for it is a widespread practice. To save space, it seems appropriate to restrict attention to price discrimination in the public utilities. The utilities usually sell services that cannot be economically resold by the buyers, and thus they are particularly likely to use price discrimination.

Water supply. An outstanding study of water supply indicates that price discrimination is widely practiced by municipal water companies, both public and private.[4] In New York City some users are unmetered, which means that they pay a flat rate with no extra charge for the heavy use of water. Obviously there is discrimination between such users and those who pay according to volume of consumption. This discrimination encourages the waste of water. In Los Angeles, on the other hand, lower rates are charged for irrigation water than for water in urban use, and the rate differentials are clearly not in proportion to the marginal costs. The result is a subsidy to farm production.

Some of the water rate differentials are in line with cost differences

---

[4] J. Hirshleifer, J. C. DeHaven, and J. W. Milliman, *Water Supply: Economics, Technology and Policy* (Chicago: University of Chicago Press, 1960).

and thus are not discriminatory in the strict definition of price discrimination. For example, most systems charge less per unit for greater volumes, a fact that may reflect the lower cost of delivering and metering the increments in volume. In Los Angeles (and many other cities) a rate differential exists between firm service and service that the water department may curtail at its convenience. Since the cost of water delivered at peak periods is greater than delivered at other times, this differential is not necessarily discriminatory—it is a way of charging for the extra load that peak users place on the system.

Gas and electricity.   Gas and electricity rates of the Consolidated Gas Electric Light and Power Company of Baltimore have been studied by Davidson.[5] Rate schedules of the Baltimore company are probably representative of those in the gas and electricity industries in general. They incorporate several kinds of price discrimination, all with the approval of the regulatory agencies. One kind of discrimination is called "peak-off-peak discrimination," which involves a failure to relate rates to the differentials in costs between peak and off-peak periods. The simplest form of such discrimination is the charging of the same rate in both peak and off-peak periods. Even when higher rates are charged peak energy users, the methods of allocating costs often fail to apply as high a proportion of capacity costs to the peak periods as is warranted, resulting in a subsidy of peak production by off-peak sales.

The study of the Baltimore Consolidated Gas Electric Light and Power Company provides illustrations of other types of price discrimination. The company makes estimates of the "value of service" to customers; rates are frequently related to such values rather than to costs. During the depression of the thirties, for example, the company set prices to meet the competition of other energy sources, cutting rates sharply for large industrial and domestic consumers. As Davidson says, "Value-of-service pricing is precisely what economists call monopolistic price discrimination, the results of which many regard as socially undesirable."[6]

The different types of rate structures which have been used in the gas and electric utilities vary in the degree of discrimination. The "simple flat rate," which was used in the early history of such utilities, was highly discriminatory, for it charged no more for high consumption than low. The "adjusted flat rate," which varied according to the number of electric lights and connected appliances, no doubt was better correlated with consumption, but it obviously did not reflect different rates of usage of the equipment.

The "straight-line rate," a uniform charge per unit of energy con-

---

[5] See R. K. Davidson, *Price Discrimination in Selling Gas and Electricity* (Baltimore: The Johns Hopkins Press, 1955), especially chap. 11.

[6] Ibid., p. 215.

sumed, requires metering. The trouble with such straight-line rates is that they do not separate charges for capacity from the charges for the use of energy. This rate thus discriminates against the large consumer (for whom the unit capacity costs are low) and against the off-peak user. The utilities, recognizing that the straight-line rates did discriminate against large users, introduced discounts for quantity consumption. These discounts have taken several forms, the most popular of which today is the block rate, in which prices of energy decrease by blocks of consumption. Many utilities using block rates require customers to pay a minimum bill to assure that at least part of the fixed customer costs are recovered. A main defect of the block rates is their failure to charge extra for consumption at the peak, discriminating against those with relatively uniform consumption over time.

To overcome some of the defects of the preceding systems, several more sophisticated rate structures have been introduced. These structures are known as "demand rate" structures. They separate the charge for energy from what is called the "demand." Note that the word "demand" in this context refers to the maximum rate of consumption over a short period of time, perhaps a quarter hour. The "demand" rate charges separately for the *maximum* "demand," which is a measure of the maximum load placed on the system's capacity.[7] The best known of the "demand" structures is the Hopkinson rate introduced in England in 1892. A typical Hopkinson rate schedule appears as follows.[8]

"Demand" charge

First 200 kw. (or less) of demand	$3.02 per kw.
Next 1,800 kw.	1.51 per kw.
Over 2,000 kw.	1.28 per kw.

Consumption charge

First 50,000 kw.-hrs.	0.94¢ per kw.-hr.
Next 250,000 kw.-hrs.	0.83¢ per kw.-hr.
Next 300,000 kw.-hrs.	0.56¢ per kw.-hr.
All over 600,000 kw.-hrs.	0.47¢ per kw.-hr.

The Hopkinson rate has one major failing. It charges for the maximum rate of consumption of the individual but does not charge for the maximum strain the individual places on the system. If the customer's peak comes at the trough of the system's load, he should be rewarded rather

---

[7] Special demand meters record the maximum demand.

[8] Taken from R. K. Davidson, *Price Discrimination in Selling Gas and Electricity,* which contains an excellent discussion of gas and electricity rate structures. Most readers will recognize the distinction between kilowatts (kw.) and kilowatt-hours (kw.-hrs.), the first being a capacity concept (power) and the second a flow concept (energy).

than penalized, for he is helping to improve the "load factor" (the ratio of actual consumption to capacity consumption). What is needed is a charge for the individual customer's contribution to the peak-load. A fuller discussion of peak-load pricing appears in a later section of this chapter.

Davidson's conclusion on all of the rate structures used in the gas and electricity industry is that "none" "conforms to the true costs of service" and "all are discriminatory."[9] Perhaps he has given too little weight to the metering costs and administrative difficulties involved in completely nondiscriminatory rates.

Railroads. The railroads are perhaps best known of all industries for the practice of price discrimination. Several varieties of rail rate discrimination are prevalent or have prevailed in the past: (1) discrimination among commodities; (2) discrimination between localities; (3) personal discrimination. The existence of discrimination among commodities is clear from the fact that some rates are as much as eight times the rates for other commodities over the same distance, as shown in Table 9–1. Only a part of this difference reflects difference in cost; the remainder is related to the ability to pay. Table 9–1 shows rates on vari-

TABLE 9–1

COMPARISON OF CARLOAD FREIGHT REVENUE FROM SELECTED COMMODITIES AND FULLY DISTRIBUTED COST, 1956*

Commodity	Percentage of Fully Distributed Cost	Commodity	Percentage of Fully Distributed Cost
Wheat	130	Iron ore	63
Corn	121	Gravel and sand (N.O.S.)	54
Flour, wheat	73	Lumber, shingles, lath	101
Cotton, in bales	135	Paint, putty, and varnish	157
Cottonseed	117	Drugs and toilet preparations	141
Cottonseed hulls	92	Agricultural implements	158
Oranges and grapefruit	78	Machinery and machines	207
Lettuce	62	Office machines	203
Potatoes	72	Automobiles, passenger	171
Cattle and calves (in single-deck cars)	74	Refrigerators	142
Eggs	100	Boots, shoes, etc.	157
Butter	112	Liquors, alcoholic	208
Anthracite coal	101	Sugar	127
Bituminous coal	80	Cigarettes	192

* Interstate Commerce Commission, Bureau of Accounts, Cost Finding and Valuation, Statement No. 6–58, *Distribution of the Rail Revenue Contribution by Commodity Groups—1956* (Washington, D.C.: U.S. Government Printing Office, 1958).

SOURCE: D. Philip Locklin, *Economics of Transportation*, 5th ed. (Homewood, Ill.: Richard D. Irwin, Inc., 1960), p. 136.

---

[9] Ibid., pp. 96–97.

ous commodities related to fully distributed cost (marginal cost would have been more suitable).

Local discrimination consists of differences in rates for equal distances, equal rates for unequal distance, and charging more for short hauls than for long hauls over the same line. One reason for such discrimination is to meet the competition of other forms of transportation, such as water and truck competition. The ICC regulates such discrimination but has made exceptions in a variety of cases.

Personal discrimination in railroad rates is rare today. In the early history of the American railroads it was a widespread practice, especially in the form of concessions or rebates to favored customers. Around the turn of the century the Standard Oil Company was able to extract such concessions and rebates by threatening to shift business to other lines or to pipelines.

PEAK-LOAD PRICING

The electricity power industry provides one example of a peak-load problem. If electric service is offered at constant prices, hourly sales quantities vary during the day and over seasons of the year due to changes in demand. Electricity cannot be stored economically in significant quantities, and the production-transmission-distribution system fails under sustained overload. Thus, peak hourly sales quantity, or peak load, determines necessary capacity of the system. Figure 9–2 shows an actual hourly load curve for one utility on the date it reached peak load for the particular year.[10]

If the sales peak is high and narrow, capacity adequate to handle peak load may be substantially greater than that needed most of the time. By increasing prices in peak periods, sales quantities (and necessary capacity) can be reduced; at the same time, quantities in off-peak periods can be increased through shifting of demand. *The problem in peak-load pricing is to determine, simultaneously, best prices in both peak and off-peak periods and "best" capacity.* Similar problems are found in distribution of gas and water and provision of telephone services.

Some general principles

It may be best to confine our attention to electricity for the time being. The electric utilities must provide capacity to meet peak loads. The question is whether they should vary rates from peak to off-peak periods. The answer of almost all economists who have studied the question is that they should charge higher rates at the peaks, since cost of producing for the peak includes cost of some capacity used only during the peak

---

[10] The illustration is from the article by Donald N. DeSalvia, "An Application of Peak Load Pricing," *Journal of Business* (October 1969), p. 460.

FIGURE 9–2

LOAD CURVE FOR DECEMBER 19, 1963

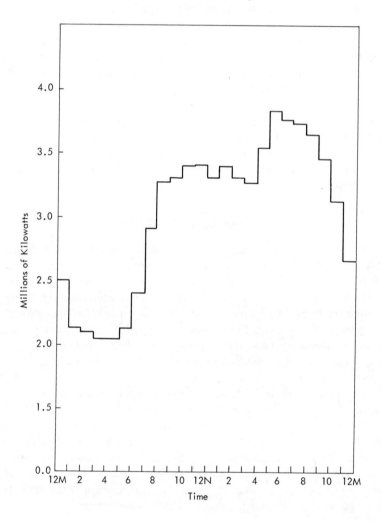

and is clearly greater than the cost for other periods.[11] *Failure to charge higher rates in peak periods causes peak consumption to be higher than it would be otherwise, and the utility must construct extra capacity to meet the peak; cost of extra capacity is then subsidized by necessarily higher rates for off-peak use.* Or, in the absence of such capacity, the

---

[11] As we shall see, the term "cost" in this connection has several alternative meanings, but the statement holds true for any of these alternatives. The statement would not hold true if we defined cost to be the energy costs plus a share of the capacity costs allocated equally to every kilowatt-hour of consumption, but this definition of cost is unacceptable to economists.

utility must engage in "load shedding" (cutting off the electricity supply of some customers), a practice which is arbitrary and inefficient.

Economists who have written on peak-load pricing are in agreement on the following two propositions:

1. Peak prices should be higher than off-peak prices for two purposes: (*a*) to allocate the limited capacity available at the peaks to those who are willing to pay most for it, and (*b*) to help cover cost of providing additional capacity required to meet that peak consumption which remains at the higher prices.

2. The only relevant costs in determination of both peak and off-peak prices are the marginal costs. (Unfortunately, some difference of opinion remains on how to measure the marginal costs.)

A graphic solution: firm peaks

Recently economists have developed what appears to be a logical solution to peak-load pricing.[12] *The solution is to equate price with marginal cost.* Figure 9–3 shows the solution for both peak and off-peak periods. This solution is based on an assumption of constant marginal cost. Although a solution for the case of increasing marginal cost is more complex, it is developed according to the same principles.

Assume for purposes of simplicity that for half of each day demand is constant at D_1D_1' and the other half constant at D_2D_2'. The kilowatt-hour charge in the low-demand period should include only the energy cost,

FIGURE 9–3

PEAK AND OFF-PEAK PRICING: THE FIRM PEAK CASE

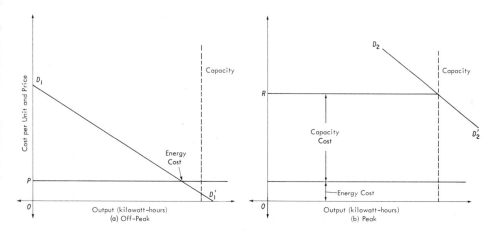

---

[12] The following discussion is based primarily on P. O. Steiner's "Peak Loads and Efficient Pricing," *Quarterly Journal of Economics,* November 1957, pp. 585–610, and J. Hirshleifer's "Comment" in August 1958 issue of the same journal, pp. 451–62.

since there is no need to add to capacity for this period. The kilowatt-hour charge in the high-demand period is equal to the energy cost plus the capacity cost. Capacity cost per kilowatt hour is total capacity cost per day divided by total kilowatt hours sold during the peak period. *The capacity cost is part of the marginal cost in the peak period, since capacity must be added to meet this demand.*

The above solution might be called the long-run equilibrium solution in which the capacity has been adjusted to the level of demand. In the shorter run, capacity may be short or in excess of equilibrium, so that the rule must be restated. In the short run the price at the peak should be such as to equate sales quantity to the capacity which is available. If capacity is in short supply the price should be set at a level higher than the sum of the capacity and energy costs, to discourage consumption by those who place low marginal values on electricity and allocate the supply to those with high marginal values. Figure 9–4a illustrates that *OS* is the appropriate price. In an excess capacity situation the price should be at *OT*, as shown in Figure 9–4b.

FIGURE 9–4

SHORT-RUN PEAK-LOAD PRICING: THE FIRM PEAK CASE

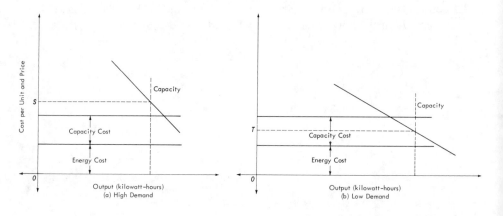

The short-run prices for the peak period are not based on full cost, but they allocate available capacity efficiently. In the first case the utility should add capacity. In the second case it should fail to replace capacity as it wears out. In both cases it should set the rate on off-peak consumption to cover only the energy cost.

A more complete discussion would consider the possibility (some economists would say the inevitability) of curvilinear costs, with rising marginal costs. For such a discussion the reader should refer to Hirshleifer's article.[13]

---

[13] Ibid., p. 455.

A graphic solution: shifting peaks

Increases in peak-period prices flatten the peak and may shift some sales to adjacent periods. Sales in other periods may then equal or even exceed those at the peak. In this case it is necessary to plot both demand curves (the high-demand and low-demand) on the same graph. Figure 9–5 illustrates. This time we add the two demands vertically to get D_c. *This combined demand curve provides estimates of how much buyers will pay for one unit of off-peak energy plus one unit of peak energy. The utility should expand capacity to the point at which D_c intersects the sum of the capacity cost (as defined in the preceding section) plus twice the energy cost.* At this point the price will cover marginal cost of energy plus marginal capacity cost (the capacity will be fully used in both periods). The prices OP_1 and OP_2 are again set to "clear the market" (use up the capacity). The result is that the capacity is fully utilized in both periods.

FIGURE 9–5

PEAK AND OFF-PEAK PRICING: THE SHIFTING PEAK CASE

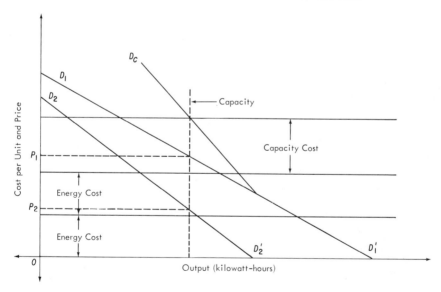

This analysis can be generalized to more than two periods and to periods which are unequal in length. The theoretical literature on peak-load pricing is in the process of extension and refinement to cover a wider range of considerations, such as indivisibilities in production and differences in plant costs.[14]

[14] O. E. Williamson, "Peak Load Pricing and Optimal Capacity under Indivisibility Constraints," *American Economic Review*, September 1966, pp. 810–27, and M. A. Crews, "Comment," in the March 1968 issue of the same journal, pp. 168–70.

Some practical problems

A number of obstacles stand in the way of actual application of the preceding analysis.

1. Demands in different periods cannot be predicted accurately.

2. Measurement of the marginal energy and capacity costs is no simple problem. Marginal costs of generation are increasing with level of output in a typical power system, due to differences in ages, locations, and types of power plants. Figure 9–6 shows DeSalvia's estimates of the relationship of marginal costs to cumulative output of an actual system in

FIGURE 9–6

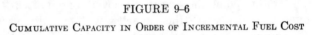

CUMULATIVE CAPACITY IN ORDER OF INCREMENTAL FUEL COST

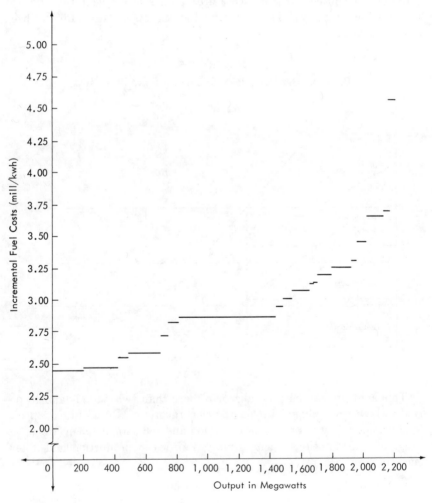

1963.[15] In this figure, the most efficient generation is used first, then the next most efficient, and so on. Off peak rates equal to marginal or energy costs that increase with cumulative output would make some contribution towards capacity cost, since these rates would exceed energy costs of the most efficient sources.

3. The proposed scheme involves flexible prices over time. This results from the necessity of using trial and error in searching for appropriate prices and from shifts in demand that cannot be exactly matched at all times by shifts in capacity. This poses serious problems for the administration of rate changes—problems which are compounded by the requirement of approval of changes by regulatory commissions. Turvey describes a controlled experiment in England and Wales to determine the effects upon consumption of electricity rate schedules containing peak-load pricing features. The experiment tested three different schedules, using three experimental groups of 890 customers each and a control group of 900 customers, and extended over a five-year period ending in winter, 1971–72.[16] Information from this experiment will be helpful in future changes toward peak-load pricing in Great Britain.

4. The public would probably react unfavorably to prices which *seem* discriminatory even though they may not be. For example, the public is not likely to understand that high rates for cooking Thanksgiving turkeys are conducive to general welfare.

5. The public would probably also react unfavorably to the instability of prices which the pricing scheme, in an extreme form, would require. They would prefer to know in advance the rates they will pay rather than be subject to sharp shifts in such rates.

The utility managers and public service commissioners are in a difficult position in the sphere of peak-load pricing. If they heed the advice of economists on marginal-cost pricing, they run the risk of public misunderstanding and charges of "unfair" pricing. Furthermore, the construction of rate schedules which meet the theoretical criteria for optimization is no easy task. But if they base their prices on full costs and try to average out rates over peaks and troughs in consumption, they are responsible for a waste of resources. By pricing peak-load consumption at its real cost and thereby deferring some capacity growth, they could reduce resource requirements (primarily investment) by substantial amounts.

Nonprice techniques for improving load factors

The use of pricing for the improvement of utility load factors has been shown to be complex and easily misunderstood. As a result, many com-

---

[15] DeSalvia, "An Application of Peak Load Pricing," p. 467.

[16] Ralph Turvey, "Peak Load Pricing," *Journal of Political Economy,* 76 (February 1968), pp. 101–13.

panies have shown a preference for marketing and other nonprice techniques which accomplish the same purpose. These consist of increased advertising in off-peak periods and the development of new markets or new products to use facilities in off-peak periods. Electric utilities have engaged in promoting the use of appliances which consume energy in off-peak periods or at least have a more stable demand. Gas companies have promoted gas-burning air conditioners.

These nonprice devices have the advantage of flexibility. Customers resent frequent changes of price but are tolerant of varying promotional activity. When advertising pushes consumption toward capacity it is easy to diminish the effort, but it is not so easy to take away a low price which has been used to promote a particular type of consumption.

Empirical studies and illustrations

Some public utilities and regulatory commissions have experimented with peak-load pricing over the years. The electric utilities used a peak-responsibility method of pricing in the early 1900s but abandoned it because of difficulties in allocating costs, in predicting when the peaks would come, and in dealing with shifts of sales to off-peak periods which created new peaks.[17] As might be expected from the intricacies of the problem, the theoretical solution was not understood. It is no wonder that the utilities found it difficult to apply the theory in practice.

Nevertheless, the electric utilities continued to experiment with methods which at least were moving in the right direction. In the 1920s, W. J. Greene introduced a schedule of rates which charged separately for consumption and demand. "Demand" in this context is referred, as we have noted above, to the customer's maximum rate of consumption. Obviously, this method does not charge the individual customer exactly for his contribution to the system's peak. His particular peak might come at the system's trough. But this method at least moved in the direction of charging for peak responsibility.

The gas industry has long charged lower rates to interruptible customers (ones whose consumption can be cut off on short notice when capacity is reached). Other examples of attempts to ease the peak-load problem through pricing are the low early morning fares of the British Railways (the fare for arrival in London before 8 A.M. is almost 50 percent below the regular fare) and the persistent experimentation of the airlines with off-season rates. An even more familiar example is the lower prices of motion pictures before 5 or 6 P.M.

Pricing is, of course, not the only way of dealing with the problem. The use of advertising and other promotional activities to improve load factors is illustrated in many industries. Florida hotels have made a great effort to stimulate occupancy in the off-season period. European countries

---

[17] Davison, *Price Discrimination in Selling Gas and Electricity,* p. 119.

have advertised the great advantages of travel in the spring and autumn when the tourists are not so much in each other's way. Some universities advertise the advantages of their summer climates in the effort to obtain greater use of their facilities in their off-peak periods.

Peak-load pricing in American utilities

Shepherd surveyed peak-load pricing in American utilities.[18] He reviewed rate schedules of 111 large private and 11 large public systems accounting altogether for over 85 percent of sales to final consumers in 1963. No true peak-load pricing was found. However, major provisions favoring off-peak usage were in the schedules of 46 large systems that had 41.8 percent of total sales in this group (about 35 percent of total sales in the nation).

Shepherd also surveyed business "message rate" pricing by telephone systems. Local telephone service usually has a broad daily peak during office hours. Therefore, office hour calls are responsible for a large share of telephone switching capacity. Message rate pricing for business telephones, with a charge for each call in excess of some base, is a step in the direction of peak-load pricing. All of the largest 8 cities (by population), and 15 of the largest 25, had message rates required for business. The 8 cities included 25 percent, and the 15 cities included 33 percent, of all telephones in the United States. Shepherd concludes that some electric systems and some telephone systems make extensive use of marginalist pricing, approaching true peak-load pricing, and that much of the measuring apparatus needed for peak-load pricing is readily available. Institutional and technical barriers can be overcome if utilities managements and regulatory commissions want to realize the resource savings of peak-load pricing, and these could be substantial.[19]

PUBLIC UTILITY RATE REGULATION

Pricing (rate making) in the public utilities presents a special problem in economic analysis. The utilities—electricity, gas, water, telephones, and public transportation—are "natural monopolies"; in any one locality a single firm tends to drive out competing firms. These are industries in which technology of production and distribution results in substantial economies of scale, which means that one large firm can produce more economically than can several firms.[20] Legislatures have recognized these

---

[18] William G. Shepherd, "Marginal-Cost Pricing in American Utilities," *Southern Economic Journal* 33 (July 1966), pp. 58–70.

[19] Ibid., pp. 58–70.

[20] It might seem that the telephone industry is an exception; a telephone company is subject to increasing costs per customer as it expands the number of customers. But if one were to measure cost per callable number, such increasing costs would no longer appear. In any case, there are obvious advantages in having a single telephone company in any single locality.

economies of scale and tendencies to monopoly by granting franchises protesting utility companies from competition and then subjecting them to rate control by regulatory commissions.

Basic pricing

Three alternative policies for pricing in the public utilities are possible: monopoly pricing, full-cost pricing, and marginal cost pricing. All are illustrated in Figure 9–7, which depicts a decreasing-cost firm. Price

FIGURE 9–7

ALTERNATIVE LEVELS OF PUBLIC UTILITY RATES

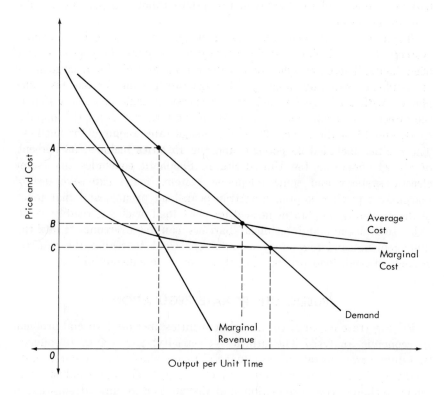

OA is the monopoly price—the price which maximizes profit. Almost all observers agree that this price is intolerable to the public. It provides a monopoly profit to firms at the expense of consumers. It results in a misallocation of resources, since the value to consumers of additional output would exceed the value of resources such additional output would use up.

Price OB *is the price sought in the usual utility regulation.* It is based on full cost—it covers fixed as well as variable costs and includes a normal return on investment. Price OB is set to provide a "fair rate of return" on the investment in the utility. The history of rate regulation is a history of controversy over what rates of returns are fair and conducive to the growth and financial strength of the utilities. It is also a history of controversy over the "rate base"—the value of the property on which the rate of return should be allowed. In periods of inflation the utilities have a strong preference for valuation at reproduction cost. They argue that the original costs, or "book costs," do not reflect the true value of the property and that returns on property valued at such costs are confiscatory. Some regulatory commissions, on the other hand, favor original cost, or a variation of original cost known as "prudent investment," not only because this practice holds down utility rates but also because original cost is easier to determine objectively. Considerable litigation often results from estimates of reproduction cost; accounting conventions reduce the amount of litigation that is possible over original cost.

The issue of original cost, reproduction cost, or other variations, such as "fair value," is still unsettled. The state regulatory commissions have not standardized their practices in establishing the rate bases; a full discussion of this issue must be left to books on public utility economics. It is necessary to note, however, that the exact level of *OB*, the price at full cost, depends somewhat on the particular regulatory agency which has jurisdiction over the utility.

Marginal cost pricing

Price *OC* is the price at marginal cost. Much of the literature on welfare economics expresses a preference for this price. The discussion of marginal cost pricing tends to become rather involved, but the argument can be summarized in nontechnical language. It is claimed that the welfare of society is increased if the price is lowered below *OB* (because the value of the added service exceeds the marginal cost of added output); the recommended price is *OC*, the point at which the demand curve intersects the marginal cost curve. *At* OC *the value to the marginal user (measured by the price he pays for the last unit, which is also the price he pays for all units) is equal to the value of the resources used up to produce the last unit.* Any higher price and lower consumption, it is argued, means a failure to maximize welfare.

Price OC *has the disadvantage that it does not cover total costs in a decreasing cost firm.* The economists who favor marginal cost pricing recommend that the government pay a subsidy to the utility so that it can cover all costs. Some of them even recommend public ownership on the grounds that the government is not required to cover all costs out of revenues.

If the utility is subject to increasing costs, as may be true of the telephone companies, marginal cost pricing may result in prices which exceed total costs. This result is shown in Figure 9–8. The firm earns excess profits in this case, but not as high as the profits that would be possible without regulation. Special taxes could siphon off a large part of the excess profit.

Marginal cost pricing is objectionable on several grounds. Subsidies mean the loss of the control advantages of rules that revenues must cover costs. Utilities may be distracted from their main business if they have to contend with political agencies for subsidies. Their profits may depend more upon their success in demonstrating the need for subsidies

FIGURE 9–8

Marginal Cost Pricing in an Increasing Cost Industry

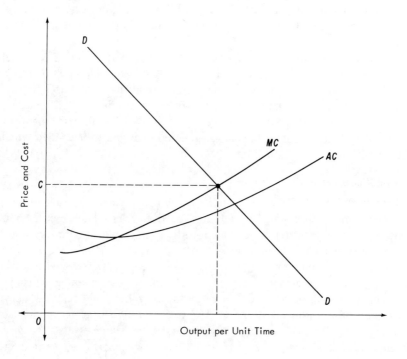

than in controlling costs. A subsidy is often a reasonable method for attaining certain social objectives, but the use of subsidies in the utilities should not be undertaken lightly. It is interesting that most nationalized utilities maintain the rule that revenues must cover costs.[21] Apparently most governments are unwilling to abandon the control advantages of requiring that costs be covered.

---

[21] Nationalized utilities are often subsidized in subtle ways, through reduced taxes or lower interest rates. And some utilities, such as the British Railways, operate with large deficits not as a matter of policy but because they have not been able to bring costs and revenues in line.

Empirical studies and illustrations

The issue of marginal cost pricing has received considerable attention in the electric utilities. Few utilities apply marginal cost pricing on an overall basis, though some of them may approach marginal costs in pricing some special services. The low electricity rates of the TVA might be rationalized as moving toward marginal cost pricing, though it does not appear that the literature on the subject was a great influence on TVA rate making. The TVA's low rates result in large part from such subsidies as low tax rates (the payments in lieu of taxes made to local and state governments are far below the rates private utilities would be required to pay) and low interest rates on funds owed the federal government.

A survey of electricity pricing in Europe suggests that marginal-cost pricing is not widely used there.[22] France and Sweden are the leaders in attention to marginal cost pricing. The Électricité de France, a nationalized concern, has been a pioneer in this respect, though it has used marginal costs more in determining particular prices than in determining the general level of rates. It has even revised particular rates when there is a "deficit between income and expenditures." This suggests that the movement towards marginal cost pricing has been quite cautious. Sweden apparently is more willing to apply the marginal cost principle when marginal cost is above average cost than in the opposite case. In explanation of this position, it is stated that it may be true, theoretically, that electricity rates ought to correspond to marginal costs even when these are lower than average costs. But if this were applied in practice, the losses incurred would have to be borne by some agency other than the electricity undertakings; e.g., the State.[23]

In other countries covered by the survey—Austria, Belgium, Italy, Norway, the Netherlands, the United Kingdom, and Switzerland—average cost pricing (full-cost pricing) appears to predominate, modified by examples of price discrimination in favor of special segments of the market.

Turning now to the United States, all the regulatory agencies, federal and state, follow a full-cost rule for overall pricing. The objective in rate regulation is to allow revenues that will cover all expenses, including depreciation, and leave a fair return on investment. The regulatory agencies vary, however, in the rates of return which they allow and in determination of the rate base.

American regulatory commissions consider four major criteria in de-

---

[22] *The Theory of Marginal Cost and Electricity Rates* (Paris: Organisation for European Economics Co-operation, 1958).

[23] Ibid., p. 76.

termining the fair return.[24] The first is the *capital-attraction* criterion.
Most commissions are concerned with allowing returns which permit the
utilities to attract capital for needed expansions and which contribute to
the financial soundness of those utilities. Another criterion is that of
efficiency of management. Some commissions make it a policy to approve
higher returns to utilities which demonstrate outstanding performance
in controlling costs and improving services. Such a policy should stimulate
greater managerial efficiency. A third criterion is that of *stable rates*.
Commissions prefer not to revise rates with each change in demand and
costs, on the grounds that constant changes would be inconvenient to
both customers and management. The last criterion is that of *fairness to
rate payers and investors*. This criterion is perhaps the most nebulous and
most difficult to apply in practice. Commissions are not in agreement,
for example, on the extent to which public utilities should take part in
the general increase in profits earned in competitive industries in periods
of inflation. Some of them are quite restrictive in this respect, on the
grounds that the owners of the utilities have, like the purchasers of bonds,
taken the risk that their earnings might not keep up with prices. Questions
of fairness will continue to lead to controversy and litigation in public
utility regulation.

Over the history of American public utility regulation, determination
of the rate base has been even a greater source of litigation than has
determination of the fair rate of return. The problem becomes especially
acute in periods of inflation, in which book values (original costs) are
below reproduction or replacement costs. The Federal Power Commission
and most of the state commissions stress an original cost or prudent investment rate base and give little regard to increasing replacement costs
until the utilities actually purchase a new plant at the higher costs. Their
preference for original cost is based on its administrative convenience.
Original costs are readily determined from the accounts and make possible the rapid disposition of rate cases with reduced expenses and more
precise results. The supporters of original cost claim that it reduces the
costs of regulation and litigation. Another argument for original cost is
that it reduces uncertainty and thus is more conducive to credit maintenance.

An important minority of American regulatory commissions lean toward what is known as the "fair value" rate base. The definition of "fair
value" is rather difficult, in view of the long history of controversy over
it since 1898 when the Supreme Court in *Smyth* v. *Ames* made it the
law of the land.[25] (The Hope Natural Gas Case[26] of 1944 ended the

---

[24] This discussion is based on J. C. Bonbright, *Principles of Public Utility Rates*
(New York: Columbia University Press, 1961).

[25] *Smyth* v. *Ames,* 169 U.S. 468 (1898).

[26] *Federal Power Commission* v. *Hope Natural Gas Company,* 320 U.S. 591 (1944).

supremacy of the "fair value" rule and left it to the individual jurisdictions to determine their own principles of rate base valuation.) In general, the "fair value" rate base is a compromise, incorporating both original cost and reproduction cost and still other considerations. In actual practice, however, some of the commissions which are bound by "fair value" statutes devote primary attention to original cost, with minor deviations to take other factors into account.

According to Bonbright, when it comes to actual practice, *all* of the commissions use versions of original cost, with minor deviations.[27] He claims that the important differences in regulation lie more in different degrees of liberality in rates of return than in determinations of the rate base. This conclusion suggests that regulation should concentrate on the determination of rates of return most appropriate for the growth and financial strength of the utilities and most conducive to the public interest, with a diminished attention to controversies over the valuation of the property. Nevertheless, some authorities would dissent and would argue for a valuation of property more in line with reproduction cost. It may at some time be possible to find an objective technique for determining reproduction cost which will reduce the costs of litigation and delay in administering rate changes.

MULTIPLE-PRODUCT PRICING

Multiple-product price and output determination must cope with product interdependency in production. Interdependency can take the form of joint products, in which one product cannot be produced without the other. Or it can take the form of alternative products, in which output of one product must be decreased to obtain increases in output of another, in the short run.

Joint products: fixed proportions

Figure 9–9 illustrates pricing and output determination for joint products produced in fixed proportions. Only one marginal cost curve is shown, since the costs of the products are indivisible. Two demand curves are shown, one for each of the two products. MR_1 indicates the marginal revenue derived from sales of the first product. MR_2 shows the marginal revenue for the second product. MR_{1+2} is the *vertical* sum of MR_1 and MR_2. The difference between Figures 9–9 and 9–1 (which illustrated price discrimination) is that the marginal revenues are summed vertically rather than horizontally. The reason for this is that *an increase of one unit on the horizontal scale means an increase in units of a package consisting of quantities of each product.* (This package is one unit of product

---

[27] Bonbright, *Principles of Public Utility Rates*, p. 283.

FIGURE 9–9

MAXIMIZATION OF PROFITS—TWO JOINT PRODUCTS

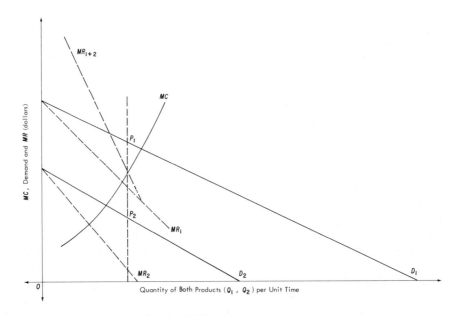

plus some amount of the other product; thus, the quantity axis of Figure 9–9 is denominated in units of the first product. The demand and marginal revenue curves for the other product must be appropriately transformed.) Added revenues result from both products and it is the sum of the revenues that should be compared with marginal costs. The optimum is at the point of intersection between marginal cost and the *aggregate* marginal revenue curve. P_1 and P_2 represent the most profitable prices for the two commodities.[28]

Figure 9–10 represents a slight alteration in the situation. Here MR_2 becomes negative before MR_{1+2} reaches the marginal cost curve. The firm will not maximize profits if it keeps on reducing the price on product 2 to get rid of it; the negative marginal revenue means a loss in total revenue. Product 2 will be sold up to the point at which its marginal revenue is zero, with P_2 the appropriate price. But it is profitable to produce more packages, until MR_1 equals the marginal cost. The excess units of product 2 will be destroyed, since their appearance on the market will depress prices.

Other variations in the situation may be worked out by the reader. These could include a case in which one of the products is sold in a purely

---

[28] For a fuller analysis, see M. R. Colberg, "Monopoly Prices under Joint Costs: Fixed Proportions," *Journal of Political Economy,* February 1941, p. 109. Also see M. R. Colberg, W. C. Bradford, and R. M. Alt, *Business Economics: Principles and Cases,* rev. ed. (Homewood, Ill.: Richard D. Irwin, Inc., 1957), pp. 299–302.

FIGURE 9–10

MAXIMIZATION OF PROFITS—JOINT PRODUCTS WITH DESTRUCTION
OF PART OF ONE PRODUCT

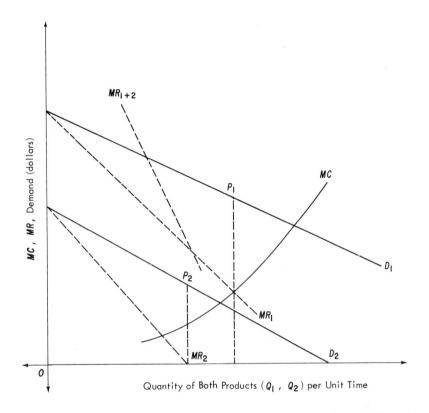

Quantity of Both Products (Q_1 , Q_2) per Unit Time

competitive market or one in which both are sold in such a market. Another interesting variation is the case in which there is a cost of destruction.

Alternative products

Figure 9–11 illustrates output and price determination for alternative products.[29] All of these products require services of some facility that will be fully utilized. Therefore, output of any one product can be increased only by cutting back output of other products.

The quantity axis in Figure 9–11 measures total use of the facility; i.e., hours per week. The demand curves for the several products have been restated in terms of equivalent demand for hours of facility use per week.

---

[29] This discussion of multiple-product pricing is adapted from Eli W. Clemens, "Price Discrimination and the Multiple-Product Firm," *Review of Economic Studies* 19 (1950–51), pp. 1–11.

FIGURE 9–11

Maximization of Profit—Alternative Products

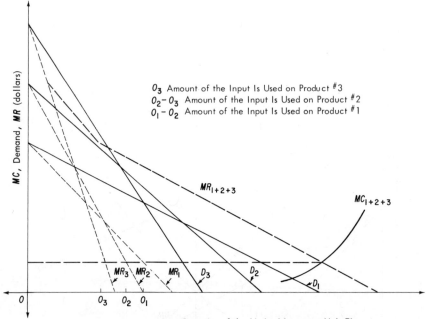

O_3 Amount of the Input Is Used on Product #3
$O_2 - O_3$ Amount of the Input Is Used on Product #2
$O_1 - O_2$ Amount of the Input Is Used on Product #1

Quantity of the Limited Input per Unit Time

The marginal cost curve in Figure 9–11 assumes that variable cost depends only on hours of plant operation and does not change as the plant is switched from product to product. The firm maximizes profit if it selects a product mix such that the marginal revenues (per unit of facility use) are equal across the various products and also equal to marginal cost (per unit of facility use) at total output. Prices of facility use for various products can be converted into equivalent market prices for the products.

The above analysis can be extended to cases in which variable costs differ from product to product (demands must be net of product-specific variable costs), in which marginal cost is constant up to some limit of plant use (in this latter case, marginal "rents"—the differences between marginal revenues and marginal costs—are equated), and to a special case in which there is excess (economically redundant) plant capacity.

Empirical examples

Decisions on multiple products are relatively unsophisticated in most firms. The construction of models which reflect the important interrelations is a difficult and costly task. Therefore, most managers rely mainly on experience and trial and error. We would expect that such a rough and ready approach will often provide approximations to the theoretical optima.

The classic example of joint costs is that of meat production. The meat packer sells products to both the food chains and the leather tanners. His prices are governed by demand and not individual product costs. The objective is to set prices at levels that will clear the market for both meat and hides. Output will be at levels that will equate the marginal revenue from both meat and hides to the marginal cost of producing both.

The grocery, in turn, must determine what price to charge for the different cuts of meat it obtains from the carcass. As Holdren states, "the elasticity of demand rather than carcass cost dominates the determination of the relative prices of different cuts of meat.[30] In the supermarkets which he studied, the average price of round steak was 85 cents per pound, rib roast was 55 cents per pound, chuck roast, 42 cents, and hamburger, 30 cents (July 1954 prices). In all of the stores hamburger and chuck roast were sold below the average cost of the carcass. He found that as beef prices rose the range of prices on different cuts narrowed, the customer substituting cheaper cuts for more expensive ones. Such substitutionary relations in demand complicate the determination of the most profitable prices.

Holdren found that the individual store managers tended to keep their prices on chuck, hamburger, and round steak competitive with prices in other stores. They followed "the get rid of" principle in pricing the other cuts. They bought enough carcasses to fill the demand for round steak and chuck roast and altered the prices of other cuts (except hamburger) until the market was cleared. In other words, the stores did not use anything approaching a mathematical model reflecting the demand and cost conditions. They instead followed a series of decision-making rules: imitate the price of other stores on some cuts; purchase quantities according to the demand for those cuts at the imitative prices; and price the other cuts to get rid of the quantity which results from the previous rules. These rules are rather uninformative on how the prices which are imitated are themselves established, a question which cannot be answered by studying one or a few stores at a time.

TRANSFER PRICING

Large, multiple-product, multiple-process companies develop complex patterns of intracompany transfers of goods. For example, an integrated international petroleum company acquires vast amounts of crude oil from hundreds of sources, allocates the heterogeneous raw material to dozens

---

[30] Bob R. Holdren, *The Structure of a Retail Market and the Market Behavior of Retail Units* (Englewood Cliffs, N.J.: Prentice-Hall, Inc., 1960), pp. 121–22.

of refineries that produce industrial goods and consumer products in varying proportions, and routes output through complex marketing channels that include thousands of retail outlets. In any week, a great many decisions must be made within such a firm. These include level of output, product mix, input combinations, pricing, scheduling, routing, and inventory accumulation and depletion, and they must be made at many plants and for many products.

A huge firm such as the one described above must be organized into numerous divisions that are allowed considerable autonomy in day-to-day decision making. The divisions transfer goods among themselves. The prices at which these goods are transferred affect divisional decision making, and wrong decisions (relative to overall company objectives) can be expected if transfer prices understate or overstate values and costs.

For purposes of decision making, intracompany transfers should be priced at marginal cost. Of course, marginal cost is the market price (opportunity cost) if there is an external market for the good. Otherwise, it is explicit marginal cost as determined within the supplying division.

The simplest case: a specialized intermediate product with excess capacity in the supplying department

Let us consider a hypothetical company with two departments—a supplying department and a using department. The letter S will represent the supplying department and U the using department. P_s will represent the price charged by the supplying department—this is the transfer price. P_u will represent the final price charged by the using department to outside purchasers. In the present example we assume *excess capacity* in S, the supplying department. That is, S can meet all the needs of U for the intermediate product.

This simplest case of transfer pricing requires an additional assumption. The intermediate product is specialized and is used only within the company. All of it is transferred to the using department. None of it is sold on the outside. Another way of stating this assumption is that *no market for the intermediate product exists*.

Under these assumptions, the solution for the transfer price is clear. It is the marginal cost (unit incremental cost) in the supplying department.

$$P_s = MC_s$$

in which

$$MC_s = \text{marginal cost in the supplying department.}$$

This transfer price will motivate the using department to order as many units as it can use and still make a contribution to overhead and profit on each unit, including the last (marginal) unit.

Let us consider a hypothetical example. The supplying department, S, produces at a constant marginal cost of $10.

$$MC_s = \$10$$

The using department, U, can produce five different products each of which makes use of the same intermediate product. The five products sell at five different prices and incur different marginal costs within the using department.

$$P_{u1} = \$25.00 \qquad MC_{u1} = \$\ 7.00$$
$$P_{u2} = \$24.00 \qquad MC_{u2} = \$\ 7.50$$
$$P_{u3} = \$23.00 \qquad MC_{u3} = \$\ 7.50$$
$$P_{u4} = \$22.00 \qquad MC_{u4} = \$10.00$$
$$P_{u5} = \$21.00 \qquad MC_{u5} = \$13.00$$

It is clear that the company is adding to its profits as long as the final prices exceed the sum of the marginal costs in the using and supplying departments. This is true of the first four products.

$$P_{u1} > MC_{u1} + MC_s \qquad \$25.00 > \$\ 7.00 + \$10.00$$
$$P_{u2} > MC_{u2} + MC_s \qquad \$24.00 > \$\ 7.50 + \$10.00$$
$$P_{u3} > MC_{u3} + MC_s \qquad \$23.00 > \$\ 7.50 + \$10.00$$
$$P_{u4} > MC_{u4} + MC_s \qquad \$22.00 > \$10.00 + \$10.00$$

But the final price of the fifth product ($P_{u5} = \$21$) is less than the sum of the marginal costs

$$P_{u5} < MC_{u5} + MC_s \qquad \$21.00 < \$13.00 + \$10.00$$

The first four products should be accepted and the fifth rejected, assuming of course that there is sufficient capacity.

Another way of stating this is that the contributions of the first four products are positive and that the contribution of the fifth product is negative.

$$C_1 = \$25.00 - (\$\ 7.00 + \$10.00) = \$8.00$$
$$C_2 = \$24.00 - (\$\ 7.50 + \$10.00) = \$6.50$$
$$C_3 = \$23.00 - (\$\ 7.50 + \$10.00) = \$5.50$$
$$C_4 = \$22.00 - (\$10.00 + \$10.00) = \$2.00$$
$$C_5 = \$21.00 - (\$13.00 + \$10.00) = -\$2.00$$

It should be clear that a transfer price which includes an allocation of the supplying department's overheads or fixed costs will lead to the wrong results. If these allocated overheads were $6, the transfer price on the intermediate product would become $16 instead of $10 and the "contributions" of the third and fourth products would be negative rather than positive. The result would be a rejection of the third and fourth products and a loss of contributions on both.

Figure 9–12 is useful in summarizing the discussion up to this point. This graph is unusual in one respect. The quantity (horizontal) axis is measured in units of the *intermediate* product, not of the final products. This is because the final products are different and their quantities cannot be measured along a single axis. The intermediate product is homogeneous. We shall assume that the quantities of the sales of the five products could be as high as follows:

Product 1: 2,000 units
Product 2: 1,000 units
Product 3: 1,500 units
Product 4: 1,000 units
Product 5: 1,500 units

FIGURE 9–12

OPTIMUM QUANTITY, FIVE PRODUCTS
USING THE SAME INTERMEDIATE PRODUCT

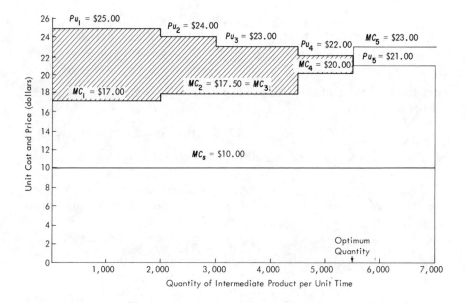

The vertical axis is the usual cost and price axis. The prices of the five products are shown. The total marginal cost in both S and U is shown.

If the overheads (fixed costs) were included in the marginal costs of the supplying department, the graph would appear as in Figure 9–13.

This graph shows that the apparent optimum would include only Products 1 and 2 and would eliminate the contributions which could be earned from Products 3 and 4.

FIGURE 9–13

FALSE OPTIMUM, SAME FIVE PRODUCTS
USING COMMON INTERMEDIATE PRODUCT

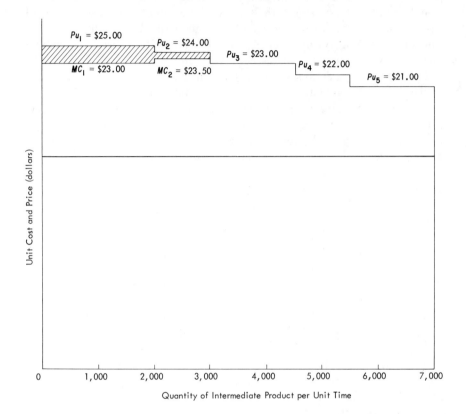

How could a company make such an error as to select the false optimum in Figure 9–13 in preference to the more profitable set of products shown in Figure 9–12? This error, which in practice must be fairly common, is a result of mixing two functions of accounting: the measurement of income and the guidance of decisions. In measuring income it seems reasonable at first glance that the transfer price should be at a level to permit the supplying department to cover its overheads. Therefore, full-cost transfer pricing, including overhead allocation, seems appropriate. At the end of each accounting period a rate of return which reflects the capacity of the department's management to control both variable and fixed costs would seem to measure performance. To allow the supplying department a transfer price which covers only its marginal costs would appear to give all the profit and all the credit to the using department.

This reasoning, attractive as it may at first be, is wrong. The profitability which is important is the company-wide profitability. To allow mere paper allocations of costs to take priority over this company-wide profitability cannot be permitted. The creation of departmental or divisional profit centers, each with its own responsibility for the control of costs, would appear to be consistent with modern ideas on decentralization of responsibility and control. But the purpose of bringing departments together under a single company framework is to achieve the advantages of integration. Decentralization must be interpreted in a way which does not defeat the very purposes of integration.

One way of making the using department contribute to the fixed expenses of the supplying department, even when the transfer price is at the marginal cost, is to require a lump sum payment for the right of access to the supplying department. The lump sum could be determined in advance; the essential point is that it must not depend on the actual volume of purchases from the supplying department.

The case of a marketable intermediate product

The first case we have discussed is that of a specialized intermediate product for which there is no external market. Now let us turn to a case in which *the intermediate product is bought and sold in a competitive market*. Now the opportunity cost concept becomes of paramount importance. In this case, the supplying department, S, should produce all of the units it can as long as it earns contributions to its overhead and profits; this includes units to be sold externally.

If, as we assumed before, the marginal cost to the supplying department is $10 ($MC_s = \$10$), production should be increased up to full capacity as long as the market will take units of the product at prices above that level.

Suppose that the market price is $16. Let us temporarily assume that transportation and outside selling costs are zero. Then the supplying department should expand production to capacity, with the result that a contribution of $6 is earned on every unit.

In this case, the rule for the transfer price is changed. It becomes $16 rather than $10. *The opportunity cost of not being able to sell to the market replaces the internal marginal cost.*

Figure 9–13 now becomes the governing graph. Only Products 1 and 2 should be produced. Products 3, 4, and 5 require costs which exceed prices. The marginal costs of these products now reflect the opportunity cost of sales on the outside. The supplying department allocates its supply of intermediate product to those uses which can pay the market price, whether these uses are internal departments or external buyers.

If external sales require certain transportation and selling costs and also risks of incurring bad debts, these should be taken into account. If the net sales price after deduction of incremental transportation and selling costs is only $13, this becomes the governing opportunity cost. In this case it will be profitable to produce Products 1, 2, and 3. The transfer price is now $13 and the first three products all make a contribution after taking this transfer price into account.

Imperfect market for final product—perfect market for intermediate product

Unfortunately, the most significant cases of transfers occur in imperfect markets. Market imperfections complicate the analysis to the point that implementation of theoretical solutions becomes almost unmanageable. It will not be possible to deal with all of the possible variations here; those who wish to study the subject in greater detail must be referred elsewhere.[31]

Let us start with a one-product firm which sells its final product in an imperfect market but can buy or sell its intermediate product in a competitive market. Figure 9–14 portrays this situation. In this case the demand curve facing the using department slopes downward to the right,

FIGURE 9–14

IMPERFECT MARKET FINAL PRODUCT
PERFECT MARKET INTERMEDIATE PRODUCT

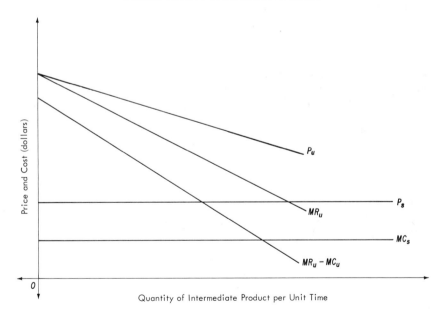

[31] The fundamental articles are Jack Hirshleifer's, "On the Economics of Transfer Pricing," *Journal of Business,* July 1956, pp. 172–84, and "Economics of the Divisionalized Firm," *Journal of Business,* April 1957, pp. 96–108. An excellent exposition of the problem, both theoretical and practical, appears in David Solomons' *Divisional Performance: Measurement and Control* (New York: Financial Executives Research Foundation, 1965).

as indicated by P_u. The marginal revenue curve, MR_u, lies below the demand curve and slopes more steeply for reasons developed in Chapter 3. In this graph it is convenient to subtract the marginal cost within the using department, MC_u, from the marginal revenue to obtain the net marginal revenue, $MR_u - MC_u$.

If there were no market for the intermediate product, the optimum would be where $MR_u - MC_u$ intersects MC_s. On all units up to that point a contribution to company-wide overhead and profits is made. The transfer price should in this subcase be MC_s. If a perfect market for the intermediate product exists at a price of P_s, the optimum is at the intersection of $MR_u - MC_u$ and P_s. Although there may be excess capacity in the using department, extra units can be sold in the open market more profitably than they can be sold to the using division. The transfer price should be at the level P_s.

The reader should work out solutions for the case in which the capacity of the supplying department is less than the using department's requirement or the case in which the marginal cost in the supplying department is increasing as output increases.

Competing demands for the intermediate product

The next step is to consider an intermediate product used by several competing using departments, each facing an imperfect market. Figure 9–15 illustrates this case.

On the consolidated diagram, we sum horizontally the quantities on the $MR_{u1} - MC_{u1}$ and $MR_{u2} - MC_{u2}$ curves. The total quantity of intermediate product is determined where this aggregate curve ($MR_{u1} - MC_{u1}$) + ($MR_{u2} - MC_{u2}$) cuts P_s. The resultant quantity of intermedi-

FIGURE 9–15

COMPETING DEMANDS—IMPERFECT MARKETS FOR FINAL PRODUCT

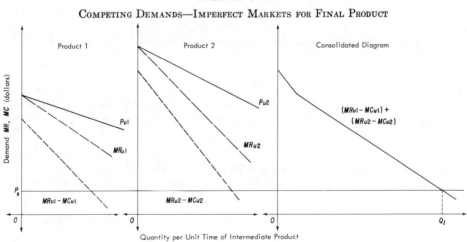

Quantity per Unit Time of Intermediate Product

ate product is then allocated to the two products. This is an application of the equimarginal principle introduced in Chapter 2.

Again the reader can work out solutions when the capacity of the supplying department is limited or when its marginal cost is rising. The marginal cost of the supplying department has been left out of Figure 9–15 for purposes of simplicity. But if MC_s is rising, the analysis is changed slightly and the company may find it profitable to buy part of its supply on the outside.

Imperfect market for the intermediate product

In the preceding section we were saved from having to determine the price of the intermediate product by the fact that a perfect market did that job for us. When the market for intermediate products is imperfect, the problem is complicated by the need to solve a large number of problems simultaneously—the quantity and price of the intermediate product as well as the quantity and price of the final products. The solution requires an application of the concepts introduced in Chapter 2—marginal costs, opportunity costs, and the equimarginal principle.

It is tempting to leave this problem for more advanced treatises. But the fact appears to be that this case is the most relevant one; to abandon the subject at this point would give a misleading impression of the ease with which transfer prices can in fact be established.

For the present discussion it is desirable to introduce an additional assumption: that the marginal cost of the intermediate product MC_s is rising. A solution to the problem when the marginal cost is constant up to capacity can be introduced later.

FIGURE 9–16

IMPERFECT MARKETS FOR BOTH FINAL AND
INTERMEDIATE PRODUCT—RISING MARGINAL COSTS

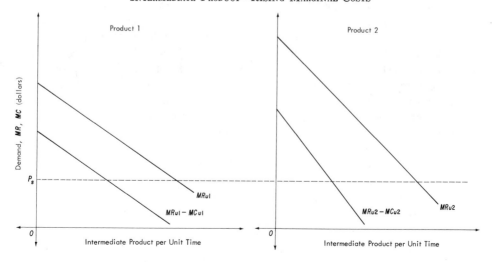

FIGURE 9-16 *(Continued)*

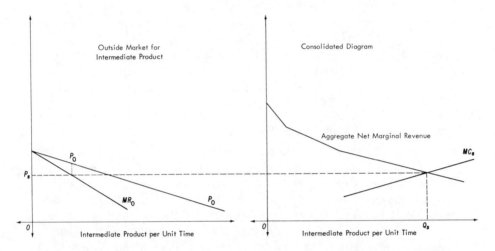

Figure 9–16 summarizes the solution to the imperfect market, rising marginal cost case. The net marginal revenues are summed horizontally, but this time the marginal revenue in the outside market is included. The supplying department produces a quantity of the intermediate product where the aggregate net marginal revenue equals the marginal cost. It should be noted that P_s is the transfer price to be charged to the using department; it is *not* the price which should be charged outside purchasers. The price to outsiders will be found on the demand curve directly above the intersection of the transfer price (marginal cost) with MR_o.

Pricing transfers for inventory valuation

Divisional inventories of raw materials, goods-in-process, and finished goods accumulate and deplete, sometimes by plan and sometimes through errors of judgment. To determine net income and net worth according to conventional accounting standards, inventories should be valued at full cost including allocated overhead. Valuation of inventories at explicit marginal cost would lead to understatement of income and net worth if there were an inventory buildup and to overstatement of these two values if there were inventory depletion. On the other hand, valuation of inventories at opportunity costs (market values greater than full cost) would lead to reporting of net income not yet realized.

Thus intracompany transfers should be priced at *full cost including allocated overhead* for purposes of income and net worth determination. Two sets of transfer prices appear to be necessary. *Marginal costs* are the appropriate prices to use as *guides in decentralized decision making*, whereas *full costs* are the proper prices for use in *determining conventional income and net worth* for the whole firm.

Decentralized control without "profit centers"

Many large firms have attempted to use a management concept in which the various divisions are viewed as "profit centers" and managerial performance is measured in terms of return on investment. If there are substantial interdivisional transfers of goods for which external market prices do not exist, there is no satisfactory basis for establishing transfer prices to support the profit center concept.

Henderson and Dearden have proposed a system for decentralized control without calculating profit or attempting ROI measurement.[32] The system is based on three budgets for each division: a contribution budget, a fixed and managed-cost budget, and a capital budget. The contribution budget is of principal interest here. This budget is negotiated annually between the division manager and his superior, in the well-known method of management by objectives, and is based on expected revenues less variable costs. If all revenues are from expected sales to other divisions of the same firm using transfer prices based on constant marginal cost, budgeted contribution is zero. (Budget contribution could be above zero if marginal cost were increasing with output.)

Henderson and Dearden show that "variances" from zero contribution budgets are more satisfactory for control and performance measurement than variances from profit budgets when the "profit" is based on arbitrary transfer prices. Thus, profit centers and ROI measurement are not necessary—indeed, they are not even desirable—for control of decentralized decision-making.

Empirical studies and illustrations

An excellent study of transfer pricing appears in a study by David Solomons.[33] Solomons not only reviews the theoretical literature but supplies a number of illustrations of sound and unsound practices in the area of transfer pricing. He provides several illustrations of companies which attempt to treat each department as if it were a separate business. The transfer prices from manufacturing to sales departments were computed on the basis of full cost without regard to whether the manufacturing department was operating at capacity. One company in this group raised the transfer price if the firm was not provided with "optimum production runs," apparently without regard to external prices. Solomons comments that this "is not how independent businesses operate. As an independent concern the factory would probably charge lower, not higher prices if it were short of work."

Solomons also cites the case of an oil company which faced the allo-

[32] Bruce D. Henderson and John Dearden, "New System for Divisional Control," *Harvard Business Review,* September 1966.

[33] David Solomons, *Divisional Performance: Measurement and Control* (New York: Financial Executives Research Foundation, 1965), p. 163.

cation of the impact of gasoline price wars. A firm transfer price was established between the refining and the marketing departments, roughly at market price less a small deduction per gallon negotiated between the two departments. This meant that the marketing department suffered the impact of price wars. At an earlier date a fixed unit margin was guaranteed the marketing department, which left the production department with the problem of fluctuating prices.

Another oil company found the problem of transfer pricing so difficult that it treated three departments, refining, marketing, and marine transportation, as a single profit center. In this way it helped make certain that arbitrary transfer prices did not stand in the way of sound decisions.

Another company set transfer prices at the "best price given any outside customer, less (a) division selling expense and (b) freight, allowances, cash discount, etc., allowed such customer." This rule applied when the product was sold "regularly and in reasonable volume to outside customers." This rule was reasonable, but a similar rule was applied even when the product was not sold on the outside—in this case a deduction from the competitive price was not made for selling expenses. As a result, using divisions might buy on the outside even when internal supplying division costs were lower. An "escape clause," however, permitted the negotiation of lower prices.

Studies of the problem show that determination of the "market price" is far from simple. For differentiated products no markets in the usual sense may exist. Discounts and terms of payment make comparisons difficult. Apparently the market price solution to the transfer pricing problem can be applied in only a minority of cases. Nevertheless, the marginal cost solution is still relatively unused. This suggests that considerable progress is yet to be made in the area of transfer pricing. Many companies achieve something in the direction of marginal cost solutions by encouraging their divisions to negotiate prices between them.

PROBLEMS FOR CHAPTER 9

1. Overseas Industries serves both a domestic and a European market from New York City. The demand in the two markets differs:

$$P = 500 - 8Q \quad \text{for domestic}$$
$$P = 400 - 5Q \quad \text{for Europe}$$

All sales of Overseas' product are on an f.o.b. New York basis. The total cost function for the company is:

$$TC = \$10,000 + 20Q$$

a. If the markets can be kept segmented, what quantities and prices are applicable to each market?

b. If the markets were not separable, what should the overall quantity be? At what price?

c. Compare the total profit under a to that under b. Is price discrimination profitable?

2. Alchemy, Inc. produces two products from a single raw material. Product X is considered to be the byproduct of the manufacture of Y. The demand equations of the two products are:

$$Q_y = 500 - 5P_y$$
$$Q_x = 2,500 - 10P_x$$

Three units of X are produced for every unit of Y. Total cost is

$$TC = 200 + Q_y$$

a. What quantity of Y should be produced? At what price should it be offered for sale?

b. What percent of X production will be sold if it is priced appropriately?

c. How would the answer in b change if the production ratio of X to Y were 6 to 1?

d. If the production ratio were flexible, what would be the optimal ratio?

3. The Ajax Company produces and distributes trash cans. In round figures, Ajax produces the cans for about $2.00 variable cost and wholesales them for $6.00. Fixed costs are about $850,000 dollars a year. Currently, operations are running about 80 percent of budgeted capacity. Ajax has been offered a contract which would absorb most of the excess capacity, but the negotiations are at a standstill over the price. The contracting firm has offered a bid of $5 per unit.

a. Should Ajax seriously consider the bid?

b. How would the decision be tempered by economic prospects? Antitrust legislation?

4. Eatmore Foods, Inc. maintains its own farms for the production of cereal grains used in the company's breakfast products. Recently Eatmore was divisionalized by the board of directors in an effort to eliminate coordination problems within the corporation. The problem has arisen, however, as to what prices the Farming Division will charge the Breakfast Foods Division for cereal grains. Wheat, for example, could be sold to the outside market in virtually any quantity for $2.10 a bushel. Assume wheat may also be purchased for $2.10 per bushel. The cost function of the wheat farming operation is:

$$TC = 90,000 + .0005Q^2{}_W$$

The Breakfast Foods Division can process wheat into a product which will cost $3.30 per bushel, exclusive of the cost of the wheat. Assume one bushel of wheat goes into each bushel of finished product. The demand equation for this product is:

$$P = 6.50 - .0000115Q_P$$

a. What price should the Farming Division charge the Breakfast Foods Division for wheat?

b. How much wheat should Eatmore produce? To whom should it be sold?

c. How much breakfast product should be produced? At what price should it be offered for sale?

5. The Acme Company is divisionalized into the Foundry and the Machine Shop Divisions. The Machine Shop Division produces and sells a patented part for which it needs a custom casting. The demand equation for the final product is:

$$P = 15.40 - .0035Q_P$$

Finishing operations on the casting cost $3.10 per unit.
The Foundry Division has estimated its cost for producing the casting as:

$$TC = 420 + .0015Q^2{}_C$$

a. What quantity of the final product should be produced? At what price?

b. What should the Foundry Division charge for the castings?

6. A monopolist sells a homogeneous product in two distinct markets. His estimated demand relations are $P_1 = 300 - 2.5Q_1$ and $P_2 = 500 - 15Q_2$ and his cost relation is $TC = 2,500 + 45Q + .5Q^2$. If the monopolist is a profit maximizer. determine the price and quantity in each market and his total profit.

7. Assume that in Problem 6 above the monopolist is forced by law to sell the product at the raw price in each market. What is the price and quantity sold in each market and what is the firm's profit?

8. A firm produces the product q and sells it in a perfectly competitive market for $10 per unit. His total cost function is $C = q^3 - 9q^2 + 25q + 10$. What should his production be? What is his ATC, MC, MR and Profit at this point?

9. The manager of a firm producing rope for a perfectly competitive market is presently having the firm produce 50 units of rope for sale at $50 a unit. He determines the following schedule.

Units of Rope	TC
48	2,395
49	2,450
50	2,500
51	2,545
52	2,585
53	2,630
54	2,680
55	2,735
56	2,795

Determine his best production level and draw a graph to show cost and revenue situation.

10. A firm has a monopoly in the production of q. The firm has determined that the demand function for the product is $q = 600 - 2p$ and its long-run total cost function is $TC = 2q^2 + 15q - 20Kq + 100K^2$ where K is the plant size. What is the optimum long-run plant size and what lot quantity of q should it produce? What is its profit? (Hint: minimize TC with respect to K).

11. Given the short-run curves below, what do $OADq$, $OBCq$, and $ABCD$ represent? What does the area under the MC curve from (O,q) represent?

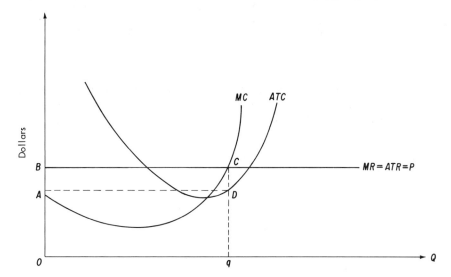

12. Given the short-run curves, what do $OACq$, $OPBq$, $APBC$, and the area under the MR curve from 0 to q represent?

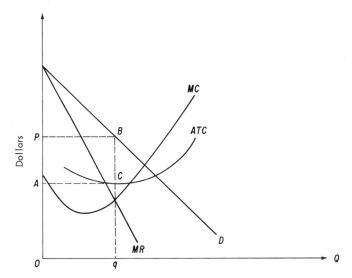

13. A firm sells its product in two separate markets. Given the following price and cost structures, what are the prices and quantities he will choose for each market? What is the total quantity produced?

#1		#2			
Q	P	Q	P	Q	TC
1	10	1	15	1	6
2	9.5	2	14	2	7
3	8	3	13	3	9
4	7	4	12	4	18
5	6	5	11	5	28
				6	40

14. A monopolist has two separate plants, both capable of producing widgets for sale in a single market. The cost and revenue schedules are as follows. How much does each plant produce and what is the price at which he sells his tota output?

P	Q	TC_1	TC_2
24	1	50	35
23	2	55	43
22	3	59	49
21	4	62	53
20	5	64	55
19	6	65	60
18	7	67	69
17	8	77	79
16	9	92	90
15	10	110	102
14	11	130	115
13	12	151	129
12	13	173	144
11	14	196	160

Cases for part four

Pricing has always been a central interest in managerial economics. Many managers who are engaged in pricing decisions are somewhat baffled by the problem. They find it difficult to organize their thoughts in some kind of pattern. A few managers may refer to the standard works on price theory but find little guidance there in bridging the gap between theory and practice.

The cases in this section provide an opportunity to develop skills in relating economic theory to pricing decisions. It will soon become apparent, however, that traditional economic theory by itself is not sufficient to deal with the complexities of the pricing situation. The cases involve environmental considerations such as antitrust and antidiscrimination legislation. They involve problems of internal organization. In all of them, the pervasiveness of uncertainty about demand, competition, and cost stands in the way of a simple application of theoretical concepts.

CASE CONCRETE PRODUCTS

Case Concrete Products is located in a medium-size city. Prior to June 1956 the firm's principal product was concrete burial vaults. The product line also included lintels, patio stones, and bird baths. The firm enjoyed a local monopoly in the manufacture of these products. There was competition from metal burial vaults; however, the price differential was large enough to reduce the importance of competition.

The basis for the price of burial vaults and other items was full cost plus a markup. The full-cost estimates were determined as follows:

```
Labor  .............................................. $X
Materials  ........................................... X
Overhead (10% of labor and materials)  ................. X
       Total cost  ...................................... $X
Markup (100% of total cost)  ........................... X
Selling price  ......................................... $X
```

The owner, Mr. Case, spent a great deal of time revising the cost estimates as costs changed. For example, he gave a general hourly wage
increase and revised the costs estimates of all products and increased
the selling prices.

In order to arrive at the cost estimates, Mr. Case ran crude time studies on the workmen, recording the time that each spent on a particular
product. The overhead rate of 10 percent had been suggested at a trade
association meeting which Mr. Case attended several years before. He
had never verified that overhead was actually 10 percent of direct labor.
The firm did not have a job order cost accounting system which would
accumulate the cost of each product; rather the cost estimates were
checked only periodically against actual costs.

In June 1956 the firm was considering a new product, concrete septic
tanks. The manufacture of this product was well suited to the present
production scheme. Also there was only one supplier of septic tanks in
the city at the time, and Mr. Case believed that the building boom was
creating a market large enough to support two producers. The molds and
a delivery truck would require an investment of $3,700, which would be
financed from internal funds. In order to arrive at some estimate of costs,
the firm manufactured a pilot model. The cost estimate was:

```
Materials  ...................... $26.85
Labor  .........................   9.00
Overhead  ......................   3.60
                                 $39.45
```

Applying the same pricing policy used on the other products would result in a price of $78.90; however, the established producer's price was
only $65. Mr. Case decided that his initial price should be the same as
his competitor's. The competitor did not retaliate by lowering his price;
later, however, he did initiate discounts for certain customers. Mr. Case
did not grant discounts, partly because the volume of sales was "satisfactory" and partly because he feared that if he were too aggressive the
competitor might begin producing concrete burial vaults.

1. *Does the full cost plus a markup formula make economic sense?*
2. *Why was the formula not used in pricing septic tanks. Was this wise?*
3. *Why did not the firm grant discounts on septic tanks? Was this refusal wise?*

THOMAS DENTON, CONTRACTOR

Thomas Denton is a small builder. He normally builds six to eight homes in the $20,000 to $30,000 price bracket each year, and gives his personal attention to the details of construction. He subcontracts much of the specialized work, such as plumbing and wiring, but he employs his own carpenters.

Mr. Denton classifies his business into two types from the point of view of pricing: (1) a house to be constructed in the future on which he is asked to submit a bid; (2) a house built "on speculation" to be sold when completed or partially completed. Approximately 70 percent of his business is in the second category. Mr. Denton normally charges more for the first type because of the probability that the customer will require many time-consuming changes before the house is complete.

Mr. Denton does not follow the practice of some other builders in pricing on a square footage basis. He believes that such pricing does not reflect the variations in materials, fixtures, and his own time required from house to house. Instead he makes a detailed estimate of the labor and materials required in a house, using the form shown as Exhibit 1. Mr. Denton does not charge a percentage markup on cost. Instead he adds a sum for his own time, which is indicated at the bottom of Exhibit 1.

Mr. Denton's charge for his own time varies from job to job. One consideration is the amount of time required in the construction of the particular house. He will vary this charge somewhat with business conditions. For example, in 1958, when business in this locality was slow, he reduced this charge to speed up the sale of houses already completed. The need to finance the construction of new houses out of the profits from those already built sometimes puts him under pressure to shade prices. In 1958, he had held two houses for over a year before reducing price. Mr. Denton is slow in starting new houses until he has sold old ones, largely because he does not like to be heavily in debt and does not like to be under extreme pressure to reduce prices because of a large inventory of unsold houses.

Mr. Denton also reduces his bids on houses to be constructed in the winter. He believes that his time is not so valuable in this period of low activity. He also wants to keep his force of carpenters together as much as possible on a full-year basis, since it is difficult to acquire first-grade carpenters. Furthermore he can hire workers at lower rates in the winter. One last consideration in pricing is Mr. Denton's estimation of the customer's personality. If he appears to be a person who is demanding of continual changes in the plan and details of the house, Mr. Denton will raise his bid.

EXHIBIT 1   THOMAS DENTON

JOB_____   DATE_____
LOCATION_____

Lot	Towel bars, etc.
Plans	Stone labor
Taxes	Plumbing
Insurance binder	Extras
Comprehensive insurance	Sump pump
Stamps	Wiring
Water	Extras
Gas	Light fixtures
Electricity	Painting
Excavation	Extras
Footings	Caulking
Labor	Sanding floors
Form work	Concrete front porch
Foundation	Steps
Waterproofing	Walk
Drain tile	Concrete back porch
Back fill	Steps
Concrete basement floor	Walk
Steel post	Plastering
Steel basement sash	Lath
Aeroways	Lath labor
Steel girders	Corner rite
Steel bolts	Furnace
Framing lumber	Duct work
¾" Storm siding	Flashing and gutter work
Rock wool	Linoleum in kitchen
Inside doors	Linoleum in bath
Outside doors	Tile in bath
Windows	Medicine cabinets
Glazing	Kitchen cabinets
Screens	Ironing board
Storm and screen doors	Attic fan
Plywood	Exhaust fan
Kitchen and bath subfloor	Dishwasher
Flooring	Disposal
Building paper	Weatherstripping
Finish lumber	Grading and bulldozer
Carpenter labor	Extra dirt
Extras	Sod
Social security	Shrubs
Nails	Drive
Hardware	Venetian blinds
Roofing	Wallpaper
Garage material	Labor
Garage doors	Cleaning house
Brick chimney	Coach light
Mantle	Fence
Fire brick and tile installation	Freight
Brixment	Hauling expense
Sand	Shutters
Cut stone sills	Flower box
Brick	Advertising
Brick labor	Real estate commission
Angle irons	Miscellaneous
Stone	Contractor's fee
SUB TOTAL $_____	GRAND TOTAL $_____

Mr. Denton has never heard of incremental costs, opportunity costs, or demand elasticities. He faces the competition of 10 or 12 builders very much like himself. He is not fearful of retaliation to reductions in his prices from such competitors, for it is difficult to compare houses and most price reductions are secret. One way of reducing price is to offer to do additional work, such as paneling a basement, without charge. Mr. Denton does admit, however, that his prices are influenced by the prices he thinks other builders are asking. Mr. Denton frequently sells his houses through real estate agents, paying the normal commission on new houses. He sometimes reduces his price for a direct sale to a customer which avoids the real estate commission. The real estate agents claim that this practice is unethical, but they continue to do business with Mr. Denton.

1. *Does Mr. Denton use full-cost pricing? Discuss.*
2. *Does Mr. Denton use going-rate pricing? Discuss.*
3. *Does Mr. Denton use incremental reasoning? Discuss.*

SPRAGUE COLLEGE STORE

Sprague College, a small private school, owns a store which competes with several groceries, clothing stores, drugstores, and stores specializing in school supplies. The store has a monopoly on the sale of textbooks in the town of 10,000 in which it is located.

The store management establishes a target return on sales for each of the four departments: books, groceries, clothing, and school supplies. An annual budget estimates the volume of business and the expenses necessary to handle that volume. On the basis of this budget, the management determines what departmental margins are necessary to cover overhead and allow the target return. Each department is given a margin to maintain which should result in the desired margin for the store as a whole. The departments report their achieved margins each week and this serves as an internal control. If a department's volume were to decrease, the average margin required on each item would increase, even though the department might be able to reduce some costs (by reducing the sales force, for example).

In 1960, at the time of the case interviews, the markup on textbooks was 13.6 percent of selling price for both new and used books. The cost of new books is 80 percent of list price, but the store sells below list. The store buys only used books that are to be reused; its markup on such used books is much lower than is usual in college bookstores. The margin in 1960 did not cover the estimated overhead (15.5 percent of revenue). The manager gave this reason for his policy on textbooks: "If I am going to give students a break on anything, why not do it on something they must have?"

Margins on the other merchandise vary considerably. Coffee, for example, is a highly competitive item on which only a 3 to 5 percent margin is possible; higher prices would result in a transfer of business elsewhere. Higher margins on less competitive goods help compensate for the low margins on coffee and books. The store makes a careful survey of the grocery prices of competitors and tries to keep its prices in line with competition.

The target net profit on sales is approximately 2.5 percent. This results in a return on investment which is higher than the average return on the other college investments. Inventory control, with an emphasis on maintaining the minimum inventory and the highest possible turnover, is essential in attaining the target return. The management maintains detailed inventory records on each item in stock; these records help the control of inventory and serve as a guide in buying.

1. *Does the store use full-cost pricing? Discuss.*
2. *Does the store use going-rate pricing? Discuss.*
3. *Does the store use target-return pricing? Discuss.*
4. *Does the store use incremental reasoning in pricing? Discuss.*
5. *Why does the store "give the students a break" in textbooks?*

INTERNATIONAL HARVESTER COMPANY[1]

International Harvester has a diversified product line, consisting of agricultural equipment, construction machinery, motor trucks, and miscellaneous equipment. The company wishes to achieve several objectives in pricing these products: (1) a target return on investment of around 10 percent after taxes; (2) maintenance of a reputation for high quality and durable products; (3) growth, without becoming so dominant that price competition is undermined. The company succeeded in earning the target return in the years immediately after World War II, but more recently has experienced lower profits after taxes.

The company's position of leadership in the market varies from one product to another. In 1947 it led an effort to resist inflation by lowering prices on farm equipment; in other years its increases in farm equipment prices have been followed by competitors. On light trucks International Harvester has followed the product and price policies of the major automobile companies, and has been able to achieve only a low return on investment. On heavy trucks the company is in a stronger position. In 1955 the company abandoned the production of refrigerators and freezers because of an inability to obtain the volume that would provide a profit. The company's traditional emphasis on quality and durability appeared to be inconsistent with the need to cut costs so that the company could compete in the refrigerator and freezer market.

[1] Based on A. D. H. Kaplan, J. B. Dirlam, and R. I. Lanzillotti, *Pricing in Big Business* (Washington, D.C.: The Brookings Institution, 1958), pp. 69–79, 135–42.

The company's market share of agricultural equipment had steadily declined from 44 percent in 1922 to 23 percent in 1948. Its share varied from about 20 percent on combines, and 30 percent on tractors, to 65 percent on cotton pickers. The company wished to maintain a reputation for quality on farm equipment. It also wished to set prices that would permit farmers to earn the initial investment in a satisfactory pay-back period, which varied from three to ten years, depending upon the product. The company also wished to keep prices on the various models in a reasonable proportion to each other, modified to some extent by the desire to meet competitive conditions in the different markets.

International Harvester's costing practices were similar to those of the large automobile companies. The main stress in pricing was on "normal costs," which are full costs, including current material and labor, plus overhead computed on the basis of "normal" operations. The overhead was prorated on the basis of direct labor costs; sales, service, collection, and administrative costs were allocated in proportion to total sales value. In addition to the normal costs the company estimated the "season's costs," which were the "actual" unit costs accumulated during the season. If the season's costs indicated that the normal costs were unrealistic, the company might revise its prices. The company also measured "specific costs," especially for service parts. Specific costs included only the actual cost of material, direct labor costs, and the direct overhead resulting from the particular item.

The practice in pricing a new product is of interest. The management started with a price based on competitors' prices and the estimated value to the farmer. It then worked back to estimating a "target cost" which, at the given price, would provide the target return on investment. The equipment designers then tried to develop models consistent with such target costs. Exhibit 1 shows the actual experience with three products introduced in 1956.

While the company's profit objective of 10 percent on investment would suggest a target return on sales of about 7 percent (sales are usually about 40 percent higher than invested capital), the company modified the target on particular products according to the competitive situation, the originality of the product, and the value to the farmer. The company recognized the need to maintain a full line, which means carrying some products that do not permit the usual markup. The company also set higher prices when it had an advantage (perhaps because of a superior product) over competition.

As Exhibit 1 suggests, the company modified its introductory prices as it accumulated experience in the actual market. Competition might force it to lower price; costs might exceed the preliminary estimates. When the profit was as low as on product C in Exhibit 1, the company might redesign the product to reduce costs, might increase price, or might abandon the line.

EXHIBIT 1

PRICE-COST ANALYSIS, REPRESENTATIVE FARM IMPLEMENTS INTRODUCED IN 1956

	Product A			Product B			Product C		
	Target	Intro-ductory	Actual	Target	Intro-ductory	Actual	Target	Intro-ductory	Actual
List price	$592.60	$592.60	$592.60	$455.85	$455.85	$455.85	$687.40	$691.35	$691.35
Trade discount—23 percent	136.30	136.30	136.30	104.85	104.85	104.85	158.10	159.00	159.00
Dealer price	$456.30	$456.30	$456.30	$351.00	$351.00	$351.00	$529.30	$532.35	$532.35
Cash discount—2 percent	9.13	9.13	9.13	7.02	7.02	7.02	10.60	10.65	10.65
Net from dealer	$447.17	$447.17	$447.17	$343.98	$343.98	$343.98	$518.70	$521.70	$521.70
Sales and administrative expense* ..	67.08	67.08	67.08	51.60	51.60	51.60	77.81	78.26	78.26
Net	$380.09	$380.09	$380.09	$292.38	$292.38	$292.38	$440.89	$443.44	$443.44
Manufacturing cost†	270.00	274.97	359.43	214.00	217.42	232.62	380.00	395.33	462.38
Profit margin (dollars)	$110.09	$105.12	$ 20.66	$ 78.38	$ 74.96	$ 59.76	$ 60.89	$ 48.11	($ 18.94)
Profit margin as percent of:									
Manufacturing cost	40.8%	38.2%	5.7%	36.6%	34.5%	25.7%	16.0%	12.1%	−4.5%
Total unit (6) + (8)	32.6	32.5	4.8	29.1	27.9	21.0	13.3	10.2	−3.1
Net from dealer	24.6	23.5	4.6	22.3	21.8	17.4	11.7	9.2	−3.6

* Allocated as normal percentages (15 percent) of net from dealer.

† Target and introductory prices based on normal manufacturing cost, including plant overhead.

SOURCE: A. D. H. Kaplan, J. B. Dirlam, and R. F. Lanzillotti, *Pricing in Big Business* (Washington, D.C.: The Brookings Institution, 1958), p. 72.

Several specific examples will give insight into the company's pricing practices:

1. In May 1957 it raised the retail price on a product from $218 to $228 because of dissatisfaction with the profit. The new price was still in line with competition. The profit position would still be unsatisfactory, but the management doubted the feasibility of even higher prices.

2. In March 1957 the company reduced the price of another product from $525 ($397.17 to the dealer) to $490. The cost to manufacture was $264.35. Management was dissatisfied with the volume on this item and wished to reduce prices to the range charged by two smaller competitors.

3. The company's cotton pickers sold at a price which yielded the target return or better. The product had a high value to potential users. The company was the first to introduce this product; the more recent entrance of competitors had not undermined the company's ability to obtain the target return.

4. The company priced "captive parts" (manufactured only by Harvester) at a price yielding a target return on normal unit costs.

5. The company priced other parts which competed with parts produced by General Motors, Ford, and Mack Truck at prices designed to meet competition. These prices did not show any consistent relationship to unit costs or target returns. The company might continue to produce and sell such parts even though the price covered only the specific costs; such a policy helped the company maintain a full line and spread its overhead burden.

The company gave the same discount from list prices to all dealers. It also gave volume discounts, which varied from 2.25 to 4 percent. The list price was a "suggested price," and some dealers sold at much less.

1. *What is the meaning of "normal costs" in this case? Should these costs be the basis of pricing?*
2. *What is the meaning of "specific costs" in this case? Should they be the basis of pricing?*
3. *What is "target cost" in this case? How does it relate to pricing?*
4. *Does International Harvester price to earn a "target return"? Or is the target return a measure of what the market permits it to earn?*
5. *Does International Harvester use full-cost pricing, going-rate pricing, target-return pricing, incremental reasoning in pricing, or what? Use Exhibit 1 to prove your point.*

SEARS, ROEBUCK AND COMPANY[1]

The merchandising organization of Sears, Roebuck has the primary responsibility for pricing. The company's 420 buyers initiate prices under the supervision of the merchandise supervisors (in charge of the 50

[1] Based on Kaplan, Dirlam, and Lanzillotti, ibid., pp. 188–98, 237–39.

buying departments) and the vice president in charge of merchandising. The pricing for mail-order selling is more centralized than that for the retail stores. The buyers and merchandise supervisors generally add a predetermined percentage or dollar markup based on the custom of the trade, modified by attention to competitors' prices. The vice president normally approves the price recommendations of the merchandise supervisors, though he does give more attention than they to the prospective return on investment that might result from larger volumes at lower prices or smaller volumes at higher margins.

At the same time, the buyers recommend retail prices for the 35 retail zones in which Sears operates. These prices are suggested retail prices; each store manager may revise prices to fit local conditions and competition. Over 90 percent of the time the store managers follow the recommendations of the parent organization. The central office determines the prices for the regular seasonal and special mail-order sales. The retail store managers determine the time of their sales. On the whole there is considerable centralization of the pricing decisions.

The objectives of the company's price policy are several: (1) to provide the maximum level of sales consistent with a target return on investment of 10 to 15 percent after taxes; (2) to maintain and increase the company's share of the national market; (3) to contribute to the company's reputation for low prices.

Pricing and buying are closely interwoven in the Sears organization. The objective of buying is to obtain merchandise at low costs that will permit low retail prices. The company owns about 22 factories, manufacturing commodities such as stoves and plumbing fixtures which at some previous time it could not obtain on satisfactory terms from outside manufacturers. The company also owns part interest in other suppliers. No doubt the company's ability to manufacture itself exerts a downward pressure on costs. Sears' contracts with outside firms normally cover direct costs to the manufacturer and a margin to cover overhead plus a profit comparable to that of Sears. Even so these contracts include a "competitive clause" that permits a transfer to lower-cost suppliers. Sears works closely with the suppliers to help them hold down distribution costs and to aid them in technical and design problems. One objective is to obtain a large volume which will reduce unit costs.

The result of these practices is selling prices ranging from about 15 to 30 percent below the list prices of competitors. These competitors' prices, however, are suggested retail prices and are less rigidly maintained than Sears' suggested prices. In fact, in recent years the differential between Sears' prices and those of competitors has narrowed on many items. Sears tries to meet this competition by emphasis on brand name (the brand name is connected in the consumer's mind with low prices), by attracting customers with low-price "stripped" models and "trading up" to more expensive models providing a higher margin, and by selling last year's models at lower prices.

Sears generally follows customary "price-points" on soft goods such as men's shirts and women's garments. Thus shirts sell at $2.95 or $3.95, rather than at some intermediate price such as $3.30, which many customers might interpret as a high price for a $2.95-quality shirt rather than a low price for a $3.95 shirt. The result is an inflexibility in price which may require a variation in quality to meet rising costs.

Sears generally maintains a differential on mail-order prices below retail prices to allow for differences in selling costs, mailing costs, and delays in delivery. Decisions on both retail and mail-order prices are based on knowledge of traditional markups and price-points, on estimates of the price differentials needed to obtain volume, expected price changes of competitors, comprehensive reviews of competitive prices, shopping surveys, quality testing, and changes in the company's share of the market for different products. On some lines of merchandise, such as tires, paint, refrigerators, and other large appliances, the company wishes to avoid starting price wars; it avoids price-slashing promotions on these lines.

1. *Does the store use full-cost pricing? Discuss.*
2. *Does the store use going-rate pricing? Discuss.*
3. *Does the store use incremental reasoning in pricing? Discuss.*
4. *Would you describe the market structure for Sears as competitive, monopolistic, or oligopolistic? Discuss.*
5. *What are the arguments for and against decentralization of pricing by Sears?*

FULGRAVE PRINTING COMPANY*

Mr. Prescott, President of the Fulgrave Printing Company, believed that few printers had an accurate method of determining the cost of an individual job. He felt that the result was price cutting and deterioration of industry profits, which in 1959 averaged 2.5 percent of sales. The Fulgrave Printing Company had installed a modern cost system which combined forecasted and actual costs and developed data to serve as a basis for pricing. Mr. Prescott believed that other firms should adopt a similar system.

Background

The Fulgrave Printing Company, one of over 100 firms in a metropolitan area of over 800,000 population, employed over 300 and was located in a modern air-conditioned plant. Competition was intense, though printers tended to specialize in particular kinds of work. On some

---

* This case was prepared by W. W. Haynes and J. L. Gibson of the University of Kentucky as the basis for class discussion. All names and locations have been disguised.

kinds of printing the Fulgrave company competed with printers in other cities. The company was a "commercial printer," producing a wide variety of jobs, but avoiding short runs and small volumes that were of interest to smaller firms. Exhibit 1 illustrates the production process of job order print shops and is applicable to the Fulgrave Printing Company.

EXHIBIT 1

Production Flow Diagram for Job Order Printing

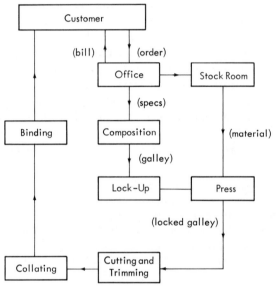

Suggested by William Green, *Wellesley Press, Inc., Case Study,* Harvard Business School, 1958.

The company's cost system: hourly machine rates

The budgeted cost system required the estimation of hourly machine costs for the coming period. The company accountants estimated total labor and overhead costs for the next year; they also estimated the volume of sales and the number of machine-hours required for those sales. These cost and hour estimates became the basis for the hourly machine rate on each machine, group of machines, or other cost centers in the plant. The hourly machine rates included overhead costs which were distributed to the various machines. Exhibit 2 shows how hourly costs were estimated for one press.

The budgeted cost system required 45 different hourly machine rates. These rates were sometimes revised during the year to bring them in line with actual experience. In theory the rates might be revised slightly every 60 or 90 days. In the 12 months preceding June 1960, however, only ten rates had been revised. In June 1960, itself, Mr. Green, the company vice president, revised 14 additional rates. Mr. Green had the primary responsibility for rate revisions.

In the establishment of the hourly machine rates, seasonal fluctuations in sales were ignored. The objective was to set rates for the year as a whole. Mr. Green stated that it did not make sense for the company to set higher rates in the low season simply because the fixed costs had to be distributed over a smaller volume; nor was it reasonable to compute lower hourly machine rates in the peak seasons.

EXHIBIT 2

DETERMINATION OF HOURLY COST FOR VERTICAL PRESS

Investment: $10,000
Floor area: 300 square feet
52 weeks × 40 hours = 1 full-time man = 2,080 hours to be paid for
52 weeks × 40 hours = 2,080 maximum possible working hours
Less: 10 days vacation = 80 hours (10 days × 8 hours)
Less: 6 days holidays = 48 hours (6 days × 8 hours)
100 percent production = 2,080 hours − 128 hours = 1,952 hours

1. Direct costs
    Labor: 2 men at $1.75 × 2,080 hours .... $ 7,280.00
    F.O.A.B. Unemployment (percent of labor) 254.80
    Workmen's compensation 21.84
    Power (1,600 K.W.H. at $.04) 64.00
    Depreciation (10% of investment) 1,000.00
    Repairs (1% of investment) 100.00
    Total direct costs .... $ 8,720.64

2. Indirect costs
    Rent (300 sq. ft. × $3) .... $ 900.00
    Insurance (½% of investment) 50.00
    Taxes (1% of investment) 100.00
    Administrative costs (80% of direct costs) 6,976.51
    Total indirect costs .... $ 8,026.51

3. Total cost for one year (next 12 months) $16,747.15

4. Hourly rates
    100% production (1,952 hours) .... $ 8.58
    80% production (1,562 hours) 10.72
    60% production (1,171 hours) 14.30
    40% production (781 hours) 21.44
    20% production (390 hours) 42.94

Costing individual jobs

The hourly machine rates were the chief but not the only factor in pricing individual jobs. In estimating the cost of a job, specialized estimators accumulated the costs on a job for each machine or other cost center through which it would pass. For this purpose time standards were required. In 1960 the company was engaged in estimating time standards on the basis of its own experience. Prior to this time it had relied on time standards or norms published by national agencies. Even when internal time standards were established, the company maintained records showing comparisons with the outside norms to see how its own experience measured up.

Thus the estimated cost in each cost center consisted of the time standard multiplied by the predetermined hourly cost. The full cost of the total job was the sum of such costs on every process used in the production of the order, plus the cost of materials. The charge for materials depended on the quantity used in the individual order. The company usually did not pass on to the customer any savings resulting from consolidating orders in the purchase of materials; quantity discounts were not passed on to the customer unless his order was large enough in itself to result in such a discount. An estimated price for a job is illustrated in Exhibit 3.

EXHIBIT 3*
Price Estimate for an Individual Job

Materials (including the markup on materials)

1,000 sheets 17 × 22, 20 lb. white Howard Bond 50 lbs. @ $.30	$ 15.00
½ lb. Bronze blue ink @ $1.90	.95

Production

Composition—2 hours × $7.86 hourly cost	15.72
Lock-up—½ hour × $8.15 hourly cost	4.08
Press, vertical—5 hours × $10.72 hourly cost	53.60
Cutting—1 hour × $5.60 hourly cost	5.60
Total cost	$ 94.95
Markup on total cost (20%)	19.00
Selling price	$113.95

* This exhibit does not represent any actual job priced by the firm on which this case is based.

Pricing individual jobs

In principle the company followed the practice of pricing on the basis of full cost plus a predetermined markup. A special markup was applied to outside materials before their inclusion in the total cost of the work to which the profit markup was added. However, a certain amount of judgment entered into pricing; it was not merely a mechanical procedure. The authority over pricing was delegated to the sales department, though Mr. Green sometimes had an influence over pricing decisions.

The company officials believed firmly in pricing on the basis of full costs. They believed the failure of some companies to adhere to this practice accounted for the severe competition in the industry. In fact, they believed other pricing procedures were unethical and referred to price-cutters as "chiselers."

The predetermined markups varied from one category of business to another. The Fulgrave company divided its business into five categories, each with a different markup percentage as indicated by Exhibit 4.

Company officials did not apply the markups mechanically. They used judgment in modifying the estimates. Sometimes the estimators themselves had an influence over the final price; they might estimate a low machine cost on a particular job because a fast worker would be assigned to it. Mr. Green, the vice president, did not approve of this practice, which was based on the estimators' misunderstanding of company policy. He argued that the time standards on any job should be

EXHIBIT 4

MARKUP SCHEDULE*

Type of Job	*Markup on Cost*
Class #I: The first run of any job requiring speculative creative work. Any job requiring outside purchases of over 60 percent of the final price.	20 percent markup on outside materials plus 20 percent markup on the total cost including outside materials.
Class #II: Reruns of jobs originally in Class #I. First runs of jobs not requiring speculative creativity.	15 percent markup on outside materials plus 20 percent markup on total cost.
Class #III: Reruns of jobs originally in Class #II.	15–15 percent
Class #IV: Jobs which are a part of a total program and which will result in additional business.	10–15 percent
Class #V: Magazines and other special publications.	10–10 percent

* Although the job classes are those of Fulgrave Printing Company, the markups are hypothetical.

based on average performance, not on the speed of the particular employee who might work on a job. He believed that the sales force sometimes put pressure on the estimators to come up with low estimates. In some cases judgment on the part of the estimators was justified. For example, they might know that a particular customer's job would flow expeditiously through the plant and that a reduction in actual cost would result.

Higher markups on brokering

Class No. 1, with the highest markups, included what is known in the printing business as "brokering." This consisted of jobs which were produced largely on the outside, with only a minority of the work done by the Fulgrave company. Not all printing companies charged a higher markup on such jobs; in fact some companies reduced their markups to get such jobs. Mr. Green was certain that the Fulgrave policy was sound, even though the higher markup was applied to the entire job and not merely to the "value added." He gave the following reasons for this position:

1. Since brokering jobs require a relatively small amount of machine time, they absorb only a small amount of overhead. (As noted earlier, the overhead is allocated through the hourly machine rates.) A high markup was needed to assure that the sales commissions were covered.

2. Brokering jobs usually require more work on design and more special contact with the customer.

3. Brokering jobs are frequently speculative; an extra charge would help compensate for the extra risk.

Price competition versus nonprice competition

Mr. Green stated that a high proportion of printing costs were fixed for short-run changes in volume. For example, labor costs did not vary greatly in proportion to volume because of the difficulty of retaining printers if they were laid off during the lulls in business. Mr. Green estimated that only 45 or 50 percent of the costs were variable. He recognized that the low level of variable costs created a temptation to cut prices; in fact, this was one reason for the cutthroat competition in the industry. Nevertheless, the Fulgrave company resisted pricing below full cost. Mr. Green stated several reasons for this policy:

1. Prices below full cost depress the market and result in low industry profits. Such prices are unethical.

2. Regular customers might be offended by special prices on irregular business. They preferred to deal with a company with consistent and stable price policies.

3. While it might seem desirable to get "fill-in" business to make use of idle capacity, there was no assurance that the capacity would in fact be idle when the jobs were ready to be run. Delays in starting jobs were frequent and unpredictable. Low-price jobs might interfere with the flow of regular work.

Mr. Green also stated that if the volume of business were down for a considerable period, it would be possible to pare some of the so-called fixed costs. For example, the labor force would be contracted. It was true that other costs such as depreciation would run on anyway, but these were a small percentage of the total. The president of the company, Mr. Prescott, admitted that the company might have to adjust to competition if idle capacity became a serious problem. In the period of the 1940s and 1950s, however, there had been no prolonged periods of substantial idle capacity.

The company preferred to rely on nonprice competition to win customers. The company stressed good customer relations. For example, if a customer's order turned out to be for a larger volume than was originally intended, the company would pass on half of the savings in

unit costs. Mr. Green believed that such a practice helped retain customers. Sometimes the company provided special services to the customer
without charge. For example, Mr. Green spent part of his evenings doing
editorial work on a customer's manuscript.

1. *Does the company use full-cost pricing? Discuss.*
2. *What is the significance of the high proportion of fixed costs in the company's operations?*
3. *Should the hourly rates be higher, lower, or the same in low seasons? Use Exhibit 2 to prove your points.*
4. *Would the company be better off to transfer attention from hourly machine rate to incremental costs?*
5. *Evaluate the reasons for not pricing below full costs.*

FALL RIVER NURSERY

The Fall River Nursery was the second largest garden nursery and
landscaping firm in its locality, a city of 150,000. The firm was a family
concern founded about 1910, with a continual reputation for quality and
service. In 1961 four partners cooperated in managing the firm.

The firm grew most of its own materials on its 500-acre plot, but
purchased a few plants from wholesalers. The firm also sold a small
fraction of its materials at wholesale; the local climate and soil conditions gave it an advantage on some plant varieties. Most of the sales
were at retail at the company's garden center. The mail-order business
was relatively small. One of the partners was in charge of the landscaping service as well as service work and spraying, another in charge of
growing and propagation, and a third in charge of the garden center.

Pricing policies and practices

The firm did not appear to have a definite policy on pricing. The
officials were skeptical of systematic approaches to pricing. They did not
maintain a cost accounting system and doubted that it would be useful.
In fact one of the partners stated that most experiments in cost accounting in other nurseries had failed and had been abandoned. He claimed
that uncertainty about the weather, plant diseases, and soil conditions
made it impossible to predict the cost of growing a particular plant
variety. The long period it took to produce plants also made it difficult
to estimate costs.

The same official stated that the firm's plants are priced "according
to the market, just as wheat and corn are priced." The firm's prices were
a little higher than prices of nurseries to the south, where labor costs
were lower, but lower than prices in the large metropolitan areas. The
firm did not maintain systematic records of what other firms were
charging, though it did have a file of catalogues of other nurseries. This

file was not kept up to date, and it apparently was not used often. In fact the company officials did not appear to know except vaguely what the price differentials from firm to firm were. Thus, if the firm's prices were based on the market, it was on a subjective evaluation of market forces rather than on any kind of statistical analysis.

The officials believed that the firm's prices were slightly on the low side in the local market, if one excluded the prices at some of the large chain groceries. They pointed to some advertisements in the local newspaper showing higher prices at a competitive firm.

Changes in prices

Price changes on plants were infrequent. Prices were established in the summer for the coming year. These prices were published in a catalogue in September. The partners believed that price changes during the year were undesirable; they did not even revise their mimeographed wholesale price during the season. The main exception to this rule was pricing for the end-of-season sale in May, at which time two categories of plants were marked down:

1. Dormant materials that had been dug up the previous fall and winter. These materials including fruit trees, hedges, and shrubs would have to be destroyed if not sold in May.

2. Block clearance items, mostly evergreens. If a few evergreens are occupying a block of land, it is desirable to sell them off at reduced prices to clear the land. Some of these materials may be of lower quality, but usually this is not the case.

From one season to the next the partners revised prices. In 1959, for example, they took into account an increase in labor costs in changing their prices upward.

Round-number pricing and promotional pricing

The company officials have traditionally preferred round numbers in pricing, such as $6 or $7 per plant, though they often used prices such as $6.50 or $8.25. In 1959 they broke away from this policy when they adjusted prices for labor cost changes. For example, they increased one price from $6.75 to $6.95 in the belief that a $7 price would develop customer resistance. In 1960 the firm returned to prices such as $7.25 and $9.25. A plant's price was the same regardless of how the plant was sold —by telephone, by purchase at the garden store, or by mail order.

The partners believed that round-number pricing was consistent with the atmosphere of quality and dignity that the company tried to maintain. They did not want to be classified with the chain stores and mass mail-order firms which sometimes had a poorer reputation. In 1961, however, the firm experimented with prices of $1.11, $2.22, or $4.44 on distress items in oversupply. In 1961 the partners also experimented with a two-for-one sale which permitted a customer to purchase a second plant for $1 upon purchase of the first plant at the regular price. In addition, bulbs, fertilizers, and other items purchased on the outside were being sold at odd prices in 1961. Expert merchandisers and speakers at trade meetings had convinced the partners that some experimentation with promotional pricing might be desirable in building up volume. But the catalogue prices were kept on a round-number basis; the promotional odd prices were the exception rather than the rule.

In 1962, the partners were not yet certain that the experiments with promotional pricing had been successful. They were planning several new "traffic builders," however. For example, they planned to offer to give one popular rose bush free to the purchaser of five rose bushes. The trend appeared to be toward more specials of this sort, but these specials were still the exception.

The pricing of particular plants

The firm did not have control over all of its prices. Some plants were patented; the firm holding the patent set the price and collected a royalty from individual nurseries. The markups on such plants were usually higher than the Fall River Nursery's markups on plants of similar size and variety.

In spite of the general inflation in costs and prices in the 1950s, the prices on some plants were lower than in earlier years. For example, *Juniperus excelsa stricta* (15 to 18 inches) was selling at $2.50 instead of the $3 of a decade earlier. The reasons for the price decline were the reduction in demand for this variety and the fact that it was more readily available. The company officials were uncertain whether they were making money on this variety at such low prices, but they continued to grow it. One partner, however, stated that the company would not continue to grow a plant that did not return a profit in the long run.

Another plant that had fallen in price was *Taxus cuspidata browni*. This plant was in short supply in 1952–53, but supply had caught up with demand by 1960 and prices had reached a more normal level.

Some of the company's prices were 25 percent or even 50 percent below prices in the large metropolitan markets. The company grew some plants especially adapted to the local climate in large blocks, with resultant economies of scale.

The prices of some plants at first appeared to be out of line with the size of the plant. An example was globe *Taxus*. The officials explained that this plant requires special shearing to give it the desired shape. Thus the labor costs were higher, and it took more years for the plant to grow to a given size. The officials doubted that they were making as great a profit on these plants as on the same variety left unsheared.

EXHIBIT 1
PRICES OF SELECTED PLANTS, 1948–60

Plant and Size	1948–49	1950–51	1952–53	1954–55	1956–57	1958–59	1959–60
Juniperus excelsa stricta							
15 to 18 inches	3.00	N.L.*	N.L.	2.50	2.50	2.50	2.50
18 to 24 inches	N.L.	3.00	3.00	3.00	3.00	3.00	3.00
2 to 2½ feet	N.L.	4.00	4.00	4.00	4.00	4.00	4.00
2½ to 3 feet	N.L.	5.50	N.L.	N.L.	N.L.	N.L.	5.00
3 to 3½ feet	N.L.	7.00	N.L.	N.L.	N.L.	N.L.	N.L.
Juniperus chinensis glauca hetzi							
15 to 18 inches	N.L.	3.50	3.50	3.00	N.L.	N.L.	N.L.
18 to 24 inches	N.L.	4.00	4.50	4.00	N.L.	N.L.	N.L.
2 to 2½ feet	N.L.	N.L.	5.50	5.00	5.50	N.L.	N.L.
2½ to 3 feet	N.L.	N.L.	7.00	6.50	7.00	7.00	N.L.
Taxus cuspidata							
15 to 18 inches	4.00	4.00	4.50	N.L.	N.L.	5.25	5.50
18 to 24 inches	5.00	5.00	6.00	6.00	6.50	6.95	7.25
2 to 2½ feet	6.50	7.00	8.00	8.00	8.50	8.95	9.25
2½ to 3 feet	8.00	9.00	11.00	11.00	12.00	12.00	12.50
3 to 3½ feet	N.L.	12.00	14.00	14.00	15.00	15.00	16.00
3½ to 4 feet	N.L.	N.L.	N.L.	18.00	20.00	20.00	22.50
4 to 4½ feet	N.L.	N.L.	N.L.	N.L.	N.L.	25.00	30.00
Taxus baccata repandens							
15 to 18 inches	N.L.	N.L.	N.L.	5.50	6.00	6.25	N.L.
18 to 24 inches	N.L.	7.00	N.L.	7.50	N.L.	8.25	8.50
2 to 2½ feet	N.L.	N.L.	N.L.	N.L.	10.00	N.L.	9.75
Taxus cuspidata browni							
15 to 18 inches	N.L.	N.L.	6.00	5.50	5.50	5.25	5.50
18 to 24 inches	5.00	5.00	6.00	7.00	7.00	6.95	7.25
2 to 2½ feet	6.50	8.00	10.00	9.00	9.00	8.95	9.25
2½ to 3 feet	8.00	N.L.	N.L.	N.L.	N.L.	N.L.	N.L.
Tsuga hemlock							
2 to 2½ feet	3.50	N.L.*	N.L.	N.L.	N.L.	N.L.	N.L.
2 to 3 feet	N.L.	N.L.	N.L.	N.L.	N.L.	4.00	4.00
2½ to 3 feet	4.00	4.00	5.00	5.00	5.00	N.L.	N.L.
3 to 3½ feet	4.50	5.00	6.00	6.00	6.00	N.L.	N.L.
3 to 4 feet	N.L.	N.L.	N.L.	N.L.	N.L.	6.00	6.00
3½ to 4 feet	5.00	5.00	7.00	7.00	7.00	N.L.	N.L.
4 to 4½ feet	6.00	6.00	8.00	9.00	9.00	N.L.	N.L.
4 to 5 feet	N.L.	N.L.	N.L.	N.L.	N.L.	8.00	8.00
4½ to 5 feet	7.00	7.00	9.00	11.00	11.00	N.L.	N.L.
5 to 6 feet	8.00	8.00	10.00	N.L.	15.00	11.00	11.00
6 to 7 feet	10.00	10.00	12.50	N.L.	N.L.	15.00	15.00
7 to 8 feet	12.00	12.00	16.00	N.L.	N.L.	20.00	20.00
8 to 9 feet	N.L.	N.L.	20.00	N.L.	N.L.	N.L.	N.L.
11 to 12 feet	25.00	N.L.	N.L.	N.L.	N.L.	N.L.	N.L.
Taxus cuspidata capitata							
2 to 2½ feet	N.L.*	N.L.	N.L.	N.L.	N.L.	8.00	8.00
2½ to 3 feet	7.00	7.00	7.50	7.50	N.L.	9.50	9.50
3 to 3½ feet	8.00	8.00	9.00	9.00	10.00	11.00	11.00
3½ to 4 feet	10.00	10.00	11.50	10.75	12.00	13.00	13.00
4 to 4½ feet	12.50	12.50	13.50	12.75	14.00	15.00	15.00
4½ to 5 feet	15.00	15.00	17.00	15.00	17.50	17.50	18.00
5 to 5½ feet	17.50	17.50	20.00	18.00	21.00	21.00	22.00
5½ to 6 feet	20.00	20.00	23.50	21.00	24.00	24.00	25.00
6 to 7 feet	25.00	25.00	27.50	25.00	28.00	28.00	30.00
7 to 8 feet	N.L.	N.L.	N.L.	N.L.	35.00	35.00	40.00

* N.L.: not listed.

EXHIBIT 1—*(Continued)*

PRICES OF SELECTED PLANTS, 1948–60

Plant and Size	1948–49	1950–51	1952–53	1954–55	1956–57	1958–59	1959–60
Columnar *Taxus hicksi*							
2½ to 3 feet	N.L.	7.00	8.00	8.00	N.L.	N.L.	N.L.
3 to 3½ feet	N.L.	8.00	10.00	10.00	N.L.	N.L.	N.L.
3½ to 4 feet	N.L.	12.50	12.50	12.50	N.L.	N.L.	N.L.
4 to 4½ feet	N.L.	15.00	15.00	15.00	N.L.	N.L.	N.L.
4½ to 5 feet	N.L.	17.50	17.50	N.L.	N.L.	N.L.	N.L.
5 to 6 feet	N.L.	20.00	20.00	N.L.	N.L.	N.L.	N.L.
Globe *Taxus*							
15 to 18 inches	N.L.	N.L.	N.L.	N.L.	N.L.	N.L.	6.50
18 to 24 inches	N.L.	7.00	N.L.	N.L.	8.00	8.00	8.00
2 to 2½ feet	N.L.	9.00	N.L.	N.L.	10.00	10.00	N.L.
2½ feet	N.L.	N.L.	N.L.	N.L.	15.00	15.00	15.00
3 feet	N.L.	N.L.	N.L.	N.L.	20.00	20.00	20.00
3½ feet	N.L.	N.L.	N.L.	N.L.	N.L.	25.00	25.00
4 to 4½ feet	N.L.	N.L.	N.L.	N.L.	N.L.	30.00	30.00

Exhibit 1 shows the record of prices of some selected items over the period from 1948 to 1960.

/1. How does cost relate to the nursery's pricing?

2. How does demand relate to the nursery's pricing?

✓ 3. How does the contribution concept relate to the nursery's pricing?

4. How does the opportunity-cost concept relate to the nursery's pricing?

✓ 5. What changes in pricing do you recommend?

TELEPHONE CHARGES TO AUXILIARY ACTIVITIES*

In 1961 the Vice President of Business Administration at the University of Kentucky requested one of his assistants to make a study of telephone charges made to auxiliary activities attached to the University. These activities were not included in the regular University budget but were connected to the central campus PBX. It was desirable that these agencies be charged their share of the total bill paid by the University to the General Telephone Company of Kentucky.

The auxiliary agencies included the Campus Bookstore, the Athletics Department (which had a separate budget), the Experiment Station (largely financed out of federal funds), and the various dormitories. In 1960 the University billed each agency at the rate of $10 per month for each main extension (MEX) and $4 per month for each bridged extension (BEX). (A bridged extension is simply a second telephone attached to the same MEX with the same extension number.) In addition, each

---

* This case was prepared by Bernard Davis under the supervision of W. W. Haynes of the University of Kentucky as a basis for class discussion.

agency paid any special charges resulting from its operations, such as the cost of installing a telephone, and recurrent monthly charges for buzzer systems, wiring plans, horns, additional listings, and special illumination. The question was whether any revisions of these charges were warranted.

The assistant made a careful analysis of the telephone expenses paid by the University, which amounted to over $13,000 per month. He found that the costs common to the whole PBX system amounted to $3,609.65 per month, as shown in Exhibit 1.

EXHIBIT 1

COMMON COSTS

Central office trunks	$1,466.40
Toll terminals	112.80
Station lines	1,477.00
Attendants' cabinets (positions)	300.00
Other charges	253.45
Total common costs	$3,609.65

The wages paid the PBX operators directly by the University were another large expense which might be considered a common cost. These wages amounted to $3,647 per month.

In addition, the telephone company charged $1.85 per month for each main extension (MEX) and another $1.85 per month for each bridged extension (BEX). The system included 680 main extensions and 635 bridged extensions. Most of the special charges of $4,010 per month for buzzers, horns, and illumination were not at stake, since everyone agreed that each agency should pay those expenses for which it was directly responsible. The one exception was the substantial charge for "mileage," a charge proportional to the distance of the lines from the PBX to the main extensions. This charge (included in the $4,010) was $734 per month. It would be difficult to allocate this expense to individual extensions because of the difficult bookkeeping problem of recording the lengths of line and keeping up with changes as new extensions were added. Furthermore, it was not clear that an agency should be charged more because it was at a greater distance from the PBX. None of the above figures includes the costs to the University accounting office for recording and distributing these expenses.

The assistant making the study found that a special statistical study would be required to determine the impact of added bridged extensions. Most of the common costs would not be affected by adding more bridged extensions. In fact, the adding of 1 or 10 bridged extensions would result in only the extra charge of $1.85 per phone. But the addition of, let us say, 300 bridged extensions might require an added attendant's cabinet and, more important, additional PBX operators. There were no records to indicate how much bridged extensions added to the total load of telephone calls.

The addition of main extensions would have a clearer impact on costs, requiring added mileage, added attendants' cabinets, and added PBX operators. Again it would make a difference whether a few or a great number of main extensions were contemplated.

Of the total number of telephones in the system, 505 (or 38 percent) were being charged to auxiliary services. Of this total, 322 were main extensions and 183 bridged extensions.

1. *Estimate the marginal cost of a main extension and a bridged extension.*
2. *Estimate the added cost per extension for an increment of 300 extensions and an increment of 300 bridged extensions.*
3. *How do marginal and full costs relate to pricing in this case?*
4. *What revisions should the university make in its telephone charges?*

AIR-INDIA (D)*

Tariffs

Air-India, like the other members of the International Air Transport Association (IATA), does not have full control over its own tariffs. Instead, the company and the Government of India have acceded to the decisions of the Traffic Conferences of IATA in which the rule of unanimity applies. Nevertheless Air-India does have a policy and a point of view with regard to tariffs. The Company *favors lower fares* and its representatives at the Traffic Conferences press for a fairly sharp reduction in tariffs, as opposed to the gradual reductions in fares favored by some other airlines and governments.

Air-India's position was expressed in its 1962–63 Annual Report as follows:

Air-India's voice at Traffic Conferences, such as it is, has generally been in favour of lower fares with the object of achieving a mass market. Because of its lean and efficient operations, resulting in almost the lowest costs in the industry, Air-India is well placed to absorb the initial impact of lower fares and benefit from the resulting expansion of the market.

The International Air Transport Association

IATA was formed in 1945 by the International airlines of countries in most parts of the world. It was given a legal existence by a special Act of the Canadian Parliament in 1945. It was associated closely with another organization, the International Civil Aviation Organization

---

* Case material of the Indian Institute of Management, Ahmedabad, is prepared as a basis for class discussion. Cases are not designed to present illustrations of either correct or incorrect handling of administrative problems. Copyright © 1964 by the Indian Institute of Management, Ahmedabad.

(ICAO) which was established in 1945 as an agency for governments which wished to establish international standards for the regulation of civil aviation.

Membership in IATA is open to any airline providing scheduled air services licensed by a government eligible for membership in ICAO. The international airlines are active members, while the domestic airlines may join as associate members.

The voting procedures of IATA are unusual when compared with those of other international organizations. Each airline has a single vote regardless of its size. All decisions must be unanimous. No decisions are effective without the approval of the interested governments. Thus any single airline or any single government has the power to veto any decision.

IATA is concerned with much more than traffic matters. It has committees dealing continuously with technical, medical, legal, and financial issues. IATA, through these committees, promotes standards of safety, comfort and efficiency. Rules and procedures govern airlines in all parts of the world. An effort is made to simplify and standardize the documents which must flow from one airline to another. The Association publishes manuals of *Revenue Accounting Practices* which aim at the standardization of the reporting of costs, profits, and losses. The IATA Clearing House in London settles monthly accounts for interline revenue transactions, making it possible for each airline to pay and collect debts in a single settlement. This case is concerned, however, with the rate-making aspects of IATA which are perhaps the most complicated and controversial matters with which the organization must deal.

The IATA traffic conferences

The steps in establishing tariffs on international routes are different from those of domestic routes. Before the tariffs are filed with the respective governments for approval, the airlines meet together to agree on a pattern of rates. These rates apply to all the carriers concerned. Unless all agree, no decision is binding. And the governments have the final say on whether the agreements can be maintained. The normal practice is for the airlines to reach an agreement after considerable give-and-take in the Traffic Conferences and for the governments to approve those agreements. Occasionally the Conferences fail to reach an agreement or one or more governments fail to sanction the agreements, but such failures are the exception rather than the rule. Furthermore, soon after a conference has failed to achieve an agreement, the airlines and governments become quite uncomfortable with the possible anarchy in rates which might ensue; thus they soon reconvene to avoid this possibility. It is also the practice of each airline to refrain from vetoing an agreement affecting territories outside its main routes.

The world is divided into three areas for the purposes of the Conferences. Area No. 1 covers the Americas. Area No. 2 covers Europe, the Middle East and Africa; and Area No. 3 covers the rest of the world. Meetings deal separately with the relations between Area No. 1 and Area No. 2, No. 2 and No. 3, and No. 3 and No. 1. But the most important work takes place in the Composite Conference covering the whole world, usually held every two years. Individual airlines make recommendations of tariff changes at these Conferences. Traffic working groups and cost committees make careful studies of prospective traffic and costs of operation. The agreement reached by past conferences consists of over 1,000 resolutions covering rates between 60,000 pairs of points in the world network.

Among the criteria of rate-making considered by the Conferences are the following: (*a*) operating costs; (*b*) traffic potential; (*c*) local economic conditions; (*d*) type of traffic to be moved; (*e*) seasonal nature of the traffic; and (*f*) competition from non-IATA carriers such as the steamship companies.

Conference crises

From time to time crises over specific issues require the adjournment and reconvenement of the Conferences. In October 1959, for example, the delegates failed to agree on fares and facilities in several parts of the world. Six months later the issue was resolved. As one commentator observed the agreement was "accomplished by special excursion and direction fares and group discounts on those international routes where they were needed, by applying cabotage fares on certain others, and sealing of the repercussive effects on other routes. . . . by measures of noncombinability and the like."[1]

Another crisis took place in 1960 and 1961 over cargo rates on the North Atlantic. It took three Conferences to settle this issue, but the fear of the consequences of an "open" rate system brought about an agreement.

The 1962–63 crisis on North Atlantic fares

Although the North Atlantic run was relatively new among Air-India routes, the Company took a great interest in the 1962–63 controversies over rates from New York to Europe. The crisis arose from the failure of one Government to approve the agreements reached by the Traffic Conference of October 1962 at Chandler, Arizona, on North Atlantic rates. Most of the 19 airlines involved on the transatlantic run favored a 5 percent increase in the round trip rates in the form of a reduction in the transatlantic return discount. The American and Canadian airlines

---
[1] W. Gordon Wood, *The IATA Traffic Conferences: An Airline Man's View*, (Montreal: IATA, n.d.).

did not oppose this rate increase. The crisis was brought to a head finally by the refusal of the United States Civil Aeronautics Board to accept the new rates. In fact the United States Civil Aeronautics Board threatened action against Pan American Airways and Trans World Airlines if they complied with the IATA recommendations. The American government was forced to back down when several European countries threatened not to permit American aircraft to land. Thus the new high rates went into effect in April 1963.

In the period from April to October, 1963, various proposals for reduced fares were publicized. Pan American Airways proposed a "thrift-class" fare on the North Atlantic which would be over 40 percent below the existing rates. BOAC pressed for a 25 percent reduction in first-class fares and extensions of existing excursion rates.

One of the main factors contributing to the controversy over rates was the upsurge in capacity resulting from reequipment with jet aircraft. The development of new national airlines added to the capacity. Some leaders in the industry argued that a restriction of capacity was essential to profitable operation. The shipping industry had been able to control capacity through a conference system; the same principle might be applied to the airlines.

The IATA Traffic Conference which reconvened in Salzburg on October 22, 1963, was faced with the following specific proposals: (*a*) reduce the one-way, first-class, transatlantic fare from $475 to $400; (*b*) reduce the one-way economy fare from $263 to $210; (*c*) introduce a round trip excursion fare, valid for 21 days, at $300.

Two of the smaller lines, Aer Lingus of Ireland and El Al of Israel, opposed these proposals, which included an abolition of "group rates" for members of clubs.

Air-India's position on passenger fares

As has already been mentioned, Air-India was a strong advocate of lower passenger fares. Company officials did not believe gradual decreases in fares would do much to stimulate traffic. They thought that the reductions must be substantial to be felt by the traveling public.

One reason for Air-India's position was the large amount of excess capacity on all of the airlines, including Air-India. Exhibit 1 presents information on the capacity offered and the capacity utilized since Air-India was established in 1953. In recent years the capacity had outrun the usage so that the load factor had fallen below 50 percent. It was hoped that lower fares would stimulate traffic and raise the load factor.

One might ask why the company continued to increase capacity when the load factor was so low. One reason company officials gave was that Air-India must increase its frequency of service if it was to win over customers. For example, they would like to build up a daily service

EXHIBIT 1

AIR-INDIA (D)
(total capacity offered and utilized for schedules service only)

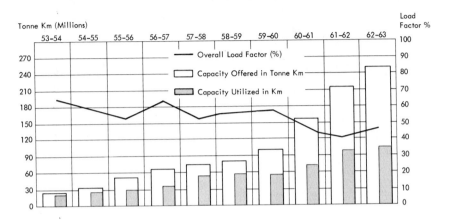

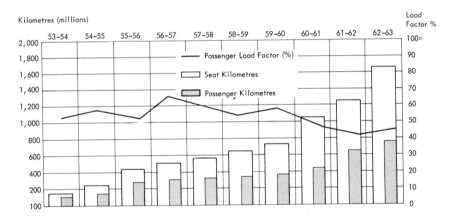

across the Atlantic to New York so that potential customers would not have to worry about whether Air-India was operating on a particular day. Extension of the Bombay–London service to New York which took place in May 1960 could be justified on several grounds: it would feed traffic into the other company lines; it would help establish the company's reputation as an international carrier; and to some extent it would use planes which otherwise would be idle in London waiting for the turn-around. Company officials also believed that an airline which failed to expand its capacity might stagnate. In any case the company had added rapidly to its capacity, as Exhibit 1 clearly demonstrates.

Another related argument for lower rates was that the added costs of

EXHIBIT 2

Air-India (D)
(operating expenses, 1962–63)

Particulars	In Indian Rupees	
1. A. Flying operations:		
a. Pay, allowances and provident fund contributions	7,639,978	
b. Staff and other general insurance	210,169	
c. Other staff costs	2,271,537	
d. Fuel and oil	31,384,512	
e. Aircraft insurance	8,894,439	
f. Aircraft landing, housing and parking fees	7,765,239	
g. Hire of aircraft	53,401	
h. Other operational expenses	1,612,537	
		59,831,812
B. Flying training:		
a. Pay, allowances and provident fund contributions	394,707	
b. Fuel, landing fees, cost of materials and insurance	1,028,405	
c. Training by third parties .	—	
		1,423,112
2. Flight equipment maintenance and overhaul:		
a. Pay, allowances and provident fund contributions	12,132,569	
b. Staff insurance	11,012	
c. Other staff costs	795,163	
d. Materials consumed including outside repairs and services	14,042,794	
e. Charges for technical handling by other operators	1,034,763	
f. Insurance of equipment and stores	210,865	
g. Other engineering expenses	2,175,714	
		30,402,880
3. Traffic, sales and publicity:		
a. Pay, allowances and provident fund contributions	14,734,370	
b. Staff and other general insurance	59,839	
c. Other staff costs	2,832,873	
d. Booking agency commission	16,603,058	
e. Publicity and sales promotion	13,798,220	
f. Charges for traffic handling by other operators	5,363,622	
g. Other traffic expenses, including rent, rates, printing and stationery, postage and telegraphs, telephones, etc.	11,381,106	
		64,773,088
4. Passenger and cargo services:		
a. Pay, allowances and provident fund contributions	3,072,762	
b. Staff and other general insurance	55,657	
c. Other staff costs	2,727,549	

EXHIBIT 2 *(Continued)*

AIR-INDIA (D)
(operating expenses, 1962–63)

Particulars		In Indian Rupees	
d. Food service including hotel accommodation and cabin service amenities		7,345,444	
e. Liability insurance		1,021,309	
f. Other expenses		585,733	
			14,808,454
5. Surface transport:			
a. Pay, allowances and provident fund contributions		1,029,115	
b. Staff and other general insurance		134,672	
c. Other staff costs		47,572	
d. Fuel and oil		438,898	
e. Materials and outside repairs		357,030	
f. Hire of transport		749,649	
g. Other expenses		253,396	
			3,010,332
6 A. General administration:			
a. Pay, allowances and provident fund contributions:			
i. Finance and accounts	3,828,824		
ii. Personnel and security	653,947		
iii. Administrative and planning	614,144		
		5,096,915	
b. Staff and other general insurance		45,631	
c. Other staff costs		353,364	
d. Board members' fees and expenses		8,880	
e. Auditors' fees and expenses		46,235	
f. Legal charges		144,888	
g. Other expenses		1,552,815	
			7,248,728
B. Staff welfare:			
a. Pay, allowances and provident fund contributions		369,128	
b. Other expenses (Net)		102,695	
c. Depreciation		233,320	
			621,015
			182,119,421

filling up the aircraft would be negligible. Company officials believed that practically all of the costs were fixed. Exhibit 2 presents figures on the operating expenses in 1962–63.

On the revenue side, the company's position was that passenger traffic would respond very sharply to rate reductions. One company official expressed the view that the demand was highly elastic in all parts of the world if the rate reductions were large enough to be noticed. Perhaps Air-India would benefit more than the average airline for several reasons:

The Asia market provided a great pool of potential customers who could not afford the higher rates. The large numbers of Indians in such places as East Africa would like to visit their homeland and would like to save travel time if they could pay the air fares.

Air-India did not have to worry quite so much as some other lines, such as KLM, about the impact on chartered services of lower fares on scheduled services. Only 1 percent of the company's revenues came from chartered services (see Exhibit 3).

EXHIBIT 3

Air-India (D)

Particulars	Rupees in Millions	Percent
How every rupee was earned		
What the corporation earned:		
Passengers	159.57	65.1
Mails	26.45	10.8
Freight including excess baggage	36.68	14.9
Charters	3.10	1.2
Contract services	4.09	1.7
Incidental Revenues	15.37	6.3
Total operating revenue	245.27	100.0
How every rupee was spent		
What the corporation spent:		
Employees	44.42	21.1
Traffic and passenger service	44.04	20.9
Operations	44.04	20.9
Depreciation	25.94	12.3
Engineering	18.05	8.5
Booking agency commission	16.60	7.9
Insurance	10.72	5.1
Administration	5.07	2.4
Surface transport	1.85	0.9
Total operating expenses	210.73	100.0

At the same time, one company official noted a factor which was holding down the elasticity of demand for Air-India's passenger services. Under India's exchange controls Indian citizens could not travel abroad without P-forms. The number of P-forms issued by the Indian government was not influenced by whether fares were high or low. Approximately half of Air-India's traffic was by Indian nationals.

The arguments for higher fares emphasized the heavy capital outlay and rapid obsolescence involved in aircraft, the great economic and political uncertainties, the high cost of fuel, landing fees, taxes, and other expenses. In the late 1950s and early 1960s the international air fares were inadequate to provide a profit for most airlines—let alone to permit a profit which would compensate for the risks.

Air-India officials tended to prefer special discounts to stimulate traffic, including seasonal discounts and discounts for large groups. In the latter case it was necessary to provide special safeguards to assure that the group rates were used only by bona fide groups. In some cases, Air-India sometimes charged less for segments of a particular route than would be consistent with the rate over the entire route. IATA permitted this practice when the competition from non-IATA lines made it necessary.

Air-India's position on cargo rates was not so strong, partly perhaps because only 15 percent of its revenue came from that source. Air-India favored the practice of relating the cargo rates to the value of the cargo and of providing special rates to move cargo which otherwise would not move by air. Company officials recognized that this last practice might lead to demands for rate reductions from other shippers. All in all, they seemed less convinced that cargo traffic would respond as much to rate reductions as passenger traffic would.

The issues in 1963

Air-India had made a profit in 1961–62 and 1962–63 despite the reduction of its load factor to 45 percent and despite the fact that most of the international airlines were unprofitable. The question was what stand the company should take on the North Atlantic fares, on fares in other parts of the world, on proposals to restrict capacity, and on the IATA system in general.

1. *How do cost considerations affect Air-India's policy toward rates?*
2. *How do demand considerations affect the policy toward rates?*
3. *Should Air-India press for rate reductions?*
4. *How does market structure affect pricing of international air travel?*

STEEL PRICES IN 1962

The most famous pricing decision in recent years was that of the U.S. Steel Company on April 9, 1962, a decision that was rescinded on April 13, 1962. The strong opposition of President John F. Kennedy, along with the refusal of several steel producers to follow the lead of U.S. Steel, resulted in this rapid reversal of price policy.

The publicity at the time of the decision and its reversal stressed cost considerations. The United Steel Workers had signed a contract with the industry in early April which limited wage increases to the estimated rate of annual increase in national productivity. The agreement provided an increase in fringe benefits costing about 10.9 cents an hour, about a $2\frac{1}{2}$ percent increase in hourly wage costs. The contract was widely hailed as noninflationary and as indicating a growing maturity of union-management relations. President Kennedy praised the agreement as "industrial statesmanship of the highest order" and said that it "should provide a solid base for continued price stability."[1] Steel officials, however, were concerned not merely with the 10.9 cent wage cost increase in 1962, but with the approximate 50 cents per hour increase in employment costs since 1958, the time of the last price increase. Furthermore, they noted that the increase in productivity in the steel industry had been only 1.7 percent per year since 1940, which was lower than the contemplated increase in employment costs. Steel officials were disturbed by their reduced profit position—the low profits resulted in part from the reduced demand in 1960 and 1961 but also from rising costs. The profits of U.S. Steel in 1961 were 36 percent below those in 1958, a recession year. Exhibit 1 presents data on steel output and prices in the years from 1957 to 1961.

The decision of U.S. Steel to increase steel prices by an average of $6 per ton, about 3.5 percent, came as a surprise to many observers, who had assumed that the moderate union demands would mean no increase in prices. No doubt the officials of U.S. Steel tried to take into account not only the rising costs and reduced profits already mentioned, but also the political repercussions and the probable price policies of competitors. It is clear that these officials made an incorrect evaluation of the political repercussions. But some observers would argue that they may also have misjudged the elasticity of demand.

The measurement of the elasticity of the demand for steel is complicated by the fact that steel is not a homogeneous product and that it is sold in a variety of markets at a variety of prices. The fact that steel can be stored means that a distinction must be made between the response to temporary price changes and permanent price changes. Secret price concessions mean that published price data are not always reliable.

Several bits of evidence would suggest that the demand for steel is inelastic. Theodore Yntema's statistical study for the U.S. Steel Corporation presented to the Temporary National Economic Committee (TNEC) in 1938 indicated extremely low demand elasticities.[2] The steel industry used this study to argue that a reduction in steel prices would make little contribution to employment in the depression of the 1930s. One might object to using a depression study in the evaluation of demand in 1962. But the fact that the demand for steel is a derived demand would support the argument that it is inelastic. For example, the price of steel would appear to be a minor factor in determining how much steel is used in the production of automobiles.

On the other hand, the growing competition from steel producers abroad and from substitutes for steel might suggest that the demand for

---

[1] In *Business Week,* April 7, 1962, p. 29, Mr. Roger Blough, Chairman of the Board of U.S. Steel denied that U.S. Steel had made any commitment on prices before, during or after the wage negotiations. See his article in *Look* magazine, January 29, 1963.

[2] See United States Steel Corporation, *T. N. E. C. Papers,* Vol. 1. pp. 169ff.

EXHIBIT 1

IMPORTANT STATISTICS ON THE STEEL INDUSTRY, 1951–61

| | U.S. STEEL COMPANY (MILLIONS OF DOLLARS) | | | | | | | | ENTIRE INDUSTRY | | |
| | Products and Services Sold | Employ-ment Costs* | Income | | Dividends | | Reinvested in Business | Average Number of Employees | Steel Products Shipped (Net Tons) | Ingot Production (Net Tons) | Ingot Operating Rate |
Year			Amount	% of Sales	Preferred Stock	Common Stock					
1951	3,524.1	1,374.5	184.3	5.2	25.2	78.3	80.8	670,700	78,928,950	105,199,848	100.9
1952	3,137.4	1,322.1	143.6	4.6	25.2	78.3	40.1	653,700	68,003,612	93,168,039	85.8
1953	3,861.0	1,569.2	222.1	5.8	25.2	78.3	118.6	682,800	80,151,893	111,609,719	94.9
1954	3,250.4	1,387.0	195.4	6.0	25.2	85.5	84.7	611,000	63,152,726	88,311,652	71.0
1955	4,097.7	1,614.9	370.1	9.0	25.2	122.9	222.0	657,600	84,717,444	117,036,085	93.0
1956	4,228.9	1,681.0	348.1	8.2	25.2	144.9	178.0	653,400	83,251,168	115,216,149	89.8
1957	4,413.8	1,862.0	419.4	9.5	25.2	161.3	232.9	656,700	79,894,577	112,714,996	84.5
1958	3,472.1	1,488.5	301.5	8.7	25.2	161.4	114.9	551,000	59,914,433	85,254,885	60.6
1959	3,643.0	1,576.2	254.5	7.0	25.2	161.8	67.5	538,800	69,377,067	93,446,132	63.3
1960	3,698.5	1,700.0	304.2	8.2	25.2	162.0	117.0	601,600	71,149,218	99,281,601	66.8
1961	3,336.5	1,622.7	190.2	5.7	25.2	162.3	2.7	N/A	66,125,505	98,014,492	N/A

* Employment costs include pensions and social security taxes and also include payments for insurance and other employee benefits.

SOURCE: United States Steel Corporation, *Annual Report 1961*; *Annual Statistical Reports*, American Iron and Steel Institute. The number of employees represents total wage and salaried employees engaged in the production and sale of iron and steel products reported to American Iron and Steel Institute by companies comprising 93 to 97 percent of the steelmaking capacity of the steel industry adjusted to 100 percent of the industry steelmaking capacity.

steel produced within the United States was becoming more elastic in the 1960s. In fact, this was one of the arguments used by the steel industry for moderation in wage demands—high domestic costs were hurting the United States' international trade position. In 1956 and 1957 the United States had exported four to five times the steel that it imported. Since 1958 imports had exceeded exports. Competition with Western Europe had become extremely severe, with the disappearance of most of the U.S. exports in Europe but with imports from Europe of over 2 million tons per year.[3] *Business Week* reported that companies in the European Coal and Steel Community were offering products at 10 to 15 percent below United States company prices in European markets. (Exhibits 2, 3, and 4 present data on the export situation.)

Probably even more important were the inroads that competing metals were making into steel markets. Aluminum had become particularly important as a substitute for steel; no doubt many purchasers made careful comparisons between the cost of aluminum and the cost of steel.

The elasticity of demand facing individual firms such as U.S. Steel was influenced in large part by the extent to which other steel companies followed the price increases of the leader. President Kennedy and other government officials exerted a great effort to prevent an industry-wide increase and thus had an important influence on the elasticity of demand. Two companies, the eighth and ninth in size, announced that they would not increase their prices. Soon thereafter, Bethlehem Steel, the second largest steel company, rescinded its price increase. U.S. Steel followed with restoration of its original prices.

Mr. Roger Blough, Chairman of the Board of U.S. Steel, made these comments on competition.[4]

There was no doubt that a price increase was necessary and we reviewed again all of the competitive factors involved. We did not—and could not—know, of course, whether other major steel producers would also raise their prices if we made the attempt; but from their published annual reports we could assume that they were suffering as we were from steadily rising costs and that they needed, as we did, the profits necessary to pay for the replacement and modernization of worn-out and obsolete facilities.

We were aware, too, that should other companies go along with the price increase, competition with substitute materials and foreign sources of steel might even add temporarily to our competitive difficulties. But the continued improvement in the economy as well as some improvement in the demand and consumption of steel indicated that a moderate price increase might be competitively possible; and, in view of the need, it was our judgment that we should delay no further in testing the market.

So on Tuesday, April 10, we announced an increase of three-tenths of a cent

---

[3] *Business Week,* March 24, 1962, pp. 100–102.

[4] *The U.S. Steel Quarterly,* May 1962, p. 5.

EXHIBIT 2
Total World Steel Trade and U.S. Steel Exports

Source: United Nations Economic Commission for Europe and U.S. Department of Commerce as reprinted in American Iron and Steel Institute, *The Competitive Challenge to Steel*, 1961.

EXHIBIT 3
Relative Importance of Direct Steel Exports and Imports

Source: American Iron and Steel Institute, *Foreign Trade Trends*, 1961.

per pound in the general level of our steel prices. This amounted to about 3½ percent and would cover only a little more than half of the 6 percent net increase in over-all costs which had occurred since 1958. Therefore, it would not restore, by any means, the cost-price relationship that had existed four years ago; but it would at least assist in meeting the competitive needs of our company, as our President, Mr. Worthington, pointed out in his statement announcing the price action. He said:

"If the products of United States Steel are to compete successfully in the market place, then the plants and facilities which make those products must be as modern and efficient as the low-cost mills which abound abroad, and as

EXHIBIT 4
U.S. Exports and Imports of Steel Related Products

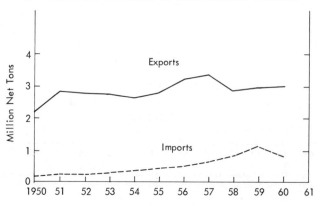

Source: American Iron and Steel Institute, *Foreign Trade Trends,* 1961.

the plants which turn out competing products here at home. Only by generating the funds necessary to keep these facilities fully competitive can our company continue to provide its customers with a dependable source of steel, and to provide its employees with dependable jobs. . . .

"The financial resources supporting continuous research and resultant new products as well as those supporting new equipment, are therefore vital in this competitive situation—vital not alone to the company and its employees, but to our international balance of payments, the value of our dollar, and to the strength and security of the nation as well."

In another article Mr. Blough commented on competitive pressures at the time of the steel price controversy. He stated that the competitive limitations of the market had restricted U.S. Steel to a 3.5 percent price increase instead of the 6 percent increase in costs. The order by Secretary of Defense Robert S. McNamara to defense contractors to buy steel only from companies which had not raised prices, along with long-distance calls by the President and his associates urging other steel companies not to raise prices, had made it difficult to maintain the 3.5 percent price increase. While eight of the companies had raised prices, the "rest of the steel companies were still selling at $6 lower, and manifold Government pressures were being exerted."[4] When Inland Steel and Kaiser Steel announced against price increases it was obvious that the "eight steel companies that had raised prices would have to lower them in order to survive." Mr. Blough also commented that no firm "has yet discovered a way to sell steel in a buyer's market at $6 a ton more than his competition."

---

[4] "My Side of the Steel Price Story," *Look* magazine, January 29, 1963, by Roger Blough as told to Eleanor Harris.

Mr. Blough believed that one favorable outcome of the steel price controversy was a public awareness "that, in the absence of Government intervention, steel prices are determined by the competitive forces of the marketplace—not by the decision of one company. Perhaps the public also realized that the market alone is the infallible arbiter of prices, and if error is made, the market itself will correct it."

The steel controversy involved broad questions about the relationship between government and business. President Kennedy stated that a few steel executives had shown "utter contempt for the interests of 185 million Americans." He apparently believed that the government had the right to intervene to protect the "public interest." Mr. Blough, on the other hand, took the position that "it is the duty of Government to protect each [individual] . . . in the pursuit of his lawful interests, to insure that force and coercion do not intrude upon those interests, and to guarantee that each individual not intrude upon the lawful interests of others." He therefore denied that it was in the public interest for the President "to substitute his own action for the action of the marketplace by trying to set prices for any competitive products."

1. *How do cost considerations affect U. S. Steel's price policy?*
2. *How do demand considerations affect the company's pricing?*
3. *Is the steel industry competitive? If so, how is it able to increase prices in the face of low demand and excess capacity? If not, why were the steel companies not able to maintain the 1962 price increases?*
4. *Which position on the "public interest" is correct: that of President Kennedy or that of the steel companies?*
5. *Should U. S. Steel have raised prices April 9, 1962? Should they have rescinded the increase on April 13, 1962?*

UTAH PIE COMPANY v. CONTINENTAL BAKING CO. (et al.)*

This case was argued Jan. 17, 1967; decided April 24, 1967; a rehearing was denied June 5, 1967. Mr. Justice White delivered the opinion of the Court.

This suit for treble damages and injunction under § § 4 and 16 of the Clayton Act, 38 Stat. 731, 737, 15 U.S.C. § § 15 and 26[1] was brought by petitioner, Utah Pie Company, against respondents, Continental Baking Company, Carna-

---

* 87 *Supreme Court Reporter* 1327; 386 U.S. 687.

1 15 U.S.C. § 15 provides that:

"Any person who shall be injured in his business or property by reason of anything forbidden in the antitrust laws may sue therefor in any district court of the United States in the district in which the defendant resides or is found or has an agent, without respect to the amount in controversy, and shall recover threefold the damages by him sustained, and the cost of suit, including a reasonable attorney's fee."

15 U.S.C. § 26 provides injunctive relief for private parties from violation of the antitrust laws.

tion Company, and Pet Milk Company. The complaint charged a conspiracy under § § 1 and 2 of the Sherman Act, 26 Stat. 209, as amended, 15 U.S.C. § § 1 and 2, and violations by each respondent of § 2(a) of the Clayton Act as amended by the Robinson-Patman Act, 49 Stat. 1526, 15 U.S.C. § 13(a).[2] The jury found for respondents on the conspiracy charge and for petitioner on the price discrimination charge.[3] Judgment was entered for petitioner for damages and attorneys' fees and respondents appealed on several grounds. The Court of Appeals reversed, addressing itself to the single issue of whether the evidence against each of the respondents was sufficient to support a finding of probable injury to competition within the meaning of § 2(a) and holding that it was not. We reverse.

The product involved is frozen dessert pies—apple, cherry, boysenberry, peach, pumpkin, and mince. The period covered by the suit comprised the years 1958, 1959, and 1960 and the first eight months of 1961. Petitioner is a Utah corporation which for 30 years had been baking pies in its plant in Salt Lake City and selling them in Utah and surrounding States. It entered the frozen pie business in late 1957. It was immediately successful with its new line and built a new plant in Salt Lake City in 1958. The frozen pie market was a rapidly expanding one: 57,060 dozen frozen pies were sold in the Salt Lake City market in 1958, 111,729 dozen in 1959, 184,569 dozen in 1960, and 266,908 dozen in 1961. Utah Pie's share of this market in those years was 66.5%, 34.3%, 45.5%, and 45.3% respectively, its sales volume steadily increasing over the four years. Its financial position also improved. Petitioner is not, however, a large company. At the time of the trial, petitioner operated with only 18 employees, nine of whom were members of the Rigby family, which controlled the business. Its net worth increased from $31,651.98 on October 31, 1957, to $68,802.13 on October 31, 1961. Total sales were $238,000 in the year ending October 31, 1957, $353,000 in 1958, $430,000 in 1959, $504,000 in 1960 and $589,000 in 1961. Its net income or loss for these same years was a loss of $6,461 in 1957, and net income in the remaining years of $7,090, $11,897, $7,636, and $9,216.

Each of the respondents is a large company and each of them is a major factor in the frozen pie market in one or more regions of the country. Each entered the Salt Lake City frozen pie market before petitioner began freezing dessert pies. None of them had a plant in Utah. By the end of the period in-

---

[2] The portion of § 2(a) relevant to the issue before the Court provides:
"That it shall be unlawful for any person engaged in commerce, in the course of such commerce, either directly or indirectly, to discriminate in price between different purchasers of commodities of like grade and quality, where either or any of the purchases involved in such discrimination are in commerce * * * where the effect of such discrimination may be substantially to lessen competition or tend to create a monopoly in any line of commerce, or to injure, destroy, or prevent competition with any person who either grants or knowingly receives the benefit of such discrimination, or with customers of either of them . . .

[3] Respondent Continental by counterclaim charged petitioner with violation of § 2(a) in respect to certain sales. On this issue the jury found for Continental, and although petitioner failed to move for a directed verdict on the counterclaim before its submission to the jury, the trial judge granted petitioner's motion for judgment notwithstanding the verdict. The Court of Appeals reversed the judgment notwithstanding the verdict on the counterclaim, and remanded the issue for a new trial. No question concerning the counterclaim is before the Court.

volved in this suit Pet had plants in Michigan, Pennsylvania, and California; Continental in Virginia, Iowa, and California; and Carnation in California. The Salt Lake City market was supplied by respondents chiefly from their California operations. They sold primarily on a delivered price basis.

The "Utah" label was petitioner's proprietary brand. Beginning in 1960, it also sold pies of like grade and quality under the controlled label "Frost 'N' Flame" to Associated Grocers and in 1961 it began selling to American Food Stores under the "Mayfresh" label. It also, on a seasonal basis, sold pumpkin and mince frozen pies to Safeway under Safeway's own "Bel-air" label.

The major competitive weapon in the Utah market was price. The location of petitioner's plant gave it natural advantages in the Salt Lake City marketing area and it entered the market at a price below the then going prices for respondents' comparable pies. For most of the period involved here its prices were the lowest in the Salt Lake City market. It was, however, challenged by each of the respondents at one time or another and for varying periods. There was ample evidence to show that each of the respondents contributed to what proved to be a deteriorating price structure over the period covered by this suit, and each of the respondents in the course of the ongoing price competition sold frozen pies in the Salt Lake market at prices lower than it sold pies of like grade and quality in other markets considerably closer to its plants. Utah Pie, which entered the market at a price of $4.15 per dozen at the beginning of the relevant period, was selling "Utah" and "Frost 'N' Flame" pies for $2.75 per dozen when the instant suit was filed some 44 months later.[4] Pet, which was offering pies at $4.92 per dozen in February 1958, was offering "Pet-Ritz" and "Bel-air" pies at $3.56 and $3.46 per dozen respectively in March and April 1961. Carnation's price in early 1958 was $4.82 per dozen but it was selling at $3.46 per dozen at the conclusion of the period, meanwhile having been down as low as $3.30 per dozen. The price range experienced by Continental during the period covered by this suit ran from a 1958 high of over $5 per dozen to a 1961 low of $2.85 per dozen.[5]

We deal first with petitioner's case against the Pet Milk Company. Pet entered the frozen pie business in 1955, acquired plants in Pennsylvania and

[4] The prices discussed herein refer to those charged for apple pies. The apple flavor has been used as the standard throughout this case, without objection from the parties, and we adhere to the practice here.

[5] The Salt Lake City sales volumes and market shares of the parties to this suit as well as of other sellers during the period at issue were as follows:

	1958				*1960*	
Company	*Volume (in doz.)*	*Percent of Market*		*Company*	*Volume (in doz.)*	*Percent of Market*
Carnation	5,863	10.3		Carnation	22,371.5	12.1
Continental	754	1.3		Continental	3,350	1.8
Utah Pie	37,969.5	66.5		Utah Pie	83,894	45.5
Pet	9,336.5	16.4		Pet	51,480	27.9
Others	3,137	5.5		Others	23,473.5	12.7
Total	57,060	100.0		Total	184,569	100.0
	1959				*1961*	
Carnation	9,625	8.6		Carnation	20,067	8.8
Continental	3,182	2.9		Continental	18,799.5	8.3
Utah Pie	38,372	34.3		Utah Pie	102,690	45.3
Pet	39,639	35.5		Pet	66,786	29.4
Others	20,911	18.7		Others	18,565.5	8.2
Total	111,729	100.0		Total	226,908	100.0

California and undertook a large advertising campaign to market its "Pet-Ritz" brand of frozen pies. Pet's initial emphasis was on quality, but in the face of competition from regional and local companies and in an expanding market where price proved to be a crucial factor, Pet was forced to take steps to reduce the price of its pies to the ultimate consumer. These developments had consequences in the Salt Lake City market which are the substance of petitioner's case against Pet.

First, Pet successfully concluded an arrangement with Safeway, which is one of the three largest customers for frozen pies in the Salt Lake market, whereby it would sell frozen pies to Safeway under the latter's own "Bel-air" label at a price significantly lower than it was selling its comparable "Pet-Ritz" brand in the same Salt Lake market and elsewhere. The initial price on "Bel-air" pies was slightly lower than Utah's price for its "Utah" brand of pies at the time, and near the end of the period the "Bel-air" price was comparable to the "Utah" price but higher than Utah's "Frost 'N' Flame" brand. Pet's Safeway business amounted to 22.8%, 12.3%, and 6.3% of the entire Salt Lake City market for the years 1959, 1960, and 1961, respectively, and to 64%, 44%, and 22% of Pet's own Salt Lake City sales for those same years.

Second, it introduced a 20-ounce economy pie under the "Swiss Miss" label and began selling the new pie in the Salt Lake market in August 1960 at prices ranging from $3.25 to $3.30 for the remainder of the period. This pie was at times sold at a lower price in the Salt Lake City market than it was sold in other markets.

Third, Pet became more competitive with respect to the prices for its "Pet-Ritz" proprietary label. For 18 of the relevant 44 months its offering price for "Pet-Ritz" pies was $4 per dozen or lower, and $3.70 or lower for six of these months. According to the Court of Appeals, in seven of the 44 months Pet's prices in Salt Lake were lower than prices charged in the California markets. This was true although selling in Salt Lake involved a 30- to 35-cent freight cost.

The Court of Appeals first concluded that Pet's price differential on sales to Safeway must be put aside in considering injury to competition because in its view of the evidence the differential had been completely cost justified and because Utah would not in any event have been able to enjoy the Safeway custom. Second, it concluded that the remaining discriminations on "Pet-Ritz" and "Swiss Miss" pies were an insufficient predicate on which the jury could have found a reasonably possible injury either to Utah Pie as a competitive force or to competition generally.

We disagree with the Court of Appeals in several respects. First, there was evidence from which the jury could have found considerably more price discrimination by Pet with respect to "Pet-Ritz" and "Swiss Miss" pies than was considered by the Court of Appeals. In addition to the seven months during which Pet's prices in Salt Lake were lower than prices in the California markets, there was evidence from which the jury could reasonably have found that in 10 additional months the Salt Lake City prices for "Pet-Ritz" pies were discriminatory as compared with sales in western markets other than California. Likewise, with respect to "Swiss Miss" pies, there was evidence in the record from which the jury could have found that in five of the 13 months during which the "Swiss Miss" pies were sold prior to the filing of this suit, prices in

Salt Lake City were lower than those charged by Pet in either California or some other western market.

Second, with respect to Pet's Safeway business, the burden of proving cost justification was on Pet and, in our view, reasonable men could have found that Pet's lower priced, "Bel-air" sales to Safeway were not cost justified in their entirety. Pet introduced cost data for 1961 indicating a cost saving on the Safeway business greater than the price advantage extended to that customer. These statistics were not particularized for the Salt Lake market, but assuming that they were adequate to justify the 1961 sales, they related to only 24% of the Safeway sales over the relevant period. The evidence concerning the remaining 76% was at best incomplete and inferential. It was insufficient to take the defense of cost justification from the jury, which reasonably could have found a greater incidence of unjustified price discrimination than that allowed by the Court of Appeals' view of the evidence.[6]

With respect to whether Utah would have enjoyed Safeway's business absent the Pet contract with Safeway, it seems clear that whatever the fact is in this regard, it is not determinative of the impact of that contract on competitors other than Utah and on competition generally. There were other companies seeking the Safeway business, including Continental and Carnation, whose pies may have been excluded from the Safeway shelves by what the jury could have found to be discriminatory sales to Safeway. What is more, Pet's evidence that Utah's unwillingness to install quality control equipment prevented Utah from enjoying Safeway's private label business is not the only evidence in the record relevant to that question. There was other evidence to the contrary. The jury would not have been compelled to find that Utah Pie could not have gained more of the Safeway business.

Third, the Court of Appeals almost entirely ignored other evidence which provides material support for the jury's conclusion that Pet's behavior satisfied the statutory test regarding competitive injury. This evidence bore on the issue of Pet's predatory intent to injure Utah Pie. As an initial matter, the jury could have concluded that Pet's discriminatory pricing was aimed at Utah Pie; Pet's own management, as early as 1959, identified Utah Pie as an "unfavorable factor," one which "d[u]g holes in our operation" and posed a constant "check" on Pet's performance in the Salt Lake City market. Moreover, Pet candidly admitted that during the period when it was establishing its relationship with Safeway, it sent into Utah Pie's plant an industrial spy to seek information

---

[6] The only evidence cited by the Court of Appeals to justify the remaining 76% of Pet's sales to Safeway was Safeway's established practice of requiring its sellers to cost justify sales that otherwise would be illegally discriminatory. This practice was incorporated in the Pet-Safeway contract. We are unprepared to hold that a contractual obligation to cost justify price differentials is legally dispositive proof that such differentials are in fact so justified. Pet admitted that its cost-justification figures were drawn from past performance, so even crediting the data accompanying the 1960 contract regarding cost differences, Pet's additional evidence would bring under the justification umbrella only the 1959 sales. Thus, at the least, the jury was free to consider the 1960 Safeway sales as inadequately cost justified. Those sales accounted for 12.3% of the entire Salt Late City market in that year. In the context of this case, the sales to Safeway are particularly relevant since there was evidence that private label sales influenced the general market, in this case depressing overall market prices.

that would be of use to Pet in convincing Safeway that Utah Pie was not worthy of its custom. Pet denied that it ever in fact used what it had learned against Utah Pie in competing for Safeway's business. The parties, however, are not the ultimate judges of credibility. But even giving Pet's view of the incident a measure of weight does not mean the jury was foreclosed from considering the predatory intent underlying Pet's mode of competition. Finally, Pet does not deny that the evidence showed it suffered substantial losses on its frozen pie sales during the greater part of the time involved in this suit, and there was evidence from which the jury could have concluded that the losses Pet sustained in Salt Lake City were greater than those incurred elsewhere. It would not have been an irrational step if the jury concluded that there was a relationship between price and the losses.

It seems clear to us that the jury heard adequate evidence from which it could have concluded that Pet had engaged in predatory tactics in waging competitive warfare in the Salt Lake City market. Coupled with the incidence of price discrimination attributable to Pet, the evidence as a whole established, rather than negated, the reasonable possibility that Pet's behavior produced a lessening of competition proscribed by the Act.

Petitioner's case against Continental is not complicated. Continental was a substantial factor in the market in 1957. But its sales of frozen 22-ounce dessert pies, sold under the "Morton" brand, amounted to only 1.3% of the market in 1958, 2.9% in 1959, and 1.8% in 1960. Its problems were primarily that of cost and in turn that of price, the controlling factor in the market. In late 1960 it worked out a co-packing arrangement in California by which fruit would be processed from the trees into the finished pie without large intermediate packing, storing, and shipping expenses. Having improved its position, it attempted to increase its share of the Salt Lake City market by utilizing a local broker and offering short-term price concessions in varying amounts. Its efforts for seven months were not spectacularly successful. Then in June, 1961, it took the steps which are the heart of petitioner's complaint against it. Effective for the last two weeks of June it offered its 22-ounce frozen apple pies in the Utah area at $2.85 per dozen. It was then selling the same pies at substantially higher prices in other markets. The Salt Lake City price was less than its direct cost plus an allocation for overhead. Utah's going price at the time for its 24-ounce "Frost 'N' Flame" apple pie sold to Associated Grocers was $3.10 per dozen, and for its "Utah" brand $3.40 per dozen. At its new prices, Continental sold pies to American Grocers in Pocatello, Idaho, and to American Food Stores in Ogden, Utah. Safeway, one of the major buyers in Salt Lake City, also purchased 6,250 dozen, its requirements for about five weeks. Another purchaser ordered 1,000 dozen. Utah's response was immediate. It reduced its price on all of its apple pies to $2.75 per dozen. Continental refused Safeway's request to match Utah's price, but renewed its offer at the same prices effective July 31 for another two-week period. Utah filed suit on September 8, 1961. Continental's total sales of frozen pies increased from 3,350 dozen in 1960 to 18,800 dozen in 1961. Its market share increased from 1.8% in 1960 to 8.3% in 1961. The Court of Appeals concluded that Continental's conduct had had only minimal effect, that it had not injured or weakened Utah Pie as a competitor, that it had not substantially lessened competition and that there was no reasonable possibility that it would do so in the future.

We again differ with the Court of Appeals. Its opinion that Utah was not damaged as a competitive force apparently rested on the fact that Utah's sales volume continued to climb in 1961 and on the court's own factual conclusion that Utah was not deprived of any pie business which it otherwise might have had. But this retrospective assessment fails to note that Continental's discriminatory below-cost price caused Utah Pie to reduce its price to $2.75. The jury was entitled to consider the potential impact of Continental's price reduction absent any responsive price cut by Utah Pie. Price was a major factor in the Salt Lake City market. Safeway, which had been buying Utah brand pies, immediately reacted and purchased a five-week supply of frozen pies from Continental, thereby temporarily foreclosing the proprietary brands of Utah and other firms from the Salt Lake City Safeway market. The jury could rationally have concluded that had Utah not lowered its price, Continental, which repeated its offer once, would have continued it, that Safeway would have continued to buy from Continental and that other buyers, large as well as small, would have followed suit. It could also have reasonably concluded that a competitor who is forced to reduce his price to a new all-time low in a market of declining prices will in time feel the financial pinch and will be a less effective competitive force.

Even if the impact on Utah Pie as a competitor was negligible, there remain the consequences to others in the market who had to compete not only with Continental's 22-ounce pie at $2.85 but with Utah's even lower price of $2.75 per dozen for both its proprietary and controlled labels. Petitioner and respondents were not the only sellers in the Salt Lake City market, although they did account for 91.8% of the sales in 1961. The evidence was that there were nine other sellers in 1960 who sold 23,473 dozen pies, 12.7% of the total market. In 1961 there were eight other sellers who sold less than the year before— 18,565 dozen or 8.2% of the total—although the total market had expanded from 184,569 dozen to 226,908 dozen. We think there was sufficient evidence from which the jury could find a violation of § 2(a) by Continental.

The Carnation Company entered the frozen dessert pie business in 1955 through the acquisition of "Mrs. Lee's Pies" which was then engaged in manufacturing and selling frozen pies in Utah and elsewhere under the "Simple Simon" label. Carnation also quickly found the market extremely sensitive to price. Carnation decided, however, not to enter an economy product in the market, and during the period covered by this suit it offered only its quality "Simple Simon" brand. Its primary method of meeting competition in its markets was to offer a variety of discounts and other reductions, and the technique was not unsuccessful. In 1958, for example, Carnation enjoyed 10.3% of the Salt Lake City market, and although its volume of pies sold in that market increased substantially in the next year, its percentage of the market temporarily slipped to 8.6%. However, 1960 was a turnaround year for Carnation in the Salt Lake City market; it more than doubled its volume of sales over the preceding year and thereby gained 12.1% of the market. And while the price structure in the market deteriorated rapidly in 1961 Carnation's position remained important.

We need not dwell long upon the case against Carnation, which in some respects is similar to that against Continental and in others more nearly resembles the case against Pet. After Carnation's temporary setback in 1959 it instituted a new pricing policy to regain business in the Salt Lake City market. The new policy involved a slash in price of 60¢ per dozen pies, which brought Carnation's price to a level admittedly well below its costs, and well below the other prices prevailing in the market. The impact of the move was felt immediately, and the two other major sellers in the market reduced their prices. Carnation's banner year, 1960, in the end involved eight months during which the prices in Salt Lake City were lower than prices charged in other markets. The trend continued during the eight months in 1961 that preceded the filing of the complaint in this case. In each of those months the Salt Lake City prices charged by Carnation were well below prices charged in other markets, and in all but August 1961 the Salt Lake City delivered price was 20 to 50¢ lower than the prices charged in distant San Francisco. The Court of Appeals held that only the early 1960 prices could be found to have been below cost. That holding, however, simply overlooks evidence from which the jury could have concluded that throughout 1961 Carnation maintained a below-cost price structure and that Carnation's discriminatory pricing, no less than that of Pet and Continental, had an important effect on the Salt Lake City market. We cannot say that the evidence precluded the jury from finding it reasonably possible that Carnation's conduct would injure competition.

Section 2(a) does not forbid price competition which will probably injure or lessen competition by eliminating competitors, discouraging entry into the market or enhancing the market shares of the dominant sellers. But Congress has established some ground rules for the game. Sellers may not sell like goods to different purchasers at different prices if the result may be to injure competition in either the sellers' or the buyers' market unless such discriminations are justified as permitted by the Act. This case concerns the sellers' market. In this context, the Court of Appeals placed heavy emphasis on the fact that Utah Pie constantly increased its sales volume and continued to make a profit. But we disagree with its apparent view that there is no reasonably possible injury to competition as long as the volume of sales in a particular market is expanding and at least some of the competitors in the market continue to operate at a profit. Nor do we think that the Act only comes into play to regulate the conduct of price discriminators when their discriminatory prices consistently undercut other competitors. It is true that many of the primary line cases that have reached the courts have involved blatant predatory price discriminations employed with the hope of immediate destruction of a particular competitor. On the question of injury to competition such cases present courts with no difficulty, for such pricing is clearly within the heart of the proscription of the Act. Courts and commentators alike have noted that the existence of predatory intent might bear on the likelihood of injury to competition. In this case there was some evidence of predatory intent with respect to each of these respondents. There was also other evidence upon which the jury could rationally find the requisite injury to competition. The frozen pie market in Salt Lake City was highly competitive. At times Utah Pie was a leader in moving the general level of prices down, and at other times each of the respondents also bore responsibility for the downward pressure on the price structure. We believe that the Act reaches price discrimination that erodes competition as much as it does price discrimination that is intended to have immediate destructive impact. In this case, the evidence shows a drastically declining price structure which the jury could rationally attribute to continued or sporadic price discrimination. The jury was entitled to conclude that "the effect of such discrimination," by each of these respondents, "may be substantially to lessen competition . . . or to injure, destroy, or prevent competition with any person who either grants or knowingly receives the benefit of such discrimination. . . ." The statutory test is one that necessarily looks forward on the basis of proven conduct in the past. Proper application of that standard here requires reversal of the judgment of the Court of Appeals.

Since the Court of Appeals held that petitioner had failed to make a prima facie case against each of the respondents, it expressly declined to pass on other grounds for reversal presented by the respondents. 349 F.2d 122, 126. Without intimating any views on the other grounds presented to the Court of Appeals, we reverse its judgment and remand the case to that court for further proceedings. It is so ordered. Reversed and remanded.

The Chief Justice took no part in the decision of this case. Mr. Justice Stewart and Mr. Justice Harlan joined in dissenting:

I would affirm the judgment, agreeing substantially with the reasoning of the Court of Appeals as expressed in the thorough and conscientious opinion of Judge Phillips.

There is only one issue in this case in its present posture: Whether the respondents engaged in price discrimination "where the effect of such discrimination may be substantially to lessen competition or tend to create a monopoly in any line of commerce, or to injure, destroy, or prevent competition with any person who either grants or knowingly receives the benefit of such discrimination. . . ."[7] Phrased more simply, did the respondents' actions have the anticompetitive effect required by the statute as an element of a cause of action?

The Court's own description of the Salt Lake City frozen pie market from 1958 through 1961, shows that the answer to that question must be no. In 1958 Utah Pie had a quasi-monopolistic 66.5% of the market. In 1961—after the alleged predations of the respondents—Utah Pie still had a commanding 45.3%, Pet had 29.4%, and the remainder of the market was divided almost equally between Continental, Carnation, and other, small local bakers. Unless we disregard the lessons so laboriously learned in scores of Sherman and Clayton Act cases, the 1961 situation has to be considered more competitive than that of 1958. Thus, if we assume that the price discrimination proven against the respondents had any effect on competition, that effect must have been beneficial.

That the Court has fallen into the error of reading the Robinson-Patman Act as protecting competitors, instead of competition, can be seen from its unsuccessful attempt to distinguish cases relied upon by the respondents. Those cases are said to be inapposite because they involved "no general decline in price structure," and no "lasting impact upon prices." But lower prices are the hallmark of intensified competition.

---

[7] Section 2(a) of the Clayton Act as amended by the Robinson-Patman Act, 15 U.S.C. § 13(a).

The Court of Appeals squarely identified the fallacy which the Court today embraces:

". . . a contention that Utah Pie was entitled to hold the extraordinary market share percentage of 66.5, attained in 1958, falls of its own dead weight. To approve such a contention would be to hold that Utah Pie was entitled to maintain a position which approached, if it did not in fact amount to a monopoly, and could not exist in the face of proper and healthy competition."

I cannot hold that Utah Pie's monopolistic position was protected by the federal antitrust laws from effective price competition, and I therefore respectfully dissent.

1. *Did the competitors engage in price discrimination? Were these practices illegal? Should they be considered illegal?*
2. *Does the fact that Utah Pie Company is a small independent firm, facing large competitors, influence your appraisal of the case?*
3. *Is the market structure competitive, monopolistically competitive, or oligopolistic?*
4. *Did the ruling in the case reduce competition or protect it?*

BIRCH PAPER COMPANY*

"If I were to price these boxes any lower than $480 a thousand," said James Brunner, manager of Birch Paper Company's Thompson division, "I'd be countermanding my order of last month for our salesmen to stop shaving their bids and to bid full cost quotations. I've been trying for weeks to improve the quality of our business, and if I turn around now and accept this job at $430 or $450 or something less than $480, I'll be tearing down this program I've been working so hard to build up. The division can't very well show a profit by putting in bids which don't even cover a fair share of overhead costs, let alone give us a profit."

Birch Paper Company was a medium-size, partly integrated paper company, producing white and kraft papers and paperboard. A portion of its paperboard output was converted into corrugated boxes by the Thompson division, which also printed and colored the outside surface of the boxes. Including Thompson, the company had four producing divisions and a timberland division, which supplied part of the company's pulp requirements.

For several years each division had been judged independently on the basis of its profit and return on investment. Top management had been

---

* This case was prepared by William Rotch under the direction of Neil E. Harlan of the Harvard University Graduate School of Business Administration as a basis for classroom discussion rather than to illustrate either effective or ineffective handling of administrative situations. Copyright © 1956 by the President and Fellow of Harvard College. Used by specific permission.

working to gain effective results from a policy of decentralizing responsibility and authority for all decisions but those relating to overall company policy. The company's top officials believed that in the past few years the concept of decentralization had been successfully applied and that the company's profits and competitive position had definitely improved.

Early in 1957 the Northern division designed a special display box for one of its papers in conjunction with the Thompson division, which was equipped to make the box. Thompson's staff for package design and development spent several months perfecting the design, production methods, and materials that were to be used; because of the unusual color and shape, these were far from standard. According to an agreement between the two divisions, the Thompson division was reimbursed by the Northern division for the cost of its design and development work.

When the specifications were all prepared, the Northern division asked for bids on the box from the Thompson division and from two outside companies. Each division manager was normally free to buy from whatever supplier he wished; and even on sales within the company, divisions were expected to meet the going market price if they wanted the business.

In 1957 the profit margins of converters such as the Thompson division were being squeezed. Thompson, as did many other similar converters, bought its paperboard and its function was to print, cut, and shape it into boxes. Although it bought most of its materials from other Birch divisions, most of Thompson's sales were made to outside customers. If Thompson got the order from Northern, it probably would buy its linerboard and corrugating medium from the Southern division of Birch. The walls of a corrugated box consist of outside and inside sheets of linerboard sandwiching the fluted corrugating medium. About 70 percent of Thompson's out-of-pocket cost of $400 for the order represented the cost of linerboard and corrugating medium. Though Southern had been running below capacity and had excess inventory, it quoted the market price, which had not noticeably weakened as a result of the oversupply. Its out-of-pocket costs on both liner and corrugating medium were about 60 percent of the selling price.

The Northern division received bids on the boxes of $480 a thousand from the Thompson division, $430 a thousand from West Paper Company, and $432 a thousand from Eire Papers, Ltd. Eire Papers offered to buy from Birch the outside linerboard with the special printing already on it, but would supply its own inside liner and corrugating medium. The outside liner would be supplied by the Southern division at a price equivalent of $90 a thousand boxes, and would be printed for $30 a thousand by the Thompson division. Of the $30, about $25 would be out-of-pocket costs.

Since this situation appeared to be a little unusual, William Kenton, manager of the Northern division, discussed the wide discrepancy of bids with Birch's commercial vice president. He told the vice president, "We sell in a very competitive market, where higher costs cannot be passed on. How can we be expected to show a decent profit and return on investment if we have to buy our supplies at more than 10 percent over the going market?"

Knowing that Mr. Brunner had on occasion in the past few months been unable to operate the Thompson division at capacity, it seemed odd to the vice president that Mr. Brunner would add the full 20 percent overhead and profit charge to his out-of-pocket costs. When asked about this, Mr. Brunner's answer was the remark that appears at the beginning of the case. He went on to say that having done the developmental work on the box, and having received no profit on that, he felt entitled to a good markup on the production of the box itself.

The vice president explored further the cost structures of the various divisions. He remembered a comment that the controller had made at a meeting the week before to the effect that costs that for one division were variable, could be largely fixed for the company as a whole. He knew that in the absence of specific orders from top management, Mr. Kenton would accept the lowest bid, which was that of the West Paper Company for $430. However, it would be possible for top management to order the acceptance of another bid if the situation warranted such action. And though the volume represented by the transactions in question was less than 5 percent of the volume of any of the divisions involved, other transactions could conceivably raise similar problems later.

1. *How does the theory of transfer pricing relate to this case?*
2. *Is there a conflict in the case between the needs of decisions on pricing and the needs of profit determination? Explain.*
3. *What price should be set on the special display boxes? Discuss.*

PART FIVE / Strategy formulation
and capital budgeting

10 / Long-range forecasting

This chapter discusses forecasting for strategic planning. Strategy has a long-run time perspective, since it extends beyond the expected useful life of much of the firm's plant and equipment. Strategic planning selects a future "business to be in," specified in terms of product mix, markets in which the products will be sold, and competitive advantages that the firm expects to achieve.

The chapter begins with a brief description of a process of formulating strategy. This gives an overview of uses of long-range forecasts in strategic planning. The chapter then discusses social forecasting, technological forecasting, and resource forecasting. It concludes with examples of economic analyses in strategic planning by business and nonprofit organizations.

FORMULATION OF CORPORATE STRATEGY

The game of chess provides an example of a need for strategy. Success— i.e. winning—requires planning ahead for at least a few plays. One chess player may have an offensive strategy requiring concentration of powerful pieces for a thrust down the middle of the board. Another may have a defensive strategy requiring early "castling" with a buildup of a deep defense in front of the king's castle. Strategy suggests most of the early moves of each player. Further, every move, even an opportunistic play, is evaluated in terms of its contribution toward the player's overall strategy.

Businesses are formulating strategy when they make decisions about the general direction and scope of their desired growth. Delineation of a future "business to be in" suggests priorities for present resource allocations to technological research, market development, management recruiting and training, plant and equipment expenditures, and mergers and acquisitions. Many contemporary decisions of line managers and staff specialists are partially formed by their relationships to the firm's long-term strategy.

The ongoing, never-ending process of strategy formulation includes specification of objectives, evaluation of the firm's strengths and weaknesses, a forecast of trends in the environment, delineation of economic threats and opportunities, and a search for synergy (economic complementarity among potential activities of the firm).[1]

Objectives and goals

Conventional microeconomic theory asserts that a business firm always acts in such a way that it maximizes profits. Some writers have suggested that firms attempt to maximize sales rather than profits.[2] Others have hypothesized that firms simply attempt to "satisfice"—i.e., reach some "satisfactory" level of profits and sales.[3] Still others have hypothesized that the primary objective of the firm is survival,[4] or that the firm is primarily interested in growth in order to survive.[5] The assumption in this chapter is that firms do attempt to maximize profits over the long run.

A broadly stated goal such as long-run profit maximization is not very helpful in the strategy formulation process. Goals must be more specific. For example, a firm may establish some target rate of *return on total assets used* over the next three to ten years. Ansoff says that even this specific goal must be decomposed into a set of subsidiary objectives relating to external competitive strengths and internal operating efficiency. Figure 10–1 illustrates an operationally useful set of long range objectives. Note that all of these goals are quantifiable, so that the firm can measure the extent to which its aspirations are being met.

In addition to those objectives related to return on assets used, the firm has a set of objectives related to flexibility. *Internal flexibility* is provided by *liquidity; external flexibility* is attained through *diversification.*[6] Both methods help ensure that the business will not be overcome by a single adversity. A business with reserve borrowing power can meet the threat

---

[1] The concept of strategy follows the concept of H. Igor Ansoff, *Corporate Strategy* (New York: McGraw Hill, 1965). Ansoff's book contains many important concepts and techniques not mentioned here.

[2] William J. Baumol, *Economic Theory and Operations Analysis,* 3d ed. (Englewood Cliffs, N.J.: Prentice-Hall, 1972), p. 320.

[3] Richard M. Cyert and James G. March, *A Behavioral Theory of the Firm* (Englewood Cliffs, N.J.: Prentice-Hall, 1963).

[4] Peter Drucker, "Business Objectives and Survival Needs: Notes on a Discipline of Business Enterprise," *Journal of Business,* 31 (1958), pp. 81–90.

[5] John Kenneth Galbraith, *The New Industrial State,* 2d ed. (Boston: Houghton Mifflin Company, 1971), pp. 171–72.

[6] Ansoff, *Corporate Strategy,* pp. 50–53.

FIGURE 10–1

A Set of Long-Range Objectives

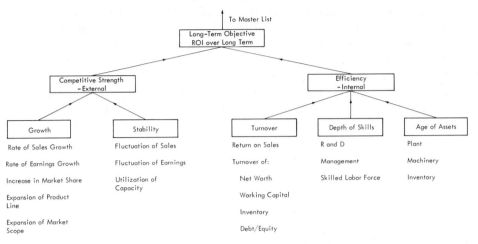

Source: H. Igor Ansoff, *Corporate Strategy* (New York: McGraw-Hill, 1965), p. 53.

of an unexpected product improvement by a competitor. A firm that is diversified across several product lines is not dependent upon the buying power of any one group of customers.

The objectives of profitability and flexibility are conflicting, so that trading off less of one for more of the other is necessary. For example, a reduction in plant and equipment expenditure will allow an increase in assets that are quickly convertible to cash. Furthermore, both objectives are subject to self-imposed responsibilities and institutional constraints. For example, management may feel responsible for provision of steady employment and job security to long-time employees. As another example, a large firm such as General Motors will not likely pursue growth within a single product line to the point that competition is wiped out and countervailing actions by the Antitrust Division of the Justice Department are stimulated.

Selecting the "business to be in"

The firm selects an evolving product mix and a corresponding set of markets that appear to offer the best prospects for achieving its objectives. It compares *various possible deployments* of its *limited* (but possibly *unique*) *set of resources* and *organizational competences*. Strategy formulation requires appraisal of the firm's strengths and weaknesses, determination of the particular business competences that are essential for success in various avenues of expansion, and forecasts of the results of successful operation in each line of activity.

The firm's *relative strengths and weaknesses* can be appraised by (1) an examination of past performance to locate patterns of success or failure, and (2) direct comparison of the firm's skills and capacities with those of major competitors. In the words of Quinn, "The purposes of such exercises should be: to identify and exploit the comparative weaknesses of competitors, to marshal sufficient resources into specific subareas of the company's operations to dominate them, to recognize where competitive strengths allow the company wider latitude in pricing or product policies than competitors, and to pinpoint the company's own weaknesses for more aggressive action or purposeful withdrawal."[7] Appraisal of the firm's strengths and weaknesses should cover all of the resources and

TABLE 10–1

OUTLINE FOR INTERNAL APPRAISAL AND INDUSTRY ANALYSIS

1. Product-Market Structure
   a. Products and their characteristics
   b. Product missions
   c. Customers
2. Growth and Profitability
   a. History
   b. Forecasts
   c. Relation to life cycle
   d. Basic determinants of demand
   e. Averages and norms typical of the industry
3. Technology
   a. Basic technologies
   b. History of innovation
   c. Technological trends—threats and opportunities
   d. Role of technology in success
4. Investment
   a. Cost of entry and exit-critical mass
   b. Typical asset patterns in firms.
   c. Rate and type of obsolescence of assets
   d. Role of capital investment in success
5. Marketing
   a. Means and methods of selling
   b. Role of service and field support
   c. Roles and means of advertising and sales promotion
   d. What makes a product competitive
   e. Role of marketing in success
6. Competition
   a. Market shares, concentration, dominance
   b. Characteristics of outstanding firms, of poor firms
   c. Trends in competitive patterns
7. Strategic Perspective
   a. Trends in demand
   b. Trends in product-market structure
   c. Trends in technology
   d. Key ingredients in success

SOURCE Ansoff: *Corporate Strategy*, p. 146.

---

[7] John B. Quinn, "Technological Strategies for Industrial Companies," *Technological Forecasting and Corporate Strategy*, edited by Gordon Wills, David Ashton, and Bernard Taylor (New York: American Elsevier Publishing Company, 1969), p. 58.

competences required in its present business, plus any other capabilities that it has or can reasonably expect to acquire. Table 10–1 lists a few examples of the kinds of organizational characteristics that are considered.

Requirements for business success in various industries are determined through (1) listing the technological, marketing, financial, and management capabilities required by the nature of each industry and (2) developing "competitive profiles" of the most successful firms in each industry. Then, in Ansoff's words, "Superposition of our firm's competence profile with the competitive profiles measures the 'fit' with each new industry and hence the chances of a successful entry."[8]

Forecasts of results of successful business operations in the various industries are obviously needed in choosing a "portfolio" of "businesses to be in." The firm needs estimates of growth prospects, return on assets used, and year-to-year variability in sales and income, assuming a competent organization, in each line of business. Such estimates cannot be made without projections and analysis of trends affecting demand for products and services, competition, the institutional and legal environment, timing and nature of technological changes, availability and relative cost of resources, and increases in industry capacity.

An overview of long-range forecasting

Long-range forecasting is still a primitive art. It deals with dimly perceived forces that interact in complex ways. For example, changing cultural values could lower birth rates; reduced birth rates diminish prospective future demands for goods and services used in the public schools; in the more distant future, the reduced number of new workers entering the labor market may tend to lift wages and thus increase the demand for capital goods. On the other hand, changing cultural values could eventually reduce the institutional pressure for complete retirement at age 65; the increase in older workers continuing part-time employment could tend to depress wages and thus decrease the demand for capital goods.

There are no adequate formal models around which the whole process of long-range forecasting can be organized. However, the forecasting process can be broken into phases and carried out in a logical sequence:

1. *Projecting, extrapolating, or constructing trends and potential breakthroughs and developments in the principal environmental forces, one at a time.*
2. Assessing the potentials for interaction (reinforcement or interference) among the various trends and *adjusting the forecasts to take interactions into account.*

---

[8] Ansoff, *Corporate Strategy*, p. 101.

3. *Considering the probable ecological ramifications* of simultaneous environmental changes resulting from the adjusted trends.

4. *Appraising potential social feedback* upon progress of the trends and control of their ecological ramifications.

5. *Developing the apparent range of alternative states of the future business environment* in the light of possible relationships of social action to the evolving ecology.[9]

SOCIAL FORECASTING

Three areas have been selected for attention in this section. Boundaries of these areas are not well defined, but using them facilitates discussion and allows emphasis of some key interrelationships among the areas. These areas, or groupings, are: cultural trends, political trends, and demographic trends.

Cultural trends

Culture consists of beliefs, values, customs, and attitudes exhibited by members of a society. Culture is learned by these members. Over time, culture changes and so does the behavior of the people, both as consumers of goods and services and as suppliers of personal services and capital needed by businesses. Thus, changes in culture can have profound effects upon demands for products and suppliers of inputs. Some discernible trends in American culture and their implications for long-range planning are discussed below.

The easy life. Puritan and frontier virtues—hard work, thrift, and individualism—are on the decline. In Philip Kotler's apt phrases, Americans want the "soft life," the "sweet life," the "social life," and the "safe life."[10] Thus, demands can be expected to burgeon for products that increase convenience and leisure time (example: convenience foods), that provide luxury and recreation (example: motor homes), that mark the user as a person of "good taste" and conventional opinions (example: memberships in social clubs), and that increase confidence and security (example: variable annuity forms of life insurance). Simultaneously, workers are becoming less and less willing to endure jobs that are dirty, noisy, dangerous, monotonous, and physically arduous.

A secular, this-world, here-and-now-attitude. Americans are placing less and less relative value on deferred satisfactions. Even the religious concept of eternal life is receiving decreased emphasis in most denominations. Thus, a sales appeal which reminds consumers that they "only

---

[9] Adapted from the statement by Otis D. Duncan "Social Forecasting—the State of the Art," *The Public Interest* 17 (Fall 1969), p. 115.

[10] Philip Kotler, *Marketing Management: Analysis, Planning & Control* (Englewood Cliffs, N.J.: Prentice-Hall, Inc., 1967) pp. 82–87.

go around once in life," and therefore should make the most of it (with the assistance of a particular product) has been effective. Many consumers are willing to build up heavy loads of debt rather than defer purchases until they can pay cash.

Broader perspective—living in a "larger world." Faster transportation and better communication broaden the perspective of the relevant world. Daniel Bell provides the examples of coast-to-coast travel in five hours and a hundred million persons simultaneously watching the Kennedy funeral.[11] Simultaneously, there is increasing interdependence and competition among people and their activities. Effects of an individual firm's actions upon the environment of other firms and persons (external effects) are becoming more important and better understood. Thus, there is an increasing tendency to look to governmental agencies for protection of the environment and of the interests of various groups through regulation of privately owned businesses and through directly providing some goods and services. Kotler lists several problem areas that make high-growth markets for direct sales to state and local governments (examples were provided by the present author): population growth (example: contraceptives); poverty (example: subsidized housing); urbanization (example: law enforcement equipment); air and water pollution (example: pollution measurement devices); congested transportation (example: rapid transit systems); agriculture (example: supplies for disease and pest eradication programs).[12]

Decreased importance of values associated with the traditional concept of "family." There is a decline in the relative authority and influence of parents compared to children, an increasingly permissive attitude toward sexual interests and activities, and decreased delineation of male and female roles. These trends bring greater emphasis upon products designed for young people or to make consumers look or feel younger. Large markets for pornographic materials have been opened. There is a move to "unisex" looks in men's and women's clothing. In the labor market, sexual rigidity is breaking down; there are now female airline pilots and male telephone operators.

Cultural values of individuals affect their behavior as consumers, producers, and voters. Thus, changing cultural values propel and shape the trends in political institutions. These trends are discussed in the next section of this chapter.

Political trends

Futuristic books like George Orwell's *1984*[13] or Aldous Huxley's *Brave*

---

[11] Daniel Bell, "The Study of the Future," *The Public Interest*, 1 (Fall, 1965), pp. 120–121.

[12] Kotler, *Marketing Management: Analysis, Planning & Control*, pp. 146–49.

[13] George Orwell, *1984* (New American Library, 1971).

New World[14] use the increasing importance of the role of government in daily life of the population as a major theme. General trends in the role of government include: (1) the increased absolute size of governmental budgets and employment; (2) increased use of public planning and regulation; (3) increased emphasis on income redistribution; (4) increasing importance of international affairs.

Size and composition of budgets. In 1972, expenditures by federal, state, and local governments in the United States amounted to 372 billion dollars, or *32.1 percent of the gross national product.*[15] Changes in the composition of these expenditures can cause large shifts in demand and in the cost of various inputs. For example, the decision to build the interstate highway system had enormous impact upon builders of earth-moving equipment, such as Caterpillar, and upon producers of cement. A future political decision to subsidize large-scale expansion of rapid transit would have similar impact upon a different set of suppliers.

Planning and regulation. So far, the United States has not used public economic planning as much as have France and some other European countries.[16] However, there has been increasing use of such powers as stockpiling of materials for later resale to stabilize prices. Further, the unprecented use of price controls in peacetime, during the period 1971 to this writing, indicates the extent to which governmental regulation of the economy has become accepted, even demanded, by the general public. Antitrust and labor legislation and the manners of their enforcement have important bearings upon the nature and result of business behavior. Consumer and environmental protection legislation also affect business practices and opportunities.

Income redistribution. Programs designed to provide minimum incomes, or even those intended to provide minimum requirements for food and health care, affect private firms on the demand side through consumption changes and on the production cost side through their effects on work attitudes.

International affairs. Governmental policy concerning international trade and finance have tremendous effects upon firms with substantial participation in importing or exporting. Diplomatic recognition of the Federal Republic of China and the opening of trade with the Soviet Union will allow American firms some opportunity to compete for product exporting and importing and raw material purchases in two large economies that have enormous potential for the future. Tariffs, quotas, subsi-

---

[14] Aldous Huxley, *Brave New World* and *Brave New World, Revisited* (Harper Row, 1958).

[15] From preliminary data published in the *Economic Report of the President* (Washington: United States Government Printing Office, 1972).

[16] See Andrew Schonfield, *Modern Capitalism* (New York: Oxford University Press, 1965).

dies, rates of exchange, and loan guarantees are examples of governmental policies and activities that determine the potential for exporting and the intensity of competition from imports.

Demographic trends

Demography is the study of changes in population, its composition by age groups and various other classifications, and the spatial distribution of population groupings. Demography is concerned with changes in such factors as death rates, birth rates, marriage rates, and geographic mobility. Demographic forecasts are helpful in projecting demand for products and availability of labor.

After individuals are born, their progress through the schools and into the labor force can be projected with considerable confidence. For example, the United States currently has over four million people per year who are reaching age 18. These are the babies born after World War II. Their needs for jobs, housing, automobiles, and other durable goods are among the most probable forecasts that can be made in business planning.

Estimates of the numbers of people who will be born in future years are subject to wider errors. "Zero population growth" may or may not become a widely accepted objective; it requires a birth rate of 2.11, and no one knows whether or when this rate will be attained and sustained. A fall in birth rate would be felt by manufacturers of children's clothing and school equipment, by textbook publishers, by teachers, and by educational institutions. Then would come the successive impacts upon producers of teen-age goods, the residential construction industry, and producers of durable goods needed after family formation.

Projected locations of population groups are of much interest in business planning. In any given year, about one fifth of the population moves. In general, the population is becoming increasingly concentrated in large urban areas. It is estimated that by 1980 the 100 largest metropolitan areas will contain 57 percent of the total population and more than 60 percent of the total purchasing power.[17] However, metropolitan areas are growing at different rates and this increases the usefulness of demographic studies in projecting sales by product mixes and markets and in planning plant sizes and locations.

An example of social forecasting: General Electric Company

"If . . . sociopolitical forecasting is done comprehensively and successfully, on both a short- and long-term basis, a business is not so likely to be taken by surprise by shifting public needs, changing aspirations of employees or customers and legislative or administrative action by government." These words are from a sociopolitical forecast originally

---

[17] Kotler, *Marketing Management: Analysis, Planning & Control*, p. 106.

prepared for the General Electric Company.[18] The methodology of this study includes: (1) interviews with more than 60 prominent educators and representatives of business, research administrators, press, and government; (2) a review of a considerable amount of futurist literature; and (3) a synthesis which takes into account at least part of the interactions among the individual ideas and predictions.

The General Electric Study forecast that social change in the United States during the 1970s would result from interaction of eight forces:

Increasing affluence. Real income would double from 1965 to 1980. Increasing percentages of income would be spent on travel, leisure, culture, and self-improvement. The authors forecast developing public impatience with circumstances leading to individual hardships—poverty, unemployment, expenses of sickness and accidents, meager income after retirement, and strikes. Money, they thought, would be more and more taken for granted and less and less useful as a motivator.

Economic stabilization. The authors expected that the swing in unemployment during the 1970s would be kept in the range 3.0–4.5 percent and that recession cutbacks in industrial production would be no greater than 5 percent. The greater stability was expected from more use of contracyclical monetary and fiscal policy and certain structural changes in the economy.

Rising tide of education. The forecasters expected spending on education to increase from about 6 percent of 1970 GNP to about 10 percent of the greater 1980 GNP. Two or three years of college, provided free to the student, would become the norm. Content of education would shift in the direction of preparation to accept change. The better-educated population would become less tolerant of authoritarianism and develop higher expectations of what it wants out of its work experience.

Changing attitudes toward work and leisure. The authors thought the character of work would be changing (from manufacturing to services, from blue-collar to white-collar, from tools to automation) and that the structure of work would also be changing (more work/study programs, more sabbaticals, more part-time work). They suggested the opportunity for an increase in modular work scheduling allowing employees greater flexibility in selecting the number of hours to work.

Growing interdependence of institutions. The United States is becoming a national, rather than a regional, economy and society. Local problems have national importance because of communication that brings them to the attention of people in other places. There is an expansion of the government role and greater meshing of all levels of governmental activity because of the awareness of these problems. At the same time, there is increasing willingness to use private enterprise in solving social

[18] Earl B. Dunckel, William K. Reed, and Ian H. Wilson, *The Business Environment of the Seventies* (New York: McGraw-Hill, 1970).

problems. Traditional boundaries between the public and the private sector are becoming blurred.

Emergence of the postindustrial society.   More and more of GNP will be produced in education, professions such as law and medicine, governments, and nonprofit institutions. With the relative decline in profit-making–consumer-oriented operations, new measures of social output will be needed.

Pluralism and individualism.   There is growing realization that the federal government cannot by itself cope with such problems as poverty and pollution. The authors forecast a strengthening of local and state governments, along with growth of regional authorities to deal with such problems as rapid transit and metropolitan zoning. They thought that social and organizational patterns would be shaped in the 1970s by a wave of individualism that would emphasize equality, personal worth, and the supremacy of individual rights over those of the organization.

The urban-minority problem.   The authors expected urban minorities to press for power over their own services and institutions. Particular targets would be schools, welfare, police and fire services, sanitation, recreation, banks, supermarkets, and lending agencies.

The study goes on to project effects of the above trends upon institutions in the socioeconomic-political system and upon the value system of the population. With respect to the effects upon business, they forecast the following:

1. Increased concern for continuing education and development of employees
2. Increased expectations of safety and other qualities of products
3. Increased insistence that business pay more of the social cost of problems it helps create (pollution, congestion)
4. Increased expectations that business will have long-range goals that are consistent with the national interest
5. Increased opposition to conglomerate forms of business
6. Increased pressure for "consumer protection," extending to packaging and advertising and possibly to quality and utility of products
7. Increased governmental regulation of plant location
8. Increased governmental regulation of hiring, testing, and training, to promote national manpower policies
9. Stricter control of mergers by large companies
10. Increased involvement of private business in the social needs markets, with business and government cooperating in organizational patterns similar to those of National Aeronautics and Space Agency and Atomic Energy Commission
11. Increased use of project task force organization in business
12. Increased participation in effective decision-making in business by professional and technical experts

13. Increasing difficulty in motivating individuals toward organizational goals
14. Increasing emphasis on autonomy, creativity, and inherently gratifying work.[19]

Future social trends will be propelled and formed partially by technological changes. For example, present attitudes toward sexual behavior have been deeply affected by availability of "the pill," which provides effective and inexpensive contraception. On the other hand, many future technological changes will be brought into place in response to changing private and social needs. For example, food needs will likely lead to a technology of ocean farming. Thus, social forecasting and technological forecasting, the subject of the section which follows, are closely related.

TECHNOLOGICAL FORECASTING

Although technological forecasting must have been attempted throughout the industrial era, formal methods of forecasting have been developed only very recently. Most of the techniques have been introduced since the early 1960s. This section describes some ways of forecasting technological change and appraises their present use and limitations.

General approaches to technological forecasting

There are two views of technological change. The *ontological* view sees inventions as coming on the scene independently of external circumstances or needs. The view leads to *exploratory* forecasting, in which one begins with existing technology, projects potential future progress, and then considers how these changes may affect the nontechnical business environment. In other words, exploratory forecasting is started by *mapping technological possibilities out toward their limits.*

The contrasting *teleological* view of technological change sees it as a response to external social forces that create new demands. This view leads to *normative* forecasting in which the forecaster starts by predicting the future needs and objectives of society. He then works back to the current state of technology to *determine the gaps that must be closed to permit meeting social aspirations.*[20]

Normative forecasts have been criticized on the basis that even widely recognized needs do not necessarily call forth an invention, but they extend farther into the future than exploratory methods. On the other hand, exploratory forecasts have been criticized for their refusal to take into account the probable future desires of society, but they are simpler and do focus on technological issues. The most reasonable approach appears

---

[19] Dunckel, Reed, and Wilson, *The Business Environment of the Seventies,* pp. 75–79.

[20] These concepts are taken from Robert V. Ayres, *Technological Forecasting and Long Range Planning* (New York: McGraw-Hill Book Company, 1969).

to be a combination of the two methods.[21] Jantsch says, "A complete technological forecasting exercise . . . always constitutes an interactive process between exploratory and normative forecasts . . . it constitutes a feedback cycle in which both opportunities and objectives are treated as adaptive inputs."[22]

Specific techniques for technological forecasting

The purpose of technological forecasting is not to predict specific forms that technology will take at some exact date in the future. Instead, the primary interest is in determining the probability that selected end results will be achieved and to evaluate their significance. Quinn points out that technology is knowledge systematically applied; this knowledge improves in small increments and what appears to be a "breakthrough" is often simply an accumulation of small advances that add up to a significant change.[23] It should also be kept in mind that there may be several technologies that can accomplish a given mission.

Intuitive forecasting techniques include the Delphi method and scenario writing. *Delphi method* was developed by Olaf Helmer at Rand Corporation.[24] It develops forecasts based on a consensus of experts without permitting personal interactions. "Bandwagon" effects, "halo" effects, and ego involvements with publicly expressed positions are reduced. At the outset, several experts respond to a written questionnaire. Summaries of the forecasts are returned to the experts with a request to modify or defend deviating forecasts. Modifications and defenses are fed back to the panel iteratively until a relative consensus develops or the issues causing disagreement are clearly defined. Figure 10–2 illustrates a Delphi consensus on the timing of selected technological end results.

Scenario writing produces narrative, time-ordered, logical sequences of events. Each such scenario is a description of a possible evolving future environment. Scenarios can be used as inputs to a forecasting technique or as vehicles for communication among forecasters. Scenarios are, strictly speaking, predictions rather than forecasts, since each scenario takes the form, "If (some set of things) then (some other set)." Among the prominent practitioners of scenario writing are Herman Kahn and his associates at Hudson Institute.[25]

---

[21] John P. Dory and Robert J. Lord, "Does TF Really Work?" *Harvard Business Review* (Nov.-Dec., 1970), p. 20.

[22] E. Jantsch, "Technological Forecasting in Corporate Planning" in *Technological Forecasting and Corporate Strategy*, edited by Gordon Wilts, David Ashton, and Bernard Taylor (New York: American Elsevier Publishing Company, 1969), p. 21.

[23] John B. Quinn, "Technological Forecasting," *Harvard Business Review* (March-April, 1967), p. 99.

[24] Olaf Helmer, *Social Technology* (New York: Basic Books, 1966).

[25] Herman Kahn and A. J. Weiner, "The Next Thirty-Three Years: A Framework for Speculation," in *Business Strategy*, edited by H. Igor Ansoff (Middlesex, England: Penguin Books Ltd., 1969), pp. 75–106. Also by the same authors, *The Year 2,000* (New York: McMillan, 1967).

FIGURE 10–2
A DELPHI CONSENSUS OF SCIENTIFIC BREAKTHROUGHS

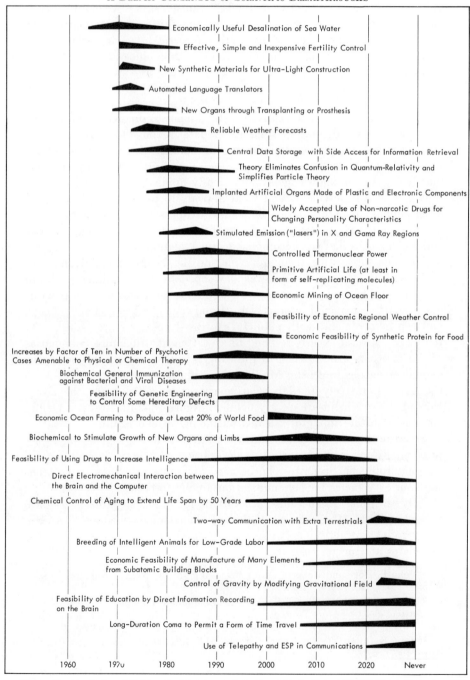

SOURCE: Gordon, R. J. and Helmer, O., *Report on a Long Range Study*, Report P–2982, Rand, September 1964.

More analytical techniques of technological forecasting include morphological analyses, several forms of trend fitting (s-curves, envelope forecasting, correlations), and system approaches. *Morphological analysis* is an attempt at identification and enumeration of all possible means of arriving at a given objective. The analyst tries to find new and feasible methods that do not violate scientific principles. For example, given the objective "propel a vehicle," Ayres enumerates possible energy sources ranging from kinetic to nuclear with numerous intermediate steps in energy conversion.[26] Since the purpose of morphological analysis is to find previously overlooked solutions to problems, it is not, strictly speaking, a forecasting device but rather a method of generating inputs for the forecasting process.

Trend fitting is especially suited to forecasting future capabilities, such as man's ability to transmit information or man's rate of travel. Several kinds of curves may be used; perhaps most common are "s-curves." These show slow growth until the potential of a technology is recognized, rapid growth as this potential is exploited, and then deceleration of growth as the curve approaches a limiting value for the particular technology.

Envelope forecasting is based on a smooth curve drawn tangential to a family of s-curves, as illustrated in Figure 10–3. The implicit assumption of the envelope method is that some new technology will allow the technological trend to continue until some absolute limit, such as speed of sound or speed of light, is approached.

Correlation relates a trend in one technical parameter to a trend or trends in one or more other variables. For example, speed of commercial air transport tends to increase (with a time lag) as speeds of military aircraft are increased, since research and development for the military sector spill over into the design of commercial equipment. Thus, one trend leads and forecasts the other.

Systems analyses put entire operating systems under scrutiny to pinpoint weaknesses in present technology. For example, an analysis of railroad passenger travel revealed, among other problems, that the rail cars weighed 2,000 pounds per passenger and that passengers were uncomfortable in high-speed turns. Existing technology could be used to lighten cars to 600 pounds per passenger and to bank the cars in turns. Another form of systems analysis assumes new technology and asks what would be its affect on present systems. For example, what would be the effect of a time-shared computer system with 200 terminals, 20,000-character program capacity, virtually unlimited memory, and $300 per hour total user cost? Some consequences: small businesses could handle all accounting and tax reporting for $100 per week; all interested students in five

---

[26] Ayres, *Technological Forecasting and Long Range Planning,* pp. 75–77.

FIGURE 10–3
TREND FITTING (S-CURVES)

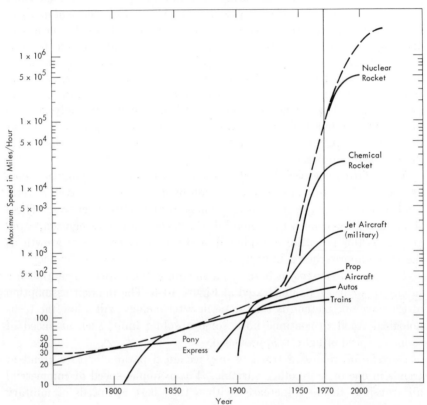

Source: Robert V. Ayres, *Technological Forecasting and Long Range Planning* (New York: Mc-Graw-Hill Book Company, 1969); reprinted in Arthur Gerstenfeld, "Technological Forecasting," *Journal of Business*, 44, No. 1, pp. 10–18.

major institutions could be provided relatively unlimited access to the computer; many present data-processing installations would be obsolete.[27]

Acceptance and some limitations of formal technological forecasting

A survey by Gerstenfeld, summarized in Table 10–2, showed that substantial percentages of firms responding to the questionnaire were using at least one specific method of technological forecasting and that the mean of their forecast horizons was approximately seven years into the future.[28] Although any corporate planner must use some form of tech-

---

[27] Examples are from Quinn, "Technological Strategies for Industrial Companies," p. 94.

[28] Arthur Gerstenfeld, "Technological Forecasting," *Journal of Business* 44, No. 1, pp. 10–18.

nological forecasting, he should avoid engaging in science fiction fantasies that involve technological developments beyond the relevant planning horizon. Furthermore, it should be kept in mind that there are unavoidable pitfalls in forecasting. Quinn lists: (1) unexpected interactions of several coincidental and apparently unrelated advances; (2) unprecedented demands, such as the "need" for atomic energy for military purposes; (3) major discoveries of entirely new phenomena, such as lasers; and (4) inadequate data concerning scientific resources committed to various lines of research and development.[29]

TABLE 10–2

NUMBER OF COMPANIES, BY INDUSTRY, USING TECHNOLOGICAL
FORECASTING, AS RELATED TO GROWTH

Industry (1)	No. of Company Respondents per Industry (2)	Companies Using at Least One Specific Forecasting Method (3)		Industry Growth Rate* (4)	Mean No. of Years into the Future (5)
		No.	% of Industry		
Transportation equipment ...	13	8	(61.5)	5.0	7.15 ($N = 8$)
Chemicals and allied products	27	18	(66.6)	8.3	6.52 ($N = 17$)
Electrical machinery, equipment, and supplies	21	15	(71.5)	6.4	7.75 ($N = 15$)
Fabricated metals	10	7	(70.0)	4.7	5.50 ($N = 7$)
Primary metals	7	1	(14.3)	3.6	5.00 ($N = 1$)
Food and kindred products ..	27	14	(52.0)	3.2	7.15 ($N = 13$)
Paper and allied products ...	8	5	(62.5)	4.9	7.00 ($N = 5$)
Scientific instruments	5	4	(80.0)	5.5	5.25 ($N = 4$)
Machinery, except electrical .	18	11	(61.0)	5.8	7.69 ($N = 11$)
Petroleum refining and related industries	14	7	(50.0)	3.2	10.00 ($N = 7$)
Stone, clay, and glass	4	2	(50.0)	3.5	7.50 ($N = 2$)
Textile mill products	8	3	(37.5)	3.5	5.00 ($N = 3$)
Total	162	95	– –	– –	7.06†($N = 93$)

* 1957–60 to 1960–65 (annual percent). Growth rates based on Federal Reserve Production Indexes for Industries, U.S. Department of Commerce, Bureau of the Census.

† Average years.

SOURCE: Bureau of the Census, U.S. Department of Commerce, *Long-Term Economic Growth* (Washington, D.C.: Government Printing Office, October 1966); reprinted in Arthur Gerstenfeld, "Technological Forecasting," *Journal of Business* 44, No. 1, p. 16.

Technological developments are sensitive to changes in relative prices of natural resources. If some resources begin rising in price because of relative scarcity, a search for *substitutes* and for other methods of reducing requirements for the scarce inputs is set in motion. If other re-

[29] Quinn, "Technological Strategies for Industrial Companies," pp. 101–103.

sources begin to have falling prices because of abundance, a search for *new technological uses* of the plentiful inputs is undertaken. Thus, resource forecasting, the subject of the section to follow, is complementary to technological forecasting.

RESOURCE FORECASTING

In resource forecasting, it is necessary to consider both "needs" and "availabilities" or, in economic terms, "demands" and "supplies." These are the forces that will determine relative prices of inputs and thereby affect choices of production techniques and relative prices of products. For example. costs of many products include substantial proportions of energy. Expected future availability and relative prices of oil, coal, gas, electricity, and nuclear energy at various places will affect choices of plant locations, production techniques, and product mixes.

Only the largest business firms will make original studies of resource prospects, since these investigations are complex and expensive. Most firms will adapt projections from outside sources to fit their own needs and circumstances. This section describes one of the generally available resource forecasts and discusses some considerations in evaluating and adapting the results of the study.

"Resources in America's Future": methods and findings

Resources in America's Future and other publications by the organization called Resources for the Future, Inc., are the products of a large-scale, continuing study of economic growth of the United States with emphasis on the role of natural resources.[30] *Resources in America's Future* contains projections of demand and supply of natural resources to the year 2000 for the United States.

The authors of *Resources in America's Future* emphasize that their numerical results are *projections* rather than forecasts. These projections are based on a set of *assumptions;* most of these are carefully specified. Some of the principal methods are: (1) *trends in consumption are extrapolated* with some modification to reflect informed judgment—these changes usually have the effect of flattening the consumption growth curves; (2) substitutions among materials and more efficient utilization of materials through *expected technological changes were incorporated* if the implications of such changes could be quantified; (3) *sector inter-*

---

[30] Hans H. Landsberg, Leonard L. Fischman, and Joseph L. Fisher, *Resources in America's Future* (Baltimore: Johns Hopkins Press, 1963). Other RFF publications include: Sam H. Schurr, et. al., *Energy in the American Economy 1850–1955;* Marion Clawson, et.al., *Land for the Future;* Harold J. Barnett and Chandler Morse, *Scarcity and Growth: The Economics of Natural Resource Availability;* Harvey S. Perloff, et.al., *Regions, Resources, and Economic Growth.*

relationships, along the lines emphasized in the discussion of input-output, *were taken into account to some extent,* although input-output analysis as such was not used; (4) *three projections were usually made*—these included a probable or medium level plus a low projection and a high projection.

The forecasts were also based on an implicit assumption that the future cultural-political environment would be similar to that of the early 1960s. The book includes virtually no consideration of possible future concerns about pollution. There were explicit assumptions about advances in technology, world trade, and public policy affecting the search for and the use and conservation of natural resources.

The outcome of the study was "the prospect of substained economic growth supported by an adequacy of resource materials." Although no general shortage of materials was expected, some particular resources were projected to become relatively scarce. This would imply relatively higher prices for these resources as the years pass, although the book does not get into the outlook for prices.

Evaluating and adapting resource forecasts

A user of the resource projections in *Resources in America's Future* could begin by examining the explicit and implicit assumptions about future technological change, future world trade conditions, and future social and political trends. His own assumptions might be different and these differences could suggest modifications in the resource forecasts. Note that business planners could be especially interested in forecasts of *changes in relative prices of inputs:* the task of price forecasting is left for the user of the book.

The user of resource forecasts should be conscious of the pitfalls inherent in projections. For example, in 1963, Resources for the Future projected probable use of 19.3 trillion cubic feet of natural gas in 1970 with proved reserves of 301 trillion cubic feet.[31] Industry testimony before a congressional committee in 1972 includes estimates that actual use in 1970 was 21.8 trillion cubic feet (a little under the "high" projection of the RFF study) and that actual 1970 year-end reserves were 260 trillion cubic feet.[32]

Resource forecasting requires consideration of sector interrelationships. To illustrate, as the demand for automobiles increases, demand for steel (thus for ore and heat) will obviously increase. Less obvious, there will be an impact upon demand for power from such sources as hydroelectric generation, coal, or nuclear energy; steel production requires large

---

[31] Landsberg, et. al., *ibid.,* p. 408.

[32] "Natural Gas Policy Issues", *Hearings Before the Committee on Interior and Insular Affairs—U. S. Senate,* 92nd. Congress, 2nd. Session, February 25 and 29 and March 2, 1972.

amounts of power. However, the relative impact of increased demand upon each of the several sources will depend upon their relative prices, and these will be largely determined by other demands for the same resources. Intersector relationships would be of particular interest to most users of resource forecasts, since most firms must look to other sectors for product demands and supplies of inputs.

FORECASTING JOINT AND DERIVED DEMANDS: INPUT-OUTPUT ANALYSIS

Social forecasting is concerned with long-range trends affecting demands for final products and supplies of labor and capital. Technological forecasting focuses on trends and potential breakthroughs in conversion of inputs into products, and upon the technical possibilities for entirely new products. Resource forecasting concentrates upon trends in resource discovery, use, conservation, and scarcity, and upon technical possibilities for resource substitution. All of these forecasts yield projections for broad sectors of the socio-political-economic system. Further work is required to relate changes in the broad sectors to prospects for the smaller aggregations or subsectors that are of interest to particular firms.

Input-output analysis, discussed in some detail in Chapter 4, can be a useful tool in making long-range forecasts for particular subsectors, or industries. This section reviews such an analysis.

"The American Economy to 1975": methods and findings

In 1966, Clopper Almon, Jr. published a forecast titled *The American Economy to 1975* which was derived with the aid of input-output techniques.[33] The approach involved constructing an input-output table for the forecast year. The table was based on projections of labor force size and the composition of final demand in 1975, and upon projected input-output coefficients in 1975. Trends in work habits, consumption, and technology were incorporated in these projections.

By comparing projected industry outputs in 1975 with those estimated for 1963 (the most recent data available at the time of the study) Almon obtained projected growth rates for the various industries. Some of these results are shown in Figure 10–4.

Evaluation and adaptation of input-output forecasting

Estimates of the level and composition of final demand are crucial assumptions in long-range forecasting by the input-output technique. For example, Almon assumed that defense procurement would decline about 1 percent a year from 1963 to 1975. Subsequent involvement of the United

---

[33] Clopper Almon, Jr., *The American Economy to 1975* (New York: Harper and Row, 1966).

FIGURE 10-4

HISTORY AND FORECAST OF INDUSTRY OUTPUTS
(The American economy to 1975; history: 1950–63; forecast: 1964–75)

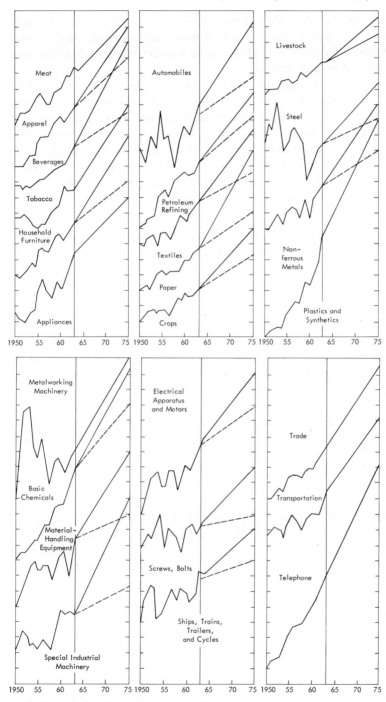

In the vertical scale one division equals 10 percent of 1963 output; dashed line is historical trend; solid line is projection.

SOURCE: Clopper Almon, Jr., *The American Economy to 1975* (New York: Harper and Row, 1966), pp. 10–11.

States in Southeast Asia during the 1965–73 period caused defense procurement to be much greater than Almon had assumed. Assumptions about future technology, including future productivity of labor, are also crucial in input-output analysis.

Input-output technique has the virtues of requiring explicit assumptions and of taking intersector relationships into account in a methodical way. It has the disadvantages that much effort and expense are involved and that final results are still in terms of industry sectors that are usually much larger than the markets and sources of supply of a particular firm. Furthermore, such a forecast may contain little or no regional detail, although individual firms usually need to break down prospects for sales growth into market outlook by areas.

AN EXAMPLE OF STRATEGY FORMULATION: RADIO CORPORATION OF AMERICA

Radio Corporation of America (RCA) began developing electronic data processing equipment for the U. S. Army in the mid-1950s, and was producing a fairly broad line of data equipment that had finally begun producing a profit by 1964. In December 1964 RCA announced a new line of computer equipment—the Spectra 70. The history of this product illustrates one firm's formulation of strategy as it entered and subsequently exited from the computer industry.

The computer industry, dominated by IBM Corporation, is characterized by high technology, capital intensity, extensive user services and technical assistance. There are high risks and long waits for payoffs.[34] RCA's entry into the computer industry was intended to offset declining profits from color television. The specific goal was to capture 10 percent of the market and stand second in the industry after IBM. The Spectra would be compatible with IBM equipment but lower priced, and improved marketing was expected to move RCA into second place.[35]

By 1970, RCA did have 7.5 percent of the market, but the computer line was still losing money. A major defect in RCA's strategy was the failure to anticipate how competitors would react to RCA's marketing tactics. IBM countered with new technological breakthroughs and reduced prices on peripheral equipment just as RCA was increasing prices on similar machinery.

In 1971, RCA reshaped its corporate strategy. Massive investments with long waits for payoff were to be avoided. The computer line was dropped. However, the business base was to be broadened through other

---

[34] William F. Sharpe, *The Economics of Computers* (New York: Columbia University Press, 1969).

[35] Allan T. Demarce, "RCA After the Bath," *Fortune,* September 1972.

avenues of diversification, and research and development were to be brought more closely in line with marketing objectives.

RCA's new strategy was designed to take advantage of its existing strong marketing position in home entertainment products, to smooth the cyclical results of durable goods industries by diversifying into such activities as automobile rentals and frozen foods, and to move with expected major cultural and social changes.

SOME EXAMPLES OF LONG-RANGE FORECASTING FOR NONPROFIT ORGANIZATIONS

This chapter closes with an examination of the ways that various techniques have been used and could be used in appraising the future of a particular "industry," higher education. Although this industry does not have goals identical with private enterprise, it does share the long-run objective of survival.

In the case of the state universities, survival depends upon behavior that is acceptable to the state legislators. The state legislatures are facing many urgent and increasing needs for funds and can be expected to keep a closer and closer watch on university budgets. In particular, they can be expected to pay attention to costs and benefits of the relatively expensive graduate programs. Thus, university administrators need to consider projections of costs of producing Ph.D.s and of prospective demands for these graduates.

Trends in costs of producing Ph.D.s.

Trends from 1956–57 to 1962–63 in costs of educating various categories of students in land grant colleges and universities were studied by Southwick in an article published in 1969.[36] Southwick classified the output of these institutions as undergraduate students, graduate students, and research (measured in dollars). He then estimated the relationships of changes in each of the above outputs to changes in inputs: numbers of administrators, amount of capital, number of librarians, number of senior teaching faculty, number of junior teaching faculty (i.e., teaching assistants) and number of researchers. The general result was a finding that higher education is becoming more labor intensive; no substantial steps are being undertaken to reduce the ratio of teachers, librarians, and administrators to students.

Southwick then examined trends in unit costs of the various inputs and projected these to 1975. Examples: he expected cost per librarian (including acquisitions of materials and cost in materials handling) to

---

[36] Lawrence Southwick, Jr., "Cost Trends in Land Grant Colleges and Universities," *Applied Economics,* 1(3), pp. 167–172.

rise to $54,000; he projected a 1975 cost of $18,200 per member of the senior teaching staff.

The final phase of Southwick's study involved projecting the 1975 unit cost of a year of undergraduate education and a year of graduate education. He did this by multiplying projected required amounts of each input by their unit costs and summing. Results are shown in Table 10–3.

TABLE 10–3

PROJECTED 1975 COSTS PER YEAR OF UNDERGRADUATE AND GRADUATE
EDUCATION IN LAND GRANT COLLEGES AND UNIVERSITIES

	Inputs					
Outputs	*Adminis-tration*	*Capital*	*Library*	*Teaching*	*Research*	*Total*
Per undergraduate	$544	$185	$216	$1,225	$0	$ 2,180
Per graduate	$340	$440	$0	$2,840	$12,500	$16,170

SOURCE: Lawrence Southwick, Jr., "Cost Trends in Land Grant Colleges and Universities," *Applied Economics*, 1 (3) pp. 178–79.

In appraising Southwick's study, two comments are in order. First, although there was no decrease from 1956–57 to 1962–63 in the ratio of 0.09 professional person per undergraduate, there are unexploited technological possibilities in higher education for economic substitution of capital for labor (audiovisual aids, programmed instruction, computer-assisted instruction, etc.). This kind of substitution could be expected to increase if legislatures tightened the appropriations of the universities. Second, graduate education is a joint product; it produces both graduates and completed research. The graduate cannot be produced without research, but research could be produced without the graduates (if it were done by full-time research personnel instead of the students). There is no way to know whether legislatures would want the same amount of research if graduate education were decreased. Assuming that they would, the projected 1975 net cost (to the state governments) of graduate education is $3,670 per year, and assuming that the average Ph.D. requires three years of graduate education beyond the baccalaureate, the projected 1975 cost (to the state) of producing a Ph.D. is about $11,000.

Trends in Demand for Ph.D.s and Output of Ph.D.s

In a study published in 1972, Cartter projected the demand for Ph.D.s and the output of Ph.D.s by years through 1990.[37]

---

[37] Allan M. Cartter, "Faculty Needs and Resources in American Higher Education," *Annals of American Academy of Political and Social Science*, vol. 404 (November, 1972) pp. 71–87.

Demand for Ph.D.s in Academia. Demographic data were used in projecting the demand for Ph.D.s in academic employments. The first step was to project the numbers of persons in the 18 to 21 age group by years (these peak in 1978 and then decline to a 1988 low which is under the 1970 level), the percentages of youths graduating from high school (Cartter assumed an increase from 80 percent in 1972 to 90 percent in 1982), and the percentage of high school graduates entering college (Cartter assumed an increase from 61 percent in 1972 to 70 percent in 1982).

It was necessary to make assumptions about future student/faculty ratios and the future proportions of faculty for which the Ph.D. degree will be required. Cartter assumed a continuation of a 20 to 1 ratio for students to faculty and calculated results for faculty proportions holding the Ph.D. that ranged from the 1972 level of 44 percent to a maximum of 75 percent.

Supply of Ph.D.s. Cartter projected the annual supplies of Ph.D.s as consisting of the initial stock, less retirements and deaths, plus new additions. Because of the rapid buildup of college and university enrollments and faculties in the 1960s, faculty age distributions are heavily weighted in the lower ages. Thus, projected annual depletions due to retirement and death are small percentages of total faculty during the 1970s (about 1.8 percent in 1970, for example).

New additions to the stock of Ph.D.s in future years were hard to project, since some socio-economic forces would support continued increases in annual output (from 29,436 in 1970 to 56,700 in 1985) and others would taper the rate of growth (to a level of 43,000 in 1985). Cartter made projections using both the higher and the lower rates of growth in output.

Cartter's projected annual production of Ph.D.s is compared to his projected annual requirements for new Ph.D.s in Figure 10–5. The rapidly widening gap after 1975 leads to his statement that "after 1975 it seems unlikely, even under the most optimistic assumption of high employment standards, that anywhere close to half of new doctorates will find teaching positions in higher education."[38]

Nonacademic demand for Ph.D.s. Cartter does not make a detailed study of prospective growth in nonacademic demand for holders of the doctorate. However, he cites Department of Labor projections of annual increases in private industry averaging 4.2 percent (or about 1,600 Ph.D.s per year). This rate would absorb only a tiny fraction of the projected excess of output compared to the academic requirements.

Appraisal. In appraising Cartter's study, the relevance of sociopolitical forecasts should be noted. The so-called counterculture, which rejects

---

[38] Cartter, "Faculty Needs and Resources in American Higher Education," p. 82.

FIGURE 10–5

PROJECTED DOCTORATES AWARDED AND NEW COLLEGE TEACHERS REQUIRED

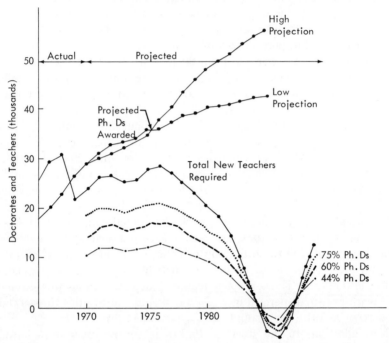

SOURCE: Alan M. Cartter, "Faculty Needs and Resources in American Higher Education," *Annals of American Academy of Political Social Science*, vol. 404 (November, 1972), p. 82.

many values associated with higher education, will decrease the demand for college teachers (to the extent that it grows). Increasing social concerns on the part of young people will also affect the composition of demand for higher education, with greater emphasis on the humanities and social sciences and perhaps less emphasis upon engineering and physical sciences.

Political trends affect the total funding of research and, through this, the demands for college and university faculty members. Similarly, political trends affect composition of this demand, since one administration may emphasize development of advanced hardware for military and space efforts and another may place more priority on solutions of domestic social problems.

Changing relative prestige of occupations, a sociological phenomenon, affects composition of the demand for higher education. For example, if the prestige of businessmen is falling relative to that of governmental employees, there will be some shifting of demand away from business administration courses and into the public administration curriculum.

Input-output techniques could be very helpful in projecting future demand for college and university faculty. Various sectors of the economy require differing compositions of specializations at the baccalaureate level and have differing growth rates. Thus, input-output methods could be used to derive the projected *composition* of the total demand for faculty, by years.

From a larger view, the examples of the Southwick and Cartter studies show that the forecast techniques used in long-range business planning can also be applied in planning for nonprofit organizations.

11 / Capital budgeting

Capital budgeting (capital-expenditure planning) is allocation of capital among alternative investment opportunities. Capital budgeting has profound effects upon the competitive position of the firm, the rewards it can provide, and the managerial responsibilities it imposes. Capital-expenditure planning is regarded as one of the important functions of general management.

The capital budgeting process also requires knowledge, skills, and judgment of people in various functional occupations, such as engineering, production, marketing, personnel, finance, accounting, risk, transportation and real estate. Thus, these specialists should also understand how business investment planning is done. Indeed, anyone intending to make a managerial career in business or in nonprofit organizations needs competence in capital budgeting.

Capital budgeting incorporates many concepts introduced in earlier chapters. Demand, cost, and pricing concepts are essential tools in forecasting investment results. Incremental reasoning is used in separating out projected cash flows that would be associated with each of the various opportunities. Cash flows in various future time periods must be discounted to their present values. Finally, investment in a project is justified only if it provides a return equal to or greater than opportunity cost of the capital.

CENTRAL ROLE OF CORPORATE STRATEGY

Many investment opportunities are uncovered in the ordinary course of business. Needs to replace machinery that is wearing out and to expand departments that are overworked seem obvious and urgent. Numerous suggestions for using capital can be expected to come up from operating levels of the firm. Without deliberate effort, most firms discover more capital expenditure proposals than can be accepted. Indeed, there is usually a backlog of apparently worthy projects.

An entrepreneurial management is not content simply to select among investment proposals arising in the spontaneous manner described above. Instead, it stimulates, directs, and coordinates capital budgeting by formulating an explicit statement of the corporate strategy. Corporate strategy includes delineation of the business(es) in which the firm intends to engage, a statement of its attitudes toward business and financial risks, and a plan for achieving competitive advantages. Strategy is not frozen; as time passes and circumstances change, strategy evolves.

Corporate strategy focuses the search for investment opportunities, coordinates long-range planning of line and staff managers, uncovers opportunities for synergy among future activities of the firm, and concentrates resources into the "critical masses" needed for success in competition. Ansoff has provided a particularly useful framework for strategy formulation along with partial development of a theory embedding capital budgeting in the larger planning process.[1]

At any given time, strategy is management's concept of the best future use(s) of the firm's resources and competences in the light of opportunities and hazards expected to result from general economic, social, and political trends. Strategy delineates the set of "businesses to be in" in terms of various product-market specializations. For each of these, it lists specific objectives by periods out to the planning horizon. The objectives include numbers and kinds of customers, product mix, market share, product development, rate of growth, flexibility of production and marketing posture, level and stability of return on capital, and nature of intended competitive advantages.

Corporate strategy is also an implicit statement of "businesses that the firm will *not* be in." By foregoing allocations of capital and management into projects that are incompatible with strategy, the firm concentrates its capital and know-how into "critical masses." Scale of effort and depth of resources are kept sufficient to carry the firm across the thresholds of business success: it is able to develop products, penetrate markets, endure startup costs, and so forth.

For present purposes, the following relationships of corporate strategy to capital budgeting should be kept in mind:

1. Although many opportunities for investment are uncovered in the ordinary course of business, this spontaneous discovery process has no "sense of direction"; in contrast, corporate strategy stimulates a deliberate search for opportunities and directs the growth of the firm along a desired set of "expansion vectors."

---

[1] H. Igor Ansoff, *Corporate Strategy* (New York: McGraw Hill, 1965).

2. Projects that are clearly not compatible with corporate strategy are rejected, and projects that are clearly essential in implementing the strategy receive priority; decisions about these two groups of projects do not require forecasts of profitability of the individual projects.

3. Many other projects will be proposed that are compatible with strategy but not essential to it; capital budgeting is concerned with choices among projects in this group, and these decisions do require forecasts and discounting of individual project costs and returns.

FORECASTING "CASH FLOW" OF A PROJECT

Incremental revenues and costs are the relevant values in comparing investment proposals. Engineering methods can be used to forecast technical input-output relationships. These estimates can be combined with economic forecasts of input and product prices to obtain expected incremental impacts of the project upon the firm's future expenses and revenues. Careful analysis is needed to overcome effects of arbitrary factors for overhead allocations and historical asset valuations upon the accounting data used in capital-expenditure planning.

It is useful to distinguish between two types of investments. The first type consists of *cost-reducing* projects. An example is replacement of one machine by another more productive machine that decreases required labor. "Cash flow" produced by such a project consists of expected net reductions in operating expenses of future periods.

Another type of investment includes *revenue-increasing* projects. An example is an increase in advertising expected to allow a price increase. "Cash flow" resulting from such a project would be the expected net increases in revenues of future periods. Some projects combine elements of cost reduction and revenue expansion. An example would be simultaneous modernization and expansion of a plant, expected to yield future reductions in unit cost as well as allowing increased rate of output.

Depreciation is *not* subtracted from revenue in estimating cash flow for a project. The objective is to estimate net cash inflow in each period subsequent to the initial outlay at the outset of the project. Note that if a project should provide total cash inflow no greater than total depreciation, we would say that the project provides a return *of* the initial outlay over a period of years, but that it provides no return *on* capital while it is tied up in the project.

A numerical example will help clarify the process of estimating cash flow. Suppose we are considering a labor-saving machine. The machine is priced to us at $23,000 and there will be a $2,000 installation cost; the initial outlay totals $25,000. Suppose the machine will also provide a higher-quality product on which price can be increased, so that annual revenue is expected to increase $1,500. The machine is expected to reduce annual direct labor expenses by $5,500 a year, but maintenance labor expenses will be increased by $500.

Suppose that in its cost accounting the firm normally estimates indirect labor at 30 percent of direct labor and overhead at 110 percent of direct labor. In the case of the new machine, direct labor will be reduced but indirect labor and overhead will not be affected. Therefore, the factors normally used for overhead allocation must be disregarded. Straight-line depreciation on the machine over a five-year period amounts to $5,000 per year. However, depreciation is not a cash expense and will *not* be deducted in projecting pre-tax cash flow.

There are tax considerations. Assume taxes are 50 percent of profits. The new machine will increase profits and thus increase taxes; the increase in taxes must be deducted in determining incremental cash flow. Depreciation *will* be subtracted from pre-tax net cash flow in determining taxable income and the amount of taxes.

Suppose the machine is expected to last for seven years and to have no salvage value. A disposal cost of $1,160 (remove and haul away) is projected. The cash flows of the seven years would be projected as shown in Table 11–1.

The estimated project results are a net post-tax cash inflow of $5,750 in each of the first five years, $3,250 in the sixth, and $2,670 in the seventh

TABLE 11–1

CASH FLOWS FROM HYPOTHETICAL PROJECT

Year 1:

Incremental revenue	$1,500
Net labor savings	5,000
Pre-tax net cash inflow	$6,500
Less: Taxes at 50% ($6,500 − $5,000)	750
Post-tax net cash inflow	$5,750

Years 2, 3, 4, and 5:
Same as Year 1

Year 6:

Incremental revenue	$1,500
Net labor savings	5,000
Pre-tax net cash inflow	$6,500
Less: Taxes at 50% ($6,500)	3,250
Post-tax net cash inflow	$3,250

Year 7:

Incremental revenue	$1,500
Net labor savings	5,000
	$6,500
Less: Disposal cost	1,160
Pre-tax net cash inflow	$5,340
Less: Taxes at 50%	2,670
Post-tax net cash inflow	$2,670

year. Total estimated cash inflow is $34,670, which is more than the initial outlay of $25,000. Clearly, there is some return *on* capital tied up in the project as well as a recovery *of* the entire initial outlay. However, the total cash inflow is not directly comparable with the initial outlay. As they stand, these numbers ignore the time value of money. This must be taken into account to determine whether it is desirable to exchange the initial outlay for the expectation of receiving a larger total amount which will be distributed over a period of seven years.

ALTERNATIVE MEASURES OF PROJECT PROFITABILITY: PROFITABILITY INDEX, INTERNAL RATE OF RETURN, REINVESTMENT-ADJUSTED RATE OF RETURN

Present value of the entire cash flow expected from an investment project can be determined by summing discounted cash flows of the individual periods. Various present values can be calculated for any given cash flow, depending upon the rate used in discounting. Opportunity cost of capital is the appropriate rate, since the objective is to determine whether the project has returns to capital that are equal to or greater than its cost. Cost of capital is discussed later in this chapter.

Discounting cash flows to present value

The formula for determining present value of a stream of cash flow is:

$$V = \frac{R_1}{(1+i)} + \frac{R_2}{(1+i)^2} + \cdots + \frac{R_N}{(1+i)^N} + \frac{S}{(1+i)^N}$$

in which

$V =$ present value
$i =$ interest rate
$R_1, R_2 \ldots R_N =$ after-tax cash flow in years, $1, 2, \ldots N$
$N =$ project duration (conventionally tied to life of asset)
$S =$ salvage value of the asset in year N.

For the illustration given in Table 11–2, computations would be set up as follows assuming a 6 percent rate of interest:

$$V = \frac{\$5,750}{(1.06)} + \frac{\$5,750}{(1.06)^2} + \frac{\$5,750}{(1.06)^3} + \frac{\$5,750}{(1.06)^4} + \frac{\$5,750}{(1.06)^5} + \frac{\$3,250}{(1.06)^6} + \frac{\$2,670}{(1.06)^7}$$

Arithmetic involved in the above calculations is simple in principle but time-consuming.

Use of discount tables. Fortunately, discount tables (present-value tables) can be used to simplify the calculations involved in determining present values. Discount tables are widely available in banks and other lending institutions, and a set of tables is provided in Appendix A at the back of this book.

Refer to the table for 6 percent rate of interest in Appendix A. The cash flow of $5,750 in Year 1 is discounted to its present value by multiplying it by the present-value factor of 0.94340, which is found in Column (1) of the 6 percent discount Table, opposite Period 1. The result, rounded to the nearest dollar, is $5,425.

Results for all seven years are summarized in Table 11–2.

TABLE 11–2

DISCOUNTED CASH FLOWS

(6 percent)

Year	Cash Flow		Factor for Present Value	Present Value
1	$ 5,750	×	.94340	$ 5,424
2	5,750	×	.89000	5,117
3	5,750	×	.83962	4,828
4	5,750	×	.79209	4,555
5	5,750	×	.74726	4,297
6	3,250	×	.70496	2,291
7	2,670	×	.66506	1,776
	$34,670			$28,288

$= 1.13 = PI$

$25,000$

Note that the total present value of the projected cash flows is $28,288, much less than their total of $34,670 before discounting. However, the reduced amount of $28,288 is still greater than the initial outlay of $25,000 (this shows that the project has a return on capital that is greater than the 6 percent value used in discounting in Table 11–2). Thus, the present value of cash flow exceeds initial outlay. There is a *net present value* of $3,288.

Profitability index (PI). A present value greater than initial outlay tells us that a project is profitable if capital can be obtained for the project at the rate used for discounting. The ratio of present value to initial outlay, called *profitability index*, is sometimes used as a measure of relative profitability of projects. For the example in Table 11–2, the profitability index is $28,288/$25,000 or 1.13. The profitability index measures results *per dollar* of initial outlay, which is desirable in comparing projects involving different amounts of initial outlay.

Decomposition of discounted cash flow. Suppose the firm can freely borrow and lend funds at a market rate of 6 percent. If it invests in the project in Table 11–2, the cash flow results can be decomposed as shown in Table 11–3.

Tables 11–2 and 11–3 are both based on *discrete* discounting, rather than continuous. In other words, cash flows of various years are assumed

TABLE 11–3

DECOMPOSITION OF CASH FLOWS

(6 percent)

Year	Project Balance	Cash Flow	Interest at 6 Percent	Partial Return of Capital	New Project Balance
1	$25,000	$5,750	$1,500	$4,250	$20,750
2	20,750	5,750	1,245	4,405	16,245
3	16,245	5,750	975	4,775	11,470
4	11,470	5,750	688	5,062	6,408
5	6,408	5,750	385	5,365	1,043
6	1,043	3,250	63	3,187	−2,144
7	−2,144	2,670	−129	2,799	−4,943

to be received in lump sums at the *end* of these years, rather than as steady streams during the years. During Year 1, there is an amount of $25,000, called the *project balance,* tied up in the project. Cash flow is $5,750; subtracting $1,500 for interest on the project balance at 6 percent leaves $4,250, which can be viewed as a partial return of the initial outlay, or a reduction of the project balance. Thus, the new project balance is $20,750.

By similar reasoning, cash flows of Years 2–6 can be decomposed into interest (return *on* capital) and reductions of project balances (return *of* capital). At the end of Year 6, project balance is — $2,144; this means the project has returned $2,144 over and above the initial outlay in addition to paying 6 percent on the project balance in each period.

In Year 7, the negative project balance is lent out at a rate of 6 percent to yield $129; this "negative interest" is then combined with cash flow produced by the original project to drive the project balance to — $4,943 at the end of Year 7. This projected net *terminal* value of $4,943, discounted at 6 percent, has a net *present* value of $3,287 as viewed from the outset of the project. Thus, we could say that a decision to go into the project increases present value of the firm by $3,287. This amount is (except for rounding error) identical with the "net present value" of $3,288 calculated at the end of the preceding section.

Note that the arithmetic of the net present value method of measuring project profitability implicitly assumes that *negative* project balances are invested (lent) at the interest rate used for discounting. However, the arithmetic of the method does not contain any implicit assumption about the rate of return on reinvestment of cash flows received in periods when the project balance is *zero or above.*

Internal rate of return (IRR).   Let us discount the cash flows of Table 11–1 at a higher rate. This time, we shall use the discount table for 10 percent. The arithmetic can be simplified even further than in the preceding example by using factors that cumulate results over a period of years. Column 3 of the discount table shows that a cash flow of $1 per year for five years has a present value of **$3.7908** at a 10 percent rate of discount. (This is the sum of the first five present value factors in column 1 of the table). Therefore, the present value computations can be simplified as shown in Table 11–4.

TABLE 11–4

DISCOUNTED CASH FLOWS
(10 percent)

Year	Cash Flow		Factor for Present Value	Present Value
1–5	$5,750	×	3.79080	$21,797
6	3,250	×	.56447	1,835
7	2,670	×	.51316	1,370
				$25,002

The total present value of the cash flows is **$25,002**. Except for rounding error, this is just equal to the initial outlay of **$25,000**. There is no net present value. We can conclude that the project has an *internal rate of return* of 10 percent, since net present value is *zero* if the cash flows are discounted at this rate.

In Table 11–5, the cash flows of the preceding example have been separated into annual returns *on* project balances at 10 percent (project balance is initial outlay less cumulative recovery) and partial returns *of* initial outlay.

TABLE 11–5

DECOMPOSITION OF CASH FLOWS
(10 percent)

Year	Project Balance	Cash Flow	Interest at 10 Percent	Partial Return of Initial Outlay	New Project Balance
1	$25,000	$5,750	$2,500	$3,250	$21,750
2	21,750	5,750	2,175	3,575	18,175
3	18,175	5,750	1,818	3,932	14,243
4	14,243	5,750	1,424	4,326	9,917
5	9,917	5,750	992	4,758	5,159
6	5,159	3,250	516	2,734	2,425
7	2,425	2,670	242	2,428	−3

During Year 1, there is a balance of $25,000 tied up in the project. Interest at 10 percent is $2,500; subtracting this interest from the cash flow of

$5,750 leaves $3,250 to be applied toward reduction of the project balance. The project balance for Year 2 is $21,750. Thus, we can think of the cash flow of Year 1 as consisting of $2,500 return on capital tied up in the project during the year plus $3,250 return of a portion of the initial outlay.

Note that the project balance at the end of Year 7 is (except for a small rounding error) zero. The initial outlay has been just recovered, so that the terminal value of the project is zero. The project has provided a 10 percent return on the amount of capital tied up in each period. Thus, the *internal rate of return* for the project is 10 percent; note again that *net present value is brought to zero if the cash flows of a project are discounted at the internal rate of return*. Present value equals initial outlay.

Table 11–5 demonstrates that decomposition of cash flows is very helpful in analyzing the results of a project with cash flow over the project life. The column titled "Partial Return of Initial Outlay" partitions initial outlay into seven parts. The amount of $3,250 at the top of the column stays invested in the project only one year, the amount of $3,575 in the second row is tied up in the project for two years, and so on; the amount of $2,428 at the bottom of the column is the only part of initial outlay that remains invested over the entire seven-year life of the project.

The hypothetical project in Table 11–5 provides an annual return of 10 percent on each of the above amounts, but this rate is earned only for the period that each amount stays invested. Thus, the internal rate of return measure of profitability does not take into account results of reinvestment of cash flow of any periods when project balances are zero or above. (Unusual patterns of cash flow can produce one or more negative project balances during the life of a project; in such cases the arithmetic of the internal rate of return method does require an assumption that *negative* project balances are reinvested to yield the internal rate.)

Compounding cash flows to terminal values

If explicit assumptions about returns from reinvestment of cash flow are made, a third measure of project profitability can be calculated. This measure is based on total terminal value of the project's cash flows compounded to a common time horizon. Cash flow of each period is compounded to the horizon at the expected *marginal rate of return* on capital invested *in that period*. Compounding generates a terminal value for each cash flow and a total terminal value for the project with reinvestment of cash flow.

Reinvestment-adjusted rate of return (RRR). In comparing projects involving different amounts of investment, it is desirable to have a measure of project profitability *per dollar* of investment. Such a measure is easily calculated from terminal value of a project. The ratio of the terminal value to the initial outlay is the factor by which each dollar of initial outlay is increased at the time horizon. An interest rate corresponding to this factor and the number of years involved is easily interpolated from the compound interest tables. This rate is the project's *reinvestment adjusted rate of return.*

The RRR method of measuring project profitability is illustrated in Table 11–6. Terminal values depend on assumed rates of return on reinvested cash flows. The terminal values in Table 11–6 are calculated for the now familiar hypothetical project using constant rates of 6, 8, and 10 percent, respectively, on reinvestment.

TABLE 11–6

TERMINAL VALUES WITH REINVESTMENT AT VARIOUS RATES

| Year | Cash Flow | Terminal Values at End of Year 7 with Reinvestment at Various Rates | | |
		6%	8%	10%
1	$5,750	$ 8,156	$ 9,125	$10,187
2	5,750	7,695	8,448	9,260
3	5,750	7,279	7,823	8,419
4	5,750	6,848	7,243	7,653
5	5,750	6,461	6,707	6,957
6	3,250	3,445	3,510	3,575
7	2,670	2,670	2,670	2,670
		$42,534	$45,526	$48,721
Terminal value/$25,000		1.7014	1.8210	1.9488
Reinvestment—adjusted rate of return		7.9	8.9	10.0

Table p. 618

The column of terminal values with all cash flows reinvested at 6 percent totals $42,534 in Table 11–6. This terminal value corresponds to an initial outlay of $25,000. Each dollar of initial outlay has increased by the ratio $42,534/$25,000, or by a factor of 1.7014. This factor is slightly less than the value of 1.7138 at seven years in column (2) of the 8 percent compound interest table in this book. Therefore, initial outlay is increased at a rate of nearly 8 percent compounded annually. By interpolation, the project's adjusted rate of return with reinvestment of cash flows at 6 percent is found to be close to 7.9 percent.

Flexibility of assumptions about rates of return on reinvested cash flows. Rates of returns on reinvested cash flow can be compounded at rates that vary, period by period, if the analyst wishes. Flexibility of the explicit assumptions about returns on reinvestment of cash flow is an advantage of the RRR method over the PI method under conditions often encountered in capital planning. Returns from marginal opportunities for reinvestment of cash flow may vary from period to period as will be discussed below.

THEORY OF EXPANSION OF THE FIRM

This section provides a theoretical model for determination of composition and amount of the firm's investment. The model is organized around the principle that the firm should increase current investment until the incrementally decreasing rate of return becomes equal to the increasing marginal cost of capital.

The investment opportunities schedule (RRR)

Schedule RRR in Figure 11–1 depicts projects ranked on the basis of their rates of return adjusted for reinvestment of cash flows to a common

FIGURE 11–1
Investment Opportunities Schedule (rrr)

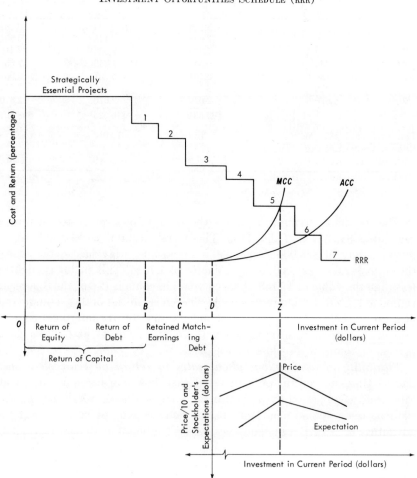

time horizon. Choices of assumed rates of return on reinvested cash flows would affect both the project rankings and the cutoff level of total investment; factors considered in assumptions about rates of return on reinvestment will be discussed below.

Strategically essential projects are placed first in the schedule at an assumed arbitrary rate higher than the return on any of the remaining projects. Thereafter, the strategically compatible but nonessential projects are positioned in order of their RRRs. The resulting *investment opportunities schedule* shows the relation of incrementally decreasing RRR to the amount of investment in the current period.

Marginal cost of capital schedule (MCC)

In the discussion that follows, it is assumed that *management has selected a ratio of debt to equity* that is expected to *minimize the firm's total cost of capital,* and that *this ratio is to be maintained* in the firm's future capital structure.[2] Average cost of capital is a weighted average of the rate of interest on the debt portion and the "stockholder's expectation" on the equity portion. *Stockholder's expectation, E',* is the expected total annual result of holding the stock—the dividend plus the capital gain—expressed as a compounded percentage of the stock's current price.

Increments of capital, in ascending order of *average cost* per unit, are depicted along schedule *ACC* in Figure 11–1. The first increment *OB* is the return of capital portion of the firm's cash flow from existing projects. It is approximately equal to the accounting valuation of depreciation. Return of capital is usually retained for reinvestment, since the firm does not ordinarily use it to repurchase stock or to pay off *permanent debt.* (Permanent debt is maintained in the desired ratio of debt to equity through replacement borrowing—refunding—as principal amounts of old debt come due for payment.)

The second increment *BD* is the sum of retained earnings plus new debt that maintains the desired debt-equity ratio. Retention of earnings would be based on management's belief that the cost of this capital (i.e., opportunity returns to stockholders in alternative investments) is below the rate of return that the firm can earn on internal investment.

Average cost of capital over the range *OD* would likely be approximately constant. An annual increment of capital to the right of point *D* can be obtained through sale of new equity combined with new borrowing that maintains the desired debt-equity ratio. The size of the increment can be varied over a wide range, but average cost per unit will eventually

---

[2] The theoretical relationship of cost of capital to capital structure is a controversial topic. Some of the leading experts in the field of corporation finance have been in disagreement about it. Empirical determination of optimum capital structure appears to be very difficult. Cost of capital may not be very sensitive to *gradual* changes in the debt-equity ratio over a fairly wide range.

be increasing with increases in the increment. The *increase in cost* with *increases in rate of current investment* will reflect *increasing risk premiums* on the part of both the *stockholders* and the *lenders*. Note that if the average cost is rising, *marginal cost* of capital is above average cost and rising more steeply.

Optimum rate of investment

For the time being, assume that the firm expands to the limit of profitability. If the schedule RRR is sufficiently far to the right, the optimum rate of investment will be at a point on the rising portion of the marginal cost of capital curve. This condition is depicted at optimum investment amount Z in Figure 11-1.

A close look at cost of capital. Average and marginal costs of capital are at first elusive concepts; careful study is required to understand them. Increasing average cost per dollar of debt with increases in the firm's current expansion is easy to see—it is the increase in interest rate, reflecting rising risk premiums of lenders. On the other hand, increasing average cost per dollar of equity is a very subtle concept. Consider carefully: increase in average cost of equity can be associated with both increases and decreases in the price at which the firm could sell each new share of common stock. How can this happen?

Note first that the average cost of equity which is relevant to decision making is management's *estimate* of the ratio, E'/P, expressed as percentage (E' is the expected annual dividend plus expected annual capital gain; P is the market price per share). Note second that a rising risk premium on the part of the stockholders, accompanying an increase in the firm's rate of current expansion, takes the form of an increase in the above ratio (through reduction in the price that will be paid for any given E'). E' will tend to be closely associated with expected earnings per share, E, the root source of both dividends and capital gains over the long pull, although there may not be one-to-one correspondence of these values at any given time.

Now refer to the supplementary diagram in the lower right portion of Figure 11-1. Management expects earnings per share to rise as the firm increases current period investment up to the optimum level Z; earnings per share would fall thereafter. In a well-informed market, the stockholders' expectation, E', would also tend to rise to a peak at optimum investment level Z.

Risk discounts of stockholders take the form of reduction in the ratio P/E' (or increase in the ratio E'/P) as depicted in the supplementary diagram. Stock price and the stockholders' expectation both rise to a peak at the optimum investment level and then fall off, but the ratio E'/P steadily increases. This ratio is the cost of equity capital as viewed by management. Thus, cost of equity can rise steadily as potential price per share first increases and then decreases with expansion of planned investment in the current period.

Capital rationing. If management is not willing to sell enough additional equity and engage in enough additional borrowing to carry the current period expansion to the limits of profitability, as described above, the firm is operating in a condition of internal capital rationing. The firm depicted in Figure 11–1 would be in this condition at a level of investment short of amount $Z;$ for example, current period investment might be limited to OD. When a firm is under internal capital rationing, the marginal project undertaken may have a return that is well above marginal cost of market-supplied capital; attention then focuses upon the marginal opportunity rate of return (ORR), the rate of return that could be earned in the best project foregone because of the capital rationing condition.

Marginal rates of return on reinvested cash flow

Figure 11–1 illustrates one of the fundamental ideas in the theory of capital budgeting—the concept of marginal rate of return on reinvested cash flow. For a firm that expands to the limits of profitability, the rate of return on the marginal project is equal to the marginal cost of capital. In this case, cash flow reinvested *at the margin* is simply replacing market-provided capital and thereby providing a return (i.e., a cost reduction) equal to the marginal cost of capital.

The situation is different under capital rationing. In this case cash flow reinvested *at the margin* can earn the marginal opportunity rate of return on capital.

Clearly, the marginal rate of return on reinvested cash flow can vary from period to period. The RRR schedule shifts from period to period, reflecting changes in the firm's opportunities due to shifts in tastes and preferences, changing technology, resource discovery, changes in public policy, changes in income and employment, and so on. The MCC curve moves with changes in supply and demand conditions in capital markets. Because of shifts in the two schedules, the marginal values may shift from period to period. For example, marginal cost of capital may be relatively high at the time capital expenditure planning is being done, although it is expected to move to lower levels in later periods. As another example, management may be operating under internal capital rationing at the time capital expenditure planning is being done, although it expects to escape this condition in subsequent periods.

Of course, it *may* be reasonable to assume that marginal rate of return on reinvested cash flow will be the same in later periods as it is in the period when capital budgeting is being done. Even though such an assumption may often be satisfactory, it is a *special* case; this distinction is important because the assumption that there will be constant future marginal rate of return on reinvested cash flow, and that this rate will be equal to marginal cost of capital in the current period, is implicit in a decision to use present value techniques of capital budgeting. For this reason, present value techniques are not theoretically correct in the *general* case. This point is clarified below.

CAPITAL BUDGETING

This section discusses techniques for determining project composition and total value of the firm's investment portfolio in the current period. The fundamental concept of project profitability at the margin of the portfolio is discussed first. Then comes an examination of the general case of capital budgeting in which decisions are based on reinvestment-adjusted rates of return (RRR). The special (but perhaps quite common) case in which decisions can be based on net present values and profitability indices (PI) is taken up next. Brief attention is given to the unsatisfactory ranking technique based on internal rates of return (IRR). Use of incremental analysis in choosing between mutually exclusive projects is discussed. The section concludes with a critique of the payback period technique.

Project profitability at the margin of the portfolio

Figure 11–1 is again useful. Current period investment cutoff is determined at the point where the schedule of investment opportunities (RRR) intersects the marginal cost of capital function (MCC). Consider the marginal project (Project 5 in Figure 11–1). This project is marginal in the light of the *combined result* of its internal rate of return and the return on reinvested cash flow; its marginal character is based on terminal value at the planning horizon with all cash flow assumed to be reinvested *at the margin of the portfolio in each future period*. In other words, reinvestment in future periods is at the assumed opportunity rates of return, which will equal marginal costs of capital if the firm expands to the limits of profitability.

Since it cannot be known at the outset of the capital budgeting process which of the projects will eventually be marginal in the current period portfolio, it is necessary to rank the projects by a rate of return criterion that is based on the assumption that the cash flow of *each* project to be ranked will be reinvested *at the margin* of the portfolios of future periods.

Project ranking using RRR

The method of calculating RRR has been explained. The RRR criterion requires explicit assumptions about rates of return at the margin of the portfolio in each future period. Although future rates of return are forecasts that most managers will consider difficult, there is no method of capital budgeting in which these assumptions about return on reinvestment can be avoided. In the RRR method, it is possible to assume that marginal rates vary from period to period.

The RRR method of project ranking correctly compares projects of varying lengths because it is based on their terminal values at a common horizon, and it correctly compares projects of varying sizes because it is an annual rate per dollar of investment.

After RRRs are calculated for each of the projects, the projects can be arranged to produce schedule RRR and the cutoff for the current period can be determined by comparing schedule RRR with the estimated marginal cost of capital schedule. Note that terminal values of each of the projects as calculated for project rankings are based on the assumption of cash flow reinvestment at the margin of future period portfolios; *since most of the cash flow will actually be reinvested at better rates than are found at the margin, the expected terminal value of the entire current period investment portfolio is greater than the sum of the terminal values as calculated for project ranking.*

Project ranking using PI

The method of calculating the profitability index (PI) has been explained; it is the ratio of present value of future cash flows to the initial outlay for the project. If the current level of cost of capital is viewed as "normal" and there is no reason to believe it will be different in future periods, and if the current RRR schedule is also viewed as "normal" (i.e., there is neither a dearth nor a surfeit of profitable projects), the analyst may be willing to assume that investment portfolios of future periods will have a constant marginal rate of return equal to the current marginal opportunity rate and the current marginal cost of capital. This is the special case in which PI is a satisfactory technique for project ranking because the effect of reinvestment of cash flow can be disregarded (compounding forward to a terminal value at some rate of increase and then discounting back to present value at that same rate does not change present value or the value of the PI criterion; therefore, this step can be bypassed).

Clearly, a decision to use the PI criterion for project ranking implies acceptance of the assumption of constant future marginal rates of return on reinvested cash flows at a level equal to current marginal cost of capital. The first part of this chapter demonstrates that the assumption is implicit in the decision to use this criterion; it is not generally implicit in the arithmetic of calculating present value (although there is in the arithmetic such an assumption with respect to reinvestment of negative project balances). The present value-profitability index technique is recommended by much of the finance literature and appears to be widely used in actual practice.

A critique of IRR

Calculation of internal rate of return (IRR) has been explained. It is that rate of discount which makes present value of cash flows equal to initial outlay. The concept of IRR is quite useful for certain purposes in economic theory, but it is not satisfactory for project ranking in capital budgeting. It does not take results of reinvestment of cash flow into account (with the exception of the assumption, implicit in the arithmetic, that negative project balances are reinvested at the project's internal rate). Thus, it cannot provide proper comparisons of projects with unequal durations and/or dissimilar patterns of cash flow.

Choosing among mutually exclusive projects

It is sometimes necessary to choose between mutually exclusive projects, where a project involving a greater amount of initial outlay has a somewhat lower rate of return. For example, it may be necessary to make a choice between two ways of doing the same job, where one of the alterna-

TABLE 11–7
INCREMENTAL ANALYSIS OF MUTUALLY EXCLUSIVE PROJECTS

	Project A		Project B	Project B-A	
Year	Cash Flow	Terminal Value	Cash Flow	Incremental Cash Flow	Terminal Value
1	$ 5,750	$12,326 (10%)	$ 2,000	$—3,750	$—8,038 (10%)
2	5,750	9,854 (8%)	4,000	—1,750	—2,999 (8%)
3	5,750	8,156 (6%)	12,000	6,250	8,865 (6%)
4	5,750	7,695 (6%)	16,000	10,250	13,716 (6%)
5	5,750	7,259 (6%)	14,000	8,250	10,415 (6%)
6	3,250	3,871 (6%)	12,000	8,750	10,421 (6%)
7	2,670	3,000 (6%)	10,000	7,330	8,236 (6%)
8	——	——	8,000	8,000	8,480 (6%)
9	——	——	3,000	3,000	3,000 (6%)
Total Terminal Value		$52,161			$ 52,096
Initial outlay		25,000	$55,000		30,000
TV/IO		2.0864			1.7365
RRR		8.5%			6.3%

tives involves more investment, has a different expected life, and has a dissimilar cash flow. The appropriate analysis is based on *incremental differences in cash flows* and views these as a result of the *incremental difference in initial outlay.*

Table 11–7 shows how to carry out an incremental analysis for two hypothetical mutually exclusive projects. Project A is already familiar to the reader; Project B is larger, has a longer life, and a different pattern of cash flows. Project B-A is the incremental initial outlay, resulting in incremental cash flows. Cash flows for Project A and the incremental cash flows for Project B-A are compounded to terminal values assuming that the marginal opportunity returns on reinvestment are 10 percent for the first period cash flow, 8 percent for the second period cash flow, and a uniform 6 percent for cash flow of all subsequent periods. The reinvestment adjusted rate of return for Project A is 8.2 percent and that for Project B-A is 6.2 percent. If the latter value of 6.2 percent is above the cutoff for the current period portfolio, Project B (equivalent to Project A *plus* Project B-A) should be selected rather than Project A.

If there are numerous mutually exclusive or interdependent projects, the mathematical programming approach to capital budgeting may be required. This topic is beyond the scope of the present book. A primary reference on the topic is a book by Weingartner.[3]

Critique of payback period

A technique of project evaluation known as payback period is often encountered in business practice. Payback period is the number of years required to recover initial outlay from cash flow. Payback period gives no consideration to cash flows beyond the recovery point, to the pattern of cash flow during the payback period, nor to results of cash flow reinvestment. Although the use of payback period has sometimes been defended on the basis that there is greater uncertainty about cash flows of more distant years, it discounts the future excessively by implicitly assigning zero probability to projected cash flows beyond the recovery point. Because of its shortcomings, it is losing ground to the techniques described earlier in this chapter.

Adjustments for risk and uncertainty

To this point, the discussion of capital budgeting has treated the cash flows of projects as if they were certain. However, each projected cash flow is actually the *mean* of the *expected values* in a *subjective probability distribution*. If these subjective distributions take the *normal* form, variability of project results can be quantified by calculating *coefficients of variation,* where each such coefficient is the *ratio* of the *standard deviation* of expected cash flows to the *mean* of these expectations. The greater the coefficient of variation, the greater the riskiness of the project.

The possibility *of differences in riskiness* among projects must now be dealt with. An example of a comparison of project variability is shown in Figure 11–2, in which two projects have the same means of the probability distributions of expected terminal values, but the distribution of expected results for Project B has a larger standard deviation than that of Project A. Since most stockholders are risk averse (i.e., prefer less risk to more risk, other things being equal), management should choose Project A over

---

[3] H. Martin Weingartner, *Mathematical Programming and the Analysis of Capital Budgeting Problems* (Englewood Cliffs, N.J.: Prentice Hall, 1963).

Project B if the two projects require the same initial outlay. Furthermore, it is possible that management should prefer Project A even if it involves *greater* initial outlay. In this example, it is easy to see that some kind of *risk adjustment* is being made in comparing the results of Project B with those of Project A.

FIGURE 11–2
COMPARISON OF PROJECT VARIABILITY

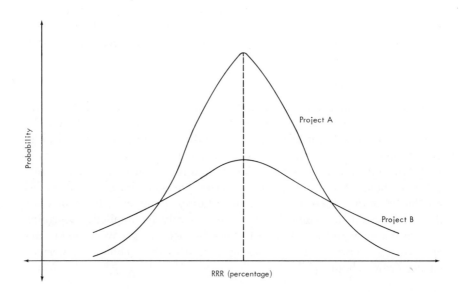

Adjustments needed in comparing projects of varying riskiness can take either of two forms. One approach consists of *lump sum adjustments in the expected terminal values* of higher-risk projects. The calculated reinvestment adjusted rates of return for the projects are thereby reduced and their relative rankings in the schedule of investment opportunities are changed accordingly. The second approach consists of *direct adjustments of the calculated rates of return;* rates of return are reduced on higher-risk projects. The approach of lump sum adjustment can also be applied to cash flows period by period; in this case, it provides clean analytic separation of effect of risk from the effect of time value of money, since the adjustment for risk can be varied over time in any desired manner. On the other hand, the approach of directly adjusting calculated rates of return implicitly assumes that risk will increase with time at a constant rate.[4]

---

[4] A. A. Robichek and S. C. Myers, "Conceptual Problems in the Use of Risk-Adjusted Discount Rates," *Journal of Finance,* 21 (December 1966), pp. 727–30.

Most managers find it easier to use the approach of direct adjustments in rates of return. It has the advantages that the managers are already accustomed to thinking in terms of rates of return and that the risk adjustment can be related to differences in money market rates of return for securities with varying degrees of risk.

The objective is to adjust for differences in riskiness of projects under consideration by the individual firm. Some companies establish classes of risk, such as high, medium, and low; there may be a need for additional categories of "extremely high" risk and "extremely low" risk. The premiums or discounts to be used in adjusting projects for differences in their class of risk can be developed by consensus and stated as policy of the company. If this is done, the handling of risk is reduced to determination of the risk class to which each project will be assigned.

Risk classification is usually intuitive but the process can be assisted by *sensitivity analysis* using optimistic, best, and pessimistic estimates of such planning data as equipment life, input and product prices, and rates of output. It is possible to develop probability distributions of project outcomes by *simulation* if the various planning data listed above are represented as probability distributions.[5]

EMPIRICAL STUDIES

Do firms actually use the capital-budgeting techniques discussed in this chapter? The answer is that few small firms use them but that these techniques are now widely used in larger firms. A 1963 study covering approximately 60 small firms uncovered no instances of the use of present-value or discounted-rate-of-return formulations, and only one manager who was even aware of such methods.[6] On the other hand, a 1960 study of 127 "well-managed" firms showed that 38 of these used discounted cash flow in making investment decisions.[7]

A 1970 study of 369 larger firms (each making at least $1 million of investment annually) showed that 57 percent of the firms were making some uses of discounted cash flow techniques in 1970, whereas only 38 percent had used these in 1964 and only 19 percent had used them in 1959.[8]

---

[5] David B. Hertz, "Risk Analysis in Capital Investment," *Harvard Business Review* January–February, 1964), pp. 94–106.

[6] Martin B. Solomon, Jr., *Investment Decisions in Small Business: Theory and Practice* (Lexington: University of Kentucky Press, 1963).

[7] James H. Miller, "A Glimpse at Practice in Calculating and Using Return on Investment," *N. A. A. Bulletin,* June 1960.

[8] Thomas Klammer, "Empirical Evidence of the Adoption of Sophisticated Capital Budgeting Techniques," *Journal of Business,* 45 (July, 1972), pp. 387–97.

PROBLEMS FOR CHAPTER 11

1. What is the discount factor for each of the following:
   a. A sum due in 1 year discounted at 6 percent? At 10 percent?
   b. A sum due in 2 years discounted at 6 percent? At 10 percent?
   c. A sum due in 5 years discounted at 6 percent? At 10 percent?
   d. A sum due in 10 years discounted at 6 percent? At 10 percent?
   e. A sum due in 30 years discounted at 6 percent? At 10 percent?

2. What are the total amount and the present value of each of the following:
   a. $100 per year for 10 years, discounted at 10 percent, with each annual amount being received at the end of the year?
   b. $100 per year for 10 years, discounted at 10 percent, with each annual amount being received as a continuous flow during the year?
   c. $100 per year for 20 years, discounted at 10 percent, with each annual amount being received at the end of the year?
   d. $100 per year for 20 years, discounted at 10 percent, with each annual amount being received as a continuous flow during the year?
   e. $100 per year for 30 years, discounted at 10 percent, with each annual amount being received as a continuous flow during the year?

3. What is the compounding factor for each of the following:
   a. A sum invested for 5 years at a rate of 6 percent? At 10 percent?
   b. A sum invested for 10 years at a rate of 6 percent? At 10 percent?
   c. A sum invested for 30 years at a rate of 6 percent? At 10 percent?

4. What are the total amount and the terminal value of each of the following:
   a. $100 per year for 10 years, compounded at 10 percent, with each annual amount being received at the end of the year?
   b. $100 per year for 10 years, compounded at 10 percent, with each annual amount being received as a continuous flow during the year?
   c. $100 per year for 20 years, compounded at 10 percent, with each annual amount being received at the end of the year?
   d. $100 per year for 20 years, compounded at 10 percent, with each annual amount being received as a continuous flow during the year?

5. An amount of $1,000 was invested for 7 years and accumulated to a terminal value of $2,000. What was the compound annual rate of return? Use interpolation to get the approximate rate.

6. A project that requires an initial outlay of $50,000 is expected to produce the following cash flows (received at the end of each year):

Year	Cash Flow
1	$11,500
2	11,500
3	11,500
4	11,500
5	11,500
6	6,500
7	5,340

Determine the present value of the cash flows discounted at 8 percent. Determine the net present value. Calculate the profitability index.

7. Decompose the cash flows of the above project, using an 8 percent rate. (Table 11–3 is the desired format.)

   Determine the net terminal value of the project.

   Determine the net present value of the project by discounting the net terminal value at 8 percent. Compare this net present value with that determined in Problem 6.

8. Decompose the cash flows in Problem 6 using a 10-percent rate. What is your conclusion?

9. Determine terminal value of the project in Problem 6, assuming that cash flow will be reinvested in year 1 at 10 percent, in year 2 at 8 percent, and in the remaining years at 6 percent; use a planning horizon ten years out. Calculate the reinvestment-adjusted rate of return (RRR).

Cases for part five

The cases in this section focus attention on long-range forecasting and capital budgeting. Analysis of actual capital investment problems provides insights which no text discussion can provide. In the abstract it is easy to determine the appropriate type of analysis; in practice one must compromise with theory to make it applicable to the complexities and uncertainties of reality; one frequently does not have all the data he needs.

Topics covered by the cases in this section range from relatively simple problems such as the determination of the present value of an income stream to a very complicated case involving a new type of business which involves long-range forecasting and capital budgeting in a relatively uncertain environment. Other cases involve determining such things as a fair rate of return, the cost of capital, and accounting and economic profit.

WALDO, SMITH, AND MAXEY

Fred Waldo, John Smith, and Thomas Maxey were partners in a sign business. Each had other business interests; the sign firm was a sideline for all of them. After they returned from the Armed Forces in 1946, they started buying up small sign companies in towns of populations under 15,000. This venture had proved highly successful, as shown in Exhibit 1. A comparison of Exhibits 1 and 2 indicates an extremely high return on the original investment (most of the capital consisted of plowed-back earnings). Exhibits 3 and 4 provide additional information on company operations.

In 1959 and 1960 several major decisions were required of the partners. One concerned the purchase of additional sign companies located in several towns scattered in nearby states. The partners knew that such com-

EXHIBIT 1

COMPARATIVE STATEMENT OF INCOME AND EXPENSE
(years ended December 31, 1954 through 1959)

	Dec. 31, 1959	Dec. 31, 1958	Dec. 31, 1957	Dec. 31, 1956	Dec. 31, 1955
Income					
Gross sales	$109,790	$114,163	$104,212	$79,124	$68,675
Other income	3,068	742	340	0	1,139
Capital gains	396	5,046	2,210	658	0
Total income	$113,254	$119,951	$106,762	$79,782	$69,814
Operating Expenses					
Cost of material	$ 4,385	$ 2,698	$ 4,264	$ 4,066	$ 4,329
Wages and salaries	20,043	25,698	19,878	13,467	12,142
Agency commissions	12,830	13,591	11,060	10,106	9,042
Transportation expenses	4,823	5,050	5,433	4,059	3,806
Insurance	7,049	1,719	1,306	915	934
Depreciation	13,237	14,223	10,148	8,309	7,920
Rent	6,240	4,894	4,509	2,827	2,268
Office supplies	2,338	2,066	918	834	849
Maintenance	1,442	2,116	2,429	1,919	1,890
Taxes and licenses	2,960	2,275	1,814	1,202	901
Professional services	366	6,123	804	200	249
Travel expenses	346	303	6,316	3,036	2,546
Other expenses	8,360	13,446	12,093	6,532	2,893
Total material cost and expense	$84,419	$94,202	$80,972	$57,472	$49,769
Net profit before manager's salary	28,835	25,749	25,790	22,310	20,045
Manager's salary	4,800	4,800	4,213	4,160	4,160
Net profit	$24,035	$20,949	$21,577	$18,150	$15,885

panies were available at prices of from five to six times earnings. On the basis of past experience the partners had established a rule of thumb that they would not pay more than five times earnings. They had never paid more than this amount in the past.

The partners knew of one small company which was available at a price of five times earnings. The company had allowed its equipment to run down, so that considerable repairs might be necessary. Mr. Waldo believed that the profits could be increased by raising rentals from the existing level by 20 percent immediately and by another 20 percent at a later date. For example, the company might raise the rate on a medium-size sign from $10 per month to $12 per month and eventually to $15 per month. The firm's experience in the past was that improved service would permit increased rates.

In establishing rates the company was influenced somewhat by the rates in other small towns. The prevailing rate on the size sign already

EXHIBIT 2

BALANCE SHEETS, 1955–59
(March 31)

	1959	1958	1957	1956	1955
ASSETS					
Cash	$ 4,756	$ 4,630	$ 2,182	$ 3,337	$ 1,626
Accounts receivable	11,384	8,446	12,366	6,150	7,419
Notes receivable	824	0	0	0	0
Inventories	2,450	2,711	3,349	3,359	2,698
Total current assets	$19,414	$15,787	$ 17,897	$12,846	$11,743
Fixed assets	77,819	77,546	88,334	45,854	43,084
Other assets	1,333	1,995	1,748	1,257	477
Total Assets	$98,566	$95,328	$107,978	$59,957	$55,304
LIABILITIES AND CAPITAL					
Current liabilities					
Notes payable	$14,293	$14,088	$ 20,800	$ 5,000	$10,000
Accounts payable	2,718	3,382	3,730	1,692	474
Accrued expenses	780	989	1,162	178	142
Federal tax withheld	311	311	264	130	154
Other	45	21	827	12	155
Total current liabilities	$18,147	$18,791	$ 26,777	$ 7,012	$10,925
Long-term notes	4,400	8,800	17,688	0	0
Total liabilities	$22,547	$27,591	$ 44,465	$ 7,012	$10,925
Capital					
Mr. Maxey	$25,340	$22,579	$ 21,171	$17,648	$14,793
Mr. Waldo	25,339	22,579	21,171	17,648	14,793
Mr. Smith	25,339	22,579	21,171	17,648	14,793
Total capital	$76,018	$67,737	$ 63,514	$52,945	$44,378
Total Liabilities and Capital	$98,566	$95,328	$107,978	$59,957	$55,304

discussed was $15 per panel, though some rates went as low as $12. Rates were almost double in cities of 50,000 population or above.

Before purchasing a new sign company, the partners did research into its potential volume and costs. Outside organizations supplied traffic data which could be used to establish average daily circulation. It was necessary to obtain cost and profit data from the potential seller or from an analysis of Waldo, Smith, and Maxey's own experience.

Mr. Waldo expressed the view that six times earnings was too much to pay for sign companies in small towns. He knew of some companies that might be available at that price but wasn't much interested in following up on such opportunities.

In 1960 another issue arose. Mr. Maxey wished to sell his interest in the firm to the other partners. The partners wished to set a price that was fair and that recognized Mr. Maxey's one-third financial contribution to the firm.

EXHIBIT 3

ADDITIONS TO FIXED ASSETS

	1958–59	1957–58	1956–57	1955–56
Land	$ 0	$ 0	$ 3,800	$ 0
Signs	12,800	10,860	48,608	9,770
Trucks	902	820	1,720	1,142
Buildings	0	101	142	214
Machinery	356	0	1,039	302
Office equipment	97	337	558	118
Total Additions	$14,154	$12,118	$55,867	$11,546

EXHIBIT 4

FIXED ASSETS AND RESERVES FOR DEPRECIATION

	Balance 4–1–58	Additions	Retirements	Balance 3–31–59
Assets:				
Land	$ 6,193	$ 0	$ 0	$ 6,193
Signs	104,182	12,800	10,148	106,834
Autos and trucks	8,281	902	2,400	6,783
Buildings	8,316	0	0	8,316
Machinery and equipment	2,338	356	0	2,694
Office equipment	2,155	97	62	2,190
Totals	$131,465	$14,155	$12,610	$133,010
Reserves for Depreciation:				
Signs	$43,274	$11,273	$ 9,620	$44,926
Autos and trucks	6,149	713	2,300	4,563
Buildings	2,023	438	0	2,461
Machinery and equipment	1,325	538	0	1,863
Office equipment	1,148	274	46	1,376
Totals	$53,919	$13,236	$11,966	$55,189

1. Is the rule of buying companies at five times earnings but not as six times earnings a reasonable one? Discuss.
2. The partners were able to borrow large sums of money for new ventures at 6 percent. Assuming this to be the cost of capital and assuming a 15-year life of a sign business beyond the time of the case, estimate the present value of the Waldo, Smith, and Maxey firm. Compare this value with a price of five times earnings.
3. The partners had access to investment opportunities which in recent years had returned more than 20 percent profit (before taxes). Assuming the opportunity cost of capital to be 20 percent, estimate the present value of the firm. Compare this value with a price of five times earnings.
4. Which cost of capital estimate (6 percent or 20 percent) is appropriate? Discuss.
5. Discuss the way in which you handled depreciation in your computation.

6. *Should Waldo, Smith, and Maxey buy the small sign company mentioned in the case? Discuss.*
7. *What would be a fair price to pay Mr. Maxey for his one-third interest in the company?*

AVELLA, INC.*

Avella, Inc. was a well-established company engaged in the manufacture of various rubber and plastic goods. The products were generally inexpensive, and a high volume of sales had to be maintained to enable the company to recover its fixed costs. The management consciously avoided taking on any products which could be characterized as novelties or fads likely to have a relatively brief period of prosperity. Avella had been fortunate in maintaining a stable pattern of sales over the years and had developed a strong customer loyalty. The company had gained a reputation through its production of a relatively complete line of quality products. There was some competition from the producers of specialties, but no other business in the industry offered competition with such a complete line.

Mr. Edgar A. Gordon, who had recently retired as chairman of the board, was firmly convinced that the company should maintain a strong working capital position and finance its resources primarily with equity capital. This policy, he believed, would place the company in a favorable position to exploit opportunities when they arose and would have the further advantage of providing protection during prolonged periods of general economic decline.

This policy was being carefully reviewed. Many of the officers and directors believed that a restrictive cash policy had checked the growth of the company and had resulted in the loss of many favorable opportunities for profitable investment. There was no desire, however, to make rapid changes. The position of the firm and its policies and procedures were being currently examined.

The company had maintained a minimum cash balance of approximately $1,500,000 at all times. Throughout the year, cash needs were carefully budgeted and plotted on a broken-line graph as shown in Exhibit 1.

Any cash flow in excess of what was required in order to finance current operations was invested in short-term government securities. This investment was adjusted up or down according to the seasonal

---

*This case was prepared by Professor Carl L. Moore of Lehigh University as a basis for class discussion. This case is not designed to present illustrations of either correct or incorrect handling of administrative decisions. Copyright 1959 by Carl L. Moore.

EXHIBIT 1

Cash Position Budget (as of September 20)

———————— Actual Cash and Securities
-------- Budgeted Cash and Securities
///////// Investment in Short-Term Government Securities

needs for cash. Careful budgeting had resulted in stabilizing the cash balance at about the desired level.

During 19—, Avella, Inc., increased its working capital by $1,310,000.

Source of net working capital
Net income before depreciation charges of $1,302,994 .... $3,510,050
Uses of net working capital
Dividend payments $1,250,100
Fixed asset additions 959,950
Total $2,200,050
Net increase in working capital $1,310,000

The statement of financial position at December 31, 19—, and the condensed operating statement for the year 19—, as given in Exhibit 2, were considered by the controller to be typical. The gross cost of the plant and equipment at the end of the fiscal year was $24,362,130. After deducting the accumulated depreciation of $16,740,630, there was a remaining net book value of $7,621,500.

The controller of the company, Mr. Charles A. Penberthy, was in the process of reviewing the way in which business investment opportunities were evaluated to determine their economic feasibility. Mr. Penberthy was well acquainted with the various activities of the company through his long years of service in production, sales, and financial administration.

Investment proposals were initiated by a new products committee which worked closely with the director of research. Possible projects were carefully screened as to market potential, their relationship to existing product lines, and production possibilities. The controller and his staff assisted in this screening process. As a general rule, a project

EXHIBIT 2

STATEMENT OF FINANCIAL POSITION
(December 31, 19—)

Current assets
Cash	$ 1,707,269
U.S. government securities at cost including accrued interest	3,111,398
Accounts receivable	7,818,592
Inventories	8,616,133
Prepaid expenses	309,380
Total current assets	$21,562,772

Current liabilities
Accounts payable	$ 1,141,834
Accrued taxes, wages, and miscellaneous expenses	1,788,636
Estimated federal income tax liability less U.S. Treasury notes of $1,080,000	183,301
Total current liabilities	$ 3,113,771

Net working capital	$18,449,001

Other assets
Miscellaneous investments	$ 590,417
Real estate, machinery, and equipment at cost less depreciation	8,420,152
Net assets	$27,459,570

Capital
Common stock	$ 7,413,480
Capital in excess of par value	2,527,242
Reinvested earnings	17,518,848
	$27,459,570

STATEMENT OF EARNINGS
(for the year ended December 31, 19—)

Sales and other income	$48,654,260

Cost and expenses
Cost of products sold	$30,232,458
Selling, administrative and general expenses	13,535,720
Federal income tax, estimated	2,479,017
Total costs and expenses	$46,447,204
Net earnings	$ 2,207,056

was not accepted unless analysis revealed that the project would probably yield a rate of return upon investment of at least 30 percent before taxes. The 30 percent rate of return had been established as a guide on the basis that the company had been earning approximately that rate on its investment in machinery and equipment over the years. For example, the company earned $4,686,073 before taxes during 19—. The total cost of the machinery and equipment (without allowance for depreciation) at the end of the year was $15,654,257. Relatively insignificant acquisitions or replacements and obvious cost saving possibilities did not go through such a rigorous screening process.

After the project had been accepted by the new products committee, it was reviewed by the marketing committee of the board of directors.

$$\frac{\text{Net dollar advantage before taxes}}{\text{Average annual investment}} = \text{Rate of return}$$

Both the net additional revenue and the direct cost savings to be derived from the project were considered in arriving at the net dollar advantage before taxes. The net additional revenue was the gross revenue anticipated from the project as reduced by the cost of goods sold and estimated selling and administrative expenses. The cost of goods sold was computed in the conventional manner, including the cost of direct materials, direct labor, and manufacturing overhead. Manufacturing overhead, including depreciation, was applied to the products on a predetermined rate basis as a percentage of direct labor cost. An allowance of 17 percent of the estimated gross revenue was deducted for selling and administrative expenses. This percentage had been established from past experience studies which showed that the selling and administrative expenses which should be identified with a product were approximately 17 percent of sales. Finally, depreciation computed on a straight-line basis on the facility cost and on what was called the capital corollary was deducted to arrive at the net dollar advantage before taxes.

NET DOLLAR ADVANTAGES BEFORE TAXES

1. Direct cost savings before depreciation .... $
2. Increased revenue
   Sales .... $
   Cost of goods sold .... _____
   Gross profit .... $
   17 percent allowance for selling and administrative expenses _____
   Net revenue addition .... _____
3. Gross dollar advantage [(1) + (2)] .... $
4. Less depreciation of facility cost and capital corollary .... _____
5. Net dollar advantage before taxes [(3) − (4)] .... $

The capital corollary represented the allocated investment in floor space used. Mr. Penberthy maintained that each machine had to absorb a portion of the cost of space used. If the allocated plant costs such as depreciation, taxes, and insurance were not considered, the building

expansion required to accommodate additional equipment would be unfairly charged against the last piece added, when in reality all additional
pieces helped bring about the need for building expansion. The corollary
investment was estimated to amount to 70 percent of the cost of the equipment. Some time in the past a study was made over a period of time to
determine the relationship between plant costs and investment. As a
result of this study, it was found that the allocated plant costs would
amount to about 70 percent of the investment in equipment.

The total average annual investment was then computed. The cost
of the equipment itself was divided in half to arrive at an average. The
capital corollary cost amounting to 70 percent of the equipment cost
was similarly averaged. Furthermore, a provision was made for the increase in working capital which would be required to support the project.

A study had been made showing that approximately 9 percent of the
estimated gross revenue was held as accounts receivable, 21 percent of
the estimated cost of goods sold was invested in inventories, and 5 percent
of the estimated cost of goods sold was held as a minimum cash balance.

Accordingly, these percentages were applied to the expected gross
revenue and cost of goods sold resulting from the project to arrive at
the additional investment held in the form of working capital.

INVESTMENT

```
One-half facility estimated cost .................... $
One-half capital corollary ........................
Total working capital ...........................    _____
     Total average annual investment ............. $
```

As an example, an evaluation of a proposal to manufacture a certain
type of air mattress to be used in swimming pools is given in Exhibit 3.

Projects which were accepted were subject to a postcompletion audit.
If the results did not come close to expectations, a decision was reached
as to whether or not an additional audit was to be made. In certain
cases it was believed that if more time were allowed, the project would
eventually meet the requirements. On the other hand, some projects
might show that there was little opportunity for improvement and that
additional audits would not be justified. An unsuccessful project might
be liquidated, or it might be continued as a sort of necessary evil which
had to be tolerated. For example, a project might be maintained, which
did not justify itself, in order to round out the product line.

Mr. Penberthy and his staff were actively investigating the possibility
of improving the method by which business investment proposals were
evaluated. Both Mr. Penberthy and his staff had been reading current
literature on the subject and had attended various conferences dealing
with this topic.

EXHIBIT 3

ECONOMIC EVALUATION OF FACILITY ACQUISITION PROPOSAL
(net dollar advantages before taxes)

Increased revenue

Sales	$793,278	
Cost of goods sold	558,774	
Gross profit	$234,504	
17% allowance for selling and administrative expenses	134,857	
Net revenue increase		$ 99,647
Gross dollar advantage		$ 99,647
Less depreciation of facility cost and capital corollary		25,730
Net dollar advantage before taxes		$ 73,917

overhead (margin annotation next to 17% line)

INVESTMENT

One-half facility estimated cost		$ 75,675
Capital corollary		
One-half other fixed assets		52,973
Total working capital		216,677
Total average annual investment		$345,325

$$\frac{\text{Net dollar advantage before taxes—\$73,917}}{\text{Total average annual investment—\$345,325}} = 21.4\% \text{ Rate of return}$$

Explanatory notes

Total facility cost	$151,350	
(Est. life of 10 years, no residual salvage value)		
Capital corollary (70% of $151,350)	$105,945	
Sales	$793,278	
Cost of goods sold	$558,774	
Selling and administrative expenses (17% of $793,278)		$134,857
Total working capital		
Accounts receivable (9% of $793,278)	$ 71,395	
Inventories (21% of $558,774)	117,343	
Cash (5% of $558,774)	27,939	
Total working capital		216,677
Depreciation [10% of ($151,350 + $105,995)]		25,730

1. *Evaluate the capital budgeting procedures of the Avella Company, including the following specific considerations:*
   a. *The amount of working capital on hand.*
   b. *The cut-off rate.*
   c. *The cost of capital to the company.*
   d. *The formula for computing the rate of return.*
   e. *The treatment of overhead in the computations.*
   f. *The treatment of depreciation in the computations.*
   g. *The use of capital corollary concept.*
   h. *The provision for working capital.*
2. *Would the capital budgeting procedures described in this case be equally applicable to replacement investments and to investments in entirely new facilities? Discuss.*

AIR-INDIA (E)*

Purchase of Boeing 707s

In early 1956 the Chairman of Air-India, Mr. J. R. D. Tata, visited the United States to discuss the purchase of jet aircraft with the Douglas Aircraft Co. and the Boeing Co. Up to that time, Air-India had also been considering turbo-propeller aircraft but had determined that they were

EXHIBIT 1

ORDERS BOOKED AS OF END OF APRIL 1956

Customer	*No.*	*Option*		*Model*	*Delivery Date*
Boeing 707					
Pan American	23		(6)	120	December 1958 to
			(17)	320	November 1959
American Airlines	30	5		120	From March 1959
Braniff	5			120	From October 1959
Continental	4	1		120	1959
Air France	10	7		320	November 1959 to
					November 1960
Sabena	4			320	From December 1959
TWA	8	22		120	From April 1959
Lufthansa	4	4		320	Spring 1960
Total	88 +	39 options			
Douglas DC–8					
Pan American	21			J–57 & J–75	From December 1959
United Airlines	30		(15)	J–57	From May 1959
			(15)	J–75	
National	6			J–57	Midsummer 1959
K.L.M.	8	4		J–75	From March 1960
Eastern Airlines	18	8	(6)	J–57	May 1959
			(12)	J–75	March 1960
JAL	4			J–75	1960
SAS	7			J–75	1960
Panagra	4			J–75	Early 1960
Swissair	2			J–75	Spring 1960
Delta Airlines	6			J–57	June 1959
TCA	6			RR–505	
Total	112 +	12 options			

uneconomical and less acceptable to the travelling public as compared with the jets. The management had also investigated the Comet IV type jet, but had found that it did not have the range required for the Bombay–Cairo or Atlantic sectors. Mr. Tata found that most of the international airlines of the world were placing orders for either the DC–8 or the Boeing 707 for delivery in the period from 1959 to 1961 (see Exhibit 1).

---

* Copyright 1964 by the Indian Institute of Management, Ahmedabad.

Mr. Tata discussed the jet purchase proposal at the Board meetings on March 5, 1956, and May 25, 1956. He noted that the carrying capacity of the jets would be equivalent to three or three-and-a-half Super-Constellations, the type of aircraft which the airline was using in 1954. They would cruise at about 500 miles per hour. Mr. Tata noted that introduction of the new aircraft would raise a number of difficult operational and economic problems, but nevertheless came out strongly for the purchase stating:

If the Corporation was to remain in business in competition with the other carriers on its routes, it would seem to be left with no option but to place an order for one of these two makes in the very near future in order to have a reasonable place in the queue. If orders were placed within the next three months or so, the Corporation would be able to get its aircraft in the second half of 1960 at approximately the same time as other carriers who had already placed their orders.

Mr. Tata also remarked that the minimum number of jets which should be purchased was three, which would be the equivalent to 10 of the existing Super-Constellations. The total cost including spare engines would be about Rs. 120 million. The Corporation could give consideration to the sale of some of its present fleet.

The Second Five-Year Plan made provision for Rs. 100 million for new aircraft. Of this amount over Rs. 20 million were committed to Super-Constellations on order. Thus, not enough was left to finance the purchase of three jets. Mr. Tata believed that the problem could be met by deferred payments or by a loan from the Import-Export Bank, the World Bank, or some other financial institution. Furthermore, delivery of even the first of the jets would come near the end of the Second Five-Year Plan period.

There appeared to be little to choose technically between the DC–8 and the Boeing 707. It would be difficult, however, to get delivery of a DC–8 before 1961. The Boeing Company had three positions open for delivery in 1960. Other airlines were in the market for these three, but Air-India could secure the three positions if it acted rapidly.

As of May 25, 1956, Air-India was one of the few international lines not to have placed an order. Mr. Tata stated that the issue was urgent since the only alternatives were to go out of business or to give up first- and tourist-class traffic and concentrate on third-class or coach traffic.

On June 6, 1956, company officials circulated a formal memorandum on purchase of the jets, most of which appears below:

Proposal for the purchase of jet aircraft—
Boeing 707 intercontinental model

1. Ever since its inception in 1947, and with the approval of the Government of India both before and after nationalization, Air-India International have followed the consistent policy of equipping their fleet with the latest and most competitive type of aircraft available. The original Constellation 749's were

changed within three years for 749A's. This was followed by the purchase of 1049 Super-Constellations, culminating with the order for three 1049G's and for two Mark III Comets (subsequently cancelled). This policy has enabled Air-India International to be from the start and to remain fully competitive with much larger, older, and better known carriers. In the view of the management, such a policy is essential to the success of any small international airline operating in a highly competitive market. In pursuance of this policy, the development of commercial jet aircraft has been closely watched by the Corporation and its predecessor ever since the early 1950's when the de Havilland Comet first came on the scene.

2. During the [preceding] nine months or so, two much larger types of American jet aircraft, almost identical in design, price, and technical characteristics, have been announced for delivery from 1959 onwards. One is the Douglas DC–8 and the other is the Boeing 707. In carrying capacity and all-up weight these American jets will be approximately twice the size of the Mark IV Comet and approach a take-off weight of 300,000 pounds. Their four engines will total over 60,000 pounds of thrust as against about 40,000 for the Comet. Their range will be such as to enable pay-loads in excess of 30,000 pounds to be carried on nonstop services over such extreme sections as the Atlantic. They will be capable of carrying up to 140 passengers although the number will be restricted to about 118 in the mixed configuration (28 standard and 90 tourist) of the aircraft proposed to be ordered by the Corporation.

3. Since October 1955, when the first orders were announced by Pan American Airways, practically every major airline in the world has ordered one or the other of these two types and a total of well over 200 has been ordered up to now with correspondingly lengthening deliveries.

4. The advent of this new generation of great jet airplanes offers to the air transport industry immense potentialities for profitable expansion and, at the same time, poses some serious problems. Substantial increases in cruising speed in air transport have in the past invariably generated new strata of air traffic which did not exist before and these increases in traffic have been achieved without any decrease in surface transport. There is every reason to expect that this greatest of all jumps in cruising speeds—from about 300 to 500 mph—will have the same effect. The fact that the increased speed will be coupled with the elimination of intermediate landings on extra long sections will still further accelerate travel from the passengers' point of view. Other features which will attract passengers will be the extraordinarily smooth conditions of flying at extreme altitudes and the freedom from vibration inherent in turbine engines.

5. From the operational point of view, the higher speeds will produce important economies in flight personnel, out-station expenses and overhead expenses, while the elimination on the one hand of propellers, with their heavy gearing, complicated controls, and feathering devices, and on the other of vibration, which is one of the principal causes of wear and tear, will result in considerable simplification and lower maintenance costs. As against these favorable factors are admittedly some unfavorable ones, amongst which are (a) heavy capital cost, (b) high fuel consumption at low altitudes, and (c) need for long runways for takeoff at high all-up weights.

6. While the cost of these aircraft is high, the capital cost per unit of trans-

portation produced will actually be lower than in the case of Super-Constellation or DC–7 aircraft. In annual ton miles of capacity, one of these jet aircraft will be equivalent to approximately 3.75 Super-Constellations, whereas its capital cost is only 2.5 times that of the Super-Constellation.

7. Although fuel consumption per mile is undoubtedly high at low altitudes, jet aircraft spend very little time at such altitudes while the combination of high cruising speed and low turbine fuel prices results in fuel cost per seat-mile or ton-mile being lower than that of piston-engined, propeller-driven airplanes. It is true that potentially the propeller-driven turbine engine (Turbo-prop) aircraft have a fuel consumption considerably below that of the pure jets under almost all comparable flight conditions, but no long-range turbo propeller aircraft, competitive with the coming big jets, is available.

8. The need for long runways for takeoffs at high all-up weight, particularly in the Tropics where conditions of high temperature and humidity prevail, places some financial burden on Government, but this is a problem which every country must eventually face. In the case of India, the additional expenditure will be heavy only at Bombay, where a good deal of cutting, filling, and culvert construction will be required. The only other cities at which relatively small expenditure will be required are Delhi and Calcutta. The Director-General of Civil Aviation and his experts have been informed of the requirements, and estimates of cost are under preparation. It is respectfully submitted that with the whole world entering the Jet Age in civil aviation, India cannot possibly remain out of it on the ground of the extra expenditure of 20 or 30 million rupees on aerodrome.

9. With the general background, the main features of the project may now be specifically discussed. On the main principle of jet operation, there is today no choice before Air-India International. The matter was generally discussed at the two last meetings of the Board and it was agreed in principle that the Corporation must enter the field of jet operations if it is to remain in business at all. The possible alternative of giving up first- and tourist-class traffic on the Corporation's main routes and concentrating exclusively on coach or third-class traffic is not considered either a practical proposition or a financially prudent one, as coach operations are likely to be extremely marginal. Assuming therefore, that Government accept the view recommended by the Corporation that jet aircraft must be ordered, the main points to be decided are (*a*) the number of aircraft to be ordered, (*b*) the type to be purchased, (*c*) the type of engines to be fitted, (*d*) deliveries, and (*e*) financial arrangements.

10. *Number of aircraft:* The minimum number of aircraft in a fleet which it is practical to operate on long routes is three, four being a more satisfactory figure. In view of the heavy cost of these aeroplanes and their high work capacity, it is proposed to limit the initial fleet to three.

11. *Type of aircraft:* The technical personnel of the Corporation, assisted by a Government of India expert, have recently undertaken a fairly detailed comparative study of both the Douglas DC–8 and the Boeing 707 on the basis of specifications and explanations furnished by representatives of the two manufacturers. Simultaneously, confidential enquiries were made with a number of other international airlines which have ordered jets. From the Corporation's own studies and the confidential reports received from other airlines, it is clear that

there is, to all intents and purposes, nothing to choose between the two types on technical grounds and that either will be suitable for operation on the Corporation's main present and future routes. There is also nothing to choose in price as the price of both the types is almost identical. The choice of engines in both cases is also the same. Consequently, it has become clear that the ultimate choice must depend on other than technical or financial considerations, such as the reputation and experience of the manufacturer and delivery.

12. *Comparison of Douglas and Boeing Companies:* The Douglas Aircraft Company, one of the world's three giants in aircraft production, has an unequalled reputation in the civil transport field, having since 1934 brought out a series of transports, beginning with the DC–2 and ending with the DC–7, all of which have proved an operational and commercial success. On the other hand, they have never produced a large jet aircraft of their own although they have built a large number of Boeing Jet bombers under license. Their immense technical and other resources, however, are such that no doubt is entertained as regards the technical and operational soundness of the DC–8 when built.

13. The Boeing Company is also one of the largest aircraft manufacturers in the world. While they have produced only three multi-engined transport types in their history, including the Stratocruiser, which is still in use on intercontinental routes, they have for years been one of the largest producers of heavy military aircraft—bombers, tankers, and freighters—and are today the only producers of heavy and super-heavy jet bombers. They have built themselves over a thousand B–47 jet bombers, the all-up weight of which approximates or exceeds that of the proposed transports, and are today in full production of the B–52 bomber which is a considerably bigger and heavier aircraft than the 707 jet transport. Their unique experience in the heavy jet field is, in the management's opinion, more than adequate to compensate for their small experience in the civil aircraft field.

14. *Delivery:* As the reputation and experience of both manufacturers are found equally satisfactory, the final choice would seem to boil down to considerations of delivery, and here there is a considerable difference between the two. While DC–8 aircraft will be available for delivery only in the winter of 1960–61, three Boeing 707 aircraft, equipped with Rolls Royce Conway engines, are today offered, subject to prior sale, for delivery in the first quarter of 1960. A reference to engine types will be made later in this memorandum.

15. As in the past, the Corporation is anxious to initiate operations with an entirely new type at the beginning of summer and not in the winter when flying conditions are more difficult and traffic less abundant. Delivery in early 1960 would, therefore, enable the Corporation to inaugurate jet operations a whole year sooner than originally thought possible. The advantages of the time gained would be enormous as the Corporation would have virtually no competition on its U.K. route for at least a year, during which it would be able to establish a strong position while securing highly profitable payloads from the start. The only drawback to the early delivery offered is that, being subject to prior sale and having been offered also to other airlines, like BOAC and Qantas, it necessitates an almost immediate decision on the part of the Corporation and Government if the three open positions in January, February, and March, 1960, are to be secured. Because the advantages of the earlier delivery

are so great, while the risks involved are so small, the management of Air-India International and the undersigned have no hesitation in recommending to the Board and to Government the grant of the earliest possible sanction to the issue to the Boeing Company of a Letter of Intent for the purchase of three Boeing 707/420 aircraft for delivery in the months mentioned above. The reason why an immediate decision is considered to involve no risk whatsoever is that in the unlikely event that within the next two or three years the Corporation or Government were to change their mind in regard to jet operations in general or to the purchase of these aircraft in particular, there would be no difficulty in disposing of the order to some other airlines not only at no loss but, in view of the past experiences, with the probability of a considerable profit.

16. *Choice of engines:* Both the manufacturers have offered their aircraft with a choice of two engines—the American Pratt & Whitney J-75 and the British Rolls Royce Conway. Both the engines have about the same thrust rating of about 16,000 pounds. In favor of the Conway are the facts that (*a*) it is about 1,400 pounds lighter in weight, (*b*) it has a specific fuel consumption lower by 2 to 4 percent, (*c*) it is paid for in sterling, and (*d*) it is available earlier. In favor of the J-75 is the fact that the large majority of the airlines which have ordered Boeing and Douglas jet transports have preferred it to the Conway. The main reason for this is attributed to the fact that the bulk of the orders are from American operators who naturally prefer an American engine. The J-75 will, however, not be available with full thrust for delivery in time for the Corporation to begin operations during the summer of 1960. Up to now, Trans-Canada Airlines alone have ordered the Conway engine but it is considered certain that when BOAC and Qantas finalize their orders for one or the other of these jet transports, they will specify the Conway engine.

17. While the Corporation is anxious to start operations with jets in 1960 rather than 1961, it attaches great importance to the engine chosen for its aircraft being in use in sufficiently large numbers to ensure that the resale value of its aircraft is not adversely affected and also to ensure the maximum of future improvement and development. It is recommended, therefore, that the Conway engine be ordered on the condition, if Boeing and Rolls Royce can be induced to accept it, that it will, within a period of one year, have the right to switch its order to the Pratt & Whitney J-75 at the cost of delayed delivery if necessary. Such a condition would give sufficient time to the Corporation to satisfy itself thoroughly about the Conway engine and about its adoption by other airlines.

18. *Terms of payment and finance:* The Second Five-Year Plan, as approved by Government in Parliament, has made a provision of Rs. 100 million for purchase by Air-India International of new aircraft during the period of the Plan. Out of this amount, a sum of about Rs. 25 million will be utilized for meeting a part of the cost of two 1049G's on order.

19. The total cost of the Boeing jet project will be a little over Rs. 110 million, as detailed in Exhibit 2. This exceeds capital funds available for the Second Five-Year Plan period by about Rs. 35 million. About two thirds of the total expenditure will actually be incurred during the last year of the Plan period and the aircraft will be used throughout the Third Five-Year Plan period. If the Government finds it impossible to make the additional amount available prior

to the Third Five-Year Plan period, it is considered that there would be no difficulty in arranging for short- to medium-term credit facilities, either in India or abroad, for the amount of Rs. 35 million to Rs. 40 million. Such a loan could, for instance, be obtained from the Export-Import Bank, the amount being repayable over a period of three to five years. Such an arrangement would in effect carry over the project into the Third Five-Year Plan period.

20. *Profitability:* As will be seen from the summarized data and estimates covering the projects appended to this memorandum (see Exhibits 2, 3, and 4), a net profit, subject only to taxes and interest on capital, of about Rs. 9.51 million per year is expected to be made from the operation of three aircraft

EXHIBIT 2

Air India (E)
(estimates of capital cost for Boeing 707 & DC–8)

Particulars	Boeing 707		DC–8	
	$	Rs.	$	Rs.
Cost of aircraft	15,450,000	73,388,000	15,750,000	74,812,000
Cost of 9 spare engines @ $225,000 each	2,025,000	9,619,000	2,025,000	9,619,000
Radio, galley, etc.	200,000	950,000	200,000	950,000
Cost of special equipment including engine overhaul facilities and test cell	1,800,000	8,550,000	1,800,000	8,550,000
Cost of simulator	1,000,000	4,750,000	1,000,000	4,750,000
Initial provisioning for rotational units and other spares for a one period	2,000,000	9,500,000	2,000,000	9,500,000
	22,475,000	106,757,000	22,775,000	108,181,000
Import duty @ 2.5% (preferential rates of duty as applicable to aircraft and engines have been assumed)	562,000	2,669,000	569,000	2,704,000
Flight and ground training expenses	239,000	1,135,000	239,000	1,135,000
Delivery charges of 3 aircraft @ $26,300 or Rs. 125,000 per aircraft	79,000	375,000	79,000	375,000
Total Capital Cost	23,355,000	110,936,000	23,662,000	112,395,000

proposed to be purchased. These estimates have been prepared on a conservative basis. For instance, the estimated cost of fuel, which forms the biggest single item of operating expenditure, has been increased by a safe margin for tolerances and increased consumption and, in addition, 20 percent has been added to the existing price per gallon of this type of fuel. Similarly, the estimated cost of stores, materials, and labor per hour of operation has been increased by about 20 percent. On the revenue side, estimates have been based on an average passenger load of 15 first class and 49 tourists, as against 28 first class and 90 tourist seats available, equivalent to a passenger load factor of 55 percent. With the estimates for mail and cargo calculated on the basis of what we actually expect to carry in the light of our existing experience, the overall load factor has been estimated at only 49 percent. Considering the very large carrying capacity and revenue earning potentiality of these big jets during peak seasons, the management believes that the estimated financial results will be improved upon in practice.

EXHIBIT 3

AIR-INDIA (E)
(estimates of operating cost of the Boeing 707)
A. *Operational Summary*

1. Frequencies: 6 times weekly Bombay/London/Bombay and 2 times weekly London/New York/London *during season* (once weekly during off-season)
2. Hours: 8,135
3. Miles: 3,687,000
4. Cargo Ton Miles: 61,400,000

B. *Summary of Operating Cost*

	Total Cost Rs.	Cost per Hour Rs.	Cost per Mile Rs.
1. Crew	1,857,000	228.27	0.504
2. Fuel & oil	19,386,000	2,383.04	5.258
3. Engineering labor for maintenance & overhaul of aircraft & engines	4,653,000	572.00	1.262
4. Materials & spares for maintenance of aircraft & engines	10,331,000	1,270.00	2.802
5. Landing fees	1,592,000	195.70	0.432
6. Depreciation & obsolescence	9,990,000	1,228.03	2.710
7. Insurance of aircraft	3,869,000	475.60	1.049
8. Route diversions, practice & test flights	1,050,000	129.07	0.285
9. Total direct operating cost	52,728,000	6,481.71	14.302
10. Indirect cost at 100% of the direct operating cost excluding fuel & oil item 2: (This percentage is generally applied in preparing cost estimates. In case of 1049 operations the indirect cost ratio is 82.5%)	33,342,000	4,098.59	9.043
11. Total operating cost	86,070,000	10,580.30	23.345
Revenue (see Exhibit 4)	95,580,000	11,749.23	25.924
Estimated profit	9,510,000	1,168.93	2.579
Comparative Unit cost for Super-Constellation 1049s		3,775	14.953

21. The annual turnover of the jet fleet of three Boeings, shown in the estimates at Rs. 95 million, is higher than the total turnover of the Corporation in the current year, estimated at Rs. 80 million with a fleet of five Super-Constellations and three Constellations. With the addition of the 1049G to replace the Constellation lost in the China Sea, and the possible retention of one of the two

1049Cs, for the replacement of which two 1049Gs have been ordered, the estimated revenues for 1957–58 will probably be about Rs. 100 to 105 million. Thus the addition of the three jets in 1960 will require doubling the Corporation's turnover. While this may at first appear optimistic, no serious difficulty is expected in reaching such a target for the following reasons:

EXHIBIT 4

AIR-INDIA (E)

(estimates of revenue for operation of
jet aircraft Boeing 707 or DC–8)

	Millions of Rs.	Millions of Rs.
*Passenger revenue:**		
1. Bombay/London		
15 Std. passengers × Rs. 4080 × 312 flights	19.09	
49 Tourist passengers × Rs. 2834 × 312 flights	43.33	
Less off-season fare differential on tourist revenue for 5 months, est. Rs.		
18,050,000 @ 15%	2.71	40.62
2. London/New York		
15 Std. passengers × Rs. 3564 × 78 flights	4.17	
49 Tourist passengers × Rs. 2348 × 78 flights	8.97	
	13.14	
Less off-season differential on total revenue for 5 months or a pro rata revenue of		
Rs. 550,000 @ 7.5%	.41	12.73
Mails:		
1. Bombay/London 3000 lbs. × Rs. 12.5 ×		
312 flights	11.70	
2. London/New York 1000 lbs. × Rs. 7.5 ×		
78 flights		.59
Cargo:		
1. Bombay/London 8000 lbs. × Rs. 4.10 ×		
312 flights	10.23	
2. London/New York 3200 × Rs. 2.46 ×		
78 flights		.61
Total Bombay/London Revenue	81.65	
Total London/New York Revenue		13.93
Total Revenue	81.65 +	13.93
	= 95.58	

* Passenger fares: single fares less 15% to cover round trip rebate, concessional fares, etc. Double the amount is taken for a round trip fare.

a. Unless there is a significant change in the existing traffic trends, which have lasted for many years, the normal growth of traffic may be expected to account for an increase of 50 percent to 60 percent in the next four years.

b. The rapid development of tourist passengers and the introduction of a third-class or "coach" fare on main routes in the next year or two are expected to create an additional demand. By the time the big jets come into operation it is anticipated that the pattern of international air transport will be that first-class and tourist services on main trunk routes will be operated with jets, while "coach" traffic and traffic on secondary routes will be operated with turbo-propeller and piston-engined aircraft.

c. The Corporation intends, before 1960, to open some new routes, including the Atlantic.

If, however, the Corporation's expectations were not to materialize to the full extent and the Corporation finds that it could not economically use the whole of its piston-engined fleet with the addition of the jets, there should be no difficulty in the disposal, at prices well above their then value in the Corporation's books, of some of its Constellations or Super-Constellations.

22. In conclusion, the Government is requested kindly to grant urgent approval to the following proposals:

a. General approval to the project for the purchase of three 707/420s equipped with Rolls Royce Conway engines or three Boeing 707/320s equipped with Pratt & Whitney J-75, at a total estimated cost (including spare engines, initial spares, customer-finished equipment, flight simulator, import duty, delivery, and training expenses and contingencies) not exceeding Rs. 115 million is requested.

b. Authority is requested to issue a Letter of Intent to the Boeing Company for the purchase of the above aircraft at a cost ex-factory, excluding customer-finished and radio equipment, of $15,450,000, payable as follows:[1]

5% within 10 days of issuing the Letter of Intent	$ 772,500
28% in 12 quarterly installments terminating six months prior to delivery	$ 4,326,000
67% on delivery	$10,351,500
100%	$15,450,000

The above figures are based on aircraft equipped with Pratt & Whitney J-75 engines and are subject to a slight downward revision, and substitution of sterling for dollars, in respect of the engines if Rolls Royce Conway engines are purchased.

c. Sanction is requested of an advance by the Government during the current financial year of a sum of Rs. 8,806,000 made up as follows:

5% down payment	$ 772,500	Rs. 3,669,000
Three quarterly payments	$1,081,500	Rs. 5,137,000
Total requirement for 1956–57	$1,854,000	Rs. 8,806,000

1. *What criteria were used by Air-India in evaluating the purchase of jets? Were these criteria quantitative or qualitative in character? Should a more exact quantitative approach have been applied?*
2. *In evaluating the jets from the financial point of view what measure did Air-India use: payback period, discounted rate of return, present value, or some other alternative? Was this the appropriate measure?*

---

[1] $1.00 = Rs. 4.76 at the time of this case. It is simpler to use the rate $1.00 = Rs. 5.00; the resulting error is not large.

3. *What attention was given the cost of capital in the decision? Should more or less attention have been given this factor?*

4. *What revisions in the capital budgeting procedures of Air-India might be appropriate?*

5. *At the time of this case, foreign exchange was in extremely short supply in India. In fact, one could call the situation a foreign exchange crisis. How is your analysis influenced by this fact?*

6. *Should Air-India have purchased the Boeing 707s as outlined in the proposal of June 9, 1956?*

7. *How would you evaluate Air-India procedures in dealing with large equipment purchases?*

WHITE CASTLE TRUCKING CO.*

"I'm sorry I can't agree with you Jim. I still believe we should pay for the trucks we have before we go out on a limb and overextend ourselves by committing most of our revenue to meeting time payments." George Pike and his brother, Jim, thus continued their argument over the expansion policy of the White Castle Trucking Company.

This company had come into existence in the spring of 1958 as the result of a casual remark made by the owner of a ready-mix concrete company: "I surely could use some extra 12-yard dump trucks this summer."

Following upon this remark, George and Jim Pike made a study of the costs and revenues involved in the dump-truck leasing business with the following results:

1. New 12-yard 10-wheel dump trucks cost between $15,000 and $22,000 each. Used trucks in fair operating condition could be purchased for between $3,500 and $10,000 depending upon their age and condition. Many methods were used to depreciate used trucks. The most common method was to depreciate them on an eight-year basis from January 1 of the model year (i.e., a 1953 truck purchased on April 1, 1957, would be depreciated over three and three-quarter years from April 1, 1957).

2. State license fees and insurance would amount to about $625 per truck per year.

3. As each truck had 10 wheels, tire repair and replacement costs would be a major consideration. Trucks were used over rough ground and the experiences of other truck leasing companies indicated that about half of the tires had to be replaced each year. Some of the tires could be recapped which would reduce replacement costs. New tires cost about $225 each. It was estimated that with careful driver maintenance it would cost approximately $800 a year for tires on a per truck basis.

---

* This case was prepared by Professor Frederic A. Brett of the University of Alabama as a basis for class discussion.

4. At current prices, the cost of gasoline and oil to operate a truck on an eight-hour basis amounted to between $15 and $18.

5. There were no general figures available for repair and maintenance costs with the exception that a complete overhaul of a truck engine would cost between $1,000 and $1,300. Other truck leasing companies had found a direct relationship between repair costs and the care given to trucks by drivers. Some companies found it necessary to completely overhaul each truck on an annual basis. Other companies, using a wage incentive plan, had reduced the annual repair and maintenance costs to as little as 40 percent of the cost of a complete overhaul.

6. Truck-with-driver lease rates were $8.50 to $9.50 per hour depending upon location (county) and road surface conditions. Road construction companies usually paid $75 per truck on a daily lease basis. It was common practice for ready-mix concrete companies to lease truck with driver for $60 per day when gasoline and oil were supplied by the lessee.

7. In order to lease trucks to most companies in the area, it was necessary to employ only union drivers. The going rate for drivers was $3.12½ per hour or $25 for an eight-hour day. However, because of competition for jobs, many union drivers worked for a flat $20 per day. These "cut-rate" drivers were considered a risk by many of the companies, which found that repair costs mounted when these drivers were used.

The Pike brothers discussed their findings and decided to start a dump-truck leasing business if they could get a firm contract from one of the concrete ready-mix companies. They contacted Carl Manning who had given them the idea of starting the business by his casual remark earlier in the year. Manning agreed to give them a contract for five trucks at $60 per truck per day (five days a week) for the period May 15 to October 15 and that he would supply gasoline and oil for the trucks. It was further agreed that if a truck started work on a particular day and, at the option of the lessee, worked less than four hours it would be paid for on the basis of one-half day; if it worked more than four hours, it would be considered as having worked a full day. If a truck broke down due to mechanical trouble, it would be docked on an hourly rate ($7.50) until repaired and put back in service. Time required for tire changes or minor repairs would not be charged against the truck unless down time ran over one hour, at which time the $7.50 deduction rate would go into effect.

On May 7, 1958, four used trucks were bought from Eastern Mack Trucks Inc., a local truck dealer, for $16,500. Terms of the purchase contract called for a down payment of $4,000 and monthly payments of $754 for 18 months. A used three-quarter ton pickup truck was also purchased for $500 cash. This vehicle was to be outfitted and used as a service truck. State license plates for the four trucks amounted to $960 and one-year premiums for liability and property damage insurance cost $1,527.84. The license plate for the pickup cost $24.50 and the insurance premium amounted to $151.70.

On May 10, a fifth truck was purchased for $7,500. Time payments of $388 per month for 18 months and a down payment of $1,000 was the best deal they could make. The annual insurance premium for this truck amounted to $381.96 and the license plate cost $240.

Drivers were hired for four of the trucks and Jim decided to give up his job as an automotive parts salesman and drive the fifth truck as well as manage the company. George would devote only part of his time to the new business. The drivers agreed to work for $20 a day until the new firm got on its feet, at which time they would expect to receive union wages. Jim decided to drive a 1954 International which was in pretty poor condition with the hope that he could "baby it along" until the cash account was improved and funds were available for needed repairs.

All five trucks reported for work on Wednesday, May 14. During the next month and a half, total revenue amounted to $8,160 of which $240 was receivable in accordance with the practice of making lease payments on Saturday of each week. During this same period, cash payments amounted to $6,458, of which $1,142 went for time payments on the trucks, $2,720 for driver's pay, $1,230 for tire repair and replacement, and $816 for truck repairs.

Analyzing the operations for the first six weeks, George and Jim came to the following conclusions:

1. Trucks had operated at only 83 percent efficiency because of down time for repairs. On a total basis, this had resulted in the loss of 29 truck-days at $40 per day or $1,160 ($60 rental less $20 driver pay).

2. The calculated risk of buying the cheaper trucks which were in rather poor operating condition had resulted in high repair costs as well as reducing potential revenue. This condition would have a reverse trend as soon as trucks were overhauled.

3. The high cost of tire repair and replacement would not continue once all worn tires had been replaced.

4. One driver had quit because he lost too much time while his truck was being repaired. The other drivers were not too happy about losing time when their trucks broke down. They felt that as long as they were working for less than union wages they should have full-time trucks to drive.

After a lengthy discussion, George and Jim decided on a new operating policy as follows:

1. Drivers would be hired at $20 a day on a five-day week basis. If their trucks were out of service due to mechanical breakdown, they would be paid at half-rate to assist in the repair work. It was believed that this policy would encourage drivers to take better care of their trucks in

order to earn full pay. Another benefit would be that driver morale would be higher because of the minimum $10 per day wage rate.

2. Repair costs had been high, and it was thought that if a suitable location could be had at a reasonable price, it would be cheaper in the long run to employ a full-time mechanic to work on the trucks at a company-owned garage.

George surveyed the area and on August 1 a service station, located near the edge of town on a little-traveled road, was leased for one year. The station was equipped with a grease rack and a wash shed which could be used as an enclosed repair shop. The station was on a large lot which could park about 50 vehicles. It was thought some revenue could be earned through leasing parking space to independent truckers and thus reduce the overhead for the operation.

On September 30, 1958, the following financial data were taken from the books of the company:

Truck rental income		$23,688
Operating expenses:		
Drivers' wages (1)	$8,460	
Tire repair and replacement	2,389	
Truck repair (2)	2,178	
Insurance (3)	2,337	
Interest and bank charges	363	
Gasoline and oil, etc. (4)	274	
Taxes (5)	1,998	
Other cash expenses	966	
Total expenses before depreciation		18,965
Profit before depreciation		$ 4,723

(1) Includes regular driver pay for Jim.
(2) Includes rent on service station and mechanic's pay.
(3) Includes annual insurance premiums on trucks.
(4) Supplied for special jobs worked on Saturdays.
(5) Includes annual truck license fees and social security taxes.

Jim was elated over the $4,723 profit the company had made since it was formed in May. George, however, was a bit worried when he realized that the cash account had increased only $501 because of the principal payments on the trucks of $4,222 ($4,568 less $346 interest included in above statement). George was also concerned about the contract's running out on October 15 with no assured work for the trucks during the winter months.

The weather during October and the early part of November was favorable for work and White Castle was able to work 32 days after October 1 before Manning closed down operations for the winter. During this period, $8,060 was collected for truck rentals. The remainder of the winter was a very trying time for the new company. On an overall average, only one truck was kept busy from November 17 until May 4, 1959, resulting in rental income of only $6,420. Operating expenses before depreciation charges for the period October 1, 1958, to May 4, 1959, were:

Drivers' wages (1)	$ 4,880
Tire Repair and replacement	737
Truck repairs (2)	3,160
Taxes (3)	1,682
Other cash expenses (4)	1,442
Total cash expenses	$11,901

(1) Drivers hired on a daily basis during winter months.
(2) The winter months were used to overhaul trucks. Other independent truckers used repair shop and receipts from these jobs were used to offset repair costs.
(3) Includes truck license fees due January 1 of each year.
(4) Includes interest payments of $641.

The company had been in a very poor cash condition during the winter months and George had had to borrow a total of $1,500 from a local bank to make the March and April payments on the trucks. George was further concerned about the insurance premiums of $2,061.50 and time payments of $1,142 due in May.

On May 4, 1959, all five trucks were leased out to Manning at the same rates as the previous year. Manning stated that he could use twice as many trucks and Jim thought it would be a good idea to refinance the old trucks, which were in good operating condition after the winter repair work was completed, and buy several more trucks for the 1959 season. He reasoned that with only six more payments to be made on the trucks, they could cut the payments to a point where three or four new trucks would not be any more of a burden than the five trucks had been the previous year. In addition, the added revenue from the additional trucks would ease the entire cash position of the company.

George was very much against the idea and voiced his opinion that the old trucks should be paid for before any new time payment commitments were made. If no new obligations were undertaken, the old trucks would be paid for before the slack winter season set in and they wouldn't have to worry about the heavy drain on cash during the winter months.

Jim believed that this conservative approach would stunt the growth of the company and favored a policy of rapid expansion for the new company. To prove his point of view, Jim had their accountant project their cash position for the period June 1, 1959, to May 31, 1960, using the following assumptions:

1. Three additional trucks would be purchased for a total of $15,000. The down payment would amount to $3,000 and monthly payments of $776 for 18 months would complete the contract.

2. The five old trucks would be refinanced for a total of $412 per month for 18 months.

3. Trucks would rent for $60 a day (gasoline and oil to be supplied by lessee) and drivers would be paid on the same basis as last year.

4. Truck repair expense, which would include net service station operations, would not cost more than an estimated $300 per month.

5. Tire repair and replacement would not run more than $500 per truck per year. This lower than average estimate was based on the fact that trucks were used on hard surface roads about 90 percent of the time.

6. An additional $2,500 would be used during the winter months to overhaul the new trucks. This amount was in addition to repair costs considered under #4 above.

7. All trucks would operate at 85 percent efficiency between June 1 and September 30. Two trucks would be kept busy for the other months on a five-day week basis. This estimate was based upon last year's experience and a snow removal and sanding contract which Jim was assured of for the coming winter.

Jim considered these estimates very conservative, since revenue was being understated for May and October when the company had a good chance of operating above 25 percent efficiency.

1. *Was the original investment in the company a sound one? Discuss. What criteria are relevant in evaluating this question?*
2. *Would the company have been better off to have invested in new rather than second-hand trucks? Discuss.*
3. *Estimate the economic profit for the company in the period up to September 30, 1958. Estimate the economic profit for the period up to May 4, 1959.*
4. *Should the company have purchased additional trucks in May 1959?*
5. *Develop a cash budget based on the assumptions listed at the end of the case. Is this budget useful in making the decision on the purchase of additional trucks?*
6. *Would it be useful to compute the present value or discounted rate of return in this case? What cost of capital would be relevant?*

AMERICAN TELEPHONE AND TELEGRAPH COMPANY*

The Federal Communications Commission has jurisdiction over interstate telephone services and rates. In this area it has been able to follow, for many years, a policy of regulation based on continuous surveillance. The Commission has maintained continuing studies of extensive financial and operating data which it requires the Bell System companies to submit in monthly, annual, and special reports. Through its field offices located in New York City, St. Louis, and San Francisco, the Commission's staff conducts on-the-spot investigations of the companies' books and associated records. The Commission also keeps itself informed of the companies' plans for new constructions and financing, as well as of the Commission

---

* This case is based primarily on official FCC proceedings on September 19 and 20, and December 13, 1962, and January 4, 1963.

Staff and the Bell System views concerning the level of earnings required, by means of periodic informal meetings.

Following this process the Commission has taken action to secure over-all rate reductions where it thought such reductions warranted. Since 1934, numerous rate reductions have been made and one general rate increase has been allowed. Based on 1962 volumes of traffic the net effect of the major rate changes during this period have resulted in savings to the public of over $1 billion annually.

The Commission has not been committed, however, exclusively to informal procedures. In several instances where agreement could not be reached informally, the Commission instituted formal rate reduction proceedings through show-cause orders. In each instance, this action led to a satisfactory resolution of the matter without the need to proceed with the hearings. The Commission also has initiated formal hearings dealing with specific rates and services. At one time recently, there were 31 formal cases involving the Bell System before the Commission.

The Commission held a series of informal conferences between September 1962 and January 1963, concerning the level of earnings required from the interstate telephone operations of the Bell System. In addition to explaining its plans for new construction and financing, the company presented testimony supporting its view that an 8 percent return was both within the range of reasonableness and required to encourage the greatest development of its communications services at the lowest cost to the users over the long term. Conversely, an expert retained by the Commission staff testified that a rate of return of 6.1 percent would be adequate.

The cost of capital: Professor Friend's testimony

One of the Company's expert witnesses, Professor Irwin Friend of the Wharton School of Finance and Commerce, testified that the cost of capital to the AT&T was more than $7\frac{1}{2}$ percent. Such a figure would cover the 3.9 percent of "embedded" debt cost and a 9.2 percent cost of equity, assuming a capital structure of 35 percent debt and 65 percent equity.

Professor Friend concentrated most of his analysis on the cost of equity. He rejected both past earnings-price ratios and past dividends-price ratios as measures of the cost of capital. These measures, he said, would apply only if investors were expecting no change in earnings, dividends, or market prices. The fact is that investors buy common stocks in the expectation of growth in earnings and dividends, so that a provision for growth must be included in the cost of capital.

Professor Friend presented a formula for the computation of the cost of equity capital. The formula is

$$i_e = g + E/P \, (1 + g)d$$

in which i_e is the cost of equity capital, g is the expected growth in earnings per share, E/P is the earnings-price ratio, and d the expected dividend payout ratio. One assumption Dr. Friend made with respect to AT&T stock is that the investor expects the E/P ratio will be the same at the termination of his investment as at the beginning. Therefore he found that the cost of equity for AT&T is the sum of the expected growth rate in earnings plus the dividend-price ratio adjusted for growth.

Professor Friend stated as a fundamental that the price-earnings ratio used in the formula must be consistent with the growth rate. Exhibit 1

EXHIBIT 1

RELATIONSHIP BETWEEN GROWTH AND PRICE/EARNINGS MULTIPLES, MOODY'S INDEXES*

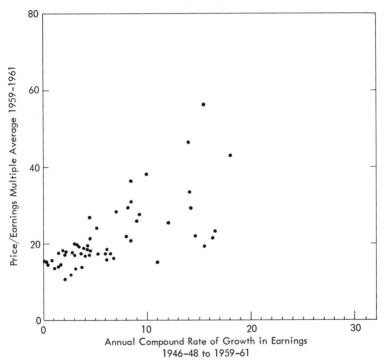

* Moody's "20 Income Stocks, 20 Growth Stocks and 24 Utility Stocks."

shows a relationship between growth rates and price-earnings ratios for a group of income stocks, growth stocks, and utility stocks. This demonstrates that a low growth rate is accompanied by a low price-earnings multiple (a high earnings-price ratio). It would be "improper to combine a high growth rate with a low price-earnings multiple or on the other hand a high price-earnings ratio with a low rate of growth."

Exhibit 2 provides some evidence on AT&T growth rates and price-earnings multiples. The period from 1946 to 1950 was atypical, being a period of depressed earnings and low interest rates. The price in 1947 seemingly was held up by the expectation of increased earnings; when the increased earnings did not materialize the price-earnings multiple declined.

The price-earnings multiple for the period 1950–58 averaged about 13½ times. Earnings per share in this period increased about 4 percent per annum. In the period 1958–62 the growth rate in earnings per share was 5½ percent which goes far to explain the rise in the price-earnings multiple in that period. Professor Friend concluded from this analysis

EXHIBIT 2

AT&T STOCK: EARNINGS PER SHARE AND PRICE/EARNINGS MULTIPLES

EARNINGS PER SHARE*

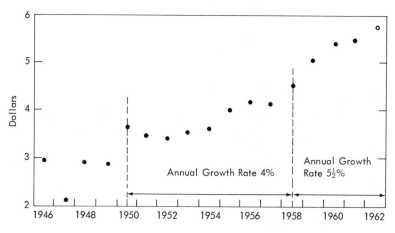

PRICE/EARNINGS MULTIPLE

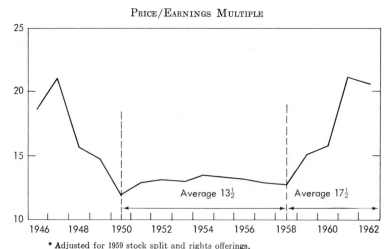

* Adjusted for 1959 stock split and rights offerings.

that a 1962 investor would expect an average price-earnings multiple of 18 times and a growth rate of 5 percent for the foreseeable future. Even higher expected growth rates, he believed, might be justified on the basis of the postwar evidence.

Exhibit 3 shows Professor Friend's computation of the cost of equity capital. He assumed a 65 percent payout even though the recent AT&T payout had been somewhat below that figure. In the bottom half of the exhibit, he made an adjustment for the "underpricing" of the stock— that is for the fact that the proceeds to the company on a sale of new stock would be 10 percent below the market price. The result was an estimated cost of equity capital of 9.2 percent.

EXHIBIT 3

Cost of AT&T Common Equity

Investors' Capitalization Rate

Reasonable expectations for AT&T stock:

annual growth in earnings per share 5%
price earnings multiple 18
dividend payout 65%

$$\text{Capitalization rate} = 5\% + \frac{1.05 \times 65\%}{18} \text{ or } 8.8\%$$

Cost to Company

Investors' capitalization rate adjusted for difference between market price and proceeds to company on sale of new shares.
Reasonable expectations for AT&T stock:
Proceeds on new shares 10% below market price

$$\text{Cost} = 5\% + \frac{1.05 \times 65\%}{18 \times 90\%} \text{ or } 9.2\%$$

Professor Friend used a cost of debt capital of 3.9 percent in his computation of the overall cost of capital. This estimate was low because it was well below the current costs of *new* debt. These are higher than the "embedded" costs which are weighted heavily by the low interest rates in the 1940s and early 1950s. A weighted average of the 9.2 percent cost of equity and the 3.9 percent cost of debt resulted in an overall cost of 7.4 percent. An adjustment for the low cost of debt and for the use of book value weights instead of market value weights would raise the estimate to over 7½ percent.

Professor Friend denied that an increase in debt financing would lower the cost of capital. While it is true that debt carries a lower cost than equity, any attempt to increase the debt-equity ratio would bring an increase in investor risk, and thus in both the interest rate and cost of equity. The tax-exempt status of interest on debt would not result in a significant saving in cost.

The cost of capital: Mr. Kosh's testimony

One of the FCC's consultants, Mr. Kosh, differed from Professor Friend in two major respects. First, he made use of recent earnings-price ratios with only a minor provision for growth. Second, he used a debt ratio of 50 percent on the grounds that the Commission should use a theoretical "optimum" capital structure in its computations even though the actual ratio was 35 percent. In his opinion a 50 percent debt ratio was safe for the telephone company even under conditions of depression. The failure to increase the debt to that level meant a failure to take full advantage of the "leverage" principle. The result of his computations was a 6.1 percent overall cost of capital instead of over 7.5 percent which Dr. Friend found.

The comparable earnings test

Another AT&T argument for an 8 percent of return presented by Mr. J. J. Scanlon, a vice president of AT&T, was based on a comparison of

EXHIBIT 4

AVERAGE INCREASE, 1946 TO 1960, IN
225 MANUFACTURING COMPANIES AND 96 ELECTRICS
(classified by growth in book equity and dividends per share)

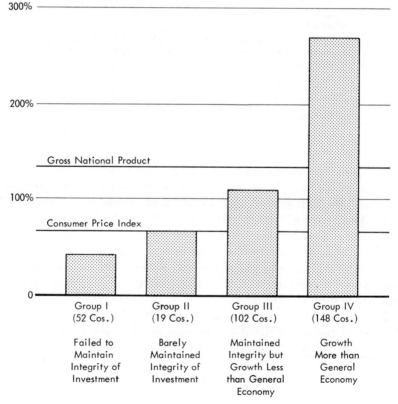

equity earnings with a broad cross-section of both regulated and unregulated companies. Exhibit 4 shows how these companies were selected.

They were the firms whose growth both in dividends and the book equity per share was greater than the increase in the Consumer Price Index, but did not exceed the growth in real GNP. The claim was that the long-term risk for AT&T is at least as great as the risk in these companies and that differences in short-term risks are equated by their differing capital structures. On this basis comparable rates of return on equity would be justified. Exhibits 4 and 5 show that the selected firms earned an average of 10.4 to 12.5 percent on equity, leading to the conclusion that the Bell System requires equity earnings at least of 10½ to 11 percent.

EXHIBIT 5

AVERAGE EARNINGS ON COMMON EQUITY, 1946–60
(groups of companies per exhibit 4)

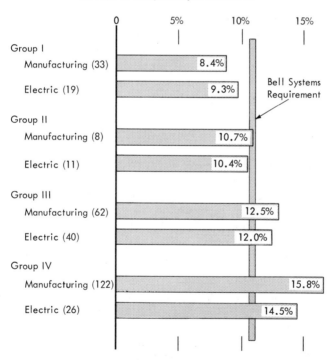

Professor James C. Bonbright of Columbia University, another consultant retained by the FCC, was critical of the comparable earnings test. He admitted that the Bell System did face competition for many of its services, but he noted that consumers had no choice but to use the Bell System if they were to make telephone calls. He also argued that industrial companies are subject to greater risks and therefore did not provide a sound basis for comparison.

Other considerations

The hearings on AT&T's earnings also covered several other issues. Professor Bonbright was concerned with the ratio of market value to book value of the AT&T stock. He would concede a rate of return which in prosperity would allow the company a market value "well in excess of book value." But when the market value reached a price double that of book value, as was the case in 1962, he became skeptical.

Witnesses at the hearings also went into the effects of rate regulation on the national economy. Dr. Paul W. McCracken, of the University of Michigan, who was formerly on the President's Council of Economic Advisors, expressed fear that a reduction in the rate of return, with a consequent reduction in the market value of AT&T stock, would have an unsettling effect on the national economy. He, as well as Dr. Joseph Kieper of New York University, also claimed that an adequate return would stimulate the AT&T construction and equipment program which would help bolster the economy. The profitable companies, they claimed, were the ones making the greatest contribution to economic growth. This position would mean that the FCC should be concerned with much more than the cost of capital. Professor Bonbright, however, maintained that the FCC should confine itself mainly to the task of finding a rate of return which would attract capital.

The record on the FCC proceedings was closed out on January 4, 1963. It resulted in an announcement that interstate station to station toll rates would be reduced to a maximum of $1.00 coast to coast after 9:00 P.M. This reduction, offset in part by an increase in person to person rates which had gotten out of line with increasing labor costs, resulted in a net $30 million annual saving to the public and a cutback of about 0.3 percent in the return the company was earning. The FCC believed, however, that technological change and an increased market for telephone service would permit the company to maintain a level of earnings within the 7 to 8 percent range realized by it since the last rate reduction in 1959.

1. *In your opinion what was the cost of capital to AT&T in 1962–63? Discuss.*
2. *What is the significance of Exhibit 1? What is its relevance in determining the cost of capital?*
3. *What is the relevance of Exhibit 2 in determining the cost of capital?*
4. *Develop the logic behind the computations in Exhibit 3.*
5. *Evaluate the comparable earnings test. In that connection evaluate Exhibits 4 and 5 as to pertinence in rate regulation.*
6. *Make a list of the other factors considered in this rate case and give your opinion on their significance and relevance.*
7. *Should the reduction of "after 9" long-distance rates have been instituted in 1963?*

PART SIX / Managerial economics
in nonprofit organizations

12 / Cost-effectiveness and benefit-cost analyses

Interests and activities of business firms and public agencies are closely intertwined. The government is the regulator and rule maker for the conduct of business and, at the same time, a major customer for business outputs. Businesses supply most of the nonlabor inputs used in public production, but they, in turn, are major demanders of public services. Hence, the profit and nonprofit sectors are important to each other from the point of view of both supply and demand. Government agencies and nonprofit enterprises have been growing in relative importance as producers of goods and services, and there is need for more attention to their management problems. This chapter shows how managerial economics is used in the public sector, and introduces additional concepts and techniques that have been developed primarily for use in planning and decision making in governmental and nonprofit organizations.

Two important differences between public agencies and business firms can be noted at the outset. *First, constituency of the public agency is much larger than that of the business firm.* A private enterprise may either confer benefits or impose costs upon the general public, but its responsibilities to employees, customers, and stockholders must be given priority if the firm is to continue producing and investing. Interests of stockholders and the general public may diverge, as in the case of pollution-creating processes, but pressure of competition usually does not allow a business firm to assume more social responsibility than the law requires. For a public agency, however, the well-being of those indirectly helped or harmed by its activities may be as important as that of the direct users of the agency's services. For example, the highway department is as responsible to those whose lives are disrupted by highway construction as it is to potential travelers of the route. Decision-making and investment analysis for government agencies takes into account and fully weighs the interests of all individuals and groups that will be affected.

A second peculiarity of public management is that many products or services are not sold directly for a price, and many others are priced at less than average cost. Those principles of pricing which are applicable to public agencies must be tailored somewhat to the public viewpoint. Furthermore, the guides to production and investment decisions that market prices provide to businessmen are not fully available to public managers.

Despite the above distinctions between private and public enterprise, both kinds of organizations can use profit as a test of efficiency in resource allocation. In public choices it is necessary to redefine the concept of profit somewhat, and it is perhaps useful to rename it "net social benefit." *In order to maximize public profit (net social benefit), a public service is expanded until decreasing marginal benefits become equal to marginal costs.* The concept of *social benefit* is quite similar to that of private revenue—it is the *value of agency outputs* to the various beneficiaries. Owing to the public viewpoint, the concept of *social cost* embraces the *value of all opportunities foregone by the constituent population* as a result of the activity of the agency.

Economic concepts used in maximizing private profits can be transferred, subject to the above types of amendments, to the public sector. They allow systematic analysis of public programs and public investments. The most widely used forms of this approach are *cost-effectiveness analysis* and *benefit cost analysis.* An introduction to these two techniques and a discussion of the role of prices in managing the public sector are the main business of this chapter.

ESTIMATING DEMAND AND EVALUATING BENEFITS

Demands for public services

The value of services provided by a public agency derives ultimately from citizen demands, which some agencies can determine in essentially the same way as a private seller would. These agencies provide information, water, postal delivery, health care, camp sites, and a variety of other services to direct users for fees that are assessed on a partial- or full-cost, pay-as-you-go basis. However, most government activities produce nonpriced outputs. Demand for nonpriced outputs is a meaningful concept, but the demand functions must be estimated in a special way (if they can be estimated at all).

Consider the example of outdoor recreation. A "free" recreation or park area actually has a "price" per visit in the form of extra costs (travel time, meals and lodging, vehicle operation, and so on) that must be incurred by the user. This price would vary directly with the distance traveled by each prospective visitor, so that the rate of visits as a proportion of the total population of surrounding cities would tend to vary with distance from the park. Analysts have used this relationship to derive estimates of demand for outdoor recreation sites.[1] The demand curve is constructed by relating visit rates of each (distance) zone to simulated increases in cost and multiplying by the relative populations in each zone. Accuracy of such demand estimates depends upon proper estimation (or simulation) of all costs which would not have been incurred save for the visit to the park. In addition, nonprice factors affecting demand, such as availability of other parks and income variations within the region, should be taken into account.

Marginal value of public services

The public agency manager may have great difficulty in estimating demand functions for his agency's services, if there are no charges for them. It may be more practical to estimate the maximum amount users would be *willing* to pay to obtain *additional* service. Notice that this approach is framed in marginal terms. With public as well as with private services, it is the willingness to pay for increments that determines value. The city water department need not do a sophisticated analysis to determine that it provides a valuable product. But the marginal value of water may be very small for most users, and this is the relevant value for decisions about additions to capacity.

Options, external benefits, and public goods

Some benefits from public programs are not as direct as those to campers, irrigators, or patients in public hospitals. As examples, persons who do not visit Yellowstone, or ride the Bay Area Rapid Transit, or swim in the Santa Barbara Channel may place some value on the knowledge that the facilities are available for their possible future use. Nonusers may be willing to pay something for such *options to use* facilities that are created and preserved by public action. Furthermore, driving in San Francisco may be more tolerable because of the construction of BART, and West Coast seafood may be much better to eat because of the enforcement of pollution controls on offshore drilling. Such "third party" benefits are called *externalities* because they are external to the direct objectives of the program. In some cases, option demands and externalities may be worth more than the benefits provided to the direct clientele of programs.

For some government programs, it may be difficult to identify any direct users. The outputs of these programs, called *public goods*, are

---

[1] See Jack L. Knetsch and Robert K. Davis, "Comparison of Methods for Recreation Evaluation," in A. V. Kneese and Stephen C. Smith, eds., *Water Research* (Johns Hopkins Press, 1960).

available to everyone in a region, and no individual's use detracts from the amount available to others. The classic example of a public good is national defense. If one person is made safer because of the Minuteman missile, that does not in the least detract from another's safety. Furthermore, the Pentagon could not deprive any individual citizen of the benefits of Minuteman (short of deporting him to an adversary nation) if he refused to buy his share. City planning, pollution control, consumer-product testing, and many other government services have similar characteristics. An efficiency-conscious government will wish to estimate the marginal value of public goods, since changing the level of these programs does use or save resources. Value of options, externalities and public goods, defined as maximum marginal willingness to pay at various levels of service, is not conceptually different from market prices for goods that have direct users, although it may be much more difficult to measure.

Enumerating benefits

The first step in evaluating a particular government program is to *enumerate specific ways in which various groups are benefited*, whether these are in the form of direct uses, externalities, options to use, or public goods. In this undertaking, the pitfalls to avoid are (1) counting benefits to some individuals or groups that are offset by costs imposed upon others and (2) counting the same benefits twice.

Suppose the objective is to list the benefits of a new highway. The primary benefit is time and expenses saved by those who travel the new road, net of possible increases in costs to others who use only feeder roads which have become more congested. External benefits may accrue to travelers using parallel routes that have become less congested because of the diverting of traffic. These motorists may also place some value on the option of an alternate route.

Any improvement in production possibilities of producers of goods and in net consumer satisfaction qualifies as net benefits. However, there is no net benefit from those side effects that simply alter resource or goods prices without changing physical production or consumption possibilities. For example, a new highway will improve profitability of service stations, restaurants, motels, and the like along its route; however, much of this improvement is offset by reduced incomes to other facilities affected by traffic reductions along previously existing roads. A new highway will also increase values of adjacent land suited for facilities rendering services to travelers, but these increases are simply capitalizations (present values) of potential additions to future income production on the sites. Listing both the current increases in land values and the current increases in incomes would be double counting.

It is sometimes difficult to make a clear distinction between benefits and costs. To do so, the agency must specify a target population for which the program is intended. Benefits often fall to persons outside the target group—construction contractors, for example—at the expense of those within it—the region's taxpayers. A similar point of view applies to increased employment, at possibly higher pay, of local construction workers. Their gains are also at the expense of the area's taxpayers. In both examples, the payoff from the program is the *difference* between the *value of the services* and the *cost of producing them.*

Evaluation of direct benefits

Simple enumeration of benefit categories and their incidence is only a beginning. *Choice of the best level* for a program and *choice among competing programs* requires *measurement of benefits,* usually in terms of money. The ideal measurement would be monetary value of total utility to all beneficiaries of a program. This value may be illustrated conceptually by means of Figure 12–1. Curve *D* represents demand of all beneficiaries for the output of a program. That is, it indicates, at every level of the program, the marginal value to all beneficiaries of that program. Now suppose it is proposed to expand in a large "jump" from Q_0 to Q_1. The value of *marginal* units will fall from V_0 to V_1. The total monetary

FIGURE 12–1

CONSUMERS' SURPLUS IN COMPARISON OF PROGRAMS

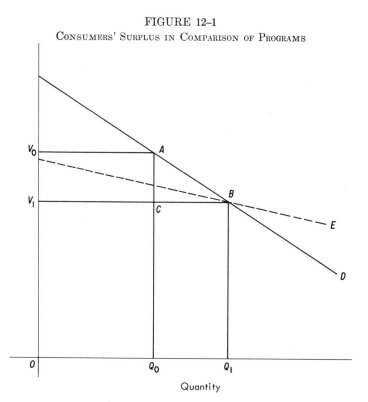

Quantity

value to users of this expansion is $Q_0 ABQ_1$. However, if the output is priced at V_1, revenue is less than the increase in monetary value of benefits provided (by the amount ABC). The area ABC is called "consumers' surplus" because the price, OV_1, which just rations the increased output, is below the consumers' marginal evaluations of those quantities acquired in moving up to the greater output at Q_1.

To illustrate the implications of the consumers' surplus approach to benefit evaluation, suppose an analyst attempts to put a value on use of a congested facility by measuring the amount of time that users will voluntarily sacrifice by waiting in line. Expansion of the facility by some substantial proportion would reduce this "price" for all. To value all output at the new price ignores the fact that some users of the increased capacity would be willing to wait longer (pay a higher price) than they actually do.

The concept of consumers' surplus is helpful in choosing among programs. For example, if demand for some other service, represented by Curve E in Figure 12–1, were more elastic, postexpansion price times quantity or consumer expenditure OQ_1BV_1 would be the same as for service D at price V_1. However, note that there is greater consumers' surplus for the expansion from Q_0 to Q_1 in the case of service D. Thus, expansion of D would be preferable to expansion of E at the same cost, and possibly preferable even if expansion of Program D has the greater cost of the two.

Full estimation of consumers' surplus may be impractical, because it requires that the entire demand curve be estimated. Consumer expenditure, which is much easier to estimate, will not be a serious underestimate of monetary value of benefits if demand is highly elastic or if the project adds only marginally to the amount of service available.

Sometimes the immediate output of a public program is a capital good expected to yield a stream of benefits over a period of years. Such is the case in most education, vocational training and rehabilitation, and other "manpower" programs. The final product of these programs is the trainee's increased productivity (which is sold in the labor market by the recipient rather than by the government). If the expected increase in future earnings of a trainee measures improvement in his productivity, the present (discounted) value of this stream of additional earnings is the appropriate measure of current benefits.

Indirect-estimation techniques

External benefits, public goods, and unpriced direct benefits must be evaluated through *indirect estimation* of consumer demands. The three most common strategies, all illustrated below, are: (1) to observe changes in prices for land (or other complementary goods) affected by the project;

(2) to obtain prices paid for close private substitutes; or (3) to estimate reductions in costs made possible by the project.

Each of these techniques can be illustrated by reference to Jerome Rothenberg's study of urban renewal projects.[2] The principal efficiency objective of urban renewal is to improve productivity of land in and around the renewal site. Assembly of a number of separately owned parcels into one large tract allows a developer, public or private, to build better housing that is not exposed to the value-depressing effects of surrounding slums. Increased rentals (net of increased costs) are capitalized in higher land values for those sites that are sold to private interests for highest bids. Increase in land values, therefore, constitutes a dollar measure of part of the direct benefits of the project.

A typical urban renewal project will also increase attractiveness of real estate in adjoining neighborhoods. Hence, the increase in market values of land surrounding the project is a partial measure of external benefits of the project. Another type of external benefit which may result from the project is reduction in fire hazard to nearby neighborhoods. A portion of this benefit accrues to the public in the form of lower costs of fire protection services, and, perhaps, lower insurance premiums. This is an example of measuring benefits by reductions in associated costs.

Finally, there may be a problem of estimating the value of public housing built as part of the project, where this property is not sold at competitive market prices. If such housing does not constitute a large portion of the total supply in the community, then its value may be estimated by using the value of nearby private housing with similar characteristics.

The above illustration does not give a complete accounting of benefits from urban renewal. Actual estimates of changes in values and costs due to a program and the identification of private substitutes for unpriced benefits will often require a good deal of ingenuity. Rothenberg was only able to estimate changes in land values.

PRODUCTION, COST, AND COST-EFFECTIVENESS

Project outlays

Estimates of program costs should take the form of *projections of outlays for each year* of the project life on the basis of *current market prices of inputs*. Even in cases where construction of all facilities is completed in the first year, total project outlays will probably include subsequent expenditures for operation and maintenance of facilities.

---

[2] Jerome Rothenberg, *Economic Evaluation of Urban Renewal* (Washington, D.C.: Brookings Institution, 1967).

General increases in input prices need not be projected, since they affect all alternatives alike, but estimates of future expenditures should reflect anticipated changes in *relative* prices of inputs.

Project outlays are only a starting point. Social cost may be substantially different from explicit financial outlay. *Social cost* is the opportunity cost (the value in the best alternate use) *of all resources used in the project.* Many such costs may not show up in agency financial outlays because they involve unpriced resources, or underpriced intragovernmental transfers, or use of existing agency-owned facilities, or because the costs are imposed upon and borne by activities external to the agency. A full accounting of project costs will include implicit agency costs and external costs in addition to the explicit costs to the agency.

Project costs

The concept and measurement of implicit costs was discussed in Chapter 2. *Implicit costs are the amounts by which opportunity costs exceed explicit costs.* Capital resources owned by a public agency have opportunity costs, as do inventories of materials and goods in process. In addition, a public agency should estimate the full value of any unpriced or underpriced resources used and add this value to project costs even though all or part of the incidence of cost is external to the agency.

As an example of the variety of relevant costs, consider an urban highway project. The immediate explicit costs are site acquisition, planning, and construction of facilities. Future explicit costs of the project include operation and maintenance of the facilities over their estimated useful lifetime. If a portion of the right-of-way is already under government ownership, value of this land in its otherwise most productive use constitutes an opportunity cost to the government. However, the highway project may also have external costs. Construction involves disruption of established travel patterns and dislocation of residents along the right-of-way. Moreover, to the extent that it encourages an increase in vehicle-miles of auto travel within the jurisdiction, there are future increases of air pollution and noise. Unless reimbursements of affected individuals is specifically required by law or by agency policy, external costs are not borne by the agency, but they are still relevant costs from the point of view of the welfare of a target population.

An illustration of the need for careful handling of implicit cost is given by a study of graduate education in management in India.[3] From the student's point of view, the largest *private* cost of management education is the value of foregone earnings from postponement of full-time employment. Of course, his projected gross earnings would be reduced by indirect taxes, sales taxes, property taxes, and excise taxes to obtain his *net* private

---

[3] S. Paul, "An Application of Cost-Benefit Analysis to Management Education" in W. A. Niskoven, et al. eds., *Benefits, Cost and Policy Analysis: 1972* (Chicago, Illinois: Aldine Publishing Company, 1973).

sacrifice. However, under assumptions of competition in the labor market and full employment, the student's *gross* earnings represent *social* cost of the sacrifice of his contribution to production. On the other hand, if there is a pool of educated underemployed, as was found in Paul's study of India, there may be little social cost of the student's withdrawal from the labor force. In this case, a series of workers "move up" to better jobs, and most of these are about as productive as the person they replace.

Project outlays that are based upon market prices of inputs may need to be adjusted for effects of unemployment, monopoly elements, government controls, price supports, or other conditions that cause market prices to diverge from marginal social costs of the resources. For example, consider the case in which some unemployed resources are expected to gain employment as a result of a project. The social cost of such resources is much less than their prices, since they would otherwise produce nothing. Note that adjustments for unemployment are appropriate only if the condition is expected to exist at the time that the resource is to be used. Project analysis usually concerns some future period, and it is probably not reasonable to assume that mass unemployment will persist year after year.

Monopoly prices and government-supported prices may overstate opportunity cost of resources required by a project. Unfortunately, there are no reliable rules of thumb for making the necessary adjustments in such cases. Since the unadjusted market prices do represent marginal evaluation of those resources (at inefficient usage levels), they may be the best estimates available to the analyst.

Cost-effectiveness analysis

Cost evaluation is usually considerably easier than evaluation of benefits, since inputs are more often subject to pricing in the market than are public outputs. It is sometimes feasible to make explicit dollar comparisons among alternative programs *only in terms of costs,* thus bypassing the difficult problems of benefit estimation. If the programs to be compared are *alternative ways of reaching the same objective,* this procedure obviously yields useful results. The alternative which has lowest cost is judged most effective. Notice also that both explicit and implicit *costs that are common to all alternatives can be disregarded* in cost-effectiveness analysis.

This type of approach is commonly used in highway planning. A variety of alternate routes between origin and destination may result in similar benefits and the major categories of benefits are time saving and safety improvements, both of which are difficult to evaluate in dollars. Common standards can be set in terms of average speeds, lives saved, and property damage avoided; comparison of alternatives can then be based only upon quantifiable costs.

Even in cases where performance specifications of alternatives are not identical, comparison of costs may be useful in clarifying the issues involved in choice. For example, an increase in average speed of two miles per hour may be shown to be attainable on Route A which will cost one million dollars more than alternate Route B. These values can be combined with traffic projections to derive an estimate of the value that must be placed on each hour of time saved in order to justify the additional cost of Route A. *Note that cost-effectiveness analysis cannot indicate the efficient level of a particular program, nor is this technique useful in choosing among programs with dissimilar benefits.* Nonetheless, because it requires less information than benefit-cost analysis and is less demanding of the time and expertise of agency personnel, it has become a regular part of the planning process in most federal agencies and in many states and localities.

PRICES, CHARGES, AND SUBSIDIES

Public agencies produce a wide variety of outputs, some of which might properly be termed "private goods." These are goods which, in contrast to "public goods," can be enjoyed independently and exclusively by individuals. That is, one person's use reduces the amount available to others but does not otherwise affect their well-being. Such goods can be divided and offered to individuals in varying amounts. Among such services commonly provided by governments are parking, water, recreation facilities, and limited-access highways. It is feasible for public agencies to impose direct charges for private goods.

Pricing of public services helps in the efficient rationing of scarce supplies. Demand for a "private good" that is provided free is likely to outrun the available supply. This is so because the good will be consumed up to the level at which marginal units are worth nothing to users, without regard to the additional cost of providing increased service. For example, on warm, summer days there are never enough free public swimming pools. As a consequence, such facilities are usually rationed by *exclusion rules,* such as time limits or residence requirements, and/or by *queues.* More efficient *price rationing* of such goods can be achieved by using the rule that price should equal marginal cost.

Marginal-cost pricing

Marginal-cost pricing can be illustrated by the example of a congested highway. Variable costs of highway transportation include highway maintenance, traffic control, vehicle maintenance and operating costs, and the travel time, effort, discomfort, and safety hazard incurred by travelers. Most of these costs (per vehicle) increase as the traffic flow increases. A toll set equal to marginal cost (in place of the present system of gas taxes set at levels that cover average costs) would cause each user to compare the *value of his benefits* from use of a congested highway with *all costs* of his addition to traffic, including those costs *imposed on others.* If the toll exceeds marginal benefit for a particular trip, then the trip will not be made (at least not by this route) thus reserving the highway for others who value their trips more highly. Hence, a system of tolls that vary with changes in traffic levels could potentially improve economic well-being of highway users. This is the same concept of peak-load pricing that was discussed in Chapter 9.

User charges do not just *ration scarce facilities;* they also *provide guides to decision about investment in additional capacity.* In the simplest case where expansions may be made in small increments and production exhibits constant returns to scale, expansion is justified whenever total revenues exceed total costs. In other words, positive net revenue is evidence that expansion will yield benefits in excess of additional costs. In the absence of user charges, there are no such direct measures of the benefits of expanded facilities.

A more general rule for expansion of a program that has direct user charges is that expansion should continue until long-run marginal cost equals demand price. An agency that wished to apply this rule would need to estimate marginal cost for a variety of program sizes and then estimate the number of users at a charge equal to marginal costs. If scale economies are present, the optimal solution would result in losses, so that the "profitability" test does not hold. Conversely, decreasing returns to scale imply that total charges would exceed costs even at optimum program size. These are the same problems of marginal cost pricing that were discussed in Chapter 9.

In some cases, it may be appropriate for an agency to deliberately charge less than marginal cost. Recall that many public services are of the type which have important external benefits to nonusers. Such nonusers might reasonably be said to have demands for (that is, place value upon) the services. A user charge that decreases frequency of residential trash collection increases the unsightliness and health hazard that must be tolerated by those who are passing by. A charge on direct users which completely covers costs will result in an undersupply of services to the indirect users. Since indirect benefits accrue to taxpayers collectively (as public goods), subsidization of services to the fee-paying direct users by appropriations from general tax revenues can raise total community well-being as compared to full-cost pricing.

Indirect charges

A number of public outputs have not normally carried direct charges, despite their basically private character, because of the *high cost of collecting* from users. This condition holds for most streets and highways and many recreation facilities. However, indirect methods of charging may be feasible. These may take the form of *licenses* or of *taxes on private goods that are complementary* with the public outputs. For example, hunting and fishing license fees can finance wildlife conservation programs; taxes on gasoline can pay for transportation facilities.

Since the tax is tied to use of the service, these "benefit levies" serve some rationing function as well as providing revenue. On the other hand, such charges do not follow the principle of marginal cost, since the user pays nothing for additional units of the associated government service. In particular, taxes on complementary goods do not ration efficiently if the public output is subject to peak-load congestion. For example, marginal costs of highway use fluctuate widely among locations and hours of the day. These differences can not be reflected in the amount of gasoline tax, since gasoline purchase is largely independent of the time and place of highway use.

Prices of "bads": penalties

A type of government-administered "price" which has been receiving increased attention is the *penalty* for *damage to the environment*. Examples are proposed taxes on leaded gasoline and sulfurous fuels. These

FIGURE 12–2

INDUSTRIAL PLANT'S RESPONSE TO EFFLUENT CHARGES

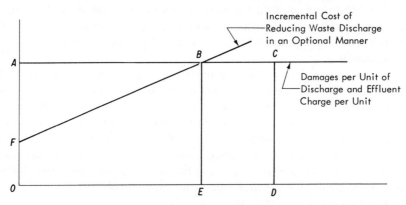

OD: Units of waste discharge if no charge levied on effluent.
OA: Damages per unit of waste discharge and effluent charge per unit.
OACD: Total damages associated with unrestricted waste discharge, i.e., no effluent
      charge levied.
OE: Reduction of waste discharge with effluent charge *OA*.
OFBE: Total cost of reducing effluent discharge to *ED*.
OFBCD: Total cost associated with waste disposal with *ED* waste discharge, i.e., re-
      sidual damage costs plus cost of reducing discharge.
OABE: Total damages avoided.
ABF: Net reduction in waste disposal associated costs by reducing waste discharge
      by *OE,* i.e., *OABE* minus *OFBE*.

would be incentives to *reduce production* of *underpriced,* or unpriced, *"bads."* As another example, suppose the waste from a plant were tested periodically for concentration of a harmful chemical, and a charge equal to the value of damages were levied per unit of discharge of this effluent. A profit-maximizing firm would respond to this charge according to its cost of controlling the waste. Allen V. Kneese has shown the effect of this policy by means of Figure 12–2.[4] Costs associated with waste disposal are minimized at E rather than at point D, where the latter represents the level of waste disposal when use of the stream is free to the firm. The institution of the charge induces the firm to adopt socially optimal waste disposal methods, reducing but not eliminating pollution; note that further treatment would require resources (equipment, location changes, or processes) that outweigh in value the additional improvement.

Subsidies

In a similar way, *subsidies* may be used to encourage *increased production* of goods that are overpriced in private markets because the *suppliers cannot collect the value of externalities.* Higher education, low-income housing, and commuter railroads are among the goods which may be produced privately and sold to direct users, but also provide significant benefits to others. One means to improve social welfare in such cases is to leave production in private hands, but to provide a public subsidy that will allow the private firm to set the price to direct users below the average cost.

Pricing and efficiency

Charges and subsidies will usually increase *efficiency of resource use* as compared to rationing by prohibitions, regulations, or other direct controls. Consider again the case of water pollution. The natural capacity of water to cleanse itself is an important resource. This resource can be overused, and it almost certainly will be if it is entirely free, but outright prohibition of its use would require some waste treatment with cost in excess of benefits. Cost of control varies widely among effluent-producing activities, and efficiency requires that any given level of water quality should be attained at the lowest possible total cost. Rules restricting the absolute quantity of effluent from each source do not take into consideration the varying costs of waste treatment. By contrast, effluent charges leave the choice of type and level of waste treatment to the polluting firm. As shown above, each firm would expand waste treatment up to the point where marginal treatment cost is just equal to the effluent charge. Any

---

[4] Allen V. Kneese, "Discharge Capacity of Waterways and Effluence Charges," in Selma Mushkin, ed., *Public Prices for Public Products* (Washington, D.C.: Urban Institute, 1972) p. 143.

desired level of water quality can be achieved by this method depending upon the level of the effluent charge. The choices of the individual firms then minimize total social cost of achieving any given level of water quality.

Summary

Since we have been stressing the importance of the pricing mechanism in properly allocating resources, it is appropriate to review the situations under which charges are justifiable or questionable. The following list is by Professors John F. Due and Ann F. Friedlander:

Use of the pricing mechanism where possible instead of free distribution with financing by taxation is regarded as most justifiable when:

1. Benefits are primarily direct, so that charges will not cause significant loss of externalities.
2. Demand has some elasticity, so that the use of prices aids resource allocation and eliminates excessive utilization.
3. Charges do not result in inequities to lower income groups, on the basis of accepted standards.
4. Costs of collection of charges are relatively low or alternate taxes measured by use can be employed.

Use of charges is more questionable when:

1. Externalities are significant and will be lost in part if charges are made.
2. Demand is perfectly inelastic, so that resource allocation is insensitive to the pricing system. Even so, charges may be regarded as warranted on equity grounds.
3. Equity standards require that the lower income groups be assured of obtaining the services.
4. Collection costs are relatively high and alternative tax measures related to usage cannot be devised.[5]

BENEFIT-COST ANALYSIS

Benefit-cost analysis is a set of techniques for comparing alternative programs or projects that are expected to yield returns over a period of years. To a considerable extent, benefit-cost studies follow the same principles of cost and return estimation that are used in private investment decisions. They are intended to provide for the public sector the kinds of guides to investment policy that are given to private firms by market prices and considerations of competition.

---

[5] John F. Due and Ann F. Friedlander, *Government Finance*, 5th ed. (Homewood, Ill.: Richard D. Irwin, Inc., 1973), p. 101. Also, for an excellent discussion of the economics of "pricing" services by public agencies the reader is referred to Alice John Vandermeulen, "Reform of a State Fee Structure," *National Tax Journal,* 17, No. 4, p. 394.

Competition can be *simulated* in decisions about public projects by the specification of a number of *alternative production techniques, levels of service, and combinations of output.* This list of alternatives will also probably include the possibility of no additional government program at all (the "status quo" alternative). The purpose of systematic analysis is not only to *justify government expenditure* to advance a certain objective, but also to find the *most efficient means* to that objective and to determine the *best level of service to provide. Comparisons among alternatives* may be largely *technical,* having to do with alternate types of equipment, or they may involve more fundamental questions of *priority* such as whether to build more job training centers vs. more research libraries.

Definition of the outputs or objectives of the project is the first necessary step in any benefit-cost analysis. These may be simple and obvious, as in the case of a bridge, or quite complex, as in the case of multiple-purpose water resources projects. In the latter case the outputs could be electric power, recreation, irrigation water, domestic and industrial water, flood control, and pollution control. Each of these outputs can be produced at different levels, but their production can not be considered independently. In other cases, project objectives may be quite intangible. Consider the problem of defining "outputs" of a correctional institution.

After objectives are stated and feasible alternative means and program levels are formulated, the goal of benefit-cost analysis is to estimate net improvement in the well-being of the target population for each of the alternatives. This suggests beginning with careful evaluations of both benefits and costs, using methods discussed in Sections 1 and 2 above.

Discounting benefits and costs

In practice, most studies of this type deal with large, durable projects from which benefits and costs will accrue over a period of years. This requires that evaluation of both costs and benefits take account of timing as well as absolute amounts of dollar magnitudes. The methods for dealing with time streams of costs and returns—compounding to terminal values, or discounting to present values—were discussed in Chapter 11. The same type of reasoning applies to government projects. For example, building of a dam will require government financing which, either by raising resource prices or increasing taxes, will take resources away from other public investment, such as roads, or from private sector investment, such as factories. Since the time streams of costs and returns will be different for these competing alternatives, discounting is required so that the projects can be compared in terms of present values.[6]

The appropriate rate of discount is the *estimated rate of return on*

---

[6] Present-value techniques are satisfactory in analysis of public investment, if the assumption of constant marginal social opportunity return on capital is accepted.

alternative investment which must be foregone in order to carry out the project under evaluation. The importance of correct choice of a discount rate may be shown by the following example.

Consider two potential government housing projects. The first, alternative A, would be built over two years at a level annual cost of $100,000 and is expected to produce benefits worth $30,000 per year beginning in year 3 and ending after ten years of use, whereupon it is replaced by a more productive land use. Alternative B would take three years to build at $100,000 per year, but would generate benefits of $30,000 per year for 20 years before it, too, becomes obsolescent. The following table compares the net present values for these two projects under three different discount rates.

Project	NPV Discounted at 5%	NPV Discounted at 7%	NPV Discounted at 10%
A	$25,383	$ 3,465	$—23,330
B	29,661	—3,205	—62,474

Notice that the choice of the discount rate is crucial in determining (1) whether a public project is warranted as compared to private investment or other uses of public funds, and (2) whether long-term or short-term investments will be favored. At 10 percent, neither project is justified. At 7 percent, project A is justified but B is not. At 5 percent, both projects are justified, but B is preferable to A. *Increases in the discount rate simultaneously improve the relative position of shorter-term alternatives, and disqualify a greater number of projects.*

Choosing the discount rate

Public agencies should use a discount rate which assures that public investments at the margin yield at least the opportunity rate of return on marginal private alternatives. The most common measures of "opportunity cost of capital" are the various market borrowing and lending rates. Which of these is most relevant to public investments? Actual government practice of recent years has favored using the rates which the governments must pay to borrow funds. Since public and private securities compete for the same lenders, these rates are related to private investment opportunities. However, a private investment that used the same resources would pay corporate income taxes; total social return is greater than the net private yield. In addition, the rate paid on government bonds is subsidized by granting personal income tax advantages to lenders. For these reasons, governments are able to borrow at rates that are well below marginal social return on private investments. Commercial rates, on the other hand, include the effects of financial risks that are relevant for investment by individual firms, but not for the expected return from all private investment taken together.

Considering these factors, suppose that corporations are paying 8 percent to obtain capital, using their optimal blend of debt and equity financing. Because of risk, a private firm might be willing to pay this rate to finance a project only if its expected return after taxes were substantially greater than the cost of capital. Corporate profits are taxed at approximately 50 per cent in the United States, but (depending upon the proportion of debt finance) this tax is partially offset by deductibility of interest. For example, a before-tax return of 15 percent with a 50–50 ratio of 6 percent bonds to new equity would be an after-tax yield of 9 percent.[7] If firms regard this as sufficient return to offset risk, then the 15 percent *before-tax* return would represent the contribution of the marginal private investment to the value of national output. Using this as the discount rate for government investment decisions would equalize marginal returns in the public and private sectors.

Now suppose that benefit and cost streams are quantified as accurately as possible in dollar terms for each feasible alternative, and a discount rate is chosen. Estimated net benefits in each year may then be discounted to present values and a total discounted net benefit may be determined for each project.

In the simplest case, all projects under consideration would be independent of one another (in terms of the resources to be used or the outcomes expected) and funds would be available for all worthy projects. In this case, *all projects with net discounted benefits greater than zero should be undertaken*. This is equivalent to recommending adoption of any "lumpy" project whose internal rate of return exceeds the discount rate, or increasing size of any continuously variable project with marginal rate of return above discount rate. Under this criterion, if marginal private investments are yielding a 10-percent before-tax return, any public project (or incremental increase in a project) that promised a greater return would be adopted and revenues would be raised to finance it.

But real public agencies are seldom able to undertake every project and every expansion that they can justify on net benefit grounds. Usually the budgetary limitation will be expressed in *maximum dollars available* rather than as a *required rate of return*. These conditions complicate the choice process. A foolproof choice criterion can still be simply stated— "approve that set of independent projects that maximizes discounted net

---

[7] An investment of $1 returns 15 cents in year one and incurs an interest charge of 3 cents (6 percent on 50 cents). Taxable profit is therefore 12 cents and taxes are 6 cents, leaving a 9-cent profit after taxes.

benefits without exceeding the budget constraint." However, if the list of projects is long and the number of mutually exclusive sets is large, project ranking requires mathematical programming techniques.

Appraisal of benefit-cost analysis

The foregoing is intended to indicate that benefit-cost analysis has firm basis in economic theory and that it has been subject to continuing refinement and expansion. However, use of the benefit-cost approach in government decision making has attracted substantial criticism. One strand of criticism is that *benefit and cost evaluations are solemnly totalled and compared regardless of what individuals or groups comprise the beneficiaries and who is requested to bear the costs.* For example, a lush recreation area accessible mainly to the well-to-do and designed to accommodate their motorized campers may outrank neighborhood playgrounds in the inner city on strict net benefit grounds. This is so because dollar evaluations of benefits depend upon the incomes of the beneficiaries as well as upon their relative preferences among goods and services. In benefit-cost analysis, the weights applied to outputs are the estimated potential dollar offers of the beneficiaries. These may not always be regarded as appropriate weights for public decisions.

A second line of criticism attacks benefit-cost analysis on pragmatic grounds of the *difficulties of implementation.* Determination of shadow prices and the appropriate discount rate, specification of a target population, the importance of "nonquantifiable" benefits, price adjustments for underemployment and market imperfections, and the approach to uncertainty of outcomes are all largely unsettled aspects of the practice of making benefit-cost studies. For these reasons, some observers have suggested that a reasonably imaginative analyst could produce positive benefits for *any* project without violating the established rules.

Research, additional practice, and an increase in the number of people who are familiar with the basic techniques may blunt the latter type of criticism. But critics of the concept will continue to have a point—no economic analysis is a substitute for basic value judgments, such as whether the poor should pay for services to the rich or vice versa. As a habit of mind, comparison of benefits against opportunity costs is fundamental to all rational choices. But as a set of practical techniques, benefit-cost analysis is likely to remain most useful *where the issues are narrow* (as in the choice of alternative hardware to produce a specified output), *where most outputs are privately consumed* (as with power production, waste disposal, or health care), and *where the program in question is sufficiently large or sufficiently simple to justify the costs of the analysis.* Even these kinds of analyses should not stand by themselves. Benefit-cost studies should always be accompanied by studies of the *incidence of benefits and costs* upon various groups.

MULTIPLE OBJECTIVES AND GROUP DECISION

Most of the foregoing discussion of government decision-making has dealt with the problem of improving efficiency of resource use. Except for the brief consideration of intergroup equity in the discussion of benefit-cost analysis, we have been assuming that all parties to any decision regard efficiency as the primary goal. In reality, efficiency of resource use may not be the only, or even the most important, concern, and it may not be fully compatible with other objectives.

In addition to attempts to improve efficiency and to make the distribution of benefits and cost as equitable as possible, an agency or budget bureau may be charged with responsibilities for (1) the prosperity, growth, and stability of the overall economy (the stabilization objective); (2) the economic development of particular regions or sectors of the country (the regional objective); (3) and/or the relationship of the nation to other nations (the international objective). Obviously these three types of goals will affect much of the decision making in the domain of the federal government.

Consider a federal program to encourage exploration for domestic sources of oil. A benefit-cost study would be aimed at answering whether federal dollars would generate more valuable benefits in this or some other use. However, even if net benefits are positive, some may object that benefits accrue narrowly to producers and marketers of oil and to large oil consumers at the widely distributed expense of typical taxpayers. In addition, many people will have an interest in the impact of the employment- and income-generating effects of the program. Still others will be interested in which regions of the country are helped most (and which, if any, are hurt). Finally, there will be concern for the effect of increased domestic oil capacity on national military preparedness, international political power, and the balance of international payments. Benefit-cost analysis alone is not suited to considering all these objectives at one time.

Conceptually, an optimal decision in the case of multiple goals requires that those goals be given explicit decision weights. Suppose, for example, that *efficiency* is measured in terms of net dollar benefits, *equity* in terms of the number of dollars transferred from those above the median family income to those below it, *regional development* as the dollar addition to gross product of a region (e.g., the Southwest), and *international affairs impact* by net change in the domestic trade balance. If weights can be assigned according to the relative importance of each goal, and the weighted outcomes can be regarded as additive, it is possible to produce a single number with which to compare alternative programs. For example, one might have as the overall objective to maximize $.4E + .3Q + .1R + .2I$, where E stands for efficiency, Q for equity, R for regional development and I for international affairs as measured above.

A somewhat more sophisticated and realistic procedure for dealing with problems of this type is given by "goal programming." *Goal programming* is an extension of linear programming which allows the setting of target minimum values for each goal with relative priorities specified among them. For example, goals for a program might be to achieve $5 million of priority net benefits, $2 million of redistribution, $1 million of regional development and $2 million of improvement in the balance of payments. The priorities are then simply the relative importance of the targets in case they are not all simultaneously attainable. The advantage of this method is that the setting of *target values* may be easier or more politically feasible than explicit determination of *relative weights* of goals categories.

In the public agency, perhaps more so than in private business, the decision-analyst must be aware that economic consequences will not entirely rule the final choice. The decision models described in this chapter handle economic variables imperfectly, and other variables, such as political costs, are not dealt with at all. Nevertheless, benefit-cost analysis and related techniques provide systematic organization of available economic information and some guide to the relative importance of information that is not yet at hand.

Cases for part six

GENERAL PASSENGER FARE INVESTIGATION*
CIVIL AERONAUTICS BOARD

Decided: November 25, 1960

OPINION

BY THE BOARD:

This proceeding was instituted in order to determine whether the general level of passenger fares of the domestic trunkline carriers is unjust or unreasonable, and if so, to determine what overall percentage change in the fare level should be permitted or required.

After due notice, extensive public hearings were held before Examiner Ralph L. Wiser, who, on May 27, 1959, issued his Initial Decision. The ultimate conclusion reached in the Initial Decision was that fares should be increased 12 percent above the pre-February 1958 fare level. The basic findings may be briefly summarized. With respect to the return element, the Initial Decision found that the carriers could attract capital and accomplish the required financing for their jet reequipment programs if allowed a rate of return on a prudent investment base, including equipment deposits, of 10.6 percent for the industry. The traffic, revenue, and load factor forecasts of the carriers were found to be reasonable, and the carriers' estimates of expenses, including their computation of normalized Federal income tax expense, were generally accepted as proper. However, the carriers' cash expense estimates were found to be somewhat high, and it was also found that their flight equipment depreciation estimates should be adjusted to reflect straight-line depreciation based upon specified service lives and residual values. The recommended 12 percent fare increase, to be accomplished by a $1 surcharge, and any necessary percentage adjustment, was found to bring fair earnings to the bulk of the industry, on a fulcrum-rate basis, and not substantially to affect the movement of traffic.

---

* This case is a condensation of a Civil Aeronautics Board Decision.

The original objective of this proceeding was "(1) to develop appropriate and well-defined standards as to the earnings which are required by the 12 domestic trunkline carriers for proper development consistent with the public interest; and (2) based on such standards, to require or permit such overall decreases or increases in domestic fares as circumstances may warrant."[1] Upon consideration of the record, the contentions of the parties, and Form 41 data for recent years, we conclude that the record before us is inadequate to permit the fixing of the fare level. However, the record does permit us to formulate significant standards which will contribute to the regulation of fares.

Our difficulty in attempting to prescribe the just and reasonable fare level from the present record is very basic. Neither the carriers nor Bureau Counsel have submitted forecasts of operations, revenues, and expenses which we find are reliable indicia of what future results will be. In addition, there is an absence of data in the record presenting the experience of operations with the new turbine-engine aircraft which are becoming an ever-larger element of the industry's operations. In these circumstances, it would be futile to attempt to prescribe the appropriate fare level on the basis of the record herein.

However, much has been gained from this proceeding in the development of standards. Thus, we are setting standards herein for passenger fare regulation in four basic areas: profit element, rate base, depreciation, and taxes. These standards will be used in assessing future fare proposals of the carriers, and in assisting the Board in evaluating the reported results of the carriers so that the Board may determine when action on its own motion should be taken.

Rate of Return

The Examiner found that the industry return should be regulated by the conventional test of rate of return on investment. The carriers' proposal to measure earnings by the operating ratio or its complement, the return margin,[2] was considered but rejected. A primary contention of the carriers is that the operating ratio method provides the proper measure of risk for the investor. The carriers argue that airline risks are more closely associated with the magnitude of annual expenses and the width of return margins than with the long-term capital investment. However, we agree with the conclusion in the Initial Decision that "No other measure than rate of return on investment . . . provides a direct and positive measure of risk." Although he recognized that capital turnover[3] and return margin[4] affect the degree of risk, the Examiner correctly

---

[1] Annual Report of the Civil Aeronautics Board, 1956, p. 9.

[2] The return margin, or margin of return, is the ratio of return to revenue, computing return after all expenses including depreciation and taxes but before interest on debt. The operating ratio, or all-expense ratio, is the ratio of expenses to revenue.

[3] The rate of capital turnover, or the ratio of annual revenues to capital employed to produce those revenues, is typically less than 0.5 for ordinary utilities, including railroads; averaged for the airlines 1.66 for the years 1946–56 and 1.78 for the years 1951–56; and was 1.76 for certain industrials for the years 1946–56.

[4] The return margin for the period 1950–56 was 14.4 percent for natural gas operating utilities, 10.2 percent for Class I railroads, 5.8 percent for 20 selected manufacturers, and 5.3 percent for the trunk airlines.

pointed out that the amount at risk is limited to the amount invested. Even as to the degree of risk, capital turnover and return margin alone were properly found to provide no meaningful measure of risk that is recognized in the market place.

A related contention made by the airlines is that they cannot safely afford to operate with the margin of return produced by an otherwise fair rate of return. Asserting that low return margins and rapid capital turnover mean variability of profits, the carriers insist that only the operating ratio approach can assure that their margin of return will not be eliminated by moderate changes in expenses or revenues. The Examiner, however, correctly declined to accept the carriers' contentions. He found that a fair return on investment will afford an adequate cushion against changes in business conditions by providing an opportunity to build up a surplus in good times which would be sufficient to tide the company over bad times. The Examiner also noted that variability of profits is not wholly dependent upon the width of profit margins, but is affected by variability in the volume of business and by ability to adjust costs to changes in revenues and revenues to changes in costs.

We find ourselves in basic agreement with the Initial Decision. The reasonableness of the decision is further underscored by recognition that the carriers' computed margin of return substantially understates their margin of safety between operating revenues and expenses. Although the carriers have figured the operating ratio with income tax included as an expense, the accurate measure of earnings protection is indicated by the operating ratio computed before, not after, taxes. The 52 percent corporate income tax expense declines as taxable income declines: and net income after taxes declines in an amount only about half that of net income before taxes. The result is that the real protective margin between revenues and expenses is nearly double that shown by the "all-expense" operating ratio.

Further exaggeration of the vulnerability of earnings stems from the failure to take account of the adaptability of revenues and expenses. For the airlines, significant factors in the protection of profits are the ability to offset increases in costs through revenue growth and to decrease costs to compensate for decreases in revenues. Thus the steady enlargement of the air traffic market has made the level of the margin of return less crucial, since it has meant that, over the long term, increases in expenses are accompanied by corresponding increases in revenues. Similarly, because a substantial portion of expenses is directly responsive to the volume of capacity offered and traffic carried, airlines are markedly able to blunt the effects of a slackening of revenue growth upon return margins by a substantial contraction of expenses. These considerations, in our view, lend persuasive weight to the Examiner's conclusion that the safety of airline earnings is not truly endangered by inadequate return margins.

A further contention of the carriers, not directly dealt with by the Examiner, relates to certain economic characteristics of airlines that are said to be more like those of unregulated industrials than like those of traditional utilities. Along with the asserted hazards of low return margin and high capital turnover mentioned above, special risks are attributed to such airline traits as vigorous competition, variable demand, and rapid technological change and obsolescence.

These factors, according to the carriers, make inappropriate the rate-of-return approach to revenue regulation.

On the record before us, we cannot conclude that retention of the traditional rate-of-return approach conflicts with the economic realities of the air transport industry. Although comparative risk of different industries may be a consideration in determining the reasonableness of a specific return to capital, we find that the indicia of relative risk cited from this record furnish no guide in themselves to the particular formula that should be employed to reach that end result. The rate-of-return standard, in our view, is sufficiently flexible to permit pragmatic adjustments to account for all risk factors, and, as is clear from the Examiners' findings adopted herein, was applied to do so here.

In sum, we conclude that only the rate of return on investment indicates the appropriate end result: earnings sufficient to compensate for all costs of service, including a reasonable but not exorbitant return to capital. Although useful for certain limited purposes, the operating ratio fails to measure the full costs of service, for the cost of capital can be determined only with respect to the amount of capital invested.

The inability of the operating ratio to approximate the return required to attract capital is clear upon this record. As found by the Examiner, the investor's ultimate test of the adequacy of earnings, in the light of all risks, is the return on his capital commitment. This means that rate of return, which keys return to the capital investment, is directly related to the investor's criterion of earnings adequacy; in contrast, the operating ratio approach, which relates return to revenues, gives no clue to the supply price of capital. For the foregoing reasons, we cannot accept the operating ratio or its complement, the return margin, as a measure of fair and reasonable earnings.

Cost of Capital. In determining the fair and reasonable return, as that term is judicially defined, the Board must reach an end result which provides earnings sufficient to cover all the costs consistent with the furnishing of adequate and efficient air transportation. Among these costs must be included a return to the owners of the enterprise which is not only comparable to the results of similar undertakings, but which will insure the retention and attraction of capital in amounts adequate to foster economic health and development.

Although the supply price of capital is a paramount consideration in finding the fair return, enlightened ratemaking for a future period depends not upon the application of any fixed historical formula, but upon the exercise of informed judgment. As the Board has stressed even with regard to rates for past periods, the cost of capital computation is only one of the elements upon which conclusions as to the proper rate of return may be based.

Following this basic approach, we have computed the fair rate of return with full regard for all the factors of record which affect the price at which capital can be retained and attracted. Our conclusion is that the industry requires a 10.5 percent rate of return. Although this result approximates the 10.6 percent figure reached by the Examiner, it rests upon different conclusions concerning the cost of equity and the appropriate capital structure for cost of capital computations. Set forth below are our findings concerning these matters, as well as the proper cost of debt.

Cost of Debt. The Examiner concluded on a judgment basis that a reasonable estimate of the cost of debt during the future period is 4.5 percent for the Big Four and 5.5 percent for the Intermediate Eight. Higher as well as lower estimates made by four cost-of-capital witnesses were considered, but rejected.

Cost of Equity. Considering all the data of record, the Examiner found on a judgment basis that the cost of equity is 15 percent for the Big Four and 17 percent for the Intermediate Eight. Weight was given to a number of factors, including the Big Four earnings-price ratios of approximately 13 percent, and the relative risk of the airlines.

After considering the contentions of the parties, we find ourselves in fundamental agreement with the Examiner's refusal to rely solely upon earnings-price ratios, and with his attempt to resolve the issue by resort to all the reliable evidence of record. Our examination, however, leads us to conclude that the supply price of equity is 16 percent for the Big Four and 18 percent for the smaller trunklines—a result for each group one point above that reached in the Initial Decision. The factors we have considered and our conclusions are set forth below.

1. Turning first to a consideration of airline earnings-price ratios, we begin with the finding that the Big Four earnings-price ratios centered about 13 percent, including allowances for costs of acquisition. Although the Initial Decision accepted the earnings-price ratio as the "most significant single indicator of capital cost," it nonetheless found that the ratio "is subject to many deficiencies."

Bureau Counsel insists that "The Examiner erred in not accepting the cost of equity as developed by the method of earnings-price ratios." In essence this is a contention that the cost of equity is precisely equivalent to an adjusted earnings-price ratio. We believe this contention is unsound, and fails to assign a proper role to the earnings-price ratio in the determination of equity cost.

The first approximation of the cost of equity capital, or the rate of earnings which will retain or attract the investor's dollar, may be gained by relating the earnings of the enterprise to the contemporaneous market price for common stock. Although the resulting earnings-price ratio has the allure of mathematical exactitude, it may not reflect the investor's real asking price. For, while the basis upon which the investor pays the market price is not past but anticipated earnings, the ratio of current earnings to price does not reveal what prospective earnings rate the investor anticipates, or to what extent he is influenced by prospects of corporate growth or investment appreciation.

Nevertheless, for long-established utilities with stable earnings, a concurrent earnings-price ratio may furnish a rather precise indicator of the actual cost of capital. This is because the reported earnings are approximately the same as the prospective income which the investor expects at the time he purchases the stock, and the market price of the stock therefore represents the investor's evaluation of the present worth of prospective income.

In contrast, the instability of airline earnings has led to relatively erratic earnings-price ratios which do not invariably reflect a market appraisal of future earnings literally translatable into a cost of equity capital. The instability of airline earnings, as compared with those of long-established utilities, is evident from the following table.

The result of earnings instability is that the investor in airline securities does not rely upon reported earnings as the yardstick of future prospects and investment worth to the same extent as does the investor in utility stocks. This is

ANNUAL EARNINGS PER SHARE

Year	Moody's 24 Public Utilities	12 Trunklines: Net Operating Income
1950	$2.62	$3.62
1951	2.44	5.64
1952	2.62	4.48
1953	2.78	4.19
1954	2.94	4.98
1955	3.21	5.30
1956	3.35	4.06
Year ended 6/30/57	3.34	2.82

shown by the failure of airline stock prices to respond closely to changing earning reports, with a consequent instability in airline earnings-price ratios. As illustrated in the table below, the airline earnings-price ratios fluctuated more widely in past years than did the ratios of the conventional utilities.

INDUSTRY EARNINGS-PRICE RATIOS

Year	12 Trunklines	Moody's 24 Public Utilities
1950	12.89%	8.39%
1951	12.33	7.50
1952	12.51	7.38
1953	14.17	7.35
1954	13.66	6.64
1955	8.78	6.52
1956	8.50	6.75
Year ended 6/30/57	7.20	6.71

The importance of stability in the earnings-price ratios was stressed by the expert witnesses, and even Bureau Counsel's rate-of-return expert agreed that "the more erratic an earnings-price ratio is over a period of time, the less reliable it is." Yet, as is evident from the foregoing discussion, airline earnings-price ratios are dissimilar, dispersed, and markedly changeable from year to year. The result is that, although analysis of the ratio is helpful as a starting point in determining the area of equity supply prices, any single average of these ratios is not reliable as the sole yardstick of the supply price of equity and can be meaningfully employed only as tempered by other available data concerning capital cost.

2. Having found that airline earnings-price ratios are not precise indicators of capital cost, we must decide whether the Examiner correctly concluded that the ratios substantially understate the cost of equity. For this purpose, we must relate the ratios to the risks of the enterprise which presumptively influence the price demanded by equity investors.

There is little controversy that investors have considered airline returns insufficient to compensate for the risks of the industry. Even apart from the abundant evidence that meager earnings caused "a flight of capital from the airlines" and left "airline stocks in disrepute among investors," the unanimous testimony of professional investors establishes that airline securities are not attractive investment opportunities at the yields expressed in the historic earnings-price ratios.

Inadequacies in the return shown by earnings-price ratios were found by witness Foster, a consulting economist, who compiled a rate of return study which, among other things, appraised airline earnings-price ratios in the light of comparative risks. After examining airlines and other industries, witness Foster testified that "The earnings-price ratios for common stocks of trunklines, if averaged over a term of years, are below any reasonable rate of return required to compensate for risk of investment in airline stocks."

This conclusion was derived from a comparison of industries according to indicia of relative risk. Using a technique consistent with our goal of "a return to the owners of the enterprise which is . . . comparable to the results of similar undertakings," the witness compared airlines with other utilities and with industrials with regard to three indicia of risk: deviation of annual rates of return; ratio of retained earnings to total earnings; and fluctuation of common stock prices.

The results of this study tend to support the quoted conclusion of the witness which, in turn, rested upon his view that "The earnings-price ratio averages, equated for differences in investment risk, are below the averages for water and electric utility stocks." Thus, taking the 1950–56 percentage price fluctuations of common stock as one index of relative risk, the measure of risk for the Big Four trunklines exceeded that of seven electric and seven water utilities by more than three and less than four times, respectively, although Big Four earnings-price ratios were less than twice those of either group. Similar computations with other indicia of relative risk, and with other industries, yield conclusions differing in detail but still indicating that airlines earnings-price ratios do not reflect fully the risks which presumptively influence the rate of earnings required by investors.

3. Although computations of the bare costs of capital can delimit the range of reasonable returns, the precise point within that range can be fixed only after consideration of special traits which affect the trunklines' ability to attract capital. Some of these factors, including the $2 billion accelerated jet reequipment program, were adverted to by the experts and, in part, appear to have been taken into the account by the Examiner.

In addition, we believe that substantial weight must be accorded to the unique risk which arises from our decision to gear fare regulation generally to the needs of the bulk of the industry, rather than to the needs of each individual carrier. Our reasons for adopting an industry-wide unit of ratemaking are sound, are necessary, and are legally proper; but the result is the risk that, because of competitive disadvantages, an individual carrier will be unable to earn the weighted average return found reasonable. This is illustrated in the following table, showing the overall rates of return which individual carriers would have earned in 1958 under the Examiner's recommended 10.6 percent for the industry.

HYPOTHETICAL RATES OF RETURN RESULTING FROM
10.6 PERCENT INDUSTRY RATE OF RETURN: 1958

Carrier	*Rate of Return*
Northeast	3.30%
Continental	6.09
Eastern	7.64
National	8.13
Northwest	9.11
TWA	9.39
Western	9.83
Braniff	10.20
Capital	12.00
Delta	12.63
United	12.78
American	13.95
Industry weighted average	10.60%

The disparity in earning power shown above, in general, couples the carriers whose earnings needs are highest with the returns which are lowest. Although this paradox cannot be resolved through ratemaking alone, we believe that where rates are set for the industry as a whole but it is apparent that many of the member enterprises will fall below the line of the average rate of return, a rate of return at the upper limits of the range of reasonableness is fair and reasonable.

4. After reviewing the foregoing factors which point towards the cost of equity, we conclude that the appropriate supply price must be recognized at 16 percent for the Big Four and 18 percent for the Intermediate Eight.

Capital Structure. The Examiner found that the overall rate of return should be computed on the basis of the actual capital structure, rather than on a hypothetical or optimum structure. Adopting the study submitted by Bureau Counsel, the Examiner found that the debt ratios planned for the period covered by carrier estimates are 45 percent for the Big Four and 50 percent for the Intermediate Eight.

We conclude that the Initial Decision correctly based the overall return upon an actual capital structure; but we find that the actual debt ratio will exceed the estimate accepted. Examination of the record in the light of actual reported results, which we officially notice, satisfies us that the percentage of debt in the capital structure will approximate that present at the end of 1959. Accordingly, we will premise our rate of return upon a capital structure containing 50 percent debt for the Big Four and 55 percent debt for the Intermediate Eight.

Increased undertakings of debt will continue during the immediate future to exceed any increment to equity by way of retained earnings or otherwise. We will, therefore, modify the Examiner's conclusions concerning the precise debt ratios which will be typical for the carriers.

Overall Returns. Application of the costs for debt and equity to the capital structure found reasonable, results in overall rates of return of 10.25 percent for the Big Four and 11.125 percent for the Intermediate Eight. Based upon the Examiner's finding that the Big Four account for two thirds of industry investment, the weighted average return appropriate for the industry is 10.5 percent. These computations are shown in the following table.

OVERALL RATES OF RETURN

Industry Unit	Security	Capitali-zation	Security Cost	Weighted Cost
Twelve trunks				10.5%
Big Four				10.25
	Debt	50%	4.5%	2.25%
	Equity	50	16.0	8.00
Other Eight				11.125
	Debt	55	5.5	3.025%
	Equity	45	18.0	8.1

For the reasons stated, we find that these returns are fair and reasonable for the carriers.

The foregoing analysis demonstrates that the determination of capital costs involves the exercise of judgment with respect to a substantial number of issues. In resolving each of these issues, we have done so, after full consideration of the evidence of record. While judgments can reasonably differ on the various subsidiary issues treated herein, it is the "end-result," in the last analysis, which must stand the test of reasonableness, and we are convinced that the overall returns determined herein fulfill that test.

Rate Base

In prescribing an appropriate rate base, the Initial Decision included all investments represented by the total capitalization of the enterprise, including equipment purchase deposits. The Examiner refused, however, to increase stated capitalization by adding thereto reserves for referred taxes or an increment for the effects of inflation.

After considering the exceptions filed by the parties, we find ourselves in disagreement with the Initial Decision's failure to adopt a depreciated assets rate base which excludes certain additional investments and special funds. Otherwise, we agree with the findings and conclusions.[5] We will limit our discussion to adjustments of the rate base and to certain exceptions.

Adjustments. The Initial Decision adopted a rate base computed from the right-hand side of the balance sheet by adding net worth to long-term debt. It was held that exclusions from this invested-capital or prudent-investment rate base should be limited to dishonest, wasteful, or imprudent expenditures, and the entire domestic portion of the stated capitalization was included in the rate base since "There is no contention . . . that any investment . . . does not constitute exercise of reasonable judgment."

Bureau Counsel contends that stated capitalization is not the proper yardstick of rate base determination. Bureau Counsel advocates adoption of a de-

---

[5] As a matter of principle, we would classify notes due beyond three months as long-term debt.

preciated assets rate base, figured from the left-hand side of the balance sheet. A rate base so computed would be less in amount than the sum of net worth plus long-term debt, since Bureau Counsel would limit recognized investment to the domestic allocation for net working capital (current assets and certain deferred charges less current liabilities and certain deferred credits), net operating property and equipment (after deducting depreciation and overhaul reserves), and other used and useful assets.

We find that Bureau Counsel's exception is well-taken. The stated capitalization method tends to result in burdening the rate base with investments not productively employed in the public service. Although exclusion of such assets from the rate base is not dependent upon the side of the balance sheet examined, adherence to the conventional depreciated assets technique properly focuses analysis upon the purpose to which investment is devoted by the enterprise.

The need for adjustment of the rate base is clear upon this record and uncontested by any party. Among the assets represented by the stated capitalization, and thus considered as part of the rate base by the Initial Decision, are a substantial number of investments which do not constitute contributions by corporate owners to the public service. These assets consist of several types: investments and special funds not used and useful to domestic certificated operation; nonoperating property and equipment not used and useful to domestic certificated operations; reserves accrued by charges to operating expense; unamortized discount and expense on debt; and property acquisition adjustments.

There can be no question that ratepayers should not be obliged to pay a return on investments and special funds or on nonoperating property and equipment which are not used and useful. Such assets, which include National's investment in a Miami television station, do not benefit air transportation or its ratepaying users. Although investors are free to receive a return on investments not beneficially dedicated to the utility enterprise, they must extract their profit from sources other than the traveling public. For this reason, we find that these investments must be excluded from the rate base, just as earnings from such assets must be excluded from calculation of carrier earnings.

Prevention of double-charging requires that we reduce the rate base by reclassifying as operating reserves those reserves, accrued by charges to operating expense, which appear on the balance sheet as surplus reserves. Through the expense allowance, these items have already been recovered by charges to the ratepayer. Since the investor is entitled to a return only upon his contributions to the enterprise, and not upon those supplied by the ratepayer, these reserves derived from charges to expense may not be included in the rate base.

Avoidance of duplicating charges to ratepayers also requires exclusion of unamortized discount and expense on debt. These expenses have already been recognized in the computations of debt costs and are compensated by inclusion in cost of capital. No further burden upon ratepayers is necessary or proper.

Rate Level

The unreliability of the expense and revenue forecasts in the record makes it impossible to determine the proper fare level in this proceeding. We have therefore confined ourselves in this opinion to the fixing of the standards which will be employed in regulating future fare levels. There remains for consideration the question of the method of employing these standards in future cases.

Essentially, the major problems of application of the standards fall into two categories: (*a*) the extent to which the fare level should be based upon results to be anticipated over an extended period, and (*b*) the extent to which fares should be regulated on an industrywide basis.

a. No party has suggested that we attempt to regulate fares so as to produce a particular rate of return for every 12-month period. It is manifest that in an industry in which costs and revenue factors tend to fluctuate and are difficult to forecast precisely for any short-term period, any attempt to maintain a constant rate of return would be futile. There is thus general agreement among the parties that the fare levels must be regulated to produce a reasonable return over an extended period of time.

This is not to say that short-term considerations need always be ignored. For example, if fare relief is necessary to prevent financial ruin to the bulk of the industry, we would clearly not be justified in refusing such relief on the ground that the adverse factors responsible for the industry's condition were merely of a temporary nature. Thus, the extent to which short-term factors would be influential in affecting the fare level must depend on the length of time those factors are expected to remain operative and the magnitude of their impact on the carriers' operating results.

From the foregoing it is apparent that the problem of determining when and for what periods fare adjustments should be made cannot be relegated for solution to any mechanical device. For this reason we do not believe that the five-year moving average formula proposed in the Initial Decision is practicable. Rather, the determination of when to permit fare adjustments and the length of the future period which should be considered in making these adjustments can be resolved only on a case-by-case basis, applying informed judgment to the task of balancing the relevant factors.

b. The second major problem in the application of standards relates to the so-called unit of ratemaking. Section 1002 (e) (5) sets forth, as one of the factors to be considered in ratemaking, "the need of *each* air carrier for revenue sufficient to enable such air carrier under honest, economical, and efficient management, to provide adequate and efficient air service." While we are thus enjoined to take into consideration "each" carrier's need, we are also faced with the facts that a large part of the domestic route structure is served by two or more carriers in competition, and that fares must be uniform as between them, notwithstanding that one carrier's revenue need may be less than another's. In short, we must reckon with the vexing problem of how to reconcile the statutory mandate to consider the need of "each" carrier with the hard fact that fares cannot be regulated on an individual basis. Specifically, shall fares be fixed to meet the needs of the carriers as a group, of the smaller trunks, of the poorest situated carrier or possibly even of the most favorably situated?

The Initial Decision concluded that fares should be set at levels which would meet the average of the costs, including return, of the bulk of the industry. In effect, the entire domestic trunkline industry would be treated as a single unit and would be regulated so as to produce an over-all rate of return to the industry equal to 10.6 percent, the weighted average of the returns which were found reasonable in the Initial Decision for the Big Four and Medium Eight carriers, respectively. The parties disagree among themselves as to the propriety of this "bulk-line" approach. Some of the carriers and Bureau Counsel agree that the nature of the industry requires that fare levels be set on the basis of the industry as a whole, whereas other carriers and the GSA argue that the Initial Decision method violates the requirement of Section 1002 (e) (5) that we consider the need of "each" carrier. We agree in general with the result, although we reach that result by somewhat different means and would subject it to some qualifications.

The Initial Decision is based in large part on the theory that regulation should strive toward achieving the same kind of results that would obtain in the open market-place, and upon the belief that fixing fares at the level proposed in the Initial Decision would substantially achieve that result. But conformance with results under hypothetical free competitive conditions is not one of the stated policy objectives of the Act, nor is it one of the statutory ratemaking standards. We would not be justified in refusing to consider the need of each individual carrier merely because a "bulk-line" concept may more nearly approach the results under free competition. Nor can we read Section 1002 (e) as authorizing the Board to ignore the need of each carrier in favor of the need of the carriers as a group. As the excepting parties have pointed out, the statute does not speak in terms of groups of carriers but rather of individual carriers. The fact that we cannot regulate fares so as to provide precisely for the need of each individual carrier does not authorize us to refuse to take such need into consideration.

On the other hand, we clearly are not required to establish fare levels to meet the need of the most poorly situated carrier as Eastern contends we must. The statutory requirements that we "consider" the need of each carrier is only one of five ratemaking factors which we are required to weigh. Consideration of the other ratemaking standards of Section 1002 (e), particularly the effect of rates on movement of traffic (Sec. 1002 (e) (1)) and the need in the public interest for transportation at the lowest cost (Sec. 1002 (e) (2)) militates against the adoption of the least profitable carrier as the standard for fixing rates. Moreover, the standard pressed upon us by Eastern would be inconsistent with the need factor itself. Thus, were we to base fares on the results of the poorest situated carrier we would of necessity be ignoring the need of every other carrier, contrary to the mandate that we consider the need of each of them. Finally, to use the most poorly situated carrier as the unit of ratemaking would result in the vast majority of the public paying rates greatly in excess of the cost of furnishing the transportation and would unjustly enrich the great majority of the air carriers.

By the same token, we obviously cannot fix fare levels on the basis of the need of the most favorably situated carrier. Such a standard could have a disastrous impact upon many of the other carriers and upon the development of transportation generally. It is thus clear that the proper fare level must be found at some point between the needs of the most profitable and least profitable carriers and that the determination of the unit to which the standards shall be applied must be based upon informed judgment. Insofar as the need standard is concerned, this determination can only be made after testing any fare proposal against the needs of the industry as a whole, smaller groups of carriers, and each individual carrier.

The approach recommended by Bureau Counsel appears to us to accommodate reasonably the practical problems of industrywide regulation with the requirements of the statute. The Bureau would first examine the results of the carriers as a group by taking the weighted average of the relationship of yield per passenger-mile to cost per passenger-mile (including return on investment). This industry average, although not controlling, is entitled to great weight. It indicates the extent of the general fare adjustment needed to produce a reasonable return for the industry as a whole. The Bureau would then test the resulting fare level against the needs of the individual carriers and of groups of carriers. Thus, consideration is given to the extent to which the fare level meets the costs of the Big Four and the Medium Eight carriers; the relative number of passenger-miles accounted for by the various carriers; the extent by which each carrier deviates from the norm; the effect of such deviation on the group and industry averages, etc.

In the absence of special circumstances, the record indicates that rates which meet the needs of the domestic trunkline industry as a whole would reflect a balancing of the needs of the high cost and low cost carriers. Where the bulk of the carriers fall within a reasonable range of the rates of return found herein to be proper, and industry figures are not distorted by the unrepresentative results of carriers who are in extremely poor or extremely favorable situations, fare adjustments should normally be based upon the results for the industry as a group.

Inevitably, under an industrywide system of regulation some carriers may fall below the standard rate of return. That a given carrier may earn less than the standard during a particular period is not by itself a cause for concern since, as we have previously discussed, the reasonableness of earnings must be judged over an extended period of time. On the other hand, even failure to earn the standard return for an extended period does not necessarily mean that the particular carrier will be unable to compete, grow, and prosper. Our findings on rate of return demonstrate that the rates of 10.25 and 11.125 percent which we have adopted as standards are not minimum returns below which confiscation would result. Rather, we have deliberately adopted rates of return which are above the minimum returns but within the broad range of reasonableness. In arriving at these rates, we have taken into consideration the circumstances that fares cannot be fixed on an individual carrier basis because of the competitive nature of our domestic rate structure and that some carriers will of necessity earn less than the average standard of return. Thus, in view of the level of the rate of return standards established, we would not regard a carrier's earnings to be deficient unless those earnings fell significantly below the standards for an extended period.

The problem of accommodating the requirements of the weak and strong carriers is, of course, one of the most difficult to be found in regulation. Clearly, general fare increases cannot be regarded as the panacea capable of solving the problem. There are other tools which are more appropriate for use in dealing with the less profitable carriers. First, an over-all examination of the general passenger fare structure, an issue excluded from this proceeding, might well result in bringing the costs and revenues of the individual carriers into closer alignment. Second, as the Examiner pointed out, carriers whose needs are not met by general fare level adjustments can seek higher fares, although competitive aspects would preclude them from charging such fares except on some few noncompetitive segments (assuming, of course, that such fares are otherwise lawful). A third tool is that of route realignments designed to produce a more balanced competitive structure. Finally, we are authorized by Section 406 of the Act to grant subsidy payments where we find that such compensation is required in the interests of commerce, the Postal service, and national defense. Whether, and to what extent, any of these approaches should be used will, of course, depend on all surrounding circumstances. Suffice it to say, however, that the Board has available to it a number of techniques for dealing with problems not amenable to solution by regulation of the general level of commercial fares.

We have considered all the exceptions to the Initial Decision, and we find that, except to the extent indicated, they should not alter our decision herein.

An appropriate order will be entered.

Gillilland, Chairman, Gurney, Vice Chairman, and Boyd, Member of the Board, concurred in the above opinion. Minetti, Member, filed the attached concurring and dissenting opinion. Bragdon, Member, did not take part in the decision.

MEMBER MINETTI, CONCURRING AND DISSENTING:

While I agree with most of the majority's determinations, I cannot concur in its resolution of three basic issues. The effect of the majority's decision on these issues is to burden the traveling public with (1) an excessive rate of return applied to (2) an inflated investment base, and (3) an allowance for fictitious federal income taxes. As a result, the uses of air transportation will be charged in the neighborhood of $80 million annually in excess of a reasonable fare level, based upon 1958 results.

| | Domestic Trunklines | |
	Per Majority (000)	Per Dissent (000)
Investment	$1,091,741	$ 923,691
Rate of return	(10.536%)	(9.04%)
Return element	$ 115,029	$ 83,483*
Interest expense	23,768	23,768
Income tax	98,866	50,827
Return and taxes	213,895	134,310
Operating costs, passenger	1,387,925	1,387,925*
Passenger revenue required	$1,601,820	$1,522,235

* Does not include provisions for return on, and amortization of, capitalized interest on purchase funds, the data being unavailable.

With respect to rate of return, I conclude that rates of approximately 8.75 percent for the Big Four and 9.6 percent for the Intermediate Eight would be reasonable and ample and that the returns of 10.25 percent and 11.125 percent found by the Board are not supported by the record. With respect to the investment base, it is my opinion that, in recognizing equipment purchase funds and deposits which are related to airplanes not yet delivered, the Board is charging today's airline passengers with part of the costs of operating tomorrow's airplanes, a result which is at war with the weight of regulatory precedent, is unfair to present passengers, and may well impede the development of traffic.

1. *Rate of return.* The rates of return adopted by the Board in this proceeding, so far as I am aware, are higher than those allowed by any other government agency in history. This fact alone would be no more than an interesting sidelight to this proceeding if the high rates of return were in fact supported by the record. In my opinion they are not.

My basic disagreement with the majority is with respect to its findings on the cost of equity capital. The majority has found that the fair returns on equity are 16 percent for the Big Four and 18 percent for the Intermediate Eight. These rates exceed the recommendations of the Examiner and of every expert witness who testified on rate of return in this proceeding.

The majority constructs its cost of equity on the basis of the earnings-price ratios of airline common stocks to which the usual allowance for flotation costs and underpricing is added. According to all of the experts, this method produces a cost of equity of approximately 13 percent for the Big Four. Had the majority stopped at this point, I would have no cause to complain. But the majority adds three percentage points to the objectively determined 13 percent on the basis of "judgment." It is here that we part company. In my opinion, the three-point allowance results in double compensation to the investor for risks which are actually reflected in the earnings-price ratios.

The majority supports its three-point increment on the ground that the earnings-price ratios, while they provide an appropriate starting point for determining cost of equity, are nevertheless unreliable. According to the majority "the instability of airline earnings has led to relatively erratic earnings-price ratios which do not invariably reflect a market appraisal of future earnings literally translatable into a cost of equity capital." It may be conceded that the earnings-price ratios for airlines do not follow as consistent a pattern as the data for the more stable public utilities, and it is therefore incumbent upon us to use such data with the utmost care. But the fact that the data may have some infirmities does not prove that the data *understates* the cost of equity capital. On the contrary, the majority's conclusion that the earnings-price ratios must be adjusted upwards is not only unsupported by the record but is at war with the logic of the situation.

In reaching its conclusion that airline earnings-price ratios understate the cost of equity, the majority relies heavily upon the testimony of witness Foster who concluded that the earnings-price ratios "are below any reasonable rate of return required to compensate for risk of investment in airline stocks" and that "the earnings-price ratio averages, equated for differences in investment risk, are below the averages for water and electric utility stocks." Although the majority states that Foster's conclusions are supported by certain studies which he placed in the record, I have found nothing in these studies which would tend to support the conclusions. These studies merely show that in terms of common stock price fluctuations and other indicia of risks, airline equity securities are riskier than water and electric utility stocks. But this proves nothing, since the airline earnings-price ratios are in fact substantially higher than the utility ratios. Foster's studies in no way substantiate his bare assertion that the high airline earnings-price ratios do not fully reflect airline risks.

In my opinion, the record if anything supports the conclusion that the earnings-price ratio data used by the witnesses and the Board *overstates* rather than understates investor earning requirements. The crucial factor which leads me to this conclusion is the fact that the period from which the ratios were drawn was the period of the highest sustained earnings level in the history of the industry. As a result, the earnings-price ratios, which were also at peak levels during this period, overstate the cost of equity. This was so because, as the majority states, "the basis upon which the investor pays the market price is not past but anticipated earnings [and] the ratio of current earnings to price does not reveal what prospective earnings rate the investor anticipates. . . ." Therefore, when earnings in any particular period are higher than those which the investor can reasonably expect will be the long term average future earnings, the earnings-price ratio developed for such a period will tend to be excessive in relation to the actual investor earnings requirements. And yet, the period from which the earnings-price ratios are drawn was a period of unusual prosperity for the carriers.

The earnings-price ratio data was drawn primarily from the period 1950–56. During a large part of this period, airline earnings were at a high level as a result of the Korean war boom and the post-Korean shortage of aircraft. For the period 1950 to 1956, the earnings on equity for the Big Four averaged 18.51 percent, *the highest sustained level of earnings in their history.* This compared to a loss of 1.94 percent during the post-war years 1946–49. In view of the economic conditions prevailing during most of 1950–56, the markedly inferior earnings of earlier periods and the characterization by this Board in 1953 of the then current earnings of the air carriers as "excessive when measured by any reasonable standard applicable to a regulated industry," it cannot be supposed that the investor expected Big Four earnings to maintain the high 1950–56 level indefinitely. It can only be concluded that the investor expected that the long term earnings of the carriers would average out to something less than the 1950–56 high. If the earnings-price ratios were adjusted for this factor a reduction of the rate of return somewhat below the majority's 13 percent starting point would be indicated.

1. *What are the most controversial issues in this case?*
2. *To what extent has the Civil Aeronautics Board followed the usual approaches to rate regulation discussed in Chapter 9?*
3. *Why was the Board unable to fix fare levels in this case?*
4. *Evaluate the operating rate method for fixing rates. Why did the airlines prefer this method?*
5. *Are the airlines more or less risky than other regulated industries? Should this factor influence rate decisions? Discuss.*
6. *Evaluate the estimates of the cost of capital in this case.*

7. *Why was there controversy about the determination of the rate base?*
8. *Was the decision of the Board generous or restrictive? Discuss.*

THE AUTO-WRECKING INDUSTRY

The auto-wrecking industry is comprised of approximately 15,600 small to medium-sized companies whose primary business is the taking in of damaged, junked, or abandoned motor vehicles, stripping them of useful parts, and selling those materials. Secondarily, they dispose of the scrap metal residue. The industry employs almost 100,000 workers, equivalent to the fabricated structural steel industry. However, 70 percent of the firms employ five or less people, 17 percent being one-man operations.

The auto-wrecking industry provides a highly valuable service. Were it not for the used auto parts made available in this manner, many older cars would have to be discarded once the manufacturer quit supplying new replacement parts. The total value of this operation is out of proportion with the junk yard image. For instance, in 1968, the auto-wrecking industry took in 9,033,000 automobiles and trucks. The average price was $334; the average resale value of the parts was $587 per vehicle, yielding an overall gross revenue of $5.3 billion. The following table compares this figure with other industries' experience:

COMPARISON OF AUTO WRECKING INDUSTRY REVENUE
WITH SHIPMENTS IN SELECTED MANUFACTURING INDUSTRIES

SIC Code	Industry	1967 Value of Shipments (Millions of Dollars)
3722	Aircraft engines and parts	5,320
2834	Pharmaceutical preparations	4,743
2042	Prepared animal feeds	4,640
3522	Farm machinery and equipment	4,428
3651	Radio and TV receiving sets	3,929
	Auto wrecking/dismantling	5,296

Source: Except for auto-wrecking-dismantling industry estimates, all data are from *Census of Manufacturers, 1967, Summary Series, Preliminary Report,* Bureau of the Census, U.S. Department of Commerce, April 1969.

The average for each of the 15,600 members of the industry was about $339,000.

Some other industry figures for 1968 point up some important considerations for the future of the industry. In that year, an estimated 8.4 million motor vehicles were abandoned or junked. However, more than 9.0 million autos were taken in by the industry. The 600,000 difference between these figures is the amount by which wreckers chewed into the backlog, as it were, of junked and abandoned autos. Estimates of the number of vehicles spread across the countryside range from 10 to 30 million. The sources of these vehicles is portrayed below:

AUTO-WRECKING INDUSTRY INVENTORY SOURCES

Source	Percent
Individuals	38
Auto and truck dealers, new/used	26
Insurance companies	21
State and local agencies	12
Other	3
Total	100

Source: *Automobile Disposal: A National Problem,* Bureau of Mines, Department of the Interior, Washington, D.C. 20240, 1967, p. 11.

Disposal of scrap and waste is the most pressing problem in the industry today. Although there would seem to be a ready market for automotive scrap iron and steel, certain economic factors work against profitable disposal. The auto hulk must be stripped, processed, and shipped to a point where the metal is saleable. Processing in this case means the preparation of the auto hulk for use by the steel industry. This usually consists of rendering the metal into bales, slabs, or shreds so that it is easily handled or moved.

One of the more common methods of processing auto hulks is the use of a baler. The auto hulk is dropped in a compartment wherein hydraulic rams reduce it to a cube weighing approximately 1,200 pounds. This is the No. 2 bundle, the basic item in auto scrap. Even so, the No. 2 bundle is not especially desired by the steel industry as it is quite easy to contaminate the metal with nonferrous or even nonmetallic substances. The exact number of balers in operation is not known. However, a 1968 Business and Defense Services Administration report indicated that at least 293 companies had installed such equipment.

A piece of equipment which produces a more easily inspected product is the slab shear. The process begins by compressing the auto hulk into a rectangular block 2 feet by 2 feet by up to 20 feet. This "scrap log" is then automatically fed through a shear which slices and compresses the metal into pillow-shaped slabs. The pieces are of very high density and are easily transported. The primary advantage is that it is easy to inspect the slabs for contaminants such as copper, zinc, chrome, stainless steel, rubber, plastic, and glass.

The machinery which poses the greatest promise for the wrecking industry is the scrap shredder. This piece of equipment chews up auto hulks into small-sized pieces, some at rates of up to 120 cars per hour. Some advantages of the method include the ability to magnetically separate the resulting scrap into ferrous and nonferrous metals and the ease of handling. However, such a machine represents a substantial investment. Prices range from about $500,000 for a small unit handling up to 100 tons per hour or more. Aside from price, the main disadvantage of the shredders is their appetite. They often can lay idle because of their efficiency and the costs of transporting hulks to the work site.

For all processing methods, the auto hulks must be stripped before they can be effectively processed. Stripping involves removing nonferrous metals. The cost may range from $3.00 to $5.00 per car, depending on wage rates and worker efficiency. A particularly difficult problem is removing the residual copper wire from the hulk. Copper in even very small quantities is a serious contaminant of steel and iron products. The average hulk weighs about 1,200 pounds of which maybe 4 pounds is copper wiring in mostly inaccessible places. Over half of this wire must be removed if the copper content of a baled or slabbed hulk is to have less than the .15 percent required by steel processors. This problem is less urgent when a shredder comes into play.

The process of stripping can be somewhat improved by the burning of the auto hulk. By incinerating the car body, various contaminants can be removed. Such might include rubber, plastic, paint, and upholstery. Incinerators may be of the pit, batch (or garage), or continuous operation type. The incinerator of the pit type is simply a covered cavity into which the hulk is placed to be burned. When the exhaust gases are caught and fed into an afterburner, the incinerator is termed a small-batch incinerator. Larger units, of the batch type, are more often of the garage type, resembling an oven, with an accompanying afterburner. The pit-type incinerator has a capacity of 8–10 autos per day, the garage type of 40–45. In addition, continuous-operation incinerators may achieve rates of 50 autos per day. They operate by hauling bodies through a tunnel on a continuous conveyor.

In 1970, however, because of stronger air-pollution-abatement regulations and uneconomical operating conditions, almost none of the pit- and garage-type incinerators were in use. All of the continuous-operation type units were shut down at that time for similar reasons. Of particular import for the larger units—of all types—was lack of utilization. It would be necessary for a number of wreckers to use the same facility in order to achieve an economical utilization of the equipment. However, many members of the industry did not express a willingness to utilize the incinerators available, mainly for economic reasons. One economically feasible alternative to incineration was open-air burning, but air-pollution-abatement regulations have now removed this alternative from practical consideration.

Another serious problem in disposing of scrap metal is the matter of transport to the point of sale. The wrecker usually does not shred or

bale his own scrap. After stripping the hulk, he flattens the body for shipment to a collection point where shredding or baling may take place.
Exhibit 1 indicates what the wrecker may have to pay to transport the
flattened hulks to a scrap salvage.

EXHIBIT 1

ESTIMATED COST OF HAULING FLAT AUTO SCRAP

REPORTED RATES FOR COMMON CARRIER AND PRIVATE/CONTRACT CARRIER FOR
TRANSPORT VIA TRUCK OF 35 FLAT SCRAP AUTO BODIES
(approximately 40,000 pounds)

Point of Departure	Destination	Approximate Distance, Mi.	Cost			
			Common Carrier		Private/Contract	
			Total	Ton/Mile	Total	Ton/Mile
1. Amarillo, Tex. ...	Pueblo, Colo.	340	—	—	$180.00	2.6¢
	Dallas, Tex.	350	—	—	180.00	2.6¢
	Eagle Pass, Tex.	550	—	—	240.00	2.2¢
2. Memphis, Tenn. .	Nashville, Tenn.	207	$164.00	4.0¢	144.90	3.5¢
	Jackson, Miss.	214	168.00	3.9¢	149.80	3.5¢
	St. Louis, Mo.	286	196.00	3.4¢	200.20	3.5¢
3. Olathe, Kan.	Kansas City, Kan.	15	75.00	25.0¢	50.00	16.7¢
4. Elizabeth, N.J. ...	Jersey City, N.J.	10	85.00	42.5¢	25.00	12.5¢
	Philadelphia, Pa.	60	135.00	11.3¢	55.00	4.6¢
	Newark, N.J.	6	45.00	37.5¢	12.00	10.0¢

Note: Some carriers may move 35–40 flat bodies per load.
Source: Cost information submitted by selected companies; ton-mile cost computed by BDSA.

These figures indicate that freight costs can considerably eat into the
$6.00–$8.00 that the wrecker may receive for each hulk.

One of the major problems of the auto-wrecking industry is disposing
of the solid wastes left by the stripping operation. Of these materials,
tires are by far the largest single item. Over 100 million tires are consumed annually in the United States. However, there is currently no truly
feasible way to either destroy them or recycle the material. For instance,
the price paid per ton at Akron, Ohio, in 1970 was $12, about 12 cents for
the average 20-pound passenger car tire. At Eastern collection points,
prices were about $7 per ton. The cost of handling and shipping would
result in the average wrecker's incurring a loss to dispose of tires. There
is hardly an incentive to deliberately collect them. The outlook is even
more harsh with respect to the other waste materials.

All things taken into consideration, the wrecker can expect to incur a
loss from disposal of the parts of an automobile which are not salable as
repair or replacement items. This fact is lamentable because the sheer
bulk of some of these materials represents a substantial resource. For
instance, Exhibit 2 indicates the market value of the various metals found
in a junk automobile:

EXHIBIT 2

MARKET VALUE OF METALS IN JUNK AUTOMOBILE
(as of January 1967)

Metal	Weight	Price	Total Value
Steel	1.28 tons	$35.00 (ton)	$44.80
Cast iron	.2335 tons	35.00 (ton)	8.17
Lead	29 pounds	9.0¢ (lb.)	2.61
Zinc	67 pounds	6.75¢ (lb.)	4.25
Copper	31 pounds	30.0¢ (lb.)	9.30
Aluminum	31 pounds	13.5¢ (lb.)	3.87
Gross value			73.27
Per ton			41.16

Source: *Bureau of Mines Research For Utilizing Automobile Scrap,* Karl C. Dean, Bureau of Mines, Department of the Interior, Washington, D.C., 20240, 1967.

However, the auto wrecker can realize only a portion of this value, primarily due to two factors. First, there is another operator in the supply chain between the wrecker (salvage yard operator) and the market (steel maker or foundry). The other reason is that the various metals are so contaminated by one another that the value of each is appreciably lessened.

EXHIBIT 3

THE AUTO SCRAP PROCESS

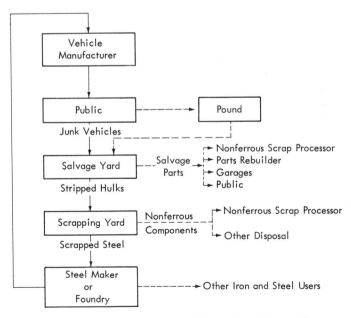

SOURCE: Copper Content in Vehicular Scrap, Ralph Stone and Company, Los Angeles, 1968, p. 41; study prepared for Bureau of Mines, Department of the Interior, Washington, D.C.

The public sector

Many state and local governments have an interest in the disposal of junked and abandoned automobiles. When an automobile is left on city streets in conspicuous, obnoxious, or hazardous places, local governments must often incur the costs of impounding and storing the vehicle until a public auction of the auto provides partial reimbursement. In rural areas, abandoned vehicles litter the countryside. The price available at most graveyards would not pay for the cost of hauling in the rotting hulks from remote rural areas.

These local governments also are concerned with the method of disposal. In the reclamation cycle, it is desirable to burn auto bodies to reduce the degree of contamination of the steel and iron to be recycled. Growing interest in ecological considerations has prompted passage of regulations all but forbidding this practice, however. At the same time, rapid disposal of existing hulks is desired in pursuit of better-looking communities. Therefore, state and local governments are asking wreckers to find a fast, clean method of processing junk autos.

To a somewhat lesser extent, the federal government is also interested in such a method. However, national interests are more concerned with the economic recycling of the scrap materials generated by the wrecking process. At present, only about 9 percent of all scrap consumed by the steel industry comes from discarded autos. The potential is much greater. There are an estimated 10 to 30 million junked automobiles scattered about the countryside which could prove to be a valuable source of iron and steel. However, at this time there is no incentive for a private agency to undertake the collection of the hulks.

The answer to many of the problems in this industry is the scrap shredder, many have said. The shredder would raise the value of scrap by more thoroughly separating ferrous and nonferrous metals. In conjunction with properly controlled incineration, more of the nonmetallic substances would also be removed without undue air pollution. Hence, the scrap salvager could afford to pay more for hulks, allowing the wrecker a wider margin. Hence, the wrecker could pay more for autos, prompting the recycling of more junked and abandoned vehicles.

Several things point to the idea that help will be needed in accomplishing the goals considered above. While the logic that the effect of higher prices will reach back to the beginning of the recycling channel is basically sound, some people feel that the differences will not be great enough to accomplish the total goal. An additional economic incentive would be needed to prompt collection of auto hulks for reprocessing. Additionally, the shredder equipment represents a substantial investment of money, up to several million dollars. These machines may have a capacity of 100 tons of scrap per hour. In order to be operated economically, the machines must be kept busy, so that a supply of up to 1,000 cars per day might be needed at a particularly large installation.

In 1970, there were 62 auto-shredder plants in operation in the United States, and 7 more were under construction. They were dispersed geographically as presented in Exhibit 4. The capacity of the plants is described in Exhibit 5.

EXHIBIT 4

LOCATION OF AUTO-SCRAP SHREDDER PLANTS IN THE UNITED STATES

Note: 1. Locations are schematic only.
2. Some symbols represent more than one installation.

EXHIBIT 5

GEOGRAPHIC DISTRIBUTION OF AUTO-SCRAP SHREDDER PLANTS IN THE UNITED STATES
(status as of April 1969)

Division	No. of Plants*	Estimated Annual Capacity (Net, Tons)	Percent of U.S. Total
New England	4	205,000	5.0
Middle Atlantic	7	480,000	11.5
East North Central	19	1,470,000	35.4
West North Central	4	252,000	6.0
South Atlantic	7	265,000	6.3
East South Central	5	261,000	6.3
West South Central	6	198,000	4.7
Mountain	7	350,000	8.4
Pacific	10	685,000	16.4
Total	69	4,163,000	100.0

* Operating, under construction or definitely planned for 1969. Note: The number may include some plants also using other than auto scrap. Source: BDSA estimates; based upon information from the Institute of Scrap Iron and Steel and auto-wrecking industry association.

Because of the discrepancies between capacity and location of scrap as presented in Exhibit 6, it has been proposed that the federal government partially subsidize the technical work necessary to build capacity for 7.5 million auto hulks annually, and to guarantee loans for the construction of the necessary plant.

EXHIBIT 6

COMPARISON OF AUTO-SCRAP SHREDDER PLANT CAPACITY
WITH MOTOR VEHICLES JUNKED IN 1968

Division	Percent of Shredder Capacity	Percent of Vehicles Junked in U.S.—1968
New England	5.0	5.7
Middle Atlantic	11.5	19.4
East North Central	35.4	24.3
West North Central	6.0	8.0
South Atlantic	6.3	13.9
East South Central	6.3	4.6
West South Central	4.7	9.6
Mountain	8.4	3.5
Pacific	16.4	11.0
Total	100.0	100.0

1. *How much additional shredder capacity is actually needed to bring it up to 7.5 million autos annually? What might it cost if an installation can operate 2,000 hours in a year? Where should the new capacity be distributed?*

2. *How might the government best encourage collection of abandoned autos? What are the economics of the situation? If auto disposal were subsidized by state and local government, what form should it take and to whom should it be given?*

Private sector: Lanier Auto Parts

A small group of businessmen is interested in starting up an auto-wrecking business in a large Southeastern metropolitan area. The team has decided to approach the situation on a different tack. The common junk yard is a large open area in which rusting hulks lie about in various stages of dismemberment. The appearance of the yard alone brings about several problems, most notably unfavorable zoning restrictions. Additionally, the haphazard stacking and aisle making use the available space very inefficiently. The cost of urban land is high enough to make the average 8–10 acre graveyard a substantial investment. As the autos lie about in the open, the elements take their toll on otherwise salable parts.

Another major area of concern is junk yard management. Most salvage companies are run and controlled by the owner in a "seat of the pants" manner. He maintains all inventory in his head, often losing out on sales because he forgets where or if he has a requested part. Records of the businesses are often inadequate. Sometimes little more is kept than is needed to satisfy the Internal Revenue Service. In many yards, even required sales information does not get into the books, especially as "under the table" transactions occur.

The management team is considering a completely enclosed operation. Auto hulks would spend a minimum time under company control before being completely stripped of all desirable parts. The rest of the hulk would be disposed of immediately. Fortunately, the entrepreneurs plan to locate their facility in a city which has a scrap shredder. All stripped parts would be tagged and recorded immediately, being distributed to bins according to part type and auto model. The stripping operation would take place in one of four stripping bays equipped with a variety of power tools.

The advantages of the proposal are relatively evident. Since salable parts are kept indoors, the effect of the elements on them has been largely reduced. Also, the mechanics who strip the hulks need not work under inconvenient space, weather, or time conditions. The saving of space is equally important. Since the hulks will be stripped and disposed of promptly, there is no need for a large investment in property. Also, the unsightly appearance is avoided, and zoning laws become less strict, allowing the location of facilities in more desirable places.

Investigating the opportunity brought certain information to light which was necessary for evaluating the feasibility of the proposal. A small survey of area wreckers showed that the daily sales of a salvage operation varied from a low of $1,000 to a high of $2,500, the average being $1,900 per day. Of that figure, the average breakdown into retail (user) and wholesale (garage dealer) sales was about $500 to $1,400. However, the number of transactions was split evenly between the two categories. Fast-moving items included engines, front ends, hoods, bumpers, fenders, and brake parts. Particularly slow items were windshields, heater cores, AM radios, and bucket seats.

The investment group considered specializing in one particular make of auto. To test this idea, they surveyed several auto dealerships and garages that handled a particular make. The monthly average purchases of these repair parts consumed from junk yards is summarized below:

	High	Low	Average
Mechanical parts	$ 800	$200	$ 500
Body parts	$1,500	$750	$1,000

Four of the ten shops interviewed kept regular accounts with at least one yard. They averaged two. All remaining shops had dealings with at least two different yards, the average being three. Eight of the ten shops responded favorably to dealing with a yard specializing in a particular make. One dealt with such a yard already. Other estimates showed that there was a potential market of $120,000 per month for used parts on the particular make in question.

The management team planned to staff the operation in the following manner. There was to be a manager, paid $250 per week, to oversee the operation, bid on junk cars, set prices, and keep adequate records. Two countermen would wait on customers. The manager would have to rely heavily on these men while acquainting himself with the workings of the operation. Thus, these men would have to be well experienced, commanding a pay rate of $200 per week. Additional personnel would include four car strippers whose skill would have to be equivalent to that of a repair mechanic. These men would expect a pay rate in the range of $125–$150 per week. Finally, the staff would include a parts man to clean, inspect, and maintain parts in the warehouse: and a delivery man to deliver parts to customers. These men would require salaries of $150 and $100 per week, respectively.

All operations were to take place indoors, in a building to be laid out as in Appendix A. Outfitting the building would require the equipment listed in Appendix B. The building, equipment, and other assets were to be insured according to the following plan:

Type	Coverage	Annual Pemium
Fire, legal liability on building	$ 30,000	$ 201.00
Fire, extended coverage on contents		$ 155.00
Workmens' Compensation, employees' liability	$100,000	$ 220.00
Public (general) liability	$100,000/300,000 BI $100,000 PD	$ 382.00
Automobile liability, covering wrecker, delivery truck, and flat bed truck	$100,000/300,000 BI $100,000 PD	$1,012.00
		$1,970.00

The building itself would be leased for a period of one or two years. Lease payments would be $12,000 annually.

The utility costs for this proposed operation would include not only the normal consumption of power and gas, but also an extensive communications network. The prospective junk dealers are considering tying into the various teletype networks which interconnect the yards throughout the Southeast. These facilities are used primarily to locate and price parts. The estimated power consumption would be $200 per month. Normal telephone service and "Yellow Pages" advertising would cost $150, while the teletype service would cost about $600 per month.

The operation startup would require two and one-half months. During this initial period, the following cash outlays would have to be made:

Cost of equipment	$15,850
Raw materials (100 cars)	50,000
Salaries (2½ months)	20,700
Rent (2½ months)	2,500
Insurance (2½ months)	410
Utilities (2½ months) (except communications)	500
License	250
Initial advertising	1,000
Total	$91,210

The group of businessmen expect that little or no revenue would accrue during this period. Hence external sources of funds would have to be relied on for operating capital in the startup period. The group found that they can raise only a small portion of the necessary capital. They expect to be able to borrow $60,000, payable over the next five years in monthly installments of $1,320.

After the original startup period, sales are expected to be in the range of $1,000 per day at first, increasing to the industry average of $1,900 per day at the end of the first year of full operations. Cost of goods sold is anticipated to be one half of the sales value of the auto parts derived from each hulk.

Assets will be depreciated on a straight line basis over a period of five years. Property taxes will be levied at about 2.0 percent of true value on fixed assets and inventories. An additional 6 percent of the payroll will have to be paid to the Social Security fund as required by law. Income taxes will be 40 percent of net income. The yard will operate five days a week.

1. *Project the cash flows of the proposed operation for the startup period and the first twelve months of full operations. Draw up a pro forma income statement and balance sheet as of the end of that period.*
2. *What are the advantages and disadvantages of specializing in one make of auto? Is it feasible to specialize? How much of the market would be necessary for the make of auto alluded to in the case?*
3. *What effect would the availability of the shredder have on operations and profitability? (If it were not available, how much more would it cost to dispose of hulks, etc.?)*

APPENDIX A

PROPOSED UTILIZATION OF WAREHOUSE SPACE, AREA—22,500 SQ. FT.

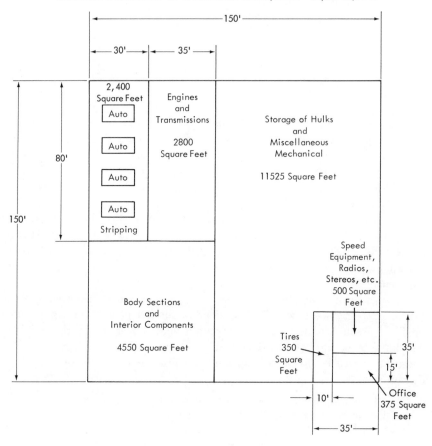

APPENDIX B

OPERATING EQUIPMENT

A. Air compressor with distribution system .... $ 1,000
B. Parts washer (for cleaning small parts) .... $ 260
C. Cutting torches: 2 @ $200 .... $ 400
D. Pneumatic impact wrenches with attachments: 4 @ $175 .... $ 700
E. Floor jacks (hydraulic, 1-ton capacity) 4 @ $150 .... $ 600
F. Jack stands: 20 @ $5 .... $ 100
G. Hydraulic crane (for removing motors) .... $ 1,000
H. Steam cleaner (for cleaning large parts) .... $ 400
I. Mechanics' tool sets, 2 @ $300 .... $ 600
J. Parts carts (for transporting parts between stripping area and storage area) 10 @ $100 .... $ 1,000
K. Material for storage bins and racks .... $ 2,000
L. Cash register (for sales area) .... $ 150
M. Tire machine (for dismounting saleable tires) .... $ 300
N. Wrecker (used) .... $ 3,000
O. Flat bed truck (for hauling off scrap) (used) .... $ 1,500
P. Material for four (4) work benches for stripping area .... $ 100
Q. Bench vices for stripping area: 4 @ $75 .... $ 300
R. Pneumatic chisel (with attachments) .... $ 200
S. Puller set .... $ 150
T. Bench grinder .... $ 100
U. Hydraulic ram set (for forcing and bending metal) .... $ 130
V. Creepers (for working under cars): 4 @ $15 .... $ 60
W. Electric saw (for removing body panels) .... $ 300
X. Pickup truck (for delivering parts) (used) .... $ 1,500

   Total $15,850

Appendix

APPENDIX / Tables useful for capital budgeting

2% Per Period

Period	(1) Present Value of $1	(2) Amount to Which $1 Will Accumulate	Present Value of $1 per Period		Amount to Which $1 per Period Will Accumulate	
			(3) Received at End	(4) Received Continuously	(5) Received at End	(6) Received Continuously
1	98039E 00	10200E 01	98039E 00	99016E 00	10000E 01	10100E 01
2	96117E 00	10404E 01	19416E 01	19609E 01	20200E 01	20401E 01
3	94232E 00	10612E 01	28839E 01	29126E 01	30604E 01	30909E 01
4	92385E 00	10824E 01	38077E 01	38457E 01	41216E 01	41627E 01
5	90573E 00	11041E 01	47135E 01	47604E 01	52040E 01	52559E 01
6	88797E 00	11262E 01	56014E 01	56573E 01	63081E 01	63710E 01
7	87056E 00	11487E 01	64720E 01	65365E 01	74343E 01	75084E 01
8	85349E 00	11717E 01	73255E 01	73985E 01	85830E 01	86685E 01
9	83676E 00	11951E 01	81622E 01	82436E 01	97546E 01	98518E 01
10	82035E 00	12190E 01	89826E 01	90721E 01	10950E 02	11059E 02
11	80426E 00	12434E 01	97868E 01	98844E 01	12169E 02	12290E 02
12	78849E 00	12682E 01	10575E 02	10681E 02	13412E 02	13546E 02
13	77303E 00	12936E 01	11348E 02	11461E 02	14680E 02	14827E 02
14	75787E 00	13195E 01	12106E 02	12227E 02	15974E 02	16133E 02
15	74301E 00	13459E 01	12849E 02	12977E 02	17293E 02	17466E 02
16	72845E 00	13728E 01	13578E 02	13713E 02	18639E 02	18825E 02
17	71416E 00	14002E 01	14292E 02	14434E 02	20012E 02	20212E 02
18	70016E 00	14282E 01	14992E 02	15141E 02	21412E 02	21626E 02
19	68643E 00	14568E 01	15678E 02	15835E 02	22841E 02	23068E 02
20	67297E 00	14859E 01	16351E 02	16514E 02	24297E 02	24540E 02
21	65978E 00	15157E 01	17011E 02	17181E 02	25783E 02	26040E 02
22	64684E 00	15460E 01	17658E 02	17834E 02	27299E 02	27571E 02
23	63416E 00	15769E 01	18292E 02	18475E 02	28845E 02	29132E 02
24	62172E 00	16084E 01	18914E 02	19102E 02	30422E 02	30725E 02
25	60953E 00	16406E 01	19523E 02	19718E 02	32030E 02	32350E 02
26	59758E 00	16734E 01	20121E 02	20322E 02	33671E 02	34006E 02
27	58586E 00	17069E 01	20707E 02	20913E 02	35344E 02	35697E 02
28	57437E 00	17410E 01	21281E 02	21493E 02	37051E 02	37420E 02
29	56311E 00	17758E 01	21844E 02	22062E 02	38792E 02	39179E 02
30	55207E 00	18114E 01	22396E 02	22620E 02	40568E 02	40972E 02

Source: J. Bracken and C. J. Christenson, *Tables for Use in Analyzing Business Decisions* (Homewood, Ill., Richard D. Irwin, Inc., 1965) pp. 24, 26, 28, 30, 32, 34, 37, 40, 42, 47, 52.

4% PER PERIOD

Period	(1) Present Value of $1	(2) Amount to Which $1 Will Accumulate	Present Value of $1 per Period		Amount to Which $1 per Period Will Accumulate	
			(3) Received at End	(4) Received Continuously	(5) Received at End	(6) Received Continuously
1	96154E 00	10400E 01	96154E 00	98064E 00	10000E 01	10199E 01
2	92456E 00	10816E 01	18861E 01	19236E 01	20400E 01	20805E 01
3	88900E 00	11249E 01	27751E 01	28302E 01	31216E 01	31836E 01
4	85480E 00	11699E 01	36299E 01	37020E 01	42465E 01	43308E 01
5	82193E 00	12167E 01	44518E 01	45403E 01	54163E 01	55239E 01
6	79031E 00	12653E 01	52421E 01	53463E 01	66330E 01	67648E 01
7	75992E 00	13159E 01	60021E 01	61213E 01	78983E 01	80552E 01
8	73069E 00	13686E 01	67327E 01	68665E 01	92142E 01	93973E 01
9	70259E 00	14233E 01	74353E 01	75831E 01	10583E 02	10793E 02
10	67556E 00	14802E 01	81109E 01	82721E 01	12006E 02	12245E 02
11	64958E 00	15395E 01	87605E 01	89345E 01	13486E 02	13754E 02
12	62460E 00	16010E 01	93851E 01	95715E 01	15026E 02	15324E 02
13	60057E 00	16651E 01	99856E 01	10184E 02	16627E 02	16957E 02
14	57748E 00	17317E 01	10563E 02	10773E 02	18292E 02	18655E 02
15	55526E 00	18009E 01	11118E 02	11339E 02	20024E 02	20421E 02
16	53391E 00	18730E 01	11652E 02	11884E 02	21825E 02	22258E 02
17	51337E 00	19479E 01	12166E 02	12407E 02	23698E 02	24168E 02
18	49363E-00	20258E 01	12659E 02	12911E 02	25645E 02	26155E 02
19	47464E-00	21068E 01	13134E 02	13395E 02	27671E 02	28221E 02
20	45639E-00	21911E 01	13590E 02	13860E 02	29778E 02	30370E 02
21	43883E-00	22788E 01	14029E 02	14308E 02	31969E 02	32604E 02
22	42196E-00	23699E 01	14451E 02	14738E 02	34248E 02	34928E 02
23	40573E-00	24647E 01	14857E 02	15152E 02	36618E 02	37345E 02
24	39012E-00	25633E 01	15247E 02	15550E 02	39083E 02	39859E 02
25	37512E-00	26658E 01	15622E 02	15932E 02	41646E 02	42473E 02
26	36069E-00	27725E 01	15983E 02	16300E 02	44312E 02	45192E 02
27	34682E-00	28834E 01	16330E 02	16654E 02	47084E 02	48020E 02
28	33348E-00	29987E 01	16663E 02	16994E 02	49968E 02	50960E 02
29	32065E-00	31187E 01	16984E 02	17321E 02	52966E 02	54019E 02
30	30832E-00	32434E 01	17292E 02	17636E 02	56085E 02	57199E 02

6% PER PERIOD

Period	(1) Present Value of $1	(2) Amount to Which $1 Will Accumulate	Present Value of $1 per Period		Amount to Which $1 per Period Will Accumulate	
			(3) Received at End	(4) Received Continuously	(5) Received at End	(6) Received Continuously
1	94340E 00	10600E 01	94340E 00	97142E 00	10000E 01	10297E 01
2	89000E 00	11236E 01	18334E 01	18879E 01	20600E 01	21212E 01
3	83962E 00	11910E 01	26730E 01	27524E 01	31836E 01	32782E 01
4	79209E 00	12625E 01	34651E 01	35680E 01	43746E 01	45046E 01
5	74726E 00	13382E 01	42124E 01	43375E 01	56371E 01	58046E 01
6	70496E 00	14185E 01	49173E 01	50634E 01	69753E 01	71825E 01
7	66506E 00	15036E 01	55824E 01	57482E 01	83938E 01	86432E 01
8	62741E 00	15938E 01	62098E 01	63943E 01	98975E 01	10192E 02
9	59190E 00	16895E 01	68017E 01	70038E 01	11491E 02	11833E 02
10	55839E 00	17908E 01	73601E 01	75787E 01	13181E 02	13572E 02
11	52679E 00	18983E 01	78869E 01	81212E 01	14972E 02	15416E 02
12	49697E-00	20122E 01	83838E 01	86329E 01	16870E 02	17371E 02
13	46884E-00	21329E 01	88527E 01	91157E 01	18882E 02	19443E 02
14	44230E-00	22609E 01	92950E 01	95711E 01	21015E 02	21639E 02
15	41727E-00	23966E 01	97122E 01	10001E 02	23276E 02	23967E 02
16	39365E-00	25404E 01	10106E 02	10406E 02	25673E 02	26435E 02
17	37136E-00	26928E 01	10477E 02	10789E 02	28213E 02	29051E 02
18	35034E-00	28543E 01	10828E 02	11149E 02	30906E 02	31824E 02
19	33051E-00	30256E 01	11158E 02	11490E 02	33760E 02	34763E 02
20	31180E-00	32071E 01	11470E 02	11811E 02	36786E 02	37878E 02
21	29416E-00	33996E 01	11764E 02	12114E 02	39993E 02	41181E 02
22	27751E-00	36035E 01	12042E 02	12399E 02	43392E 02	44681E 02
23	26180E-00	38197E 01	12303E 02	12669E 02	46996E 02	48392E 02
24	24698E-00	40489E 01	12550E 02	12923E 02	50816E 02	52325E 02
25	23300E-00	42919E 01	12783E 02	13163E 02	54865E 02	56494E 02
26	21981E-00	45494E 01	13003E 02	13389E 02	59156E 02	60914E 02
27	20737E-00	48223E 01	13211E 02	13603E 02	63706E 02	65598E 02
28	19563E-00	51117E 01	13406E 02	13804E 02	68528E 02	70564E 02
29	18456E-00	54184E 01	13591E 02	13994E 02	73640E 02	75828E 02
30	17411E-00	57435E 01	13765E 02	14174E 02	79058E 02	81407E 02

8% PER PERIOD

Period	(1) Present Value of $1	(2) Amount to Which $1 Will Accumulate	Present Value of $1 per Period		Amount to Which $1 per Period Will Accumulate	
			(3) Received at End	(4) Received Continuously	(5) Received at End	(6) Received Continuously
1	92593E 00	10800E 01	92593E 00	96249E 00	10000E 01	10395E 01
2	85734E 00	11664E 01	17833E 01	18537E 01	20800E 01	21621E 01
3	79383E 00	12597E 01	25771E 01	26789E 01	32464E 01	33746E 01
4	73503E 00	13605E 01	33121E 01	34429E 01	45061E 01	46840E 01
5	68058E 00	14693E 01	39927E 01	41504E 01	58666E 01	60983E 01
6	63017E 00	15869E 01	46229E 01	48054E 01	73359E 01	76256E 01
7	58349E 00	17138E 01	52064E 01	54120E 01	89228E 01	92751E 01
8	54027E 00	18509E 01	57466E 01	59736E 01	10637E 02	11057E 02
9	50025E 00	19990E 01	62469E 01	64936E 01	12488E 02	12981E 02
10	46319E-00	21589E 01	67101E 01	69750E 01	14487E 02	15059E 02
11	42888E-00	23316E 01	71390E 01	74209E 01	16645E 02	17303E 02
12	39711E-00	25182E 01	75361E 01	78337E 01	18977E 02	19726E 02
13	36770E-00	27196E 01	79038E 01	82159E 01	21495E 02	22344E 02
14	34046E-00	29372E 01	82442E 01	85698E 01	24215E 02	25171E 02
15	31524E-00	31722E 01	85595E 01	88975E 01	27152E 02	28224E 02
16	29189E-00	34259E 01	88514E 01	92009E 01	30324E 02	31522E 02
17	27027E-00	37000E 01	91216E 01	94818E 01	33750E 02	35083E 02
18	25025E-00	39960E 01	93719E 01	97420E 01	37450E 02	38929E 02
19	23171E-00	43157E 01	96036E 01	99828E 01	41446E 02	43083E 02
20	21455E-00	46610E 01	98181E 01	10206E 02	45762E 02	47569E 02
21	19866E-00	50338E 01	10017E 02	10412E 02	50423E 02	52414E 02
22	18394E-00	54365E 01	10201E 02	10604E 02	55457E 02	57647E 02
23	17032E-00	58715E 01	10371E 02	10781E 02	60893E 02	63298E 02
24	15770E-00	63412E 01	10529E 02	10945E 02	66765E 02	69401E 02
25	14602E-00	68485E 01	10675E 02	11096E 02	73106E 02	75993E 02
26	13520E-00	73964E 01	10810E 02	11237E 02	79954E 02	83112E 02
27	12519E-00	79881E 01	10935E 02	11367E 02	87351E 02	90800E 02
28	11591E-00	86271E 01	11051E 02	11487E 02	95339E 02	99103E 02
29	10733E-00	93173E 01	11158E 02	11599E 02	10397E 03	10807E 03
30	99377E-01	10063E 02	11258E 02	11702E 02	11328E 03	11776E 03

10% Per Period

Period	(1) Present Value of $1	(2) Amount to Which $1 Will Accumulate	Present Value of $1 per Period		Amount to Which $1 per Period Will Accumulate	
			(3) Received at End	(4) Received Continuously	(5) Received at End	(6) Received Continuously
1	90909E 00	11000E 01	90909E 00	95382E 00	10000E 01	10492E 01
2	82645E 00	12100E 01	17355E 01	18209E 01	21000E 01	22033E 01
3	75131E 00	13310E 01	24869E 01	26092E 01	33100E 01	34729E 01
4	68301E 00	14641E 01	31699E 01	33258E 01	46410E 01	48694E 01
5	62092E 00	16105E 01	37908E 01	39773E 01	61051E 01	64055E 01
6	56447E 00	17716E 01	43553E 01	45696E 01	77156E 01	80953E 01
7	51316E 00	19487E 01	48684E 01	51080E 01	94872E 01	99540E 01
8	46651E-00	21436E 01	53349E 01	55974E 01	11436E 02	11999E 02
9	42410E-00	23579E 01	57590E 01	60424E 01	13579E 02	14248E 02
10	38554E-00	25937E 01	61446E 01	64469E 01	15937E 02	16722E 02
11	35049E-00	28531E 01	64951E 01	68147E 01	18531E 02	19443E 02
12	31863E-00	31384E 01	68137E 01	71490E 01	21384E 02	22437E 02
13	28966E-00	34523E 01	71034E 01	74529E 01	24523E 02	25729E 02
14	26333E-00	37975E 01	73667E 01	77292E 01	27975E 02	29352E 02
15	23939E-00	41772E 01	76061E 01	79803E 01	31772E 02	33336E 02
16	21763E-00	45950E 01	78237E 01	82087E 01	35950E 02	37719E 02
17	19784E-00	50545E 01	80216E 01	84163E 01	40545E 02	42540E 02
18	17986E-00	55599E 01	82014E 01	86050E 01	45599E 02	47843E 02
19	16351E-00	61159E 01	83649E 01	87765E 01	51159E 02	53676E 02
20	14864E-00	67275E 01	85136E 01	89325E 01	57275E 02	60093E 02
21	13513E-00	74003E 01	86487E 01	90743E 01	64003E 02	67152E 02
22	12285E-00	81403E 01	87715E 01	92031E 01	71403E 02	74916E 02
23	11168E-00	89543E 01	88832E 01	93203E 01	79543E 02	83457E 02
24	10153E-00	98497E 01	89847E 01	94268E 01	88497E 02	92852E 02
25	92296E-01	10835E 02	90770E 01	95237E 01	98347E 02	10319E 03
26	83905E-01	11918E 02	91609E 01	96117E 01	10918E 03	11455E 03
27	76278E-01	13110E 02	92372E 01	96917E 01	12110E 03	12706E 03
28	69343E-01	14421E 02	93066E 01	97645E 01	13421E 03	14081E 03
29	63039E-01	15863E 02	93696E 01	98306E 01	14863E 03	15594E 03
30	57309E-01	17449E 02	94269E 01	98908E 01	16449E 03	17259E 03

12% PER PERIOD

Period	(1) Present Value of $1	(2) Amount to Which $1 Will Accumulate	Present Value of $1 per Period		Amount to Which $1 per Period Will Accumulate	
			(3) Received at End	(4) Received Continuously	(5) Received at End	(6) Received Continuously
1	89286E 00	11200E 01	89286E 00	94542E 00	10000E 01	10589E 01
2	79719E 00	12544E 01	16901E 01	17895E 01	21200E 01	22448E 01
3	71178E 00	14049E 01	24018E 01	25432E 01	33744E 01	35730E 01
4	63552E 00	15735E 01	30373E 01	32161E 01	47793E 01	50607E 01
5	56743E 00	17623E 01	36048E 01	38170E 01	63528E 01	67268E 01
6	50663E 00	19738E 01	41114E 01	43534E 01	81152E 01	85929E 01
7	45235E-00	22107E 01	45638E 01	48324E 01	10089E 02	10683E 02
8	40388E-00	24760E 01	49676E 01	52601E 01	12300E 02	13024E 02
9	36061E-00	27731E 01	53282E 01	56419E 01	14776E 02	15645E 02
10	32197E-00	31058E 01	56502E 01	59828E 01	17549E 02	18582E 02
11	28748E-00	34786E 01	59377E 01	62872E 01	20655E 02	21870E 02
12	25668E-00	38960E 01	61944E 01	65590E 01	24133E 02	25554E 02
13	22917E-00	43635E 01	64235E 01	68017E 01	28029E 02	29679E 02
14	20462E-00	48871E 01	66282E 01	70183E 01	32393E 02	34299E 02
15	18270E-00	54736E 01	68109E 01	72118E 01	37280E 02	39474E 02
16	16312E-00	61304E 01	69740E 01	73845E 01	42753E 02	45270E 02
17	14564E-00	68660E 01	71196E 01	75387E 01	48884E 02	51761E 02
18	13004E-00	76900E 01	72497E 01	76764E 01	55750E 02	59032E 02
19	11611E-00	86128E 01	73658E 01	77994E 01	63440E 02	67174E 02
20	10367E-00	96463E 01	74694E 01	79091E 01	72052E 02	76294E 02
21	92560E-01	10804E 02	75620E 01	80072E 01	81699E 02	86508E 02
22	82643E-01	12100E 02	76446E 01	80947E 01	92503E 02	97948E 02
23	73788E-01	13552E 02	77184E 01	81728E 01	10460E 03	11076E 03
24	65882E-01	15179E 02	77843E 01	82426E 01	11816E 03	12511E 03
25	58823E-01	17000E 02	78431E 01	83048E 01	13333E 03	14118E 03
26	52521E-01	19040E 02	78957E 01	83605E 01	15033E 03	15918E 03
27	46894E-01	21325E 02	79426E 01	84101E 01	16937E 03	17934E 03
28	41869E-01	23884E 02	79844E 01	84544E 01	19070E 03	20192E 03
29	37383E-01	26750E 02	80218E 01	84940E 01	21458E 03	22721E 03
30	33378E-01	29960E 02	80552E 01	85294E 01	24133E 03	25554E 03

15% PER PERIOD

Period	(1) Present Value of $1	(2) Amount to Which $1 Will Accumulate	Present Value of $1 per Period		Amount to Which $1 per Period Will Accumulate	
			(3) Received at End	(4) Received Continuously	(5) Received at End	(6) Received Continuously
1	86957E 00	11500E 01	86957E 00	93326E 00	10000E 01	10733E 01
2	75614E 00	13225E 01	16257E 01	17448E 01	21500E 01	23075E 01
3	65752E 00	15209E 01	22832E 01	24505E 01	34725E 01	37269E 01
4	57175E 00	17490E 01	28550E 01	30641E 01	49934E 01	53592E 01
5	49718E-00	20114E 01	33522E 01	35977E 01	67424E 01	72363E 01
6	43233E-00	23131E 01	37845E 01	40617E 01	87537E 01	93950E 01
7	37594E-00	26600E 01	41604E 01	44652E 01	11067E 02	11877E 02
8	32690E-00	30590E 01	44873E 01	48160E 01	13727E 02	14732E 02
9	28426E-00	35179E 01	47716E 01	51211E 01	16786E 02	18015E 02
10	24718E-00	40456E 01	50188E 01	53864E 01	20304E 02	21791E 02
11	21494E-00	46524E 01	52337E 01	56171E 01	24349E 02	26133E 02
12	18691E-00	53503E 01	54206E 01	58177E 01	29002E 02	31126E 02
13	16253E-00	61528E 01	55831E 01	59921E 01	34352E 02	36868E 02
14	14133E-00	70757E 01	57245E 01	61438E 01	40505E 02	43472E 02
15	12289E-00	81371E 01	58474E 01	62757E 01	47580E 02	51066E 02
16	10686E-00	93576E 01	59542E 01	63904E 01	55717E 02	59799E 02
17	92926E-01	10761E 02	60472E 01	64901E 01	65075E 02	69842E 02
18	80805E-01	12375E 02	61280E 01	65769E 01	75836E 02	81392E 02
19	70265E-01	14232E 02	61982E 01	66523E 01	88212E 02	94674E 02
20	61100E-01	16367E 02	62593E 01	67178E 01	10244E 03	10995E 03
21	53131E-01	18822E 02	63125E 01	67749E 01	11881E 03	12751E 03
22	46201E-01	21645E 02	63587E 01	68245E 01	13763E 03	14771E 03
23	40174E-01	24891E 02	63988E 01	68676E 01	15928E 03	17094E 03
24	34934E-01	28625E 02	64338E 01	69051E 01	18417E 03	19766E 03
25	30378E-01	32919E 02	64641E 01	69377E 01	21279E 03	22838E 03
26	26415E-01	37857E 02	64906E 01	69660E 01	24571E 03	26371E 03
27	22970E-01	43535E 02	65135E 01	69907E 01	28357E 03	30434E 03
28	19974E-01	50066E 02	65335E 01	70121E 01	32710E 03	35107E 03
29	17369E-01	57575E 02	65509E 01	70308E 01	37717E 03	40480E 03
30	15103E-01	66212E 02	65660E 01	70470E 01	43475E 03	46659E 03

18% PER PERIOD

Period	(1) Present Value of $1	(2) Amount to Which $1 Will Accumulate	Present Value of $1 per Period		Amount to Which $1 per Period Will Accumulate	
			(3) Received at End	(4) Received Continuously	(5) Received at End	(6) Received Continuously
1	84746E 00	11800E 01	84746E 00	92163E 00	10000E 01	10875E 01
2	71818E 00	13924E 01	15656E 01	17027E 01	21800E 01	23708E 01
3	60863E 00	16430E 01	21743E 01	23646E 01	35724E 01	38851E 01
4	51579E 00	19388E 01	26901E 01	29255E 01	52154E 01	56719E 01
5	43711E-00	22878E 01	31272E 01	34009E 01	71542E 01	77803E 01
6	37043E-00	26996E 01	34976E 01	38037E 01	94420E 01	10268E 02
7	31393E-00	31855E 01	38115E 01	41451E 01	12142E 02	13204E 02
8	26604E-00	37589E 01	40776E 01	44344E 01	15327E 02	16668E 02
9	22546E-00	44355E 01	43030E 01	46796E 01	19086E 02	20756E 02
10	19106E-00	52338E 01	44941E 01	48874E 01	23521E 02	25580E 02
11	16192E-00	61759E 01	46560E 01	50635E 01	28755E 02	31272E 02
12	13722E-00	72876E 01	47932E 01	52127E 01	34931E 02	37988E 02
13	11629E-00	85994E 01	49095E 01	53392E 01	42219E 02	45914E 02
14	98549E-01	10147E 02	50081E 01	54464E 01	50818E 02	55266E 02
15	83516E-01	11974E 02	50916E 01	55372E 01	60965E 02	66301E 02
16	70776E-01	14129E 02	51624E 01	56142E 01	72939E 02	79323E 02
17	59980E-01	16672E 02	52223E 01	56794E 01	87068E 02	94688E 02
18	50830E-01	19673E 02	52732E 01	57347E 01	10374E 03	11282E 03
19	43077E-01	23214E 02	53162E 01	57815E 01	12341E 03	13421E 03
20	36506E-01	27393E 02	53527E 01	58212E 01	14663E 03	15946E 03
21	30937E-01	32324E 02	53837E 01	58549E 01	17402E 03	18925E 03
22	26218E-01	38142E 02	54099E 01	58834E 01	20634E 03	22440E 03
23	22218E-01	45008E 02	54321E 01	59075E 01	24449E 03	26588E 03
24	18829E-01	53109E 02	54509E 01	59280E 01	28949E 03	31483E 03
25	15957E-01	62669E 02	54669E 01	59454E 01	34260E 03	37259E 03
26	13523E-01	73949E 02	54804E 01	59601E 01	40527E 03	44074E 03
27	11460E-01	87260E 02	54919E 01	59725E 01	47922E 03	52116E 03
28	97119E-02	10297E 03	55016E 01	59831E 01	56648E 03	61606E 03
29	82304E-02	12150E 03	55098E 01	59920E 01	66945E 03	72804E 03
30	69749E-02	14337E 03	55168E 01	59996E 01	79095E 03	86017E 03

20% PER PERIOD

Period	(1) Present Value of $1	(2) Amount to Which $1 Will Accumulate	Present Value of $1 per Period		Amount to Which $1 per Period Will Accumulate	
			(3) Received at End	(4) Received Continuously	(5) Received at End	(6) Received Continuously
1	83333E 00	12000E 01	83333E 00	91414E 00	10000E 01	10970E 01
2	69444E 00	14400E 01	15278E 01	16759E 01	22000E 01	24133E 01
3	57870E 00	17280E 01	21065E 01	23107E 01	36400E 01	39929E 01
4	48225E-00	20736E 01	25887E 01	28397E 01	53680E 01	58885E 01
5	40188E-00	24883E 01	29906E 01	32806E 01	74416E 01	81632E 01
6	33490E-00	29860E 01	33255E 01	36480E 01	99299E 01	10893E 02
7	27908E-00	35832E 01	36046E 01	39541E 01	12916E 02	14168E 02
8	23257E-00	42998E 01	38372E 01	42092E 01	16499E 02	18099E 02
9	19381E-00	51598E 01	40310E 01	44218E 01	20799E 02	22816E 02
10	16151E-00	61917E 01	41925E 01	45990E 01	25959E 02	28476E 02
11	13459E-00	74301E 01	43271E 01	47466E 01	32150E 02	35268E 02
12	11216E-00	89161E 01	44392E 01	48697E 01	39580E 02	43418E 02
13	93464E-01	10699E 02	45327E 01	49722E 01	48497E 02	53199E 02
14	77887E-01	12839E 02	46106E 01	50576E 01	59196E 02	64936E 02
15	64905E-01	15407E 02	46755E 01	51288E 01	72035E 02	79020E 02
16	54088E-01	18488E 02	47296E 01	51882E 01	87442E 02	95921E 02
17	45073E-01	22186E 02	47746E 01	52376E 01	10593E 03	11620E 03
18	37561E-01	26623E 02	48122E 01	52788E 01	12812E 03	14054E 03
19	31301E-01	31948E 02	48435E 01	53131E 01	15474E 03	16974E 03
20	26086E-01	38338E 02	48696E 01	53417E 01	18669E 03	20479E 03
21	21737E-01	46005E 02	48913E 01	53656E 01	22503E 03	24684E 03
22	18114E-01	55206E 02	49094E 01	53855E 01	27103E 03	29731E 03
23	15095E-01	66247E 02	49245E 01	54020E 01	32624E 03	35787E 03
24	12579E-01	79497E 02	49371E 01	54158E 01	39248E 03	43054E 03
25	10483E-01	95396E 02	49476E 01	54273E 01	47198E 03	51775E 03
26	87355E-02	11448E 03	49563E 01	54369E 01	56738E 03	62239E 03
27	72796E-02	13737E 03	49636E 01	54449E 01	68185E 03	74797E 03
28	60663E-02	16484E 03	49697E 01	54515E 01	81922E 03	89866E 03
29	50553E-02	19781E 03	49747E 01	54571E 01	98407E 03	10795E 04
30	42127E-02	23738E 03	49789E 01	54617E 01	11819E 04	12965E 04

25% PER PERIOD

Period	(1) Present Value of $1	(2) Amount to Which $1 Will Accumulate	Present Value of $1 per Period		Amount to Which $1 per Period Will Accumulate	
			(3) Received at End	(4) Received Continuously	(5) Received at End	(6) Received Continuously
1	80000E 00	12500E 01	80000E 00	89628E 00	10000E 01	11204E 01
2	64000E 00	15625E 01	14400E 01	16133E 01	22500E 01	25208E 01
3	51200E 00	19531E 01	19520E 01	21869E 01	38125E 01	42714E 01
4	40960E-00	24414E 01	23616E 01	26458E 01	57656E 01	64595E 01
5	32768E-00	30518E 01	26893E 01	30129E 01	82070E 01	91948E 01
6	26214E-00	38147E 01	29514E 01	33066E 01	11259E 02	12614E 02
7	20972E-00	47684E 01	31611E 01	35416E 01	15073E 02	16888E 02
8	16777E-00	59605E 01	33289E 01	37296E 01	19842E 02	22230E 02
9	13422E-00	74506E 01	34631E 01	38799E 01	25802E 02	28908E 02
10	10737E-00	93132E 01	35705E 01	40002E 01	33253E 02	37255E 02
11	85899E-01	11642E 02	36564E 01	40965E 01	42566E 02	47689E 02
12	68719E-01	14552E 02	37251E 01	41735E 01	54208E 02	60732E 02
13	54976E-01	18190E 02	37801E 01	42351E 01	68760E 02	77035E 02
14	43980E-01	22737E 02	38241E 01	42843E 01	86949E 02	97414E 02
15	35184E-01	28422E 02	38593E 01	43237E 01	10969E 03	12289E 03
16	28147E-01	35527E 02	38874E 01	43553E 01	13811E 03	15473E 03
17	22518E-01	44409E 02	39099E 01	43805E 01	17364E 03	19453E 03
18	18014E-01	55511E 02	39279E 01	44007E 01	21804E 03	24429E 03
19	14412E-01	69389E 02	39424E 01	44168E 01	27356E 03	30648E 03
20	11529E-01	86736E 02	39539E 01	44298E 01	34294E 03	38422E 03
21	92234E-02	10842E 03	39631E 01	44401E 01	42968E 03	48140E 03
22	73787E-02	13553E 03	39705E 01	44484E 01	53810E 03	60286E 03
23	59030E-02	16941E 03	39764E 01	44550E 01	67363E 03	75470E 03
24	47224E-02	21176E 03	39811E 01	44603E 01	84303E 03	94450E 03
25	37779E-02	26470E 03	39849E 01	44645E 01	10548E 04	11817E 04
26	30223E-02	33087E 03	39879E 01	44679E 01	13195E 04	14783E 04
27	24179E-02	41359E 03	39903E 01	44706E 01	16504E 04	18490E 04
28	19343E-02	51699E 03	39923E 01	44728E 01	20640E 04	23124E 04
29	15474E-02	64623E 03	39938E 01	44745E 01	25809E 04	28916E 04
30	12379E-02	80779E 03	39950E 01	44759E 01	32272E 04	36156E 04

30% PER PERIOD

Period	(1) Present Value of $1	(2) Amount to Which $1 Will Accumulate	Present Value of $1 per Period		Amount to Which $1 per Period Will Accumulate	
			(3) Received at End	(4) Received Continuously	(5) Received at End	(6) Received Continuously
1	76923E 00	13000E 01	76923E 00	87958E 00	10000E 01	11434E 01
2	59172E 00	16900E 01	13609E 01	15562E 01	23000E 01	26299E 01
3	45517E-00	21970E 01	18161E 01	20766E 01	39900E 01	45624E 01
4	35013E-00	28561E 01	21662E 01	24770E 01	61870E 01	70745E 01
5	26933E-00	37129E 01	24356E 01	27849E 01	90431E 01	10340E 02
6	20718E-00	48268E 01	26427E 01	30218E 01	12756E 02	14586E 02
7	15937E-00	62749E 01	28021E 01	32041E 01	17583E 02	20105E 02
8	12259E-00	81573E 01	29247E 01	33442E 01	23858E 02	27280E 02
9	94300E-01	10604E 02	30190E 01	34521E 01	32015E 02	36607E 02
10	72538E-01	13786E 02	30915E 01	35350E 01	42619E 02	48733E 02
11	55799E-01	17922E 02	31473E 01	35988E 01	56405E 02	64497E 02
12	42922E-01	23298E 02	31903E 01	36479E 01	74327E 02	84989E 02
13	33017E-01	30288E 02	32233E 01	36857E 01	97625E 02	11163E 03
14	25398E-01	39374E 02	32487E 01	37147E 01	12791E 03	14626E 03
15	19537E-01	51186E 02	32682E 01	37370E 01	16729E 03	19128E 03
16	15028E-01	66542E 02	32832E 01	37542E 01	21847E 03	24981E 03
17	11560E-01	86504E 02	32948E 01	37674E 01	28501E 03	32590E 03
18	88924E-02	11246E 03	33037E 01	37776E 01	37152E 03	42481E 03
19	68403E-02	14619E 03	33105E 01	37854E 01	48397E 03	55340E 03
20	52618E-02	19005E 03	33158E 01	37914E 01	63017E 03	72056E 03
21	40475E-02	24706E 03	33198E 01	37961E 01	82022E 03	93787E 03
22	31135E-02	32118E 03	33230E 01	37996E 01	10673E 04	12204E 04
23	23950E-02	41754E 03	33253E 01	38024E 01	13885E 04	15876E 04
24	18423E-02	54280E 03	33272E 01	38045E 01	18060E 04	20651E 04
25	14172E-02	70564E 03	33286E 01	38061E 01	23488E 04	26857E 04
26	10901E-02	91733E 03	33297E 01	38073E 01	30544E 04	34926E 04
27	83855E-03	11925E 04	33305E 01	38083E 01	39718E 04	45415E 04
28	64504E-03	15503E 04	33312E 01	38090E 01	51643E 04	59051E 04
29	49618E-03	20154E 04	33317E 01	38096E 01	67146E 04	76778E 04
30	38168E-03	26200E 04	33321E 01	38100E 01	87300E 04	99823E 04

Indexes

Index of Cases

Index

A

Acceleration principle
defined, 95
empirical studies and illustrations, 99–100
Accounting costs, limitations of, for decision making, 191–93
Adams, F. G., 117 n
Advertising firm, as example of use of incremental reasoning, 18
Advertising outlays
decisions about, 44–45
relation to revenue and profits, 44
Aggregate marginal revenue curve
horizontal summation to obtain, in price discrimination, 390
vertical summation to obtain, in joint product pricing, 409–10
Agricultural commodities, as example of demand estimates based on time series data, 88–89
Air conditioners, as example of "demonstration effect," 102
Aircraft manufacturing, as example
of finite production runs, 232–33
of learning curves, 234–35
Algebraic determination of optimum output, 210–11
Algebraic form of break-even analysis, 208
Algebraic form of profit-volume analysis, 209–10
Algebraic solution of basic EOQ problem, 303–4
with variable purchase costs, 304–8

Algebraic solution of a linear programming problem, 275–80
Almon, C., 498
Alt, R. M., 410 n
Alternative products, theory of price and output determination for, 411–12
Analytical (engineering) approach to estimation of cost-output relationships, 197–98, 249–58
Ansoff, H. I., 480–83
Arbitrage, 387
Arc elasticity, 74–76
Autocorrelation, 88
Automobiles
demand for, 92, 161
as example
of differentiated oligopoly, 94, 359
of durable goods, 96
income sensitivity of demand for, 98
survivorship technique, in manufacture of, 248
Average product
defined, 222
relation to total product, 222
Average total cost, relation of
to average fixed cost, 231
to average variable cost, 230–31
to marginal cost, 230–31
to total cost (diagrams), 181–85
Ayres, R. V., 490 n

B

Bank's demand for loans, as example of demand forecasting for a firm, 153–54

This book is set in 10 and 9 point #21, leaded 2 points. Part numbers and titles and chapter numbers and titles are set in 14 point Vogue Bold. The size of the type page is 27 x 45½ picas.